13th Edition

Choices in RELATIONSHIPS

We would like to dedicate this 13th edition to Emily Schacht.

—David Knox and Caroline Schacht

To my family—the reason I became a family scholar. To my dear daughters Allison and Annika—the reasons I love being a family scholar.

—I. Joyce Chang

Sara Miller McCune founded SAGE Publishing in 1965 to support the dissemination of usable knowledge and educate a global community. SAGE publishes more than 1000 journals and over 800 new books each year, spanning a wide range of subject areas. Our growing selection of library products includes archives, data, case studies and video. SAGE remains majority owned by our founder and after her lifetime will become owned by a charitable trust that secures the company's continued independence.

Los Angeles | London | New Delhi | Singapore | Washington DC | Melbourne

13th Edition

Choices in RELATIONSHIPS

David Knox
East Carolina University

Caroline Schacht
East Carolina University

I. Joyce Chang
University of Central Missouri

Los Angeles | London | New Delhi
Singapore | Washington DC | Melbourne

FOR INFORMATION:

SAGE Publications, Inc.
2455 Teller Road
Thousand Oaks, California 91320
E-mail: order@sagepub.com

SAGE Publications Ltd.
1 Oliver's Yard
55 City Road
London, EC1Y 1SP
United Kingdom

SAGE Publications India Pvt. Ltd.
B 1/I 1 Mohan Cooperative Industrial Area
Mathura Road, New Delhi 110 044
India

SAGE Publications Asia-Pacific Pte. Ltd.
18 Cross Street #10-10/11/12
China Square Central
Singapore 048423

Printed in Canada

Names: Knox, David, 1943- author. | Schacht, Caroline, author. | Chang, I-Tung Joyce, author.

Title: Choices in relationships: an introduction to marriage and the family / David Knox, East Carolina University, Caroline Schacht, East Carolina University, I. Joyce Chang, University of Cental Missouri.

Description: Thirteenth edition. | Los Angeles: SAGE, [2021] | Includes bibliographical references and index.

Identifiers: LCCN 2019032755 | ISBN 9781544379197 (paperback; alk. paper) | ISBN 9781544379203 (epub) | ISBN 9781544379180 (epub) | ISBN 9781544379173 (ebook)

Subjects: LCSH: Family life education. | Marriage—United States.

Classification: LCC HQ10 .K5 2021 | DDC 306.810973—dc23

LC record available at https://lccn.loc.gov/2019032755

Acquisitions Editor: Joshua Perigo

Content Development Editor: Alissa Nance

Marketing Manager: Zina Craft

Production Editor: Sarah Downing

Copy Editor: Lynne Curry

Typesetter: Hurix Digital

Proofreader: Sue Irwin

Indexer: Joan Shapiro

Cover Designer: Gail Buschman

This book is printed on acid-free paper.

20 21 22 23 24 10 9 8 7 6 5 4 3 2 1

BRIEF CONTENTS

DETAILED CONTENTS

Chesnot /Getty Images Europe

Barcroft Media/ Getty

Barcroft Media/Getty

Barcroft Media/Getty

Vladimir Gerdo/TASS/Getty

Chapter 8: Communication and Technology in Relationships 161

Chapter 9: Sexuality in Relationships 181

Nur Photo/Getty

Robert Daemmrich Photography/Corbis News/Getty

Chapter 10: Violence and Abuse in Relationships   205

Mikhail Tereshchenko/TASS/Getty

Barcroft Media/Getty

Chapter 12: Diversity in Parenting   253

Chapter 13: Money, Work, and Relationships   277

Hero Images Inc./Alamy Stock Photo

Bloomberg/Getty

Chapter 14: Stress and Crisis in Relationships   295

iStockphoto.com/Adene Sanchez

Chapter 15: Divorce, Remarriage, and Stepfamilies 319

Robert Alexander/Archive Photos/Getty

SELF ASSESSMENTS

Authors Knox and Schacht welcome I. Joyce Chang as a coauthor to the 13th edition. Dr. Chang is Professor of Child and Family Development, University of Central Missouri, Warrensburg, and has won awards in both teaching and research. She is active in one of the most prestigious professional organizations in the field, the National Council on Family Relations. In addition to her cutting-edge insights and input throughout the text, Dr. Chang wrote the new Technology sections featured in each chapter.

While technology continues to have a major impact in relationships, our primary focus remains on the choices we make in reference to relationships, marriages, and families. These choices have consequences for the happiness, health, and well-being of ourselves, our partners, our marriage, our parents, and our children. By making deliberate informed choices, everyone wins. Not to take our relationship choices seriously is to limit our ability to enjoy deep, emotionally fulfilling relationships—the only game in town.

This new edition is based on state-of-the-art research with 885 new references, new technology sections—for example, "Robots Are Here"; new Self-Assessment scales, such as "Effective Communication Scale"; new Applying Social Research boxes—for example, "The Experience of Casual Sex"; and new Family Policy inserts like "Childhood Vaccinations—Public Policy and Parental Rights," which continue the cutting-edge format for which *Choices in Relationships* is known. In addition, in the "The Future of..." section at the end of each chapter, we predict, based on trends found in the latest research studies, what the future is likely to hold for marriage, singlehood, parenting, divorce and remarriage, and other chapter topics. Other new content added to each chapter includes the following.

NEW TO THE 13TH EDITION: CHAPTER BY CHAPTER

Chapter 1: Choices in Relationships: An Introduction to Marriage, Family and Diversity

Individualized marriage—new term to describe current marriages

Applying Social Research: Impact of Religion on Love, Relationships, and Sexuality

African American clergy committed to marriage preparation

Supreme Court ruling redefining marriage

Human Ecology Framework

Couple and Family Technology Framework

Transnational families

Marriage—Then and Now

Ghost marriage

Is marriage obsolete?

Generation Z

Technology and the Family: Robots

Japan's rent-a-family industry

Fictive kin

Impact of time on social media and relationship satisfaction

Impact of religiosity on staying married to a partner who cheated

Automatic acceptance of same-sex marriage by offspring of parents has not occurred.

Autoethnology

American policies separating children from their families

AI will continue in family life but most are wary of intrusiveness

Socioeconomic/minority status impact on use of technology influences careers/relationships

Mischievous responders as research caveat

How homeless youth view "family"

Chapter 2: Love Relationships

Importance of and meaning of love today

Technology and Love: The Digital Language of Love

Outcome of swinging on relationship quality

Love Directions—heteroromantic, homoromantic, aromantic

Letting love die and moving on

Referents to feeling loved include feeling loved by a pet.

Benefits and drawbacks of polyamory families

Google searchers on nonmonogamy

Primary mate ejection

Love feelings for an android?

Gaslighting

Chapter 3: Gender and Diversity

Chapter 4: Singlehood, Cohabitation, and Living Apart Together

Chapter 5: Selecting a Partner

Effect of conflictual/neglectful parents on one's own relationship

Effect of new relationship for someone on the rebound

Continuum of arranged marriage

Settling

Social anhedonia

Future of partner selection

When there are discrepancies in attraction, love, commitment

Catfishing

Ghosting

Desire for a romantic relationship sets stage for reality of involvement in a relationship

Social anhedonia—no interest in social relationships and no pleasure in social interaction

Chapter 6: Diversity in Marriage Relationships

Immigrant families

Poly families—definitions, benefits and difficulties

Self-Assessment: Satisfaction in Couple Relationship Scale

Family Policy: Ending Child Marriages

After the wedding/new marriage—12% of wives in one study reported clinical depression

Family and Technology: The Downsides of "Smart" Devices

Technoference

African American Families

Hispanic population—fastest growing minority

Asian American Families

Transnational families

Secret lives of international students while in the U.S.

Marital generosity

Up Close: My College Marriage

Forced Marriages

Applying Social Research: Happiness and Power in Relationship

Infidelity data during deployment

Sex frequency drops off significantly the second year of a relationship

Managing the emotions of one's partner and one's self for enhanced marital quality

Interracial spouses have children at a similar rate to same race couples.

Extended kin support is perceived as lacking for White mother with a minority child.

MEES (mundane extreme environmental stress) theory

Non-materialistic couples happier

Biracial children

Immigrants—about half (45%) do not want immigrants moving into their country.

Hologram marriage

Use of Love EveryDay app

A genetic variation referred to as OXTR rs53576 is associated with happy marriages.

Chapter 7: LGBTQIA Relationships

American Psychiatric Association removal of homosexuality as a mental disorder

New sexual orientation category of "mostly heterosexual" attracted to same sex partners

Technology and Sex Reassignment Surgery

Applying Social Research: Trans partner relationships: A qualitative exploration

Asexuality

Ally development model

Benefits of same sex monogamy

Positive experiences of LGBT individuals

Five stages couple goes through when there is disclosure in mixed orientation relationship

Rearing a gender variant (GV) child

Parental gender differences reaction to child's coming out

Gay fathers

Lower sexual satisfaction among non-heterosexuals than heterosexuals

Negative aspects of same-sex marriage—unrealistic expectations of family life

Parents are challenged to give up the idea of a biological grandchild from gay offspring.

Parents of lesbian and gay children seek schools which are racially diverse and gay friendly.

Class rather than the Black church may be more influential in homophobia attitudes.

Mate preferences of transgender individuals

The experience of transgender youth in middle school

"Bear" as a gay male identity

Religion may further complicate one's gay identity resulting in worse mental health.

Resistance to rape associated with decreased rape completion

California affirmative consent law

Spring Break at the Beach

Avoiding mixing alcohol types and using "protective behavioral strategies"

Triggers for leaving an abusive relationship

CPV—Child Parent Violence

Cyberstalking

Male rape

Cultural militarism creates context for making violence normative.

Some parents in Egypt arrange for their children to "marry" tourists to circumvent laws against having sex with children.

Relationship context in which abuse occurs

Teenagers whose parents are abusive are more likely to be abusive in their own relationships.

A woman who elopes or marries against the consent of the family may be killed in what is called an honor crime.

Revenge porn

Abuse of robots

Chapter 11: Planning for Parenthood

The narrative about having children has changed from "when" to "whether"

"Missing females" due to sex selection technology

Comparison of gay and heterosexual desire to have children

Co-parenting among teens

Family size and obesity of the children

Applying Social Research: Are male children still preferred?

Effect of infertility on individual and couple well-being

Experience of child born into lesbian family

Experience of children from Eastern Europe adopted by American parents

Effect on different causes of infertility on female sexual dysfunction

Why child-free by choice individuals changed their minds

Child-free viewed as least warm and most troubled

Cost of attending college in 18 years for one's child

Transnational commercial surrogacy

Acceptance of male contraceptive pill

China's one child policy

Fewer children for those who have children and for those now child-free

Regrets in having children are both circumstantial and specific to the child.

Embryo adoption

Having a child as an unmarried adult is now culturally approved of.

Chapter 12: Diversity in Parenting

The "Good Enough" Parent

Millennials as parents themselves

Safe Haven/Baby Moses Law

Personal Choices: Co-Sleeping with Ones Infant?

Family Policy: Childhood Vaccinations: Public Policy and Parental Rights

Parental empowerment

Drop in sexual satisfaction of first-time parents following birth of child

Comparison of time spouses with and without children spend together/impact on marriage

Comparison of child care work hours for egalitarian relationships

Parental warmth—trajectory across adolescents for fathers, mothers, grandparents, aunts

Trade-off for parents who teach children to think independently

American Academy of Pediatrics guidelines for screen time of children

Primary reason for adult children leaving and returning to family home

Effect of child under five on sex frequency of single parent mother

Changes in couple's relationship that are in period of empty nest

Following the rules to stay Facebook friends with your children

Texting symbols teenagers use

Fewer economic assets and fewer savings when adult children live with parents

Percent of parents monitoring teen's online activity

Quality time

Parenting foci differs

Mexican parents whose offspring emigrate to the United States do not become depressed.

Chapter 13: Money, Work, and Relationships

Chapter 14: Stress and Crisis in Relationships

Women's sleep is troubled by children in the house; men's sleep is troubled by unemployment and worry about household finances.

Low marital quality, loneliness, and Internet infidelity

Opioid use

Conditions under which an affair is associated with life satisfaction

Psychosocial treatment of opioid use has not been effective.

Substance abuse as "White drug exceptionalism" whereby White women are rarely portrayed as victims of drug culture

Undergraduates identified three major ways to avoid cheating, but were largely unsuccessful in using them.

Having cheated or been cheated upon is associated with identifying more behaviors—both emotional and sexual—as cheating.

Emotional and sexual infidelity are regarded as equally unacceptable.

Suicide attempts among the mentally ill are associated with experiencing lifetime trauma.

Chapter 15: Divorce, Remarriage, and Stepfamilies

High conflict divorce

Relationship with one's romantic partner after romantic relationship terminated

Discernment counseling—spouses on the brink of divorce reconcile/remain married

Percent of separations that end up as reconciliations

Number of years after wedding most couples divorce

Applying Social Research: Romantic Breakup: Difficult Loss of Some/Not Others

Self-Assessment: Positive and Negative Ex-Relationship Thoughts Scale

Technology and Postdivorce Co-Parenting

Estrangememt

Positive aspects of divorce as identified by undergraduates

Validity of "staying married for the children"

Adult children reacting to the late-life divorce of their parents

Postdivorce relationships with former stepparents

Conscious uncoupling as new approach to divorce

Stigmatization of divorce in Saudi Arabia

Same-sex divorce

Calling off the divorce

Economic resources provided by nonresident father and time spent with children

Mistakes divorcing individuals report that they made in getting married and selecting a partner

There is no one age one should marry to avoid divorce and have high marital satisfaction.

Shared parenting by high-conflict divorcing parents results in poorer adjustment for children

The ambivalence of divorce

Unequal housework is associated with divorce

Romantic heartbreak is associated with sexual values becoming more liberal

Annulments

Chapter 16: The Later Years

Education and international travel reduce filial piety

Effect of taking care of frail elderly in one's own home

Loneliness

Elderly who have "completed life" and no longer find meaning in life

Characteristics of lifestyle of the elderly in the "blue zone"

Effect of grandchild on decision of woman to retire

Cultural reframing of "the elderly" to be more affirming

Self-Assessment: Attitudes Toward Taking Care of Elderly Parents Scale

Support groups should be sought by those taking care of the mentally ill aging parent

What if? What if your parent's marriage is worse than divorce?

Living apart together is becoming an increasingly chosen option for the elderly.

New romantic love partner for 14 divorced or widowed women, 65-84

The younger the child, the more likely grandparents are to spend time with the grandchild.

Grandsons want support and advice from grandparents; granddaughters want friendship.

Daily exercise by the elderly has benefits for marital satisfaction.

Midlife emotional connection and support for autonomy continues into later life marriages.

A content analysis of "Hot in Cleveland" revealed sex as desirable for women over 50.

Physical exercise is associated with the stabilization of depression among the elderly.

While prevalent among the advanced elderly (e.g., 84), insomnia is generally mild.

Sexuality changes in elderly women

Older Tanzanian men report the difficult expectations of sexual masculinity

Effect of chronic low back pain on individuals and their partners

Reverse retirement occurs more often for those with children under 30 and mortgage debt.

"Successful aging" often used interchangeably with "healthy aging"

Drinking patterns of elderly spouses often mirror each other.

Elderly women not integrated into extended family networks were looking for love.

Applying Social Research: The Psychosocial Sources of Sexual Interest in Older Couples

Self-neglect cases—the elderly who live alone and are a danger to themselves

Chinese rural elderly who have cell phone happier than those with no cell phone

Less sex with aging does not translate into having a diminished marriage in terms of success.

Elderly siblings have limited contact with each other after their parents die.

Men are becoming more involved in the care-giving role.

Communication technology in residential care for the elderly can decrease loneliness.

Changing norms in China regarding putting one's parents in a nursing home

Dying alone is viewed differently by survivors and the soon-to-be deceased.

UNIQUE FEATURES OF THE TEXT

In addition to being student friendly, *Choices in Relationships* has several unique features that are included in every chapter.

Culture and Diversity

Rather than one chapter on diversity and inclusiveness, these themes are woven throughout the respective chapters. Examples include references to national and international data as well as culture and diversity. Some chapters emphasize diversity more than others. Chapter 6 on "Diversity in Marriage Relationships" includes sections on African American families, Hispanic/Latino families, Asian American families, immigrant families, poly families, military families, interracial marriages, international marriages, age-discrepant relationships and marriages, college marriages, and forced marriages.

Technology and the Family

From how people meet, whether through apps or online, to divorce and taking down Facebook images of the happy couple or family, technology impacts relationships. Each chapter features a Technology insert relevant to the topic of the chapter—for example, Love, Gender, Sexuality, and so forth—and how these advances require choices which have positive outcomes for individuals, couples, and families. Examples of these technology sections include "The Digital Language of Love," "Shebot, Hebot or Itbot?" and "Sexual Enhancement Products."

Self-Assessment Scales

Each chapter features one or more self-assessment scales that allow students to measure a particular aspect of themselves or their relationships. These are presented after Special Topic II on page 371.

Applying Social Research

To emphasize that *Choices in Relationships* is not a self-help trade book but a researched-based college textbook, we present a research application feature in every chapter and specify how new research may be applied to one's interpersonal relationships. Examples of new Applying Social Research features in this edition include "The Impact of Religion on Love, Relationships, and Sex," "Romantic Loss: Difficult Loss of Some/Not Others," and "Trans Partner Relationships: A Qualitative Exploration."

Family Policy

Congress is concerned about enacting policies that benefit families. In each chapter we review policies relevant to marriage and the family. Examples include men's health, singlism, and child marriage.

Personal Choices

An enduring popular feature of the text is the Personal Choices—detailed discussions of personal choice dilemmas. Examples include: "Who is the Best Person for You to Marry?" "Should I Get Involved in a Long-Distance Relationship?" and "How Much Do I Tell My Partner About My Past?"

Original Data

To supplement national and international data, the text provides original data from over 13,000 respondents collected by the authors and their colleagues.

Chapter Summaries

Each chapter ends with a summary, formatted as questions and answers, with each question relating back to the Learning Objectives listed at the beginning of every chapter.

Key Terms

Boldface type indicates key terms, which are defined and featured in the margin of the text as well as the glossary at the end of the text.

Web Links

The Internet is an enormous relationship resource. Internet addresses are provided at the end of each chapter. These have been checked at the time of publication to ensure that they are "live."

Special Topics

This edition features the Special Topics section on marriage and family careers and state-of-the art information about contraception and STIs.

SAGE edge for instructors

A password-protected resource site available at edge. sagepub.com/knox13e supports teaching, by providing high-quality content to create a rich learning environment for students. The SAGE edge for this book includes the following instructor resources:

- **Test banks** built on Bloom's Taxonomy provide a diverse range of test items.
- Editable, chapter-specific **PowerPoint slides** offer flexibility for creating a multimedia presentation for lectures
- **Lecture notes** align with the PowerPoint slides and summarize key concepts to help with preparation for lectures and class discussion
- Carefully selected **video and multimedia content** enhance exploration of key topics

- **Chapter-specific discussion questions** help launch engaging classroom interaction while reinforcing important content
- **Sample course syllabi** provide suggested models for structuring your course
- **Tables and figures** from the book are available for download
- **SAGE coursepacks** provide easy LMS integration

SAGE edge for students

The open-access companion website helps students accomplish their coursework goals in an easy-to-use learning environment, featuring:

- **Learning objectives** reinforce the most important material
- **eQuizzes** encourage self-guided assessment and practice
- **eFlashcards** hat strengthen understanding of key terms and concepts.
- Carefully selected **video and multimedia content** enhance exploration of key topics

SAGE Coursepacks

SAGE coursepacks make it easy to import our instructor and student resource content into your school's learning management system (LMS) with minimal effort. Intuitive and simple to use, **SAGE coursepacks** gives you the control to customize course content to meet your students' needs. The SAGE coursepacks are customized and curated for use in Blackboard, Canvas, Desire2Learn (D2L), and Moodle.

In addition to the content available on the Edge site, the coursepacks include:

- **Pedagogically robust assessment tools** that foster review, practice, and critical thinking:
- **Chapter tests** identify opportunities for student improvement, track student progress, and ensure mastery of key learning objectives.
- **Instructions** on how to use and integrate the comprehensive assessments and resources provided.
- **Assignable video and corresponding assessments** bring concepts to life to increase student engagement
- **Integrated links to the eBook version** make it easy to access the mobile-friendly version of the text, which can be read anywhere, anytime.

ACKNOWLEDGMENTS

Texts are always a collaborative and collective product. Josh Perigo (Acquisitions Editor) who signed the text and assembled a seasoned team to bring the manuscript to print, Sarah Downing (Production Editor) who oversaw the various stages of production, Alissa Nance (Content Development Editor) whose recommendations were most timely/helpful, Lynne Curry (Copyeditor) whose attention to detail was relentless, and to Zina Craft (Marketing Manager) who demonstrated her skill in putting the text in orbit. Others who provided support included Andrea Fulle (references), Noelle Cumberbatch (Editorial Assistant), and Taylor Hilliard (research). All were superb, and we appreciate their professionalism and attention to detail. We would also like to thank numerous photographers, including Trevor Werb, Chelsea Curry Edwards, and Maria McDonald for their superb photographs.

Reviewers for the 13th Edition

Sampson Lee Blair, The State University of New York – Buffalo

Rhonda Buckley, PhD, Texas Women's University

Christopher Chacha, Alabama Agricultural and Mechanical University

Chara Doyle, M.S.W., Rowan College at Glouchester County

Wendy Grab, Wilmington College

Dr. Heather Griffiths, Fayetteville State University

Terry Hatkoff, PhD, California State University Northridge

Sheldon Hefling, College of the Canyons

Rose Malcolm, University of Toledo

Dan Moen, PhD, LMFT, CFLE, Minnesota State University, Mankato

Claudia Porras Pyland, Associate Professor and Master's Director Counseling Psychology Program, Texas Women's University

Nancy Reeves, Rowan University

Loreen Wolfer, University of Scranton

We love the study, writing, and teaching of marriage and the family and recognize that no one has a corner on relationships. We welcome your insights, stories, and suggestions for improvement in the next edition of this text. We check our e-mail frequently and invite you to send us your thoughts. We will respond.

David Knox, Knoxd@ecu.edu

Caroline Schacht, CSchacht@suddenlink.net

I. Joyce Chang, Chang@ucmo.edu

ABOUT THE AUTHORS

David Knox, PhD, is professor of sociology at East Carolina University, where he teaches courtship and marriage, marriage and the family, and sociology of human sexuality. He is a relationship therapist and the author or coauthor of twelve books and over 130 professional articles. He regularly presents new research at annual conferences with undergraduates, graduate students, and colleagues. He and Caroline Schacht are married with three children and five grandchildren.

Caroline Schacht, MA in both sociology and family relations, is formerly an instructor of sociology at East Carolina University where she taught courtship and marriage, introduction to sociology, and the sociology of food. Her clinical work includes marriage and family relationships. She is a certified Romana Pilates instructor.

I. Joyce Chang, PhD is professor of Child and Family Development at the University of Central Missouri (UCM). Dr. Chang received her doctorate in human development and family sciences and master's degree in interdisciplinary studies (psychology, women studies, and statistics) from Oregon State University. Dr. Chang's primary research interests are high-risk behaviors, relationship development, and impacts of technology on families. She has received awards for teaching, research, and service. Dr. Chang has also taught and lectured in Sweden, Taiwan, and the Netherlands.

1

Choices in Relationships

An Introduction to Marriage, Family, and Diversity

*May your choices reflect your hopes,
not your fears.*

—Nelson Mandela

Learning Objectives

1.1.   Review facts about a "choices" view of relationships and various influences on those "choices"

1.2.   Describe the theoretical frameworks for studying marriage and the family

1.3.   Identify the elements, benefits, and types of marriage relationships

1.4.   Understand the definition and types of family

1.5.   Explain the distinction between marriage and family

1.6.   Summarize the research process and its caveats

1.7.   Identify changes in marriage and the family in the future

Master the content at
edge.sagepub.com/knox13e

With all the swiping and talk of Tinder, "friends with benefits," and cohabitation, one wonders why a text and course about marriage and the family? Are marriage and family done for? No. All polls and surveys provide essentially the same finding—that most individuals seek a marital and family context for their adult lifestyle (James-Kangal et al., 2018).

The reason? Marriage and family are the contexts of sustained emotional connections. Thus, this text focuses on human connections and relationship choices. Few experiences are more important. It is something all of us have in common—the search for meaningful love connections which result from deliberate, thoughtful, considered choices in one's relationships. Many of these intense and sustained love relationships end up in marriage and having a family—the bedrock of society. All individuals were born into a family—however one defines this concept—and most will end up in a family of their own.

"Have a happy marriage" remains the top value reported by 13,119 undergraduates with 44% selecting this value, 32% choosing "have career I love," and 21% opting for "have financial security" (Hall & Knox, 2019). In this chapter we review the definitions, types, and frameworks for viewing marriage and the family. We begin with the principle framework for this text—choices in relationships.

CHOICES IN RELATIONSHIPS— VIEW OF THE TEXT

Whatever your relationship goal, in this text we encourage a proactive approach of taking charge of your life and making wise relationship choices.

Making the right choices in your relationships, including marriage and family, is critical to your health, happiness, and sense of well-being. Your times of greatest elation and sadness will be in reference to your love relationships.

The central theme of this text is choices in relationships. Although we will make over 100 relationship decisions, among the most important are whether to marry, whom to marry, when to marry, whether to have children, whether to remain emotionally and sexually faithful to one's partner, and whether to protect oneself from sexually transmitted infections and unwanted pregnancy. Though structural and cultural influences are operative, a choices framework emphasizes that individuals have some control over their relationship destiny by making deliberate choices to initiate, nurture, or terminate intimate relationships.

Facts About Choices in Relationships

The facts to keep in mind when making relationship choices include the following:

Not to Decide Is to Decide

Not making a decision is a decision by default. If you are sexually active and decide not to use a condom, you have made a decision to increase your risk for an unwanted pregnancy and possibly contracting a sexually transmitted infection (STI). If you don't make a deliberate choice to end a relationship that is unfulfilling or going nowhere, you have made a choice to continue that relationship and eliminate the possibility of getting into a more positive and flourishing relationship. If you don't make a decision to be faithful to your partner, you have made a decision to be vulnerable to cheating. See the Personal Choices section for more examples of taking charge of your life by making deliberate choices.

Relationships thrive on unique experiences like sharing the sunset together.
Courtesy of Trevor Werb

If your feet don't move, you'll never get there.
Ann Marie Antenucci,
recalling the words of her immigrant grandmother

Action Must Follow a Choice

Making a decision but not acting on it is tantamount to no decision at all. You must pull the trigger. If you decide to only have safe sex, you must buy condoms, have them available, and use them.

Choices Involve Trade-Offs

By making one choice, you relinquish others. Every relationship choice you make will have a downside and an upside. If you decide to hook up with someone, you may enjoy the sexual excitement, but you may feel regretful in the morning and decide that the night will not result in a relationship. If you decide to marry, you will give up your freedom to pursue other emotional or sexual relationships or both. But, your marriage may result in a stable lifetime of shared memories.

Any partner that you select will also have characteristics that must be viewed as a trade-off. One woman noted of her partner, "he doesn't do text messaging or e-mail… he doesn't even know how to turn on a computer. But he knows how to build a house, plant a garden, and fix a car… and he loves me… trade-offs I'm willing to make."

Some Choices Require Correction

Some of our choices, although they seem correct at the time that we make them, turn out to be disasters. Once we realize that a choice has consistently negative consequences, it is important to stop defending it, make new choices, and move forward. Otherwise, we remain consistently locked into continued negative outcomes for a "bad" choice. The analogy is that no matter how far you have gone down the wrong road, you can always turn back.

It all depends on how we look at things, and not on how they are in themselves.
Carl G. Jung, psychoanalyst

PERSONAL CHOICES

Relationship Choices—Deliberately or by Default?

It is a myth that you can avoid making relationship decisions, because by default, not making a decision is a decision. Some examples follow:

- If you don't make a decision to pursue a relationship with a particular person, you have made a decision (by default) not to have a relationship with that person.

- If you do not decide to do the things that are necessary to improve your current relationship, you have made a decision to let the relationship slowly disintegrate.

- If you do not make a decision to be faithful to your partner, you have made a decision to be open to situations and relationships which may result in infidelity.

- If you do not make a decision to delay having intercourse, you have made a decision to have intercourse early in a relationship. Research suggests less regret with delaying the first intercourse (Farvid & Braun, 2017).

- If you are sexually active and do not make a decision to use birth control or a condom, you have made a decision to expose yourself to getting pregnant or to contracting an STI.

Throughout the text, as we discuss various relationship choices, consider that you automatically make a choice by being inactive—that not to make a choice is to make one. We encourage a proactive style whereby you make deliberate relationship choices. ●

TABLE 1.1

Five Generations in Recent History

	BORN	MAJOR LIFE EVENTS	HABITS	PERCENTAGE OF THE U.S. POPULATION
Traditionalists/Silent Generation	(1913-1945)	Years of the Great Depression, World War II veterans and civilians.	Traditional values	10%
Baby Boomers	(1946-1964)	Children of WWII Traditionalists.	Questioning of traditional values.	23%
Generation X	(1965-1979)	Generation of change, MTV, AIDS, diversity.	Children of boomers.	20%
Generation Y (Millennials)	(1980-1996)	Boomerang generation, delay marriage.	Loyalty to corporations is gone, frequent job changes.	23%
Generation Z	(1997-2012)	Grew up in context of terrorism. Skyrocketing college costs.	Also known as Plurals, App Generation, Homelanders, "Always on"	24%

Choices Include Selecting a Positive or a Negative View

As Thomas Edison progressed toward inventing the light bulb, he said, "I have not failed. I have found ten thousand ways that won't work."

In spite of an unfortunate event in your life, you can choose to see the bright side. Regardless of your circumstances, you can opt for viewing a situation in positive terms. A partner breaking up with you due to lack of love can be viewed as an opportunity to become involved in a new, mutual, love relationship. The discovery of your partner cheating on you can be viewed as an opportunity to open up communication channels with your partner and to develop a stronger connection. Discovering that you have a sexually transmitted infection can be viewed as a challenge to face adversity with your partner. It is not the event but your view of it that determines its effect on you.

Most Choices Are Revocable; Some Are Not

Most choices can be changed. For example, a person who has chosen to be sexually active with multiple partners can decide to be monogamous or to abstain from sexual relations in new relationships. People who have been unfaithful in the past can elect to be emotionally and sexually committed to a new partner.

Other choices are less revocable. For example, backing out of the role of parent is very difficult. Social pressure keeps most parents engaged, but the law, such as forced child support, is the backup legal incentive. Hence, the decision to have a child is usually irrevocable. Choosing to have unprotected sex may also result in a lifetime of coping with a sexually transmitted infection like herpes.

Choices of Generation Y

Generations vary and social scientists study and compare these cohorts, focusing on their habits and how they differ from previous generations (see Table 1.1). Much attention has been given to **Generation Y**, more commonly known as **millennials**, and their choices. Numbering about 80 million, they represent 23% of the U.S. population. The choices of this generation reveal a focus on enjoyment and flexibility. Rather than fixating on marriage, they "hang out," "hook up," and live together. Research shows that they aren't in a hurry to find "the one," to marry, or to begin a family (Klinenberg, 2012). Instead, many enjoy living alone. Their focus is on their educations and careers, and enjoying their freedom in the meantime. These changes are notable from previous generations, where marriage and childbearing were considered obligatory. Such trends may contribute to the negative stereotype that millennials are self-absorbed individuals. Another notable change in this generation stems from technology. Generation Y has been greatly influenced by technology, and the following generation, Generation Z, is the "always on" technology generation (Dimock, 2019). We will discuss how technology affects their choices in subsequent chapters.

Choices About the Use of Technology

Since the use of technology may have positive or negative consequences depending how it is used, individuals may be deliberate in their choices to maximize desired outcomes. For example, those in

Millennials: persons born between 1980 and 1996.

a new relationship make the choice whether to continue texting their previous partner, spouses make the choice to send a text message thanking each other for a previous behavior or lash out at a perceived miscue, and parents decide how much screen time for their children. Heterosexual spouses view interactive technology, such as cell phones, the Internet, and social networking sites, as both facilitating distraction as well as providing a mechanism for connection (Vaterlaus & Tulane, 2019). Individuals on the job market also make choices to "clean up their social media" from embarrassing photos. Individuals must also deal with issues of cell phone or game addiction or both, stalking, and ghosting.

Parents also decide about vlogging—the frequent recording and uploading of personal videos. *Family Fun Pack* is created by two teachers, Kristine and Matt. They have six kids and their Family Fun Pack video has 5.2 million subscribers and 9.4 billion views. While a substantial income can be gained from such uploading, the degree to which one should submit his or her children to growing up in public is an issue some families wrestle with (Luscombe, 2017).

Choices Are Influenced by the Stage in the Family Life Cycle

The choices a person makes tend to be individualistic or familistic, depending on the stage of the family life cycle—formally a series of stages individuals progress through, such as married couple, childbearing, and preschool age. The concept, though, doesn't apply to everyone since some never marry, don't have children, and so forth.

However, for the young, single person, individualism characterizes his or her thinking and choices. These individuals are concerned only with their own needs. Should they marry and have children, familistic values ensue as the needs of a spouse and children begin to influence behavioral choices. For example, evidence of familistic values and choices is reflected in the fact that spouses with children are less likely to divorce than spouses without children.

Global, Structural, Cultural, and Social Media Influences on Choices

Choices in relationships are influenced by global, structural, cultural, and media factors. This section reviews the ways in which globalization, social structure, and culture impact choices in relationships. Although a major theme of this book is the importance of taking active control of your life in making relationship choices, it is important to be aware that the social world in which you live restricts and channels such choices. For example, social disapproval for marrying someone of another race

is part of the reason that over 85% of adults in the United States are married to someone of the same race. Behler (2017) also found that high status males in high school have a greater opportunity to attract the partner of their choice; conversely, lower status males are more limited in their partner alternatives. The point is that social factors operate independent of individual factors of desire. Finally, the gender composition of a high school impacts the willingness of one to become involved in a romantic relationship. For example, Harknett and Cranney (2017) analyzed the behavior of 12,617 high school students and noted that when female classmates were more numerous than male classmates—thus giving the males the upper hand from a bargaining standpoint—the males were less likely to express desire for a romantic relationship, and hence, less commitment. Hence, love is impacted just by the numbers of specific genders in one's social world. Of course, social media allows individuals to interact and connect with a much broader pool of potential partners, so the disadvantage of gender ratios in high school may become irrelevant.

Globalization

Families exist in the context of globalization. Economic, political, and religious happenings throughout the world affect what happens in your marriage and family in the United States. When the United Kingdom voted to leave the European Union (Brexit), the stock market in the United States dropped 900 points in two days. Negative economic conditions are associated with reduced interest in social approval for getting married—the thinking is that stable economic conditions (e.g., a job) provide a more positive context for the marriage to flourish (Gassman-Pines et al., 2017). Schneider (2017) noted that marriage and family choices impacted by the recession in 2008 included a lower fertility rate, less relationship happiness, and fewer divorces.

The country in which you live also affects your happiness and well-being. For example, in the World Happiness Report, citizens in 150 countries were asked to indicate their level of life satisfaction on a scale from 1 (worst possible life for you) to 10 (best possible life for you). Citizens in Denmark, Switzerland, and Iceland averaged 7.5; those in Syria averaged 3.0; and those in the United States averaged 7.1 (Helliwell et al., 2016). The Internet, social media, and various news outlets provide global awareness so that families are no longer isolated units.

Social Structure

The social structure of a society consists of institutions, social groups, statuses, and roles.

1. **Institutions.** The largest elements of society are social **institutions**, which may be defined as established and enduring patterns of social relationships. The institution of the family in the United States is held as a strong value, as reflected by tax deductions for parents, family-friendly work policies, and government benefits for young mothers and their children (e.g., the WIC—Women, Infants and Children—program).

In addition to the family, major institutions of society include the economy, education, religion, and government. Institutions affect individual decision-making. For example, you live in a capitalist society where economic security is important. In effect, the more time you spend focused on obtaining money, the less time you have for relationships. You are now involved in the educational institution that will impact your choice of a mate—for example, college-educated people tend to select and marry one another. Religion also affects relationship choices: Devout members select each other as a life partner. Spouses who "believe in the institution of the family" are less likely to divorce.

2. **Social groups.** Institutions are made up of social groups, defined as two or more people who share a common identity, interact, and form a social relationship. Most individuals spend their days going between social groups. You may awaken in the context of a social group of a roommate, partner, parents, siblings or spouse. From there you go to class with other students, lunch with friends, and work with other employees. These social groups have various influences on your choices. Your roommate influences what other people you can have in your room for how long, your friends may want to eat at a particular place, your fellow workers will ignore you or interact with you, and your parents may want you to run an errand if you live at home or want you to come home for the weekend if you live at school.

Students sometimes argue that they—as individuals—make choices. In reality, the choices they make are only the ones the social context permits. For example, a Mormon woman married to a Mormon man in the Mormon Church has almost no choice to be "child-free." Change her context so that she is no longer a member of the Mormon Church and is married to a non-Mormon who wants to be child-free. She is now able to be child-free but only because her context has changed. Individuals are not important—their context is (Zusman, 2019).

While on campus, your interpersonal choices are influenced mostly by your partner and peers. Thus, selecting a partner and peers is important.

For example, partner selection among heterosexual individuals is often influenced by the mating gradient. The **mating gradient** is a norm that gives social approval to men who seek out younger, less educated, and less financially secure female partners and to women who seek out male partners that are older, more educated, and more financially secure. High-status men benefit the most from the mating gradient, while high-status women and low-status men may be penalized. These dynamics often play out on college campuses, where first-year female students seem to have more viable options than those that are available to fourth-year female students. Based on women's tendency to date older men and vice versa, the pool of eligible partners each year appears to decrease for women and increase for men. Their choices are affected by social structure and class rank.

Social groups may be categorized as primary or secondary. **Primary groups**, which tend to involve small numbers of individuals, are characterized by interaction that is intimate and informal. A family is an example of a primary group. Persons in our primary groups are those who love us and have lifetime relationships with us. In contrast to primary groups, **secondary groups,** which may be small or large, are characterized by interaction that is impersonal and formal. Your classmates, teachers, and coworkers are examples of individuals in your secondary groups. Unlike your parents, siblings, and spouse, members of your secondary groups do not have an enduring emotional connection with you and are more transient.

3. **Statuses.** Just as institutions consist of social groups, social groups consist of statuses. A status is a position a person occupies within a social group. The statuses we occupy largely define our social identity. The statuses in a family may consist of mother, father, child, sibling, and stepparent. In discussing family issues, we refer to statuses such as teenager, partner, and spouse. Statuses are relevant to choices in that many choices can significantly

....

Institution: established and enduring pattern of social relationships (e.g., the family).

Mating gradient: norm which gives social approval to men who seek out younger, less educated, less financially secure women and vice versa.

Primary groups: small numbers of individuals among whom interaction is intimate and informal.

Secondary groups: groups in which the interaction is impersonal and formal.

change one's status. Making decisions that change one's status from single person to spouse to divorced person can influence how people feel about themselves and how others treat them.

4. **Roles.** Every status is associated with many roles, or sets of rights, obligations, and expectations. Our social statuses identify who we are; our roles identify what we are expected to do. Roles guide our behavior and allow us to predict the behavior of others. Spouses adopt a set of obligations and expectations associated with their status. By doing so, they are better able to influence and predict each other's behavior.

Because individuals occupy a number of statuses and roles simultaneously, they may experience role conflict. For example, the role of the parent may conflict with the role of the spouse, employee, or student. If your child needs to be driven to the math tutor, your spouse needs to be picked up at the airport, your employer wants you to work late, and you have a final exam all at the same time, you are experiencing role conflict.

5. **Socioeconomic status and minority status.** Ball et al. (2019) noted differential use of technology in reference to socioeconomic status and minority status and emphasized the concept of emotional cost. Some individuals, such as those with lower socioeconomic and minority status, are anxious and stressed when presented with digital technology, which results in lower use. This lower use not only impacts career paths with fewer STEM (science, technology, engineering, and mathematics) career options but, by extension, may also impact relationships since the person is not "plugged" into the technological system of communicating with others, such as, text messaging.

Culture

Just as social structure refers to the parts of society, culture refers to the meanings and ways of living that characterize people in a society. Two central elements of culture are beliefs and values.

1. **Beliefs.** Beliefs refer to definitions and explanations about what is true. The beliefs of an individual or couple influence the choices they make. For example, unmarried emerging adults who have less confidence and think divorce is likely are slower to get married (Arocho, 2019). Couples who believe that young children flourish best with a full-time parent in the home will make greater adjustments in their work life to accommodate having a parent in the home than those who feel that day care offers opportunities for enrichment.

2. **Values.** Values are standards regarding what is good and bad, right and wrong, desirable and undesirable. Values influence choices. Valuing **individualism** leads to making decisions that serve the individual's interests rather than the family's interests (**familism**). Forty-four percent of 13,111 undergraduates agreed that "I would divorce my spouse if I fell out of love" (Hall & Knox, 2019). Allowing one's personal love feelings to dictate the stability of a marriage is a highly individualistic value. "What makes me happy?" is the focus of the individualist, not "What makes my family happy?" (familism). Different questions from different cultural contexts result in different answers and different outcomes. Routledge (2019) suggested that there is a connection between our increasingly individualistic society and social media use: "The more socially disconnected or alienated people feel as a result of the individualistic worldview that privileges personal freedom and independence over social duty and interdependence, the more they may look to social media to meet their basic social needs, even if online connections are poor substitutes for deeper in-person relationships."

Related to familism is **collectivism,** which emphasizes doing what is best for the group, not specific to the family group; collectivism is characteristic of traditional Asian, South American, and African families. Park et al. (2017) also emphasized that individualism and personal fulfillment were influential in decreasing the percent, now at 57%, of South Koreans who stated that marriage was desirable. Those who live together, who seek a child-free lifestyle, and who divorce are more likely to be operating from an individualistic perspective than those who do not live together before marriage, rear children, and stay married, a familistic value. Because families are so important in collectivist societies, the selection of marriage partners is a crucial event for both the partners and their families. Collectivistic values are

....

Individualism: making decisions that serve the individual's interests rather than the family's.

Familism: value that decisions are made in reference to what is best for the family.

Collectivism: pattern in which one regards group values and goals as more important than one's own values and goals.

at play when a partner ends the relationship because his or her partner goes against the families' wishes.

These elements of social structure and culture play a central role in making interpersonal choices and decisions. One of the goals of this text is to emphasize the influence of social structure and culture on your interpersonal decisions. Sociologists refer to this awareness as the **sociological imagination** or sociological mindfulness. For example, though most people in the United States assume that they are free to select their own sex partner, this choice—or lack of it—is heavily influenced by structural and cultural factors. Most people hang out with, date, have sex with, and marry a person of the same racial background. Structural forces influencing race relations include segregation in housing, religion, and education. The fact that African Americans and White Americans live in different neighborhoods, worship in different churches, and often attend different schools makes meeting a person of a different race unlikely. When such encounters occur, prejudices and bias may influence these interactions to the point that individuals are hardly "free" to act as they choose. Hence, cultural values transmitted by parents and peers may not support or promote mixed racial interaction, relationship formation, or marriage. Consider the last three relationships in which you were involved, the racial similarity, and the structural and cultural influences on your choices.

Other Influences on Relationship Choices

Aside from structural and cultural influences on relationship choices, other influences include one's family of origin, the family in which you were reared, and one's family of procreation, individual personality, previous choices, and hormones. We discuss these first two below.

> The cascade of hormones that rains down on humans when they first fall in love can sometimes blind them to their poor choices.
>
> Belinda Luscombe, journalist/novelist

Family of Origin (FOO)

Your family of origin is a major influence on your relationship choices. Coming from a family whose parents are married and who love each other predicts not only the positive meanings you attach to marriage (Barr & Simons, 2018) but the happiness for your own relationships with both your spouse and

Religion has an enormous influence on relationship choices.

children. Experiences in one's family of orientation have also been instrumental in influencing adolescents to make wise choices and stay out of trouble (Animosa et al., 2018). For example, adolescents whose parents divorce have a temporary increase in delinquent behavior (Boccio & Beaver, 2019).

One's siblings in the family of origin are also influential in one's relationship choices. Killoren et al. (2019) examined the messages about dating and sexuality shared by 62 sister dyads which confirm the importance of sisters in the socialization of each other. For example, a 19-year-old told her younger sister about the importance of similar values in a partner:

> Find someone who's like you. I think it comes down to your values being the same. If we didn't agree about religious or political things…I couldn't do that. I'm pretty outspoken about that kind of stuff and so if you can't take me being outspoken about it and be out-spoken with me, we have an issue.

Sociological imagination: the influence of social structure and culture on interpersonal decisions.

The Impact of Religion on Love, Relationships, and Sex

Religion is considered one of the most influential social institutions that impact the daily lives of individuals. Scholars have argued that secularization among emerging adults is rapidly occurring within our society. However, findings from this study indicate that religion still impacts beliefs and values within young adults that translate into life's choices.

Data

Analysis of data on 6,068 undergraduates who completed an Internet survey revealed how religiosity was associated with choices about love, relationships, and sexuality. The sample was 82% White, 55% female, and heterosexual (22%). The average age of the respondents was 19.91 years (Hall & Knox, 2019).

Findings

Respondents identified their religiosity along a continuum including very religious (5), moderately religious (4), about midway (3), moderately not religious (2) and not religious at all (1). Those significantly more likely to report being "very" or "moderately" religious were Black and heterosexual. There were no significant differences between women and men.

Higher religiosity was also significantly associated with certain beliefs. For example, agreeing with the statement "I believe that there is only one true love that never comes again" corresponded with being more religious. Religion encourages the idea that love is destined and that one may be destined to have only one true love in a lifetime. Praying for one's soul mate reflects a belief that there is one soul mate per person.

Being religious was significantly related to unwillingness to divorce if one fell out of love, revealing a strong connection between the level of self-identified religiosity and commitment to marriage. Religion encourages lifetime commitment ("until death do us part")—just because one may have fallen out of love was not viewed as an acceptable reason for divorce.

Being religious was also significantly related to less willingness to end a relationship with a cheating partner, perhaps revealing the value for forgiveness. A willingness to live with a nonmarital partner was also lower for religious respondents since religion encourages individuals to avoid premarital sex or cohabitation or both before marriage. Previously, persons who lived together before marriage were referred to as "living in sin."

Respondents who were religious were also significantly less likely to have looked for a partner on the Internet. Religion encourages individuals to look to divine sources for one's partner (e.g., "I have prayed to God to send me someone") rather than to rely on technology which suggests one's life partner is not "heaven sent" or "divinely selected." ●

Source: Adapted and abridged from K. Fox, D. Knox, S. S. Hall, and Douglas Kuck. 2019. RELIGIOSITY: Impact on love, relationships and sexual values/behaviors. Poster, Southern Sociological Society, Annual meeting, Atlanta, April.

Personality

One's personality—whether introverted, extroverted, passive, or assertive—also influences choices. For example, people who are assertive are more likely than those who are passive to initiate conversations with someone they are attracted to at a party. People who are very quiet and withdrawn may never choose to initiate a conversation even though they are attracted to someone. Similarly, certain personality traits can affect the quality of one's relationship. Having a partner who is lazy or dishonest may lead individuals to be unhappy and end their relationship.

Social Media

Involvement on social media has an impact on relationship choices. Abbasi and Alghamdi (2018) noted how spending a lot of time on social media is related to lower relationship satisfaction and openness to infidelity. Not only is time spent on social media time not spent with one's partner, it is time that individuals may spin up alternative relationships via interacting with persons they meet on social media.

THEORETICAL FRAMEWORKS FOR VIEWING MARRIAGE AND THE FAMILY

Although we emphasize choices in relationships as the framework for viewing marriage and the family, other conceptual theoretical frameworks are helpful in understanding the context of relationship decisions. All **theoretical frameworks** are the same in that they provide a set of interrelated principles designed to explain a particular phenomenon and provide a point of view. In essence, theories are explanations.

Social Exchange Framework

The **social exchange framework** is one of the most commonly used theoretical perspectives in marriage and the family. The framework views interaction and choices in terms of cost and profit.

The social exchange framework also operates from a premise of **utilitarianism**—the theory that individuals rationally weigh the rewards and costs associated with behavioral choices. A social exchange view of marital roles emphasizes that spouses negotiate the division of labor on the basis of exchange. For example, one partner may spend more time on child care in exchange for the other earning an income.

Family Life Course Development Framework

The **family life course development** framework emphasizes the important role transitions of individuals that occur in different periods of life and in different social contexts. For example, a young unmarried couple may become cohabitants, then parents, grandparents, retirees, and widows. While the family life course development framework identifies traditional stages through which most individuals pass, not all do so.

The family life course developmental framework has its basis in sociology—for example, role transitions—whereas the **family life cycle** has its basis in psychology, which emphasizes the various developmental tasks family members face across time, such as marriage, childbearing, preschool, school-age children, teenagers, and so on. If developmental tasks at one stage are not accomplished, functioning in subsequent stages will be impaired. For example, one of the developmental tasks of early American marriage is to emotionally and financially separate from one's family of origin. If such separation from parents does not take place, independence as individuals and as a couple may be impaired.

....

Theoretical frameworks: a set of interrelated principles designed to explain a particular phenomenon.

Social exchange framework: views interaction and choices in terms of profit and loss.

Utilitarianism: individuals rationally weigh the rewards and costs associated with behavioral choices.

Family life course development: the stages and process of how families change over time.

Family life cycle: stages that identify the various developmental tasks family members face across time.

Structure-Function Framework

The **structure-function framework** emphasizes how marriage and family contribute to society. Just as the human body is made up of different parts that work together for the good of the individual, society is made up of different institutions—family, religion, education, economics— that work together for the good of society. Functionalists view the family as an institution with values, norms, and activities meant to provide stability for the larger society. Such stability depends on families performing various functions for society.

First, families serve to replenish society with socialized members. Because our society cannot continue to exist without new members, we must have some way of ensuring a continuing supply. However, just having new members is not enough. We need socialized members—those who can speak our language and know the norms and roles of our society.

The case of Genie Wiley is a classic example of why socialization is important in our society. Genie is a young girl who was discovered in the 1970s; she had been kept in isolation in one room in her California home for 12 years by her abusive father. She could barely walk and could not talk. Although provided intensive therapy at UCLA and the recipient of thousands of dollars of funded research, Genie progressed only slightly. Today, she is in her late 50s, institutionalized, and speechless. Her story illustrates the need for socialization; the role of institutions like parenthood and the obligation to nurture

---

CULTURE AND DIVERSITY

Aware that the family, which consists of a woman and a child, is the primary source of new members for an expanding group, Boko Haram kidnapped 276 girls at the Government Secondary School Chibok, Borno State, Nigeria, in 2014 in an act of sexual and gender-based violence (SGBV) against women. Boko Haram construes women as the bearers of their future despite its brutality toward them—mass rape of women, consequent impregnation and kidnapping the offspring (Oriola, 2017). Hence the goal of Boko Haram was to replace the family and bring up the girls to believe in their values and norms. Due to some of the girls escaping and others being exchanged by the Nigerian government for the release of five Boko Haram commanders, about half have been returned. With the presidential bid of Obiageli Ezekwesili, who began the Bring Back Our Girls campaign, there is hope to find and return the missing girls to their "real" family contexts (Nugent, 2018).

....

Structure-function framework: emphasizes how marriage and family contribute to society.

and socialize offspring ensure that this socialization will occur.

Second, marriage and the family promote the emotional stability of the respective spouses. Marriage ideally provides a context for people to share their lives and experiences and help each other cope during difficult times. While a partner is not a stand-in for a therapist, he or she can provide emotional support.

Children also need people to love them and to give them a sense of belonging. This need can be fulfilled in a variety of family contexts, including two-parent families, single-parent families, and extended families. The affective function of the family is one of its major benefits. No other institution focuses so completely on meeting the emotional needs of its members as marriage and the family.

Third, families provide economic support for their members. Although modern families are no longer self-sufficient economic units, they provide food, shelter, and clothing for their members. One need only consider the homeless in our society to be reminded of this important function of the family.

In addition to the primary functions of replacement, emotional stability, and economic support, other functions of the family include the following:

- **Physical care**—Families provide the primary care for the adults, their infants, children, and aging parents.

- **Regulation of sexual behavior**—Spouses in many societies are expected to confine their sexual behavior to each other, which reduces the risk of having children who do not have socially and legally bonded parents.

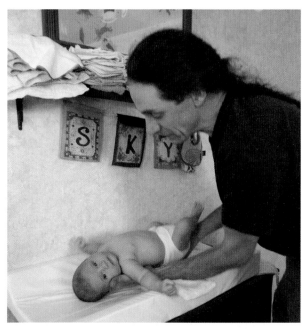

Parents are on the front line providing basic physical care.

- **Status placement**—Being born into a family provides social placement of the individual in society. One's family of origin largely determines one's social class, religious affiliation, and future occupation. The Kennedy family provides an example of multiple children being born into high status families, many of whom became politicians.

- **Social control**—Spouses in high-quality, durable marriages provide social control for each other that results in less criminal behavior. Parole boards often note that the best guarantee against recidivism is a nonconvicted spouse who expects the partner to get a job and avoid criminal behavior and who reinforces these behaviors (Andersen et al., 2015).

Conflict Framework

Conflict framework views individuals in relationships as competing for valuable resources like time, money, and power. Conflict theorists recognize that family members have different goals and values that create conflict. Adolescents want freedom, while parents want their child to get a good night's sleep, stay out of trouble, and excel academically.

Conflict theorists also view conflict not as good or bad but as a natural and normal part of relationships. They regard conflict as necessary for the change and growth of individuals, marriages, and families. Cohabitation relationships, marriages, and families all have the potential for conflict. Cohabitants are in conflict about commitment to marry, spouses are in conflict about the division of labor, and parents are in conflict with their children over rules such as curfew, chores, and their choice of friends.

Conflict theory is also helpful in understanding choices in relationships with regard to mate selection and jealousy. Singles are in competition with other singles for a desirable mate. Such conflict is particularly evident in the case of older, often widowed women in competition for the few elderly men.

Symbolic Interaction Framework

The **symbolic interaction framework** views marriages and families as symbolic worlds in which the various members give meaning to one another's behavior. Human behavior can be understood only by the meaning attributed to behavior. The term *symbolic interaction* refers to the process of

....

Conflict framework: the view that individuals in relationships compete for valuable resources.

Symbolic interaction framework: views marriages and families as symbolic worlds in which the various members give meaning to each other's behavior.

interpersonal interaction and involves the concepts of the definition of the situation, the looking-glass self, the self-fulfilling prophecy, and taking the role of the other.

Definition of the Situation

Two people who have just spotted each other at a party are constantly defining the situation and responding to those definitions. Is the glance from the other person (1) an invitation to approach, (2) an approach, or (3) a misinterpretation—was he or she looking at someone else? The definition each partner has will affect their interaction.

Looking-Glass Self

The image people have of themselves is a reflection of what other people tell them about themselves. People develop an idea of who they are by the way others act toward them. If no one looks at or speaks to them, they will begin to feel unsettled. Similarly, family members constantly hold up social mirrors for one another into which the respective members look for definitions of self. Parents are particularly intent on holding up positive social mirrors for their children when they say, "You are a good student and we are proud of you."

Self-Fulfilling Prophecy

Once people define situations and the behaviors in which they are expected to engage, they are able to behave toward one another in predictable ways. Such predictability of behavior affects subsequent behavior. If you feel that your partner expects you to be faithful, your behavior is likely to conform to these expectations. The expectations thus create a self-fulfilling prophecy.

Taking the Role of the Other

"The ability to put oneself in the role of the other. . .to be empathic about what another is experiencing. . . is related not only to one's ability to cope with difficulties but enhances one's relationship satisfaction" (Levesque et al., 2014). Hence, having the ability of understand emotionally what another is experiencing has both individual and relationship payoffs.

Family Systems Framework

The **family systems framework** views each member of the family as part of a system and the family as a unit that develops norms of interacting, which may be explicit. For example, parents specify when their children must stop texting for the evening and complete homework. Or the family norms may be implicit: spouses expect fidelity from each other. These rules serve various functions, such as the allocation of keeping the education of offspring on track and solidifying the emotional bond of the spouses.

Rules are most efficient if they are flexible. For instance, they should be adjusted over time in response to a child's growing competence. A rule about not leaving the yard is appropriate for a 4-year-old but inappropriate for a 16-year-old.

Family members also develop boundaries that define the individual and the group and separate one system or subsystem from another. A boundary may be physical, such as a closed bedroom door, or social, such as expectations that family problems will not be aired in public. Boundaries may also be emotional, such as communication, which maintains closeness or distance in a relationship. Some family systems are cold and indifferent; others are warm and nurturing.

Family systems may be open, in that they are receptive to information and interaction with the outside world, or closed, in that they feel such contact is harmful. The Amish have a closed family system and, in the past, have had minimal contact with the outside world. More recently the Amish have begun to use cell phones and watch reality TV.

Human Ecology Framework

The **human ecology framework**, also known as the ecological perspective, looks at family as an ecosystem which interacts with the environment. The well-being of individuals and families cannot be considered apart from the well-being of the environment. For example, nutrition and housing are important to the functioning of families. If a family does not have enough to eat or adequate housing, it will not be able to function at an optimal level. The human ecology framework also includes how individuals and couples interact in the various environments of the home, school and workplace.

Feminist Framework

Although a **feminist framework** views marriage and family as contexts of inequality and oppression for women, today some feminists seek equality in their relationships with their partners. There are many different feminist perspectives, including lesbian feminism, emphasizing oppressive heterosexuality;

Family systems framework: views each member of the family as part of a system and the family as a unit that develops norms of interaction.

Human ecology framework: views the family and the environment as an ecosystem.

Feminist framework: views marriage and family as contexts of inequality and oppression for women.

psychoanalytic feminism, focusing on cultural domination of men's phallic-oriented ideas and repressed emotions; and standpoint feminism, stressing the neglect of women's perspective and experiences in the production of knowledge (Lorber, 1998). Regardless of which feminist framework is being discussed, all feminist frameworks have the themes of inequality and oppression. In addition, this framework has been adapted to examine other inequalities and oppressions such as sexism, lookism, and heterosexism.

Couple and Family Technology Framework

In response to the explosion of technology, the couple and family technology framework (CTF) focuses on the roles, rules, and boundaries in the respective contexts (Cravens, 2015; Hertlein & Blumer, 2013). This theory suggests that technology impacts the structure and process of couples and families. For example, what roles are partners and spouses to play in regard to each others' texts, emails, blogs, Internet surfing, and Facebook, Instagram, Twitter, and Snapchat accounts?

What are the rules about the use of technology in regard to adult sites? And what are the boundaries in regard to interacting with others? Earlier we noted how social media can leave a "social trail" that may need to be "cleaned" from being visible to potential employers who can use technology to screen applicants. The CFT framework emerged since the existing frameworks did not address the new issues brought on by new technology in communication. As the title of this text and the technology features in every chapter suggest, the CFT framework will be evident throughout.

The major theoretical frameworks for viewing marriage and the family are summarized in Table 1.2.

TABLE 1.2

Theoretical Frameworks for Marriage and the Family

THEORY	DESCRIPTION	CONCEPTS	LEVEL OF ANALYSIS	STRENGTHS	WEAKNESSES
Social Exchange	In their relationships, individuals seek to maximize their benefits and minimize their costs.	Benefits Costs Profit Loss	Individual Couple Family	Provides explanations of human behavior based on evaluation of outcome.	Assumes that people act rationally and all behavior is calculated.
Family Life Course Development	Families pass through stages.	Stages Transitions Timing	Institution Individual Couple Family	Families are seen as dynamic rather than static. Useful in working with families who are facing transitions in their life course.	Difficult to adequately test the theory through research.
Structure Function	The family has several important functions for society.	Structure Function	Institution	Emphasizes the relation of family to society, how families affect and are affected by the larger society.	Families with nontraditional structures (single-parent, same-sex couples) are not accounted for.
Conflict	Conflict in relationships is inevitable, due to competition over resources and power.	Conflict Resources Power	Institution Individuals	Views conflict as a normal part of relationships and as necessary for change and growth.	Sees all relationships as conflictual, and does not acknowledge cooperation.
Symbolic Interaction	People communicate through symbols and give meaning to the behavior or others.	Definition of the situation Looking-glass self Self-fulfilling prophecy	Individual Couple	Emphasizes the perceptions of individuals, not just objective reality.	Ignores the larger social interaction context and minimizes the influence of external forces.

(Continued)

TABLE 1.2 (Continued)

Family Systems	The family is a system of interrelated parts that function together to maintain the unit.	Subsystem Roles Rules Boundaries Open system Closed system	Couple Family	Very useful in working with families who are having serious problems (violence, alcoholism). Describes the effect family members have on each other.	Based on work with systems, troubled families, and may not apply to nonproblem families.
Feminism	Women's experience is central and different from man's experience of social reality.	Inequality Power Oppression	Institution Individual Couple Family	Exposes inequality and oppression as explanations for frustrations in women's experience.	Multiple branches of feminism may inhibit central accomplishment of increased equality.
Human Ecology	Family as ecosystem which interacts with the environment.	Ecosystem Interaction	Individual Couple Environment	Emphasizes interaction of humans and environment	Linkages sometimes seem contrived
Couple and Family Technology	Impact of use of technology on relationships	Roles Rules Boundaries	Individual Couple Family	Emphasizes need for communication related to technology use	Limited research to suggest optimum guidelines

MARRIAGE

While young adults think of marriage in terms of love and a committed life together, the federal government regards marriage as a legal relationship that two individuals of either sex work together for the reproduction, physical care, and socialization of children. Beginning in 2015, this legal definition changed from one man and one woman to include same-sex partners marrying each other. Each society works out its own details of what marriage is.

In the United States, **marriage** is a legal contract between two people of any sexual orientation and the state in which they reside. That contract specifies the economic relationship between the couple: they become joint owners of their income and debt.

On June 26, 2015, the Supreme Court of the United States ruled that state laws prohibiting same-sex marriage were unconstitutional, thus legalizing marriage for sexual and gender minorities (SGM). Persons of all sexual orientations now have access to legal marriage and are included in the definitions of marriage and the family.

The frequency of marriage is changing in the United States. Of all adults in the United States, 50% are married. This percent is down from 72% in 1960. But most of those not currently married will eventually marry. Women are delaying marriage until age 28; men, 30 (Geiger & Livingston, 2019). However, marriage is still quite common. About 2.25 million marriages occur every year in the United States. (National Center for Health Statistics, Marriage and Divorce, 2018). Of adult women and men in the United States over the age of 65, 96% have married at least once (Wang, 2018). The decision to marry is generally not taken lightly as it's viewed as a lifelong commitment. To assess your own views of marriage, refer to the Self-Assessment: Attitudes Toward Marriage Scale on page 371. Various elements implicit in the marriage relationship in the United States are discussed in the following section.

Elements of Marriage

No one definition of marriage can adequately capture its meaning. Rather, marriage might best be understood in terms of its various elements. Some of these include the following:

Legal Contract

Marriage in our society is a legal contract into which two people of different or the same sex and legal age may enter when they are not already married to someone else. The age required to marry varies by state and is usually from 16 to 18, although most states set 17 or 18 as the requirement.

In some states (e.g., Alabama) individuals can marry at age 14 with parental or judicial consent. In California, individuals can marry at any age with parental consent. The marriage license certifies that a legally empowered representative of the state performs the ceremony, often with two witnesses present. The marriage contract gives power to the state

....

Marriage: a legal relationship that binds a couple together for the reproduction, physical care, and socialization of children.

over the couple—should they decide to divorce, the state can dictate the terms—who gets custody of the children, division of property, and child support. One of the reasons some individuals cite for not marrying is to "keep the government out of my business."

Under the laws of the state, the license means that spouses will jointly own all future property acquired and that each will share in the estate of the other. In most states, whatever the deceased spouse owns is legally transferred to the surviving spouse at the time of death. In the event of divorce and unless the couple has a prenuptial agreement, the property is usually divided equally regardless of the contribution of each partner. The license also implies the expectation of sexual fidelity in the marriage. Though less frequent because of no-fault divorce, infidelity is a legal ground for both divorce and alimony in some states.

The marriage license is also an economic authorization that entitles a spouse to receive payment from a health insurance company for medical bills if the partner is insured, to collect Social Security benefits at the death of one's spouse, and to inherit from the estate of the deceased. Spouses are also responsible for each other's debts. One mother warned her son, "If you marry her, you are taking on her $50,000 in student loan debt."

Though the courts are reconsidering the definition of what constitutes a "family," the law is currently designed to protect spouses, not lovers or cohabitants. An exception is **common-law marriage**, in which a heterosexual couple who cohabits and presents themselves as married will be regarded as legally married in those states that recognize such marriages. Common-law marriages exist in fourteen states (Alabama, Colorado, Georgia, Idaho, Iowa, Kansas, Montana, New Hampshire, Ohio, Oklahoma, Pennsylvania, Rhode Island, South Carolina, and Texas) and the District of Columbia. Even in these states, not all persons can marry by common-law—they must be of sound mind, be unmarried, and must have lived together for a certain period of time, such as three years. Persons married by common law who move to a non-common-law state are recognized as being married in the state to which they move.

Emotional Relationship

Ninety-three percent of married adults in the United States point to love as their top reason for getting married. Other reasons include making a lifelong commitment (87%), having companionship (81%), and having children (59%) (Cohn, 2013). American emphasis on love as a reason to marry is not shared throughout the world. Individuals in other cultures, such as India, do not require feelings of love

Common-law marriage: a heterosexual cohabiting couple presenting themselves as married.

Kissing is one way of expressing emotional intimacy.
Courtesy of Stacy Huff

to marry—love is expected to follow, not precede marriage. In these countries, parental approval and similarity of religion, culture, education, and family background are considered more important criteria for marriage than love. While love is an important motivation for marriage, it is companionship in the United States which promotes a couple in courtship to remain committed and move toward marriage (Ogolsky et al., 2016).

Sexual Monogamy

Marital partners generally expect sexual fidelity. Over two thirds (68%) of 13,111 undergraduates agreed with the statement, "I would divorce a spouse who had an affair" (Hall & Knox, 2019). There is also a stigma associated with couples who are nonmonogamous (Cohen, 2016).

Legal Responsibility for Children

Although individuals marry for love and companionship, one of the most important reasons for the existence of marriage from the viewpoint of society is to legally bind a male and a female for the nurture and support of any children they may have. In our society, child rearing is the primary responsibility of the family, not the state.

Marriage is a relatively stable relationship that helps to ensure that children will have adequate care and protection, will be socialized for productive roles in society, and will not become the burden of those who did not conceive them. Even at divorce, the legal obligation of the noncustodial parent to the child is maintained through child-support payments.

Public Announcement

The legal binding of a couple in a public ceremony is often preceded by an engagement announcement. Following the ceremony there is a wedding announcement in the newspaper. Public knowledge of the event helps to solidify the commitment of the partners to each other and helps to marshal social and economic support to launch the couple into married life.

Types of Marriage

There are different types of marriage. Monogamy is the legal form in our country. With high marriage, divorce, and remarriage rates, some scholars may perceive our system as serial monogamy. Although we think of marriage in the United States as involving one man and one woman, other societies view marriage differently. **Polygamy** is a generic term for marriage involving more than two spouses. Polygamy occurs "throughout the world … and is found on all continents and among adherents of all world religions" (Zeitzen, 2008). Polygamy is against the law in America and Canada—individuals are prosecuted who have multiple legal wives. Polygamists often evade the law by have only one legal wife, the rest being social wives. There are three forms of polygamy: polygyny, polyandry, and pantagamy.

Polygyny in the United States

Polygyny involves one husband and two or more wives and is practiced illegally in the United States by some religious fundamentalist groups. These groups are primarily in Arizona, New Mexico, and Utah as well as Canada and have splintered off from the Church of Jesus Christ of Latter-day Saints, commonly known as the Mormon Church. To be clear, the Mormon Church does not practice or condone polygyny; the church outlawed it in 1890. Those that split off from the Mormon Church represent only about 5% of Mormons in Utah. The largest offshoot is called the Fundamentalist Church of Jesus Christ of the Latter-day Saints (FLDS). Members of the group feel that the practice of polygyny is God's will. Joe Jessop, an elder of the FLDS had five wives, 46 children, and 239 grandchildren. Although the practice is illegal, polygynous individuals are rarely prosecuted because a husband will have only one legal wife while the others will be married in a civil ceremony. Women are socialized to bear as many children as possible to build up the "celestial family" that will remain together for eternity.

It is often assumed that polygyny in FLDS marriages exists to satisfy the sexual desires of the man, that the women are treated like slaves, and that jealousy among the wives is common. In most polygynous societies, however, polygyny has a political and economic rather than a sexual function. Polygyny, for members of the FLDS, is a means of having many children to produce a celestial family. In other societies, a man with many wives can produce a greater number of children for domestic or farm labor. Wives are not treated like slaves, although women have less status than men in general; all household work is evenly distributed, and each wife is given her own house or private sleeping quarters. In FLDs households, jealousy is minimal because the female is socialized to accept that her husband is not hers alone but is to be shared with other wives "according to God's plan." The spouses work out a rotational system for conjugal visits, which ensures that each wife has equal access to sexual encounters, while the other wives take care of the children.

Independent of polygynous marriage, some couples want a three-way marriage. Examples have existed in Brazil and the Netherlands whereby one male was "married" to two females. While these are not legal marriages, they reflect the diversity of lifestyle preferences and patterns. Theoretically, the arrangement could be of any sex, gender, and sexual orientation. The example in the Netherlands was of a heterosexual man "married" to two bisexual women.

Polyandry

Tibetan Buddhists foster yet another brand of polygamy, referred to as **polyandry**, in which one wife has two or more (up to five) husbands. These husbands, who may be brothers, pool their resources to support one wife. Polyandry is a much less common form of polygamy than polygyny. The major reason for polyandry is economic. A family that cannot afford wives or marriages for each of its sons may find a wife for the eldest son only. Polyandry allows the younger brothers to also have sexual access to the one wife that the family is able to afford.

Pantagamy

Pantagamy is a formal arrangement that was practiced in communes, such as the one in Oneida, New York, in the 19th and 20th centuries which involves a group marriage in which each member of the group is "married" to the others. Pantagamy is, of course, illegal in the United States. Some polyamorous individuals see themselves in a group marriage.

Our culture emphasizes monogamous marriage and values individuals staying together to care for each other and their children. One cultural

---

Polygamy: a generic term for marriage involving more than two spouses.

Polygyny: type of marriage involving one husband and two or more wives.

Polyandry: type of marriage in which one wife has two or more husbands.

Pantagamy: a group marriage in which each member of the group is "married" to the others.

expression of this value is the existence of family policies—not to be confused with social policies—in the form of laws, policies, and services designed to support the family (Cherlin, 2019).

Benefits of Marriage

Most adults in America eventually marry. Doing so has enormous benefits. Researchers Knopfli et al. (2016) noted that spouses report greater health than those who are single or divorced. Superior health is only one of several advantages for being married (see Table 1.3 for a comparison of the never married with the married). The advantages of marriage over singlehood have been referred to as the **marriage benefit** and are true for first as well as subsequent marriages.

Explanations for the marriage benefit include economic resources, such as higher income, wealth, and the ability to afford health care; and social

An example of the degree to which marriage is regarded as critical to one's life, even after death, is the concept of **ghost marriage 冥婚**—marriage of the dead. The ghost marriage has been documented throughout Chinese history and is still practiced in certain regions. Parents who had children who never married and who died may arrange a ghost marriage for their deceased children. The marital union is believed to bring peace to their deceased children in the afterlife (Wang, 2016). The wedding ceremony for the ghost marriage can be arranged for two deceased people or between a living person and a dead person. The living person of the ghost marriage usually chooses to get married in real life. Chinese ghost marriage is a folk tradition without legal bond.

TABLE 1.3

Benefits of Marriage and the Liabilities of Singlehood

	BENEFITS OF MARRIAGE	LIABILITIES OF SINGLEHOOD
Health	Spouses have fewer hospital admissions, see a physician more regularly, and are sick less often. They recover from illness and surgery more quickly.	Single people are hospitalized more often, have fewer medical checkups, and are sick more often.
Longevity	Spouses live longer than single people.	Single people die sooner than married people.
Happiness	Spouses report being happier than single people.	Single people report less happiness than married people.
Sexual satisfaction	Spouses report being more satisfied with their sex lives, both physically and emotionally.	Single people report being less satisfied with their sex lives, both physically and emotionally.
Money	Spouses have more economic resources than single people.	Single people have fewer economic resources than married people.
Lower expenses	Two can live more cheaply together than separately.	Cost is greater for two singles than one couple.
Drug use	Spouses have lower rates of drug use and abuse.	Single people have higher rates of drug use and abuse.
Connected	Spouses are connected to more individuals who provide a support system—partner, in-laws, and so forth.	Single people have fewer individuals upon whom they can rely for help.
Children	Rates of high school dropouts, teen pregnancies, and poverty are lower among children reared in two-parent homes.	Rates of high school dropouts, teen pregnancies, and poverty are higher among children reared by single parents.
History	Spouses develop a shared history across time with significant others.	Single people may lack continuity and commitment across time with significant others.
Crime	Spouses are less likely to be involved in crime.	Single people are more likely to be involved in crime.
Loneliness	Spouses are less likely to report loneliness.	Single people are more likely to report being lonely.

Marriage benefit: the advantages of marriage over singlehood, including married persons being healthier and happier.

Ghost marriage: A marriage between two deceased parties or one deceased party with a living person. The Chinese ghost marriage is a folk tradition which does not involve a legal bond between the parties.

control with spouses—for example, ensuring partners moderate their alcohol or drug consumption or both, and don't ride motorcycles. The marriage benefit also involves spouses providing social, emotional, and psychosocial support as an in-resident counsellor and loving and caring partner (Rauer, 2013; Tumin & Zheng, 2018).

However, being married is not beneficial to all individuals in that marriage is associated with obesity (Rauer, 2013). In addition, people in self-assessed poor marriages are miserable and much less happy than unmarried people (Chapman & Guven, 2016).

Marriage—Then and Now

In her landmark book, *The Way We Never Were: American Families and the Nostalgia Trap*, Stephanie Coontz (2016) explained the myths we perpetuate about marriages and families which disappear under factual scrutiny. She also discussed her

Couple Preparation and Relationship Education

Whether couple preparation is known as marriage preparation, premarital counselling, or marriage education, the federal government has a vested interest in couple relationship or couple education programs. The estimated societal costs of divorce and family instability on communities, states, and the nation are a minimum of $33 billion; the economic cost for the couple getting divorced is between $15,000 and $20,000 (Clyde & Hawkins, 2019). The philosophy behind marriage preparation education is that building a fence at the top of a cliff is preferable to putting an ambulance at the bottom. To the degree that people select a mate wisely and have the skills to manage conflict, communicate, and stay married, there is greater economic stability for the family and less drain on social services in the United States for single-parent mothers and the needs of their children.

African American clergy have been particularly involved in marriage preparation. In a study comparing 141 members of seven primarily African American denominations with 793 clergy from the 15 largest, predominantly White, congregations. African American clergy were significantly more likely than clergy in the comparison group to address premarital content, to use a skills-based approach, to require a longer waiting period, more sessions, and more homework assignments, and to consider marriage preparation an important part of their ministry (Wilmoth & Blaney, 2016).

Kanter and Schramm (2018) emphasized the efficacy of "brief interventions" for marriage education and found 12 such programs amid large databases. These interventions included issues such as self-esteem, distress related to conflict, and gratitude that promoted healthy relationship functioning. The researchers concluded that such brief interventions can be helpful for promoting healthy relationships. McGinnis and Burr (2018) also found a correlation between couple relationship education and relationship satisfaction.

Over 2,000 public schools nationwide offer a marriage preparation course. In Florida, all public high school seniors are required to take a marriage and relationship skills course. Persons who have done so get a $32.00 discount on their marriage license and may skip the three-day waiting period. Persons seeking a marriage license in Florida may also take a premarital course online which provides 21 chapters to choose from. Individuals can choose any of the chapters if they meet a four-hour minimum requirement. Ten states—Florida, Oklahoma, Maryland, Minnesota, Tennessee, Georgia, South Carolina, Texas, West Virginia, and Utah—promote marriage education of their residents by, for example, offering a discount on the marriage license, which results in about 15,000 fewer divorces annually (Clyde & Hawkins, 2019).

Significant positive increases in attitudes, knowledge, communication and conflict management skills result when adolescents, undergraduates, and emerging adults experience these programs (McElwain et al., 2016; Duncan et al., 2016; Cottle et al., 2015; Cottle et al., 2014). Job et al. (2017) assessed the value of a CRE (Couple Relationship Education) program for 234 couples and found a reduction in conflict for those that had the lowest pretest satisfactions. However, for couples with higher satisfaction ratings, there was no change or deterioration.

In spite of the benefits, there is opposition to marriage preparation education in the public school system. Opponents question using school time for relationship courses. Teachers are viewed as overworked, and an additional course on marriage seems to press the system to the breaking point. In addition, some teachers lack the training to provide relationship courses. However, many schools already have programs in family and consumer sciences, and teachers in these programs are trained in teaching about marriage and the family. A related concern with teaching about marriage and the family in high school is the fear on the part of some parents that the course content may be too liberal. Some parents who oppose teaching sex education in the public schools fear that such courses lead to increased sexual activity (in Chapter 9 we address sex education policies). ●

historical review of family life on the past, present, and future of marriage (Leviton, 2016). For example, there is the idea that family values, defined as the most important focus in one's life, was the primary value during colonial times. But that was never the case. "Early Americans believed you had responsibilities to the larger community. They did not talk about 'The Christian Family,' because it was too narrow and too exclusive" (Leviton, 2016, p. 5). Indeed, there was no state sponsorship of one religion but all religions including Jews, Hindus, and Muslims. "The highest value was to make yourself available to the public" (p. 5).

Another myth about marriage in American history is the idea of the male breadwinner— that he would bring home the bacon to the wife at home. In reality, men and women both worked on the farm, rearing and slaughtering hogs together. "In the American colonies, if a couple ran an inn together, and the wife died, the authorities would revoke the man's business license until he remarried" on the premise that he could not run a business without help (p. 6).

Is Marriage Obsolete?

As noted earlier, marriage remains the dominant goal for most individuals. While there has been a decline in the percentage of individuals choosing to marry, Schneider et al. (2018) identified, among other factors, the reduced economic prospects of men and the increased wage opportunities of women as explanations. The researchers also noticed the influence of the waning normative imperative to marry and the acceptability of alternative family forms. It should also be kept in mind that lower marriage rates are primarily in reference to those without college degrees. As income and education increase, so do marriage rates.

Rather than being obsolete, the meaning of marriage has changed. **Individualized marriage** is the term which describes the blending of two cultural forces in America—the individualistic need to be autonomous and the need to be grounded in traditional family structure such as marriage. Lindemann (2017) observed this phenomenon in her study of commuter marriages whereby spouses chose to be married although they were separated in much of their work lives. They were adamant that they were "together" even though they were physically separated. They used digital technology to keep them "virtually together."

....

Individualized marriage: blending of two cultural forces in America; the individualistic need to be autonomous and the need to be grounded in traditional family structure such as the marriage.

FAMILY

Starting a family is often viewed as synonymous with having children. While children may precede marriage, most individuals both want and have children (Chang et al., 2018). However, the definition of what constitutes a family is sometimes unclear. This section examines how families are defined, their numerous types, and how marriages and families have changed in the past fifty years.

> *Call it a clan, call it a network, call it a tribe, call it a family. Whatever you call it, whoever you are, you need one.*
> Jane Howard, the late English novelist

Definitions of Family

The answer to the question "Who is family?" is important because access to resources such as health care, Social Security, and retirement benefits is involved. The U.S. Census Bureau defines family as a group of two or more people related by blood, marriage, or adoption. This definition has been challenged because it does not include foster families or long-term couples who live together. Unless cohabitants are recognized by the state in which they reside as in a "domestic partnership," cohabitants are typically not viewed as "family" and are not accorded health benefits, Social Security, or retirement benefits of the partner. Indeed, the "live-in partner" may not be allowed to see the beloved in the hospital, which may limit visitation to "family only." Being the same sex and being excluded from being with one's hospitalized partner was another motivating factor for legal approval of same-sex relationships.

CULTURE AND DIVERSITY

Dragojlovic (2016) interviewed 24 women from Europe, Australia, and the United States who had vacationed in Bali, fallen in love with a Balinese man, and had one or more children. Although there were variations in the various patterns of commitment and relationships, a common theme was that these women were "playing family" by living and rearing their children in their native land while maintaining a relationship with the father of the children. Even though he was often married and had other children with a Balinese woman, the woman would visit annually to maintain the relationship with the partner and father of the child. These non-conventional **transnational families** challenge the nuclear family norm.

....

Transnational family: family in which the mother and child live in another country from the father.

The definition of who counts as family is being challenged. In some cases, families are being defined by function rather than by structure—for example, what is the level of emotional and financial commitment and interdependence between the partners? How long have they lived together? Do the partners view themselves as a family? Are single parent families a "real family" or only those with two parents in one residence?

CULTURE AND DIVERSITY

Hawaii has a cultural tradition of "hanai adoptions" which allows a child to be "hanai'd out"—the child may be adopted by someone in the extended family or by a childless couple. Typically, no papers are signed, but the new adoptive parents love, nurture, rear, and educate the child as though he or she were a biological child. In addition, the relationship between the child and the birth parents is not only permitted but encouraged.

Sociologically, a **family** is defined as a kinship system of all relatives living together or recognized as a social unit, including adopted individuals. This definition includes same sex couples with or without children as well as single parents. The family is regarded as the basic social institution of society because of its important functions of procreation and socialization; the family is found in some form in all societies. **Fictive kin**, also called families of choice, voluntary kin, discretionary kin, and nonconventional kin, refers to nonbiological and nonlegal relationships that are close, meaningful, and supportive. In the Netherlands, 35% of those aged 61-79 years old are more likely to include fictive kin in their networks (Voorpostel, 2018). Parker and Mayock (2019) surveyed homeless youth in terms of how they viewed "family." Four themes emerged, including "family as reliable and supportive; family as interrupted and 'broken'; family as fragile and elusive; and family as fluid and ambiguous—revealing the unfolding nature of young people's constructions of family and family relationships" (p.540).

Before same-sex marriage couples, some same-sex couples sought a **civil union** which was to provide some benefits to the couple. In reality, recognition of a civil union provided few benefits and only at the state level. Even less was provided at the federal level: The federal tax rates and Social Security

----

Family: a group of two or more people related by blood, marriage, or adoption.

Fictive kin: nonbiological and nonlegal relationships that are close, meaningful and supportive.

Civil union: a pair-bonded relationship given legal significance in terms of rights and privileges.

This couple drove with these three dogs from Chicago to Florida for the winter and back again in the Spring. They "won't leave home without them."

and medical benefits were not available to those in civil unions.

While less important since same-sex marriage became a legal option, **domestic partnerships** are relationships in which cohabiting individuals are given some kind of official recognition by a city or corporation so as to receive partner benefits, such as health insurance. Domestic partnerships do not confer any federal recognition or benefits.

Friends

Friends sometimes become family. Due to mobility, spouses may live several states away from their respective families. Although they may visit their families for holidays, they often develop close friendships with others on whom they rely locally for emotional and physical support. Persons in the military who are separated from their parents and siblings or deployed spouse often form close "family" relationships with other military individuals, couples, and families.

Pets

Ninety-five percent of 1,010 adult responses to Purina's Dog Survey (2018) viewed their dog as part of the family (Grandstaff, 2016, 4b). Examples of treating pets like children include owners requiring a fenced-in backyard for where they rent or buy an apartment or house, staying only in pet friendly motels, or feeding the pet a special diet, hanging a stocking or buying presents for the pet at Christmas or both (Smith & Bravo, 2016). Other owners buy "clothes" for the pet and leave money in one's will for the care of one's pet. Some cohabitants get a puppy which symbolizes their commitment to "family." Some pet owners buy accident insurance for their pets. In divorce, custody is assigned, parental responsibility to pay for

----

Domestic partnerships: relationships in which cohabiting individuals are given some kind of official recognition by a city or corporation so as to receive partner benefits.

upkeep and medical care is identified and custody is given on the best interests of the pet.

Hodges (2019) revealed that dogs function as protection, such as a guard dog, as a companion, or as a status symbol depending upon one's socioeconomic status. The higher one's socioeconomic status, the more likely the owner viewed his or her dog as a sort of status symbol, and the lower one's socioeconomic status, the more likely the owner viewed his or her dog as an object fulfilling a specific purpose such as protection. Owners of dogs and cats are likely to experience greater symptoms of depression and anxiety as well as poorer quality of life when their pet has a chronic or terminal disease (Spitznagel et al., 2017).

> ### CULTURE AND DIVERSITY
>
> The age at which a citizen is allowed to marry varies by country. Most countries identify 18— China is the exception with marriage allowed at 21— as the minimum age to marry though some permit marriage earlier—13 in Columbia—with parental consent. Being able to "rent" a family member is available in Japan. Japan's rent-a-family industry involves one's ability to rent a wife, husband, child, sibling, you name it. Indeed, a Japanese woman who wants a traditional wedding but who has no man in her life can rent a stand-in groom, bridesmaids, ushers, and so forth. She need only show up with her parents to have the event of her lifetime—the cost is $47,000. Grieving widows and widowers can also rent a spouse, parents who are estranged from their children can rent engaged children, and the elderly can rent grandchildren. One such company is called Family Romance, founded by Yuichi Ishii who has 1,200 freelance actors from which to choose. Ishii has played the husband to 100 women. These are social, not sexual, relationships (Batuman, 2018).

Types of Families

There are various types of families.

Family of Origin

Also referred to as the **family of orientation**, this is the family into which you were born or the family in which you were reared. It involves you, your parents, and your siblings. When you go to your parents' home for the holidays, you return to your **family of origin**. Siblings in one's family of origin also provide a profound influence on one another's behavior, emotional

development, adjustment, and happiness (Incerti et al., 2015). The relationship with one's siblings, particularly the sister-sister relationship, represents the most enduring relationship in a person's lifetime.

Edwards and Martinez (2018) emphasized gathering data from one's entire family history via autoethnography to better understand various choices and histories as they interact with intersectional positions. Persons of color may particularly benefit from an awareness of how racial issues have been treated in their past family history. To find out about one's personal genetic ancestry breakdown, over five million individuals have turned to "23andMe," a genomics and biotechnology company based in Mountain View, California. The company is named for the 23 pairs of chromosomes in a normal human cell. Individuals send off for a kit, provide a saliva sample, and are sent a report in six weeks about their DNA history.

Family of Procreation

The **family of procreation** represents the family that you will begin should you marry and have children. Of U.S. citizens living in the United States 65 years old and over, 96% have married with most establishing their own family of procreation (Wang, 2018). Across the life cycle, individuals move from the family of orientation to the family of procreation.

Nuclear Family

The **nuclear family** refers to either a family of origin or a family of procreation. In practice, this means that your nuclear family consists either of you, your parents, and your siblings or of you, your spouse, and your children. Generally, one-parent households are not referred to as nuclear families. They are binuclear families if both parents are involved in the child's life, or single-parent families if only one parent is involved in the child's life.

Sociologist George Peter Murdock (1949) emphasized that the nuclear family is a "universal social grouping" that is found in all of the 250 societies he investigated. The nuclear family converts and channels the sexual energy between two lovers so as to reproduce, care for, and socialize children to be productive members of society.

Traditional, Modern, and Postmodern Family

There are three central concepts of the family. The **traditional family** is the two-parent nuclear family,

---

Family of orientation: also known as the family of origin, the family into which a person is born.

Family of procreation: the family a person begins typically by getting married and having children.

Nuclear family: consists of you, your parents, and your siblings or you, your spouse, and your children

Traditional family: the two-parent nuclear family, with the husband as breadwinner and the wife as homemaker.

When Families Are Destroyed by the Government

In Australia, between 1885 and 1969, between 50,000 and 100,000 "half-caste"— people with one White parent— Aboriginal children were taken by force from their parents by the Australian police. The White society wanted to convert these children to Christianity and to destroy their Aboriginal culture, which was viewed as primitive and without value. The children were forced to walk or were put on a camel or a train and taken hundreds of miles away from their parents to church missions. Australian government destruction of Aboriginal families is the theme of *Rabbit-Proof Fence*, a movie available on DVD.

One of the children, Bob Randall, taken from his parents at age 7 wrote of his experience:

> *Instead of the wide open spaces of my desert home, we were housed in corrugated iron dormitories with rows and rows of bunk beds. After dinner we were bathed by the older women, put in clothing they called pajamas, and then tucked into one of the iron beds between the sheets. This was a horrible experience for me. I couldn't stand the feel of the cloth touching my skin (Randall 2008, p. 35).*

The Australian government subsequently apologized for the laws and policies of successive parliaments and governments that inflicted profound grief, suffering, and loss on the Aborigines. However, Randall noted that the Aborigines continue to be marginalized and that nothing has been done to compensate them for the horror of taking children from their families.

America is also guilty of separating children from their parents. In 2018-2019, 2,800 children, including toddlers, were separated from their illegal immigrant parents who were incarcerated awaiting trial, which could take three months. Records were often not kept regarding which child belonged to which parents, so that reconnection of the children with their parents was difficult (Jervis & Gomez, 2019). A historical look at such a practice in America reveals that not only were children separated from their parents during slavery—fathers were sold off to different plantation owners—but Native American children as young as five were taken from their families in order to "civilize" them in White boarding schools or non-Indian families—a practice that lasted more than 100 years and formally ended only with the Indian Child Welfare Act of 1978. ●

with the husband as breadwinner and the wife as homemaker. The **modern family** is the dual-earner family, in which both spouses work outside the home. **Postmodern families** include same-sex couples and their children as well as mothers who are single by choice. Polyamorous families are also an example of this category.

Binuclear Family

A **binuclear family** is a family in which the members live in two separate households. This family type is created when the parents of the children divorce and live separately, setting up two separate units, with the children remaining a part of each unit. Each of these units may also change again when the parents remarry and bring additional children into the respective units called a **blended family**. Hence, the children may go from a nuclear family with both parents, to a binuclear unit with parents living in separate homes, to a blended family when parents remarry and bring additional children into the respective units.

Extended Family

The **extended family** includes not only the nuclear family or parts of it but other relatives as well. These relatives include grandparents, aunts, uncles, and cousins. An example of an extended family living together would be a husband and wife, their children, and the husband's parents, the children's grandparents. The extended family is particularly important for African-American, Asian-American, and Latino-American families. Extended families, such as aunts ("tias") and uncles ("tios"), frequently play an active role in the parenting (Ansion & Merali, 2018). We earlier made reference to fictive kin, which may also become part of one's extended family.

Modern family: the dual-earner family, in which both spouses work outside the home.

Postmodern family: lesbian or gay male couples or parents and mothers who are single by choice, which emphasizes that a healthy family need not be the traditional heterosexual, two-parent family.

Binuclear family: a family in which the members live in two households.

Blended family: a family created when two individuals marry and at least one of them brings a child or children from a previous relationship or marriage. Also referred to as a stepfamily.

Extended family: the nuclear family or parts of it plus other relatives such as grandparents, aunts, uncles, and cousins.

CULTURE AND DIVERSITY

Asians are more likely than White Americans to live in extended families. Among Asians, the status of the elderly in the extended family derives from religion. Confucian philosophy, for example, prescribes that all relationships are of the superordinate–subordinate type—that is, husband-wife, parent-child, and teacher-pupil. For traditional Asians to abandon their elderly rather than include them in larger family units would be unthinkable. However, commitment to the elderly may be changing as a result of the westernization of Asian countries such as China, Japan, and Korea. Indeed, there have been reports on the news to the effect that over 1,000 elderly Chinese parents, including a 94-year-old, have sued their children for lack of financial support. A specific example is a mother who sued her son for rearing him and paying for his dental training. The Taiwan court ordered the son to pay his mother almost US$1 million (https://www.bbc.com/news/world-asia-42542260).

DIFFERENCES BETWEEN MARRIAGE AND FAMILY

Marriage can be thought of as a social relationship that sometimes leads to the establishment of a family. Indeed, every society or culture has mechanisms for guiding their youth into permanent emotional, legal, or social relationships that are designed to have and rear offspring. Although the concepts of marriage and the family are sometimes used synonymously, they are distinct. The late sociologist Lee Axelson noted some of the differences in marriage and the family (Table 1.4).

Changes in Marriage and the Family in the Last 70 Years

Various researchers have noted the enormous changes that have occurred in marriage and the family. A basic

change has been in the reasons for marriage. The most basic purpose for marriage in history has been to acquire the advantages of having in-laws and to expand the family labor source (Coontz, 2016). Marriage today is about emotional intimacy and companionship and a context for self-discovery, self-esteem, and personal growth (Finkel, 2019). Other changes since the 1950s are identified in Table 1.5.

TABLE 1.4

Differences Between Marriage and the Family in the United States

MARRIAGE	FAMILY
Usually initiated by a formal ceremony	Formal ceremony not essential
Involves two people	Usually involves more than two people
Ages of the individuals tend to be similar	Individuals represent more than one generation
Individuals usually choose each other	Members are born or adopted into the family
Ends when spouse dies or is divorced	Continues beyond the life of the individual
Sex between spouses is expected and approved	Sex between near kin is neither expected nor approved
Requires a license	No license needed to become a parent
Procreation expected	Consequence of procreation
Spouses are focused on each other	Focus changes with addition of children
Spouses can voluntarily withdraw from marriage	Parents cannot divorce themselves from obligations via divorce to children
Money in unit is spent on the couple	Money is used for the needs of children
Recreation revolves around adults	Recreation revolves around children

TABLE 1.5

Changes in Marriages and Families—1950 and 2020

	1950	2020
Family Relationship Values	Strong values for marriage and the family. Individuals who wanted to remain single or child-free were considered deviant, even pathological. Husband and wife should not be separated by jobs or careers.	Individuals who remain single or child-free experience social understanding and sometimes encouragement. Single and child-free people are no longer considered deviant or pathological but are seen as self-actuating individuals with strong job or career commitments. Husbands and wives can be separated for reasons of job or career and live in a commuter marriage. Married women in large numbers have left the role of full-time mother and housewife to join the labor market.

(Continued)

TABLE 1.5   (Continued)

Gender Roles	Rigid gender roles, with men dominant and earning income while wives stay home, taking care of children.	Egalitarian gender roles with both spouses earning income and involved in parenting children.
Sexual Values	Marriage was regarded as the only appropriate lifestyle in middle-class America. Living together was unacceptable, and children born out of wedlock were stigmatized. Virginity was expected or exchanged for marital commitment.	Focus on having safe sex has taken precedence over the marital context for sex. Virginity before marriage is rare. Cohabitation has become a stage in a couple's relationship that may or may not lead to marriage. Having children outside of marriage is acceptable. Hooking up is normative among singles.
Homogamous Mating	Strong social pressure existed to date and marry within one's own racial, ethnic, religious, and social class group. Emotional and legal attachments were heavily influenced by approval of parents and kin.	Dating and mating reflect more freedom of the individual to select a partner outside his or her own racial, ethnic, religious, and social class group. Pairings are less often influenced by parental approval.
Cultural Silence on Intimate Relationships	Intimate relationships were not an appropriate subject for discussion in the media.	Interviews on television and features in magazines reveal intimate details of the lives of individuals. Survey results in magazines are open about sexuality and relationships.
Divorce	Society strongly disapproved of divorce. Familistic values encouraged spouses to stay married for the children. Strong legal constraints kept couples together. Marriage was forever.	Divorce has replaced death as the end point of 40-50% of marriages. Less stigma is associated with divorce. Individualistic values lead spouses to seek personal happiness. No-fault divorce allows for easy severance. Increasing numbers of children are being reared in single-parent homes.
Familism versus Individualism	Families were focused on the needs of children. Mothers stayed home to ensure that the needs of their children were met. Adult concerns were less important.	Adult agenda of work and recreation has taken on increased importance, with less attention given to children. Children are being reared in day care centers due to dual career parents. Some parents are helicopter parents.
LGBTQ	LGBTQ emotional and sexual relationships were culturally hidden phenomena. These relationships were invisible and stigmatized.	LGBTQ individuals are more open about their identity and relationships. Same-sex marriage is legal in every state in the United States.
Scientific Scrutiny	Aside from the Kinsey Report, a study of sexuality, few studies were conducted on intimate relationships.	Acceptance of scientific study of marriage and intimate relationships. The Society for the Scientific Study of Sex has an annual conference, journal, and so forth.
Family Housing	Husbands and wives lived in the same house.	Husbands and wives may "live apart" (LAT), which means that, although they are emotionally and economically connected, they—by choice—maintain two households, houses, condos, or apartments.
Communication Technology	Nonexistent, except phone.	Smart phones, texting, sexting, Facebook, Instagram, and other social media permeate the lives of individuals, couples, and families.

TECHNOLOGY AND THE FAMILY

Robots Are Here

Oxford dictionary defines technology as an "application of scientific knowledge for practical purposes, especially in industry." There are also different types of technology including information communication, biomedical engineering, robotics, artificial intelligence, entertainment media, and space and energy. In the family and technology sections of this text, the term technology is used to include any practical use, translation or application of scientific knowledge which can include design, products, or services. We begin with robots.

The term robot is defined as a machine with *humanlike* features which is able to sense, think, and act. Robots can be categorized according to their mobility such

"Pepper" is being used for companionship of the elderly in some countries such as Japan.

BSIP/Universal Images Group/Getty

as stationary, wheeled, and so forth; they can also be divided into categories based on their application such as industrial, domestic and household, rehabilitation, and entertainment. Misselhorn (2018) notes that robots are "flying airplanes or drones; they are trading high-frequency stocks; and they are controlling our working and living environment" (p. 161).

The term "personal robots" is used to describe robots that serve as personal assistants to the user, and may serve multiple functions or reside with the user and families. Personal robots, which have been developed to perform domestic tasks such as vacuuming and laundry folding, have received increasing attention. The United States and other countries, such as Japan, Italy, and France, have launched projects to explore the use of robots as personal assistants for elderly people and people with disabilities (Marx, 2018; Güttler et al., 2015). Robots have also been used in rehabilitation (Mekki et al., 2018; Chemuturi et al., 2013) and to protect property. Regarding the latter, Knightscope is a five-foot high, 400-pound security bot hired to patrol the grounds of an animal shelter in the Mission District of San Francisco (Marx, 2018).

The development of robots to function in home settings is a unique challenge. In addition to functionality, the appearance of personal robots must be acceptable to users. The extent to which robots have become lifelike is uncanny. Hanson Robotics ("Why human-like robots") has created strikingly realistic humanlike robots including those with a full range of human facial expressions, such as anger, surprise, and so forth. The charming Sophia ("Being Sophia"), Hanson Robotics' latest robot, has appeared in many shows and interviews around the world and become a media celebrity.

Will robots be considered as "family"? The U.S. Census Bureau defines a family as "a group of two or more people who are related by birth, marriage, or adoption and residing together; all such people are considered members of one family." Using this definition, only humans will be considered as family members. However,

what if future personal robots not only perform domestic tasks and share the same dwelling, but also socialize our children, take care of our aging parents, and serve as an important source of intimate relations? Is it possible to have a deep, meaningful, and reciprocal relationship between humans and robots? Although some individuals view advancements in technology, including the use of robots, as important to an improved quality of life, others are apprehensive about such a future. The fear of being replaced by robots is real. It has been predicted that by 2030, between 30% and 47% of our jobs will be replaced by robots (Marx, 2018).

Artificial Intelligence expert Noel Sharkey reported that teenagers risk losing their virginity to sophisticated humanoid robots (Roxby or Rocky True Companion) and that the new companion for children may be robots with whom they may bond. Companies in South Korea and Japan are manufacturing and marketing "child care" robots that will likely enter mainstream use within a few years. In addition, "companion" humanoid units like Pepper or Paro are being used to provide companionship to elderly people in Asian countries such as Japan (Marx, 2018). What choices will individuals, couples, and families make about the use of this technology in their own lives? If a robot can provide companionship to an elderly parent in another city, will the offspring still choose to visit? Will parents get a dog for their children or will this choice be replaced with a robotic dog such as CHiP)?

To what degree are robots accepted by undergraduates? Forty-four percent of 345 undergraduates reported that they could view robots in the home as family members who performed chores (Chang, Huff, & Knox, 2019). According to a survey of 1,000 adults, 77% of Americans think it will be normal to have a robot in their home within 20 years (Smith & Loehrke, 2017). Over two thirds, about 68%, of 2,001 millennial respondents in a Prudential Financial survey reported that they fully expect the next generation to establish emotional relationships with the robots that serve them (Smith & Loehrke, 2018).

Dr. David Levy, an expert on artificial intelligence and the author of *Love and Sex with Robots*, has predicted a new type of family in the future. According to Levy, this new nuclear family will consist of human parents, robot parents, and human-robot children (Levy, 2017).

The use, function, service, and capability of robots will continue to expand. Roboethics which investigate implications and consequences of robotic technology will become increasingly important. The morality and ethics of artificial intelligence has already surfaced (Misselhorn, 2018). For example, should the vacuuming robot Roomba kill a ladybug or go around it? How much monitoring of an elderly person should occur that is reported to concerned adult children? The morality, ethics, and choices regarding robots in the family elicit new questions which future research may address.

RESEARCH PROCESS AND CAVEATS

Hughes et al. (2018) emphasized the absence of research methods content in marriage and family textbooks. A content analysis of the major leading texts revealed that only 1% of the content included the science of research. "Aren't we social scientists?" asked Robert Hughes. Why don't we talk about our *science?!*

Research is valuable since it helps to provide evidence for or against a hypothesis. For example, it is assumed that hookups do not become monogamous love relationships. But almost a fourth of couples, about 23%, in one study who reported having hooked up also noted that they transitioned into a long-term romantic relationship with their hookup partner (Erichsen & Dignam, 2016). Researchers follow a standard sequence when conducting a research project and there are certain caveats to be aware of when reading any research finding.

> *Google is not a synonym for research.*
> Dan Brown, *The Lost Symbol*

Steps in the Research Process

Several steps are used in conducting research.

1. **Identify the topic or focus of research.** Select a subject about which you are passionate. For example, are you interested in studying social media and relationships, which has become a new focus for family researchers (Dworkin et al., 2018)? Give your project a title in the form of a question—"Do People Who Use Social Media Have Happier Relationships Than Those Who Do Not?"

Researchers present their new research at professional conferences like the National Council on Family Relations which is included in textbooks.

2. **Review the literature.** Go online to the various databases of your college or university and read research that has already been published on social media use. Not only will this prevent you from "reinventing the wheel"—you might find that a research study has already been conducted on exactly what you want to study—but it will also give you ideas for study.

3. **Develop hypotheses. A hypothesis** is a suggested explanation for a phenomenon. For example, you might hypothesize that high social media use is associated with lower relationship satisfaction because the individuals look to external secondary group contexts for interaction and affirmation of closer informal primary group contexts.

4. **Decide on type of study and method of data collection.** The type of study may be **cross-sectional**, which means studying the whole population at one time—in this case, finding out from persons about their current use of social media—or **longitudinal**, which means studying the same group of individuals across time—in this case, collecting data for each of four years of college. The method of data collection varies: It could involve using archives with secondary sources such as journals, surveys, interviews with one or both partners, or a case study that focuses on one couple. A basic difference in research methodology is quantitative, which relies on surveys or archival material for data collection, or qualitative where interviews and case studies are conducted.

5. **Get IRB approval.** To ensure the protection of people who agree to be interviewed or who complete questionnaires, researchers must obtain IRB approval by submitting a summary of their proposed research to the Institutional Review Board (IRB) of their institution. The IRB reviews the research plan to ensure that the project is consistent with research ethics and poses no undue harm to participants. When collecting data from individuals, it is important that they are told that their participation is completely voluntary, that the study maintains

Hypothesis: a suggested explanation for a phenomenon.

Cross-sectional: analysis of data representing one point in time. For example, infidelity the first year of marriage in contrast to longitudinal data which would look at infidelity throughout the marriage.

Longitudinal: analysis of data on a phenomenon over time. For example, infidelity over the years of a marriage in contrast to cross-sectional data which would look at infidelity at one point in time.

TABLE 1.6

Potential Research Problems in Marriage and Family

WEAKNESS	CONSEQUENCES	EXAMPLE
Sample not random	Cannot generalize findings	Opinions of college students do not reflect opinions of other adults.
No control group	Inaccurate conclusions	Study on the effect of divorce on children needs control group of children whose parents are still together.
Age differences between groups of respondents	Inaccurate conclusions	Effect may be due to passage of time or to cohort differences.
Unclear terminology	Inability to measure what is not clearly defined	What is definition of cohabitation, marital happiness, sexual fulfillment, good communication, quality time?
Researcher bias	Slanted conclusions	A researcher studying the value of a product should not be funded by the organization being studied. (Ornstein & Thomas, 2018).
Time lag	Outdated conclusions	Often-quoted Kinsey sex research is over 70 years old.
Distortion	Invalid conclusions	Research subjects exaggerate, omit information, recall facts or events inaccurately, or do all of these actions. Respondents may remember what they wish had happened.
Deception	Public mislead	Researchers change research data to continue receiving economic support of sponsors (Google scientific misconduct).
Mischievous responders	Invalid data	Respondents mislead researcher by providing extreme or untruthful responses to be "funny" (Cimpian et al., 2018)

their anonymity, and that the results are confidential. Respondents under age 18 need the consent of their parents. Rinehart et al. (2017) confirmed that collecting research from undergraduates on "sensitive topics" such as rape does not increase participant distress unduly. Indeed, subjects may benefit from their participation in research. Bay-Chen (2017) found increased sexual self-esteem from participants who reviewed their sexual history.

6. **Collect and analyze data.** Various statistical packages are available to analyze data to discover if your hypotheses are true or false.

7. **Write up and publish results.** Writing up and submitting your findings for publication are important so that your study becomes part of the academic literature.

Caveats to Consider in Evaluating Research Quality

"New Research Study" is a frequent headline in popular magazines which promises accurate information about "hooking up," "what women want," "what men want," or other relationship, marriage, and family issues. As you read such articles, as well as the research in texts such as these, be alert to their potential flaws. Many of the various issues to keep in mind when evaluating research are identified in Table 1.6.

FUTURE OF MARRIAGE

While marriage will remain the lifestyle choice for 85% of adults in the United States, the delay for some in getting married, postponing it until their late 20s or early 30s, will continue. Hooking up, friends with benefits, and cohabitation will be experiences for many, but the goal of marriage to one person with children will be the destination context for today's youth. The 15% who elect never to marry will become not only a growing but less stigmatized segment of our population.

Pearce et al. (2018) emphasized the increasing diversity and complexity of family structures—those who are single parents, divorced, cohabiting, same-sex couples/parents, living with parents/grand-parents, widowed, and those who have never been married. Increasingly, while individuals will have different family experiences as a result of growing up in varied contexts, the emotional function of connectedness and support will remain a unique benefit of family life.

Although the Supreme Court legalized same-sex marriage, social acceptance will increase slowly. Indeed, even acceptance in one's own family will be slow (Kennedy et al., 2018).

The visibility of immigrant families in the United States will increase. Political policies such as separating children from parents according to administration rulings will be challenged in court, and immigrant families, now 13.5% of the U.S. population, will increase (Radford & Budiman, 2018).

Finally, technology and the use of artificial intelligence (AI) will continue to become a part of family living. However, while experts note that AI will improve the lives of most people, there are concerns about how advances in AI will affect what it means to be human, to be productive, and to exercise free will (Anderson & Rainie, 2018).

SUMMARY

What is the view or theme of this text?
A central theme of this text is to encourage you to be proactive—to make conscious, deliberate relationship choices to enhance your own well-being and the well-being of those in your intimate groups. Some of the important choices are whether to marry, whom to marry, when to marry, whether to have children, whether to remain emotionally and sexually faithful to one's partner, and whether to use a condom. Important issues to keep in mind about a choices framework for viewing marriage and the family are that (1) not to decide is to decide, (2) some choices require correcting, (3) all choices involve trade-offs, (4) choices include selecting a positive or negative view, (5) making choices produces ambivalence, and (6) some choices are not revocable. Most emerging adults are in no hurry to find "the one," to marry, and to begin a family.

What are the theoretical frameworks for viewing marriage and the family?
Nine theoretical frameworks were discussed. The most commonly used are the family systems framework, the human ecology framework, the symbolic interaction framework, and the social exchange framework. The newest framework is the couple and family technology framework.

What is marriage?
Marriage is a system of binding adults together to have, care for, and socialize offspring if they choose to. The federal government regards marriage as a legal contract between a couple and the state in which they reside that regulates their economic and sexual relationship. Other elements of marriage involve emotion, fidelity, and a formal ceremony. Types of marriage include monogamy and polygamy. Various forms of polygamy are polygyny, polyandry, and pantagamy.

What is family?
The U.S. Census Bureau defines family as a group of two or more people related by blood, marriage, or adoption. In recognition of the diversity of families, the definition of family is increasingly becoming two adult partners whose interdependent relationship is long-term and characterized by an emotional and financial commitment. The family of origin is the family into which you were born or the family in which you were reared. The family of procreation represents the family that you will begin should you marry and have children. Central concepts of the family are traditional, modern, and postmodern. Types of family include nuclear, binuclear, extended, and blended.

What are the steps in the research process and what caveats should be kept in mind?
Steps in the research process include identifying a topic, reviewing the literature, deciding on methods and data collection procedures, ensuring protection of subjects via getting IRB (Institutional Review Board) approval, analyzing the data, and submitting the results to a journal for publication.

Caveats that are factors to be used in evaluating research include a random sample where the respondents providing the data reflect those who were not in the sample; a control group where the group is not subjected to the experimental design for a basis of comparison; objectively defined terminology being used to study the phenomenon; researcher bias which is present in all studies; time lag which takes two years from study to print; and distortion or deception of data, which, although rare, some researchers do. Few studies avoid all research problems.

What is the future of marriage?
Marriage will continue to be the lifestyle of choice for the majority, about 85%–90%, of U.S. adults. Individuals will increasingly delay getting married until their late twenties to early thirties in order to complete their educations, launch their careers, or become economically independent or all of those. And there will be an increase in those who never marry.

WEB LINKS

Institute for Family Studies
https://ifstudies.org/

National Council on Family Relations
http://www.ncfr.org/

U.S. Census Bureau
http://www.census.gov/

Get the tools you need to sharpen your study skills. SAGE edge offers a robust online environment featuring an impressive array of free tools and resources.
Access practice quizzes, eFlashcards, video, and multimedia at **edge.sagepub.com/knox13e**

2 Love Relationships

I don't want to live—I want to love first and live incidentally.

—Zelda Fitzgerald

Learning Objectives

2.1.   Review the various meanings of love

2.2.   Explain the theories of love

2.3.   Describe the contexts in which love is socially controlled

2.4.   Summarize the conditions in which people fall in love

2.5.   Illustrate the various ways in which love is a context for problems

2.6.   Recognize the sources, consequences and coping mechanisms of jealousy

2.7.   Review the advantages and disadvantages of polyamory

2.8.   Identify future changes to love in relationships

Master the content at
edge.sagepub.com/knox13e

Love is a compelling emotion. Thirty-one percent of 12,785 undergraduates reported that if they were "really in love," they would marry someone they had known for only a short time (Hall & Knox, 2019). Abundant research documents the positive effects of love promoting one's mental (Stanton & Campbell, 2014), physical (Rauer et al., 2014) and marital well-being (Reis et al., 2014). In a survey of 2,000 U. S. adults, "finding love" was of the utmost importance—78% of respondents reported that it was more important than being wealthy (Smith & Loehrke, 2018).

In contrast to the benefits of love, when love goes awry, data confirm that one's mental health is at risk in terms of severe depression, suicide ideation, and suicide attempts (Soller, 2014). Watkins and Beckmeyer (2018) noted that there is stress, anxiety, and depression associated with wanting a romantic relationship and being unable to achieve or sustain it. There are similar deteriorations in one's physiological health, such as increased blood pressure and mortality. When partners have lived together for 50 plus years, and one dies, the other has a shortened life span.

In this chapter, we examine the various meanings of love, styles, and theories. Along the way we ask the basic question about how you fall in love. We begin by reviewing the various meanings we attribute to love.

THE MEANINGS OF LOVE TODAY

A common class exercise among professors who teach marriage and the family is to randomly ask class members to identify one word they most closely

And when I talk about love, I'm talking about something that's great, though, brother. I'm talking about something that will sustain you.

Cornel West, American philosopher

associate with love. Invariably, students identify different words—commitment, feeling, trust, altruism—suggesting great variability in the way we think about love. Lomas (2018) regarded love as polysemous, or something with multiple meanings, and examined its nature and presence across the world's cultures reflected in published and Internet sources. He found 609 words associated with "love" which he grouped into fourteen categories representing fourteen "flavors" of love. Examples included familial love, passionate love, compassionate love, possessive love, and star-crossed love. Still other categories included experiential love, aesthetic love, playful love, and momentary love. Heshmati et al. (2019) surveyed 495 adults to identify common behavioral references to the experience of feeling loved. Results revealed both romantic and nonromantic contexts. Love can be shown when someone is compassionate toward you in a moment of crisis, when a child snuggles up next to you, or when your pet is happy to see you.

Two major meanings of love are those of it being romantic or realistic.

Romantic Love

Also referred to as passionate love, **romantic love** may be described as *"A state of intense longing for the union with another"* (Hatfield et al., 2012). This type of love is not unique to Western society but is a universal emotion (p. 154). Love is also viewed as critical for beginning a marriage but less important for maintaining it (Sprecher & Hatfield, 2017).

....

Romantic love: an intense love whereby the lover believes in love at first sight, only one true love, and love conquers all.

Conjugal or Realistic Love

Conjugal love, also known as realistic love, is the love between married people characterized by companionship, calmness, comfort, and security. Conjugal love is in contrast to romantic love, which is characterized by excitement and passion. Stanik et al. (2013) interviewed 146 couples who had been married from three to 25 years and confirmed a decrease in the intensity of love feelings across time. Hence, romantic love which may develop quickly from a love at first sight experience gradually becomes conjugal or realistic love.

Love may be described as existing on a continuum from romanticism to realism (refer to the Self-Assessment on Love Attitudes on page 372).

> *Love is a force that cannot be contained. . . it has the power to change the world.*
> Janelle Monáe, singer and actress

For some people, love is romantic; for others, it is realistic. Romantic love, said to have appeared in all human groups at all times in human history (Berscheid, 2010), is characterized in modern America by such beliefs as "love at first sight," "one true love," and "love conquers all." Regarding love at first sight, 36% of 2,971 undergraduate males and 24% of 9,812 undergraduate females reported that they had experienced love at first sight (Hall & Knox, 2019). One explanation for men falling in love more quickly than women is that from a biological and evolutionary perspective, men must be visually attracted to young, healthy females to impregnate them. This biologically-based reproductive attraction is labeled and interpreted as a love attraction so that the male feels immediately drawn to the female. Zsok et al. (2017) found that "love at first sight" is not love but an attraction that is labeled as love. In regard to love at first sight, Barelds and Barelds-Dijkstra (2007) studied the relationships of 137 married couples or cohabitants and found that the relationship quality of those who fell in love at first sight was similar to that of those who came to know each other more gradually. Huston et al. (2001) found that, after two years of marriage, the couples who had fallen in love more slowly were just as happy as couples who fell in love at first sight.

An openness to falling in love and developing an intimate relationship is Erik Erikson's sixth stage of psychosocial development. He noted that between the ages of 19 and 40, most individuals move from "isolation to intimacy," wherein they seek to establish committed loving relationships. Failure to do so leaves one vulnerable to loneliness and depression.

The magic of romantic love is a cherished experience. It has existed in couples throughout history.
Courtesy of Isabel Lima Dahl

The expectation for feeling chemistry in a relationship is relatively high. One third of 5,509 Match.com (2017) respondents reported that they expected to feel romantic chemistry on the first date.

Lust and Infatuation

Lust is about sexual desire and is biologically driven. The word **infatuation** comes from the same root word as *fatuous,* meaning "silly" or "foolish," and refers to a state of passion or attraction that is not based on reason. Infatuation is characterized by euphoria (Langeslag et al., 2013) and by the tendency to idealize the love partner. People who are infatuated magnify their lovers' positive qualities by saying, for example, "My partner is *always* happy," and overlook or minimize their negative

CULTURE AND DIVERSITY

The theme of American culture is individualism, which translates into personal fulfillment, emotional intimacy, and love as the reason for marriage. In Asian cultures the theme is familism, which focuses on family considerations and obligations, love is secondary. While arranged marriages are and have been the norm in Asian societies, love marriages are becoming far more frequent (Allendorf, 2013). In a comparison of marriages in which the spouses chose each other versus their parents selected their spouse (arranged marriage), those in the self-selected marriages reported more love. Wives in the self-selected marriages also reported feeling like more a partner with their husbands (Olcay et al., 2019).

Conjugal love: the love between married people characterized by companionship, calmness, comfort, and security.

Lust: sexual desire.

Infatuation: intense emotional feelings based on little actual exposure to the love object.

Using Your Heart or Your Head?

Lovers are frequently confronted with the need to make decisions about their relationships, but they are divided on whether to let their heart or their head rule in such decisions. We asked students in our classes to fill in the details about deciding with their heart or their head. Some of their answers follow:

Heart

Those who relied on their hearts for making decisions—women more than men—felt that emotions were more important than logic and that listening to their heart made them happier. One sophomore female said:

> In deciding on a partner, my heart knows what I want, what would make me most happy. My head tells me what is best for me. But I would rather have something that makes me happy than something that is good for me.

Head

Some undergraduates make relationship choices based on their head as some of the following comments show:

> In deciding on a mate, I feel my head should rule because you have to choose someone that

you can get along with after the new wears off. If you follow your heart solely, you may not look deep enough into a person to see what it is that you really like. Is it just a pretty face or a nice body? Or is it deeper than that, such as common interests and values? The "heart" sometimes can fog up this picture of the true person and distort reality into a fairy tale.

Some individuals feel that both the head and the heart should rule when making relationship decisions.

> When you really love someone, your heart rules in most of the situations. But if you don't keep your head in some matters, then you risk losing the love that you feel in your heart. I think that we should find a way to let our heads and hearts work together.

There is an adage, "Don't wait until you find the person you can live with; wait and find the person that you can't live without!" In your own decisions you might consider the relative merits of listening to your heart or head and moving forward recognizing there is not one "right" answer for all individuals on all issues. ●

ones, such as "My partner doesn't have a problem with alcohol but just likes to have a good time."

Love Styles

Theorist John Lee (1973, 1988) identified a number of styles of love that describe the way lovers relate to each other. Keep in mind that individuals may view love in different ways at different times. These love styles are also independent of one's sexual orientation.

1. **Ludic.** The **ludic love style** views love as a game in which the player has no intention of getting seriously involved. The ludic lover refuses to become dependent on any one person and does not encourage another's intimacy. Two essential skills of the ludic lover are to juggle several partners at the same time and to manage each relationship so that no one partner is seen too often.

These strategies help to ensure that the relationship does not deepen into an all-consuming love. Don Juan represented the classic ludic lover, embodying the motto of "Love 'em and leave 'em." Tzeng et al. (2003) found that whereas men were more likely than women to be ludic lovers, ludic love characterized the love style of college students the least.

2. **Pragma.** The **pragma love style** is the love of the pragmatic—that which is logical and rational. Pragma lovers assess their partners on the basis of assets and liabilities. One undergraduate female hung out with a guy because he had a car and could drive her home on weekends to see her boyfriend. An undergraduate male dated his partner because she would write his term papers and do his laundry.

Ludic love style: views love as a game where the player has no intention of getting involved.

Pragma love style: love style that is logical and rational. The love partner is evaluated in terms of pluses and minuses and is regarded as a good or bad "deal."

Eros, the love style of most college students, reflects great joy and contentment.
Courtesy of Trevor Werb

3. **Eros.** Just the opposite of the pragmatic love style, the **eros love style,** also known as romantic love, is imbued with passion and sexual desire. Eros is the most common love style of college women and men (Tzeng et al., 2003) and has been associated with higher relationship satisfaction (Vedes et al., 2016).

4. **Mania.** The **mania love style** is the out-of-control love whereby the person "must have" the love object. Being jealous, possessive, dependent, and controlling are symptoms of manic love. One must be careful of becoming involved with a manic lover since these may turn into stalkers when the relationship ends.

5. **Storge.** The **storge love style,** also known as **companionate love,** is a calm, soothing, nonsexual love devoid of intense passion. Respect, friendship, commitment, and familiarity are characteristics that help to define the storge love relationship. The partners care deeply about each other but not in a romantic or lustful sense. Their love is also more likely to endure than a fleeting romance. One's grandparents who have been married 50 years are likely to have a storge type of love. Neto (2012) compared love perceptions by age group and found that the older the individual, the more important love became and the less important sex became.

Eros love style: also known as romantic love, the love of passion and sexual desire.

Mania love style: the out-of-control love whereby the person "must have" the love object. Obsessive jealousy and controlling behavior are symptoms of manic love.

Storge love style: also known as companionate love, a calm, soothing, nonsexual love devoid of intense passion.

6. **Agape. Agape love style,** also known as **compassionate love,** is characterized by a focus on the well-being of the person who is loved, with little regard for reciprocation. The love parents have for their children is often described as compassionate love and is associated with positive parenting (Miller et al., 2015). Key qualities of agape love are not responding to a partner's negativity and not expecting an exchange for positives but believing that the other means well and will respond kindly in time.

Triangular View of Love

Sternberg (1986) developed the "triangular" view of love, which consists of three basic elements: intimacy or emotional connectedness, passion or physical attraction, and commitment or the desire to maintain the relationship. The presence or absence of these three elements creates various types of love experienced between individuals, regardless of their sexual orientation. These various types include the following:

1. **Nonlove**—the absence of intimacy, passion, and commitment. Two strangers looking at each other from afar are experiencing nonlove.

2. **Liking**—intimacy without passion or commitment. A new friendship may be described in these terms of the partners liking each other.

3. **Infatuation**—passion without intimacy or commitment. Two people flirting with each other in a bar may be infatuated with each other.

4. **Romantic love**—intimacy and passion without commitment. Two individuals connect at the emotional level and also find each other sexually attractive.

5. **Conjugal love**, also known as realistic love—intimacy and commitment without passion. A couple married for 50 years illustrates this type of love.

6. **Fatuous love**—passion and commitment without intimacy. Couples who are passionately wild about each other and talk of the future but do not have an intimate connection with each other have a fatuous love.

7. **Empty love**—commitment without passion or intimacy. A couple who stay together

Agape love style: also known as compassionate love, characterized by a focus on the well-being of the love object, with little regard for reciprocation.

for social—for example, children—and legal reasons but who have no spark or emotional sharing between them have an empty love.

8. **Consummate love**—combination of intimacy, passion, and commitment; Sternberg's view of the ultimate, all-consuming love.

Individuals bring different combinations of the elements of intimacy, passion, and commitment—the triangle—to their relationship. One lover may bring a predominance of passion, with some intimacy but no commitment—romantic love—whereas the other person brings commitment but no passion or intimacy—empty love. The triangular theory of love allows lovers to see the degree to which they are matched in terms of passion, intimacy, and commitment in their relationship.

Love Languages

The **five love languages** have become part of American love culture (Chapman, 2010). These five languages are gifts, quality time, words of affirmation, acts of service, and physical touch.

....

Five love languages: concept made popular by Gary Chapman, these languages are gifts, quality time, words of affirmation, acts of service, and physical touch.

Chapman encourages individuals to use the language of love most desired by the partner rather than the one preferred by the individual providing the love. Bland and McQueen (2018) studied the love languages in 100 couples and found that congruent love languages between the partners was associated with their reporting less distress in their relationship. In a previous study, Bunt and Hazelwood (2017) compared love languages in 67 heterosexual couples and found that 61% had the same primary love language. However, there was no significant relationship between having the same love language and reported relationship satisfaction. Rather it was the self-regulation, the adaptability in adjusting to the different perceptions, particularly for women, that was associated with relationship satisfaction.

Acts of service are related to the concept of sacrifice and putting a partner's needs above one's own. Johnson et al. (2019) analyzed data on 3,405 participants and their unmarried partners and found that commitment by the partner and security in the partner's love were the conditions under which sacrifice and putting the partners' needs above one's own had the highest frequency.

TECHNOLOGY AND THE FAMILY

The Digital Language of Love

The first text message, "Merry Christmas," was sent on December 3, 1992 (Kelly, 2012). Little did we know, it would eventually revolutionize how we communicate with each other. Text messaging, or texting, originally denoted brief electronic message exchanges between people using computers or portable devices. Current messaging not only involves texts, but also emoticons, photos, videos, websites, and audio content. With the advent of smart phones, texting has become pervasive. According to the Pew Research Center (2019), 96% of Americans own a cell phone. Sending text messages is the most frequent use and typically occurs throughout the day between partners in beginning or established relationships.

Research examining the effects of text messaging on relationships has yielded mixed results. Human communication is complicated, and texting can be easily misinterpreted in the absence of tone, facial expression, body language and emotion. A large-scale study with participants from Australia, the United Kingdom, and the United States revealed that text messaging was

negatively associated with relationship satisfaction (Goodman-Deane et al., 2016). The use of emoticons was found to facilitate playfulness (Hsieh & Tseng, 2017). However, greater relationship satisfaction was reported when text messaging was used to convey affection or positive emotions (Brody & Peña, 2015). Equity in text messaging may be expected and even considered as a way to show commitment. Similarity in texting behavior, frequency, and initiation between partners can predict relationship satisfaction among young adults (Ohadi et al., 2017).

To maximize positive outcomes from texting, there are various choices to make. Not only might couples make clear how often they expect a text message from a partner but what content is appropriate—for example, no sex "pics" or content about former partners. Milne (2015) noted other suggestions including: (1) Text on noteworthy occasions, such as "I had a great time yesterday" and "good luck on your interview today." (2) Call if talking would be better. (3) Flirt with caution. (4) Avoid texting at odd hours. And (5) drunk texting is a no-no. ●

Social Media and a Couple's Love Relationship

Facebook postings and readings are pervasive in the lives of many individuals and couples. Northrup and Smith (2016) studied how Facebook time is associated with a couple's romantic relationship. They found that "couples who engage in more Facebook maintenance tend to experience less love towards each other, and couples who feel more love towards each other engage in less relationship maintenance via Facebook" (p.249). The researchers suggested that "healthy couples who engage in face-to-face relationship maintenance find that relationship maintenance via Facebook is not needed" (p. 249). "Why would couples who engage in more Facebook maintenance seem to experience less love? The answer may be that couples who feel less love for each other may feel the need to present to friends and family online as if everything is fine, and therefore engage in more relationship maintenance via Facebook." (p. 249). (See the insert of Technology and Love)

SOCIAL CONTROL OF LOVE

The ultimate social control of love is **arranged marriage**—mate selection pattern whereby parents select the spouse of their offspring. The practice of "arranged marriage" is still common in 40% of the world's population in countries such as India and Pakistan. In most countries in Asia, marriage is regarded as the linking of two families; the love feelings of the respective partners are irrelevant. Love is expected to follow marriage, not precede it.

Arranged marriage: mate selection pattern whereby parents select the spouse of their offspring. A matchmaker may be used but the selection is someone of whom the parents approve.

Arranged marriages not only help to guarantee that cultural traditions will be carried on and passed to the new generation, but they also link two family systems together for mutual support of the couple. Parents may know a family who has a son or daughter whom they would regard as a suitable partner for their offspring. If not, they may put an advertisement in the newspaper identifying the qualities they are seeking. The prospective mate is then interviewed by the family to confirm his or her suitability. Or a third person—a matchmaker—may be hired to do the screening and introducing.

Selecting a spouse for a daughter may begin early in the child's life. In some countries, such as Nepal and Afghanistan, child marriage occurs whereby young females from ages 8 to 12 are required to marry an older man selected by their parents. Suicide is the only alternative "choice" for these children. While parents in countries such as India exercise direct control by selecting the partner for their son or daughter, American parents do their own "arranging." They influence mate choice by moving to certain neighborhoods, joining certain churches, and enrolling their children in certain schools, colleges, or universities. Doing so increases the chance that their offspring will "hang out" with, fall in love with, and marry people who are similar in race, religion, education, and social class. Parents want their offspring to meet someone who will "fit in" and with whom they will feel comfortable.

Diamond (2003) emphasized that individuals are biologically wired and capable of falling in love and establishing intense emotional bonds with members of their own or opposite sex. Discovering that one's offspring is in love with and wants to marry someone of the same sex is a challenge for many parents. The social control of love may also occur in the workplace (see the Family Policy section).

Love in the Workplace

With increasing numbers of working women (approximately 47% of the workface), delaying the age of first marriage until their late 20s, and spending eight or more hours with coworkers every day, the workplace has become a predictable context for romantic relationships to develop. More future spouses may meet at work than in academic, social, or religious settings. In a survey of over 700 adults in the workforce, 30% of respondents aged 18-21 and 72% of those over the age of 50 reported having been involved in an office romance (Vault Survey, 2019).

Although such relationships are most often between peers, sometimes a love relationship develops between individuals occupying different status positions. And it can get ugly. Such was the case of Harry Stonecipher, a 68-year-old married man and head of Boeing, and a 48-year old divorcee employee, which resulted in Stonecipher being fired. His dismissal was not because of the affair but because of the negative publicity he brought to the company when his sexually explicit e-mails became public. These types of love relationships are sometimes problematic in the workplace. Four-star

(Continued)

(Continued)

general David Petraeus had an affair with a woman he met at work. He was later demoted.

Advantages of an Office Romance

The energy that both fuels and results from intense love feelings can also fuel productivity at work. If the coworkers eventually marry or enter a nonmarital but committed, long-term relationship, they may be more satisfied with and committed to their jobs than spouses whose partners work elsewhere. Working at the same location enables married couples to commute together, go to company-sponsored events together, and talk shop together. Workplaces such as academia often try to hire both spouses since they are likely to become more permanent employees.

Recognizing the potential benefits of increased job satisfaction, morale, productivity, creativity, and commitment, some companies encourage love relationships among employees. Aware that their single employees are interested in relationships, in Tokyo, Japan, Hitachi Insurance Service provides a dating service for its 400,000 employees, many of whom are unmarried, called Tie the Knot. Those interested in finding a partner complete an application, and a meeting or lunch is arranged with a suitable candidate through the Wedding Commander. In America, some companies hire two employees who are married, reflecting a focus on the value of each employee to the firm rather than on their love relationship outside work.

Disadvantages of an Office Romance

However, workplace romances can also be problematic for the individuals involved as well as for their employers. When a workplace romance involves a supervisor and subordinate relationship, other employees might make claims of favoritism or differential treatment. In a typical differential-treatment allegation, an employee, usually a woman, claims that the company denied her a job benefit because her supervisor favored another female coworker—who happens to be the supervisor's girlfriend.

If a workplace relationship breaks up, it may be difficult to continue to work in the same environment and others at work may experience the fallout. A breakup that is less than amicable may result in efforts by partners to sabotage each other's work relationships and performance, to instigate incidents of workplace violence and harassment, or make allegations of sexual harassment or do all of these actions.

Company Policies on Office Romances

Some companies such as Walt Disney, Universal, and Columbia have "anti-fraternization" clauses that impose rules on workers talking about private issues or sending personal e-mails. Some British firms have "love contracts" that require workers to tell their managers if they are involved with anyone in the office. Other companies, have anti-nepotism policies prohibiting married couples working in the same department.

Most companies do not prohibit romantic relationships among employees. However, the company may have a policy prohibiting open displays of affection between employees in the workplace and romantic relationships between a supervisor and a subordinate. Most companies have no policy regarding relationships at work and generally regard romances between coworkers as "none of their business." There are some exceptions to the general permissive policy regarding workplace romances. Many companies have written policies prohibiting intimate relationships when one member of the couple is in a direct supervisory position over the other. These policies may be enforced by transferring or dismissing employees who are discovered in romantic relationships. ●

THEORIES ON THE ORIGINS OF LOVE

Various theories have been suggested with regard to the origins of love.

Evolutionary Theory

Love has an evolutionary purpose by providing a bonding mechanism between adults who become parents during the time their offspring are dependent infants. Love's strongest bonding lasts about four years after the birth of a child, the time during which children are most dependent and when two parents are most beneficial to the developing infant. "If a woman was carrying the equivalent of a twelve-pound bowling ball in one arm and a pile of sticks in the other, it was ecologically critical to pair up with a mate to rear the young," observed anthropologist Helen Fisher (Toufexis, 1993). The "four-year itch" is Fisher's term for the time at which parents with one child are most likely to divorce—the time when the woman can more easily survive without parenting help from the male. If the couple has a second child, doing so resets the clock, and "the seven-year itch" is the next most vulnerable time.

Learning Theory

Learning theory emphasizes that love feelings develop in response to behaviors of each partner toward the other. Individuals in a new relationship who smile at each other, compliment each other, touch each other endearingly, and do things for each other are engaging in behaviors that encourage the development of love feelings. When these positive behaviors occur in a relationship context with no negative behavior toward each other and there is no competing love relationship, love feelings may flourish.

Sociological Theories

Rusu (2018) reviewed classic sociological views of love including that of Max Weber. Weber viewed love as a means of sensual salvation in an increasingly rationalized social world based on impersonal formal relationships. Another sociological theory of love is the wheel model which focuses on the social context in which love feelings develop; it has four stages—rapport, self-revelation, mutual dependency, and fulfillment of personality needs (Reiss, 1960). In the rapport stage, each partner has the feeling of having known the partner before, feels comfortable with the partner, and wants to deepen the relationship.

Such desire leads to self-revelation or self-disclosure, whereby each reveals intimate thoughts to the other about oneself, the partner, and the relationship. Such revelations deepen the relationship because it is assumed that the confidences are shared only with special people, and each partner feels special when listening to the revelations of the other. As the level of self-disclosure becomes more intimate, feelings of mutual dependency develop. Each partner is happiest in the presence of the other and begins to depend on the other for creating the context of these euphoric feelings. "I am happiest when I am with you" is the theme of this stage.

The feeling of mutual dependency involves the fulfillment of personality needs. The desires to love and be loved, to trust and to be trusted, and to support and be supported are met in the developing love relationship.

Psychosexual Theory

According to psychosexual theory, love results from blocked biological sexual desires. In the sexually repressive mood of his time, Sigmund Freud (1905-1938) referred to love as "aim-inhibited sex." Love was viewed as a function of the sexual desire a person was not allowed to express because of social restraints. In Freud's era, people would meet, fall in love, get married, and have sex. Freud felt that the socially required delay from first meeting to having sex resulted in the development of "love feelings." By extrapolation, Freud's theory of love suggests that love dies with marriage, which offers unlimited access to one's sexual partner.

Biochemical Theory

"Love is deeply biological" wrote Carter and Porges (2013), who reviewed the biochemistry involved in the development and maintenance of love. **Oxytocin** is released from the pituitary gland during the expulsive stage of labor that has been associated with the onset of maternal behavior in lower animals, but oxytocin may be manufactured in both women and men when an infant or another person is present —hence it is not dependent on the birth process (Carter & Porges, 2013). Oxytocin has been referred to as the "cuddle chemical" because of its significance in bonding. Later in life, oxytocin seems operative in the development of love feelings between lovers during sexual arousal. Oxytocin may be responsible for the fact that more women than men prefer to continue cuddling after intercourse.

Phenylethylamine (PEA) is a natural, amphetamine-like substance that makes lovers feel euphoric and energized. The high that they report feeling just by being with each other is from PEA that the brain releases into their bloodstream. The natural chemical high associated with love may explain why the intensity of passionate love decreases over time. As with any amphetamine, the body builds up a tolerance to PEA, and it takes more and more to produce the special kick. Hence, lovers develop a tolerance for each other. "Love junkies" are those who go from one love affair to the next to maintain the high. Alternatively, some lovers break up and get back together frequently as a way of making the relationship new again and keeping the high going.

The neurobiology of love emphasizes that romantic love and maternal love are linked to the perpetuation of the species. Romantic love bonds the male and female together to reproduce, take care of, and socialize new societal members, whereas maternal love ensures that the mother will prioritize the care of her baby over other needs. Because of the social functions of these love states, neurobiologists have learned via brain imaging techniques that both types of attachment activate regions of the brain that access the brain's reward system, areas rich in oxytocin and vasopressin receptors. Both lovers and mothers are very happy and focused. They are on a biological mission, and the reward center of their brain keeps them on track.

Attachment Theory

The outcry in response to separating immigrant children from their parents in 2018 has solid empirical support that enforcing that policy has negative long-term consequences. The attachment theory of love emphasizes that a primary motivation in life is to be emotionally connected with other people. Children

TABLE 2.1

Love Theories and Criticisms

THEORY	CRITICISM
Evolutionary—love is the social glue that bonds parents with dependent children and spouses with each other to care for offspring.	The assumption that women and children need men for economic and emotional survival is not true today. Women can have and rear children without male partners.
Learning—positive experiences create love feelings.	The theory does not account for (1) why some people share positive experiences but do not fall in love, and (2) why some people stay in love despite negative behavior by their partner.
Psychosexual—love results from blocked biological drive.	The theory does not account for love couples who report intense love feelings and have sex regularly.
Sociological—the wheel theory whereby love develops from rapport, self-revelation, mutual dependency, and personality need fulfillment.	Not all people are capable of rapport, revealing oneself, and so on.
Biochemical—love is chemical. Oxytocin is an amphetamine-like chemical that bonds mother to child and produces a giddy high in young lovers.	The theory does not specify how much of what chemicals result in the feeling of love. Chemicals alone cannot create the state of love; cognitions are also important.
Attachment—primary motivation in life is to be connected to others. Children bond with parents and spouses to each other.	Not all people feel the need to be emotionally attached to others. Some prefer to be detached.

abandoned by their parents and placed in foster care or separated due to immigration policies are vulnerable to having their early emotional attachment to their parents disrupted and developing "reactive attachment disorder" (Stinehart et al., 2012). This disorder involves a child who is anxious and insecure since he or she does not feel he or she is in a safe environment. As adults, these children are emotionally distant, insecure, and jealous (Knapp et al., 2014).

Each of the theories of love presented in this section can be criticized (see Table 2.1).

HOW WE FALL IN LOVE

Various social, physical, psychological, physiological, and cognitive conditions influence the development of love relationships.

Social Conditions for Love

Love is a social label given to an internal feeling. Our society promotes love through popular music, movies, and novels. These media convey the message that love is an experience to pursue, enjoy, and maintain. People who fall out of love are encouraged to try again: "Love is lovelier the second time you fall." Unlike people reared in Eastern cultures, Americans grow up in a cultural context which encourages them to turn on their radar for love.

Physical Conditions for Love

The probability of being involved in a love relationship is influenced by approximating the cultural ideal of physical appearance. Halpern et al. (2005) analyzed data on a nationally representative sample of 5,487 African-American, Caucasian, and Hispanic adolescent females and found that for each one-point increase in body mass index (BMI), the probability of involvement in a romantic relationship dropped by 6%. Hence, to the degree that a woman fulfills our society's unrealistic expectations of the "ideal" slender body type, she increases the chance of attracting a partner and becoming involved in a romantic love relationship. Body mass is also related to relationship problems among women. Skoyen et al. (2018) found that low relationship quality was associated with higher BMI in women. Similarly, high relationship quality was related to lower BMI in women.

CULTURE AND DIVERSITY

The preference for thin and trim is not universal. Two researchers compared body-mass preferences among 300 cultures throughout the world and found that 81% of cultures preferred a female body size that would be described as "plump" (Brown & Sweeney, 2009).

Psychological Conditions for Love

Psychological conditions associated with falling in love include perception of reciprocal liking, personality, high self-esteem, and self-disclosure.

Perception of Reciprocal Liking

One of the most important psychological factors associated with falling in love is the perception of reciprocal liking (Riela et al., 2010). When one perceives that he or she is desired by someone else, this perception has the effect of increasing the attraction toward that person. Having someone look at you and smile conveys the message that it is OK for you to approach the other person and say "hello."

Personality Qualities

The personality qualities of the love object have an important effect on your falling in love (Riela et al.,

A healthy self-concept is a prerequisite for falling in love. Feeling good about yourself translates into the belief that others can feel good about you too.
Courtesy of Trevor Werb

2010). Viewing the partner as intelligent or having a sense of humor are examples of qualities that makes the lover want to be with the beloved. The person who falls in love must also be available to do so. Individuals, such as artists, musicians, or poets, who are immersed in creative, artistic endeavors describe less interest in being involved in a love relationship since they may derive their emotional satisfactions from their solitary work (Campbell & Kaufman, 2017).

Self-Esteem

High self-esteem is important for falling in love because it enables individuals to feel worthy of being loved, of being positively evaluated. Feeling good about yourself allows you to believe that others are capable of loving you. Individuals with low self-esteem doubt that someone else can love and accept them. Weisskirch (2017) noted that high self-esteem is associated with less fear of being negatively evaluated by a dating partner. Experiencing reciprocal love can also enhance one's self-esteem. Feeling loved, desired, and accepted by another person may boost one's confidence, since one feels that he or she is worthy of love.

People who have never felt loved and wanted may require constant affirmation from a partner as to their worth and may cling desperately to that person out of fear of being abandoned. Such dependence—the modern term is *codependency*—may also

---

APPLYING SOCIAL RESEARCH

Taking Chances in Romantic Relationships

Making choices sometimes includes taking chances—moving in together after knowing each other for a short time, changing schools to be together, and forgoing condom usage thinking "this time won't end in a pregnancy." To assess the degree to which undergraduates take chances in their relationships, 381 students completed a 64-item questionnaire posted on the Internet. Over 80% of respondents were female and approximately 74% were White. About 53% of the respondents described their relationship status as emotionally involved with one person, with 4% engaged or married.

Findings

Of the various risk-taking behaviors identified on the questionnaire, eight were identified by 25% or more of the respondents as behaviors they had participated in. These eight are identified in Table 2.2..

Almost three fourths, about 72%, of the sample self-identified as being a "person willing to take chances in my love relationship." However, only slightly over one-third of the respondents indicated

TABLE 2.2

Most Frequent Chances Taken in a Romantic Relationship (N = 381)

RISK-TAKING BEHAVIOR	PERCENT
Unprotected sex	70
Being involved in a "friends with benefits" relationship	63
Broke up with a partner to explore alternatives	46
Had sex before feeling ready	41
Disconnected with friends because of partner	34
Maintained long-distance relationship (1 year)	32
Cheated on partner	30
Lied to partner about being in love	28

(Continued)

(Continued)

that they considered themselves as risk takers in general. This suggests that college students may be more likely to engage in risk-taking behavior in love relationships than in other areas of their lives. Both love and alcohol were identified as contexts for increasing one's vulnerability for taking chances in romantic relationships—60% and 66%, respectively. Both being in love and drinking alcohol—both love

and alcohol may be viewed as drugs—gives one a sense of immunity from danger or allows one to deny danger. ●

Source: Adapted and abridged from L. Elliott, Easterling, B., & Knox, D. (2016). Taking chances in romantic relationships. *College Student Journal, 50*(2), 241-245. The content was also presented as a poster at the annual meeting of the Southern Sociological Society in New Orleans, LA.

encourage staying in unhealthy or abusive relationships because the person may feel "this is all I deserve."

Self-Disclosure

Disclosing oneself is necessary if one is to fall in love—to feel invested in another. Ross (2006) identified eight dimensions of self-disclosure: (1) background and history, (2) feelings toward the partner, (3) feelings toward self, (4) feelings about one's body, (5) attitudes toward social issues, (6) tastes and interests, (7) money and work, and (8) feelings about friends. Disclosed feelings about the partner included "how much I like the partner," "my feelings about our sexual relationship," "how much I trust my partner," "things I dislike about my partner," and "my thoughts about the future of our relationship." Of interest in Ross's findings is that disclosing one's tastes and interests was negatively associated with relationship satisfaction. By telling a partner too much detail about what one liked or didn't, partners discovered something that turned them off and lowered their relationship satisfaction.

Trust is the condition under which people are most willing to disclose themselves. When people trust someone, they tend to feel that whatever feelings or information they share will not be judged and will be kept safe with that person. If trust is betrayed, people may become bitterly resentful and vow never to disclose themselves again. One woman said, "After I told my partner that I had had an abortion, he told me that I was a murderer and he never wanted to see me again. I was devastated and felt I had made a mistake telling him about my past."

It is not easy for some people to let others know who they are, what they feel, or what they think. Alexithymia is a personality trait which describes a person with little affect. The term means "lack of words for emotions," which suggests that the person does not experience or convey emotion. Persons with alexithymia are not capable of psychological intimacy.

Frye-Cox (2012) studied 155 couples who had been married an average of 18.6 years and found that being an alexithymic spouse is associated with lower marital quality. Alexithymia also tends to repel individuals in mate selection in that persons who seek an emotional relationship are not reinforced by alexithymics. Alexithymic individuals may also be alcohol dependent. About 49% of the 274 alcohol dependent individuals in the study by Pombo et al. (2015) were also alexithymic. Another term for alexithymic is aromantic. Two alexithymic or aromantic individuals could enjoy each other's companionship and relationship since neither expects emotional intimacy.

Physiological Condition and Timing of Love

Physical chemistry between partners is unpredictable—it does not happen between all people—but is powerful when it occurs. Partners who feel strong chemistry toward each other escalate their relationship; those who do not have less motivation to become or to stay involved. Timing of interest in love must also be right. There are only certain times in life—for example, when educational and career goals are met or within sight—when people are open to or seek a love relationship. When those times occur, a person is likely to fall in love with the person who is there and who is also seeking a love relationship. Hence, many love pairings exist because each of the individuals is available to the other at the same time—not because they are particularly suited for each other.

Keeping Your Love Alive Across Time

Ogolsky et al. (2016) analyzed how 232 couple relationships changed over a nine-month period. Twenty percent of the couples broke up by the ninth month of the study. Partners most likely to break up were "passionately in love" . . . suggesting great volatility of love. Partners interested in keeping their love alive across time might consider the following:

- **Select your partner carefully**—one who has a similar background, similar interests, values, goals, education, religion, and a personality compatible with yours makes for a good beginning.

- **Drop your expectations**—be aware of the principle of **satiation** (a stimulus loses its value with repeated exposure) and don't be shocked to discover that your partner and your relationship does not stay at the high pitch level of fun, excitement, sex, adventure, and enjoyment later in your relationship compared to earlier.

- **Expect unpredictable life events to alter everything**—death of a parent, infertility, or a serious car accident can change you, your partner, and your relationship. Allow for major life-changing events to come your way.

- **Keep yourself happy and healthy**—take care of your own needs so that you bring to your partner a happy, engaged, and healthy—exercise daily—partner. Do not expect your partner to "fulfill" or "complete" you.

- **Support your partner's interests**—facilitate whatever your partner wants or needs to make his or her own life a fulfilling one.

- **Ensure emotion and physical engagement with each other**—so that neither is vulnerable to looking outside the relationship to fulfill these needs.

- **Plan and execute new activities together**—change the context of the mundane to the new adventure. One couple went to 50 bed and breakfast experiences.

- **Be responsible and keep your relationship on track**— "If you see something, say something" means if you feel that you and your partner are drifting apart, address the issue and change your respective behaviors to put your relationship back on course. If you don't take time to nurture your relationship, you will be taking time to write out checks to your lawyer over your divorce settlement.

Letting Love Die and Moving On

Humans are serial monogamists who typically mate with the same partner for years or even decades but often mate with more than one partner over the life course (Boutwell et al. 2015). Given this trajectory, the researchers suggested that individuals have the innate capacity—evolutionary, cognitive,

neurobiological, and genetic—which allows them to eject a mate and to move on. **Primary mate ejection** can be explained as a functional device designed to transfer and focus resources from one mate to another. For males in need of making adjustments regarding where their resources are flowing, primary mate ejection could have evolved as an unconscious retraction of the affection felt between partners allowing for a redistribution of resources (p. 33).

Thank God I found the GOOD in goodbye.
Beyoncé Knowles

LOVE AS A CONTEXT FOR PROBLEMS

For all of its joy, love is associated with problems. In this section we review seven such problems.

Unrequited or Unreciprocated Love

Unrequited love is a one-sided love where one's love is not returned. An example is from the short story "Winter Dreams" by F. Scott Fitzgerald. Dexter Green is in love with Judy Jones. "He loved her, and he would love her until the day he was too old for loving—but he could not have her." Blomquist and Giuliano (2012) assessed the reactions of a sample of adults and college students to a partner who said "I love you." The predominant response by both men and women was "I'm just not there yet." Both genders acknowledged that while this response was honest, it hurt the individual who was in love.

Making Risky, Dangerous Choices

Plato said that "love is a grave mental illness," and some research suggests that individuals in love make risky, dangerous, or questionable decisions. Non-smokers who become romantically involved with a smoker are more likely to begin smoking (Kennedy et al., 2011). Similarly, couples in love and in a stable relationship are less likely to use a condom (Milhausen et al., 2018).

Ending the Relationship With One's Parents

Some parents disapprove of the partner their son or daughter is involved with to the point that they will end the relationship with their child. "They told

Satiation: a stimulus loses its value with repeated exposure.

Primary mate ejection: evolutionary device which allows one to transfer and focus resources from one mate to another.

Unrequited love: love that is not returned.

Individuals are capable of being in love with two or more people at once.
Courtesy of Trevor Werb

me I couldn't come home if I kept dating this guy, so I stopped going home," said one college student who was involved with a partner of a different race. Choosing to end a relationship with one's parents is a definite downside of love.

Simultaneous Loves

While most individuals in a dating relationship expect fidelity in their partners (Watkins & Boon, 2016), sometimes an individual is in love with two or more people at the same time. While this is acceptable in polyamorous relationships where the partners agree on multiple relationships (discussed later in the chapter), simultaneous loves may become a serious problem with a partner who expects monogamy.

One answer to the dilemma of simultaneous love is to let the clock run. Most love relationships do not have a steady course. Time has a way of changing them. If you maintain both relationships, one is likely to emerge as more powerful, and you will have your answer. Alternatively, if you feel guilty for having two loves, you may make the conscious choice to spend your time and attention with one partner and let the other relationship go in terms of actual time spent with the partner. Although you can have emotions for two people at the same time, you cannot physically be with more than one person at a time. The person with whom you choose to take to significant events is likely to be the person you love "a little bit more" and with whom your love feelings are likely to increase.

Abusive or Stalking Relationships

Twenty-four percent of 3,061 undergraduate males and 39% of 10,002 undergraduate females reported that they had been involved in an emotionally abusive relationship with a partner. As for physical abuse, 4% of the males and 11% of the females reported such previous involvement (Hall & Knox, 2019). Rejected lovers, most of whom are men, may stalk—repeated pursuit of a target victim that threatens the victim's safety—a partner because of anger and jealousy and try to win the partner back. Nineteen percent of the males and 28% of the females in the above sample reported that they had been stalked. Abusive relationships and stalking will be discussed in greater detail in Chapter 13.

Gaslighting

Gaslighting refers to being manipulated by a person who uses the context of love and hope to completely control the person and their perceptions. For example, if a person feels unloved or disrespected, the "gaslighter" will react with dismay that the interpretation is completely wrong and talk the person into discounting their own perceptions or suspicions. In reality, the person is correct but loses confidence in being able to see reality in a relationship and loses complete trust in others out of fear of being misled or emotionally abused again.

Profound Sadness and Depression When a Relationship Ends

Just as love is associated with relationship happiness (Harris et al., 2016), its end is the cause of profound sadness and depression. Fisher et al. (2010) noted that "romantic rejection causes a profound sense of loss and negative affect. It can induce clinical depression and in extreme cases lead to suicide and/or homicide." The researchers studied brain changes via magnetic resonance imaging of ten women and five men who had recently been rejected by a partner but reported they were still intensely "in love." Participants alternately viewed a photograph of the partner who rejected them and a photograph of a familiar individual interspersed with a distraction-attention task. Their responses while looking at the photo of the person who rejected them included feelings of love, despair, good, and bad memories, and wondering about why this happened. Brain image reactions to being rejected by a lover were similar to withdrawal from cocaine.

While there is no clinically recognized definition or diagnostic criteria for "love addiction," some similarities to substance dependence include euphoria and unrestrained desire in the presence of the love object or associated stimuli, a state resembling drug intoxication; negative mood and sleep disturbance when separated from the love object, which is similar to drug withdrawal; intrusive thoughts about the love object; and problems associated with love which may lead to clinically significant impairment or distress (Reynaud et al., 2011).

JEALOUSY IN RELATIONSHIPS

Jealousy is an emotional response to a perceived or real threat to an important or valued relationship. People experiencing jealousy fear being abandoned and feel anger toward the partner or the perceived competition. Jealousy may be innate in that, in most traditional contexts, it reflects one's psychological survival and well-being since one's source of interpersonal reinforcement is threatened. Jealously may also be about one's social survival since the termination of a relationship will impact one's relationships with others (e.g., friends the couple share in common).

Jealousy is a learned emotion and varies with social context. Polygynous Mormons reflect the context where wives are socialized to "share" the husband. Not only is the principle of multiple wives "God's will," but also the wives embrace the presence of other wives who help out with child care and housework. While her research findings have been questioned, Margaret Mead noted that the Samoans were absent in reporting feelings of jealousy (Freeman, 1999).

Some individuals in polyamorous or open relationships report zero feelings of jealousy for their partner's emotional and sexual relationship with others. The absence of jealousy is unusual among undergraduates. Of 12,893 undergraduates, 53% agreed with the statement, "I am a jealous person"; women were slightly more likely to report feeling jealous than men (Hall & Knox, 2019).

Types of Jealousy

Barelds-Dijkstra and Barelds (2007) identified three types of jealousy as reactive jealousy, anxious jealousy, and possessive jealousy. **Reactive jealousy** consists of feelings that are a reaction to something the partner is doing, such as texting a former lover. **Anxious jealousy** is obsessive ruminations about the partner's alleged infidelity that make one's life a miserable emotional torment. **Possessive jealousy** involves an attack on the partner or the alleged person to whom the partner is showing attention. Jealousy is a frequent motive when one romantic partner kills another.

....

Jealousy: an emotional response to a perceived or real threat to an important or valued relationship.

Reactive jealousy: jealous feelings that are a reaction to something the partner is doing.

Anxious jealousy: obsessive ruminations about the partner's alleged infidelity that can make one's life a miserable emotional torment.

Possessive jealousy: involves attacking the partner or the alleged person to whom the partner is showing attention.

Jealousy may occur when one's partner shows an interest in someone else.
Courtesy of Trevor Werb

Causes of Jealousy

Jealousy can be triggered by a number of external or internal factors.

External Causes

External factors refer to behaviors a partner engages in that are interpreted as (1) an emotional or sexual interest or both in someone or something else, or (2) a lack of emotional or sexual interest or both in the primary partner.

Internal Causes

Internal causes of jealousy refer to characteristics of individuals that predispose them to jealous feelings, independent of their partner's behavior. Examples include being mistrustful, having low self-esteem, being highly involved in and dependent on the partner, and having no perceived alternative partners available (Pines, 1992). The following are explanations of these internal causes of jealousy:

1. **Mistrust.** If an individual has been cheated on in a previous relationship, that individual may have learned to be mistrustful in subsequent relationships. Such mistrust may manifest itself in jealousy. Mistrust and jealousy may be intertwined. Indeed, one must be careful if cheated on in a previous relationship not to transfer those feelings to a new partner. Disregarding the past is not easy but constantly reminding oneself of reality—"My new partner has given me *zero* reason to be distrustful"—is important. Otherwise, the person may feel unjustly accused and want to end the relationship.

2. **Low self-esteem.** Individuals who have low self-esteem tend to be jealous because they don't believe anyone will love them.

It is devastating to a person with low self-esteem to discover that a partner has, indeed, selected someone else.

3. **Lack of perceived alternatives.** Individuals who have no alternative person or who feel inadequate in attracting others may be particularly vulnerable to jealousy. They feel that if they do not keep the person they have, they will be alone since no one else will want them.

4. **Insecurity.** Individuals who feel insecure—for example, no commitment from the partner—in a relationship may experience higher levels of jealousy. They feel at any moment their partner could find someone more attractive and desirable and end the relationship.

Consequences of Jealousy

Jealousy can have both desirable and undesirable consequences.

Desirable Outcomes

Reactive jealousy may have a positive outcome on one's relationship. Not only may reactive jealousy signify that the partner is cared for, but also the partner may learn that the development of other romantic and sexual relationships is unacceptable (Barelds-Dijkstra & Barelds, 2007).

One wife said:

When I started spending extra time with this guy at the office, my husband got jealous and told me he thought I was getting in over my head and asked me to cut back on the relationship because it was "tearing him up." I felt he really loved me when he told me this, and I stopped having lunch with the guy at work. I'm sure his jealousy kept me out of trouble.

The researchers noted that making the partner jealous may also have the positive function of assessing the partner's commitment and of alerting the partner that one could leave for greener mating pastures. Hence, one partner may deliberately evoke jealousy to solidify commitment and ward off being taken for granted. In addition, sexual passion may be reignited if one partner perceives that another might take one's partner away. That people want what others want is an adage that may underlie jealousy.

Undesirable Outcomes

Shakespeare referred to jealousy as the "green-eyed monster," suggesting that it sometimes leads to undesirable outcomes for relationships. Anxious jealousy with its obsessive ruminations about the partner's alleged infidelity can make individuals miserable. They are constantly thinking about the partner being with the new person, which they interpret as confirmation of their own inadequacy. And, if the anxious jealousy results in repeated unwarranted accusations, a partner can tire of such attacks and end the relationship with the accusing partner.

In its extreme form, jealousy may have fatal consequences. Possessive jealousy involves an attack on a partner or an alleged person to whom the partner is showing attention. In the name of love, people have stalked or killed the beloved and then killed themselves in reaction to being rejected.

Gender Differences in Coping With Jealousy

Zengel et al. (2013) studied a national sample of women and men and found that women reported higher levels of jealousy than men. The researchers also noted that heterosexual men were more jealous when their partner engaged in sexual intercourse with another man than when their partner was emotionally involved with someone else. Evolutionary theorists point out that men are wired to care about the paternity of their offspring, which is the basis of their focus on physical fidelity.

Strategies Used to Cope With Jealousy

Women tend to turn to food and men to alcohol as strategies to cope with feelings of jealously (Knox et al., 1999). Both might consider exercise as a way of relieving their stress.

POLYAMORY

Compersion, sometimes thought of as the opposite of jealousy, is the approval, indeed embracing, of a partner's emotional and sexual involvement with another person. Polyamory means multiple loves. Poly = many; amor = love. **Polyamory** is a lifestyle in which two lovers embrace the idea of having multiple lovers. By agreement, each partner may have numerous emotional and sexual relationships. Seguin (2019) confirmed wide ranging attitudes toward polyamory including 1) valid and beneficial; 2) unsustainable; 3) perverse, amoral, and unappealing; 4) acceptable; and 5) deficient. Persons more likely to identify as polyamorous are those with sexual

Compersion: the opposite of jealousy; the approval of a partner's emotional and sexual involvement with someone else.

Polyamory: a lifestyle in which two lovers embrace the idea of having multiple lovers. By agreement, each partner may have numerous emotional and sexual relationships.

These individuals are in a polyamorous relationship—while they regard their relationship as primary, each has emotional and sexual relationships with others.

minority identities, such as bisexual, pansexual, and transgender, and are previously divorced (Balzarini, et al., 2019).

About 80% of the 85 adult members of Twin Oaks Intentional Community in Louisa, Virginia, and 97% of the 30-member Acorn community next door are polyamorous in that each partner may have several emotional or physical relationships with others at the same time. Although not legally married, these adults view themselves as emotionally bonded to each other and may rear children together.

Polyamory is not **swinging**—a married or pair-bonded couple agree that each will have recreational sex with others while maintaining an emotional allegiance to each other. A qualitative study on swinging was conducted by Vaillancourt and Few-Demo (2014) whereby each spouse of ten couples responded to a series of questions over the Internet. In most cases, the husband became aware of swinging first and introduced the idea to the spouse. Over several discussions, a joint decision was made to pursue other swinging couples. Most couples were private about their swinging behavior and felt that it had a positive outcome for their relationship.

Swinging is recreational sex. A basic "rule" that swingers have with their partners is that they do not fall in love with others. In contrast, polyamorous lovers prefer enduring, intimate relationships that include sex. People in polyamorous relationships often have the goal to rid themselves of jealous feelings and to increase their level of compersion. Morrison et al. (2013) compared polyamorous and monoamorous individuals and found that the former had higher intimacy needs and interests than the latter.

Swinging: individuals in a committed relationship agree to have recreational sex with other individuals, independently or as a couple.

Advantages and Disadvantages of Polyamory

Polyamory has both advantages and disadvantages. Advantages of polyamory include greater variety in one's emotional and sexual life; the avoidance of hidden affairs and the attendant feelings of deception, mistrust, betrayal, or guilt; the avoidance of the pressure of one person meeting all the needs of the other person and the opportunity to have different needs met by different people. The disadvantages of polyamory involve having to manage one's feelings of jealousy and emotions in multiple relationships and having limited time with each partner. Of the latter, one polyamorous partner said, "With three relationships and a full-time job, I just don't have much time to spend with each partner so I'm frustrated about who I'll be with next." There is also stigma and prejudice associated with polyamory—parents may want nothing to do with their children who live this lifestyle. Finding partners to be polyamorous is also a challenge. While not specific to polyamory, Sizemore and Olmstead (2016) studied willingness to engage in consensual non-monogamy. In a sample of 549 undergraduates only 12.9% were willing to do so. Over three fourths, about 78.7%, were clear about their unwillingness to participate.

Scheff (2014) conducted extensive interviews with poly couples and parents and identified the benefits and difficulties of poly families, multi-partner relationships that raise children and function as families. Benefits included shared resources, honesty and emotional intimacy among family members and multiple role models for children. "Many parents say that their children's lives, experiences, and self-concepts are richer for the multiple loving adults in their families" (p. 201). The difficulties of poly families include social stigma and teenage leverage against poly parents where a disgruntled teen can blackmail their parents, threatening to reveal their unconventional lifestyle to authorities, employers, or teachers.

Scheff's investigation of poly families highlights that the nonsexual emotional ties that bind people in poly families together are far more important than the sexual connections between the adults (Scheff, 2014):

While the sexual relationships polys establish with each other get the most attention from the media. . . .they are not the. . . most important aspect of poly relationships. . . .Much like heterosexual families, poly families spend far more time hanging out together, doing homework, making dinner, carpooling, folding laundry, and having family meetings or relationship talks than they do having sex (pp. 206-207).

Seguin et al. (2017) examined relationship quality of 3,463 individuals in monogamous, open, and polyamorous relationships and found no significant differences in reported relationship quality and equity. The researchers concluded that "these results strongly suggest that these types of relationship agreements are equally healthy viable options."

Conley et al. (2018) compared the sexual satisfaction of individuals in monogamous and consensually non-monogamous (CNM) relationships and found slightly lower sexual satisfaction and orgasm rates among monogamous individuals. Swingers reported higher sexual satisfaction than monogamous individuals; those in open relationships had equal sexual satisfaction rates with those in monogamous relationships. In addition, relationship satisfaction did not differ between monogamous and CNM groups.

FUTURE OF LOVE RELATIONSHIPS

Love will continue to be one of the most treasured experiences in life. Love will be sought, treasured, and when lost or ended, will be met with despair and sadness. After a period of recovery, a new search will begin. Love will also continue to be associated with positive outcomes such as a sense of well-being, a buffer against stress, and the release of endorphins which are referred to as the "happy hormones" (Deepak, 2019).

As our society becomes more diverse, the range of potential love partners will widen to include those with demographic characteristics different from oneself. Hiroshi Ishiguro of Japan builds androids—"beautiful, realistic, uncannily convincing human replicas." He has suggested that developing love feelings for an android is now a possibility (Mar, 2017).

Some individuals report falling in love with robots and holograms. Researcher Neil McArthur, director of the Center for Professional and Applied Ethics at the University of Manitoba, noted that these individuals are the second-wave digisexuals, people who regard technology as integral to their sexual identity. The first wave was people who used technology such as dating apps to help them find and connect with others. The second wave does not see humans as essential to a romantic experience—they can fall in love with and enjoy a relationship with a humanoid or hologram (Sato et al., 2018).

Finally, while alternatives to monogamy are realized by a small percentage of committed couples, there has been an increased interest in consensual non-monogamy as evidenced by data searchers on Google (Moore, 2017). As diversity in relationships, individualism and relationship norms expand, such an increase may continue.

SUMMARY

What are the meanings of love?
Love remains an elusive and variable phenomenon. Researchers have conceptualized love as a continuum from romanticism—for example, belief in love at first sight, one true love, and love conquers all—to realism, as a style, such as ludic, eros, storge, and mania, and as a triangle consisting of three basic elements—intimacy, passion, and commitment.

How is love under social control?
All parents attempt to influence and control the person their children fall in love with. Love may be blind, but offspring are socialized to know what color a person's skin is—about 90% of Americans fall in love with and marry someone of their same racial background. Because romantic love is such a powerful emotion and marriage such an important relationship, mate selection is not left to chance when connecting an outsider with an existing family and peer network. Unlike Eastern parents who arrange the marriage of their children—in 40% of the world's population, marriages are arranged by the parents—American parents move to certain neighborhoods, join certain churches, and enroll their children in certain schools. Doing so increases the chance that their offspring will "hang out" with, fall in love with, and marry people who are similar in race, education, and social class.

What are the various theories of love?
Theories of love include evolutionary, love that provides the social glue needed to bond parents with their dependent children and spouses with each other to care for their dependent offspring; learning, love that is a feeling based on the positive behavior of the partner; sociological, Reiss's "wheel" theory; psychosexual, love that results from a blocked biological drive; and biochemical, love that involves feelings produced by biochemical events. For example, the neurobiology of love emphasizes that because romantic love and maternal love are linked to the perpetuation of the species, biological wiring ensures the bonding of the male and female to rear offspring and of the mother to the infant. Finally, attachment theory focuses on the fact that a primary motivation in life is to be connected with other people.

What is the process of "falling in love?"
Love occurs under certain conditions. Social conditions include a society that promotes the pursuit of love, peers who enjoy it, and a set of norms that link love and marriage. Body type is related to falling in love in that the closer one's body type or physical condition matches the cultural ideal, the more likely the person is to fall in love. Psychological conditions involve high

self-esteem, a willingness to disclose oneself to others, a perception that the other person has a reciprocal interest, and gratitude. Physiological and cognitive conditions imply that the individual experiences a stirred-up state and labels it "love." People stay in a relationship because it meets important emotional needs, such as satisfaction, they have few alternatives—for example, no place to go—and they have already invested resources like time, money, and friendship networks.

How is love a context for problems?

For all of its joy, love is associated with problems, which include unrequited or nonreciprocated love, making dangerous or destructive choices, ending the relationship with one's parents, simultaneous loves, involvement in an abusive relationship, and profound sadness and depression when a love relationship ends.

What is jealousy—the various types and consequences (positive and negative)?

Jealousy is an emotional response to a perceived or real threat to a valued relationship. Types of jealousy are reactive, where a partner shows interest in another; anxious, which involves ruminations about a partner's unfaithfulness; and possessive which means striking back at a partner or another. Jealous feelings may have both internal and external causes and may have both positive and negative consequences for a couple's relationship.

What is polyamory?

Compersion is the opposite of jealousy and involves feeling positive about a partner's emotional and physical relationship with another person. Polyamory ("many loves") is an arrangement whereby lovers agree to have numerous emotional relationships, which may include sex, with others at the same time. Persons in polyamorous relationships report similar levels of marital satisfaction to those in monogamous relationships.

What is the future of love relationships?

Love will continue to be the most important experience in life. While rates of consensual nonmonogamy will continue to be low, there will be more individuals who develop these agreements with their partners.

KEY TERMS

Agape love style, 35
Anxious jealousy, 45
Arranged marriage, 37
Compersion, 46
Conjugal love, 33
Eros love style, 35
Five love languages, 36
Infatuation, 33

Jealousy, 45
Ludic love style, 34
Lust, 33
Mania love style, 35
Polyamory, 46
Possessive jealousy, 45
Pragma love style, 34
Primary mate ejection, 43

Reactive jealousy, 45
Romantic love, 32
Satiation, 43
Storge love style, 35
Swinging, 47
Unrequited love, 43

WEB LINKS

Polyamory Society
http://www.polyamorysociety.org/

Twin Oaks
https://www.twinoaks.org/

Third Age
http://www.thirdage.com/romance/

Get the tools you need to sharpen your study skills. SAGE edge offers a robust online environment featuring an impressive array of free tools and resources.
Access practice quizzes, eFlashcards, video, and multimedia at **edge.sagepub.com/knox13e**

3

Gender and Diversity

Gender is like a Rubik's Cube with one hundred squares per side, and every time you twist it to take a look at another angle, you make it that much harder a puzzle to solve.

—Sam Killermann, Activist

Learning Objectives

3.1.   Distinguish between the terms *sex* and *gender*

3.2.   Identify five theories of gender role development

3.3.   Recall seven agents which influence gender role learning

3.4.   Discuss the consequences of gender role socialization for women and men

3.5.   Summarize how gender roles are changing

3.6.   Identify future changes to gender and gender roles

Master the content at
edge.sagepub.com/knox13e

Singer/songwriter Taylor Swift was given a boost at birth by her mother, Andrea, that would one day help her launch a career in show business. She selected the gender-neutral name for her baby girl, so that when she grew up and applied for jobs in the male-dominated society, no one would know if she were male or female. . .

Family life researchers note that one of the defining moments in an individual's life is when his or her sex is announced. Gender reveal parties have become commonplace where prospective parents gather with their close friends to share finding out about the baby's sex. Beyond the excitement of "It's a boy" or "It's a girl" is an onslaught of cultural programming affecting the color of the nursery, the name of the baby, and clothing choices.

In this chapter, we examine variations in gender roles and the choices individuals make in how they express their gender behavior. We begin by looking at the terms used to discuss gender issues.

TERMINOLOGY OF GENDER ROLES

In common usage, the terms *sex* and *gender* are often used interchangeably, but social scientists do not regard these terms as synonymous. After clarifying the distinction between *sex* and *gender*, we clarify other relevant terminology, including *gender identity*, *gender role*, and *gender role ideology*.

Sex

Sex refers to the biological distinction between females and males. Hence, to be assigned as a female or male, several factors are used to determine the biological sex of an individual:

> *But I also consider being female such a unique gift, such a sacred joy, in ways that run so deep I can't articulate them. It's a special kind of privilege to be born into the body you wanted, to embrace the essence of your gender even as you recognize what you are up against.*
>
> Lena Dunham, *Not That Kind of Girl*

- *Chromosomes:* XX for females; XY for males
- *Gonads:* Ovaries for females; testes for males
- *Hormones:* Greater proportion of estrogen and progesterone than testosterone in females; greater proportion of testosterone than estrogen and progesterone in males
- *Internal sex organs:* Fallopian tubes, uterus, and vagina for females; epididymis, vas deferens, and seminal vesicles for males
- *External genitals:* Vulva for females; penis and scrotum for males

Even though we commonly think of biological sex as consisting of two dichotomous categories—female and male—biological sex exists on a continuum. Sometimes not all of the items just listed are found neatly in one person. Rather, items typically associated with females or males might be found together in one person, resulting in mixed or ambiguous genitals; such persons are called **intersex individuals**. Indeed, the genitals in these intersex individuals, about 2% of all births, are not clearly male or female. **Intersex development** refers to congenital variations in the reproductive system, sometimes resulting in ambiguous genitals.

Gender

The term **gender** is a social construct that refers to the social and psychological characteristics associated

Sex: the biological distinction between females and males.

Intersex individuals: those with mixed or ambiguous genitals.

Gender: social construct, which refers to the social and psychological characteristics associated with being female, male, or neither.

Weightlifting is traditionally thought of as masculine, but more and more women are incorporating it into their exercise regimens.

with being female or male. Women are often thought of as soft, passive, and cooperative; men as rough, aggressive, and forceful (Clemans & Graber, 2016). In popular usage, gender is dichotomized—**gender binary**—as an either-or concept. This conception is limiting in that not all individuals fit neatly into either-or categories, suggesting that gender might be viewed along a continuum of femininity and masculinity—**gender non-binary**).

Gender is an important term in the Spanish language. For example, Latino is the masculine term and Latina is the feminine version. Recently, the word Latinx has been used as the more inclusive and gender-neutral alternative.

Some people do not like the idea that the terms "woman" and "women" include the words "man" and "men" which they feel suggests symbolically than men are needed to be "complete." In response, they prefer, the word "womyn" to avoid being a subcategory of men. Increasingly, states are adding a non-gender binary identification (X) to designate one's sex rather than M or F. The airline industry allows customers to identify themselves as M(ale), F(emale), U(undisclosed) or X(unspecified). Those who do not identify with a gender have the option of selecting "Mx." as a title. Lamm (2019) noted an increased recognition to allow one to choose one's gender identity and the removal of the category of

Gender binary: a binary that presents gender as either feminine or masculine.

Gender nonbinary: gender is viewed on a continuum and a spectrum of gender identities.

"sex" and the male/female binary from birth certificates and replacing it with the category of "gender" and "X" as the sole option at birth.

Biological Factors

Gender differences are a consequence of biological and social factors. The biological provides a profound foundation for gender role development. Evidence for this biological influence is the experience of the late John Money, psychologist and former director of the now-defunct Gender Identity Clinic at Johns Hopkins University School of Medicine, who encouraged the parents of a boy, Bruce Reimer, to rear him as a girl because of a botched circumcision that left the infant without a penis. Money argued that social mirrors dictate one's gender identity, and thus, if the parents treated the child as a girl—for example, by the name, clothing, and toys they chose—the child would adopt the role of a girl and later that of a woman. The child was castrated and sex reassignment began.

However, the experiment failed miserably; the child as an adult, now calling himself David, reported that he never felt comfortable in the role of a girl and had always viewed himself as a boy. He later married and adopted his wife's three children. In the past, this situation was used as a textbook example of how nurture is the more important influence in gender identity. Today, his case makes the point that one's biological wiring dictates gender outcome. Indeed, David Reimer noted in a television interview, "I was scammed," referring to the absurdity of trying to rear him as a girl. Distraught with the ordeal of his upbringing and beset with financial difficulties, he died by suicide in 2004.

The story of David Reimer emphasizes the power of biology in determining gender identity. Other research supports the critical role of biology, suggesting that male and female brains are different (Brizendine, 2006). However, this "hard-wired" male-vs.-female brain research has been brought into question, suggesting a less sex-linked, more flexible view as explanations for gender role behavior (Jordan-Young & Rumiati, 2012). An international research team (Joel et al., 2015) conducted a comprehensive study based on MRIs of the brains of more than 1,400 male and female subjects. From their analysis of these data and supported by documentation of the interests, behavior, and personality traits of 5,500 male and female subjects, the researchers arrived at a more nuanced and complex view. The previous sexual dimorphic model did not hold up against the new findings of extensive overlap in the characteristics of male and female gray matter, white matter, and neurological connections. The study also found that brains with consistently "male" or "female" characteristics were rare; instead, most brains comprised what the researchers called a "mosaic," with variances observed within each gender, and commonalities observed in both males and females.

Shebot, Hebot or Itbot?

The field of human-robot interaction (HRI) has received increasing cultural visibility due to advances in technology. In order to develop a truly sociable robot, both verbal and nonverbal human communications are involved (Rincon et al., 2018). Gender is also an important factor in human social interaction which impacts one's perceptions, expectations, actions, and interpretations of behavior. Although robots are machines with no gender, a robot's implied gender, such as voice and clothing, can impact human-robot interaction.

Speech is a fundamental element of human communication and has been introduced in human-computer interaction (Hussain et al., 2018). Apple's famous personal digital assistant Siri is a familiar voice assistant (Bhardwaj & Gal, 2018). Users interact with voice assistants like Siri via natural language without written commands like typing. Siri is not only equipped with the ability to interpret human speech, but is able to respond using a synthesized voice. Other popular personal digital assistants include Amazon's Alexa, Google Home Assistant, and Microsoft's Cortana (Hoy, 2018). Interestingly, manufacturers have chosen the gender default voice setting for all personal digital assistants, GPS, and many automated voice systems as female. This may be because women are often considered nurturing and helpful. More specifically, the default voice setting is a non-accented female from North America (Teitel, 2017).

There have been various speculations about the feminization of personal digital assistants. Early research suggested that a female voice was preferred. Pioneer Clifford Nass noted that the human brain favored a female voice as early as the prenatal stage (Griggs, 2011). Gender research also revealed that providing a non-authoritative female voice may lessen user's anxiety when interacting with artificial intelligence (Woods, 2018). Hence, the use of a female voice in artificial intelligence contexts is based on user bias (Steele, 2018).

Robots are machines made by humans. Since the gender gap in the field of engineering is still wide (Catalyst, 2018), robots are very likely to be created and built by men. The overpowering male representation in robotics may also contribute to robot-sexism. In films, animation, and literature, female robots are frequently over-sexualized, objectified, and idealized. The danger of creating "mechanical pinups" and depicting female robots as obedient wives and submissive sexual slaves is not only sexist, but may also fuel new types of fetishism (Kakoudaki, 2014).

Since gender is a salient factor in human interaction, should the design of robots include the ability of robots to recognize gender cues and respond to users differently according to gender? Or should all robots be made gender neutral? As human-robot interactions increase, these are questions for researchers and engineers to ponder. ●

This finding was corroborated by the study's personality analysis segment, which found that internal consistency per gender was "extremely rare." Based on these results, researchers concluded that the human brain cannot be regarded as two separate classes of male and female. Although further research is needed, this study provides compelling scientific data for the conception of gender as a cultural construct, calling into further question the biological determinism perspective.

Social Factors

Nevertheless, **socialization**—the process through which we learn attitudes, values, beliefs, and behaviors appropriate to the social positions we occupy—does impact gender role behaviors, and social scientists tend to emphasize the role of social influences in gender differences. Later in the chapter we discuss seven agents of socialization, all of which are social factors. While the degree of

....

Socialization: the process through which we learn attitudes, values, beliefs, and behaviors appropriate to the social positions we occupy.

influence of biological and social factors will continue to be debated, there is agreement that both are important.

Although her research is controversial, Margaret Mead (1935) focused on the role of social learning in the development of gender roles in her study of three cultures. She visited three New Guinea tribes in the early 1930s, and observed that the Arapesh socialized both men and women to be feminine, by Western standards. The Arapesh people were taught to be cooperative and responsive to the needs of others. In contrast, the Tchambuli were known for dominant women and submissive men— just the opposite of our society. Both of these societies were unlike the Mundugumor, which socialized only ruthless, aggressive, "masculine" personalities. The inescapable conclusion of this cross-cultural study is that human beings are products of their social and cultural environments and that gender roles are learned.

Gender Identity

"I have always thought of myself as more of a woman," said Caitlyn Jenner, (formerly Bruce Jenner), in a television interview. She was disclosing that while she had the anatomy of a male, she saw herself as a woman. **Gender identity** is the psychological state of viewing oneself as male, female, a blend of both, or neither. Some individuals are **agender** in that they do not identify as having a gender identity at all. Still others are **genderfluid** in that they change conceptions of how they feel and how they view themselves. **Genderqueer** individuals can consider themselves as non-binary—not feminine or masculine—but a blend of both. People who are **cisgender** feel that their gender identify matches their biological sex.

Some individuals prefer gender fluid terms which can be used in reference to both relationships and family. For instance, instead of referring to an individual as their "boyfriend" or "girlfriend," the couple may agree to refer to each other as their "partner" or "significant other."

The word **transgender** is a term for a person whose gender identity does not match the biological sex they were assigned at birth. Transgender individuals have the biological and anatomical sex of being male or female but the self-concept of the other sex. "I am a female trapped in a man's body" reflects the feelings of the male-to-female transsexual (MtF), who may take hormones to develop breasts and reduce facial hair and may have surgery to artificially construct a vagina. The female-to-male transsexual (FtM) is a biological and anatomical female who feels, "I am a man trapped in a female's body." This person may take male hormones to grow facial hair and deepen their voice and may have surgery to create an artificial penis. This person lives full time as a man.

Transsexual is an older term for the person who has had had hormonal or surgical intervention to change his or her body to align with his or her gender identity. Individuals need not take hormones or have surgery to be regarded as transgender. The

distinguishing variable is living full time in the role of the gender opposite one's biological sex. A man or woman who presents full time as the opposite gender is a transgender person by definition. While still used as an identity label by some, the term transgender has become the term of choice.

Transgender women and men are typically rejected as potential dating partners. Across a sample of 958 heterosexual, lesbian, gay, bisexual, queer, and trans individuals, 87.5% indicated that they would not consider dating a trans person, with cisgender heterosexual men and women being most likely to exclude trans persons from their potential dating pool (Blair & Hoskin, 2019). Swanbrow Becker et al. (2017) also found that transgender undergraduates reported higher rates of trauma and suicide compared to cisgender peers.

Cinderella,

I want to wear your shoes

Dress in pastel pink, not blues

Wear red lipstick and rouge

Maybe this year on Halloween

I'll dress up just like you

And the world will finally see me

From my own point of view

Caroline Schacht

Gender Roles

Gender roles are social norms which specify the socially appropriate behavior for females and males in a society. All societies have expectations of how boys and girls, men and women should behave. Gender roles influence women and men in virtually every sphere of life. Soltanpanah et al. (2018) found that gender role satisfaction—whether egalitarian or traditional—predicts life satisfaction.

Some gender-role differences continue to this day. A Pew Research Poll revealed that about seven-in-ten adults or 71% said it was very important for a man to be able to support a family financially to be a good husband or partner, while just 32% said the same for a woman to be a good wife or partner (Geiger & Livingston, 2019). In addition, in heterosexual marriages, men are still expected to propose. Only 5% of heterosexual marriages begin with a proposal from the woman (Cass, 2014).

Gender identity: the psychological state of viewing oneself as male, female, a blend of both, or neither.

Agender: not identifying as having a gender identity.

Gender fluid: the capacity to feel and present as a male sometimes, as a female at other times and as androgyne at still other times.

Genderqueer: individuals can consider themselves as non-binary—not feminine or masculine—but a blend of both.

Cisgender: one's gender identity matches his or her biological sex.

Transgender: abbreviated as "trans"—describes a person whose gender identity does not match the biological sex they were assigned at birth.

Transsexual: older term for the person who has had had hormonal or surgical intervention to change his or her body to align with his or her gender identity.

Gender roles: social norms which specify the socially appropriate behavior for females and males in a society.

FIGURE 3.1

Source: Trans Student Educational Resources.

Gender role expectations tend to be more traditional in Latino culture. Machismo refers to traditional masculine pride and the husband or father is expected to protect, provide, and defend his family. Marianismo refers to traditional femininity such as purity, chastity, and virtuosity.

The term **sex roles** is often confused with and used interchangeably with the term *gender roles*. However, whereas gender roles are socially defined and can be enacted by either women or men, sex roles are defined by biological constraints and can be enacted by members of one biological sex only—for example, wet nurse, sperm donor, or child bearer. You might want to complete the Self-Assessment on Gender Role Attitudes on page 373 to find out the degree to which you are traditional or egalitarian.

Sex roles: roles defined by biological constraints and enacted by members of one biological sex only: for example, wet nurse, sperm donor, child-bearer.

Gender Role Ideology

Gender role ideology refers to beliefs about the proper role of relationships between women and men in society. Expressing one's interest in initiating a date or spending time together can be conveyed verbally and nonverbally. The traditional heterosexual dating script expected women to give nonverbal cues, such as eye contact and a smile, and men to verbally ask for a date or propose marriage. Egalitarian norms and technology have provided more ways of initiating a relationship. Some high schools have the Sadie Hawkins dance where girls ask boys out to dance. Although men are usually the initiators of dates, more women are comfortable texting and asking men out.

However, the egalitarian gender role ideology is dominant. Of 12,406 undergraduates, 65% of the women and men reported equal power. Twenty percent of the women and 24% of the men reported that they had more power (Hall & Knox, 2019). Sells and

Gender role ideology: the proper role of relationships between women and men in a society.

Gender Worlds of Sex, Betrayal, and Love

In spite of egalitarian changes in our society, women and men report significantly different experiences. The table below reflects some of these differences in a large non-random sample of 12,822 undergraduates.

Percent Agreement on Sex, Betrayal And Love*

ITEM	FEMALE (N = 9,830)	MALE (N = 2,992)	SIG.
Sexual Experiences			
I have masturbated.	72%	97%	.000
I have hooked up/had sex with a person I just met.	24%	35%	.000
I regret my choice for sexual intercourse the first time.	25%	16%	.000
Betrayed			
I have been involved with someone who cheated on me.	55%	49%	.000
Love at First Sight			
I have experienced love at first sight.	24%	36%	.000

Source: Based on original data from S. Hall, & Knox, D. (2019). Relationship and sexual behaviors of a sample of 12,822 undergraduates. Unpublished data collected for this text. Department of Family, Consumer, and Technology Education Teachers College, Ball State University and Department of Sociology, East Carolina University, Greenville, NC.

Ganong (2017) presented five gender role relationship options to 451 emerging adults: (a) male-head/female-complement, (b) male-senior/female-junior partner, (c) partner-equal, (d) female-senior/male-junior partner, and (e) female-head/male-complement. The overwhelming majority selected the egalitarian model in which they projected the greatest couple satisfaction. The authors noted, "Egalitarian relationships may be viewed as more appealing and satisfying than other types of partnerships because both partners are seen as equally contributing to household duties, household income, and family decision-making." Bay-Cheng et al. (2018) studied 395 heterosexual relationships and noted that while egalitarian relationships were consistently associated with greater quality—deeper intimacy, less turmoil, more pleasure—women more often reported that they felt subordinate.

Hilliard et al. (2019) assessed feminist attitudes and found that higher scorers on the Liberal Feminist Attitude and Ideology Scale (LFAIS) varied by gender: more women achieved higher scores than men; sexual minorities, such as LGBTQ individuals, outperformed heterosexuals; people of color outscored their White counterparts; and seniors outpaced first year students. Still, traditional gender experiences have not disappeared (see the feature "Applying Social Research: Gender Worlds of Sex, Betrayal, and Love").

Traditional American gender role ideology has perpetuated and reflected patriarchal male dominance and male bias in almost every sphere of life.

Increasingly, relationships are becoming more egalitarian.

Even our language reflects this male bias. For example, the words *man* and *mankind* have traditionally been used to refer to all humans. There has been a growing trend away from using male-biased language. Dictionaries have begun to replace *chairman* with *chairperson* and *mankind* with *humankind*.

Egalitarian Relationship

Egalitarian relationship is a term often used to describe the modern relationship. While the definition may be elusive, factors involved in making up an egalitarian relationship include mutual respect where credence is given to each partners opinions and values; support for achieving each other's goals; fidelity, both emotionally and sexually; sharing power, where there is no "boss" in the relationship; open dialogue where there is a free-flowing exchange of information; and negotiation of win-win outcomes for conflictual issues. Egalitarian partners are engaged in enhancing the life of each other.

THEORIES OF GENDER ROLE DEVELOPMENT

Various theories attempt to explain why women and men exhibit different values and behaviors.

Biosocial/biopsychosocial

In the discussion of gender at the beginning of the chapter, we noted the profound influence of biology on one's gender. **Biosocial theory** emphasizes that social behaviors, such as gender roles, are biologically based and have an evolutionary survival function. For example, women tend to select and mate with men whom they deem will provide the maximum parental investment in their offspring. The term **parental investment** refers to any venture by a parent that increases the offspring's chance of surviving and thus increases reproductive success of the adult. Parental investments require time and energy. Women have a great deal of parental investment in their offspring and they tend to mate with men who have high status, economic resources, and a willingness to share those economic resources. As we will see in the parenting chapter, economic resources are not inconsequential as the average cost today of rearing a child from birth to age 18 is around $250,000.

....

Biosocial theory: also referred to as **sociobiology**; social behaviors (for example, mate selection) are biologically based and have an evolutionary survival function.

Parental investment: any investment by a parent that increases the offspring's chance of surviving and thus increases reproductive success.

The biosocial explanation, also referred to as **sociobiology**, for mate selection is extremely controversial. Critics argue that women may show concern for the earning capacity of a potential mate because they have been systematically denied access to similar economic resources, and selecting a mate with these resources is one of their remaining options. In addition, it is argued that both women and men, when selecting a mate, think more about their partners as companions to have fun with than as future parents of their offspring.

Bioecological

Urie Bronfenbrenner's bioecological model, which evolved from his ecological model, emphasizes the importance of understanding bidirectional influences between an individual's development and his or her surrounding environmental contexts. The focus is on the combined interactive influences so that the predispositions of the individual interact with the environment, culture, and society, resulting in various gender expressions. For example, the individual will read what gender role behavior his or her society will tolerate and adapt accordingly.

Social Learning

Derived from the school of behavioral psychology, the social learning theory emphasizes the roles of reward and punishment and observational learning or modeling in explaining how a child learns gender role behavior. This is in contrast to the biological explanation for gender roles. For example, consider the real-life example of two young brothers who enjoyed playing "lady"; each of them put on a dress, wore high-heeled shoes, and carried a pocketbook. Their father came home early one day and angrily demanded, "Take those clothes off and never put them on again. Those things are for women." The boys were punished for "playing lady" but later rewarded with their father's approval for boxing and playing football.

The use of makeup by females is designed to present an image that approximates the socially learned cultural image of femininity.

Reward and punishment alone are not sufficient to account for the way in which gender roles are learned. Children also learn gender roles when parents or peers offer direct instruction. In addition, many of society's gender rules are learned through modeling. In modeling, children observe and imitate another's behavior. Gender role models include parents, peers, siblings, and characters portrayed in the media.

The impact of modeling on the development of gender role behavior is controversial. For example, a modeling perspective implies that children will tend to imitate the parent of the same sex, but children in all cultures are usually reared mainly by women. Yet this persistent female model does not seem to interfere with the male's development of the behavior that is considered appropriate for his gender. One explanation suggests that boys learn early that our society generally grants boys and men more status and privileges than it does girls and women. Therefore, boys devalue the feminine and emphasize the masculine aspects of themselves.

Identification

Although researchers do not agree on the merits of Freud's theories, Freud was one of the first theorists to study gender role acquisition. He suggested that children acquire the characteristics and behaviors of their same-sex parent through a process of identification. Boys identify with their fathers, and girls identify with their mothers. The classic example is the son watching his father shave and the daughter watching her mother give herself an at-home manicure.

Cognitive-Developmental

The cognitive-developmental theory of gender role development reflects a blend of the biological and social learning views. According to this theory, the biological readiness of the child, in terms of cognitive development, influences how the child responds to gender cues in the environment (Kohlberg, 1966). For example, gender discrimination—the ability to identify social and psychological characteristics associated with being female or male—begins at about age 30 months. However, at this age, children do not view gender as a permanent characteristic. Thus, even though young children may define people who wear long hair as girls and those who never wear dresses as boys, they also believe they can change their gender by altering their hair or changing clothes.

Not until age six or seven do children view gender as permanent (Kohlberg, 1966; 1969). In Kohlberg's view, this cognitive understanding involves the development of a specific mental ability to grasp the idea that certain basic characteristics of people do not change. Once children learn the concept of gender permanence, they seek to become competent and proper members of their gender group. For example, a child standing on the edge of a school playground may observe one group of children jumping rope while another group is playing football. That child's gender identity as either a girl or a boy connects with the observed gender-typed behavior, and the child joins one of the two groups. Once in the group, the child seeks to develop behaviors that are socially defined as gender-appropriate.

AGENTS OF SOCIALIZATION

Three of the four theories discussed in the preceding section emphasize that gender roles are learned through interaction with the environment. Indeed, though biology may provide a basis for one's gender identity, cultural influences in the form of various socialization agents—parents, peers, religion, and the media—shape the individual toward various gender roles. These powerful influences, in large part, dictate what people think, feel, and do in their roles as men or women. In the next section, we look at the different sources influencing gender socialization.

Family

The family is a gendered institution in that female and male roles are highly structured by gender. The names parents assign to their children, the clothes they dress them in, and the activities they direct, such as hunting for boys and shopping for girls, all reflect gender roles.

Parents often encourage different gender socialization for their children in the toys they provide. Kollmayer et al. (2018) confirmed that when selecting toys for their children, parents rated same-gender-typed and gender-neutral toys as more desirable for their children than cross-gender-typed toys. Egalitarian parents also permit a greater range of interests and behaviors in their children than traditional parents did. Younger parents, parents with lower educational levels, and fathers reported more traditional gender role attitudes than did older parents, parents with higher educational levels, and mothers.

Reich et al. (2018) revealed how LEGOs are marketed to male and female consumers via brick colors and characters. A content analysis showed gendered messages that encourage boys to enact various skilled professions, heroism, and expertise, whereas girls are encouraged to focus on having hobbies, being domestic, caring for others, socializing, being amateurs, and appreciating and striving for beauty. Indeed, these alternatives promote stereotyped gender roles for enacting femininity and masculinity in play.

Cordero-Coma and Esping-Andersen (2018) also demonstrated that parents serve as models for the gender roles their children adopt. Analysis of data on 2,293 sons and daughters who lived with their parents at ages 18 and 19 and whose parents reported their own time spent on housework when their children were ages 8 and 11 revealed that parental division of labor increased the likelihood of sons participating in similar behavior.

In addition to parents as a family socialization agent, siblings also influence gender role learning. As noted in Chapter 1, the relationship with one's sibling, particularly in sister-sister relationships, is likely to be the most enduring of all relationships. In addition, growing up in a family of all sisters or all brothers intensifies social learning experiences toward femininity or masculinity. A male reared with five sisters and a single-parent mother is likely to reflect more feminine characteristics than a male reared in a home with six brothers and a stay-at-home dad.

CULTURE AND DIVERSITY

Samoan society and culture provides a unique example of gender role socialization via the family. The Fafafini, commonly called Fafa, are males reared as females. There are about 3,000 Fafafini in Samoa. The practice arose when there was a lack of women to perform domestic chores and the family had no female children. Thus, effeminate boys-were identified and socialized and reared as females. Fafafini represent a third gender, neither female nor male; they are unique and valued, not stigmatized. Most Samoan families have at least one Fafafini child who takes on the role of a woman, including having sex with men (Abboud, 2013).

Race

Race impacts gender roles. Regarding African American women, Floro et al. (2014) identified four stereotypes: Mammy, the Black woman who is expected to take care of others; Jezebel, the Black woman who uses sex to get what she wants; Sapphire, the Black woman who is loud and angry; and Superwoman, the Black woman who is strong and survives. These stereotypes may still be operative and, unfortunately, may influence one's perception of the desirability of the Black woman as a potential partner. The intersection between race and gender has been noted. African American mothers report holding less traditional gender role attitudes than fathers; and mothers' gender role attitudes are associated with their offsprings' gender role attitudes (Lam et al., 2018). One study suggested that African American adolescent males have more flexible gender role attitudes. Rather than a hypermasculine self-concept, African American adolescent males reported a combination of feminine and masculine gender roles (Buckley, 2018).

Peers

Although parents are usually the first socializing agents that influence a child's gender role development, peers become increasingly important. Mercer et al. (2018) observed that observation of peer behavior is related to an individual engaging in that behavior. Weymouth and Buehler (2018) also noted that peer influence, particularly for adolescents, is operative in academic performance, relationship functioning, substance misuse, and suicide. Finally, Azad et al. (2018) emphasized that peer influence is often critical in regard to entrance into deviant behavior, substance abuse, and exiting such behaviors. Hence, the decision to behave differently requires the decision to change one's social context since these contexts, particularly peers, have enormous social learning impacts.

Religion

An example of how religion impacts gender roles involves the Mormon Church which is dominated by men and does not provide positions of leadership for women. Traditional religion also emphasizes traditional marital roles for women and men. More recently, Burchardt (2018) noted how religion is being used in South Africa to resocialize men. There are the dual notions of men as dominant, oppressing women and emphasizing their headship construed as "traditional masculinity"; on the other end, versions of masculinity may focus on gender equality and be viewed as "liberal." The current impact of the Charismatic Christian and Pentecostal religions in Cape Town end up providing mixed messages and outcomes.

Education

The educational institution is another socialization agent for gender role ideology. Spinner et al. (2018) investigated the impact of stereotypic and counter-stereotypic peers pictured in children's magazines on children's gender flexibility around toy play and preferences, playmate choice, and social exclusion behavior on 82 children, ages four to seven. A girl, for example, would be shown with a toy pony versus a boy being shown with a toy car. Results revealed significantly greater gender flexibility around toy play and playmate choices among children in the counter-stereotypic condition compared to the stereotypic condition.

CULTURE AND DIVERSITY

Data comparing 109 countries on the World Economic Forum Gender Gap Index from 1 to 5 revealed that Iceland, Norway, Finland, Sweden, and Ireland rank as the top five countries with the United States ranking 25; Yemen ranks 109. In all countries, men evidence higher income, salaries, education, and political power (Nowakowski, 2017b).

Economy

The economy of the society influences the roles of the individuals in the society. The economic institution is a very gendered institution. **Occupational sex segregation** is the concentration of men and women in different occupations which has grown out of traditional gender roles. Men dominate as airline pilots, architects, and auto mechanics; women dominate as elementary school teachers, florists, and hair stylists.

Female-dominated occupations tend to involve greater flexibility. Bensidoun and Trancart (2018) noted that the reason women still earn 12% less than men is that they have different priorities. When asked if they want a stable job, one with the potential for advancement or one which provides a good "work-life" balance, the latter is chosen more often by women than men. Women prefer jobs that provide flexibility for family roles. Increasingly, occupations are becoming less segregated on the basis of gender, and social acceptance of

Occupational sex segregation: the concentration of women and men in different occupations.

nontraditional career choices has increased. Barth et al. (2016) found that females in STEM majors—science, technology, engineering and math—find romantic partners who support their major and career interests.

Mass Media

Mass media, such as the Internet, movies, television, magazines, newspapers, novels, music, computer games, and music television videos, all reflect and shape gender roles. Media images of women and men typically conform to traditional gender stereotypes, and media portrayals depicting the exploitation, victimization, and sexual objectification of women are common. A content analysis of 2,000 screenplays revealed that 60% of the dialogue was written for men (Anderson & Daniels, 2017). Chang and Ward (2017) reiterated the common gender biases in Disney films. However, a focus on appearance may be changing. A study of 12 Disney films from *Snow White* to *Frozen* revealed a decrease in compliments related to appearance and an increase in compliments related to skills (Nowakowski, 2017a).

As for the gender role influence of music, Flynn (2016) conducted a content analysis of rap, R&B, and hip-hop and found frequent references to female body objectification. Regarding novels, Arvanitak (2019) noted that while some romance novels, such as Harlequin Mills and Boon postmillennial "Modern" novels, reflect the influence of feminism, "ultimately these tales demand of these autonomous identities that the heroine is still required to be 'swept off her feet.'"

Regarding television news media, men dominate as anchors in all three major networks—CBS, NBC, and ABC. While women may substitute, men are anchors. Ouahidi (2018) noted that Moroccan news broadcasts are dominated by men. Based on a content analysis of a two-week period, "males seem to be associated more with hard and soft news than their female counterparts. In addition, both male and female reporters rely on male sources to comment on the news content they report" (p. 99).

The cumulative effects of family, peers, religion, education, the economic institution, and mass media perpetuate gender stereotypes. Each agent of socialization reinforces gender roles that are learned from other agents of socialization, thereby creating a gender role system that is deeply embedded in our culture. All of these influences affect relationship choices (see Table 3.2).

TABLE 3.2

Effects of Gender Role Socialization on Relationship Choices

WOMEN	MEN
1. A woman who is not socialized or encouraged to regard all career options for her will narrow the options she feels are "appropriate" for her gender.	1. Men who are socialized to define themselves in terms of their occupational success and income may discover that their self-esteem and masculinity are vulnerable if they become unemployed, retired, or work in a low-income job.
2. Women who are socialized to play a passive role and not initiate relationships will bypass interactions that might develop into valued relationships.	2. Men who are socialized to restrict their experience and expression of emotions are denied the opportunity to discover the rewards of emotional interpersonal involvement.
3. Women who are socialized to be passive will be less likely to require egalitarian relationships with men.	3. Men who are socialized to believe it is not their role to participate in domestic activities (e.g., child rearing, food preparation, or house cleaning) will not develop competencies in these life skills. Potential partners may view domestic skills as desirable and reject more traditional males.
4. Women who internalize society's standards of beauty and view their worth in terms of youth and appearance are likely to feel less positive about themselves as they age. Their negative self-concept may result in their "settling" and staying in unsatisfactory relationships.	4. Heterosexual men who focus on cultural definitions of female beauty overlook potential partners who might not fit the cultural beauty ideal but who would be wonderful life companions.
5. Women who are socialized to accept that they are solely responsible for taking care of their parents, children, and husband are likely to experience role overload. In this regard, some women may feel angry and resentful, which may have a negative impact on their relationships.	5. Men who are socialized to have a negative view of women who initiate relationships will be restricted in their relationship opportunities. Men who are socialized to be in control of relationship encounters may alienate their partners, who may desire equality.

CONSEQUENCES OF TRADITIONAL GENDER ROLE SOCIALIZATION

This section discusses positive and negative consequences of traditional female and male socialization in the United States.

Consequences of Traditional Female Role Socialization

In this section we summarize some of the negatives of being socialized as a woman in U.S. society. Each consequence may or may not be true for a specific woman. For example, although women in general have less education and income, a particular woman may have more education and a higher income than a particular man.

CULTURE AND DIVERSITY

Most women do not have equality with men. In 2019, only six countries had equal rights for men and women. Belgium, Denmark, France, Latvia, Luxembourg, and Sweden scored full marks of 100 in the World Bank's "Women, Business and the Law 2019" report. The average score was 74.71. The United States scored 83.75. The various issues identified in the different countries were freedom of movement, starting a job, getting paid, getting married, having children, running a business, managing assets, and getting a pension (Picheta & Mirchandani, 2019).

Negative Consequences of Traditional Female Role Socialization

There are several negative consequences of being socialized as a woman in our society.

1. **Less Income.** Although women earn more college degrees than men and about half of PhDs, they have lower academic rank and earn less money. The lower academic rank in a university job is because women often give priority to the care of their children and family over the time it takes to publish articles (the condition of promotion). Women still earn 12% of what men earn, even when their level of educational achievement is identical (see Table 3.2). Women are still more likely than men to be more family than career oriented (Fernandez-Cornejo et al., 2016). Indeed, women with young children are more likely to scale back on their work demands than men who have young children (Young & Schieman, 2018). Almost half, about 45%, of 10,006 undergraduate females in contrast to 38% of 3,055 undergraduate males identified "having a happy marriage" as their top value. Thirty-five percent of these undergraduate males in contrast to 32% of the undergraduate females identified "having a career that I love" as a top value (Hall & Knox, 2019). In a study of 738 professional women, 45% reported that having children has had a negative impact on their career (Korn Ferry Survey, 2018).

TABLE 3.3

Women's and Men's Median Income With Similar Education

	BACHELOR'S	MASTER'S	DOCTORAL DEGREE
Men	$63,269	$80,083	$101,591
Women	$41,045	$54,571	$72,018

Source: *ProQuest Statistical Abstract of the United States*, 2019, Online Edition, Table 730.

2. **Feminization of Poverty.** Another reason many women are relegated to a lower income status is the **feminization of poverty.** This term refers to the disproportionate percentage of poverty experienced by women living alone or with their children. Single mothers are particularly associated with poverty.

When head-of-household women are compared with married-couple households where both spouses are employed, the median income is $36,658 versus $106,082 (*ProQuest Statistical Abstract*, 2019). In contrast, the median income for head-of-household men is $51,568. The process is cyclical—poverty contributes to teenage pregnancy because teens have limited supervision (e.g., parents working minimum wage jobs) and few alternatives to parenthood. Such early childbearing interferes with educational advancement and restricts women's earning capacity, which keeps them in poverty. Their offspring are born into poverty, and the cycle begins anew.

3. **Higher Risk for Sexually Transmitted Infections.** Due to the female anatomy, women are more vulnerable to sexually transmitted infections and HIV; they receive more bodily fluids from men. Therefore, skills and confidence to negotiate condom use and practice safer sex are crucial for cisgender women's health.

4. **Negative Body Image.** Sharp and Keyton (2016) examined the ideologies of 496 undergraduate women and found that higher endorsement of normative romantic ideologies was associated with higher preoccupation with thinness and appearance, and preoccupation with thinness was linked to higher disordered eating. In effect, women valued involvement in a romantic relationship and were aware of the advantage a thin and trim figure afforded them in being sought by men.

The cultural emphasis on beauty is extensive. There are upwards of 4,000 beauty pageants annually in the United States. The effect for many women who do not match the cultural ideal is to have a negative body image. American women also live in a society that devalues them in a larger sense. Their lives and experiences are not taken as seriously as men's. **Sexism** is an attitude, action, or institutional structure that subordinates or discriminates against individuals or groups because of their sex. Sexism against women reflects the tradition of male dominance and presumed male superiority in American society. **Benevolent sexism** is a related term and reflects the belief that women are innocent creatures who should be protected and supported. While such a view has positive aspects, it assumes that women are best suited for domestic roles and need to be taken care of by a man since they are not capable of taking care of themselves.

5. **Less Personal and Marital Satisfaction.** An analysis of data on 707 marriages revealed that wives in traditional marriages were particularly likely to report lower marital satisfaction (Bulanda, 2011). Such lower marital satisfaction of wives is attributed to power differentials in the marriage. Traditional husbands expect to be dominant

Fishing is thought of as a "man's sport," but many women enjoy this activity.

Feminization of poverty: the idea that women, particularly those who live alone or with their children, disproportionately experience poverty.

Sexism: an attitude, action, or institutional structure that subordinates or discriminates against individuals or groups because of their biological sex.

Benevolent sexism: the belief that women are innocent creatures who should be protected and supported.

Female Genital Alteration

Female genital alteration, more commonly known as FGC (female genital cutting), female genital mutilation, female circumcision or clitoridectomy, involves cutting off the clitoris and or excising, partially or totally, the labia minora or labia majora or both. In some cases, the labia majora are also stitched together to prevent sexual intercourse or the vaginal opening is narrowed by a seal in a procedure called infibulations. The alteration is often carried out without anesthesia, resulting in potential pain, bleeding, infection, and shock (Turbitt, 2017).

Worldwide, up to 140 million women have undergone FGC (Nakku, 2019). In the United States, half a million females have had or are at risk for this procedure. Among them is Renee Bergstrom who reported that a fundamentalist Christian physician mutilated her genitals to prevent her from masturbating (Baldas, 2017). Federal law criminalizes the performance of FGC on females under 18 in the United States; however, the procedure is not unknown in this country. Dr. Jumana Nagarwala of Detroit was arrested for performing the operation (Baldas, 2017). More commonly, young women are sent back to their country of origin for the procedure. Over 90% of women from Djibouti, Egypt, Eritrea, Ethiopia, Mali, Sierra Leone, and Northern Sudan have had the procedure with 109,205 women in Egypt alone having had it done (Diop & Stewart, 2015). The American Academy of Pediatrics condemns all types of female genital cutting.

The practice of FGC is not confined to a particular religion. The reasons for the practice include the following factors:

a. Sociological and cultural—parents believe that female circumcision makes their daughters lose their desire for sex, which helps them maintain their virginity and helps to ensure their marriage ability and fidelity to their husbands. Hence, the "circumcised" female is seen as one whom males will desire as a wife. FGC is seen as a "rite of passage" that initiates a girl into womanhood and increases her bonding and social cohesion with other females.

b. Hygienic and aesthetic—female genitalia are considered dirty and unsightly so their removal promotes hygiene and provides aesthetic appeal.

c. Religious—some Muslim communities practice FGC in the belief that the Islamic faith demands it, but it is not mentioned in the Qur'an.

What is the outcome of FGC for the woman's sexuality? Abdulcadir et al. (2016) reported data on the comparison of 15 women with FGC and 15 uncut women as a control group matched by age and parity. Results revealed that women with FGC had a significantly smaller volume of the clitoris and scored significantly lower on sexual desire than women without FGC. Lien (2017) interviewed Gambian men in regard to the sexuality of their women partners who were cut and uncut. Most preferred uncut partners citing low interest, rare orgasm, and lack of responsiveness in cut women. The comments of two respondents are below:

> *There are big differences between cut and uncut women. The cut women don't have feelings, so I was not happy with them. Both partners need to have feeling. You are not 100% satisfied with them. The thing that gives them feeling is taken away. (Wolof, 34 years)*

> . . .

> *I have two wives. One is completely flat and levelled. We have sexual problems. She never becomes aroused. It is boring. I am not satisfied and she is not either. She is always dry and never wet. (Mandinka, 50 years)*

The usual treatment for vaginal pain such as suggesting other options for sexual expression would not be considered culturally appropriate (Connor et al., 2016). Changing a country's deeply held beliefs about FGC begins with increasing the education of women. In Sierra Leone, a country of six million, over 90% of the females have undergone female genital alteration. However, since 2010, an alternative Bondo ceremony is being provided for some girls which allows them to become a woman without FGA. ●

and expect their wives to take care of the house and children. Life satisfaction and relationship satisfaction are also related and variable over time (Roberson et al., 2018).

6. **Fearful of Talking About Sex.** Women are also more uncomfortable talking about sex than men. Based on interviews with 95

women ages 20-68, the researchers noted that the respondents, in general, feared being disapproved of for communicating sexual desire or talking about sexual behavior (Montemurro et al., 2015).

Before ending this section on negative consequences of being socialized as a woman, look at the Family Policy feature on female genital alteration. This is more of an issue for females born in some African, Middle Eastern, and Asian countries than

Female genital alteration: cutting off the clitoris or excising (partially or totally) the labia minora.

for women in the United States. However, the practice continues even here.

Positive Consequences of Traditional Female Role Socialization

We have discussed the negative consequences of being born and socialized as a woman. However, there are also decided benefits.

1. **Longer Life Expectancy.** Women have a longer life expectancy than men. It is not clear if their greater longevity is related to biological or to social factors. Females born in the year 2019 are expected to live to the age of 82, in contrast to men, who are expected to live to the age of 77 (Life Expectancy, 2019).

2. **Stronger Relationship Focus.** Women, compared to men, are socialized to seek and have sex in the context of an emotional relationship which results in fewer sexual partners. Mitchell et al. (2019) compared national data on British women and men who reported seven and 14 lifetime partners, respectively. Women also prioritize family over work and do more child care than men. Mothers provide more "emotion work," helping children with whatever they are struggling with.

3. **Keeps Relationships on Track.** Women are more likely to initiate "the relationship talk" to ensure that the relationship is moving forward (Nelms et al., 2012). Women are also more self-disclosing (Horne & Johnson, 2018) which is associated with emotional bonding.

4. **Bonding With Children.** Another advantage of being socialized as a woman is the potential to have a closer bond with children. In general, women—whether in heterosexual or same-sex relationships—tend to spend more time with children than men (Prickett et al., 2015). Hall and Willoughby (2019) noted in their study of emerging adults that women, compared to men, continue to emphasize marriage and parenthood as a central foci of their lives. Table 3.4 summarizes the consequences of traditional female role socialization.

5. **Higher Self-confidence Among Singles.** Seventy-three percent of single women compared to 64% of single men in the Match. com (2017) survey of 5,509 single respondents reported a higher level of confidence. This positive self-image may be a result of the cultural theme of female empowerment and higher percent of college degrees. Women are also focused on completing their training

TABLE 3.4

Consequences of Traditional Female Role Socialization

NEGATIVE CONSEQUENCES	POSITIVE CONSEQUENCES
Less income (more dependent)	Longer life
Feminization of poverty	Stronger relationship focus
Higher STD/HIV infection risk	Keeps relationships on track
Negative body image	Bonding with children
Less personal/marital satisfaction	Identity not tied to job
Fearful of talking about sex	Higher confidence

and establishing themselves economically—hence, less dependent on men for their self-worth and economic survival.

Consequences of Traditional Male Role Socialization

Male socialization in American society is associated with its own set of consequences. As with women, each consequence may or may not be true for a specific man.

Negative Consequences of Traditional Male Role Socialization

There are several negative consequences associated with being socialized as a man in U.S. society.

1. **Identity synonymous with occupation.** Ask men who they are, and many will tell you what they do. Society tends to equate a man's identity with his occupational role. Male socialization toward greater involvement in their careers often ends in their being obsessive to the point of "working 80 hours a week nonstop" noted Canadian psychologist Jordan Peterson (Luscombe, 2018).

2. **Lower educational attainment.** Owens (2016) confirmed that men, compared to women, complete fewer years of education—they drop out of high school at higher rates and have fewer years of college and college graduation. The researcher suggested that one reason may be the gender difference in early self-regulation and prosocial behaviors. Boys display higher levels of behavior problems which reduce their success in later adult educational achievement.

3. **Limited expression of emotions.** Petts et al. (2018) noted that men who mirror the traditional masculine norm of emotional stoicism may find it difficult as a father to engage children emotionally and to nurture them.

4. **Fear of intimacy.** Men are reluctant to become emotionally close since it means that they may lose control, an embarrassing quality for traditional men.

5. **Custody disadvantages.** Courts are sometimes biased against divorced men who want custody of their children. Because divorced fathers are typically regarded as career focused and uninvolved in child care, some are relegated to seeing their children on a limited basis, such as every other weekend or four evenings a month.

6. **Shorter life expectancy.** As noted above, men typically die five years sooner, at age 77, than women, who die at 82. One explanation is that the traditional male role emphasizes achievement, competition, and suppression of feelings, all of which may produce stress. Not only is stress harmful to physical health, but it may lead to compensatory behaviors such as smoking, alcohol, or other drug abuse, and dangerous risk-taking behavior (e.g., driving fast or binge drinking). (See Family Policy: Men's Health)

> *We've begun to raise daughters more like sons...but few have the courage to raise our sons more like our daughters.*
> Gloria Steinem, feminist pioneer

Positive Consequences of Traditional Male Role Socialization

As a result of higher status and power in society, men tend to have a more positive self-concept and greater confidence in themselves. In a sample of 3,069 undergraduate men, 76% noted agreement with the statement, "I have a very positive self-concept." In contrast, 73% of 10,005 undergraduate women agreed with the statement (Hall & Knox, 2019). Men also enjoy higher incomes and an easier climb up the good-old-boy corporate ladder; they are also stalked, followed, and harassed less often than women. Other benefits are the following:

1. **Greater freedom of movement.** Unlike women, who are taught to fear rape, walk in well-lit places, and not walk alone after dark, men are typically walk about as they please.

2. **Greater pool of potential partners.** Because of the mating gradient—men marry "down" in age and education whereas women marry "up"—men, particularly White men, tend to marry younger women so that a 35-year-old man may view women from 20 to 35 years of age as possible mates. However, a woman, typically a White woman, of age 35 is more likely to view men her same age or older as potential mates. As she ages, fewer men are available. As noted, these mating gradient norms are typically not operative for African Americans as Black women are open to marrying younger men and vice versa.

3. **Norm of initiating a relationship.** Men are advantaged because traditional norms allow them to be aggressive in initiating relationships with women. In addition, men tend to initiate marriage proposals and the bride more often takes the last name of her husband rather than keeping her last name. Table 3.5 summarizes the consequences of being socialized as a male.

4. **Higher general life satisfaction.** Urbano-Contreras et al. (2019) found higher general life satisfaction among men than women.

FAMILY POLICY

Men's Health

Elder and Griffith (2016) emphasized a major deficit in cultural awareness and public policy— men's health. The facts are shocking: The life expectancy at birth of males in the United States when compared to that of males in 21 other highly developed countries, such as Canada, Sweden, Japan, and so forth, is the lowest and has been for the past three decades! Compared to women, males are less likely to go to a health care provider, to be uninsured, and to avoid taking care of themselves. The culprit is regarded as men's thinking that health care is not masculine. To combat this perception, one slogan emphasized that "Real Men Wear Gowns." Elder and Griffith (2016) suggest a need to move beyond conceptions of masculinity to examine the lack of public policies which emphasize men's health. ●

Source: Adapted and abridged from Elder, K., & Griffith, D. M. (2016). Men's health and masculinity. *American Journal of Public Health, 106,* p. 1157.

TABLE 3.5

Consequences of Traditional Male Role Socialization

NEGATIVE CONSEQUENCES	POSITIVE CONSEQUENCES
Identity is work role/lower education	Higher income and occupational status
Limited emotionality	More positive self-concept
Fear of intimacy; lonelier	Less job discrimination
Disadvantaged in getting custody	Freedom of movement; more partners to select from; more normative to initiate relationships
Shorter life	Happier life satisfaction

The researchers also noted that the couple's relationship was the factor most responsible for the individual's general life satisfaction. Feeling that they were being taken care of for women and feeling that their partner was concerned when they were sad for men were the specific behaviors associated with the couples' reported life satisfaction.

CHANGING GENDER ROLES

Androgyny and gender fluidity emphasize that gender roles are changing.

Androgyny

In the past, masculinity and femininity were conceptualized as opposite ends of a spectrum. In the 1970s, Dr. Sandra Bem opposed this gender polarization and developed the concept of psychological androgyny. She conceptualized that femininity and masculinity exist on two distinct continua rather than on a single bipolar continuum (Keener & Mehta, 2017). She developed the Bem Sex Role Inventory (BMSI), which measures different hypothesized psychological gender traits. Participants who had an equal mix of both stereotypically masculine and feminine traits were categorized as androgynous. This type of androgyny is linked to positive mental health adjustment (Martin et al., 2016).

Bem's concept of androgyny challenged traditional categories of what is masculine vs. feminine. However, it's important to note that there have been

....

Androgyny: a blend of traits that are stereotypically associated with masculinity and femininity.

many changes in gender studies in the past 40 years. Later in her career, Bem recognized that her concept of androgyny overlooked the culture that created these concepts of masculinity and femininity. As a result, it "reproduced the gender polarization that it [sought] to undercut" (Bem, 1993). By failing to recognize that "masculine" and "feminine" behaviors are based on social constructs, the concept of psychological androgyny may perpetuate the idea that behavior is inherently gendered.

The modern notion of **androgyny** refers to having a combination of traditionally masculine and feminine characteristics. Someone who is androgynous is not specifically masculine or feminine, and they may identify as non-binary or genderqueer. One may present as androgynous regardless of their gender identity, and androgyny is often presented through clothing. Dressing androgynously may involve unisex clothing or individuals who present as masculine wearing traditionally feminine clothing, such as a dress and high heels.

> I am not male or female. I think I float somewhere in between.
>
> Sam Smith, singer

Genderfluid

Genderfluid abandons the notion of gender as fixed—that one's self-identity can be fluid. To be genderfluid is to feel and present as a male sometimes, as a female at other times, and as androgyne at still other times. See box on "I am Genderfluid."

I AM GENDERFLUID

I am a 22-year-old undergraduate genderfluid person who uses they/them pronouns in place of female pronouns. I was born with female genitalia, but that does not define my gender— just my sex. This means that my gender identity is made up of more than one gender. There are times (and this can vary throughout the day or from day to day) that I identify as a female, male, androgyne (an identity where I am a blend of female and male) or agender (I don't think of myself as any gender). I can't control which gender I happen to be each day or even from minute to minute.

I want to stress that sex and gender are completely different concepts. Sex is a person's anatomy- female, male, or intersex. It includes the person's internal and external sex organs, chromosomes, and hormones. Some people are intersex rather than female or male. Gender is how a person identifies or sees one's self as (seeing myself as a woman, man, etc.).

These photos reflect the gender fluidity of the person when feeling feminine to feeling masculine.
Courtesy of Trevor Werb

A lot of genderfluid people (but not all) experience dysphoria. This means that they experience severe discomfort with their body for not being the gender that they identify with.

The concepts of being pansexual and genderfluid are often confused. Pansexual is a sexual orientation whereby the person may be sexually attracted to others regardless of their sex, gender, age or race. Being genderfluid is a gender identity. (Dolan, K., 2019).

FUTURE OF GENDER ROLES

Gender role relationships are in flux. Not only has the concept of gender neutrality emerged in the culture (Saguy & Williams, 2019), Pipin and Cotter (2018) also observed that there are mixed ideologies at play with today's youth espousing egalitarian norms in the workplace, while more conventional roles in the home with the man the principal breadwinner and the woman more focused on domestic life are regaining acceptance.

Transgender issues will become increasingly visible and legal responses will vary. Nicole Maines, age 17, won a $75,000 lawsuit against her high school which required her to use the staff restroom rather than the restroom for students, signifying legal support for transgender individuals using the restroom of their gender identity. Gender fluidity and intersexuality conversations have also begun. Non-binary identification (X) to designate one's sex rather than M or F on driver's licenses has begun. Unisex bathrooms are becoming more available and Target has also removed pink and blue backing from display shelves that often signify whether a toy is meant for a boy or girl. *Kazoo* is a magazine that has emerged to widen the view of young girls and women about gender roles.

A final change is that men are changing the way they rear their sons. Faith Salie (2018) noticed that when her husband held their five-pound newborn boy in his arms he said "Hi, sweet pea." Not "buddy" or "little man." She noted that she was "witnessing her husband's commitment to raising a sweet boy, a revelation that filled her with unanticipated joy."

SUMMARY

What are the important terms related to gender?
Sex refers to the biological distinction between females and males. One's biological sex is identified on the basis of one's chromosomes, gonads, hormones, internal sex organs, and external genitals, and exists on a continuum rather than being a dichotomy. *Gender* is a social construct and refers to the social and psychological characteristics associated with being female or male. Other terms related to gender include *gender identity,* one's self-concept as a girl or boy; *gender role,* social norms of what a girl or boy "should" do; *gender role ideology,* how women and men "should" interact; and *transgender,* expressing characteristics or having a self-identity different from one's biological sex).

What theories explain gender role development?
Biosocial theory emphasizes that social behaviors, such as gender roles, are biologically based and have an evolutionary survival function. Biopsychosocial theory includes the psychological and personality dimension of gender role expression. Ecobiological emphasizes the interaction of the individual with the environment. Social learning theory emphasizes the roles of reward and punishment and observational learning in explaining how children learn gender role behavior. Identification theory says that children acquire the characteristics and behaviors of their same-sex parent through a process of identification. Cognitive-developmental theory emphasizes biological

readiness, in terms of cognitive development, of the child's responses to gender cues in the environment. Once children learn the concept of gender permanence, they seek to become competent and proper members of their gender group.

What are the various agents of socialization?

Various socialization influences include parents and siblings of different races and ethnicities, peers, religion, the economy, education, and mass media. These shape individuals toward various gender roles and influence what people think, feel, and do in their roles as women or men.

What are the consequences of traditional gender role socialization?

Traditional female role socialization may result in negative outcomes such as less income, negative body image, and lower marital satisfaction but positive outcomes such as a longer life, a stronger relationship focus, keeping relationships on track, and a closer emotional bond with children. Traditional male role socialization may result in the fusion of self and occupation, a more limited expression of emotion, disadvantages in child custody disputes, and a shorter life but higher income,

greater freedom of movement, a greater available pool of potential partners, and greater acceptance in initiating relationships.

How are gender roles changing?

In the past, masculinity and femininity were used to conceptualize opposite ends of the same continuum. Dr. Sandra Bem opposed gender polarization and conceptualized femininity and masculinity as two different axes, thus generating four quadrants (Keener & Mehta, 2017). Androgyny refers to the combination of traits that are stereotypically associated with both masculinity—assertiveness and dominance—and femininity—understanding and caring. It may also imply flexibility of traits; for example, an androgynous individual may be emotional in one situation, logical in another, assertive in another, and so forth.

What is the future of gender roles?

Gender role relationships are in flux. Transgender issues are becoming increasingly visible, which has opened a new conversation of what it means to be male and female or somewhere in between. Gender fluidity and intersexuality conversations have also begun.

KEY TERMS

Agender, 55

Androgyny, 67

Benevolent sexism, 63

Biosocial theory, 58

Cisgender, 55

Female genital alteration, 64

Feminization of poverty, 63

Gender, 52

Gender binary, 53

Gender fluid, 55

Gender identity, 55

Genderqueer, 55

Gender nonbinary, 53

Gender role ideology, 56

Gender roles, 55

Intersex individuals, 52

Occupational sex segregation, 61

Parental investment, 58

Sex, 52

Sex roles, 56

Sexism, 63

Socialization, 54

Transgender, 55

Transsexual, 55

WEB LINKS

American Men's Studies Association
http://www.mensstudies.org/

Equal Employment Opportunity Commission
http://www.eeoc.gov/

Good Men Project
http://goodmenproject.com/about/

Intersex Society of North America
http://www.isna.org/

National Organization for Women (NOW)
http://www.now.org/

Transgender Forum
http://www.tgforum.com/

Get the tools you need to sharpen your study skills. SAGE edge offers a robust online environment featuring an impressive array of free tools and resources.
Access practice quizzes, eFlashcards, video, and multimedia at **edge.sagepub.com/knox13e**

4

Singlehood, Cohabitation, and Living Apart Together

My alone feels so good, I'll only have you if you're sweeter than my solitude.

—Warsan Shire, Somali-British Writer

Learning Objectives

4.1.   Explain the types of singles and the reasons individuals give for delaying marriage

4.2.   Identify the changes in dating in the last 70 years

4.3.   Summarize the differences between hanging out, hooking up, and long-distance relationships

4.4.   Describe the types of cohabitant relationships and the relationship consequences

4.5.   Review the positives and negatives of living apart together

4.6.   Discuss the future of singlehood

The choices of single individuals are changing. Take Erika Anderson, who represents a new commitment too singlehood by marrying herself, or practicing **sologamy**. Like many single individuals, she grew tired of explaining why she wasn't married—a question that often implies that one is not complete on their own. Erika decided to marry herself in a civil ceremony. In doing so, she confirmed that she was enough and she was making an important commitment to herself, someone she loved and trusted.

While sologamy has not "caught on" as a trend, almost one in five, about 19%, of 5,509 Match.com (2017) respondents reported that they did not want a relationship and preferred to stay unattached. Today's single adults, who are interested in marriage, are in no hurry. They enjoy the freedom of singlehood and most put off marriage until their late twenties or early thirties. Previously, marriage was the only lifestyle option and delaying marriage was viewed with suspicion (Trost, 2016).

Young adults in other countries reflect the same pattern—individuals in France, Germany, and Italy are also delaying marriage. In the meantime, the process of courtship has evolved, with various labels and behavioral patterns, including hanging out, hooking up, and "situationship," which refers to those who are partners but their future is unclear. We begin with examining singlehood versus marriage.

SINGLEHOOD

In this section, we discuss the various categories of singles, why individuals are delaying marriage, the choice to be permanently unmarried, and the legal blurring of the married and unmarried.

....

Sologamy: marrying onself

> *It's not just OK to be single for both men and women—it's wonderful to be single, and society needs to embrace singlehood in all its splendiferous, solitary glory.*
>
> Chelsea Handler, actor/comedian

Categories of Singles

The term **singlehood** is most often associated with young unmarried individuals. However, there are three categories of single people: the never-married, the divorced, and the widowed.

Never-Married Singles

Today, about 20% of those ages 25 and older have not married compared to 1960 when only about 10% were single (Wang & Parker, 2014). This results in 37.3 million "never married" males and 32.8 million "never married" females age 18 and older in the United States (*ProQuest Statistical Abstract*,

This single, never married male reports an enriched and engaged life.

....

Singlehood: the relationship status of not being married.

2019, Table 57). These individuals are completing their education and building their careers, while enjoying the freedom of singlehood and its attendant companionship, sex, cohabitation, and procreation.

What are the characteristics of those who never marry? Single men are likely to be less educated (Murray, 2012) and to have lower incomes (Ashwin & Isupova, 2014) than married men. Those who are never married (both men and women) also tend to suffer from obesity (Sobal & Hanson, 2011), are at greater risk for a heart attack (Kilpi et al., 2015), and were reared in single-parent families (Valle & Tillma, 2014). Never-married singles also experience ambiguous loss in that they must cope with the uncertainty of whether or when they will meet a partner with whom they will move toward marriage (Jackson, 2018). Munsch (2015) emphasized that not all singles are stigmatized equally. Never-married singles are more stigmatized than divorced singles. And while singles in the workplace are assumed to be more competent and committed, the rewards to them compared to marrieds are not forthcoming.

The pressure to be married is worse for women. Even amid today's cultural approval of diverse lifestyles and a woman's individual choice for singlehood, Budgeon (2016) notes that while women are free to enjoy whatever sexual relationships they want, they must "undertake whatever remedial measures necessary to make a "good" relationship with a man work" (p. 414). The unmarried disproportionately live in large cities. For example, in New York, 70% of the adults are unmarried; in Washington D C, half of the adults are unmarried. These individuals are often young adults seeking adventure, careers, and relationships.

How happy are single people compared to the pair bonded? Lehmann et al. (2015) analyzed data on persons who were both in or out

While older, unmarried women in America are aware that social approval for their singlehood decreases each year, Chinese women who live in China, are over the age of 27, and are unmarried are referred to as "left-over"—they are the objects of ridicule in the media and by their own families. To escape this stigmatized social category, some of these women become involved in romantic relationships and marriages with foreign men (Zurndorfer, 2018). In Shanghai, parents who have a son or daughter they want to get married will go to the "blind date park" to advertise their children and try to find someone to take them on a date.

of a relationship. Those who were satisfied with their current relationship status—whether in a relationship or not—report higher life satisfaction. Hence, being in a relationship is not the only road to life satisfaction. In a study of 5,500 individuals who were single, over 75% reported that they were happy with their personal life (Fisher & Garcia, 2016).

McCann and Allen (2018) interviewed fourteen single women age 50 or older to ascertain their feelings about never having been married. Women who were highly integrated into an extended family network, typically their family of origin, had little interest in romance in later life. Women not integrated into a kin network were most hopeful of finding a romantic or marriage partner.

Divorced Singles

Another category of those who are single is the divorced. There are 14.6 million divorced females and 10.9 million divorced males in the United States. (*ProQuest Statistical Abstract*, 2019, Table 57). Marriages end because either one or both partners decide to divorce. Either way, the previously married are less interested in remarriage. Only 21% say they would like to marry again (Wang & Parker, 2014).

Widowed Singles

Although divorced people have often chosen to leave their spouses and be single again, the widowed are forced into singlehood. The stereotype of the widow and widower is utter loneliness, even though there may be compensations, such as escape from an unhappy marriage. There are 11.6 million widowed females and 3.2 million widowed males in the United States (*ProQuest Statistical Abstract*, 2019, Table 57).

Individuals Are Delaying Marriage Longer

Having identified the three categories of singles as never-married, divorced, and widowed, we now focus on the never-married, the largest group. A primary question is whether more people are choosing to never marry—we do not know the answer. What we do know is that individuals are *delaying marriage*. Birger (2015) suggested that one of the motivations is an oversupply of educated women—there are four college graduate women for every three college graduate men, ages 22 to 29. There is a reluctance to marry someone with a different educational level. "Classism is bigger than racism in dating," says Evan Marc Katz (Birger, 2015). Hence, with men less inclined to marry women who are more educated,

Is Singlehood for You?

Singlehood is not a one-dimensional concept. Whereas some are committed to singlehood as a permanent lifestyle, others enjoy it for now but intend to marry eventually. An essential difference between traditional marriage and singlehood is the personal, legal, and social freedom to do as you wish. Of 3,035 undergraduate males, 9% reported that maintaining their freedom and never marrying was their top life goal; out of 10,006 undergraduate females, only 6% responded in kind (Hall & Knox, 2019). Those who prefer to never marry may experience various challenges including loneliness, less money, and establishing an identity independent of being in the role of spouse. Consider the following:

1. **Loneliness?** Fifty-six percent of 5,509 Match.com (2017) respondents reported that they felt lonely about the dating landscape. Loneliness may be defined as the subjective evaluation that the number of relationships a person has is smaller than the person desires or that the intimacy the person wants has not been realized. Hansan and Clark (2017) suggested that persons who feel particularly lonely or socially isolated may over-rely on a romantic partner to fulfill a need to belong. But single individuals need not feel lonely. Sarkisian and Gerstel (2016) found that "single individuals are more likely to frequently stay in touch with, provide help to, and receive help from parents, siblings, neighbors, and friends than the married." We noted earlier that researchers McCann and Allen (2018) found that having one's social needs met by one's extended family and family of origin eliminates the negative feelings among the never married in later life about not finding a romantic partner or being in a marriage.

Nevertheless, Fokkema et al. (2012) noted that loneliness is associated with being single. However, Musick and Bumpass (2012) compared spouses, cohabitants, and non-pair-bonded singles and found few differences in terms of social ties. Indeed, singles often report having more connections. Researchers have also confirmed that social media such as Facebook provide a mechanism for individuals to connect and maintain casual relationships (Root et al, 2014).

2. **Less money.** Unmarried individuals who live alone typically have less income than married people. The median income of the single female householder with no husband is $36,658—for the male single householder with no wife, $51,568— compared to a married couple with an income of $106,082 (*ProQuest Statistical Abstract*, 2019, Table 727). The lower income of single women continues into the later retirement years (Alaminos & Ayuso, 2019).

3. **Social identity.** Having a social identity—a role— that defines who a person is, independent of being a spouse, is important. A career provides structure, relationships with others, and a strong sense of identity. "I am a veterinarian—I love my work," said one single female.

4. **Children.** Some individuals want to have a child but not a spouse. We will examine this issue in Chapter 11 in a section on Single Mothers by Choice. There are no data on single men seeking the role of parent. Although some custodial divorced men are single fathers, this is not the same as never having married and having a child. ●

there are more women who want to marry than men. In the meantime, men are involved in their work, take their time, and enjoy singlehood.

Will those who are delaying marriage eventually marry? Probably. But we need to wait until the current cohort of youth reach the age of 85 and beyond to see if our current cohort catches up to their parents (*ProQuest Statistical Abstract*, 2019, Table 57). You can evaluate your own attitude toward singlehood by referring to the "Self-Assessment: Attitudes Toward Singlehood Scale" on page 374.

Reasons for Delaying Marriage

Muraco and Curran (2012) identified thirteen reasons why individuals could delay marriage. These include the need for financial stability, inability to pay for a wedding, doubts about self as a potential spouse, doubts about partner as spouse, quality of relationship, doubts about self as parent, doubts about partner as parent, capability of being economic provider, partner capability of being economic provider, fear of divorce, infidelity, in-laws, and bringing children from own and partner's previous relationships together.

Benefits of Singlehood and Limitations of Marriage

BENEFITS OF SINGLEHOOD	LIMITATIONS OF MARRIAGE
Freedom to do as one wishes	Restricted by spouse or children
Variety of lovers	One sexual partner
Spontaneous lifestyle	Routine, predictable lifestyle
Close friends of both sexes	Pressure to avoid close other-sex friendships
Responsible for one person only	Responsible for spouse and children
Spend money as one wishes	Expenditures influenced by needs of spouse and children
Freedom to move as career dictates	Restrictions on career mobility
Avoid being controlled by spouse	Potential to be controlled by spouse
Avoid emotional and financial stress of divorce	Possibility of divorce

The single lifestyle has its advantages. When considered in combination with the limitations of marriage, it is clear why the lifestyle is attractive. Table 4.1 identifies both the benefits of singlehood and the limitations of marriage. The primary advantage of remaining single is freedom and control over one's life. Once a decision has been made to involve another in one's life, one's choices become vulnerable to the influence of that other person. The person who chooses to remain single may view the needs and influence of another person as something to avoid. "By living alone, I avoid the drama of living with someone else," noted one never-married person.

Blacks are overrepresented among the never married. Black women, particularly, report that there are few Black men who have the education and job stability they prefer in a mate. Only 48% of Black women compared to 55% of White women are married (*ProQuest Statistical Abstract*, 2019, Table 56).

Singlism

Singlism refers to stereotyping, stigmatizing, and discriminating against people who are single (DePaulo, 2018). Much of the discrimination against singles is institutional discrimination—a type of discrimination in which institutional policies result in unequal treatment of a particular group. Institutional discrimination is not necessarily intended to hurt any group. Indeed, many of the policies that discriminate against singles do not deliberately aim to hurt singles, but rather, they aim to benefit married couples. But are policies that provide privileges and benefits to married couples fair to singles? Are policies that give advantages to married people a form of discrimination against singles?

Singlism: refers to stereotyping, stigmatizing, and discriminating against people who are single.

FAMILY POLICY

Singlism—Policies That Discriminate Against Singles

Singles miss out on the more than 1,000 laws that provide legal or financial benefits to married couples. Due to various policies in government, the workplace, and the marketplace, singles typically pay more than married people for taxes, healthcare, and insurance policies, including health insurance, life insurance, home insurance, and car insurance (Arnold & Campbell, 2013). U.S tax laws at the federal and state levels give married couples the option to file taxes jointly, often saving them thousands of dollars.

Social Security policies also deny singles some of the benefits granted to married people. For example, when one married partner dies, the spouse can receive the dead spouse's Social Security if the deceased's benefits are more than the surviving spouse's benefits would be. When single people die, they cannot designate a sibling, close friend, or other loved one to be the beneficiary of their Social Security benefits. Single people who were once married can receive a portion of their ex-spouse's Social Security benefits if they are 62 or older, their marriage lasted at least ten years, and they are not entitled to Social Security based on their own employment history. But single people who do not meet these criteria cannot benefit from another person's Social Security, no matter how close the relationship.

Singles who are also child-free, known as SWOCs (single workers without children) often face discrimination at the workplace. People in this category of singles report that, "their employers assume they have no lives and therefore

(Continued)

(Continued)

can and should devote all of their waking hours to work, meaning employers expect single workers without children to travel with little notice, to work evening hours, and to be available on weekends and holidays (Jones, 2014, p. 1,255). This type of discrimination is not explicitly codified in a company policy, but there are typically no policies to protect SWOCs from this type of discrimination in the workplace.

In the marketplace, singles are also disadvantaged by policies that allow married couples to take advantage of discounted rates for couples. For example, gyms typically offer family plans to couples whereas singles cannot join a gym with a sibling, neighbor, or close friend at a discounted rate.

Policies that give advantages to married individuals and couples mean that the nearly half of U.S. adults who are divorced, widowed, or never married are being treated unfairly. Unmarried Equality is an organization that supports individuals who value being single. According

to the mission statement identified on the website of Unmarried Equality (http://www.unmarried.org/), the emphasis of the organization is to advocate

> . . . for equality and fairness for unmarried people, including people who are single, choose not to marry, cannot marry, or live together before marriage. We provide support and information for this fast-growing constituency, fight discrimination on the basis of marital status, and educate the public and policymakers about relevant social and economic issues. We believe that marriage is only one of many acceptable family forms, and that society should recognize and support healthy relationships in all their diversity.

As long as marriage is the culturally approved relationship, rewards for being married will likely continue, and singles will have to either accept the policies that, in essence, discriminate against them, or speak up to demand equal treatment. ●

CHANGES IN "DATING"

Dating in the traditional heterosexual sense has given way to "hanging out." Sometimes one individual will send a text message to another, such as "Hey—wanna hang out Thursday night at the . . . ?" The person will text back "sure." Jayson (2014) noted that there is ambiguity in whether this meeting would be a date. Indeed, 68% of a sample of 2,467 adults between the ages of 18-59 said they would be confused. However, 80% said the event would be a date if the individuals "planned a one-on-one hangout."

After the partners hang out on several occasions they will get more specific about when they will see each other again. In effect, they slide into the structure of seeing each other at predictable times rather than impose the structure initially. Whether this is called "hanging out" or "seeing someone," the couple typically spend increasing amounts of time together and become involved. Conrad and Olmstead (2014) noted that two individuals may interpret their "dating" differently—one may consider themselves exclusive, monogamous, and committed while the other may think of their relationship as a "trial" which suggests less commitment. Hanging out and hooking up will be discussed later in this chapter. For now, we look at when increasing involvement occurs, and why it might happen.

Functions of Involvement With a Partner

Meeting and becoming involved with someone have six functions: (1) confirmation of a social self;

(2) recreation; (3) companionship, intimacy, and sex; (4) anticipatory socialization; (5) status achievement and (6) mate selection.

1. **Confirmation of a social self.** In Chapter 1, we noted that symbolic interactionists emphasize the development of the self. When we are hanging out with a person, we are continually trying to assess how that person sees us: What does the person think of me? Does the person like me? Will the person want to be with me again? When the person gives us positive feedback through speech and gesture, we feel good about ourselves and tend to view ourselves in positive terms.

2. **Recreation.** The focus of hanging out and pairing off is fun. Being someone who is fun to be with is often a reason partners select each other. Individuals who just met make only small talk and learn very little about each other—what seems important is that they have fun together.

3. **Companionship, intimacy, and sex.** Beyond fun, other reasons for becoming involved are companionship, intimacy, and sex. The impersonal environment of a large university makes a secure relationship very appealing. "My last two years have been the happiest ever," remarked a senior in interior design. "But it's because of the involvement with my partner. During my freshman and sophomore years, I felt alone. Now I feel loved, needed, and secure."

4. **Anticipatory socialization.** Before puberty, boys and girls interact primarily with same-sex peers. A fifth grader may be laughed at if he or she shows an interest in someone of the other sex. Even when boy-girl interaction becomes the norm at puberty, neither sex may know what is expected of the other. "Seeing someone" provides a context for individuals to learn how to interact with a partner in a relationship. Though the manifest function of seeing someone is to teach partners how to negotiate differences—for example, how much sex and how soon—the latent function is to help them learn the skills to maintain long-term relationships, such as empathy, communication, and negotiation. In effect, pairing off involves a form of socialization that anticipates a more permanent union in one's life. Individuals may also try out different role patterns, like dominance or passivity, and try to assess the feel and comfort level of each.

5. **Status achievement.** Being involved with someone is associated with more status than being unattached and alone. In a couple's world, sometimes there is embarrassment with "I'm not seeing anyone." Some may seek such involvement because of the associated higher status. Others may become involved out of conformity to gender roles or to please family members. "My mother is always happier when I'm seeing someone" reported one of our students.

6. **Mate selection.** Finally, seeing someone may eventually lead to marriage, which remains a major goal in our society. Selecting a mate is big business. Amazon lists 80,000 "relationship books" on their website.

Finding Tinderella Tonight

The Global Positioning System (GPS) is a satellite-based navigation system originally intended for military use. Civilian use of GPS became available in the 1980s and has since impacted our daily lives. Geosocial dating apps, such as Tinder, Grindr, and Bumble, have altered the landscape of finding a partner and hooking up. Instead of meeting someone through family or friends followed by a long courtship, many young adults today find a partner for an immediate hookup using one of several apps.

Tinder is known as "the hookup app" (LeFebvre, 2018). Tinder users can gain quick access to a large pool of potential partners immediately after uploading a few pictures and answering a few questions such as age and gender preference. Swiping to the right—"liking the picture"—and swiping to the left—"not liking the picture"—in real time is a quick and easy way to find a potential partner. If the attraction is mutual, Tinder notifies the two users of a "new match" and the users may start communicating. There are approximately 50 million Tinder users worldwide, 1.6 billion swipes a day with 26 million "matches" daily (Smith, 2018). A Tinder "match" is primarily based on a user's photos. However, using the word "match" for such a superficial association may give the users a false sense of compatibility (Finkel, 2015).

Smartphone-based dating applications are prevalent among emerging adults. Sawyer et al. (2018) surveyed 509 heterosexual undergraduates, aged 18-25, and found 39.5% reported utilizing dating apps. Men were still more likely to initiate the communication (LeFebvre, 2018).

Since women were more likely to receive unwanted requests and offensive messages, the Bumble app only allows women to initiate communication with potential partners (Bivens & Hoque, 2018).

Tinder's increasing popularity has not only altered dating, but also impacted popular culture. References to Tinder can be found in art, music, literature and film worldwide. Despite Tinder's widespread influences, comparatively little is known about the motives for using such a new medium. Based on studies of 3,262 participants from the United States and Belgium, thirteen common Tinder motives were identified. The primary motive was entertainment and amusement, followed by curiosity, socialization, a quest for love, an ego boost, distraction, the ability to flirt, being able to meet people with a similar sexual orientation, feeling under pressure, the desire to travel (to be able to communicate with locals), the ability to have casual sex, forgetting about one's ex, and being cool (Timmermans & Caluwé, 2017). Hence, individuals make choices in regard to their use of Tinder. The technology is independent of the value choices of how it is used.

Traditional dating has become antiquated. Calling up someone several days ahead of time to ask for a "date," going out to eat and seeing a movie, making out in the car, and saying goodnight underneath the parents' porch light has vanished. Swiping and waiting for the "match" is the new way to find Tinderella or Mr. Tinder nearby. The choices are literally held in one's hands. ●

Changes in Dating in the Past 70 Years

There have been numerous changes to dating and marriage patterns since the 1950s. The changes include:

- an increase in the age at marriage. Marrying at age 29 rather than 22 provides more time and opportunity to hang out with more people.

- a broadening of the dating pool today with an increasing number of individuals in their thirties who have been married before. Usually divorced, these individuals often have children, which changes the context of being together from hanging out alone to watching a DVD with the kids.

- cohabitation, which, as we will note later in this chapter, has become more normative. For some couples, the sequence of seeing someone, falling in love, and getting married has been replaced by seeing someone, falling in love, and living together. Such a sequence results in the marriage of couples that are more relationship-savvy than those who dated and married just after high school in the fifties.

- gender role relationships that have become more egalitarian. Though the double standard still exists, women today are more likely to ask men out than women in the 1950s, to have sex without being in love or requiring a commitment, and to postpone marriage until meeting their own educational and career goals.

- both sexes being more cautious about practicing safe sex to avoid an STI. People are more comfortable talking about condoms and purchasing them. It's quite common to buy condoms along with one's groceries. This is a notable change from the 1950s, when people feared asking a pharmacist for condoms. In addition to being readily available at grocery stores, condoms are often available for free on campus.

HANGING OUT, HOOKING UP, AND LONG-DISTANCE RELATIONSHIPS

Whether an individual has the goal of remaining unmarried or eventually getting married, most have the goal of finding someone to have fun with and share their lives with. One of the unique qualities of the college or university environment is that it provides a context in which to meet hundreds of potential partners of similar age, education, and social class. This context will likely never recur following graduation. Although people often meet through friends, including through Facebook, or on their own in school, work, or recreational contexts, an increasing number are open to a range of alternatives including hanging out and meeting through dating apps like Tinder or websites such as Match.com or eharmony.

Hanging Out

Hanging out means going out in groups where the agenda is to meet others and have fun. Hanging out may occur in group settings such as at a bar, a sorority or fraternity party, or a small gathering of friends that keeps expanding. Friends may introduce individuals, or they may meet someone "cold," as in initiating a conversation. There is usually no agenda beyond meeting and having fun.

Hooking Up

Hooking up is a sexual encounter that occurs between individuals who have no relationship commitment. Thirty-five percent of 3,009 males and 24% of 9,923 females reported that they had "hooked up"— had oral sex or sexual intercourse with someone they just met (Hall & Knox, 2019). It's important to note here that hooking up can mean anything from kissing to having sexual intercourse with someone—in this study, "hooking up" referred to either having oral sex or sexual intercourse. Allison and Ralston (2018) noted the effect of structure on hooking up—the larger the university, the higher the rate of hooking up, and the less likely students were to partner with one another. One third of 5,509 Match.com (2017) respondents reported that they had had sex with someone before going on an official first date. This percent is no doubt higher for those meeting casually through apps such as Tinder.

Hooking up for college students is not associated with a rejection of marriage. According to an analysis of data on 248 emerging adults, James-Kangal et al. (2018) noted, "Contrary to concerns about the devaluation of marriage, results indicated that level of engagement in hooking up was not associated with expectations for involvement in future committed relationships, including marriage" (p. 706).

Which groups are more likely to hook up? Allison and Risman (2017) confirmed that delay in getting married was associated with hooking up and

Hanging out: refers to going out in groups where the agenda is to meet others and have fun.

Hooking up: a sexual encounter that occurs between individuals who have no relationship commitment.

with more partners. But such activity occurs less often for working class women, particularly Black women, and Asian men who do not benefit from the White, male more class-privileged hook up college culture. Data analysis of 3,893 undergraduates also revealed that males were more likely than females to have hooked up and to be willing to hook up if they had not done so. Across sexual identities, gay and lesbian and bisexual individuals were more likely to have hooked up than straight individuals (Hall & Knox, 2017a). Motivations for hooking up include not having a formal dating scene alternative, hoping for a serious relationship, sexual gratification, wanting to fit in, fun and adventure, and being so busy with one's education or career that there is no time for a steady relationship (Uecker et al., 2015).

For those who hook up there is generally no expectation of seeing each other again, and alcohol is often involved. Chang et al. (2012) identified the unspoken rules of hooking up—hooking up is not dating; hooking up is not a romantic relationship; hooking up is physical; hooking up is secret; one who hooks up is to expect no subsequent phone calls from their hooking up partner; and condom and protection should always occur though only 57% of their sample reported condom use on hookups. Aubrey and Smith (2013) also noted that there is a set of cultural beliefs about hooking up. These beliefs include that hooking up is shameless and fun, will enhance one's status in one's peer group, and reflects one's sexual freedom and control over one's sexuality. Implicit in these "rules" is consent—while these encounters are casual, they must be consensual.

Encounters where the partners meet at a party or bar are more likely to involve binge drinking (Kuperberg & Padgett, 2017). Anders et al. (2018) noted the influence of alcohol on the decision to hook up as decreasing one's standards— "A 7 can start looking like a 10 whenever you're drunk." The outcome of hooking up while drunk often has negative consequences. Individuals are more at risk for having sex without consent, for feeling regret and guilt, becoming depressed, and defining the experience negatively. Indeed, women must carefully navigate the stigma and double-standard associated with hooking up (See "Women Hooking Up: Navigating Stigma," Chapter 9). However, the motive of hooking up impacts the emotional outcome. Those who seek hooking up for fun, pleasure, or personal enhancement rather than as a coping mechanism are more likely to report a positive emotional outcome (De Jong et al., 2018).

Long-Distance Relationships

The primary advantages **of long-distance relationships**, defined here as being separated from a romantic partner by 500 or more miles, which precludes regular weekly face-to-face contact, include positive labeling, meaning "even though we are separated, we care about each other enough to maintain our relationship"; keeping the relationship "high" since constant togetherness may result in the partners being less attentive to each other; having time to devote to school or a career; and having a lot of one's own personal time and space. Young adults in

These individuals have been involved for six years and will be separated for two years due to different colleges and jobs. They FaceTime often and get together when they can. "We make it work" is their mantra.

Females are often stigmatized for being sexually aggressive, despite this being a common behavior.
Courtesy of Chelsea Curry

Long-distance relationship: separated from a romantic partner by 500 or more miles, which precludes regular weekly face-to-face contact.

long-distance relationships (*n*=232) and geographically close relationships completed an online survey assessing relationship and sexual outcomes, such as romantic satisfaction, sexual satisfaction, extradyadic sexual activity. Results revealed that individuals in LDRs and GCRs had similar satisfaction, a similar likelihood of engaging in extradyadic sexual activity, and perceived the impact of being in an LDR as more positive than negative (Goldsmith & Byers, 2018).

People suited for such relationships have developed their own autonomy or independence for the

---

Making Choices on How to Maintain a Long-Distance Relationship

Some individuals in long distance relationships wear a bracelet to symbolize that they are in such a relationship and not available.

There is considerable reluctance to become involved in a long-distance relationship. Of 5,509 Match.com (2017) respondents, 20% reported that they would "never" and 54% "not likely" date someone who lived in another state. Hence almost 75% were not open to a long-distance dating relationship. And, long distance relationships are more unstable—more likely to dissolve—than relationships where the partners live close together (Krapf, 2018). For couples who have the goal of maintaining their relationship and reducing the chance that the distance will result in their breaking up, some specific behaviors to engage in include the following:

1. **Use technology to stay connected.** Not only may lovers text each other throughout the day, they may Facetime or Skype to spend time together. They may also use virtual reality and apps to simulate sex and intimacy. Separated lovers can remotely control sex toys to transmit pleasure or affection to each other.

2. **Enjoy or use the time when apart.** While separated, it is important to remain busy with study, friends, work, sports, and personal projects. Doing so will make the time pass faster. Du Bois et al. (2016) found that those in long distance relationships report exercising more than those living close to their partners.

3. **Avoid arguing during phone conversations.** Talking on the phone should involve the typical sharing of events. When the need to discuss a difficult topic like trust arises, the phone is not the best place for such a discussion. Rather, it may be wiser to wait and have the discussion face to face. If you decide to settle a disagreement over the phone, stick to it until you have a solution acceptable to both of you.

4. **Stay monogamous.** Agreeing not to be open to other relationships is crucial to maintaining a long-distance relationship. Individuals who say, "Let's date others to see if we are really meant to be together," often discover that they are capable of being attracted to and becoming involved with numerous "others." Such other involvements usually predict the end of an LDR. Lydon et al. (1997) studied 69 undergraduates who were involved in LDRs and found that "moral commitment" predicted the survival of the relationships. Individuals committed to maintaining their relationships are not open to becoming involved with others. Some individuals in long distance relationships wear a bracelet to symbolize that they are in such a relationship and not available to others (see photo). About 10% of marriages began as a long-distance relationship; 40% of LDDR (long distance dating relationships) break up within five months (Miss Your Mate, 2015).

5. **Review and plan.** Jurkane-Hobein (2015) noted how long-distance partners can use the time apart to remember their good times together and plan new events together. In effect, their cognitive space is filled with thoughts of togetherness.

6. **Be creative.** Some partners in long-distance relationships watch Netflix's movies together— they each pull up the movie on their computer and talk on the phone while they watch it. Others send video links, photos, and so forth, throughout the day. One coed says "I wear his shirts" and "he has my pillow." Some find that keeping a journal of their relationship and feelings during the LDDR adventure is helpful. ●

times they are apart, have a focus for their time such as school or a job, have developed open communication with their partner to talk about the difficulty of being separated, and have learned to trust each other because they spend a lot of time away from each other. Another advantage is that the partner may actually look better from afar than up close. One respondent noted that he and his partner could not wait to live together after they had been separated—but "when we did, I found out I liked her better when she wasn't there."

The primary disadvantages of long-distance relationships include being frustrated over not being able to be with the partner and loneliness. Du Bois et al. (2016) found greater relationship stress. Other disadvantages of involvement in a long-distance relationship are missing out on other activities and relationships, less physical intimacy, spending a lot of money on phone calls and travel, and not discussing important relationship topics.

COHABITATION

Cohabitation, also known as living together, involves two adults, unrelated by blood or by law, involved in an emotional and sexual relationship, who sleep in the same residence at least four nights a week for three months. Seventy percent of first marriages begin with premarital cohabitation which lasts an average of 32 months before marriage (Kuperberg, 2019). Seventy-five percent have only one cohabitation experience with 25% being serial cohabiters (Eickmeyer & Manning, 2018).

CULTURE AND DIVERSITY

In Canada, cohabitation before marriage has become normative and is the most common way to form a first union. Furthermore, cohabitation is increasingly being used as an alternative to marriage rather than a prelude to marriage. Persons who did not finish college are more likely to live together, to have a child, and to remain unmarried (Wright, 2019).

Virtually all marriages in Sweden and Iceland are preceded by the couple living in a cohabitation relationship; however, only 12% of first marriages in Italy are preceded by cohabitation (Kiernan, 2000). Italy is primarily Catholic, which helps to account for the low cohabitation rate.

Cohabitation: two adults, unrelated by blood or by law, involved in an emotional and sexual relationship, who sleep in the same residence at least four nights a week for three months.

Stovall and Blair (2016) found that same sex couples move in relatively quickly for practical reasons like economics compared to other sex couples who move in later for reasons related to the stage of their relationship. Cohabitation has become a stage through which couples pass on their way to marriage. Sassler et al. (2018) found that a quarter of women had begun cohabitating within six months of becoming sexually involved. Women with more advantaged backgrounds were less likely to cohabit. Parental cohabitation and having a low level of family belonging are also associated with the decision to live together (Thorsen, 2017).

Reasons for the increase in cohabitation include career or educational commitments; increased tolerance of society, parents, and peers; improved birth control technology; desire for a stable emotional and sexual relationship without legal ties; avoiding loneliness and greater disregard for convention. Cohabitants are also fearful of getting divorced—67% of the cohabitants in the Singles in American Survey think of living together as a way of avoiding marriage and helping to ensure a strong and stable future marriage (Fisher, 2015).

Nine Types of Cohabitation Relationships

There are various types of cohabitation:

1. **Here and now.** These new partners have a fun relationship and are focused on the here and now, not the future of the relationship. They want to be together more often and living together is one way to do so.

2. **Testers.** These couples are involved in a relationship and want to assess whether they have a future together. Women and men cohabitants often value the relationship differently. Rhoades et al. (2012) studied 120 cohabiting couples and found women more committed than men to the relationship in about half the couples or 46%. Such discrepancy was associated with a lower-quality relationship.

3. **Engaged.** These cohabiting couples are in love and are planning to marry. Among those who report having lived together, about two-thirds or 64% say they thought of their living arrangement as a step toward marriage (Pew Research Center, 2010). Engaged cohabitant couples who have an agreed upon future report the highest level of satisfaction, the lowest level of conflict, and, in general, have a higher quality relationship than other types of cohabitants (Willoughby et al., 2012).

Transitioning a Hookup to a Committed Relationship?

Hooking up, an initial sexual encounter that occurs between individuals who have no future relationship commitment, has become a frequent behavior of undergraduates. About 60% of both women and men report having had one or more hookup experiences. For those who have not experienced hooking up, most report that they are open to such an encounter.

Two hundred and six undergraduates at a large southeastern public university completed a 50-item Internet questionnaire to reveal their frequency of hooking up and the relationship outcome for doing so. The sample was overwhelmingly female (81%), White (73%), and between the ages of 17-21.

Findings

Twenty-two percent of the participants reported that they had transitioned a hookup relationship into a committed romantic relationship. In terms of the length of time it took to transition the relationship, the most frequent time period was one to three months (n=15); the second most frequent time period was seven months to a year (n=5).

Respondents identified two main strategies for transitioning a hookup to a committed relationship: about 35% spent "out of bed" post-coital time together doing things of mutual interest, while 28% had a conversation that defined the relationship as boyfriend and girlfriend. These strategies were reported by both men and women. Examples of the transition follow:

We were "hooking up" every other day. The time we began to spend together evolved into emotion for one another. After we established this emotion for each other, it was evident that we should pursue a long-term relationship.

An additional facet of transition was repeated hookups mentioned by the majority, 71.4%, of those who transitioned. And 54.4% of respondents who transitioned also identified sexual and romantic chemistry as the strongest facilitator of transition. While 53.1% of men were the most likely to initiate commitment, only 18.7% of women were likely to initiate commitment; almost thirty percent—28.1%—indicated that the commitment process was mutual. Women were significantly more likely than men to report interest in transitioning a hookup if the partner's future aligned with their own. Comments from respondents follow:

. . .

The transition took a month and he was the one who pushed it more for us to be more exclusive. The same frequency of sex was maintained but more "couple-y" things such as dates and communicating were added into our relationship.

. . .

My hookup partner and I transitioned to a relationship because about 2-3 weeks of just hooking up, we started texting and talking more realizing we wanted a relationship. I was more interested in making the transition because just hooking up and not having a foundation is not easy for me. ●

Source: Adapted and abridged from Erichsen, K., & Dignam, P. (2016, April). *From hookup to husband: Transitioning to a committed relationship.* Paper presented to the Southern Sociological Society, Atlanta, GA.

After three years, 40% of first premarital cohabitants end up getting married, 32% are still cohabiting, and 27% have broken up. Ishizuka (2018) noted that cohabitants who marry often have the economic resources—a sufficient stable income—to do so.

4. **Money savers.** These couples live together primarily out of economic convenience. They are open to the possibility of a future together but regard such a possibility as unlikely. Sassler and Miller (2011) noted that working class individuals tend to transition more quickly than middle class individuals to cohabitation out of economic necessity or to meet a housing need.

5. **Pension partners.** These cohabitation partners are older, have been married before, still derive benefits from their previous relationships, and are living with someone new. Getting married would mean giving up their pension benefits from the previous marriage. An example is a widow from the war in Afghanistan who was given military benefits due to a spouse's death. If remarried, the widow would forfeit both health and pension benefits, but now lives with a new

partner and continues to get benefits from the previous marriage.

6. **Alimony maintenance.** Related to widows who cohabit are the divorced who are collecting alimony which they would forfeit should they remarry. To maintain the benefits, they live with a new partner instead of marrying.

7. **Security blanket cohabiters.** Some of the individuals in these cohabitation relationships are drawn to each other out of a need for security rather than mutual attraction. Being alone is not an option. They want somebody, anybody, in the house.

8. **Rebellious cohabiters.** Some couples use cohabitation as a way of making a statement to their parents that they are independent and can make their own choices. Their cohabitation is more about rebelling from parents than being drawn to each other.

9. **Marriage never (cohabitants forever).** Celebrities Goldie Hawn and Kurt Russell have lived together—never married—over 30 years. Similarly, Oprah and Graham

This couple has been living together for 12 years and plan never to marry. They feel "if it isn't broken, it does not need to be fixed" and that it feels better to want to stay together than to have social pressure to stay together to avoid a divorce

Stedman have been together, sometimes living together, for over 30 years. Hatch et al. (2017) interviewed 45 committed unmarried heterosexual couples who were committed to remaining single. Concerns over the meanings of marriage, such as it lets the government get into your business, and fears of how marriage would change the relationship were the primary reasons for never marrying and wanting to remaing single forever.

Ortyl et al. (2013) interviewed 48 long-term heterosexual cohabiters to identify their motives for cohabiting as a permanent lifestyle. Six themes emerged:

1. **Marriage free.** The largest percent—38%—believed that marriage is unnecessary to their happiness. They used the term "marriage free" much like one would use the word "child-free." Such couples may feel a moral commitment to each other and to their relationship yet have no interest in marriage (Pope & Cashwell, 2013). In some cases, the respective cohabitant partners may differ in terms of whether they want to marry. In a sample of 1,837 couples who were cohabitating, those relationships in which only one partner wanted to delay getting married and placed a lower importance on marriage were associated with less stability, poorer communication, and lower relationship satisfaction (Willoughby & Belt, 2016).

2. **Risk aversion.** The cohabitants had parents or siblings in disastrous marriages and wanted to avoid the same fate.

3. **Marriage boycott.** The cohabitants rejected the government defining marriage as heterosexual, thus supporting gays who are denied same sex marriage in all states.

4. **Sexism dissent.** Cohabitants rejected the patriarchal history of marriage which controlled women.

5. **American dreamer.** Some cohabitants saw the day when their school debts would be paid off and their career established as the day it would be OK to get married.

6. **Economic disincentives.** Cohabitants knew that marriage involves being responsible for the debts of the spouse and wanted to avoid, by living together, being economically burdened by a partner with an unstable job and a history of money problems.

In a cross-national study comparing 36, 889 individuals who were married, cohabitating, or single in 27 countries, higher levels of happiness were reported by spouses, followed by cohabitants, followed by the never married (Lee & Ono, 2012).

Some couples who view their living together as "permanent" seek to have it defined as a **domestic partnership,** a relationship involving two adults who have chosen to share each other's lives in an intimate and committed relationship of mutual caring.

Consequences of Cohabitation

Although living together before marriage does not ensure a happy, stable marriage, it has some potential advantages.

Advantages of Cohabitation

Many unmarried couples who live together report that it is an enjoyable, maturing experience.

Other potential benefits of living together include the following:

1. **Sense of well-being.** Compared to uninvolved individuals or those involved but not living together, cohabitants are likely to report a sense of well-being, particularly if the partners see a future together. They are in love, the relationship is new, and the disenchantment that frequently occurs in long-term relationships has not had time to surface. Indeed, the context of living with another intimate partner—a cohabitant or spouse—is associated with increased mental well-being (Perelli-Harris & Styrc, 2018).

2. **Delayed marriage.** Another advantage of living together is remaining unmarried— the longer one waits to marry, the better. Being older at the time of marriage is predictive of marital happiness and stability, just as being young, particularly 18 years and younger, is associated with marital unhappiness and divorce. Hence, if a young couple who have known each other for a short time is faced with the choice of living together or getting married, their delaying marriage while they

....

Domestic partnership: two adults who have chosen to share each other's lives in an intimate and committed relationship of mutual caring. These relationships are given some kind of official recognition by a city or corporation so as to receive partner benefits: for example, health insurance.

Iceland is a homogeneous country of 250,000 descendants of the Vikings. Their sexual norms include early protected intercourse, living together before marriage, and non-marital parenthood (Halligan et al., 2014). Indeed, a wedding photo often includes not only the couple but also the children they have already had. One American woman who was involved with an Icelander noted, "My parents were upset with me because Ollie and I were thinking about living together, but his parents were upset that we were not already living together."

live together seems to be the better choice. And, if they break up, the split will not go on their record as would a divorce.

3. **Knowledge about self and partner.** While living together before marriage does not make a couple immune to the increase in interpersonal conflict (Hall & Adams, 2011), it does provide couples with an opportunity for learning more about themselves and their partner. For example, a person's behavior with either family, such as calling parents daily, or with friends—having a beer on weekends with a buddy— or exhibiting certain habits like being a "neat freak," or having relationship expectations about how emotionally close or distant a partner should be are sometimes more fully revealed when living together than in a traditional dating context.

4. **Safety.** Particularly for heterosexual females, living with a partner provides a higher level of safety not enjoyed by single females who live alone—presumably the male would deter someone who broke into the apartment of the female. Of course, living with a roommate or group of friends would provide a similar function of safety.

Disadvantages of Cohabitation

There is a downside for individuals and couples who live together.

1. **More problems than spouses and higher dissolution**. When cohabitants are compared to spouses, the former report lower relationship quality (Brown et al., 2017). Cohabitants are also more likely to end the relationship with their partners than are spouses (Hognas & Thomas, 2016). Cohabitant couples with children are also more likely to dissolve than

married couples with children (Musick & Michelmore, 2018).

2. **Feeling used or tricked.** When expectations differ, the more invested partner may feel used or tricked if the relationship does not progress toward marriage. One partner said, "I always felt we would be getting married, but it turns out that he never saw a future for us."

3. **Parental problems.** Some cohabiting couples report that they must contend with parents who disapprove of or do not fully accept their living arrangement. For example, cohabitants sometimes report that, when visiting their parents' homes, they are required to sleep in separate beds in separate rooms. Some cohabitants who have parents with traditional values respect these values, and sleeping in separate rooms is not a problem. Other cohabitants feel resentful of parents who require them to sleep separately. Some parents express their disapproval of their child's cohabiting by cutting off communication, as well as economic support, from their child. Being aware of such disapproval, some adult children hide their cohabitation from their parents.

4. **Economic disadvantages.** Some economic liabilities exist for those who live together instead of getting married. In the Family Policy section on domestic partnerships, we noted that cohabitants typically do not benefit from their partner's health insurance, Social Security, or retirement benefits. In most cases, only spouses qualify for such payoffs.

Given that most relationships in which people live together are not long term and that breaking up is not uncommon, cohabitants might develop a written and signed legal agreement should they purchase a house, car, or other costly items together. The written agreement should include a description of the item, to whom it belongs, how it will be paid for, and what will happen to the item if the relationship terminates. Purchasing real estate together may require a separate agreement, which should include how the mortgage, property taxes, and repairs will be shared. The agreement should also specify who gets the house if the partners break up and how the value of the departing partner's share will be determined.

If the couple has children, another agreement may be helpful in defining custody, visitation, and support issues in the event the couple terminates the relationship. Such an arrangement may take some of the romance out of the cohabitation relationship, but it can save a great deal of frustration should the partners decide to go their separate ways.

Just as cohabitation rates are higher in European and Scandinavian countries, the rate of dissolution is also higher than among married couples in those countries. Sixty percent of cohabiting parents in France and 88% of cohabiting parents in Norway end their relationship (DeRose, 2017).

In addition, couples who live together instead of marrying can protect themselves from some of the economic disadvantages of living together by specifying their wishes in wills; otherwise, their belongings will go to next of kin or to the state. They should also own property through joint tenancy with rights of survivorship. This stipulation means that ownership of the entire property will revert to one partner if the other partner dies. Finally, the couple should save for retirement, because live-in companions may not access Social Security benefits, and some company pension plans bar employees from naming anyone other than a spouse as the beneficiary.

5. **Negative effects on children.** About 40% of children will spend some time in a home where the adults are cohabitating. In addition to being disadvantaged in terms of growing up in a home with lower parental income and education, they are also likely to experience the breakup of their parents' relationship (Hognas & Thomas, 2016). Instability in parental relationships has negative outcomes for children—higher frequencies of negative behavior and problems in school, higher frequency of teenage pregnancy, and delinquent behavior. Indeed, cohabitation parents are twice as likely to end their relationship than married parents (DeRose et al., 2017).

Pregnancy as a Precursor to Cohabitation

Getting pregnant is a precursor to moving in together, particularly if individuals are adolescents. In addition, pregnancy is associated with the cohabiting couple getting married. However, the longer a couple has been living together, the less impact the nonmarital pregnancy will have on the couple getting married (Thorsen, 2019). However, the birth of a child is also associated with the couple getting married (Cho et al., 2018) unless one of the partners already has a child (Guzzo, 2018).

Will Living Together Ensure a Durable Marriage?

Couples who live together before marrying assume that doing so will increase their chances of having a happy and durable marriage relationship. But will it? No. Based on national data over a 45-year period of women in their first marriages, those who cohabitated before marriage had higher divorce rates than those who did not do (Rosenfeld & Roesler, 2019). These higher divorce rates were not evident the first year of marriage but were from the second year going forward.

Other research suggests that those, particularly women (Manning & Cohen, 2012), who have only one cohabitation experience and marry the person they live with have a lower risk of subsequent divorce (Jose et al., 2010).

Because people commonly have more than one cohabitation experience, the term **cohabitation effect** applies. This means that those who have multiple cohabitation experiences prior to marriage are more likely to end up in marriages characterized by violence, lower levels of happiness, lower levels of positive communication, and higher levels of depression (Booth et al., 2008).

What is it about serial cohabitation relationships that predict negatively for future marital happiness and durability? One explanation is that serial cohabitants repeatedly violate social norms by living together before marriage and have a pattern of breaking up. Once they marry, they may be more willing to break another social norm and divorce if they are unhappy than are unhappily married people who tend to conform to social norms and have no history of unconventional behavior. It should be pointed out that serial cohabitation has a positive in that breaking a cohabitation before marriage is preferable to breaking a relationship after marriage. Whatever the reason, cohabitants should not assume that cohabitation will insulate them from divorce. Perelli-Harris et al. (2019) found that both marriage and cohabitation are associated with positive subjective well-being (when compared to not being in a coresidential living situation). ●

Legal Aspects of Living Together

In recent years, the courts and legal system have become increasingly involved in relationships in which couples live together. Some of the legal issues concerning cohabiting partners include common-law marriage, palimony, child support, and child inheritance. Lesbian and gay couples also confront legal issues when they live together as opposed to getting married.

Technically, cohabitation is against the law in some states. For example, in North Carolina, cohabitation is a misdemeanor punishable by a fine not to exceed $500, imprisonment for not more than six months, or both. Most law enforcement officials view cohabitation as a victimless crime and feel that the general public can be better served by concentrating upon the crimes that do real damage to citizens and their property. In reality, prosecution for these crimes does not occur.

Common-Law Marriage

The concept of common-law marriage dates to a time when couples who wanted to be married did not have easy or convenient access to legal authorities, who

Cohabitation effect: those who have multiple cohabitation experiences prior to marriage are more likely to end up in marriages characterized by lower levels of happiness.

could formally sanction their relationship so that they would have the benefits of legal marriage. Thus, if the couple lived together and wanted other people to view them as a married couple, they would be considered married in the eyes of the law.

Despite the assumption by some that heterosexual couples who live together a long time have a common-law marriage, only 14 states recognize such marriages (see Figure 4.1). In these states a heterosexual couple may be considered married if they are legally competent to marry, if the partners agree that they are married, and if they present themselves to the public as a married couple. A ceremony or compliance with legal formalities is not required.

In common-law states, individuals who live together and who prove through a shared address, bank accounts, children, checking into hotels as a married couple, and so forth that they are married "by common law" may inherit from each other or receive alimony and property in the case of relationship termination. They may also receive health and Social Security benefits, as would other spouses who have a marriage license. In states not recognizing common-law marriages, the individuals who live together are not entitled to benefits traditionally afforded married individuals. More than three-quarters of the

FIGURE 4.1

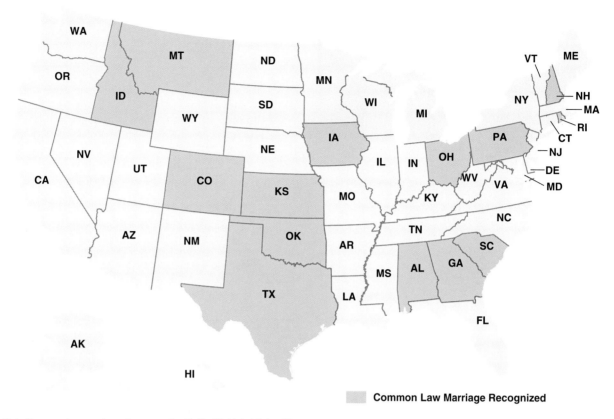

Common Law Marriage Recognized

Note: Common law marriage also recognized in the District of Columbia.

states have passed laws prohibiting the recognition of common-law marriages within their borders.

A takeoff on the word *alimony*, **palimony** refers to the amount of money one "pal" who lives with another "pal" may have to pay if the partners end their relationship. For example, comedian Bill Maher was the target of a $9 million palimony suit by ex-girlfriend Coco Johnsen.

Child Support

Heterosexual individuals who conceive children are responsible for those children whether they are living together or married. In most cases, the custody of young children will be given to the mother, and the father will be required to pay child support. In effect, living together is irrelevant with regard to parental obligations. However, a woman who agrees to have a child with her lesbian partner cannot be forced to pay child support if the couple breaks up. The Massachusetts Supreme Judicial Court ruled that their informal agreement to have a child together did not constitute an enforceable contract.

....

Palimony: refers to the amount of money one "pal" who lives with another "pal" may have to pay if the partners end their relationship.

Couples who live together or who have children together should be aware that laws traditionally applying only to married couples are now being applied to many unwed relationships. Palimony, distribution of property, and child support payments are all possibilities once two people cohabit or parent a child.

Child Inheritance and Access to Parents After Breakup

Children born to unmarried cohabitants can inherit from their respective parents. However, if there is a breakup, the biological parent has more power and will be given custody.

LIVING APART TOGETHER (LAT)

Rosalynn Carter, married over 70 years to Jimmy Carter, former president of the United States from 1980-1984, was asked, "What is your secret to a happy marriage?" "Space," she replied. She went on to say that one of the most difficult times in their marriage was when they left the White House: "It was the first time we'd been together in the house all day every

This two-story condo is where the first and second authors of your text lived for 13 years. She owned the bottom condo where she lived with her daughter while he owned the top condo for him and his children. After the children left, the couple sold the condos and moved to a house.

day. So, I got my office in what was a bedroom, and his is in the garage" (Westfall, 2014, p. 75). Some couples take the idea of "space" to a new level which may include different residences—living apart together.

The definition of **living apart together (LAT)** is a committed couple in which the partners live in separate households. Seven percent of women and 6% of men age 23 and older who are in a romantic relationship with their partner are in a living apart together arrangement in the United States (Cherlin, 2010). The Census Bureau estimates that 1.7 million married couples are living in this arrangement (Gottman, 2013). Krapf (2018) found that about three fourths or 72.9% of living apart together individuals live less than an hour from each other. Broese van Groenou et al. (2019) compared individuals in older (50 to 79) LAT relationships in the Netherlands with those in first marriages, remarriages, and cohabitation and found that LAT partners were most often involved in exchanging emotional support. Daily care was less than those who were married.

Coulter and Hu (2017) surveyed a sample of 3,112 LAT relationships in Great Britain and identified four types: 44% are nested young adults, individuals living with their parents but in a relationship with a partner outside their home; 32% are independent adults, individuals living in their own house or apartment and in a relationship with someone they did not live with; 11% are single parents; and 13% are seniors. Rather than a new family form the researchers noted that LAT was a "way to practice partnership within the context of life course circumstances."

While young adults are living apart when they meet, some choose to continue to live apart even if they could move in together as cohabitants or spouses. But for older adults, LAT is becoming a preference (Connidis et al., 2017). Those who are widowed or otherwise single, do not want to marry or

....

Living apart together (LAT): a living arrangement where partners in a committed relationship live in separate households.

CULTURE AND DIVERSITY

Another version of living apart together is the "walking marriage." High in the Tibetan Himalayas, "walking marriages" occur in the Mosuo culture (Kingdom of Women) in China, which does not have traditional marriage—no husbands or wives. Rather, in this matrilineal society, women live with other women and raise the children and men "walk by at night and visit and leave the next morning." The women and men can have as many "walking marriages" as they want with the men never living with the woman, only visiting her (Mosuo, 2010).

live together so living together apart is becoming an increasingly chosen option.

Some couples, including spouses, find that living apart together is preferable to their living in the same place (Hess, 2012). LAT is one of several alternatives being considered as alternatives to traditional marriage (Gadoua & Larson, 2014).

Living apart together is not new. Simone de Beauvoir, in 1929, had her own apartment while in a relationship with Jean-Paul Sartre for 51 years. Actor Jack Nicholson lived in a house separate from his girlfriend Rebecca Boussard with whom he had two children. He said of the housing arrangement, "I'm not good at cohabitation with Rebecca. I look at it as a two-bedroom apartment—my home and her house" (Eliot, 2013, p.249). The arrangement is not unique. In a study of 68 adults, 93% of whom were married, 7% reported that they preferred a LAT arrangement with their spouse. Forty-six percent said that living apart from your spouse enhances your relationship (Jacinto & Ahrend, 2012).

Three criteria must be met for a couple to be defined as a "living apart together" couple: (1) they must define themselves as a committed couple; (2) others must define the partners as a couple; and (3) they must live in separate domiciles. The lifestyle of living apart together involves partners in loving and committed relationships, married or unmarried, identifying their independent needs in terms of the degree to which they want time and space away from each other. While separate domiciles is the most pervasive criteria for LAT, the term is sometimes viewed as a continuum from partners who have separate bedrooms and baths in the same house to those who live in a separate place, such as an apartment, condo, or house, in the same or different cities. LAT couples are not those couples who are forced by their career or military assignment to live separately. Rather, LAT partners choose to live in separate domiciles and feel that their relationship benefits from the LAT structure. The primary reason for LAT participants to maintain separate domiciles is to preserve their autonomy, not because they are less committed to each other (Brown et al., 2016). LAT may also become more frequent among the elderly. Benson and Coleman (2016) interviewed a sample of elderly individuals in regard to their feelings about LAT. While they ranged from rejection to ambivalence to advocacy, it is clear that age was involved. One of the respondents said:

> I reasoned it out that if we were young people going to start a family, I would not do this. I would never have done this before marriage and neither would he, as a young person. But it's different because, you are not, it's not affecting the family whatsoever. You're not gonna have children, but you need this, you need this loving, and I had not had much [in my marriage].

Upton-Davis (2015) interviewed 20 women over the age of 45 who had chosen the living apart together arrangement over cohabitation. Below is an excerpt from one of the interviews:

"So, I'm curious Celia, is your LAT relationship something you sat down and talked about or did it just evolve into a LAT?"

> It definitely just evolved. Larry and I have been together 10 years now and I think at the start we were both thinking we would move in together – he was thinking that more than I was I think. But as time went by and the relationship was working out so well the way it was I thought why change it? Larry is gorgeous, generous, my family adores him, and he gets on socially with everyone. But honestly, I don't think we would last five minutes if we lived together.

"Why's that?"

> I like my space. Besides, Larry and I are very different, we like different things. He has a very nice house just a couple of suburbs away, it's very nice – but it's not my cup of tea if you know what I mean, she adds quietly. I look around her apartment, at the carefully placed, internationally acquired object d'art and can imagine what she means (Upton-Davis, 2015, p.8).

Refer to the "Self-Assessment: Living Apart Together (LAT) Scale" on page 374, which allows you to assess the degree to which this lifestyle is compatible with your needs.

The living apart together lifestyle or family form is not unique to couples in the United States. The phenomenon, for example, is more prevalent in European countries such as France, Sweden, and Norway. Jones (2015) analyzed data on LAT individuals in Bulgaria. There are both advantages and disadvantages of the living apart together arrangement.

Advantages of LAT

The benefits of LAT relationships include the following:

1. **Space and privacy.** This is a primary advantage listed by the Upton-Davis (2015) respondent. Having two places enables each partner to have a separate space to read, watch TV, talk on the phone, or whatever. This not only provides a measure of privacy for the individuals, but also for the couple. When the couple has overnight guests, the guests can stay in one place while the partners stay in the other place. This arrangement gives guests ample space and the couple private space and time apart from the guests.

2. **Career or work space.** Some individuals work at home and need a controlled quiet space to work on projects, talk on the phone, and focus on their work without the presence of someone else. The LAT arrangement is particularly appealing to musicians for practicing, artists to spread out their materials, and authors for quiet. Hemingway, for example, built a separate building where he wrote in Key West.

3. **Variable sleep needs.** Although some partners enjoy going to bed at the same time and sleeping in the same bed, others like to go to bed at radically different times and to sleep in separate beds or rooms. A frequent comment from LAT partners is, "My partner thrashes throughout the night and kicks me, not to mention the wheezing and teeth grinding, so to get a good night's sleep, I need to sleep somewhere else."

4. **Allergies.** Individuals who have cat or dog allergies may need to live in a separate antiseptic environment from their partner who loves animals and won't live without them. "He likes his dog on the bed," said one woman.

5. **Variable social needs.** Partners differ in terms of their need for social contact with friends, siblings, and parents. The LAT arrangement allows for the partner who enjoys frequent time with others to satisfy that need without subjecting the other to the presence of a lot of people in one's life space. One wife from a family of seven children enjoyed frequent contact with both her siblings and parents. The LAT arrangement allowed her to continue to enjoy her family

at no expense to her husband who lived in a separate household.

6. **Blended family needs.** LAT works particularly well with a blended family in which remarried spouses live in separate places with their children from previous relationships. An example is a remarried couple who bought a duplex with each spouse living with his or her own children on the respective sides of the duplex. The parents could maintain a private living space with their children, the spouses could be next door to each other, and the stepsiblings were not required to share living quarters—a structural answer to major stepfamily blending problems.

7. **Keeping the relationship exciting.** Zen Buddhists remind us of the necessity to be in touch with polarities, to have a perspective where we can see and appreciate the larger picture—without the darkness, we cannot fully appreciate the light. The two are inextricably part of a whole. This is the same with relationships; time apart from our beloved can make time together more precious. **Satiation** is a well-established psychological principle. The term means that a stimulus loses its value with repeated exposure. Just as we tire of eating the same food, listening to the same music, or watching the same movie, we can become satiated in a relationship. Couples in a long-distance dating relationship know the joy of missing each other and the excitement of being with each other again. Similarly, individuals in a LAT relationship help to ensure that they will not become satiated with each other but maintain excitement in seeing or being with each other.

8. **Personal and relationship enhancement.** Upton-Davis (2015) summarized the living apart together experience for the 20 women she interviewed:

The overwhelming response to the question of how LAT relationships had affected the women's view of themselves was positive, indicating autonomy, a feeling of control over their destiny, a sense of pride in living and managing to live – financially independently and in coping with everyday practical issues, freedom, joy and appreciation of the opportunity to live this way (Upton-Davis, 2015, p. 110).

9. **Self-expression and comfort.** Partners often have very different tastes in furniture, home décor, music, and temperature. With two separate places, each can arrange and furnish his or her respective homes according to his or her individual preferences. The respective partners can also set the heat or air conditioning according to their own preference and play whatever music they like.

10. **Cleanliness or orderliness.** Separate residences allow each partner to maintain the desired level of cleanliness and orderliness without arguing about it. Some individuals like their living space to be as ordered as a cockpit. Others simply don't care.

11. **Elder care.** One partner may be taking care of an elderly parent in his or her own house. The other partner may prefer not to live with an elderly person. A LAT relationship allows for the partner taking care of the elderly parent to do so while providing a place for the couple to be alone.

12. **Maintaining one's lifetime residence.** Some retirees, widows, and widowers meet, fall in love, and want to enjoy each other's companionship. However, they don't want to move out of their own home. The LAT arrangement does not require that the partners move.

13. **Leaving inheritances to children from previous marriages.** Having separate residences allows the respective partners to leave their family home or residential property to their biological children from an earlier relationship without displacing their surviving spouse.

Disadvantages of LAT

There are also disadvantages to the LAT lifestyle.

1. **Less happy, feeling stigmatized.** Lewin (2017) found lower happiness reported by older adults in LAT relationships when compared with those in cohabitation relationships, first marriages, and remarriages. Because the norm that married couples move in together is firmly entrenched, couples who do not do so are suspect. "People who love each other should want to live in their own house

---

Satiation: a stimulus loses its value with repeated exposure (e.g., lovers tire of each other if around each other all the time).

together... those who live apart aren't really committed" is the traditional perception of people in a committed relationship.

2. **Cost.** The cost of two separate living places can be more expensive than two people living in one domicile. But there are ways LAT couples afford their lifestyle. Some live in two condominiums that are cheaper than owning one larger house. Others buy housing outside of high-priced real estate areas. One partner said, "We bought a duplex 10 miles out of town where the price of housing is 50% cheaper than in town. We have our LAT context and it didn't cost us a fortune."

3. **Inconvenience.** Unless the partners live in a duplex or two units in the same condominium, going between the two places to share meals or be together can be inconvenient.

4. **Lack of shared history.** Because the adults are living in separate quarters, a lot of what goes on in each house does not become a part of the life history of the couple. For example, children in one place don't benefit as much from the other adult who lives in another domicile most of the time.

5. **No legal protection.** The legal nature of the LAT relationship is ambiguous. Currently this relationship does not have legal protection in the United States.

FUTURE OF SINGLEHOOD, COHABITATION, AND LAT

Singlehood will, in the cultural spirit of diversity, lose some of its stigma as more young adults, particularly the non-college educated, will choose this option. Individuals in the United States will continue to be in no hurry to get married. Completing their education, becoming established in their career, and enjoying the freedom of hanging out and hooking up will continue to be the modus operandi of emerging adults. Increasingly, women and men will wait until their late twenties or early thirties to marry. This trend will continue as individuals keep their options open in America's individualistic society.

Cohabitation will increase. The link between cohabitation and negative marital outcome will dissolve as more individuals elect to cohabit before marriage. Previously, only risk takers and people willing to abandon traditional norms lived together before marriage. In the future, mainstream individuals will cohabit.

Living apart together will also increase, particularly among middle and older adults who have less to gain from cohabitation or marriage. In a national study of 578 LAT participants, 61% reported that they were "very happy" and committed to their partners at a level of 4.2 on a scale of five. LAT for these couples was an end point, not a prelude to cohabitation or marriage (Brown et al., 2016).

SUMMARY

What is the status of singlehood today?
Singles consist of the never married, the divorced, and the widowed. The never married are delaying marriage in favor of completing their education, establishing themselves in a career, and enjoying hanging out and hooking up. The primary attraction of singlehood is the freedom to do as one chooses. Others fear getting into a miserable marriage or having to go through a divorce.

What are the functions of and changes in dating?
The various functions of dating include (1) confirmation of a social self; (2) recreation; (3) companionship, intimacy, and sex; (4) anticipatory socialization; (5) status achievement and (6) mate selection. The changes in dating in the last 70 years include an increase in the age at marriage, more formerly divorced in the dating pool, cohabitation becoming more normative, and women becoming more assertive in initiating relationships.

How have hanging out and hooking up replaced traditional dating?
Couples today often meet each other while hanging out and hooking up. While the latter may be a hoped-for beginning of a continuing relationship, 75% of the time it is not.

What is cohabitation like among today's youth?
Cohabitation, also known as living together, is becoming an expected stage in courtship with about two-thirds of college students reporting having lived together. Of 100 weddings in the United States almost 60% of American brides report that they had cohabited before marriage. Reasons for an increase in the number of couples living together include a delay of marriage for educational or career commitments, fear of marriage, increased tolerance of society for living together, and a desire to avoid the legal entanglements of marriage. Types of relationships in which couples live together include the here-and-now, those testing the relationships; engaged

couples, those planning to marry; and cohabitants forever or those never planning to marry.

What are the advantages and disadvantages of living together?

Although living together before marriage does not ensure a happy, stable marriage, it has some potential advantages. These include a sense of well-being, delayed marriage which allows more time to find out about one's self and one's partner, a feeling of safety, and being able to end the relationship with minimal legal hassle. Disadvantages of cohabitation include more problems and higher dissolution, feeling used or tricked, parental problems such as lying to parents, and not having the same economic benefits as those who are married. Social Security and retirement benefits are paid to spouses, not live-in partners.

What are the pros and cons of "living apart together"?

LAT means that monogamous committed partners—whether married or not—carve out varying degrees of physical space between themselves. People living apart together exist on a continuum from partners who have separate bedrooms and baths in the same house to those who live in separate apartments, condos, or houses in the same or different cities. Couples choose this pattern for a number of reasons, including the desire to maintain some level of independence, personal and work space, enjoyment of having alone time, family obligations, and keeping their relationship fresh and exciting. Disadvantages include feeling stigmatized, cost, inconvenience and lack of a shared history.

What is the future of singlehood?

Fewer individuals will marry as singlehood will lose some of its stigma. In addition, those who marry will marry at later ages when education is completed and career established. This trend shows no signs of abating as individuals continue to explore their options in today's individualistic society in the United States..

KEY TERMS

Cohabitation, 81

Cohabitation effect, 86

Domestic partnership, 84

Hanging out, 78

Hooking up, 78

Living apart together (LAT), 88

Long-distance relationship, 79

Palimony, 87

Satiation, 90

Singlehood, 72

Singlism, 75

Sologamy, 72

WEB LINKS

Unmarried Equality
http://www.unmarried.org/

Selective Search
http://www.selectivesearch.com/

Get the tools you need to sharpen your study skills. SAGE edge offers a robust online environment featuring an impressive array of free tools and resources.
Access practice quizzes, eFlashcards, video, and multimedia at **edge.sagepub.com/knox13e**

5

Selecting a Partner

It's taken me a long time to realize that the perfect partner—someone who shares my likes and dislikes, and who couldn't agree more with my political opinions and religious convictions and sexual preferences, and who'd never in a million years want to sleep with the window open when I want the window closed—doesn't exist.

—**Sy Safransky, Editor,** *Sun Magazine*

Learning Objectives

5.1. Identify the different factors operative in selecting a partner

5.2. Explain the various ways of using technology to find a partner

5.3. Describe how couples move toward a committed relationship

5.4. Summarize factors that affect a couple's decision to marry

5.5. Discuss future changes to selecting a partner

Some people spend more time making the decision to buy a car than they spend on selecting a lifetime partner. Good looks, a sense of adventure, and feeling loved are mate selection criteria typically used in the United States, unlike in Asian countries such as China, Japan, and India which use similar family background, religion and values as criteria. The results are predictable—three times the divorce rate in the United States. In this chapter we examine the factors involved in mate selection and point out those which predict well for a happy and enduring life together.

FACTORS INVOLVED IN SELECTING A MATE

Two people do not just "happen" to marry. Rather, there are sociological, psychological, sociobiological, and cultural factors operating, often without their awareness.

Sociological Factors Operative in Mate Selection

Homogamy—"like selects like"— refers to the tendency for the individual to seek a mate with similar characteristics—for example, age, race, education, and so forth. Saggino et al. (2016) analyzed data on 184 Italian married couples and found that the more the spouses had in common and were compatible, the higher their marital satisfaction. A small contingent of Japanese and Koreans believe that similarity of blood type is an important factor in selecting one's partner. For them, "what is your blood type?" is an important and appropriate question to ask a

person they consider as a potential mate. The following are factors individuals often use to find someone who is a "match" in terms of similarity.

Race

Most individuals select someone of the same racial background to marry.

Race refers to physical characteristics that are given social significance. Eighty-three percent of all newlyweds have a spouse of the same race or ethnicity (Livingston & Brown, 2017). Both heterosexuals and gays are attracted to persons of their same race and ethnicity (Brooks & Neville, 2017). In general, as one moves from dating to marriage, the willingness to marry interracially decreases. Of 2,977 undergraduate males, 34% reported that they had dated interracially; 39% of 9,804 undergraduate females had done so (Hall & Knox, 2019). But only about 17% actually marry interracially. And most of these marriages are not Black-White mergers (Livingston & Brown, 2017).

Age

Most individuals select a mate who is relatively close to them in age. Men tend to select women three to five years younger than themselves. The result is the marriage squeeze, which is the imbalance of the ratio of marriageable-aged men to marriageable-aged women. In effect, women have fewer partners to select from because men choose from not only their same age group but also from those younger than themselves. One 40-year-old recently divorced woman said, "What chance do I have with all these guys looking at all these younger women?"

Education

Educational homogamy also operates in mate selection. Not only does college provide an opportunity

---

Homogamy: the tendency for an individual to seek a mate who has similar characteristics.

Educational homogamy: selecting a partner who has a similar level of education.

Seventeen percent of all persons who marry will select someone of a different race or ethnicity.
Courtesy of Trevor Werb

to meet, hang out with, and cohabit with potential partners, it also increases one's chance that only a college-educated partner becomes acceptable as a potential cohabitant or spouse. Even students with "some college"—those who don't graduate—are more likely to marry a college educated person than those with no college (McClendon, 2018). However, as women have begun to earn more college degrees than men, they are more likely to marry a male with less than more education than in previous years (Qian, 2017).

Intelligence

Dijkstra et al. (2012) studied the mate selection preferences of the intellectually gifted and found that intelligence was one of the primary qualities sought in a potential partner. While both genders valued an intelligent partner, women gave intelligence a higher priority.

Open-Mindedness

People vary in the degree to which they are **open-minded**. Homogamous pairings in regard to open mindedness reflect that partners seek like-minded individuals. Such open mindedness translates into tolerance of various religions, political philosophies, and lifestyles.

Social Class

Social class reflects your parents' occupations, incomes, and educations as well as your residence, language, and values. If you were brought up by parents who were physicians, you probably lived in a large house in a nice residential area—summer vacations and a college education were givens. Alternatively, if your parents dropped out of high school and worked blue-collar jobs, your home was likely smaller and in a less expensive part of town, and your opportunities, such as education, were more

limited. Social class affects one's comfort in interacting with others. We tend to select as friends and mates those with whom we feel most comfortable. One undergraduate from an upper-middle-class home said, "When he pulled out coupons at Subway for our first date, I knew this was going nowhere."

The **mating gradient** refers to the tendency for husbands to be more advanced than their wives with regard to age, education, and occupational success. Indeed, husbands are typically older than their wives, have more advanced education, and earn higher incomes.

Physical Attractiveness

Physical attractiveness is the most important quality individuals use when deciding to pursue someone on a dating site or app. Forty-one percent of 5,509 Match.com (2017) respondents reported that they had judged someone based on their photo on a dating site or app. O'Connor and Gladstone (2018) emphasized the advantages of being beautiful. Being able to use one's beauty to get the partner one wants is an example.

Weight and Height

Partners select as a mate someone of similar physique in terms of weight and height. Research by Prichard et al. (2015) confirmed that the physical measurements of brides-to-be were positively correlated with those of their fiancés, although the brides were lighter and shorter than their partners. Yancey and Emerson (2016) analyzed data from Yahoo dating personal advertisements and found that women were more concerned than men about dating someone who is taller than they are. Perhaps such concern is warranted. One of our male students who was 5' 7" said that he could never go with a woman taller than him since it would give him a feeling of inferiority.

Marital Status

Never-married people tend to select other never-married people as marriage partners; divorced people tend to select other divorced people; and widowed people tend to select other widowed people.

Religion/Spirituality

Religion may be defined as a set of beliefs in reference to a supreme being which involves practices or rituals, such as communion, generally agreed upon

....

Mating gradient: the tendency for husbands to be more advanced than their wives with regard to age, education, and occupational success.

Notice the weight and height similarity and that the woman is not taller than the man.

by a group of people. Some individuals view themselves as more "spiritual"—sacred, meaningful, and personal—than "religious"—communal, codified, and cultural (Steensland et al., 2018).

Religious and spiritual homogamy is operative in that people of a similar religion or spiritual philosophy tend to seek out each other. Thirty-five percent of 2,975 undergraduate males and 42% of 9,830 undergraduate females agreed that "It is important that I marry someone of my same religion" (Hall & Knox, 2019). Such religious homogamy is associated with higher marital satisfaction and a lower chance of divorce (Olson et al., 2014). While expressing a preference for a particular religion is becoming less frequent (Hout, 2017), being committed to one's religion and its teachings and

....

Religious and spiritual homogamy: selecting a partner who has similar religious and spiritual views.

marrying someone who is also committed is associated with subsequent marital quality (Perry & Whitehead, 2016). Finally, Henderson et al. (2018) found that religiosity among the unmarried was associated with relationship satisfaction and positive attitudes toward marriage.

Politics

An analysis of national data on thousands of spousal pairs in the United States revealed that homogamous political attitudes were the strongest of all social, physical, and personality traits in regard to impact on their relationship (Alford et al., 2011). We know of a couple who disagreed about President Trump and found that their political conflicts made it intolerable for them to stay together.

Circadian Preference

Circadian preference refers to an individual's preference for morningness-eveningness in regard to intellectual and physical activities. In effect, some prefer the morning while others prefer late afternoon or evening hours.

Traditional Roles

Partners who have similar views of what their marital roles will be are more likely to be attracted to each other.

Geographic Background

Haandrikman (2011) studied Dutch cohabitants and found that the romantic partners tended to have grown up within six kilometers of each other. While the university context draws people from different regions of the country, the demographics of state universities tend to reflect a preponderance of those from within the same state.

Economic Values, Money Management, and Debt

Individuals vary in the degree to which they have money, spend money, and save money. Some are deeply in debt and carry significant educational debt. The average debt for those with a bachelor's degree is $23,000. Almost half or 48% of those who borrowed money for their undergraduate education report that they are burdened by this debt (Pew Research Center, 2011). Of 2,960 undergraduate males, 7% and 5% of 9,786 undergraduate females owed more than a thousand dollars on a credit card (Hall & Knox, 2019). Money becomes an issue in mate selection in that different economic values predict conflict. One undergraduate male noted, "There is no way I would get involved with this woman—she jokes about maxing out her credit cards. Her debt is going to be someone else's nightmare."

Psychological Factors Operative in Mate Selection

Psychological factors are also involved in the selection of a mate. Research has focused on complementary needs, exchanges, parental characteristics, and personality types with regard to mate selection.

Complementary-Needs Theory

Yes, opposites may attract! **Complementary-needs theory** states that sometimes we select mates whose needs are opposite yet complementary to our own. For example, some partners may be drawn to each other on the basis of nurturance versus receptivity. These complementary needs suggest that one person likes to give and take care of another, whereas the other likes to be the benefactor of such care. Other examples of complementary needs are responsibility versus irresponsibility, peacemaker versus troublemaker, and disorder versus order. Wang et al. (2017) found that differences in general in the "big five" personality types—neuroticism, openness, extroversion, agreeableness and conscientiousness—were associated with lower marital quality.

Exchange Theory

Exchange theory in mate selection is focused on finding the partner who offers the greatest rewards at the lowest cost. The characteristics or qualities that a person has to offer another individual influence who that person can attract. The following five concepts help to explain the exchange process in mate selection:

1. **Rewards.** Rewards are the behaviors, words, resources, and services your partner provides that you value and that influence you to continue the relationship. Similarly, you provide behaviors, words, resources, and services for your partner that he or she values. Relationships in which the exchange is equal are happiest. Increasingly, men are interested in women who offer "financial independence" and women are interested in men who "cook and do the dishes."

These spouses have been married for 27 years which, in exchange theory terms, reflects that the "rewards" each brings to the relationship are greater than the "costs" so that there is a "profit" in staying together. Each spouse was previously married which reflects that staying in those respective relationships incurred greater "costs" than "rewards," and hence a "loss."

The price of anything is the amount of life you exchange for it.

Henry David Thoreau

2. **Costs.** Costs are the unpleasant aspects of a relationship. A woman identified the costs associated with being involved with her partner: "He abuses drugs, doesn't have a job, and lives nine hours away." The costs her partner associated with being involved with this woman included "she nags me," "she doesn't like sex," and "she insists that we live in the same town as her parents if we marry."

3. **Profit.** Profit occurs when the rewards exceed the costs. Unless the couple described in the preceding paragraph derive a profit from staying together, they are likely to end their relationship and seek someone else with whom there is a higher profit margin. Profit may also refer to nonmonetary phenomena.

4. **Loss.** Loss occurs when the costs exceed the rewards. Partners who feel that they are taking a loss in their relationship are vulnerable to looking for another partner who offers a higher profit.

5. **Alternative.** Is another person currently available who offers a higher profit? In effect, you will stay in a relationship where you have a high profit at a low cost. You will leave a relationship where your costs are high and you have an alternative partner who offers you a relationship with high rewards.

Complementary-needs theory: selecting a mate whose needs are opposite and complementary to one's own needs.

Exchange theory: theory that emphasizes that relationships are formed and maintained based on who offers the greatest rewards at the lowest costs.

Role Theory

Freud's psychoanalytic **role theory of mate selection** emphasizes that a son or daughter models after the parent of the same sex by selecting a partner similar to the one the parent selected as a mate. This means that a man looks for a wife who has similar characteristics to those of his mother and that a woman looks for a husband who is very similar to her father.

Attachment Theory

The **attachment theory of mate selection** emphasizes the drive toward an intimate emotional connection. One's earliest experience as a child is to be emotionally bonded to one's parents in the family context. The emotional need to connect remains as an adult and expresses itself in relationships with others, most notably the romantic love relationship. Children diagnosed with oppositional-defiant disorder (ODD) or post-traumatic stress disorder (PTSD) have had disruptions in their early bonding and frequently display attachment problems, possibly due to early abuse, neglect, or trauma. Children reared in Russian orphanages in the fifties where one caretaker was assigned to multiple children learned "no one cares about me" and "the world is not safe." Reversing early negative or absent bonding is difficult. The "Self-Assessment: Relationship Involvement Scale" on page 376 allows you to assess your current level of involvement.

The partner one finds, selects, and ends up with is complicated. Eastwick et al. (2017) explained:

> *In principle, heterosexual individuals [the same principles apply to same sex partners] in most contemporary societies could form romantic relationships with a vast number of peers. But they will only ever meet a subset of those peers—a subset that historically has been circumscribed by a demographically specific local context. Furthermore, people experience the desire to become romantically involved with only some of the opposite sex individuals whom they know, and only a portion of this select group will reciprocate that desire. In combination, these elements whittle down each person's universe of possible pairings to a unique pool of current and ex-romantic partners (p. 855).*

....

Role theory of mate selection: theory which focuses on the social learning of roles. A son or daughter models after the parent of the same sex by selecting a partner similar to the one the parent selected.

Attachment theory of mate selection: developed early in reference to one's parents, the drive toward an intimate, social/emotional connection.

And, individuals must have a desire for romantic relationship engagement. Watkins and Beckmeyer (2018) noted that such a desire sets the stage for actual romantic involvement which typically results in such relationships and marriage.

Undesirable Personality Characteristics of a Potential Mate

Researchers have identified several personality factors predictive of relationships which are unhappy or end in dissolution or divorce (Burr et al., 2011). Potential partners who are observed to consistently display these characteristics might be avoided.

1. **Controlling.** Partners want to be supported and respected for their interests, not criticized and told how to think and behave.

2. **Narcissistic.** Individuals who are narcissistic view relationships in terms of what they get out of them. When satisfactions wane and alternatives are present, narcissists are the first to go. Because all relationships have difficult times, a narcissist is a high risk for a durable marriage relationship.

3. **Poor impulse control.** Lack of impulse control is problematic in relationships because such individuals are less likely to consider the consequences of their actions. Having an affair is an example of failure to control one's behavior to ensure one's fidelity. Such people do as they please and worry about the consequences later.

4. **Hypersensitive.** Hypersensitivity to perceived criticism involves getting hurt easily. Any negative statement or criticism is received with a greater impact than a partner intended. The disadvantage of such hypersensitivity is that a partner may learn not to give feedback for fear of hurting the hypersensitive partner. Such lack of feedback to the hypersensitive partner blocks information about what the person does that upsets the other and what could be done to make things better. Hence, the hypersensitive one has no way of learning that something is wrong, and the partner has no way of alerting the hypersensitive partner. The result is a relationship in which the partners can't talk about what is wrong, so the potential for change is limited.

5. **Inflated ego.** "You're so vain...you probably think this song is about you" are lyrics from a Carly Simon hit of long ago. They reflect a person with an exaggerated sense of self,

an inflated ego. Such a person is less likely to consider another's feelings, opinions, and preferences and, rather than negotiate differences, prefers to dictate outcomes. Such disrespect for the partner can be damaging to any relationship.

6. **Perfectionistic.** Individuals who are perfectionists may require perfection of themselves and others. They are rarely satisfied and always find something wrong with their partner or relationship. Living with a perfectionist will be a challenge since whatever one does will not be good enough.

7. **Insecure.** Feelings of insecurity also make relationships difficult. The insecure person has low self-esteem, constantly feels that something is wrong, and feels disapproved of by the partner. The partner must constantly reassure him or her that all is well—a taxing expectation over time.

8. **Controlled.** Individuals who are controlled by their parents, former partner, child, or anyone else compromise the marriage relationship because their allegiance is external to the partner and their relationship. Unless the person is able to break free of such control, the ability to make independent decisions will be thwarted, which will both frustrate the spouse and challenge the marriage. Being controlled can begin early in one's relationship. An example is a divorced man who deferred to his 8-year-old daughter who was given veto power over each new partner.

9. **Substance abuser.** Heavy drug use is associated with relationship distress and lower relationship quality.

10. **Unhappy.** Personal happiness is associated with relationship happiness. Stanley et al. (2012) noted that being unhappy in one's personal life is predictive of having an unhappy marriage. Conversely, having high life satisfaction before marriage is predictive of high relationship satisfaction once married. Hence, selecting an upbeat, optimistic, happy individual predicts well for a future marriage relationship with this person.

11. **Promiscuous.** Is one's body count or the number of previous sexual partners a relevant variable in one's acceptability as a potential romantic partner? In heterosexual relationships, Jones (2016) found that individuals with extensive sexual histories, who were currently monogamous, were more acceptable to women than to men. Hence, the double standard is operative such that women are more accepting of high numbers of previous sexual partners for men but men fixate on women's previous high number of sexual partners in spite of a shift toward monogamy.

12. **Social anhedonia.** A psychiatric term, persons who have no interest in social contact and derive no pleasure from social interactions are referred to as having **social anhedonia**. Assaad et al. (2018) found that such persons have difficulty functioning in a romantic relationship in that they express few positive sentiments toward a partner and are not accepting of emotional overtures from a partner. This phenomenon reflects the reality that some people are not wired for involvement in social or love relationships and find them aversive.

In addition to undesirable personality characteristics, Table 5.1 reflects some particularly troublesome personality disorders and how they may impact a relationship.

Female Attraction to "Bad Boys"

Carter et al. (2014) reviewed the **dark triad personality** in some men and confirmed that some women are attracted to these "bad boys." The dark triad is a term for inter-correlated traits of narcissism, those with a grandiose view of one's self; Machiavellianism, those who are deceptive; and psychopathy, those with no empathy. These men are socially skilled and manipulative, have a high number of sex partners, and engage in mate poaching. The researchers analyzed data from 128 British undergraduate females who were attracted to bad boys. Explanations for such attraction included the self-confidence of the bad boys as well as their skill in manipulating the females. Similarly, research by Giebel et al. (2015) found that women who were turned off by and avoided boring partners and who sought exciting social activities were attracted to dominant—bad boy—males. And there is the challenge associated with bad boys. "I always knew I wasn't the only one, but I wanted to be the girl that changed him," said one undergraduate who dated a bad boy. In the end, she did not change him—he broke her heart.

Social anhedonia: people who have no interest in social contact or interactions with others.

Dark triad personality: term for inter-correlated traits of narcissism, a sense of entitlement and grandiose self-view; Machiavellianism, being deceptive and insincere; and psychopathy, being callous and having no empathy.

TABLE 5.1

Personality Disorders Problematic in a Potential Partner

DISORDER	CHARACTERISTICS	IMPACT ON PARTNER
Paranoid	Suspicious, distrustful, thin-skinned, defensive	Partners may be accused of everything.
Schizoid	Cold, aloof, solitary, reclusive	Partners may feel that they can never connect and that the person is not capable of returning love.
Borderline	Moody, unstable, volatile, unreliable, suicidal, impulsive	Partners will never know what their Jekyll-and-Hyde partner will be like, which could be dangerous.
Antisocial	Deceptive, untrustworthy, no conscience, no remorse	Such a partner could cheat on, lie to, or steal from a partner and not feel guilty.
Narcissistic	Egotistical, demanding, greedy, selfish	Such a person views partners only in terms of their value. Don't expect such a partner to see anything from your point of view; expect such a person to bail in tough times.
Dependent	Helpless, weak, clingy, insecure	Such a person will demand a partner's full time and attention, and other interests will incite jealousy.
Obsessive compulsive	Rigid, inflexible	Such a person has rigid ideas about how a partner should think and behave and may try to impose them on the partner.
Neurotic	Worries, obsesses about negative outcomes.	These individuals will impose negative scenarios on their partners.

PERSONAL CHOICES

Who Is the Best Person for You to Marry?

Although no perfect mate exists, some individuals are more suited for you as a marriage partner than others. As we have seen in this chapter, people who have a big ego, poor impulse control, and an oversensitivity to criticism should be considered with great caution.

Just as important as avoiding certain partners, it is important to seek partners with certain characteristics. Someone with whom you have a great deal in common is predictive of your future marital happiness and stability. "Marry yourself" is a worthy guideline in selecting a mate. Homogamous matings with regard to race, education, age, values,

religion, social class, and marital status—for example, never-married people marry never-married people—are more likely to result in more durable, satisfying relationships. "Marry your best friend" is another worthy guideline for selecting the person you marry.

Finally, marrying someone with whom you have a relationship of equality and respect is associated with marital happiness. Relationships in which one partner is exploited or intimidated engender negative feelings of resentment and distance. One man said, "I want a co-chair, not a committee member, for a mate." He was saying that he wanted a partner to whom he related as an equal. ●

Biological Factors Operative in Mate Selection

Almost 80% of 5,509 Match.com (2017) respondents reported being open for involvement in a relationship or actively looking for a partner. Biological anthropologist Helen Fisher (2015) notes that brain scans of over 100 individuals reflect changes in brain chemistry when in love. She noted that there is an evolutionary, biochemical drive to seek a

partner for sex and romance. The same centers of the brain that activate in response to thirst, food, cocaine, nicotine, or addictive substances also light up in reference to interpersonal sexual and emotional engagement. This innate, biological drive to meet a partner operates in the context of where one lives, who one can meet, or one's Internet use, such as Match.com, to expand one's catchment area. The other person must also "swipe right" in terms of reciprocation of interest.

Sociobiological Factors Operative in Mate Selection

In contrast to the sociological and psychological aspects of mate selection, the sociobiological perspective suggests that biological or genetic factors may be operative in mate selection.

Sociobiology

Based on Charles Darwin's theory of natural selection, which states that the strongest of the species survive, **sociobiology** holds that men and women select each other as mates on the basis of their innate concern for producing offspring who are most capable of surviving.

According to sociobiologists, men look for a young, healthy, attractive, sexually conservative woman who will produce healthy children and invest in taking care of them. Women, in contrast, look for an ambitious man with stable economic resources who will invest his resources in her children. Boxer et al. (2015) studied mate preference trends over the past 25 years and found that both men and women, increasingly, placed a higher value on a mate's financial prospects and desire for home and children. The sociobiological theory of mate selection remains evident.

Criticisms of the Sociobiological Perspective

The sociobiological explanation for mate selection is controversial. Critics argue that women may show concern for the earning capacity of men because women have been systematically denied access to similar economic resources, and selecting a mate with these resources is one of their remaining options. In addition, it is argued that both women and men, when selecting a mate, think about their partners more as companions than as future parents of their offspring.

Cultural Factors of Mate Selection

The sociological and psychological aspect of mate selection occur in cultural context. Individuals are not free to become involved with or marry whomever they want. Rather, their culture and society radically restrict and influence their choice. The best example of mate choice being culturally and socially controlled is the fact that 1% of the 63.3 million marriages in the United States consist of a Black spouse and a White spouse (*ProQuest Statistical Abstract, 2019, Table 60*). Indeed, up until the late sixties, such marriages in most states were a felony and

mixed spouses were put in jail. In 1967, the Supreme Court ruled that mixed marriages—those between Whites and Blacks—were legal. Similarly, up until the Supreme Court ruling in 2015 legalizing same sex marriages, individuals were prohibited from marrying someone of their same sex. Even with the legalization of same sex marriage, continued prejudice and discrimination may deter some individuals from such a marriage. Rather, they may seek a heterosexual marriage so as to "blend in." Endogamy and exogamy are also two forms of cultural pressure operative in mate selection.

> **CULTURE AND DIVERSITY**
>
> In most cultures, mate selection is not left to chance and parents are primary in the selection of their offspring's partner. India is made up of 29 states, reflecting a range of languages, dialects, and religions. But Indian culture as a whole is largely familistic, focusing on family unity and loyalty, rather than individualistic, focusing on personal interests and freedom. Most Indian youth defer to their parents as better able to select a lifetime marital partner.

Endogamy

Endogamy is the cultural expectation to select a marriage partner within one's own social

Endogamous cultural pressure encourages individuals to select a partner from their own racial group.
Courtesy of Chelsea Curry

Sociobiology: theory which emphasizes the biological basis for all social behavior, including mate selection.

Endogamy: cultural expectation to select a marriage partner within one's own social group (e.g., race).

Exogamy is operative among the Hopi Indians, about 10,000 of whom live on reservations in Arizona. The Hopi belong to different clans, such as Bear, Badger, Rain, and so forth, and the youth are expected to marry someone of a different clan. By doing so, they bring resources from another clan into their own.

Marriage market in China.
dpa picture alliance/Alamy Stock Photo

group, such as in the same race, religion, and social class. **Endogamous pressures** involve social approval from parents for selecting a partner within one's own group and disapproval for selecting someone outside one's own group. The pressure toward an endogamous mate choice is especially strong when race is involved. Such pressure is why the overwhelming majority of individuals end up selecting someone of the same race to marry.

Exogamy

Exogamy is the cultural pressure to marry outside the family group. Incest taboos are universal; in addition, children are not permitted to marry either of their parents in any society. In the United States, siblings and first cousins are also prohibited from marrying each other. The reason for such restrictions is fear of genetic defects in children whose parents are too closely related.

Once cultural factors have determined the general **pool of eligibles**—the population from which a person may select a mate—individual mate choice becomes more operative. However, even when individuals feel that they are making their own choices, social influences are still operative, such as in receiving approval from one's parents and peers.

Continuum of Arranged Marriages

Pande (2016) revealed the continuum of arranged marriages in British-Indian London society. These included the "traditional arranged marriage" whereby the parents set up the meeting between the partners, they were not allowed to be alone, and have little input into partner choice. "Semi-arranged marriages" where those in which the parents and their offspring consulted with each other, a viable candidate was identified, and the offspring would spend time with the person in the presence of the family with the goal of falling in love. Hence, the

....

Endogamous pressures: cultural pressure to marry someone with similar demographic characteristics (e.g., race, religion, education).

Exogamy: the cultural pressure to marry outside the family group.

Pool of eligibles: the population from which a person selects a marriage partner.

partner was pre-approved and needed only the love and agreement of the offspring. "Love with arranged marriage" involved the partners meeting on their own, dating, falling in love and then asking for their parents' permission. Since the partner chosen to fall in love with had characteristics such as religion, education, age, family values, and so forth that the parents would like, in most cases the parents would sign off and the wedding plans would go forward.

Olcay et al. (2019) compared the marriages of 456 Turkish husbands and wives in self-selected and arranged marriages in terms of love and feelings of being in a partnership. Results revealed that couples who selected their partner reported more love in their marriages and greater feelings of being in a partnership than couples whose marriage was arranged.

Some Chinese parents play an active role in seeking the right match for their adult children. The photo depicts Chinese parents displaying their adult children's resume-style profiles hoping to exchange information which occurs in the "marriage markets." The Shanghai marriage market is in the People's Square in Shanghai (Feng, 2018).

FINDING A PARTNER ONLINE

Increasingly, individuals are using the Internet and apps to find partners for fun, companionship, and marriage. The Internet has become the primary mechanism through which people meet, develop friendships, and maintain family relations. See Table 5.2 regarding how individuals meet.

TABLE 5.2

How Did You Meet Your Most Recent Date? (N = 4997)

Online	26%
Through a Friend	16%
Work	9%
School	6%
Bar	6%
Church	2%

Source: Match.com

Tinder is the largest U.S. dating app, available worldwide.
Courtesy of Trevor Werb

While the Internet has become the primary mechanism to look for a partner, it is not the primary means for finding a sexual partner, at least not for LGBTQ youth. Ybarra and Mitchell (2016) analyzed national data on 5,078 youth, 13 to 18 years old self identifying as lesbian, gay, queer, bisexual, heterosexual, questioning, unsure, and youth of other sexual identities and concluded that "the Internet is not replacing in-person exploration and expression of one's sexuality and meeting sexual partners online appears to be uncommon in adolescence across sexual identities" (p. 1357).

Kreager et al. (2014) analyzed data on individuals who sought a partner online from a sample of 8,259 men and 6,274 women and found that being aggressive in contacting someone seemed to pay off for men as male initiators connected with more desirable partners than men who waited to be contacted. Female initiators connected with equally desirable partners as women who waited to be contacted. However, female-initiated contacts were more than twice as likely as male-initiated contacts to result in

a connection. There are both advantages and disadvantages for meeting someone online and through apps.

Meeting Online—Advantages

Online and app dating services have become clear in their mission—to provide a place where people go to "shop" for potential romantic partners and to "sell" themselves in hopes of creating a successful romantic relationship. A major advantage is the ease of "shopping" and finding a partner. As individuals delay getting married and move beyond contexts like college where hundreds of potential partners are available, busy people can find and connect with someone new within a few hours. They may also want to avoid smoky bars or feel that their age bracket of people is easier to reach online.

Another advantage of looking for a partner online is that it removes emotion, chemistry, and first meeting magic from the mating equation so that individuals can focus on finding someone with common interests, values, and goals. In real life, you can "fall in love at first sight" and have zero in common. To help ensure meeting someone with similar characteristics, a variety of websites target a specific demographic—Black singles on BlackPlanet.com, Jewish singles on Jdate.com, and gay singles on Gay.com. There are even sites which match people on marijuana use and what individuals do not like such as Hater.com.

While Bauman (2013) in *Liquid Love* suggested that the value for life-long partnerships has been "liquefied" by unbridled individualism and technological change, Hobbs et al. (2017) provided data from 376 respondents that the desire for long-term monogamous relationships was still preferred. In the meantime, there were benefits to using the Internet to find partners to fit into one's busy schedule. One single mother noted,

> I'd just write 'sex?' so that was very direct, and it seemed to work for me, and then everyone knew where they stood ... as a single parent you're so socially isolated [and] you're financially screwed [and] it's really tough, so you're trying to see as many people in the shortest amount of space and then you're trying to use up the time that you have to yourself, which is not that often.

Another single woman wrote of the value of Tinder for her empowerment.

> I liked the way that I could make men behave in a way that traditionally women have behaved.... I felt like I was in complete control of everything and I just wish more women could experience

that and not feel bad about themselves and their bodies. So that's what the dating apps did for me. . . . I got my power back.

Dating sites are really introduction sites. There's not a dating service on this planet that can do what the human brain can do in terms of finding the right person.

Helen Fisher, biological anthropologist

Meeting Online—The Downside

Downsides from meeting online or through apps include bait and switch, less homogamous pairings, increased potential for lying or dishonesty, falling in love too quickly, and having unlimited options. Potarca (2017) compared data on individuals who met via the Internet to those who met through various offline contexts of interaction such as through friends or family. Results revealed that the Internet couples reflected less endogamy and commonality than those who met in conventional contexts.

Lying is common in online dating. Hall et al. (2010) analyzed data from 5,020 individuals who posted profiles on the Internet who revealed several categories of misrepresentation. These included personal assets, relationship goals, personal interests, personal attributes, past relationships and physical characteristics. Men were most likely to misrepresent personal assets, relationship goals, and personal interests whereas women were more likely to misrepresent weight. Lo et al. (2013) noted that deception is motivated by the level of attractiveness of the target person—deception is higher if the target person is particularly attractive.

Shopping Online for a Partner

Matchmaking has been documented throughout human history. Early Christians believed that one's soulmate was created by God and those who found their soulmate were blessed with happiness. Matchmakers were frequently utilized to facilitate the right match since young people were considered unable to make this critical life decision. For example, parental consent was required for marriage during the Victorian era.

The rapid development of social technology and online matchmaking services has shifted matchmaking to the virtual world. Rather than finding a partner via family and friends, individuals may choose to "shop" for a partner online by entering their personal information and preferences and trust the computer algorithms to find their Mr. or Ms. Right. And the pool of potential partners is very large. In the Facebook Dating alternative, there are 200 million people in 19 countries listing themselves as single.

Physical attractiveness is the most desirable trait for both men and women (Arnocky, 2018). However, attractiveness may be decoded differently by men and women. A study by McGloin and Deneses (2018) found that males with more attractive profile pictures were perceived to be trustworthy by women, but females with more attractive profile picture were viewed as less trustworthy by men, meaning "too hot to trust." Having had some college experience can increase one's desirability in the online marriage market in that women are more likely to identify education as an important quality for a potential partner (Whyte et al., 2018).

The process of looking for a partner online can be harrowing. About 80% of men are more likely to initiate the first message, while women's reply rate is less than 20% (Bruch & Newman, 2018). However, individuals who are sensitive about being rejected are more comfortable with the online medium— more at ease of being themselves—than in face-to-face meetings (Hance et al., 2018).

Matchmaking sites often use a compatibility questionnaire or assessment as the basis for pairing their clients. The concept of compatibility is grounded in the research on homogamy, which asserts that stable committed couples are more likely to be similar in education, religion, race, and social class. However, there is no consensus on the operational definition of compatibility and the validity of compatibility tests is often unavailable. Similar backgrounds may be a good foundation, but does not guarantee attraction or love. Considerable efforts have been made in the pursuit of the perfect matchmaking algorithm. Indeed, several matchmaking tools have received U.S. patents. For example, eHarmony asserts that it is responsible for 550 marriages daily (Baird, 2018) and emphasizes its "formula for love" is based on "scientific research" to match profiles of their members (Shambora, 2010). Researchers remain skeptical about the online matchmaking formulas since an individual's needs and preferences are complex, difficult to identify, and in flux. Some individuals are also cautious as not all students feel comfortable using or choosing technology to find a partner. "It's not for me," emphasizes one of our students. ●

Some online app users also lie about being single when in reality they are married or in a relationship. However, to suggest that the Internet is the only place where deceivers lurk is to turn a blind eye to those who meet through traditional channels. It is important to be cautious of arranging a date with someone you met online or through apps. Although these are convenient venues to meet new people, they also allow someone you rejected or an old lover to monitor your online behavior. Most sites note when you have been online most recently, so if you reject someone online by saying, "I'm really not ready for a relationship," that same person can log on and see that you are still looking. Some individuals become obsessed with a person they meet online and turn into a cyber-stalker when rejected. A quarter of the respondents in the Pew Research Center study said they were harassed or made to feel uncomfortable by someone they had met online (Smith and Duggan, 2013). Some people also use the Internet to try on new identities. For example, a person who feels he or she is attracted to same sex individuals may present a gay identity online.

Other disadvantages of online and app meeting dating include the potential to fall in love too quickly as a result of intense mutual disclosure; not being able to assess "chemistry" or how a person interacts with your friends and family; the tendency to move too quickly toward marriage, without spending much time to get to know each other, and not being able to observe nonverbal behavior. In regard to the nonverbal issue, Kotlyar and Ariely (2013) emphasized the importance of using Skype, which allows one to see the partner and assess nonverbal cues, as soon as possible and as a prelude to meeting in person to provide more information about the person behind the profile. However, Skype is not a substitute for meeting in person.

The caveat is to take it slow—after connecting in an e-mail through the dating site, move to instant messages, texting, phone calls, skyping, then meet in a public place with friends nearby. In addition, be clear in your profile about what you want. If you say in your profile "Interested in casual dating" this could translate to "not interested in a relationship." If your goal is to establish a long-term relationship, you could update your profile with "Love a good time and the adventure of life but only interested in a partner who wants a long-term relationship." Most people might not respond, but those who do will be more likely to have similar relationship goals.

Another disadvantage of using the Internet to find a partner is that having an unlimited number of options sometimes results in not looking carefully at the options right in front of you. With such choice overload, people are viewed as replaceable. What is needed is a careful consideration of each person—the same attention one would hope for one's own profile. Researcher Aditi (2014) found that those who met online are more likely to be involved in casual relationships compared to those who met offline who are more likely to be married. The explanation is that people online have a lot of options and like to keep going back to the pool to get a new partner. The classic example is a person on a date with someone they met on Tinder. After 15 minutes, they become disenchanted, go to the bathroom, and swipe right. Those who meet offline tend to move slowly rather than constantly looking for a better option.

It is also important to use Internet dating sites safely, including not giving out home or business phone numbers or addresses, always meeting the person in one's own town with a friend, and not posting photos that are too revealing, as these can be copied and posted elsewhere. Many websites require detailed personal information and charge membership fees. New Jersey passed the first Internet Dating Safety Act in 2008, which required Internet dating sites to provide criminal background checks and to better protect clients' personal information. Despite the recent boom of online dating and membership fees, not all states have implemented safety policies for Internet dating. Before going out with a person, vet that individual to ensure that person is who he or she says he or she is.

Catfishing

Catfishing is the process of creating a fake social media account to lure victims into a romantic relationship with stolen pictures and false identities. Impersonating a member of the military is one of the most common scams (Allan, 2018). People who are lured into having a relationship with the catfisher and those who have their photos used by the catfish scammer are both victims (Flynn, 2018). In an interview of 27 self-identified catfish scammers, 41% mentioned being lonely and unable to connect socially with others (Vanman, 2018).

One of our students reported on how she was "catfished":

I was on the app Tinder after a bad break up with my ex. It was a horrible heartbreak so I started chatting with this guy named Adam. We hung out a few times and then things became sexual (against my better judgment). After we had sex, he completely dropped out of my life. His phone was disconnected. I tried searching him on social media. And I could not find anybody by his name from the location he said he was from. I even paid

....

Catfishing: the process of creating a fake social media account to lure victims into a romantic relationship with stolen pictures and false identities.

for a one-time phone background check and the name registered with the phone wasn't the name he gave me. He deactivated his Tinder account or deleted me off of his chat list so I couldn't contact him there. I finally was able to contact him over Snapchat, but most of the time he would read my messages then not reply. I finally irritated him enough to where he finally talked to me. I asked him why he never came back after we had sex and his excuse was because he was gay. So that was the first and the last time I ever had sex with a guy that I didn't really know.

Ghosting

Related to catfishing is ghosting. Sometimes individuals are victims of **ghosting** which means that the partner breaks off the relationship suddenly without explanation. Without warning, there is no contact, communication, texting, emails, phone calls—nothing. Not only does the person doing the ghosting stop initiating contact, he or she ignores the former partner's attempts to reach out or communicate.

Speed Dating

Dating innovations that involve the concept of speed include the eight-minute date. If both parties are interested in seeing each other again, the organizer provides contact information so that the individuals can set up another date. Speed-dating saves time because it allows daters to meet face-to-face without burning up a whole evening.

Selecting a partner (or being selected) in a speed-dating context is tricky. Sels et al. (2019) found that "the more positive (excited, interested, or happy) participants felt after one interaction partner, the less attracted they were toward a new interaction partner, and the more negative they felt (irritated or bored), the more attracted they were. The effect of negative emotions (NEs) was primarily visible in men, for whom more prior NEs even increased the chance of choosing an interaction partner at the end of the evening."

> CULTURE AND DIVERSITY
>
> In Western culture, there is the "nice guy stereotype" that men who are caring are not attractive as potential partners. Data on speed-dating among single Asian Americans revealed that this quality (both self-rated and perceived) contributed to greater speed-dating success (Wu et al., 2019).

....

Ghosting: a situation when a partner breaks off the relationship suddenly without explanation.

MOVING TOWARD COMMITMENT

As partners continue to see each other, there is need for clarity. This often involves "the talk."

Having "The Talk"

The talk is a dialogue whereby both parties reveal their feelings about each other and their commitment to the future. Nelms et al. (2012) sampled 211 undergraduates who reported various strategies for assessing the partner's feelings about the future of the relationship.

The most common strategy was a direct question—"What do you see as far as the future of our relationship?" Half of the responses to this question were a direct commitment to the future; almost a third (32.3%) was uncertainty; and not quite ten percent (9%) responded that there was no future. The effects of having the relationship talk were variable. Over a third (34.7%) of the respondents reported that the effect was "to move us closer and forward." Fourteen percent ended the relationship and 11.7% said that their relationship became strained since they had different feelings about the future. Another 10% said they were still talking about the issue.

Engagement

Engagement moves the relationship of a couple from a private love-focused experience to a public, parent-involved experience. Unlike casual dating, **engagement** is a time in which the romantic partners are sexually monogamous, committed to marry, and focused on wedding preparations. The engagement period molds the intimate relationship of the couple by means of the social support and expectations of family and friends. It is the last opportunity before marriage to systematically examine the relationship—to become confident in one's decision to marry a particular person. Some engagements happen very fast. Not all engagements end in marriage. Between a fourth and a third of formal engagements break before the wedding.

Premarital Counseling

Jackson (2011) developed and implemented a unique evidence-informed treatment protocol for premarital counseling including six private sessions and two post marital booster sessions. Some clergy require one or more sessions of premarital counseling before they agree to marry a couple. Premarital counseling is a process of discovery. Because partners might have hesitated to reveal information that feel may have met

APPLYING SOCIAL RESEARCH

When There Are Discrepancies in Love and Commitment

It is sometimes the case that partners are discrepant in their attraction to, love for, and commitment to each other. This study reported data from 640 undergraduates who completed a 40-item Internet survey on the various types of discrepancies and the outcomes for their respective relationships. Results revealed that half of the respondents had been more and half less attracted to, in love with, and committed to a partner in a current or past relationship than was true of the partner's level of attraction, love and commitment. Men were significantly more likely than women to report that they were more in love with their partner. Being less committed for men and for women was associated with more cheating, depression, and alcohol and drug abuse on the part of the less involved. Hence, not being invested in a relationship

was associated with looking elsewhere for a partner, feeling depressed, and substance abuse.

However, of discrepant relationships that continued, 44% of the respondents reported that the discrepancies did not matter and were happy in spite of the discrepancies. Hence, over four in ten relationships continued in spite of the differences such that discrepancies were not regarded as deal breakers. ●

Source: Weiser, D. T., Hilliard, T. & Knox, D. (2018, November 9). "I Thought You Loved Me too?": Correlates and outcomes of discrepant involvement among undergraduates. Poster Annual Meeting, National Council on Family Relations, San Diego, CA. Also published in *Interpersona: An International Journal on Personal Relationships, 12*(2), 267–282.

with disapproval during casual dating, the sessions provide the context to be open with the other about their thoughts, feelings, values, goals, and expectations. The Self-Assessment of the Involved Couple's Inventory on page 377 is a guide for individuals in committed relationships to learn more about each other by asking specific questions.

Visiting Your Partner's Parents

Fisher and Salmon (2013) identified the reasons individuals take their potential partners home to meet their parents—to seek parental approval and feedback and to confirm to their partner that they are serious about the relationship. They also want to meet their partner's parents—to see how their potential mate will look when older, their future health, and potential familial resources that will be available.

Seize the opportunity to discover the family environment in which your partner was reared and consider the implications for your subsequent marriage. When visiting your partner's parents, observe their standard of living and the way they interact with one another. How does their standard of living compare with that of your own family? How does the emotional closeness or distance of your partner's family compare with that of your family? Such comparisons

are significant because both you and your partner will reflect your respective family or origins. "This is the way we did it in my family" is a phrase you will hear your partner say from time to time.

If you want to know how your partner is likely to treat you in the future, observe the way your partner's parent of the same sex treats and interacts with his or her spouse. If you want to know what your partner may be like in the future, look at your partner's parent of the same sex. There is a tendency for a man to become like his father and a woman to become like her mother. A partner's parent of the same sex and the parents' marital relationship are the models of a spouse and a marriage relationship that the person is likely to duplicate.

> *A commitment means you are going to stay loyal to what you said you were going to do long after the mood you said it in has left you.*
>
> Anonymous

Prenuptial Agreement

A **prenuptial agreement** is a contract made in anticipation of marriage. Prenups must be in writing and signed by both parties. It becomes effective upon marriage and is enforceable if there has

Engagement: time in which the romantic partners are sexually monogamous, committed to marry, and focused on wedding preparations.

Prenuptial agreement: a contract between intended spouses specifying which assets will belong to whom and who will be responsible for paying for what in the event of a divorce or when the marriage ends by the death of one spouse.

been fair and reasonable disclosure of each party's financial status, the agreement reasonable, and voluntary. Some appellate courts have held that both parties must have had an opportunity to consult with independent counsel, and the agreements must be signed at least seven days prior to the marriage (Gardner, 2017).

The primary purpose of the agreement is to specify how property will be divided if the marriage ends in divorce or when it ends by the death of one partner. Prenuptial agreements may not waive child support or dictate child custody as these are decided by the court. Individuals in second marriages and those with considerable assets are likely to develop a prenuptial agreement. In effect, the value of what you take into the marriage is the amount you are allowed to take out of the marriage. Some agreements may also contain clauses of no spousal support, also called alimony, if the marriage ends in divorce, but some states prohibit waiving alimony. Prenuptial agreements are sensitive issues. They are not romantic and emphasize that relationships have a "business" side replete with assets and potential division of property.

Reasons for a prenuptial agreement include the following:

1. **Protecting assets for children from a prior relationship.** Some children encourage their remarrying parent to draw up a prenuptial agreement with the new partner so that their inheritance, house, or possessions will not automatically go to the new spouse upon the death of their parent.

2. **Protecting business associates.** A spouse's business associate may want a member of a firm or partnership to draw up a prenuptial agreement with a soon-to-be-spouse to protect the firm from intrusion by the spouse if the marriage does not work out.

Prenuptial agreements are not very romantic. But they protect the partner who has a lot of assets. Kim Kardashian was able to maintain her $175 million fortune following her divorce because she had a prenup with Kris Humphries.

Prenups may also serve as a self-fulfilling prophecy. Indeed, 22% of 2,966 undergraduate males and 24% of 9,798 undergraduate females agreed with the statement "I would not marry someone who required me to sign a prenuptial agreement." Twenty-six percent of the males and 21% of the females felt that couples who have a prenuptial agreement are more likely to get divorced (Hall & Knox, 2019). However, Maybruch et al. (2017) compared marital outcomes for individuals who did and did not sign a religious prenuptial agreement and found no differences in marital adjustment or tendency to consider divorce among those who signed the prenuptial agreement.

Prenuptial contracts are almost nonexistent in first marriages and are still rare in second marriages. Maybruch et al. (2017) analyzed data on the 2,652 Orthodox Jews in North America and found that those who signed a religious prenuptial agreement

FAMILY POLICY

Increasing Requirements for a Marriage License

Should marriage licenses be obtained so easily? Should couples be required, or at least encouraged, to participate in premarital education before saying "I do"? Given the high rate of divorce today, policy makers and family scholars are considering this issue. Data confirm the value of marriage education exposure (Childs & Duncan, 2012; Kalinka et al., 2012; Lucier-Greer et al., 2012).

Several states have proposed legislation requiring premarital education. For example, an Oklahoma statute provides that parties who complete a premarital education program may pay a reduced fee for their marriage license. In addition, in Lenawee County, Michigan, local civil servants and clergy have made a pact: they will not marry a couple unless that couple has attended marriage education classes. Other states that are considering policies to require or encourage premarital education include Arizona, Illinois, Iowa,

Maryland, Minnesota, Mississippi, Missouri, Oregon, and Washington. Proposed policies include not only mandating premarital education and lowering marriage license fees for those who attend courses but also imposing delays on issuing marriage licenses for those who refuse premarital education.

Advocates of mandatory premarital education emphasize that such courses reduce marital discord. However, questions remain about who will offer what courses and whether couples will take the content of such courses as intended. Indeed, people contemplating marriage are often narcotized with love feelings and may not take any such instruction seriously. Love myths such as "divorce is something that happens to other people" and "our love will overcome any obstacles" work against the serious consideration of such courses. ●

reported higher levels of marital satisfaction than those who did not. While some individuals are deciding whether to have a prenuptial agreement, states are deciding whether to increase marriage license requirements, this chapter's family policy issue.

IMPORTANT CONSIDERATIONS BEFORE YOU SAY "I DO"

While the Internet and apps are a valuable tool for helping to identify partners, one must then evaluate the partner and the relationship. If you and your partner have become serious about your future together, the following are some factors to consider.

Avoid Teen Marriage

The strongest predictor of getting divorced is getting married during the teen years. Individuals who marry at age 18 or younger have three times the risk of divorce than those who delay marriage into their late twenties or early thirties. Marriages in a couple's late 20s or early 30s are associated with the most durable happy marriages.

Date Partner for at Least Three Years Before Getting Married

Twenty-nine percent of 2,971 undergraduate males and 32% of 9,814 undergraduate females agreed, "If I were really in love, I would marry someone I had known for only a short time" (Hall & Knox, 2019). Impulsive marriages in which the partners have known each other for less than a month are associated with a higher-than-average divorce rate. Indeed, partners who date each other three years or more before getting married are 39% less likely to divorce than those who rush into marriage (Fisher, 2019). A short courtship does not allow partners enough time to learn about each other's background, values, and goals and does not permit opportunity to observe and scrutinize each other's behavior in a variety of settings, such as with one's close friends and family.

To increase the knowledge you and your partner have about each other, find out each other's answers to the questions in the Involved Couple's Inventory (see the Self-Assessments on page 377), take a five-day camping trip, go on a 15-mile hike together, wallpaper a small room together, or spend several days together when one partner is sick. If the couple plans to have children, they may want to offer to babysit a young child of their friends for a weekend. These scenarios may be helpful in learning more about your partner.

End an Abusive Relationship Before Marriage

Abusive lovers become abusive spouses, with predictable negative outcomes. Though extricating oneself from an abusive relationship is difficult before the wedding, it becomes even more difficult after marriage, particularly when children are involved. Abuse is a serious red flag of impending relationship doom that should not be overlooked and one should seek the exit ramp as soon as possible (see Chapter 10 on the details of leaving an abusive relationship).

Compliment Each Other Often and Avoid Criticizing Each Other

Research on couples across the first five years of marriage reveals that more negative and less positive communication before marriage is associated with subsequent divorce. In addition, the researchers emphasize that "negatives tend to erode positives over time." Individuals who criticize each other end up damaging their relationship in a way which does not make it easy for positives to erase (Markman et al., 2010).

Marry Someone Similar to You

Relentless conflict often arises from numerous significant differences. Though all spouses are different from each other in some ways, those who have similarities in key areas such as race, religion, social class, education, values, and goals report higher marital satisfaction and lower divorce rates.

Be Aware That an On-and-Off Relationship Is a Bad Sign

A roller-coaster premarital relationship, which occurred in about a quarter of relationships in one study (Hardy & Vennum, 2014), is predictive of a marital relationship that will follow the same pattern. About 60% of couples report that they have experienced a breakup and reconciliation (Lindstrom et al., 2014). Partners in cyclical relationships have developed a pattern in which the dissatisfactions in the relationship become so frustrating that separation becomes the antidote for relief. Dailey et al. (2013) identified various types of on-and-off relationships in which most of the partners had different personalities or interests or just fell back together with no changes. Only 22% improved the relationship after the breakup.

Consider Your Parents' Opinion

Approval of the parents on the mate choice of their son or daughter is associated with the subsequent marital satisfaction of the son or daughter (Parise et al., 2017; Vellucci et al., 2014). Disapproval is associated with subsequent lower marital satisfaction. It is important to give consideration to your parents' opinions since they know you very well.

Be Aware That a Good Sex Life Predicts Well for Relationship Success

Sexual satisfaction is linked to relationship satisfaction, love, and commitment. Hence, couples who are dissatisfied with their sexual relationship might explore ways of improving it either alone or through counseling.

Don't Settle

Settling is remaining in a relationship that provides a reasonable level of satisfaction with the knowledge that one is fearful of taking the chance to find someone better. Settling has several characteristics:

1. **Moderate love.** Persons who settle report feelings of love for their partner but there is an absence of passion. The partner is viewed as comfortable but does not elicit feelings of being deeply in love. The problem of "settling" for someone is that there will come a time when you will meet someone that you are really attracted to and you will be "stuck" with the person with whom you "settled."

2. **Fear.** Settling for a partner in a relationship is driven by the fear of being alone and not finding a partner at least as good as the current partner. Staying with someone out of fear of being alone is a questionable reason to maintain a relationship. Such a decision reflects a negative self-concept on your part and negative feelings about the partner.

3. **Guilt.** The partner who is settling feels guilty for not feeling passionately in love and for hiding that he or she is settling. Shakespeare's phrase "The false face must hide what the false heart doth know" captures the emotional state of the settler. You have nothing to feel guilty about. It is OK not to

feel madly in love with someone. But be slow to marry someone you aren't passionate about.

4. **Anxiety.** The partner who is settling is anxious. He or she knows that it is best to end the relationship but feels incapable of doing so. Living in a state of anxiety has negative consequences for your physical, emotional, and mental well-being.

5. **Depression.** To know what one should do but to be incapable of action coupled with being in a relationship that one is not proud to be in is depressing. Disengaging from the relationship will free you from the depression and anxiety of being on a train going nowhere. Even if a new person that you are wildly attracted to and feel good about does not surface, you have still avoided the knowledge that you settled and should not have done so.

In spite of all the above reasons, it is important to keep in mind that Americans are socialized to expect continuous excitement, love, and passion in their relationships—an unrealistic goal. There is a fine line between acknowledging the reality of a companionable day-to-day relationship and its value and not interpreting this relationship as substandard—that one is settling. A new partner may bring excitement but such excitement may not be sustained over time. One spouse said, "We were not unhappy . . . we just thought we could do better . . . we were wrong. . . we should have nurtured what we had." On the other hand, if you do not love your partner, the danger of marrying this person is that you may fall in love with someone else after you are married . . . making it difficult to stay in the marriage with the person you "settled" for.

Avoid Marrying for the Wrong Reason

Some reasons for getting married are more questionable than others. These reasons include the following.

1. **Rebound.** A rebound marriage results when you marry someone immediately after another person has ended a relationship with you. A rebound marriage is a frantic attempt to reestablish your desirability in your own eyes and in the eyes of the partner who dumped you. To marry on the rebound is usually a bad decision because the new marriage is in reference to the previous partner and not the current partner. In effect, you are using the person you intend to marry

---

Settling: remaining in a relationship that provides a reasonable level of satisfaction with the knowledge that one is fearful of taking the chance to find someone better.

to establish yourself as the "winner" in the previous relationship. However, Brumbaugh and Fraley (2015) investigated persons who were in a rebound relationship and found that those in their new relationships were more confident in their desirability and had more resolution over their ex-partner. Hence, the outcome for the person on the rebound may be positive.

But what kind of partner is the rebound partner for the new partner? Barber and Cooper (2014) used a longitudinal, online diary method to examine trajectories of psychological recovery and sexual experience following a romantic relationship breakup among 170 undergraduate students. Consistent with stereotypes about individuals on the rebound, those respondents who had been "dumped" used sex to cope with feelings of distress, anger, and diminished self-esteem. Hence, caution about becoming involved with someone on the rebound may be warranted. One answer to the question, "How fast should you run from a person on the rebound?" may be "as fast as you can." Waiting until the partner has 12 to 18 months distance from the previous relationships provides for a more stable context for the new relationship.

2. **Escape**. A person might marry to escape an unhappy home situation in which the parents are oppressive, overbearing, conflictual, alcoholic, or abusive or has some combination of these traits. Marriage for escape is a bad idea since it is often more in reference to the context one is escaping from rather than the new context one is entering. It is far better to continue the relationship with the partner until mutual love and respect become the dominant forces propelling you toward marriage rather than follow the desire to escape an unhappy situation. In this way you can evaluate the marital relationship in terms of its own potential and not as an alternative to unhappiness.

3. **Unplanned pregnancy.** Getting married because a partner becomes pregnant should be considered carefully. Indeed, the decision of whether to marry should be kept separate from decisions about a pregnancy. Adoption, abortion, single parenthood, and unmarried parenthood where the couple can remain together as an unmarried couple and have the baby are all alternatives to simply deciding to marry if a partner becomes pregnant. Avoiding feelings of being trapped or later feeling that the marriage might not have happened without the pregnancy are two reasons for not rushing into marriage because of pregnancy. Couples who marry when the woman becomes pregnant have an increased chance of divorce.

4. **Psychological blackmail**. Some individuals get married because their partner takes the position that "I will commit suicide if you leave me." Because the person fears that the partner may commit suicide, he or she may agree to the wedding. The problem with such a marriage is that one partner has resorted to harmful threats to get what he or she wants. This constitutes emotional manipulation, and the threatened partner should seek help, if possible.

5. **Insurance benefits**. Some couples marry so that their partner will have health insurance. While selecting a partner who has resources, which may include health insurance, is not unusual, to select a partner solely because he or she has health benefits is dubious. Both parties might be cautious if the alliance is more about "benefits" than the relationship.

6. **Pity**. Some partners marry because they feel guilty about terminating a relationship with someone whom they pity. The fiancée of an Afghanistan soldier reported that "when he came back with his legs blown off I just changed inside and didn't want to stay in the relationship. I felt guilty for breaking up with him...." Regardless of the reason, if one partner becomes brain-damaged or fails in the pursuit of a major goal, it is important to keep the issue of pity separate from the advisability of the marriage. The decision to marry should be based on factors other than pity for the partner.

7. **Filling a void**. A former student in the authors' classes noted that her father died of cancer. She acknowledged that his death created a vacuum, which she felt driven to fill immediately by getting married so that she would have a man in her life. Because she was focused on filling the void, she had paid little attention to the personality characteristics of the man who had asked to marry her. She discovered on her wedding night that her new husband had several other girlfriends whom he had no intention of giving up. The marriage was annulled.

Afrasiabi and Dehaghani Daramroud (2018) interviewed 31 women who had applied for divorce and asked them to identify the mistakes they made in their decision to marry and in selecting their partner to marry. The various wrong decisions they noted included marrying someone very different, escaping from a crisis situation, being destitute, and giving in to pressure. In deciding whether to continue or terminate a relationship, listen to what your senses tell you: Does it feel right? Listen to your heart—do you love this person or do you question whether you love this person? And evaluate your similarities—what do you have in common? Finally, be realistic. Indeed, most people exhibit some negative and some positive indicators before they marry.

FUTURE OF PARTNER SELECTION

In the past, the focus of selecting a partner was to share one's life in an intimate couple marriage. What has changed is an increase in individuals being focused on their own life agendas, and while they are interested and willing to become involved in an intimate long-term relationship, they are also interested in pair bonding with a partner who will facilitate their own self-actualization (Fisher, 2015). This dual focus on partner selection of intimacy, autonomy, and support for one's life agenda will increase in the future.

SUMMARY

What are the sociological factors that influence mate selection?

Sociological aspects of mate selection involve homogamy—"like attracts like"—or the tendency to be attracted to people similar to oneself. Many variables, such as race, age, religion, education, social class, personal appearance, personality, and open-mindedness, have been identified.

What are the psychological factors operative in mate selection?

Several psychological theories have been used to explain mate selection. Complementary-needs theory where "opposites attract" suggests that people select others who have characteristics opposite to their own. Exchange theory suggests that one individual selects another on the basis of rewards and costs. As long as an individual derives more profit from a relationship with one partner than with another, the relationship will continue with the "higher profit" person. Exchange concepts influence who dates whom, the conditions of the dating relationship, and the decision to marry. Freud's psychoanalytic theory suggests that individuals select a partner similar to the opposite-sex parent. Attachment theory views the bond between infant and primary caretaker as the foundation of later relationships.

Undesirable personality characteristics of a potential mate include being too controlling, being narcissistic, having poor impulse control, being hypersensitive to criticism, having an inflated ego, and so forth. Paranoid, schizoid, and borderline personality disorders may also require one to be cautious.

What are the biological factors operative in mate selection?

There is an evolutionary, biochemical drive to seek a partner for sex and romance. The same centers of the brain that activate in response to thirst, food, cocaine, nicotine, and addictive substances also light up in reference to interpersonal sexual and emotional engagement.

What are the sociobiological factors operative in mate selection?

The sociobiological view of mate selection suggests that men and women select each other on the basis of their biological capacity to produce and support healthy offspring. Men seek young women with healthy bodies, and women seek ambitious men who will provide economic support for their offspring. There is disagreement about the validity of this theory. Critics argue that women may show concern for the earning capacity of men because women have been systematically denied access to similar economic resources, and selecting a mate with these resources is one of their remaining options.

What are the cultural factors that affect your selection of a mate?

Two types of cultural influences in mate selection are endogamy—to marry someone inside one's own social group such as race, religion, social class—and exogamy, to marry someone outside one's own family.

What are the advantages and disadvantages of meeting online?

Internet dating, app dating, and speed dating are increasingly being used to find a partner. The Internet is efficient, allows one to screen multiple partners quickly, and to disappear at will. Downsides include that one cannot assess "chemistry" through a computer screen; Internet relationships allow no observation of the potential partner with his or her friends and family; and there may be considerable deception by both parties.

What factors suggest you might consider delaying the wedding?

Factors suggesting that a couple may not be ready for marriage include being in their teens, having known each other less than three years, and having a relationship characterized by significant differences or dramatic parental disapproval or both. Some research suggests that partners with the greatest number of similarities in values, goals, and common interests are most likely to have happy and durable marriages. Negative reasons for getting married include being on the rebound, escaping from an unhappy home life, unplanned pregnancy, psychological blackmail, insurance benefits, pity, and filling a void.

What is the future of selecting a partner?

Sociological, psychological, and cultural factors will continue to be involved in the selection of a marital partner. The future of mate selection will also involve the increased use of technology to find a marriage partner. Use of technology permeates the lives of today's youth such that the use of Tinder, Match.com, and other such sites will become normative and lose their stigma.

KEY TERMS

Attachment theory of mate selection, 98

Catfishing, 105

Complementary-needs theory, 97

Dark triad personality, 99

Educational homogamy, 94

Endogamy, 101

Endogamous pressure, 102

Engagement, 107

Exchange theory, 97

Exogamy, 102

Ghosting, 106

Homogamy, 94

Mating gradient, 95

Pool of eligibles, 102

Prenuptial agreement, 107

Religious and spiritual homogamy, 96

Role theory of mate selection, 98

Settling, 110

Social anhedonia, 99

Sociobiology, 101

WEB LINKS

Denver Family Institute
http://denverfamilyinstitute.org/

The Gottman Institute
https://www.gottman.com/

The Relate Institute
https://relateinstitute.com/

Get the tools you need to sharpen your study skills. SAGE edge offers a robust online environment featuring an impressive array of free tools and resources.

Access practice quizzes, eFlashcards, video, and multimedia at **edge.sagepub.com/knox13e**

6 Diversity in Marriage Relationships

You see, our glorious diversity—our diversity of faiths, and colors and creeds—that is not a threat to who we are, it makes us who we are.

—Michelle Obama

Learning Objectives

6.1.   Discuss the individual motivations for and societal functions of marriage

6.2.   Review how marriage is a commitment to one's partner, family, and state

6.3.   Identify how weddings and honeymoons are rites of passage

6.4.   Understand the changes that occur after a marriage

6.5.   Review the vast array of marriage types

6.6.   Discuss the characteristics of successful marriages

6.7.   Review the prediction for the future of marriage relationships

Individuals in their own marriage are often oblivious to the enormous variety of marriage relationships. This chapter covers differences in marriages across various demographics. While there is great variation in marriage, there are key similarities, which we'll discuss.

MOTIVATIONS FOR AND FUNCTIONS OF MARRIAGE

In this section, we discuss both why people marry and the functions that getting married serve for society.

Individual Motivations for Marriage

We have defined marriage in the United States as a legal contract between two adults that regulates their economic and sexual interaction. However, individuals in the United States tend to think of marriage in personal more than legal terms. The following are some of the reasons people give for getting married.

Love

Many couples view marriage as the ultimate expression of their love for each other—the desire to spend their lives together in a secure, legal, committed relationship. In U.S. society, love is expected to precede marriage—thus, only couples in love consider marriage. Those not in love would be ashamed to admit it.

Personal Fulfillment

We also marry because we anticipate a sense of personal fulfillment by doing so. We were born into a family, our family of origin, and want to create a family of our own, our family of procreation. We remain optimistic that our marriage will be a good one. Even if our parents divorced or we have friends who have done so, we feel that our relationship will be different.

Companionship

Although marriage does not ensure it, companionship is the greatest expected benefit of marriage in the United States. Coontz (2016) noted that companionship has become the legitimate goal of marriage.

Parenthood

Most people want to have children. In a sample of 598 undergraduates, 72% reported that they wanted children; 65% reported that they always wanted to have children (Chang et al., 2018). Although some people are willing to have children outside of marriage, such as in a cohabiting relationship or in no relationship at all, most Americans prefer to have them in a marital context. Previously, a strong norm existed in our society, particularly among Whites,

Sharing a glass of wine and a lifetime of memories together is what marriage is all about.
Courtesy of Trevor Werb

that individuals should be married before they have children. This norm is becoming more relaxed, with more individuals willing to have children without being married.

Marriage is about children. If children were not involved, marriage would not exist.

George P. Murdock, anthropologist

Economic Security

Married people report higher household incomes than do unmarried people. Indeed, almost 80% of married women work outside the home so that two incomes are available to the couple. Table 6.1 reflects the higher income of couple over single households.

TABLE 6.1

Median Income of Married Couple and Single Households

Married couple (two incomes)	$103,699
Single female household	$ 34,126
Single male household	$ 49,772

Source: *ProQuest Statistical Abstract of the United States, 2019, Online Edition.* Table 727

Psychological and Physical Well-Being

Regardless of sexual orientation, being married is associated with higher levels of psychological well-being than being single (Wright et al., 2013). Spouses not only in the United States, but in the United Kingdom and Germany too, report being happier than the unmarried (Chapman & Guven, 2016). This same finding has been revealed in a large sample of Canadians (Zella, 2016). Wadsworth (2016) asked whether marriage leads to subjective well-being or are people who feel a positive sense of well-being more likely to marry? Regarding physical well-being, Zella (2016) confirmed greater health among Canadians who were married when compared to not married.

Societal Functions of Marriage

As noted in Chapter 1, the historical functions of marriage were to provide in-laws with expanded resources and offspring for family labor. Today, important societal functions of marriage are to bind two individuals together who will raise and provide physical care for their dependent young, and socialize them to be productive members of society who will replace those who die. Marriage helps protect children by giving the state legal leverage to force parents to be responsible to their offspring whether they stay married. If couples did not have children, the state would have no interest in regulating marriage.

TABLE 6.2

Traditional Versus Egalitarian Marriages

TRADITIONAL MARRIAGE	EGALITARIAN MARRIAGE
Limited expectation of husband to meet emotional needs of wife and children.	Both spouses are expected to meet emotional needs of each other and children.
Wife is not expected to earn income.	Both spouses are expected to earn income.
Emphasis on traditional roles.	Emphasis is on companionship.
Couples do not live together before marriage.	Couples often live together before marriage.
Wife takes husband's last name.	No one must change surname. Both spouses may change last names. In some cases, he will take her last name.
Husband is dominant; wife is submissive.	Neither spouse is dominant.
Roles for husband and wife are rigid.	Roles for spouses are flexible.
Husband initiates sex; wife complies.	Either spouse initiates sex.
Wife takes care of children.	Both spouses are equal in child care and rearing.
Education is important for husband, not for wife.	Education is important for both spouses.
Husband's career decides family residence.	Career of either spouse may determine family residence.
Marriage is heterosexual, male dominated.	Marriage may be two same sex females or males as egalitarian partners.

Additional functions of marriage include regulating sexual behavior and stabilizing adult personalities by providing a companion and "in-house" counselor. In the past, marriage and family served protective, educational, economic, and religious functions for its members. These functions have been taken over by the legal, educational, economic and religious institutions of our society. Only the companionship-intimacy function of marriage and family has remained virtually unchanged (Coontz, 2016). To feel connected, loved, involved with another in an intimate long-term relationship also benefits society. Background profiles of the various shooters in malls, schools, nightclubs, theaters, and other public venues reveal disconnected, alienated individuals.

The nature of the marriage relationship has changed from being very traditional or male-dominated to being very modern or egalitarian. A contrast of traditional and egalitarian marriage is presented in Table 6.2. Keep in mind that these are stereotypical marriages and that only a small percentage of today's modern marriages have all the traditional or egalitarian characteristics that are listed. Some marriages today also consist of same sex spouses where the roles are more egalitarian since there is no one "male" to dominate.

MARRIAGE AS A COMMITMENT

Marriage represents a multilevel commitment—person-to-person, family-to-family, and couple-to-state.

Person-to-Person Commitment

Commitment is the intent to maintain a relationship. Persons express commitment by telling one another, telling friends, doing things for each other, and providing economic resources. Wilcox and Dew (2016) found that commitment to the partner and relationship was the primary factor associated with **marital generosity**—small acts of service, forgiving the spouse, displaying affection and respect. The "Self-Assessment: Satisfaction in Couple Relationship Scale" on page 381 allows you to assess satisfaction in your current relationship.

Family-to-Family Commitment

Whereas love is private, marriage is public. Whether one has a large wedding or a courthouse ceremony,

the marriage ceremony involves a couple agreeing to the marriage before a witness. When individuals marry, one's parents and extended kin also become involved.

Marriage also involves commitments by each of the marriage partners to the family members of the spouse. Married couples are often expected to divide their holiday visits between both sets of parents.

Couple-to-State Commitment

In addition to making person-to-person and family-to-family commitments, spouses become legally committed to each other according to the laws of the state in which they reside. This means they cannot arbitrarily decide to terminate their own marital agreement.

Just as the state says who can marry—not close relatives—and when—usually at age 18— legal procedures must also be instituted for the spouses to divorce. The state's interest is that a married couple with children stays married and takes care of the children. Indeed, one of the reasons the Supreme Court legalized same sex marriage is that children reared in same sex relationships would benefit from the increased stability of the relationship between the parents. There has also been a concern that no-fault divorce which allows spouses to leave marriage with relative ease and without their being a "guilty party" would increase the divorce rate.

Marital generosity: small acts of service, forgiving the spouse, displaying affection/respect.

Bride wealth: also known as bride price or bride payment, the amount of money or goods paid by the groom or his family to the bride's family for losing her as a labor source.

MARRIAGE AS A RITE OF PASSAGE

A **rite of passage** is an event that marks the transition from one social status to another. Starting school, getting a driver's license, and graduating from high school or college are events that mark major transitions in status. The wedding is another rite of passage that marks the transition from fiancée and fiancé to spouse. Preceding the wedding is the traditional bachelor party for the soon-to-be groom usually involving excessive alcohol consumption (Briggs & Ellis, 2017). Somewhat new on the cultural landscape is the bachelorette party for the soon-to-be bride, also a time of alcohol consumption. Both of these rituals convey the message that marriage is a new role with new rules and the freedom of singlehood will soon end.

Weddings

States control who is eligible for a marriage license. To obtain a marriage license, the partners must meet basic criteria such as age. In most states, the age of marriage is 18. But 4% set the age of eligibility at 15 and 1% at younger than 15. Children as young as 12 have been granted marriage licenses in Alaska, Louisiana, South Carolina, and Tennessee (Tsui, 2017). Some states require a waiting period—in Minnesota it is five days— after applying for the marriage license and they determine when the couple may obtain the license. Other states require a waiting period from the time the license is issued until the wedding may occur. In Texas, it is three days. In Oklahoma, couples must use the marriage license within ten days or it will expire. The cost of a wedding license varies from $10 to $115. Some states such as Florida waive the marriage license fee if the couple has had the premarriage course sanctioned by the state.

The wedding is a rite of passage that is both religious and civil. To the Catholic Church, marriage is a sacrament that implies that the union is both sacred and indissoluble. According to Jewish and most Protestant faiths, marriage is a special bond between the husband and wife sanctified by God, but divorce and remarriage are permitted. A member of the clergy marries 80% of couples; the other 20%, primarily couples getting remarried, go to a justice of the peace, judge, or magistrate. Some states like North Carolina require a "real clergy, pastor, priest, and so forth," not someone who "got a certificate on the Internet stating that the person is clergy."

That marriage is a public event is emphasized by weddings in which the couple invites their family and friends to participate. The wedding is a time for the respective families to learn how to cooperate with each other for the benefit of the couple. Conflicts over the number of bridesmaids and ushers, the number of guests to invite, and the place of the wedding are not uncommon. Campbell et al. (2011a) surveyed 610 spouses and found that those who had an elaborate wedding reported less present-day satisfaction and commitment, suggesting that individuals who idealize their relationship may enact elaborate weddings, and when their high relational expectations go unmet, satisfaction and commitment decline.

Brides often wear traditional artifacts: something old, new, borrowed, and blue. The old wedding artifact represents the durability of the impending marriage. The new wedding artifact, perhaps in the form of new undergarments, emphasizes the new life to begin. The borrowed wedding artifact is something that has already been worn by a currently happy bride. The blue wedding artifact represents fidelity; "those dressed in blue or in blue ribbons have lovers true." When the bride throws her floral bouquet, the single woman who catches it will be the next to be married; the rice thrown by the guests at the newly married couple signifies fertility.

Couples now commonly have weddings that are neither religious nor traditional. In the exchange of vows, the couple's relationship may be spelled out by the partners rather than by tradition, and neither partner may promise to obey the other. Vows often include the couple's feelings about equality, individualism, humanism, and openness to change. Some weddings are ultra-unique: One couple, who met on POF (a Canadian online dating service formerly known as Plenty of Fish), donned scuba gear and said their vows underwater.

Weddings can be expensive. U.S. couples spend an average of $29,200 for about 126 guests. (The Knot World Wide, 2019). The traditional wedding etiquette is for the bride's family to be responsible for wedding and reception expenses. However, the new rules of individuals getting married today is that they expect both families to contribute. If the couple has been working, the couple is expected to share the cost as well. Ways in which couples lower the cost of their wedding include marrying any day but Saturday or marrying off-season or off-locale. They may also broadcast their wedding over the Internet. Streaming capability means that the couple can get married in Hawaii and have their ceremony beamed back to the mainland where well-wishers can see the wedding without leaving home. Some couples buy wedding insurance to cover issues such as the venue going out of business, liability of someone slipping on the dance floor, and unforeseen weather.

....

Rite of passage: an event that marks the transition from one social status to another.

Honeymoons

Traditionally, another rite of passage follows immediately after the wedding—the **honeymoon,** the time following the wedding whereby the couple isolate themselves to recover from the wedding and to solidify their new status change from lovers to spouses. The functions of the honeymoon are both personal and social. The personal function is to provide a period of recuperation from the usually exhausting demands of preparing for and being involved in a wedding ceremony and reception. The social function is to provide a time for the couple to be alone to solidify their new identity, changing from that of an unmarried to a married couple.

While most spouses in new marriages report this to be the happiest time of the lives, Scott and Stafford (2018) revealed data from 152 women who had only been married six months or less: 12% of them "reported reliable and clinically meaningful increases in depressive symptoms after their wedding." These symptoms were in reference to increases in self-uncertainty, partner uncertainty, and relationship uncertainty following the wedding. While weddings and honeymoons are wonderful events for most individuals, for some, they are times of misery.

CHANGES AFTER MARRIAGE

After the wedding and honeymoon, the new spouses begin to experience changes in their legal, personal, and marital relationship.

> Marriage isn't a love affair. It isn't even a honeymoon. It's a job. A long hard job, at which both partners have to work, harder than they've worked at anything in their lives before. If it's a good marriage, it changes, it evolves. . .
>
> Rosamunde Pilcher, *Wild Mountain Thyme*

Legal Changes

Unless the partners have signed a prenuptial agreement specifying that their earnings and property will remain separate, the wedding ceremony makes each spouse part owner of what the other earns in income and accumulates in property. If the couple divorce, courts typically award to each spouse half of the assets accumulated during the marriage even

....

Honeymoon: the time following the wedding whereby the couple becomes isolated to recover from the wedding and to solidify their new status change from lovers to spouses.

though one of the partners may have contributed a smaller proportion. A prenuptial agreement could alter this pattern.

Name Change for Female

More than 70% of U.S. adults believe that after marriage, married women should take their husband's last name; half believe it should be legally required (Kitchener, 2018). The traditional practice of married women taking their husband's last name stems from historic notions of women being viewed as their husband's property. The most common reason U.S. adults believe that women should take their husband's last name is the belief that women should put their families and marriages ahead of themselves—a cultural view that persists despite gains made by feminism and the gender equality movement (Shafer, 2017).

Although the tradition of married women taking their husband's name persists, marital name changing is, itself, changing. While 97% of couples over age 55 take the husband's last name, only 72% of young married heterosexual U.S. couples follow this tradition (Khoo, 2017). There are a variety of reasons why women are choosing to keep their given surname. One reason is that doing so avoids the hassle of updating one's driver's license, social security card, passport, credit cards, bank and investment accounts, insurance policies, and other documents. Some married women keep their names as a reflection of their political or feminist values for gender equality or to maintain their professional identity or a combination of these reasons. Some married women choose to take their spouse's name legally but keep their maiden name in their professional lives.

A British study found that one in 10 men ages 18 to 34 are choosing to take their wife's last name (Khoo, 2017). In the United States, only eight states allow men to follow the standard procedure for changing one's marital name. In other states, men must petition the court and run ads in local papers notifying the public of the name change (Rapacon, 2013). In some states, rules about marital name changing are written only to apply to opposite-sex couples, creating obstacles for same-sex couples wanting to legalize a marital name change.

Some women make their surname their middle name and take their spouse's last name, as in "Hillary Rodham Clinton." Some states require going through the process of a legal name change to do this. Another variation of marital name changing is for the couple to create a new last name, such as hyphenating the two spouses' last names or blending them, creating a hybrid name. This option also requires a legal name change.

Is "Partner's Night Out" a Good Idea?

Although spouses enjoy spending time together, they also want to spend time with their friends. Some spouses have a flexible policy based on trust with each other. Other spouses are very suspicious of each other. One husband said, "I didn't want her going out to bars with her girlfriends after we were married. You never know what someone will do when they get three drinks in them." For partner's night out to have a positive impact on the couple's relationship, it is important that the partners maintain emotional and sexual fidelity to each other, that each partner have a night out, and that the partners spend nights alone with each other. Friendships can enhance a marriage relationship. Grief and Deal (2012) reported that the higher the number of couple friends, the happier the marriage. But the respective partners may also have their individual friends and enjoy time with them. Khalil Gabran said, "Let there be spaces in your togetherness." ●

Mental and Physical Health Changes

New spouses experience an array of personal changes in their lives. One consequence of getting married is a new identity. The person is now part of a couple and viewed by some as "half of one" (Soulsby & Bennett, 2017). Another change is an enhanced sense of self-esteem and sense of mastery (Chen et al., 2016). The strong evidence that your spouse approves of you and is willing to spend a lifetime with you also tells you that you are a desirable person.

Spouses also drink less alcohol but consume more food than before marriage. Liew (2016) confirmed that being married is associated with lower alcohol use. Teachman (2016) noted that both women and men put on weight after they are married.

Friendship Changes

Marriage affects relationships with others. Couples in love often spend more time with each other and less time alone with their friends. However, abandoning one's friends after marriage may be problematic because one's spouse cannot be expected to satisfy all of one's social needs. Because almost half of marriages end in divorce, friendships that have been maintained throughout the marriage can become a vital source of support for a person going through divorce. "Don't forget your friends on your way up—you'll need them on your way down" reflects the sentiment of maintaining one's friends after getting married.

Relationship Changes

Once someone else's life depends on you keeping it together, it's easier to keep it together.

Jerry Seinfeld, comedian

A couple happily married for 45 years spoke to the first author's marriage and family class and began their presentation with, "Marriage is one of life's biggest disappointments." They spoke of the difference between all the hype and the cultural ideal of what marriage is supposed to be . . . and the reality. One effect of getting married is **disenchantment,** also known as **disillusionment** —the transition from a state of newness and high expectation to a state of mundaneness tempered by reality. The change over time is for the worse in relationship qualities such as love and affection. It may not happen in the first few weeks or months of marriage, but it is almost inevitable. Whereas courtship is the anticipation of a life together, marriage is the day-to-day reality of that life together—and reality does not always fit the dream. "Moonlight and roses become daylight and dishes" is an adage reflecting the realities of marriage. In a national study of married ($N = 752$) and cohabiting ($N = 323$) couples, Niehuis et al. (2015) confirmed that disillusionment occurred in both sets of couples with the greater the disillusionment, the greater the predicted breakup. Cohabitation relationships were more vulnerable than married relationships due to fewer social and legal constraints from ending the relationship. What is disheartening is that while couples are aware of relationship boredom and what to do about it, they don't follow through with engaging in the new behaviors (Harasymchuk et al., 2017). In learning terminology, this means the partners have satiated on each other and have little motivation for trying new things with a partner they already feel bored with—a death knell for their relationship.

Disenchantment after marriage is also related to the partners shifting their focus away from each other to work or children; each partner usually gives

Disenchantment: the transition from a state of newness and high expectation to a state of mundaneness tempered by reality.

The Downsides of Smart Devices

Smart devices, such as smartphones, tablets and watches, are small portable machines connected to wireless networks. Smart devices provide Internet access and offer constant communication with others via text, voice, and video. Eighty-one percent of American people own smartphones, while an even higher percentage—96%—of young adults, ages 18-29, possess them as well (Pew Research Center, 2019).

The rapid growth of smart devices has come with a price—Americans have a less favorable view of the impacts of the Internet than previously (Jiang, 2018a). Terms such as smartphone addiction, cellphone dependency, and nomophobia—anxiety when away from one's cellphone—are being used to describe problematic behaviors. More than half of teenagers (54%) report concern about their own excessive screen time usage (Jiang, 2018b). Research has revealed that cell phone attachment and use are associated with physical health and psychological well-being (Alhassan et al., 2018; Lissak, 2018; Twenge et al., 2018; Vernon et al., 2018; Yang et al., 2018). Smart phone usage also increases one's exposure to radiation such that guidelines have been issued to keep them away from one's body (Goldsborough, 2018).

Being distracted by the use of smart devices has also been associated with auto accidents (Oviedo-Trespalacios et al., 2018). Text messaging while driving is the culprit (Ortiz et al., 2018). Distracted walking incidents due to cell phone use are also rampant, particularly in large city heavy traffic (Barin et al., 2018). Individuals are encouraged to make deliberate choices regarding the safe use of smart devices.

Smart devices also interfere with personal relationships by competing for one's time and attention (Bugatti, 2018). Ninety-eight percent of Americans report using their mobile phones during social gatherings (Perrin, 2017). A couple can be physically together but "not psychologically together" if both of them focus on their smart devices and pay zero attention to each other. A team of researchers (Misra et al., 2014) studied the "iPhone effect" by observing 100 dyads in a naturalistic face-to-face setting. The researchers concluded that conversational quality in the respective dyads was significantly higher in the absence of mobile devices. The interference of technology, also known as **technoference**—the interference of technology in the interaction between two people resulting in conflicts and negative feelings—has been associated with greater conflicts, depression, and lower relationship satisfaction (McDaniel et al., 2018; McDaniel & Coyne, 2014). Smart devices have been referred to as the electronic rival. Websites depicting "Divorcing your cell" and "Digital Detox" are available online. Of course, individuals can choose to prioritize human face-to-face interaction over focusing on technological devices. ●

and gets less attention in marriage than in courtship. College students are not oblivious to the change after marriage. Twenty-six percent of 2,962 undergraduate males and 20% of 9,794 undergraduate females agreed that "most couples become disenchanted with marriage within five years" (Hall & Knox, 2019).

In addition to disenchantment, a couple will experience numerous changes once they marry:

1. **Loss of freedom.** Single people do as they please. They make up their own rules and answer to no one. Marriage changes that as the expectations of the spouse impact the freedom of the individual.

2. **More responsibility.** Single people are responsible for themselves only. Spouses are responsible for the needs of each other and sometimes resent it.

3. **Less alone time.** Aside from the few spouses who live apart, most live together. They wake up together, eat their evening meals together, and go to bed together. Each may feel too much togetherness. "This altogether, togetherness thing is something I don't like," said one spouse.

4. **Sexual changes.** There is steep drop-off in the frequency of sex beginning with the second year of a relationship with slower declines after that (Schroder & Schmiedeberg, 2015). However, marital sex is still the most satisfying of all sexual contexts. Of married people in a national sample, 85% reported that they experienced extreme physical pleasure and extreme emotional satisfaction with their spouses. In contrast, 54% of individuals who were not married or not living with anyone said that they experienced extreme physical pleasure with their partners, and 30% said that they were extremely emotionally satisfied (Michael et al., 1994).

Technoference: the interference of technology on the interaction of two people.

5. **Power changes.** The power dynamics of the relationship change after marriage with men becoming less patriarchal and collaborating more with their wives while women defer less to their husbands' authority to challenging their authority (Huyck & Gutmann, 1992). In effect, with marriage, men tend to lose power and women gain power. However, such power changes may not always occur. In abusive relationships, the abusive partner continues the power advantage and keeps the partner under control.

6. **Use of technology.** Partners may focus more on their smart phones than each other (see Technology and the Family: The Downsides of "Smart" Devices box).

Most married couples have children who become a major focus of their lives.
Courtesy of Chelsea Curry

Parents and In-Law Changes

Marriage affects relationships with parents but having children affects the relationship even more. Aarskaug et al. (2017) surveyed 4,061 partnered individuals ages 18 to 55, of whom 31% were cohabiting, and found that having a preschool child was associated with more frequent contact with the in-laws regardless of whether the individual was married or cohabiting. Emotional separation from one's parents is an important developmental task in building a successful marriage. When choices must be made between one's parents and one's spouse, more long-term positive consequences for the married couple are associated with choosing the spouse over the parents.

DIVERSITY IN MARRIAGE

Any study of marriage relationships emphasizes the need to understand the diversity of marriage and family life. In this section, we review African American, Latino American, Asian American, Poly, and military families. We also look at other examples of family diversity: interracial and biracial, international, immigrant, college, forced, and age-discrepant marriages.

African American Families

Black families are like families in general; they are diverse. There are African American families, Caribbean families, and African families. In the literature, the terms Black and African American families are used interchangeably. Blacks represent about 43 million individuals in the United States or 13% of the U.S. population (*ProQuest Statistical Abstract*, 2019, Table 7). Black families include husband-wife families, same-sex families, single parent families,

and families headed by grandparents. Black families also are large and extended with generations of close and distant relatives helping each other. Fictive kin "play significant emotional and instrumental roles in contemporary African American family life" (Bryant, 2018).

African American families have been stereotyped as being low income, having high birthrates among unmarried mothers, having marital instability, being one-parent families, and having absentee fathers (Januário et al., 2018). Black men are often seen as frustrated and blocked from success (Abrams et al., 2018). Such a perspective, seen by some as a pathological view, is a result of researchers looking at the African American family as a deviation from the White family norm rather than viewing African American families in terms of their historical and resilient uniqueness and cultural variant, called the cultural retention approach (Dixon, 2017). In addition, Smith and Landor (2018) recommended MEES (Mundane Extreme Environmental Stress) theory be used as a way of looking at the African American experience: Mundane indicates that the stress is common and chronic; extreme shows that it impacts the consciousness of the individuals daily; environmental emphasizes that the environment and society are sources of stress; and stress is the outcome. Johnson and Loscocco (2014) also noted that, often overlooked, is the fact that aspects of the Black family are egalitarian, empowering, and pioneering.

Dixon (2017) reviewed the historical and contemporary aspects of the African American family. African Americans are the only group that came to U.S. society involuntarily and experienced 250 years of slavery, torture, segregation, and institutional racism. The inhumane treatment of Blacks by many slave owners contributed to unique family structures, spiritual expression, and social community. Family structures evolved which emphasized the mother who became and remains the core of the Black family. Related is the fact that the Black woman, independent of being a mother, is known as "strong and empowered" (Williams et al., 2016). The result is that these women want strong men as partners who bring a great deal to the table including economic resources (Debnam et al., 2017). In reference to finding such a man, Porter et al. (2017) surveyed 89 unmarried African-American women who were in the dating market who noted that there was a shortage of eligible African American men. Indeed, these women experienced considerable frustration, hopelessness, and anxiety about this shortage.

Spiritual expression also emerged in Black families to provide hope and as an outlet for the oppressive context of slavery. Social community developed out of survival needs to help each other cope with their unconscionable treatment during slavery (Dixon, 2017).

The majority of African American married couples live in one household. Although higher rates of Black female single parent families compared to White female single parent families exist, this does not reflect a disregard for marriage, but a response to the economic reality of Black men. Also accounting for the high prevalence of African American single households is the fact that half of Black women have a family member or extended family member who is in prison (Wildeman & Wang, 2017). Such incarceration speaks more to the disadvantages in social economic status and prejudice than to Black men, per se.

Unique aspects of African American families identified by Dixon (2017) include:

1. **Cultural collective.** A functional network of individuals based on their shared history, group experiences, and struggles provide a sense of cultural pride and identification. African Americans who do not know each other may greet each other with cultural handshakes—a fist bump and phrases like "Whassup?"

2. **Ethnic socialization.** Blacks emphasize their own self-respect, dignity, and pride, which counters negative stereotypes of Blacks. Parents are focused on building a strong sense of Black pride in their children.

3. **Prominence of motherhood.** Noted earlier, as a key person in Black families, mothers not only look after their own but cooperate with other Black mothers in the rearing of their children. Illustrative of the value of community mothering is the story of

Hannah, an enslaved woman who escaped, leaving her daughter behind. She was criticized as being "inhumane" for leaving an infant daughter, but cultural norms were in place that a network of mothers was always available to take care of children in the Black community. Even today, the mother remains an important parent in the home. One example is of a college football coach who told one of his star Black players that "I am sending airline tickets to your mother to attend the game on Saturday" since the coach knew that the mother's attendance would guarantee a superb performance.

4. **Firm childrearing strategies.** In addition to shared parenting, Black families are known for their firm disciplining. "My mother would smack my lips off if I even thought about sassing her," said a Black undergraduate.

5. **Social justice training of children.** To prepare children for the reality of racism, Black parents socialize their children to be alert to the cultural entrenchment of racism and to look to their own group for understanding and pride. Parents of White children do not experience racism and therefore do not socialize their children to cope with it.

6. **Religion.** In spite of the fact that religion was used to justify slavery, Blacks have embraced religion and socialize their children to do so. The church provided a coping mechanism during slavery and today is a source of hope and a context to be spiritually expressive and to bond with other Blacks and Black families. Chaney et al. (2017) emphasized that Blacks today tend to regard religion as the foundation of marriage, as a context to practice important rituals together, and as a source of strength to turn to in difficult times.

7. **Divorce.** Economic oppression and racism contribute to a higher divorce rate of 67% among Blacks versus 45% among Whites.

8. **Extended family.** Vil et al. (2018) noted four ways in which the extended family impacts on the Black married couple: extended family living, child care, advice and emotional support, and interfamilial conflict.

The above factors do not emphasize the Black father. Research has found that his presence is important to the outcome for children and adolescents. Data by Langley (2016) revealed that African American adolescents reporting a father figure had lower rates of sexual debut than those youth reporting no father figure.

Hispanic and Latinx American Families

The panethnic term *Hispanic*, also referred to as Latino, refers to both immigrants and U.S. natives with an ancestry to one of twenty Spanish-speaking countries in Latin America and the Caribbean. Hispanics represent the fastest growing minority population (Qian et al., 2018).

Hispanics number 58,947 million, about 18% of the U.S. population (*ProQuest Statistical Abstract,* 2019, Table 7). Hispanic families vary not only by where they are from but by whether they were born in the United States. About 40% of U.S. Hispanics are foreign born and immigrated here, 32% have parents who were born in the United States, and 28% were born here of parents who were foreign born.

Great variability exists among Hispanic families. Although 65% of Hispanic and Latinx people have their origin in Mexico, often rural and impoverished, these families may also come from economically developed urbanized areas in Latin America, specifically Argentina, Uruguay, and Chile. Hispanics may also refer to themselves as Mexican, Puerto Rican, and Cuban.

Hispanics tend to have higher rates of marriage, early marriage, higher fertility, nonmarital child rearing, and prevalence of female householder. They also have three micro family factors: Male power, mother centric and strong familistic values.

1. **Male power.** The husband and father are the head of the family in most Hispanic families. The children and wife respect the husband as the source of authority in the family. The wife assumes the complementary role where her focus is taking care of the home and children.

2. **Mother centric.** While the father is often the official head of the family, the mother's involvement with her children is intense. Wheeler et al. (2014) confirmed that the mother's involvement with her adolescent children is a strong influence on her marriage and family interaction (conflict, warmth). Indeed, therapists who work with Latino families might focus on the mother as the agent of family change.

3. **Strong familistic values.** The family, consisting of the parents, children and extended kin, is paramount among Hispanic families and have a moral responsibility to help family members with money, health, or transportation needs. Children are taught to respect their parents as well as the elderly. Indeed, elderly parents may live with the Hispanic family where children may address

This close-knit family enjoys traveling together.

their grandparents in a formal way. Spanish remains the language spoken in the home as a way of preserving family bonds.

Asian American Families

Asian Americans are American with ancestral origins in Asia, which is the largest and most populous continent. Asian American families are very diverse in culture, language, religion, and belief systems. There are over 20 million Asian American families in the United States representing three subgroups: East Asians from China, Japan, Korea, and Taiwan; South Asians from Afghanistan, India, and Nepal; and Southeast Asians from Cambodia, Vietnam, Indonesia, Philippines (Chen & Lewis, 2018).

While norms and family patterns are changing due to Western influences, traditional gender roles in Asian families have been noted for their hierarchal structure whereby males have been viewed for their authority, leadership, and role of provider. Family structure in Asian families may also include not only the family of origin but extended family members and, sometimes, friends. Children typically inhabit an important focus in that the parent-child relationship is often considered more important than the couple relationship. Finally, filial piety, the concept of being respectful to and taking care of elderly parents is a strong value (Chen & Lewis, 2018).

Asian Americans are sometimes burdened by the "model minority" stereotype that they are always academically advanced, economically successful, and spiritually enlightened. Human service providers might be aware that those stereotypes may prohibit seeking mental health or other services and these expectations may be sources of stress.

Immigrant Families

There are 44 million foreign-born members of the U.S. population. While over 80% of these came from Europe and Canada in the 1960s, today about a quarter of new immigrants are from Mexico, Latin America, and South and East Asia respectively (Radford & Budiman, 2018). Today, immigrants make up 13.5% of the U.S. population. While unauthorized immigrants have been the focus of much political attention, 11.3 million comprise this group (Radford & Budiman, 2018). Two million children live with at least one undocumented parent. Vesely et al. (2018) noted that immigrant families in the United States "face pressures to acculturate and become self-sufficient, yet their lives are highly regulated by restrictive and punitive policies and programs that may hinder their ability to cope with exposure to trauma and to build resilience" (p. 93). The stressors these families endure include uncertainty and threatened family separation, ecosystemic trauma and stress, limited navigational capital, and erosion of collectivism and community solidarity. The mental health difficulties, resulting in stress and trauma, and the physical health problems stemming from inadequate nutrition and chronic conditions of these immigrant families necessitate the dismantling of U. S. policies harmful to immigrant families. This would include, for example, eliminating the zero-tolerance policy whereby children can be separated from their parents (Vesely et al., 2019)

What is it like to be a U.S. college student from an immigrant family? Bakhtiari et al. (2018) provided data on 2,210 university students in the United States from immigrant families. The students noted four sources of stress—ethnic discrimination, parent–child cultural conflict, family disengagement, and family financial stress. Family disengagement was the most frequent family stress in that students were trying to navigate their exposure to new values and behavior against the backdrop of their more traditional parents. Students sometimes felt isolated, alone, and misunderstood by their parents.

Polyamorous Families

Interest in polyamory and open relationships continues to increase (Moors, 2017). **Polyamory** refers to multiple intimate sexual or loving relationships or both with the knowledge and consent of all partners involved. The term is different from polygamy which means multiple spouses. Multi-partner relationships that raise children and function as families are known as **poly families.** One study of polyamory included about 500 participants, 131 of whom were interviewed by Elizabeth Sheff (2014). The majority were white, college educated, and had a professional job such as teacher or health care professional.

Benefits of Poly Families

1. **Shared resources.** Sharing resources was the most important advantage of living in a poly family. "From shared income to increased personal time for adults and more attention for children, having numerous adults in the family allows members to distribute tasks so that ideally no one person has to take the brunt of family care" (p. 196).

2. **Honesty and emotional intimacy among family members.** In Sheff's study, "Parents emphasized honesty with their children as a key element of their overall relationship philosophy and parenting strategy" and "characterized honesty as the primary factor that cultivated emotional intimacy..." (p. 191). Sheff interviewed children and teens who valued the open and honest relationships they had with their parents. Speaking of her relationship with her parents, one daughter said,

   We have a good dialog; there is nothing I would keep from them. We are just very open people; there is no need to hide anything... Some of my friends, things are bad for them at home, they can't and don't want to talk to their parents. It is kinda sad; they don't think they can trust their parents (pp. 194-195).

3. **Multiple role models for children.** Children in poly families benefit from the multiple role models available in poly families. "Many parents say that their children's lives, experiences, and self-concepts are richer from the multiple loving adults in their families" (p. 201).

....

Polyamory: a lifestyle in which two lovers embrace the idea of having multiple lovers. By agreement, each partner may have numerous emotional and sexual relationships.

Poly families: parents in multiple families who regard each other as also parents of their own and the other children in an emotional and functional sense.

Difficulties in Poly Families

1. **Social stigma.** Due to the social stigma associated with polyamory, members of poly families may experience rejection from other family members and risk discrimination in the workplace, housing, and child custody matters. Sheff (2014) noted that, "people in poly families were...aware that the stigma of being a sexual minority made them more vulnerable to accusations of poor parenting or questionable family situations from relatives, neighbors, teachers, and Child Protective Services. . ." (p. 225). Although children ages five to eight generally were not aware that their family was different from other families, older children and teens knew that their families were different and were aware of the potential for social stigma. One child reported he did not invite friends to his house because he did not want to explain the multiple adults living in his household. A fifteen- year -old male said, "It's kind of weird to live with a secret, something you can't tell any of your friends cause they wouldn't understand" (p. 144).

2. **Teenagers' leverage against poly parents.** Raising teenagers can be challenging for any parent, but poly parents have the additional possibility that a disgruntled teen can blackmail them, threatening to reveal their unconventional lifestyle to family members, friends, or employers.

Sheff concludes that polyamory is "a legitimate relationship style that can be tremendously rewarding for adults and provide excellent nurturing for children" (p. x). She also notes that "polyamory is not for everyone. Complex, time-consuming, and potentially fraught with emotional booby traps, polyamory is tremendously rewarding for some people and a complete disaster for others" (p. ix). Sheff's investigation of poly families highlights that the nonsexual emotional ties that bind people in poly families together are far more important than the sexual connections between the adults.

Sheff found that the children in the poly families she studied "seemed remarkably articulate, intelligent, self-confident, and well adjusted". . . and "appeared to be thriving with the plentiful resources and adult attention their families provided" (p. 135). The well-being of the children could also be due, in part, to their privileged upper-middle class, predominantly White background. Does being reared in a poly family lead children to reject monogamy in their own lives? Sheff found that some teens were definitely not interested in polyamory in their own relationships, others envisioned trying polyamory in their adult lives, and still others were undecided, but "none of them reported feeling pressured to become polyamorous in the future or feeling like their choices were constrained" (p. 158).

Military Families

Approximately 2.6 million members of the U.S. military were deployed in recent U.S. interventions with 40% being deployed more than once. Over half (52%) of service members are married with most having children (Bushatz, 2018).

There are three main types of military marriages. In one type, an individual falls in love, gets married, and subsequently joins the military. A second type of military marriage is one in which one or both partners are already a member of the military before getting married. The final and least common type is known as a **military contract marriage,** in which a military person will marry a civilian or another military person to get more money and benefits from the government due to the new marital status. Their relationship is a scam and sham for the money. In some cases, the military member will keep the extra money and the civilian will take the benefit of health insurance. Contract military marriages are not common, but they do exist.

Some ways in which military families are unique include:

1. **Traditional sex roles.** Although both men and women are members of the military service, the military has considerably more men than women—85% versus 15%. In the typical military family, the husband is deployed (sent away to serve), and the wife is expected to understand his military obligations and to take care of the family in his absence. In effect, she becomes a single parent with a paycheck from her husband. Her duties include paying the bills, child care, housework, and house maintenance. The wife often must sacrifice her career to follow or stay behind in the case of deployment and support her husband in his fulfillment of military duties. Husbands who complain to the military about the burdens put on their wives when they are deployed are told "If the military had wanted you to have a spouse, they would have issued you

Military contract marriage: a military person will marry a civilian to get more money and benefits from the government.

one." In other words, having a family is your problem.

2. **Loss of control—deployment.** Military families have little control over their lives as the chance of deployment is ever-present. Where one of the spouses will be next week and for how long are beyond the control of the spouses and parents. Some deployed spouses who were exposed to combat have had their brain chemistry permanently altered and are never the same again. "These spouses rarely recover completely—they need to accept that their symptoms—for example, depression and anxiety—can be managed but not cured," noted Theron Covin (2013), who specializes in treating PTSD among the combat deployed. Spouses have a particular challenge of adjusting to their altered spouse—depression, sleep problems, substance abuse and risky behaviors such as unsafe driving, among those who have been deployed. Indeed, the mental health of the returning soldier impacted the mental health of the at-home partner upon return (Gorman et al., 2015) as well as the children (Knobloch et al., 2017). As might be expected, the adjustment of the parents to the reintegration after deployment predicts the adjustment of the children.

Wives of deployed spouses face their own challenges. Easterling and Knox (2010) surveyed 259 military wives whose husbands had been deployed and who reported feelings of loneliness, fear, and sadness. Some women had gone for extended periods of time without communicating with their husbands and in constant worry over their well-being. Talking with other military wives and friends who understood was the primary mechanism for coping with the husband's deployment (Spears et al., 2014). Getting a job, participating in military-sponsored events, and living with a family were also helpful. On the positive side, wives of deployed husbands reported feelings of independence and strength. They were the sole family member available to take care of the house and children, and they rose to the challenge.

3. **Infidelity.** Although most spouses are faithful to each other, deployment increases the vulnerability to infidelity. Balderrama-Durbin et al. (2017) surveyed the extramarital behavior of 164 U.S. Air Force soldiers during the period of one-year deployment and six to nine months after deployment. The researchers found

that 23% reported infidelity during this time compared to 6% of civilians who reported infidelity during a similar length of time. The double standard may also be operative, whereby "men are expected to have other women when they are away" and "women are expected to remain faithful and be understanding." Separated spouses use various strategies to bridge the time they are apart with text messages, e-mails, Skype, and phone calls.

4. **Frequent moves and separation from extended family.** Because military couples are often required to move to a new town, parents no longer have doting grandparents available to help them rear their children. And although other military families become an important community of support for each other, the consistency of such support may be lacking.

5. **Lower marital satisfaction.** Karney and Trail (2017) found lower marital satisfaction among a national sample of Army couples where one partner had been deployed. The first deployment was the most difficult and dissatisfactions were also related to the service member experiencing traumatic events while deployed and returning with PTSD.

Don't confuse your rank with my authority.
Wife of military husband (he had just returned from deployment)

6. **Employment of spouses.** Military spouses, primarily wives, are at a disadvantage when it comes to finding and maintaining careers or even finding a job they can enjoy. Employers in military communities are often hesitant to hire military spouses because they know that the demands that are placed on them in the absence of the deployed military member can be enormous. They are also aware of frequent moves that military families make and may be reluctant to hire employees for what may be a relatively short amount of time. The result is a disadvantaged spouse who has no job and must put his or her career on hold.

7. **Resilient military families.** In spite of these challenges, there are also enormous benefits to being involved in the military, such as having a stable job—one may get

demoted, but it is much less frequent that one is fired—and having one's medical bills paid for. In addition, most military families are amazingly resilient. Not only do they anticipate and expect mobilization and deployment as part of their military obligation, but they have responded with pride. Indeed, some reenlist eagerly and volunteer to return to military life even when retired.

Interracial Marriages

Seventeen percent of all weddings involve spouses of a different race or ethnicity (Livingston & Brown, 2017). By racial or ethnic group, the percent of newlyweds who are married interracially include 29% Asian, 27% Hispanic, 18% Black, and 11% White. Hispanic and White are 42% of the most common pairing of interracial newlyweds; the least common interracial couples are Hispanic and multiracial. Black and Whites represent 11% of all interracial newlyweds (Livingston & Brown, 2017). However interracial, of all marriages in the United States one percent are between a Black person and a White person (*ProQuest Statistical Abstract,* 2019. Table 60). Interracial relationships may not always be what they seem. Petts and Petts (2019) noted that intracial relationships (those in which the partners are the same race) may change. For example, in a sample of 2,845 respondents, 6% in intraracial relationships had inconsistent racial identities. Hence, while they were viewed by others as being the same race, the individuals may have identified themselves as being of a different racial identity.

Religious segregation where the races worship in separate churches, housing divided into White and Black neighborhoods, and separate White and Black colleges in education, not to speak of parental and peer endogamous pressure to marry within one's own race, are all factors that help to explain the low percentage of interracial Black and White marriages.

Regarding interracial pairings in general, the fewer co-racial and co-ethnic partners a person must select from, the greater the chance that the person will pair bond across racial and ethnic lines (Choi & Tienda, 2017). Establishing a friendship across racial lines may also increase the chance of interracial marriage. Such friendships are more likely to develop in contexts where individuals live in the same neighborhood and go to the same church.

Some individuals belong to religions that encourage interracial unions. The Baha'i religion, which has more than six million members worldwide and 140,000 in the United States, teaches that God is particularly pleased with interracial unions. Finally, interracial spouses may tend to seek contexts of diversity. "I have been reared in a military family, been everywhere, and met people of different races and nationalities throughout my life. I seek diversity," noted one student.

About 15% of interracial couples have children. If the mother is White and has a minority child, there is less perceived support from White extended kin (Bratter & Whitehead, 2018). The biracial identity of the offspring of mixed-race parents may also be problematic. Csizmadia and Nazarian (2014) reported a higher frequency of internalizing behavior among children identifying themselves as biracial. Durrant and Gillum (2018) noted that Black-White biracial sons reported challenges in reference to self-identification, force-choice dilemma, and appearance. The popular *This is Us* television series dealt with each of these issues. Although most mixed-race parents identify their child as having minority race status, there is a trend toward identifying their child as multiracial.

Interracial partners are more likely to experience negative reactions to their relationship resulting in depression, anxiety, and stress. Black individuals partnered with White individuals have their Blackness and racial identity challenged by other Black people. Whites partnered with Blacks may lose their White status and have their awareness of Whiteness heightened. Marital quality and stability in Black and White biracial marriages has been the focus of research. Lower quality has sometimes been reported particularly with Black husband and White spouse pairings. The divorce rate of Black and White marriages is also higher than for White and White marriages but lower than Black and Black marriages (Robinson, 2017).

International Marriages

With increased globalization, international match-making Internet opportunities, and study abroad programs, there is greater opportunity to meet and marry someone from another country. The opportunity to meet that someone on campus from another country is also increasing, as upwards of one million foreign students are studying at American colleges and universities. Stoner et al. (2019) found that almost two thirds of a sample of 111 international students in the United States were open to dating an American on campus, over a third had done so, and almost one in five was emotionally involved. Over three fourths of 2,971 undergraduate males (79%) and over two-thirds (70%) of 9,809 undergraduate females reported that they would

This couple met on a train in Paris when the American woman was studying abroad. . . she sat next to a similar aged Frenchman. They talked, began to see each other, married, and now have three children and live in Paris.

be willing to marry someone from another country (Hall & Knox, 2019).

Some people from foreign countries marry an American citizen to gain citizenship in the United States, but immigration laws now require the marriage to last two years before citizenship is granted. If the marriage ends before two years, the foreigner must prove good faith—that the marriage was not just to gain entry into the country—or he or she will be asked to leave the country. **Transnational families** are those in which the migrant parents are separated from their children. Research by Mazzucato et al. (2017) compared migrant parents with parents who live with their children. Results reveal that migrant parents were worse off than their non-transnational counterparts in terms of health, life satisfaction, happiness, and emotional well-being.

Age-Discrepant Relationships and Marriages

Although people in most pairings are of similar age, sometimes the partners are considerably different in age. In marriage, these are referred to as ADMs, or age-dissimilar marriages, and are in contrast to ASMs, or age-similar marriages. ADMs are also known as **May-December marriages.** Typically, the woman is in the spring of her youth in May whereas the man is in the later years of his life in December. Sociobiology suggests that men select younger women since doing so results in healthier offspring. Women benefit from having children with older men who have more resources for their offspring.

There are benefits for the older man but not the younger woman in the age-discrepant relationship.

....

Transnational families: families in which the migrant parents are separated from their children.

May-December marriage: age dissimilar marriage (ADM) in which the woman is typically in the spring of her life (May) and her husband is in the later years (December).

Drefahl (2010) studied the relationship between age gap and longevity and found that having a younger spouse is beneficial for men but detrimental for women. One explanation is health selection—healthier males can attract younger partners. Hence, an older male married to a younger woman may have lower mortality since he is healthier. He may also benefit since the younger woman provides health care and social support.

Women tend not to benefit as much from having younger partners since social norms are less supportive for women marrying younger men and women have more social relationships, contacts, and supports than men. Women in age-discrepant relationships who are older than their spouse tend to retire later to be more in sync with their partner's retirement (Gustafson, 2017). A 2018 study by Lee and McKinnish revealed that both men and women in the age-dissimilar marriages are more satisfied with younger spouses during the initial stage of their marriage. However, the bigger the age gap, the more dissatisfied the couple become after six to 10 years. Although less common, some age-discrepant relationships are those in which the woman is older than her partner.

More common is the older woman out to date younger men for sport. Valerie Gibson (2002), the author of *Cougar: A Guide for Older Women Dating Younger Men*, notes that the current use of the term **cougar** refers to "women, usually in their 30s and 40s, who are financially stable and mentally independent and looking for a younger man to have fun with." Gibson noted that one-third of women between the ages of 40 and 60 are dating younger men. Financially independent women need not select a man in reference to his breadwinning capabilities. Instead, these women are looking for men not to marry but to enjoy. The downside of such relationships comes if the man gets serious and wants to have children, which may spell the end of the relationship.

Alarie (2019) interviewed 55 women aged 30-60 years old who dated younger men and found that "contrary to common cultural representations of 'cougars,' very few women depicted themselves as seductresses who pursued younger men, with younger men passively waiting to be courted." Rather, it was the younger men who pursued them which allowed the women to convey that they were still "attractive/desirable."

College Marriages

Cottle et al. (2013) analyzed data from 429 currently and formerly married college students. The ages

....

Cougar: an older affluent woman who enjoys the company of or relationships with younger men.

This couple began dating in the ninth grade and married at the end of their first year in college.

ranged from 18 to 62. The newlyweds reported significantly greater life satisfaction, marital satisfaction, relationships with in-laws, communication about sex, problem solving, and so forth than the older college-married students. A major finding was that students who quit college were less likely to report satisfaction in these areas. Between 10 and 20% of undergraduates in American universities are married. See "My College Marriage" for an example of one college marriage.

UP CLOSE: MY COLLEGE MARRIAGE

I met my husband in the eighth grade and we starting dating in the ninth grade. We started sex early and have only had sex with each other. We went to the same college our freshmen year and lived in separate dorms. My husband was taking out enormous loans with high interest rates since his parents' income was considered in getting these loans. By getting married, our parents' incomes were no longer considered so we were viewed as ultra-poor and qualified for more loans at lower interest rates. Saving a lot of money was a major advantage of getting married our sophomore year. Other advantages were that we felt more committed, other people took our relationship more seriously, we always had each other to talk to and rely on, and, ultimately, we were able to be together more and have each other's back.

The disadvantages for being married while in college are that other people think we are weird since most college students are NOT married; we are defined by our marital status with people asking "Why didn't you tell me you were married?" is a common statement; people think we are a lot older than we are—we were 20 when we got married; and we have never explored what it is like to be with anyone else.

My husband is in a social fraternity so there are a lot of social events that we go to. We also spend time alone with our own same sex friends. We live

in a studio apartment with our dog. We love being together and traveling together—we have been to over 15 countries together. Life is good!

Used with the permission of Taylor Hilliard

· ·

Forced Marriages

Having little cultural visibility, some marriages are **forced marriages** in that one of the individuals has no choice in the person they marry. These are sometimes also known as child marriages where the individual is under age 18 (see Family Policy section). According to the American Community Survey, approximately 6.2 of every 1,000 children surveyed had ever been married. The incidence was higher among girls than among boys—6.8 vs. 5.7 per 1,000—and was lower among White non-Hispanic children—5.0 per 1,000—than among almost every other racial or ethnic group studied. It was especially high among children of American Indian or Chinese descent who had rates of 10.3 and 14.2, respectively. Only 20% of married children were living with their spouses; the majority of the rest were living with their parents (Koski, 2018).

Alanen (2016) gave an example of a forced marriage: the case of 8-year-old Mannal who was sold by her father for $8,000 to marry a 59-year-old man. Poverty, saving the "honor" of the family, and religious cults are reasons for forced marriages. The outcome is predictable— physical and psychological consequences for the child are disastrous and enduring.

Forced marriage occurs internationally. Frias (2017) analyzed national data on seven communities in Oaxaca and Chiapas, Mexico, and found that 4.1% of the indigenous women were obliged to marry and 4.8% were sold. The researcher pointed out that the practice of forced marriage is an expression of both family and partner abuse violence against women.

Gill and Harvey (2017) examined forced marriage in Britain, noting that young adults with parents from India and Pakistan were most affected. While youth wanted their parents' involvement, they also wanted the option of choice. Although they could prosecute their parents for forcing them into a marriage, this rarely occurred. The result was a dance of influence and pressure from parents and careful acceptance and negotiation by youth so that relationships with their parents were maintained.

· ·

Forced marriage: at least one of the spouses has no choice in the decision to marry.

Ending Child Marriages

Child marriage—marriage before the age of 18—is much more common among girls than boys. In 2018, one in five young women throughout the world reported that they were married before the age of age 18 (UNICEF, 2018a). Sayi and Sibanda (2018) noted that child marriage in Zimbabwe was related to the woman's education, wealth, religion and provincial residence. Child marriage is considered to be a violation of human rights as it compromises a girl's development due to early pregnancy, interruption of one's education, career stagnation, employment limitations, and increased risk of domestic violence (UNICEF, 2018b). In many child marriages, girls are bribed, tricked, threatened, beaten, or forced into marriage (Unchained at Last, 2018).

Although child marriage is most common in least developed countries, it occurs throughout the world, including the United States. In many states, there is no minimum age requirement to marry. In addition, in most states where the minimum legal age to marry is 18, there are exceptions that allow minors to marry if they have parental consent or approval from a judge. Unchained at Last is a national organization focused on ending child marriage in the United States by creating social,

legal, and policy changes (Unchained at Last, 2018). This organization also provides free legal services and support to help women and girls leave forced marriages. Efforts to end child marriage in the United States have had some success: in 2018, Delaware and New Jersey became the first two states to end child marriage.

Other states have passed much needed legislation. Sherry Johnson, a Floridian, was 8 when she was first raped by her church deacon. She was forced to marry him when she was 11 years old and had six children by the time she was 17 (Vasilinda, 2018). Today, Florida allows 17-year-olds to marry if they have parental consent and if the person they marry is not more than two years older than them (Vasilinda, 2018).

Although child marriage has declined globally in recent years, each year there are 12 million girls worldwide who marry before age 18 (Yi, 2018). Some are as young as 8 or 9. One of the United Nations Sustainable Development Goals is to end child marriage by 2030. Instrumental in working toward that goal is *Girls Not Brides*—a global partnership of more than 1,000 organizations that are dedicated to ending child marriage so that girls may fulfill their life potential. ●

MARRIAGE QUALITY

A successful marriage is the goal of most couples. But what is a successful marriage and what are its characteristics?

Definition and Characteristics of Successful Marriages

Marital success refers to the quality of the marriage relationship measured in terms of stability and happiness. Stability refers to how long the spouses have been married and how permanent they view their relationship to be, whereas happiness refers to more subjective and emotional aspects of the relationship. In describing marital success, researchers have used the terms *"satisfaction," "quality," "adjustment," "lack of distress,"* and *"integration."* Marital success is often measured by asking spouses how happy they are, how often they spend their free time together, how often they agree about various issues, how easily

they resolve conflict, how sexually satisfied they are, how equitable they feel their relationship is, and how often they have considered separation or divorce.

Are wives or husbands happier? Chapman and Guven (2016) reported that wives were happier than husbands across their national samples from the United States, United Kingdom, and Germany. How does relationship quality impact life satisfaction? Gustavson et al. (2016) analyzed data from 239 heterosexual couples over a three-year period and found that relationship quality predicted a positive change in life satisfaction. Similarly, DeMaris (2018) analyzed national data on 1,240 respondents over three years and found that spouses were less distressed than the unmarried.

Researchers have also identified characteristics associated with successful relationships and marriages (Sewell et al., 2017; Stafford, 2016; Harris et al., 2016) Their findings and those of other researchers include the following:

1. **Time together and intimate partner attachment.** Spending time together is basic. Flood and Genakek (2016) reviewed data from 46,883 individuals over a seven-year

Marital success: refers to the quality of the marriage relationship measured in terms of marital stability and marital happiness.

This couple has been married for 57 years.

period and confirmed that greater happiness and less stress were associated with spending time with one's spouse rather than spending time apart. Even just watching television with one's partner is associated with relationship satisfaction (Gomillion et al., 2017). In addition, emotionally attached spouses report high levels of marital satisfaction (Alder et al., 2018).

2. **Communication and humor.** Successful spouses feel comfortable telling each other what they want from each other and not being defensive at feedback from the partner. Spouses who stay together are five times more likely to lace their arguments with positives and to consciously choose to say things to each other that nurture the relationship (Gottman & Carrere, 2000). Humor is also associated with relationship satisfaction. Hall (2017) reviewed 39 manuscripts focused on humor and relationship satisfaction and found a positive correlation. Relational humor, when the partners joked and laughed together, was more valuable than when one person was the source of the humor and the other partner the audience.

3. **Common interests, positive self-concepts, and time together.** Spouses who have similar interests, values, and goals, as well as positive self-concepts, report higher marital success (Arnold et al., 2011). Spending time together is also associated with marital satisfaction (Luu, 2014).

4. **Not materialistic.** Although a couple may live in a nice house and have expensive toys, their happiness does not depend on these materialistic possessions. "You can have my things, but don't take away my people," is a phrase from one husband reflecting his feelings about his family. Leavitt et al. (2018) studied the impact of materialism on a couple's emotional and sexual relationship. They implored therapists to inform their clients of the relational and sexual costs of materialism and to encourage them to reduce their materialism.

5. **Positive role models.** Successfully married couples speak of having positive role models in their parents. Good marriages beget good marriages—good marriages run in families (Amato, 2015b). It is said that the best gift you can give your children is a good marriage.

6. **Religious and spiritual.** Strong religious values, religious homogamy and viewing one's self as religious or spiritual are associated with marital satisfaction and a lower divorce rate (McDonald et al., 2018; Stafford, 2016; Okhotnikov et al., 2016; Dilmaghani, 2018). Religion or spirituality provides spouses with a common value. In addition, religion provides social, spiritual, and emotional support from church members and with moral guidance in working out problems.

7. **Trust.** Trust in the partner provides a stable floor of security for the respective partners and their relationship (Harris et al., 2016). Neither partner fears that the other partner would leave or become involved in another relationship. "She can't take him anywhere he doesn't want to go" is a phrase from a country-and-western song that reflects the trust that one's partner will be faithful.

8. **Personal and emotional commitment to stay married.** For committed couples, divorce is never considered an option. The spouses are committed to each other for personal reasons rather than societal pressure.

9. **Sexual satisfaction.** Barzoki et al. (2012) studied wives and found that marital dissatisfaction leads to sexual dissatisfaction but that this connection can become

reciprocal—sexual dissatisfaction can lead to marital dissatisfaction. The result is that sexual satisfaction is associated with a happier, stable relationship.

10. **Equitable relationships.** Partners in equitable and egalitarian relationships report higher relationship quality than those in traditional relationships (Simpson et al., 2015).

11. **Marriage and connection rituals. Marriage rituals** are deliberate repeated social interactions that reflect emotional meaning to the couple. **Connection rituals** are those which occur daily in which the couple share time and attention. Campbell et al. (2011b) studied 129 unmarried individuals who identified 13 different types of rituals with an average of six. The most frequent was enjoyable activities with 23% participating in activities such as having meals together and watching TV together. Nineteen percent enjoyed intimacy expressions, including "taking a shower together every morning and washing each other's hair." About 14% had a communication ritual that involved sending frequent text messages and having pet names for each other. Jewish families recognizing Sabbath, the most salient tradition, report strong family and religious identity (Hatch & Marks, 2014).

12. **Absence of negative statements and attributions and selective attention.** Decreasing the frequency of negative remarks and negative interaction is associated with higher levels of relationship happiness. Sewell et al. (2017) found that fewer negative statements and behaviors increased with age, income, and education. Older couples, those with more stable incomes and those with higher education, were more likely to report more positive statements and interaction. Biological anthropologist Helen Fisher (2015) noted that happily married spouses have mastered the quality of "positive illusion" whereby they consciously choose to focus on the positive aspects of their partner and relationship and overlook the negatives.

13. **Appreciative comments.** Expressing appreciation to one's spouse is related to higher relationship quality. A study of 726

German couples found that "expressed appreciation" was an important factor for being identified as belonging to the "happy class" as opposed to the "fairly happy," "sharp declining," and "improving class." (Durtschi & Kimmes, 2014).

14. **Forgiveness.** At some time in all marriages, each spouse engages in behavior that hurts or disappoints the partner. Forgiveness, rather than harboring and nurturing resentment, allows spouses to move forward. Researchers have found that forgiving and being forgiven are related to higher marital quality (Aalgaard et al., 2016; Prabu & Stafford, 2015). Cortes et al. (2018) also found that relationship satisfaction was related to focusing on current positive behaviors and minimizing past transgressions.

Indeed, spouses who do not "drop the lowest test score" of their partner find that they inadvertently create an unhappy marital context which they also must endure. However, Woldarsky and Greenberg (2014) noted that it is not forgiveness but the perception that the partner experiences shame for the transgression that is restorative to the couple. Perhaps the two work in combination?

15. **Economic security.** Although money does not buy happiness, lower incomes are associated with higher rates of divorce. Even though lower income spouses may report similarly levels of marital satisfaction on average across time, they are subjected to more turbulence in their relationship due to external stresses (Jackson et al., 2017).

16. **Physical and emotional health.** One's physical and emotional health and the control of one's stress positively impact one's marriage (Fisher, 2015). A good marriage also has positive effects on one's health and emotional well-being (Miller et al., 2014).

17. **Flexibility.** Flexible couples accommodate as necessary to each other's schedule, make compromises as necessary, and create a "we will make it work" theme in their relationship. Hence, whatever the issue conflict, their relationship is more important.

18. **Mindset of marriage success.** Marital success may be viewed from a "growth" or a "fixed" mindset. A team of researchers confirmed that the "growth" view was associated with greater romantic love for the partner and greater hope for resolving

....

Marriage rituals: repeated social interactions that reflect emotional meaning to the couple.

Connection rituals: behaviors couples engage in to share their time and attention.

marital conflict than a "fixed" view (Buri et al., 2014).

19. **Exchange minded.** Happily married spouses ensure a high rate of positive behavior exchange with each other. Each partner is eager to do things for each other. Examples include one cooks and the other does the dishes and cleans the kitchen. Or one takes the spouse's car to have it serviced while the other cleans the partner's study. In effect, both are givers, which results in a balance—neither feels exploited.

20. **Empathy.** Being able to empathize with one's partner and what the partner is experiencing is one of the hallmarks of a successful relationship (Ulloa et al., 2017). This quality is particularly important for husbands (McDonald et al., 2018). To feel a partner's empathy is to feel understood. Since intimacy is a primary reason individuals marry, empathy in one's relationship is a factor associated with both quality and longevity.

21. **Realistic expectations**. Spouses who are unrealistic about their expectations report feeling less satisfied (McNulty, 2016). Such expectations include perpetual excitement, comfort, sexual bliss, and intellectual engagement (Perel, 2017).

22. **Managing the emotions of partner and self.** Minnotte (2017) noted the importance of managing the emotions of one's self as well as one's partner. **Integrative emotion work** is the management of one's partner's emotions, such as reacting to a partner's anger so as to diffuse rather than escalate it. Masking emotion work is controlling one's own emotional reactions and moods. Both forms of positive emotion work are related to higher marital quality.

23. **A genetic component?** A genetic variation referred to as OXTR rs5376 is associated with empathy and attachment. Spouses who have this gene report happier, more stable marriages (Monin et al., 2019).

Theoretical Views of Marital Happiness and Success

Interactionists, developmentalists, exchange theorists, and functionalists view marital happiness and success differently. Symbolic interactionists emphasize the subjective nature of marital happiness and point out that the definition of the situation is critical. Indeed, a happy marriage exists only when spouses define the verbal and nonverbal behavior of their partner as positive, and only when they label themselves as being in love and happy. Marital happiness is not defined by the existence of specific criteria like time together but by the subjective definitions of the respective partners. Indeed, spouses who work together may spend all of their time together but define their doing so as a negative. Shakespeare's phrase, "Nothing is either good or bad but thinking makes it so" reflects the importance of perception.

Family developmental theorists emphasize developmental tasks that must be accomplished to enable a couple to have a happy marriage. These tasks include separating emotionally from one's parents, building a sense of "we-ness," creating a pleasurable sex life, managing conflict, and and being faithful to each other. Exchange theorists focus on the exchange of behavior of a kind and at a rate that is mutually satisfactory to both spouses. When spouses exchange positive behaviors at a high rate with no negatives, they are more likely to feel marital happiness than when the exchange is characterized by high-frequency negative behavior and no positives. Structural functionalists regard marital happiness as contributing to marital stability, which is functional for society. When two parents are in love and happy, the likelihood that they will stay together to provide for the physical care and emotional nurturing of their offspring is increased. Furthermore, when spouses take care of their own children, society is not burdened with having to pay for their care through welfare payments, paying foster parents, or paying for institutional management in group homes.

Marital Happiness Across Time

Anderson et al. (2010) analyzed longitudinal data of 706 individuals over a 20-year period. Over 90% were in their first marriage; most had two children and 14 years of education. Reported marital happiness, marriage problems, time spent together, and economic hardship were assessed. Five patterns emerged:

1. High stable 2 (started out happy and remained so across time) = 21.5%

2. High stable 1 (started out slightly less happy and remained so across time) = 46.1%

3. Curvilinear (started out happy, slowly declined, followed by recovery) = 10.6%

4. Low stable (started out not too happy and remained so across time) = 18.3%

5. Low declining (started out not too happy and declined across time) = 3.6%

Integrative emotion work: the management of one's partner's emotions.

FIGURE 6.1

Trajectories of Marital Happiness

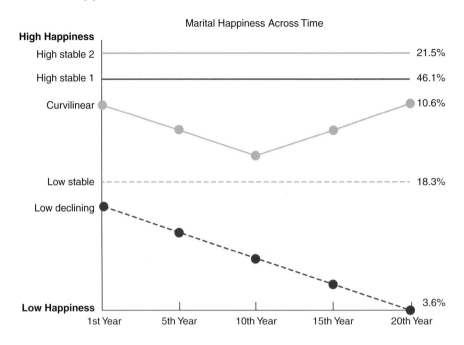

Marital Happiness Across Time

Happiness and Power in Relationships

Relationship power may be defined as the extent to which one partner can influence another and avoid being influenced by that person. This study identified happiness as related to young adult perceptions of having equal, more, or less power in one's current relationship.

Sample

A sample of 1,098 heterosexual undergraduates, who were "emotionally involved with one person" but not married, completed an online survey at both a midwestern and an eastern university and identified having less, equal, or more power in their relationship.

Findings

The undergraduates revealed 70% had "equal power," 19% had "more power," and 11% had "less power." Equal power was more likely among White than non-White respondents and more power was more likely among non-White than White respondents. Gender was not a factor distinguishing different levels of relationship power. Happier relationships were associated with equal power or more power. Individuals might avoid relationships in which they have less power. ●

Source: Hall, S. S., & Knox, D. (2017). Perceived relationship power in emerging adults' romantic relationships. *Journal of Family Studies*. Retrieved from http://dx.doi.org/10.1080/1322 9400.2016.1269660

The researchers found that, for couples who start out with a high level of happiness, they are capable of rebounding if there is a decline. But for those who start out at a low level, the capacity to improve is more limited. Spencer and Amato (2011) emphasized the importance of using a number of variables such as interaction and conflict rather than just marital happiness in the examination of marital relationships over time. Based on data from couples married over 20 years they found that marital happiness shows a U-shape distribution, but interaction declined across time. The researchers hypothesized that couples do not interact less because they are unhappy but because they have other interests. Meier et al. (2018) noted that having adolescents compared to having young children in the home is associated with the lowest levels of personal well-being and happiness, with mothers reporting more difficulty than fathers. Lampis et al. (2018) also noted that while similarity of personalities was associated with high levels of romantic relationship adjustment early in a couple's relationship, 10 to 20 years later these same personality similarities did not have the same impact. Hence, the value of similar personalities can best be evaluated with a life span view.

Other studies on marital happiness over time show, in general, a progressive decline in satisfaction. Based on an analysis of marital data on women across 35 years of marriage, James (2015) found evidence supporting a continuous decline in marital happiness with about 35% of marriages recovering in the later years, but never to the early marriage level. A "flat fishhook" was used to describe the pattern. Finkel (2015) suggested that in order to achieve marital happiness, three conversations must occur. The first is about what each partner expects of marriage in these areas: the level of emotional intimacy, commitment, and fidelity. The second conversation is about one's commitment of personal resources, such as time and money, to achieve the expectations. The third conversation involves recalibration which occurs across time —for example, investing more resources or asking less from the partner.

FUTURE OF MARRIAGE RELATIONSHIPS

Diversity will continue to characterize marriage relationships of the future. The traditional model of the husband provider, stay-at-home mom, and two children will continue to transition to other forms including more women in the work force, single parent families, same sex marriages, and smaller families. What will remain is the intimacy companionship focus that spouses expect from their marriages. Interracial, interreligious, cross-national and age-discrepant relationships will increase. The driving force behind this change will be the American value of individualism which discounts parental disapproval. An increased global awareness, international students, and study abroad programs will facilitate increased opportunities and a mindset of openness to diversity in terms of one's selection of a partner.

SUMMARY

What are the individual motivations for and societal functions of marriage?

Individual motives for marriage include personal fulfillment, companionship, legitimacy of parenthood, and emotional and financial security. Societal functions include continuing to provide society with socialized members, regulating sexual behavior, and stabilizing adult personalities.

What are three levels of commitment in marriage?

Marriage involves a commitment—person-to-person, family-to-family, and couple-to-state.

How are the wedding and honeymoon rites of passage?

While weddings are often a source of stress, they are a rite of passage that is both religious and civil. To the Catholic Church, marriage is a sacrament that implies that the union is both sacred and indissoluble. According to Jewish and most Protestant faiths, marriage is a special bond between the husband and wife sanctified by God, but divorce and remarriage are permitted. Wedding ceremonies still reflect traditional cultural definitions of women as property.

The wedding is a rite of passage signifying the change from the role of fiancé or fiancée to the role of spouse. Women, more than men, are more invested in preparation for the wedding. Most spouses report a positive wedding night experience with exhaustion from the wedding or reception often being a problem. The honeymoon is a time of personal recuperation and making the transition to the new role of spouse.

What changes might a person anticipate after marriage?

Changes after the wedding impact all aspects of a person's life: They are legal— each becomes part owner of all income and property accumulated during the marriage; personal—each has an enhanced self-concept; social—each spends less time with friends; economic— money spent on entertainment in courtship is diverted to living expenses and setting up a household; sexual—sex occurs with less frequency; and parental—each has an improved relationship with parents. The greatest change is disenchantment—moving from a state of exhilaration to a state of mundaneness. New spouses also report experiencing a loss of freedom, increased responsibility, and changes in how money is spent.

What are the downsides of the use of smart phones in marriage/family contexts?

The use of cell phones may interfere with two face-to-face partners talking with each other—the partners may be texting someone else—on feelings of closeness and connection. "Technoference" is also associated with conflicts, depression, and lower relationship satisfaction. Since smart devices can be a source of distraction, miscommunication, and lower relationship satisfaction, some couples agree on "rules" to avoid the downsides.

These rules include TTT ("Time out from Technology at the Table"), no texting about important personal issues, scheduling smart device-free nights, deleting social media apps, turning phones off after a certain time, and adjusting the notification sounds to avoid constant noise.

What are examples of diversity in marriage relationships?

There are many diversities in marriage relationships. Some marriages are forced marriages in that one of the individuals has no choice in the person they marry. About 1,500 marriages annually in United States are forced marriages. An example of a forced marriage is the case of 8-year-old Mannal who was sold by her father for $8,000 to marry a 59-year-old man. Poverty, saving the "honor" of the family, and religious cults are reasons for forced marriages. The outcome is predictable—physical and psychological consequences are disastrous and enduring.

Hispanic and Latino American families tend to marry earlier and have higher rates of marriage and higher fertility. Male power and strong familistic values also characterize Hispanic and Latino American families. Military families cope with deployment and the double standard.

Mixed marriages include interracial, interreligious, and age-discrepant. About 15% of all marriages in the United States are interracial with Hispanic–non-Hispanic the most frequent pairing. Interracial marriages are also more likely to dissolve than same-race marriages. The success of interreligious marriage is related to the degree of devoutness of the partners in the respective religions. If both are very devout, the conflict is more likely to surface. Regarding age-discrepant relationships, men who marry younger women seem to benefit in terms of living longer. Both men and women in age-dissimilar marriages are more satisfied with their younger spouses during the initial stage of their marriage. However, the bigger the age gap, the more dissatisfied the couple become after six to 10 years.

What are the characteristics associated with successful marriages?

Marital success is defined in terms of both quality and durability. Characteristics associated with marital success include intimacy, commitment, common interests, communication, religiosity, trust, forgiveness, an equitable relationship, a marriage ritual, an absence of financial hardship, flexibility, a mindset of marriage success, being exchange minded, empathy, realistic expectations, nonmaterialism, having positive role models, and managing emotions.

Married couples report the most enjoyment with their relationship in the beginning, followed by less enjoyment during the child-bearing stages, and a return to feeling more satisfied after the children leave home.

What is the future of marriage relationships?

Marriages and families will continue to be characterized by diversity. The traditional model of the family will continue to transition to other forms. What will remain is the intimacy and companionship focus that spouses expect from their marriages. Openness to interracial, interreligious, cross-national, and age-discrepant relationships will increase. An increased global awareness, international travel, and international students will facilitate a mindset of openness to diversity.

KEY TERMS

Bride wealth, 118

Connection rituals, 134

Cougar, 130

Disenchantment, 121

Forced marriage, 131

Honeymoon, 120

Integrative emotion work, 135

Marital generosity, 118

Marital success, 132

Marriage rituals, 134

May-December marriage, 130

Military contract marriage, 127

Polyamory, 126

Poly families, 126

Rite of passage, 119

Technoference, 122

Transnational families, 130

WEB LINKS

National Council on Family Relations
https://www.ncfr.org/

Groves Conference on Marriage and the Family
http://www.grovesconference.org/membership.html

Get the tools you need to sharpen your study skills. SAGE edge offers a robust online environment featuring an impressive array of free tools and resources.
Access practice quizzes, eFlashcards, video, and multimedia at **edge.sagepub.com/knox13e**

7

LGBTQIA Relationships

I'm straight, but it may just be a phase.

—Anonymous

Learning Objectives

7.1. Know the meaning of the letters LGBTQIA

7.2. Discuss the problems with identifying and classifying sexual orientation

7.3. Explain the origins of sexual orientation

7.4. Define homonegativity, homophobia, biphobia, binegativity, and transphobia

7.5. Review LGBTQ relationships and mixed-orientation relationships

7.6. Describe the struggles LGBTQ individuals face during the coming out process

7.7. Understand the pros and cons of same-sex marriage

7.8. Know the various LGBTQ parenting issues

7.9. Discuss the future for LGBTQ relationships in the United States

Master the content at
edge.sagepub.com/knox13e

Increasingly, U.S. culture reflects more acceptance of LGBTQ (lesbian, gay, bisexual, transgender, and queer or questioning) individuals and their relationships. The Supreme Court has legalized same-sex marriage, voters have elected openly gay individuals like Colorado's Jared Polis as governor, mainstream television programs have continued to feature openly gay characters (Gonzalez, 2018), and the Boy Scouts of America has lifted its ban on admitting gay people into their ranks.

BASIC TERMS

In this chapter, we discuss concerns experienced by LGBTQIA individuals. **LGBTQIA** is an initialism that has emerged to refer collectively to **l**esbians, **g**ays, **b**isexuals, **t**ransgender individuals, those **q**uestioning their sexual orientation or sexual identity or **q**ueer individuals, **i**ntersex individuals, and **a**sexual people or **a**llies who do not identify as LGBTQIA but support the rights of those who do.

Sexual Orientation

Many of the terms included in the LGBTQIA initialism relate to sexual orientation. **Sexual orientation** is an enduring emotional, cognitive, and sexual attraction or non-attraction, also known as asexuality to other people. It is generally understood to be a classification of individuals as heterosexual, homosexual, bisexual, or queer. The person's self-identity is also important. One's attraction, **sexual identity**, and sexual behavior may be different. Hence, a person may be attracted to those of the same sex, but self-identify as heterosexual and not engage in sexual activity. Sexual orientation can change or be fluid for some people. Galupo et al. (2017) noted that individuals use a diversity of terms to describe their sexual identities including "fluid," "pansexual," and "queer."

Unpacking each of the concepts above, **heterosexuality** refers to the predominance of cognitive, emotional, and sexual attraction to individuals of the other sex. **Homosexuality** refers to the predominance of cognitive, emotional, and sexual attraction to individuals of the same sex. Since the word homosexual has been used in a prejudicial context in recent years, some people may consider the word offensive. The word "homosexual" should be avoided when referring to a person with same sex preferences, as the terms "gay" or "lesbian" are preferred. **Bisexuality** is cognitive, emotional, and sexual attraction to members of both sexes, and **pansexuality** is sexual attraction to other people regardless of their biological

---

LGBTQIA (also LGBTQQIA): general term which refers to lesbian, gay, bisexual, queer, transgender individuals, those who question their sexual identity, those who are intersex, and those who are asexual or support the sexual minority movement.

Sexual orientation: an emotional, cognitive, and sexual attraction or non-attraction (asexuality) to other people.

Sexual identity: Individual's self-identification or label an individual chooses.

Heterosexuality: emotional and sexual attraction to individuals of the other sex.

Homosexuality: older prejudicial term which refers to the predominance of cognitive, emotional, and sexual attraction to individuals of the same sex.

Bisexuality: cognitive, emotional, and sexual attraction to members of both sexes.

Pansexuality: sexual attraction to other people regardless of their biological sex, gender, or gender identity.

This asexual woman enjoys intense love relationships with both men and women but is not sexually attracted to either.

This pansexual woman reports that she is attracted to people regardless of their gender or sexual orientation.

sex, gender, or gender identity. The term **lesbian** refers to women who prefer same-sex partners; **gay** can refer to either women or men who prefer same-sex partners but more often refers to a gay man.

There are about 10 million LGBTQ adults in the United States or about 4% of the 250 million in the U.S adult population with millennials most willing to self-identify (7.3%; Gates, 2017). Here is the percentage breakdown by sexual orientation per category: 1% of females self-identify as lesbian, 2% of males self-identify as gay, and 1.5% of adults self-identify as bisexual (Mock & Eibach, 2012). It's important to give visibility to these groups, as the data on LGBTQ individuals can influence laws and policies that affect LGBTQ people and their families. "The more we are counted, the more we count" is the slogan that points out the value of LGBTQ individuals being visible. However, LGBTQ individuals will no longer be included in the 2020 census, making visibility more important than ever.

Just as important as the major classifications of sexual orientation is that of asexuality. The term **asexual** refers to the absence of sexual attraction to others (ACE is slang for asexual person). However, asexual people may form emotional attachments, masturbate, and experience sexual pleasure and orgasm—what is unique is that they don't want to be sexual with someone.

Mitchell and Hunnicutt (2019) noted that asexuality (absence of sexual attraction) is virtually invisible for two reasons. One, most people are not aware that asexuality exists and two, it is easy to fake interest in sex. The Asexual Visibility and Education Network (AVEN) facilitates awareness of asexuality as an explicit identify category.

Gupta (2017) interviewed 30 asexual individuals and identified five ways they saw themselves as affected by compulsory sexuality or the idea that individuals in a relationship are usually expected to have sex with their partners. They experienced

(1) pathologization, or being treated like something was "wrong" with them; (2) isolation and being treated like they weren't wanted; (3) unwanted sex; (4) relationship conflict, which often stemmed from being pressured to have sex; (5) and the denial of epistemic authority, such as being told that they would get over being asexual and were just a late bloomer.

Gender Identity

The other terms that comprise the LGBTQIA initialism relate to gender identity. Gender identity is distinct from sexual orientation, and is one's concept of self as male, female, a blend of both, or neither. Simply put, sexual orientation is whom you go to bed *with*, and gender identity is whom you go to bed *as*. Many people identify as a different gender than what they were assigned at birth. **Genderqueer** refers to people who do not want to be defined by the gender binary term, such as female or male, and embrace fluid ideas of gender. As defined in Chapter 3, **transgender** is a term for a person whose gender identity does not match the biological sex they were assigned at birth.

Lesbian: a woman who prefers same-sex partners.

Gay: term which refers to women or men who prefer same-sex individuals as emotional and sexual partners.

Genderqueer: individuals can consider themselves as non-binary—not feminine or masculine—but a blend of both.

Transgender: abbreviated as "trans" describes a person whose gender identity does not match the biological sex they were assigned at birth.

This male to female individual says that being a woman is more "crushing" than being a transgender person.

Less than 0.6% of adults or about 1.4 million individuals in the United States self-identify as transgender (Flores et al., 2016). Under the Trump administration consideration was given to defining gender as a biological, immutable condition determined by genitalia at birth (Green et al., 2018). Kuper et al. (2012) found that 292 transgender individuals self-identified as genderqueer—their gender identity was neither male nor female—and pansexual or queer—they were attracted to men, women, or bisexuals—as their sexual orientation. Some individuals who identify as transgender undergo gender reaffirming surgery, which is discussed in "Technology and the Family."

Transsexual is an older term for transgender people. "Transsexual" differs from "transgender" in that it is not an umbrella term; many transgender people do not identify as transsexual. Some who have changed, or seek to change, their bodies through medical interventions prefer "transsexual." In the Kuper et al. (2012) sample of 292 transgender individuals, most did not desire to or were unsure of their desire to take hormones or undergo sexual reassignment surgery. Individuals need not take hormones or have surgery to be regarded as transsexuals. The distinguishing variable of a transsexual is living full time in the role of the other biological sex. A man or woman who presents full time as the other gender is a transsexual by definition.

Intersex, also known as innersex, individuals are those who are born with a variety of chromosomes, gonads, sex hormones, or genitals. Some individuals who are born intersex do identify as intersex in terms of their gender identity, but otherwise may identify as male, female, or gender non-conforming, just as non-intersex people do. They often have ambiguous

genitals at birth so that assigning them as a female or male is problematic. Hence, our society provides limited variation from the binary female or male.

Johnson et al. (2014) noted the complexity of gender, sexuality, and sexual orientation issues as experienced by transgender, queer, and questioning individuals. One of the participants in their study who identified themselves as TQQ, explained:

> *I would consider myself to be bi-gendered or gender fluid. Which is probably like the most complicated thing or decision that I have ever made . . . because there aren't very many people that understand it. Being bi-gendered makes a lot more sense for me just because like my sexuality in general is just really fluid and it's really hard to identify myself in one particular box for very long at all 'cause it's always changing.*

This participant's experiences are similar to those who identify as queer. The term **queer** is an umbrella term, which refers to people who reject binary categories of gender and sexual orientation. Traditionally, the term *queer* was used to denote a gay person, and the connotation was negative. More recently, individuals have begun using the term queer with pride, much the same way African Americans called themselves Black during the 1960s Civil Rights era as part of building ethnic pride and identity. Hence, LGBTQ people took the term queer, which was used to demean them, and started to use it with pride.

Choices in Language

Because gender identity and sexual orientation are a sensitive, complex topic, it is important to be aware of language. In recent years, there has been a push toward using gender inclusive pronouns, such as the singular "they." By not paying attention to language, you may misgender someone, by using a pronoun that does not reflect the gender identity with which that person identifies. If you are unsure what gender pronouns you should use for your friends, just ask politely. For example, ask "How would you like to be addressed?" or "Please remind me what pronouns you prefer again?" Some people include gender pronoun preferences in their e-mail signatures. For example, below your e-mail signature line, add your preferred pronouns such as "pronouns: she/her/hers." You can also include your gender pronouns when introducing yourself. For example, "Hi, my name is Terry and I am from Springfield. My pronouns are they/them/theirs." Similarly, you may also ask what terminology people

Transsexual: older term for the person who has had had hormonal or surgical intervention to change his or her body to align with his or her gender identity.

Intersex: having many of the characteristics (hormonal, physical) of both sexes.

Queer: inclusive term used by individuals desiring to avoid labels. People who labels themselves as "queer" could be gay, lesbian, bisexual, pansexual, trans, intersex, non-conforming heterosexual.

Gender Affirming Surgery

Gender affirming surgery (GAS), formerly known as gender reassignment surgery or sex reassignment surgery, is a procedure used to alter one's biological sex characteristics. The goal of GAS is to change one's sex-specific physical characteristics such as genitals, chest, face and voice (Van de Grift et al., 2018). GAS is one of the treatment choices for individuals who suffer from gender identity disorder or gender dysphoria. Gender dysphoria is "a conflict between a person's physical or assigned gender and the gender with which he, she, or they identify" (American Psychiatric Association, 2018). By transforming one's appearance and body, GAS provides people who experience the incongruence between their biological sex and preferred gender.

GAS is a complicated and prolonged process and usually includes three types of surgeries: breast surgery—for example, augmentation, implants, or mastectomy, and reduction; genital surgery, such as alternating, removing, or creating genitalia; and other aesthetic surgical interventions like shaving of the Adam's apple. In male to female (MtF) GAS, a neovagina is usually created from the individual's own genitalia or other parts of the body and additional surgery is frequently required to improve its function and appearance. Nearly 60% of total GAS surgeries are male to female transition (Global Market Insight, 2018). Compared to the MtF process, the FtM procedure is more complex. A neophallus is usually fashioned from one's own skin grafts, either from the forearm or other parts of the body. The lengthening of the female urethra to male dimensions in FtM surgery allows for FtMs to urinate standing.

Gender affirming surgery has a profound impact on the individual person and its impacts are irreversible. In making their choice, individuals considering GAS need to be aware of the physical, psychological, and social implications. According to the Standards of Care (SOC) which were outlined by the World Professional Association for Transgender Health (WPATH), the process begins with the person seeking to transition to be interviewed by mental health professionals with expertise in gender related issues to obtain a diagnosis of gender identify disorder or gender dysphoria. Next, hormonal therapy is required to stimulate the desired body growth such as breasts in a female for an MtF. Some also opt to have hormone therapy prior to puberty to stop the secondary sex growth—for example, a deep voice. In addition, a period of living in the social role of the desired gender for 12 continuous months is required. Finally, various surgeries to remove organs, alter genitalia, and construct body parts are performed. Post-GAS care and support are also important. Although the Standards of Care document has been used to review eligibility and assess readiness, it was critiqued as lacking rigorous and empirical evidence. In addition, the SOC can also be a barrier for GAS (Worth, 2018).

Post-GAS evaluation is mostly satisfactory. The advancement of medical technologies has made GAS safer (Canner et al., 2018). One study reported a 94-100% satisfaction rate during a four-to-six-year period post GAS (Van de Grift et al., 2018). GAS regret rate has been stable at about 2.3% across recent studies (Worth, 2018). Although the cost of gender affirming surgery was high and the medical interventions were complex and long, the surgery reduces one's constant struggle and improves one's quality of life (Özata Yildizhan et al., 2018).

The international prevalence and legalization of GAS reflects the growing acceptance of sexual diversity. Sweden, which legalized GAS in 1972, is known for its progressive views on gender issues. With the increasing acceptance of transgender issues and expanding insurance coverage, GAS has grown during the last decade and is forecasted to continue to rise. ●

prefer when referring to their sexual orientation. For example, do they identify as queer, gay, or bisexual? It can be a delicate topic to address, but one can be a better ally by trying to use proper language.

PROBLEMS WITH IDENTIFYING AND CLASSIFYING SEXUAL ORIENTATION

The classification of individuals into sexual orientation categories—for example, heterosexual, gay, or bisexual—is problematic for several reasons. First, many individuals conceal or falsely portray their sexual orientation to avoid prejudice and discrimination. Heterosexuality is often perceived as the "norm" and there is social stigma associated with nonheterosexual identities.

Second, not all people who are sexually attracted to or have had sexual relations with individuals of the same-sex view themselves as gay or bisexual. For example, 11%, about 26 million, of U.S. adults report experiencing same-sex attraction, a percent five times greater than the number of self-identified gay or lesbian individuals (Gates, 2011). For example, Kyper and Box (2016) proposed a new category of "mostly heterosexuals" who are also attracted to same-sex partners. This category consists of mostly

FIGURE 7.1

The Heterosexual-Homosexual Rating Scale

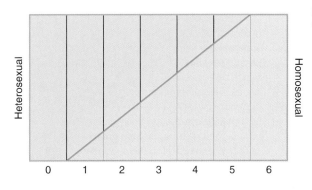

Based on both psychologic reactions and overt experience, individuals rate as follows:

0. Exclusively heterosexual with no homosexual
1. Predominantly heterosexual, only incidentally homosexual
2. Predominantly heterosexual, but more than incidentally homosexual
3. Equally heterosexual and homosexual
4. Predominantly homosexual, but more than incidentally heterosexual
5. Predominantly homosexual, but incidentally heterosexual
6. Exclusively homosexual

heterosexual women who fall between heterosexual and bisexual women in terms of sexual attraction, fantasies, and sexual behaviors. About 10% of women represent this category.

A third difficulty in labeling a person's sexual orientation is that an individual's sexual attractions, behavior, and identity may change across time. One's sexual orientation is, indeed, fluid. For example, in a longitudinal study of 156 lesbian, gay, and bisexual youth, 57% consistently identified as gay or lesbian and 15% consistently identified as bisexual over a one-year period, but 18% transitioned from bisexual to lesbian or gay (Rosario et al., 2006).

Ross et al. (2013) studied a sample of 652 men and 1,250 women and suggested that sexual orientation be conceptualized as heterosexual, gay, bisexual, and fluid. Six percent of men in the Ross et al. sample reported fluidity in terms of having sex with both women and men; 15% of the women reported having sex with both women and men. In regard to sexual fantasies, the fluidity percentages were much higher—15% of the men and 49% of the women.

The Heterosexual-Homosexual Rating Scale that Kinsey et al. (1953) developed allows individuals to identify their sexual orientation on a continuum. Individuals with ratings of 0 or 1 are entirely or largely heterosexual; 2, 3, or 4 are more bisexual; and 5 or 6 are largely or entirely homosexual (see Figure 7.1). Very few individuals are exclusively a 0 or a 6, prompting Kinsey to believe that most individuals are bisexual. It is also important to note that the Kinsey data were collected at a time when being gay was not accepted, prompting some individuals to avoid identifying themselves as a 0 or 1.

Finally, sexual-orientation classification is also complicated by the fact that sexual behavior, attraction, love, desire, and sexual-orientation identity do not always match. For example, "research conducted across different cultures and historical periods, including present-day Western culture, has found that many individuals develop passionate infatuations with same-gender partners in the absence of same-gender sexual desires . . . whereas others experience same-gender sexual desires that never manifest themselves in romantic passion or attachment" (Diamond, 2003, p.173).

ORIGINS OF SEXUAL-ORIENTATION DIVERSITY

Same-sex behavior has existed throughout human history. Much of the biomedical and psychological research on sexual orientation attempts to identify one or more "causes" of sexual-orientation diversity. The driving question behind this research is this: "Is sexual orientation inborn or is it learned or acquired from environmental influences?" Although a number of factors have been correlated with sexual orientation, including genetics (Ganna et al., 2019), prenatal hormones, gender role behavior in childhood, fraternal birth order, and child sex abuse, no single theory can explain diversity in sexual orientation.

Prior to 1973, the American Psychiatric Association listed homosexuality as a mental disorder with treatments including chemical castration, electric shock therapy, mental institutionalization, and lobotomies. The catalyst for the change was a presentation in 1972 by psychiatrist and member of the APA organization, John E. Fryer. He appeared as Dr. H. Anonymous at the annual convention in Dallas in 1972 wearing a mask, a big curly wig, and used a voice-altering microphone.

"I am a homosexual. I am a psychiatrist," he said and noted that he had to remain anonymous for fear of losing his job as an untenured professor at a major university. Earlier he had been terminated from his psychiatry residency program at the University of

Pennsylvania's School of Medicine when it was discovered he was gay.

A year after Dr. Fryer's presentation, the American Psychiatric Association removed homosexuality from the *Diagnostic and Statistical Manual of Mental Disorders* as a mental disorder.

> *Is it biology or nurture? I don't know why we can't let that debate go. We are always, at every point in time, the product of both.*
> Stephanie Sanders, senior scientist at Indiana University's Kinsey Institute.

Beliefs About What "Causes" Sexual Orientation

Aside from what "causes" same sex sexual attraction, social scientists are interested in what people *believe* about the "causes" of same sex attraction. For example, are gay individuals "biologically wired" to be attracted to each other or can they "choose" their sexual orientation? Overby (2014) analyzed Internet data of over 20,000 respondents, primarily heterosexual, and found that roughly half, about 52%, believed same sex attraction was based primarily on "biological make-up" compared to 32% who believed sexual orientation as more of a lifestyle choice. Of course, regarding whether sexual orientation is a biological imperative or a choice, one may ask of heterosexuals if they are "wired that way" or choose partners of the other sex.

Although the terms *sexual preference* and *sexual orientation* are often used interchangeably, those who believe that sexual orientation is inborn more often use the term *sexual orientation*, and those who think that individuals choose their sexual orientation use *sexual preference* more often. The term *sexual preference* can be seen as offensive to the gay community.

Can One's Sexual Orientation Change?

Individuals who believe that gay or queer people choose their sexual orientation tend to think that people can change their sexual orientation and may be proponents of conversion therapy. Various forms of **conversion therapy**, also called **reparative therapy,** are focused on changing one's sexual orientation. Some religious organizations sponsor "ex-gay ministries," which claim to "cure" and transform them into heterosexuals by encouraging them to

ask for "forgiveness for their sinful lifestyle" through prayer and other forms of "therapy."

Data confirm that conversion therapy is ineffective and misguided. Gay people are not the problem; social disapproval is the problem. In fact, these treatments may cause psychological, physical, and emotional harm. The National Association for the Research and Therapy of Homosexuality (NARTH) has been influential in moving public opinion from "gays are sick" to "society is judgmental." The American Psychiatric Association, the American Psychological Association, the American Academy of Pediatrics, the American Counseling Association, the National Association of School Psychologists, the National Association of Social Workers, and the American Medical Association agree that homosexuality is not a mental disorder and needs no cure.

The American Psychological Association (APA), American Academy of Pediatrics, and The American Counseling Association have recommended legislation to ban conversion therapy. Eleven states have such a ban and 24 other states have similar legislation in progress (Miller, 2018). In July 2017, the Church of England called on the government to ban conversion therapy and has condemned the practice as unethical and potentially harmful.

HETEROSEXISM, HOMONEGATIVITY, HOMOPHOBIA, BIPHOBIA, BINEGATIVITY, AND TRANSPHOBIA

The United States, along with many other countries throughout the world, is predominantly heterosexist. **Heterosexism** refers to "the institutional and societal reinforcement of heterosexuality as the privileged and powerful norm." Heterosexism is based on the belief that heterosexuality is superior to homosexuality. Of 12,788 undergraduates, 25% agreed, with more men concurring than women, with the statement "It is better to be heterosexual than gay" (Hall & Knox, 2019). Heterosexism results in prejudice and discrimination against gay and bisexual people. The word *prejudice* refers to negative attitudes. Prejudice begins early and judgment is given by one's peers. Farr et al. (2019) reported on 131 elementary school students (M_{age} = 7.79 years; 61 girls) who viewed images of same-sex—female and male— and

Conversion therapy: also called reparative therapy, designed on using techniques to change one's sexual orientation. Recognized as ineffective and harmful.

Heterosexism: the institutional and societal reinforcement of heterosexuality as the privileged and powerful norm. Assumes that homosexuality is "bad."

Memorial signs and flowers outside the Stonewall Inn, a gay bar in New York City's Greenwich Village, the day after the June 12, 2016 shooting at an LGBTQ nightclub in Orlando, Florida, the greatest mass shooting in U.S. history.
Dennis K. Johnson/Lonely Planet Images/Getty Images Plus

other-sex couples with a child and then were asked about their perceptions of these families, particularly the children. Results indicated participants' preferences toward children with other-sex versus same-sex parents.

Discrimination refers to behavior that denies equality of treatment for individuals or groups. Woodford et al. (2015) used the term *microaggression* to refer to subtle and covert discrimination against sexual minorities. Examples of microaggressions include hearing someone say "That's so gay" to describe something negative about a member of the LGBTQ community. Other examples of microaggressive statements include "you're not really gay," "being gay is just a phase," and "you know how gay people are" (Swann et al., 2016).

Even though the Supreme Court has legalized same sex marriage in June 2015 (Obergefell v. Hodges, 576 U.S. ___ 2015), 28 states have no laws prohibiting discrimination against same-sex individuals. Indeed, prejudice and discrimination against sexual minorities continues (Hoyt et al., 2019). In 2018, Kansas and Oklahoma passed legislation to allow state licensed child welfare agencies to cite religious beliefs for not placing children in LGBTQ homes. Twenty-one states have religious exemption laws. Previously, in the *Masterpiece Cakeshop v. Colorado Civil Rights Commission*—the "gay wedding cake" case—the Supreme Court ruled that the cake makers could refuse certain services based on the free exercise of religion, and thus, were not required to bake a wedding cake for a gay couple.

The consequences of being a victim of prejudice for being a sexual minority adult in the United States involves, relative to heterosexuals, lower social health which includes loneliness, friendship strain, familial strain, and social capital (Doyle & Molix, 2016). This finding is based on a comparison of

365 self-identified heterosexuals of which 105 were women and 214 sexual minorities of which 103 were women. In addition, since social health is related to psychological and physical health, the implications for prejudice and discrimination are devastating. From bullying, hate crime, inadequate work assignments, and prohibiting usage of bathroom to sexist jokes, discrimination can manifest itself in overt or subtle forms (Nadal, 2018). Such discrimination can lead to a hostile working environment for sexual minorities and negatively affect their employment and economic well-being.

Before reading further, you may wish to complete the Self-Assessment on page 382, which assesses the degree to which you are prejudiced toward gay men and lesbians.

Attitudes Toward Being Gay, Homonegative, and Homophobic

We got White girls and Black girls and everything in between. Straight girls and gay girls. ... It's my absolute honor to lead this team out on the field. There's no other place that I would rather be...
Megan Rapinoe, American professional soccer player and top scorer of the 2019 Women's World Cup

The term **homophobia** is commonly used to refer to negative attitudes and emotions toward people who are gay or lesbian. Homophobia is not necessarily a clinical phobia—that is, one involving a compelling desire to avoid the feared object despite recognizing that the fear is unreasonable. Other terms that refer to negative attitudes and emotions toward members of the LGBTQ community include **homonegativity**—attaching negative connotations to being LGBTQ— and **antigay bias**. The result of homonegativity is predictable: depression and anxiety in gay individuals (Puckett et al., 2017) as well as conflict and lower relationship quality in same-sex couples (Totenhagen et al., 2018). Discrimination also continues into elder and nursing home care such that some workers are not comfortable around "gays" (Leyerzapf et al., 2018). Negative social meanings associated with being gay can affect the self-concepts of LGBTQ individuals. **Internalized homophobia** is a sense of personal failure and self-hatred among

Homophobia: negative attitudes and emotions toward people who are gay or lesbian.

Homonegativity: attaching negative connotations to homosexuality.

Antigay bias: being biased against lesbians, gays, and bisexuals.

Internalized homophobia: a sense of personal failure and self-hatred among lesbians and gay men resulting from social rejection and stigmatization of being gay.

queer individuals resulting from social rejection, and the stigmatization of being gay has been linked to increased risk for depression, substance abuse and addiction, anxiety, and suicidal thoughts (McLaren, 2016). Newcomb et al. (2014) compared national samples of gay and straight youth and found higher drug use among sexual minorities. Van Bergen et al. 2013 also found higher suicide rates. Platt et al. (2018) also found that sexual minority individuals utilize mental health care professionals at higher rates than heterosexual individuals. Hu et al. (2016) compared lesbian, gay, and bi adults with heterosexual adults and found lower self-esteem and higher loneliness in the former groups. Cao et al. (2017) reviewed 32 research reports and confirmed that same sex relationships are burdened by sexual minority stress in the form of internalized homophobia—negative feelings about being gay, lesbian, bisexual or trans. Having these feelings may result in depression, anxiety, and irritability. In addition, Pepping et al. (2019) noted that minority stressors, such as internalized homophobia and difficulties accepting one's sexuality, are associated with lower relationship satisfaction via concealment motivation.

Being gay and growing up in a religious context that is antigay may be particularly difficult. Todd et al. (2013) conducted focus groups of LGBTQ individuals who confirmed that religion had a negative impact on them. One group member said, "Religion made me feel that something was wrong with me. . . it made me feel worse about myself and become depressed." Given that religion has traditionally been antigay, it is no wonder that LGBTQ college students view campus religious and spiritual spaces as less diverse, supportive, and tolerant. This finding is based on a national study of 13,776 students at 52 institutions that took part in the Campus Religious and Spiritual Climate Survey (Rockenbach et al., 2017). Finally, Rodriguez et al. (2019) also found an association with one's gay identity struggle and negative mental health. And, when religion and spirituality influences, which were typically negative, were considered, the identity struggle was ongoing and active rather than a passive cognitive conflict.

Homophobia also results in gay individuals hiding their sexual orientation for fear of negative reactions or consequences. Such hiding may also have implications for gay interpersonal relationships. Easterling et al. (2012) found that gay individuals were significantly more likely to keep a secret from their romantic partner than straight individuals. The researchers hypothesized that gay people learn early to keep secrets and that this skill slides over into their romantic relationships.

In particular, the African American community faces enormous pressure to hide homosexual behavior, resulting in some African American males being on the "down low." Black men on the **down low** are non-gay-identifying men—for example, they do not view themselves as gay—who have sex with men and women. They meet their gay partners out of town, not in a predictable context or on the Internet.

With Black men, you have to almost hide it. I think that's why the DL [down low] community was such a big deal or became so large because it's a. . . . there are certain codes or things that you have to do in order to be perceived as straight. If you don't do those things, then you're considered gay. As a Black man, you can't express . . . you can't cry, you can't be the emotional. I feel that this is the reason for the growth of the DL community. . . there are certain expectations that Black men have to do in order not to be stigmatized in society (Trahan & Goodrich 2015, p. 152).

However, in spite of the double stigma of race and sexual identity, Edwards (2016) identified 42 Black gay males, 79% of whom reported that they had been in their present relationship at least four years or longer.

Does race impact persons who identify as LGBTQ? According to the Williams Institute (2019), statistics show that 58%, more than half of the LGBT population, is White, and that figure is followed by Latino with 21%, Black with 12%, more than one race with 5%, Asians with 2%, American Indians and Alaska Natives with 1%, and Native Hawaiian and other Pacific islanders with 1%. In general, being a racial and sexual minority individual is associated with minority stress, such as discrimination and microaggression. A study of 396 self-identified gay, lesbian, and bisexual participants in New York City revealed that Black and Latino sexual minorities reported experiencing greater stigma than their Caucasian counterparts (Shangani et. al., 2019). To counter the report of negative experiences of LGBTQ individuals, Flanders et al. (2017) revealed 278 positive experiences of 91 individuals about their sexual identity via daily diaries. An example recorded by one respondent follows:

I talked more with my coworker who came out to me and he ended up saying he was poly[amorous] and pan[sexual], and I admitted I was bi rather than totally gay and he was like "rock on man, I hear you." We talked a bit about the semantics of bi vs pansexual because he's dating a transman, but all together it was a great and affirming experience. I did not expect to make a friend at work who got this stuff.

Down low: non-gay-identifying men who have sex with men and women.

Biphobia and Binegativity

Biphobia, also referred to as **binegativity**, refers to a parallel set of negative attitudes toward bisexuality and those identified as bisexual. Just as bisexuals are often rejected by heterosexuals—though men are more rejecting than women—they are also rejected by many gay and lesbian individuals. There are harmful stereotypes that bisexual people are confused about their sexual orientation or are immoral or hypersexual. Thus, bisexuals experience "double discrimination" and reveal worse mental health than their heterosexual and gay or lesbian counterparts. Minority stress and lifetime adversity contribute to this outcome (Persson & Pfaus, 2015). A related finding is by Gorman and Oyarvide (2018) who compared bisexual elders with heterosexual, gay, and lesbian elders. Bisexual elders had the lowest rates of completed schooling, lived in lower-income households, and had poorer health predictive.

Transphobia

Transgender people are targets of **transphobia,** a set of negative attitudes toward transgenderism or those who self-identify as transgender. Blosnich et al. (2016) found that transgender individuals who lived in states with employment nondiscrimination protection—about half—had a 26% lower incidence of mood disorders like depression. In regard to the school experience of transgender youth, Day et al. (2018) surveyed 31,896 youth representatives of the middle and high school population in California, one percent of which identified as transgender. Compared to cisgender youth, transgender youth were more likely to be truant from school, to experience victimization, and bias-based bullying, which did not translate into lower grades.

Effects of Homophobia, Trans Bias, and Discrimination on Heterosexuals

The antigay and heterosexist social climate of our society is often viewed in terms of how it victimizes the gay population. Moran et al. (2018) surveyed 347 LGBTQ students and found that depressive symptomology was associated with victimization of bullying such as verbal, relational, cyber, and physical abuse. Support from peers provided a buffer to lower levels of depression.

Heterosexuals are also victimized by heterosexism and antigay prejudice and discrimination. Some of these effects follow:

1. **Casualties of hate crimes.** Extreme homophobia and transphobia contributes to instances of violence against LGBTQ individuals, known as **hate crimes**. In June of 2016, the "Orlando Shooting" was a hate crime directed toward the LGBTQ community leaving 49 dead and 53 wounded. Some of these victims identified as straight. Thus, even though LGBTQ individuals may be the primary target of a hate crime, heterosexual individuals may still be affected.

2. **Concern, fear, and grief over well-being of LGBTQ family members and friends.** Many family members and friends experience concern, fear, and grief over the mistreatment of their gay or lesbian friends or family members or all of them. Heterosexual parents who have a gay or lesbian teenager often worry about how the harassment, ridicule, rejection, and violence experienced at school might affect their gay or lesbian child. Will their child be traumatized or drop out of school to escape the harassment, violence, and alienation they endure there? Will the gay or lesbian child respond to the antigay victimization by turning to drugs or alcohol?

3. **Restriction of intimacy and self-expression.** Because of the antigay social climate, heterosexual individuals, especially males, are hindered in their own self-expression and intimacy in same-sex relationships. Many men feel that they must be careful in how they interact platonically with other men, for fear that they may be perceived as gay. Homophobic scripts also frighten youth who do not conform to gender role expectations, leading some youth to avoid activities—such as arts for boys, athletics for girls—and professions such as elementary education for males.

4. **Stigmatizing one's sexual behavior.** Heterosexism may prevent individuals from fully exploring their sexual identity. Adolescents, in particular, may be affected. They may resist their own sexual desires because they've been taught that heterosexuality is the norm. Adolescent male virgins are often teased by their male

---

Biphobia: parallel set of negative attitudes toward bisexuality and those identified as bisexual.

Transphobia: a set of negative attitudes toward transgenderism or those who self identify as transgender.

Hate crime: violence motivated by prejudice including verbal harassment, vandalism, sexual assault/rape, physical assault, and murder.

peers, who say things like "You mean you don't do it with girls yet? What are you, a fag or something?" Such language can further stigmatize adolescents who do not identify as heterosexual.

5. **School shootings.** Antigay harassment has also been a factor in many of the school shootings in recent years. For example, 15-year-old Charles Andrew Williams fired more than 30 rounds in a San Diego, California, suburban high school, killing two and injuring 13 others. A woman who knew Williams reported that the students had teased him and called him gay.

Recent research has focused on how to promote more inclusive attitudes among heterosexist individuals. An **ally development model** has been suggested as a means of providing a new learning context for homophobic heterosexist students (Zammitt et al., 2015). Such a model is multilayered and involves school counselors, school social workers, and school psychologists providing programs to expose children K-12 to the nature of prejudice and discrimination toward LGBTQ individuals. In addition, LGBTQ individuals should be provided with a framework to react or perceive prejudice and discrimination. In some schools the whole culture is LGBTQ aware and supportive.

College is another context where acceptance toward LGBTQ individuals can increase. Research has demonstrated that interaction with gays and lesbians and taking courses related to these issues is associated with more accepting attitudes regarding same-sex relationships, voting for a gay presidential candidate, being friends with a feminine man or masculine woman, and comfort with a gay or lesbian roommate (Sevecke et al., 2015).

LGBTQ RELATIONSHIPS

Interviews with 36 LGBTQ couples in regard to their relationship histories revealed that LGBTQ individuals and couples noted more stress in reference to coming out—if and when—as individuals and as a couple, greater hesitancy to commit, and less family and institutional support for their relationship, and hence, more vulnerable to breaking up (Macapagal et al., 2015). Otherwise, gay and heterosexual couples are amazingly similar in regard to having equal power and control, being emotionally expressive, perceiving many attractions, and few alternatives to the relationship, placing a high value on attachment, and

sharing decision-making (Kurdek, 1994). (Refer to the Self-Assessment for same-sex couples on page 384.)

Sexuality and Commitment

Kurdek (2008) studied both partners from 95 lesbian couples, 92 gay male couples, 226 heterosexual couples living without children, and 312 heterosexual couples living with children. In studying them over a 10-year period, researchers found that lesbian couples showed the highest level of relationship quality. Like many heterosexual women, most gay or queer women value stable, monogamous relationships that are emotionally as well as sexually satisfying. Gay and heterosexual women in U.S. society are taught that sexual expression should occur in the context of emotional or romantic involvement. When lesbians and heterosexual females are compared on the value of fidelity, lesbians report being more loyal (Okutan et al., 2017).

Long term quality male-male relationships are less frequent. A common stereotype of gay men is that they prefer casual sexual relationships with multiple partners versus monogamous, long-term relationships. Gotta et al. (2011) found that gay men reported greater interest in casual sex than did heterosexual men. The degree to which gay males engage in casual sexual relationships is better explained by the fact that they are male than by the fact that they are gay. In this regard, gay and straight men have a lot in common: They both tend to have fewer barriers—no stigma— to engaging in casual sex than do women who are heterosexual or lesbian.

Contributing to this phenomenon is the use of technology. McKie et al. (2017) conducted focus groups with 43 young adult gay men in regard to Internet use and outcome. Most used the Internet, which was described as having negative outcomes—gay male porn provided unrealistic sex-focused models for gay relationships, dating sites promoted meeting for sex not for relationships, and cheating on one's partner was easy. An absence of positive models for long- term relationships was noted by one interviewee:

> There is nothing like eharmony.com for gay men, where if you are actually interested in a long-term relationship to go to . . .rather you end up on a website that by and large tends to be about sex . . .

Rosenberger et al. (2014) analyzed data from 24,787 gay and bisexual men who were members of online websites facilitating social or sexual interactions with other men. Over half of those who completed the questionnaire—61.4%—reported that they did not love their sexual partner during their most recent sexual encounter, while 28.3% reported being in love with their most recent sexual partner. Hence, most of these

---

Ally development model: emphasizes those who are supportive of the LGBTQIA movement.

men did not require love as a context to having sex. Although they are given little cultural visibility, many gay men are in long-term monogamous relationships or are interested in monogamy. Van Eeden-Moorefield et al. (2015) studied a small sample of 43 gay men and found that 72% reported a preference for traditional monogamy. Interviews with 36 gay men committed to monogamy in their relationships revealed the benefits of emotional and sexual satisfaction, trust, security, and so forth (Duncan et al., 2015).

What about the sexual satisfaction of sexual minorities? Ritter et al. (2018) compared data on 193 heterosexual and 87 sexual minority undergraduate respondents and found lower sexual satisfaction

APPLYING SOCIAL RESEARCH

Trans Partner Relationships: A Qualitative Exploration

"Trans," as used here, is a comprehensive term which encompasses individuals within the gender nonconforming population. Existing research reveals that trans individuals are among the most discriminated, marginalized, and stigmatized with high levels of mental and financial difficulties. While this study is about trans relationships, not all of the respondents were in a relationship at the time of the interview.

Methodology and Findings

Data for this study came from interviews with 38 trans individuals who self-identified as either (a) having transitioned or (b) having gender expression fluidity from male to female (MtF) or female to male (FtM). As for sexual orientation, participants identified as lesbian, bisexual, demisexual, pansexual, straight, queer, and no label. Most were White, Euro-American and the remainder African American, Hispanic, or biracial. The respondents were recruited through widely placed advertisements on trans-oriented public pages on Facebook.

The participants completed a one-hour interview via Skype during which they responded to 13 prompt questions about their lives and relationships, such as "Overall, what would you say are the pros and cons of being trans in regard to romantic relationships?". Five themes were identified in the answers from the respondents.

1. The oppressive gender binary system

Thirty-three of the 38 participants, about 87%, noted the relentless stress of living within the oppressive and narrowly defined male or female gender role system. Examples of issues trans individuals had to confront included the complexity of determining their own gender identity and how to present themselves; that is, did they want to present as a male, female, or genderqueer person? And what type partner did the other person want?

2. Coming out and disclosure decisions

Dealing with the complexity of disclosure of one's trans identity to one's current or future partners was another major issue. Dierckx et al. (2019) interviewed 17 partners of trans people who reported the various roles they had to manage were the co-parenting role, the ally role, and the romantic partner role, the latter being the most difficult.

3. Emotional and physical sexuality concerns

Participants talked about the challenges of sexual relations. Some comments included:

> It's hard for a partner to react to a body that they're not familiar with. (Cris, age 25)

4. Healthy relationships are work

Trans individuals must navigate all the issues that other couples do—where to live and questions like whether the city is trans gender friendly, work priority and schedule issues, and in-laws and extended family.

> We see them [extended family] in the summers and at Christmas time . . . So, a year ago they met me as one person and now here I am and I'm not the same person. I mean, I'm the same person, but I don't look the same, I don't have the same name, I don't even sound the same, so. . . they were quite confused. (Jake, age 37)

5. Living an authentic life

In spite of the difficulty trans individuals face, there is joy in moving out of the shadows and being true to one's self:

> So, the pros are that you're being completely authentic and I think that in a loving relationship . . . that is absolutely critical. (Aubrey, age 59)

The researchers summarized their research by noting the important issues trans individuals face in their relationships—their fears and rejections—but also their joy of authenticity.

Abridged from Platt, L. F., & Bolland, K. S. (2017). Trans partner relationships: A qualitative exploration. *Journal of GLBT Family Studies 13* 163-185. Also, see Dierckx, M., Mortelmans, D., & Motmans. J. (2019). Role ambiguity and role conflict among partners of trans people. *Journal of Family Issues, 40,* 85-110.

among the latter. Previous researchers have suggested that sexual minority relationships exist in a context of heterosexism, suppression, stigmatization, prejudice, discrimination, and violence which results in lower relationship quality. Such an impact on minority couples' satisfaction may spill over into lower sexual satisfaction.

Paine et al. (2019) interviewed 16 married midlife lesbians who reported a decrease in sexual interest over time, citing weight gain, the exhaustion of rearing children, caring for aging parents, and menopause as culprits. They also noted the positive value of a mutual understanding of menopause, and some were intent on not letting sex slide into nonexistence in their relationship. Some reported "penciling in" time for sex to make sure it happened.

Mate Preferences of Transgender Individuals

Aristegui et al. (2018) surveyed the mate preferences of 134 male to female (MtF) individuals who emphasized attractiveness and socioeconomic status in a partner; the same survey showed that 94 female-to-male (FtM) individuals were more focused on dependable character. The researchers noted that "although biological sex differences were present in both groups, providing support to the evolutionary theory, MtF individuals valued the same characteristics as both biological male and female individuals do" (p. 330).

Fein et al. (2018) noted that transgender individuals have a variety of sexual partners, predominantly cisgender, and may change sexual preference when they transition. However, transitioning can be associated with having no primary sexual partner, despite past sexual partnerships. Recognizing the unique challenge for many gender-nonconforming individuals, dating sites and apps have enabled members to select transgender or other gender-nonconforming identities in profile. Despite these changes, transgender individuals may face more challenges in finding a partner than heterosexual or queer individuals. Blaire (2019) found that across a sample of heterosexual, lesbian, gay, bisexual, queer, and trans individuals, 87.5% indicated that they would not consider dating a trans person.

Division of Labor

Compared to heterosexual couples, previous studies have found gay and lesbian couples share household labor and childcare more equally. Kelly and Hauck (2015) interviewed 30 queer participants who were cohabitating with a partner to examine how they negotiated the household division of labor in their relationship. Results revealed that their roles in

reference to housework and childcare were shaped by time availability and personal preferences as well as labor force participation and citizenship. The authors suggested that queer couples are "redoing gender" by challenging normative gender roles.

Mixed-Orientation Relationships

Mixed-orientation couples are those in which one partner is heterosexual and the other partner is lesbian, gay, or bisexual. Adler and Ben-Ari (2017) studied 46 individuals in mixed orientation marriages and found varying patterns of secrecy from complete secrecy to complete openness. Their research challenged the idea that secrecy is detrimental and openness is beneficial in the context of mixed-orientation marriages. In another study, eight heterosexual women in a relationship with a gay or bisexual partner emphasized that they were able to reframe their involvement with their partner to move toward a successful relationship (Adler & Ben-Ari, 2018). The Straight Spouse Network (www.straightspouse.org) provides support to heterosexual spouses or partners, current or former, of LGBTQ mates.

COMING OUT TO SIBLINGS, PARENTS, AND PEERS

Coming out is a major decision with which LGBTQ individuals struggle. **Coming out** can mean a series of decisions and an ongoing process for many. A person must first "come out" to oneself, then decide on who, when, where, and what to disclose. Peterson et al. (2017) found siblings were the first individuals to whom their sample of LGBTQ individuals came out and with 100% positive response. The reaction of friends is particularly important. Puckett et al. (2017) reported that LGBTQ youth who lost friends when they came out were 29 times more likely to report suicide attempts. Coming out to parents involves the parents adjusting their previous expectations—the parents must give up the idea that their offspring will either not have a biological child or will want to adopt (Jhang, 2018). Coming out to grandparents is a cautious decision based on the perception of their having conservative values (Scherrer, 2016). Coming out as a transgender individual can be particularly difficult. Brumbaugh-Johnson and Hull (2019) interviewed 20 transgender people about their coming out process. The result indicated that coming out is a strategic decision and requires thoughtful consideration for social contexts for transgender individuals.

Parents also struggle with coming out to their wives and children. A gay father—his daughter was in

....

Coming out: being open about one's sexual orientation and identity.

Risks and Benefits of "Coming Out"

In a society where heterosexuality is expected and considered the norm, heterosexuals do not have to choose whether or not to tell others that they are heterosexual. However, decisions about **"coming out,"** or being open and honest about one's sexual orientation and identity, particularly to one's parents, are agonizing for LGBTQ individuals. Whether LGBTQ individuals come out is influenced by the degree to which they are frustrated with hiding their sexual orientation, the degree to which they are pressured to come out by their partners, the degree to which they feel more "honest" about being open, their assessment of the risks of coming out, and their prediction of how others will respond.

Risks of Coming Out

1. **Parental and family members' reactions.** Rothman et al. (2012) studied 177 LBG individuals who reported that two-thirds of the parents to whom they first came out responded with social and emotional support. Their research is in contrast to that of Mena and Vaccaro (2013), who interviewed 24 gay and lesbian youth about their coming out experience to their parents. All reported a less than 100% affirmative "we love you" and "being gay is irrelevant" reaction which resulted in varying degrees of sadness or depression. Parents' reactions have a major effect on the development of the child, and parental rejection is related to suicide ideation and suicide attempts (Van Bergen et al., 2013).

2. **Harassment and discrimination at school.** LGBTQ students are more vulnerable to being bullied, harassed, and discriminated against. The negative effects are predictable: "a wide range of health and mental health concerns, including sexual health risk, substance abuse, and suicide, compared with their heterosexual peers" (Russell et al., 2011). Some communities offer charter schools which are "LGBTQ friendly" and promote tolerance; LGBTQ students as well as faculty often seek these contexts of greater acceptance.

3. **Discrimination and harassment at the workplace.** The workplace continues to be a place where 8 million LGBTQ individuals experience discrimination and harassment. Specifically, gay men are paid less than heterosexual men, LGBTQ individuals feel their potential for promotion is less than the heterosexual majority, and many remain closeted for fear of retribution. There is no federal law that explicitly prohibits sexual orientation and gender identity discrimination against LGBTQs.

4. **Hate crime victimization.** Another risk of coming out is being victimized by antigay hate crimes against individuals or their property. Such crimes include verbal threats and intimidation, vandalism, sexual assault and rape, physical assault, and murder.

Benefits of Coming Out

Coming out to parents is associated with decided benefits. D'Amico and Julien (2012) compared 111 gay, lesbian, and bisexual youth who disclosed their sexual orientation to their parents with 53 who had not done so. Results showed that the former reported higher levels of acceptance from their parents, lower levels of alcohol and drug consumption, and fewer identity and adjustment problems. ●

the first author's class—who married a heterosexual woman revealed his experience:

I had always known I was gay, but I knew coming out to my family was not an option . . . My family had always been church fixtures and a gay son would have ruined their reputation. I dated women in an attempt to turn myself and ended up getting my girlfriend at the time pregnant. I decided to marry her even though I knew it wasn't going to work in the long run because I wanted to give my child as normal of a childhood as possible.

After five years of marriage, we separated and it felt like I could maybe stop hiding who I was. My family was pressuring me to "get back out there" and after holding them off I met a woman who I believed would be my saving grace. I learned that she had been with other women during college and felt like she could be my cover up. However, after we married, it was apparent that would not be the case. I began drinking because I was ashamed of who I was and what my life had become because of it. I made the decision to end my second marriage and come out to my family. My parents and grandparents had passed away at this point so I didn't feel like I had to worry about rejection from them. Coming out to the older members of our family led to a few interesting conversations, but they all assured me that they still loved me and their opinion of me as a person and as a father to my children had not changed. Once I was honest with everyone, I felt like a huge weight had been lifted off my shoulders.

Social media is sometimes used to come out and celebrate one's sexual identify—"out and proud." Ten percent of 42 gay men who were interviewed reported using Facebook to come out. Facebook may also be a forum to be "out and discreet" whereby 57% came out to friends—for example, by controlling privacy settings—but hid this information from others. "Facebook and closeted" was another option used by a third of the interviewees who carefully manage their online profile to ensure their sexual identify is not exposed (Owens, 2017). Snapchat, Instagram and YouTube are also used in coming out. Shawn Dawson did so for seven million viewers (Couric, 2015).

LGBTQ individuals may also "go back into the closet" when they enter a new context. Svab and Kuhar (2014) identified the concept of the "transparent closet" to describe a situation in which parents are informed about a child's homosexuality but do not talk about it. . . a form of rejection. The "family closet" refers to the wider kinship system having knowledge of a child's being gay but is "keeping it quiet," a kind of denial. Because Black individuals are more likely than White individuals to view homosexual relations as "always wrong," African Americans who are gay or lesbian are more likely to face disapproval from their families than are White lesbians and gays (Glass, 2014). "We just don't talk about it," said one African-American parent.

I was recently asked in an interview what it's like to be a gay athlete in sports. I said that it's exactly like being a straight athlete. Lots of hard work but usually done with better eyebrows.

Adam Rippon, American Figure Skater

Coming out as a bisexual is different from coming out as gay or lesbian. In a qualitative study of the coming out experiences of 45 bisexuals, Scherrer et al. (2015) noted that bisexuals may come out to remove the confusion for parents. For example, explaining why one spends a lot of time with and is moving in with a same-sex person. Others feel that use of the term "gay" is easier for parents and family than "bisexual." One respondent said that her parents knew what gay was but thought bisexuals were "weird" so gay was used. Regardless of the strategy or use of term, the

Research comparing heterosexual, gay male and lesbian relationships has revealed that lesbians report higher relationship satisfaction.
Courtesy of Mia Bella Expressions

predominant reaction by parents to coming out as a bisexual was to label the new identity as a phase, as in "You are just trying this out, but you will come to your senses."

SAME-SEX MARRIAGE

My feelings for Ellen overrode all of my fear about being out as a lesbian. I had to be with her, and I just figured I'd deal with the other stuff later.
Portia de Rossi, wife of Ellen DeGeneres

In June 2015, the Supreme Court ruled that same sex marriage was legal in all 50 states. The decision was 5-4. Justice Anthony Kennedy, the pivotal swing vote, wrote the majority opinion. "They ask for equal dignity in the eyes of the law," Kennedy wrote of same-sex couples in the case. "The Constitution grants them that right." Hart-Brinson (2018) observed that the legalization of same-sex marriage was the culmination of social and political forces including a significant positive shift in the perception of gays and lesbians. Masci et al. (2017) identified five key facts about same-sex marriage:

1. Greater societal support. Every year since 2007 there has been an increase in public support for same-sex marriage. In 2017, 62% supported same sex marriage; 32% opposed.

2. Demographic differences in support. There is a demographic divide in support of same-sex marriage with religiously unaffiliated more supportive than the religiously affiliated. Younger individuals are also more supportive: 74% of millennials, now ages 18 to 36, back same-sex marriage; 65% of Generation Xers, ages 37 to 52, agree; 56% of baby boomers, ages 53 to 71, concur; and 41% of those in the Silent Generation, ages 72 to 89, also support same-sex marriages.

3. More same sex marriages. Before legalization, 38% of cohabiting same-sex couples were married. After the Supreme Court ruling, 61% of cohabiting same-sex couples are married.

4. Reasons for marriage. While both LGBTQ individuals and the general public cite love as the primary reason for marriage—84% and 88%, respectively—46% of LGBTQ individuals are more likely to cite rights and benefits as a reason for marriage compared with 23% of the general public. The abilities to become political and empowered were also motivations, identified by Lannutti (2018), for same-sex marriages.

5. The United States is one of 20 countries legalizing same-sex marriage. The first nation to legalize same-sex marriage was the Netherlands in 2000. Since then Canada, Spain, France, the Scandinavian countries, Ireland, Argentina, Brazil, Colombia, New Zealand, South Africa, Uruguay, and India have legally supported same-sex marriage. However, homosexuality is still illegal in 74 countries and punishable by death in countries such as Sudan, Iran, Saudi Arabia, Yemen, Afghanistan, and Pakistan.

By a 5-4 decision, the Supreme Court declared DOMA (The **Defense of Marriage Act**) unconstitutional on equal protection grounds, thus giving same-sex married couples federal recognition

....

Defense of Marriage Act: legislation which says that marriage is a "legal union between one man and one woman" and denies federal recognition of same-sex marriage.

and benefits. Previously Edith Windsor had sued the federal government (U.S. vs Windsor) on grounds that she did not owe $363,053 in estate taxes since she was legally married. Her deceased long-term partner, Thea Spyer, had left her entire estate to her. Windsor won. Below is a list of benefits resulting from the legalization of same-sex marriage:

*   The right to inherit from a spouse who dies without a will;

*   The benefit of not paying inheritance taxes upon the death of a spouse;

*   The right to make crucial medical decisions for a spouse and to take care of a seriously ill spouse or a parent of a spouse under current provisions in the federal Family and Medical Leave Act;

*   The right to collect Social Security survivor benefits; and

*   The right to receive health insurance coverage under a spouse's insurance plan.

Other rights bestowed on married or once-married partners include assumption of a spouse's pension, bereavement leave, burial determination, domestic violence protection, reduced-rate memberships, divorce protections such as equitable division of assets and visitation of partner's children, automatic housing lease transfer, and immunity from testifying against a spouse. All of these advantages are now available to same-sex married couples because of the Supreme Court decision. Additional effects of the legalization of same-sex marriage are lower levels of LGBTQ identity concealment, a less difficult process accepting one's LGBTQ identity, and less vigilance and isolation (Riggle et al., 2017).

A major benefit of the legalization of same-sex marriage is that it will promote relationship stability among gay and lesbian couples. In a study of the long-term dating intentions and monogamy beliefs of gay and lesbian online daters across 53 regions in eight European countries (N = 24,598), the presence of pro same-sex relationship legislation was found to be also associated with higher long-term dating intentions and stronger monogamy beliefs (Potarca et al., 2015). This higher rate is attributed to the presence of institutional support. Supreme Court recognition of same-sex marriage will result in an increase of more stable unions.

Positive outcomes for being married as a gay couple have been documented. Perales and Baxter (2018) analyzed data on 25,348 individuals in the United Kingdom, comparing same-sex couples with heterosexuals, and found similar levels of relationship quality. However, LeBlanc et al. (2018) provided data to confirm that although same sex marriage is now legal in every state, unequal recognition continues which is associated with negative mental health, such as psychological distress, depression, and problematic drinking.

One negative aspect of the legalization of same-sex marriage has been to put enormous pressure on same same-sex couples to "present an idyllic image of family." Indeed same-sex spouses facing parental separation are concerned that their divorce "would disrupt efforts to achieve social and political acceptance" (Gahan, 2018).

LGBTQ PARENTING ISSUES

Undergraduate females, friends of gays, individuals supportive of same-sex marriage and former students of a marriage and family class where same-sex issues were discussed are more likely to report favorable attitudes toward same-sex parenting (Schoephoerster & Aamlid, 2016). In regard to lesbians and gay men themselves deciding to have children, Gato et al. (2017) identified the various issues that impact their decision: sociodemographic such as gender, age and cohort, and race and ethnicity; personal, the internalization of antigay prejudice and openness about one's nonheterosexual orientation; relational, one's partner's parental motivation and social support; and contextual such as work conditions, access to LGBTQ support networks, information and resources, and social, legal, and medical barriers.

Lesbian Mothers and Gay Fathers

Fatherhood takes on a special meaning for gay males. Traditionally deprived of the role, Shenkman and Shmotkin (2016) found that gay males in contrast to heterosexual males were more likely to tie the meaning of life to the role of fatherhood. Tornello and Patterson (2018) found that when gay fathers told their children that they were gay, the children felt closer to their fathers and had a higher sense of well-being. Golombok et al. (2018) compared 40 gay father families created through surrogacy and a group of 55 lesbian mother families created through donor insemination. Results revealed that children in both family types showed high levels of adjustment with lower levels of children's internalizing problems reported by gay fathers.

Data on gay fathers also reveal that they are more likely to co-parent equally and compatibly than fathers in heterosexual relationships. Erez

and Shenkman (2016) also found gay dads happier in reported subjective well-being than heterosexual dads. The act of becoming a father has a very positive outcome on gay men's sense of self-worth. Part of this effect may be due to the fact that some gay men think that gay fatherhood was an unattainable role.

Bos et al. (2018) found no significant differences on children's well-being or problems in the parent–child relationship between mothers and fathers in same-sex and different-sex parent households. Indeed, it is the relationship that children have with their parents, not their sexual orientation that determines adult outcomes for children.

A mutual concern of lesbian mothers and gay fathers is the school their adolescent children attend. Goldberg et al. (2018) emphasized that parents of lesbian and gay youth struggle to find a school system that will minimize the exposure of their children to stigma. Seeking schools emphasizing racial diversity and gay friendliness were specific criteria.

Bisexual Parents

Power et al. (2013) surveyed 48 bisexuals who were parenting inside a variety of family structures—heterosexual relationships, same-sex relationships, co-parenting with ex-partners or nonpartners, or sole parenting—and revealed issues relevant to all parents: discipline, combining work and parenting, and so forth. The dimension of bisexuality rarely surfaced. When it did, it was in the form of being closeted to help prevent their child from being subjected to prejudice and dealing with prejudiced ex partners, in-laws, and grandparents.

There is some question about how bisexual parents socialize their children in regard to gender. Flanders et al. (2019) interviewed 25 non-monosexual-minority women in different gender relationships about their parenting practices. Results revealed that the participants expressed an openness to deviating from gender norms in the socialization of their children by providing both same- and cross-gender opportunities, as well as in being open to the potential their children would identify as trans. One respondent mother reported the following:

So I think I try really hard to let the kids be who they are, whether it's about gender or any other part of their identity, and I guess that's what's important to me and how it relates to my identity, is that I want the freedom and the latitude to be who I am, to be authentic to myself and so I want that for my kids too.

American Gordon Lake (L) and his Spanish husband Manuel Valero (R) play with their daughter Carmen.
Lillian Suwanrumpha/Stringer/AFP/Getty

Development and Well-Being of Children With Gay or Lesbian Parents

While critics suggest that children reared by same-sex parents are disadvantaged (Kirby & Michaelson, 2015), there are no data to support this fear. Cenegy et al. (2018) examined national data on the well-being of children reared in same-sex families and found poorer health that was "largely the product of demographic and socioeconomic differences rather than exposure to nontraditional family forms."

In regard to how LGBTQ parents differ from heterosexual parents, Averett (2016) found that while heterosexual parents believe that children are or should be heterosexual and encourage traditional gender socialization—for example, a ribbon in the hair for female babies—LGBTQ parents provide their children with a variety of gendered options for clothing, toys, and activities like "the gender buffet." Below is an example of "the gender buffet" revealed in comments by Latisha and Maria about the interest of their three-year-old daughter Alivia in both "boy" and "girl" things (p. 200).

Latisha:

Once Maria bought her an imitation tool set, because that's what she was interested in at the time. But she also has microphones, and she also has dolls. But, even like, with her puzzles—she is interested in castles and dragons and things like that. And so that's the puzzle that we're going to get, and we don't think about [whether it is for boys or girls].

Maria:

But then there's people's view on it, like when we bought that tool set. The cashier—it was

man—was like, "Oh, you buying this for your son?" And I was like "Actually, no, my daughter." And he was like, "Whoa! Oh, okay, that's cool!" But it, like, takes people a minute.

Rearing a Gender Variant Child

Gray et al. (2016) addressed the issues parents struggle with in parenting a gender variant (GV) child. These GV children are defined as having a "subjective sense of gender identity and/or preferences regarding clothing, activities, and/or playmates that are different from what is culturally normative for their biological sex." Interviews with eight mothers and three fathers of GV children, ages five to 13, revealed their efforts to provide a non-stigmatized childhood for their GV by trying to reduce the child's fear of stigma or hurt and advocating for a more tolerant society. An example of the former was to teach the child that prejudice exists and to minimize one's exposure. One parent said of her son, "I worry for me, and for him, about society… but he's so good at editing himself now, I think he'll get even better at it. I think it's kinda sad that he has to do it, but I think it just is a reality. And that I'm gonna encourage him to continue to do it." Other parents were more supportive of their GV child being "less stealthy."

The sentiment about changing society is revealed in a parent who said, "My view is that gender variance as we talk about it now as a 'problem' is not really the kid's problem—it's society's problem in that we have a few narrow categories." These parents were intent on educating teachers and administrators and persons who would be in leadership roles with their children—for example, the karate teacher. Pyne (2016) noted that parents of GV children and other gender nonconforming children seek to affirm their children. Theirs is "not a job, but a relationship with their children."

Parents of GV children are like other parents. Their role is to love and protect their child. This involves unconditional love, support, and respect for whom their child is and clearly communicating all of these. Since the path to adulthood will be different for GV children, parents should also make contact with transgender specialists, become involved with support groups, and get ready for the challenging parenting experience ahead.

Discrimination in Child Custody, Visitation, Adoption, and Foster Care

A student in one of our classes reported that after she divorced her husband, she became involved in a lesbian relationship. She explained that she would like to be open about her relationship to her family and friends, but she was afraid that if her ex-husband

Adoption of Children by LGBTQ Individuals and Couples?

Thousands of children in the U.S. child welfare system are waiting to be adopted. The American Psychological Association (2012) reviewed the research and noted that lesbian and gay parents are as likely as heterosexual parents to provide supportive and healthy environments for their children. In addition, the adjustment, development, and psychological well-being of children are unrelated to parental sexual orientation.

Despite the research confirming positive outcomes for children reared by gay or lesbian parents, and despite the support for gay adoption by child advocacy organizations, placing children for adoption with gay or lesbian parents remains controversial. Of 12,816 undergraduates, 18% agreed—with more men concurring than women—with the statement "Children of gay parents are disadvantaged over children of parents reared by heterosexual parents" (Hall & Knox, 2019). Prejudice against same-sex adoptions is not unique to America. In a study of Portuguese undergraduates, Gato and Fontaine (2016) found both women and men expressing more negative attitudes toward adoption by gay individuals, with increased disapproval for adoption of males into gay families. Italy remains a country in the European Union where same-sex marriages and civil unions are not legally recognized and where homosexual couples are not allowed to adopt a child (Giunti & Fioravanti, 2017).

Social policies that prohibit LGBTQ individuals and couples from adopting children result in fewer children being adopted. With the legalization of same-sex marriage, an increasing number of children will be adopted by LGBTQ individuals and couples. ●

found out that she was in a lesbian relationship, he might take her to court and try to get custody of their children. Although several respected national organizations including the American Academy of Pediatrics, the Child Welfare League of America, the American Bar Association, and others have gone on record in support of treating gays and lesbians without prejudice in parenting and adoption decisions, lesbian and gay parents are often discriminated against in child custody, visitation, adoption, and foster care.

This chapter's Family Policy section asks whether gay and lesbian individuals and couples should be prohibited from adopting.

Most adoptions by gay people are second-parent adoptions. A **second-parent adoption,** also called co-parent adoption, is a legal procedure that allows individuals to adopt their partner's biological or adoptive child without terminating the first parent's legal status as parent. Second-parent adoption gives children in same-sex families the security of having two legal parents. Second-parent adoption potentially benefits a child by:

- placing legal responsibility on the parent to support the child;
- allowing the child to live with the legal parent in the event that the biological or original adoptive parent dies or becomes incapacitated;
- enabling the child to inherit and receive Social Security benefits from the legal parent;
- enabling the child to receive health insurance benefits from the parent's employer; and
- giving the legal parent standing to petition for custody or visitation in the event that the parents break up (Clunis & Green, 2003)

Second-parent adoption is not possible when a parent in a same-sex relationship has a child from a previous heterosexual marriage or relationship unless the former spouse or partner is willing to give up parental rights.

FUTURE OF LGBTQ RELATIONSHIPS

While heterosexism, homonegativity, biphobia, and transphobia have historically been entrenched in American society, moral acceptance and social tolerance and acceptance of gays, lesbians, bisexuals, and transgender people as individuals, couples, and parents will increase. Corporate America will lead the way. American Airlines is an example of a major airline to implement both sexual orientation and gender nondiscrimination in the workplace. As a result of a more accepting culture, more LGBTQIA individuals will come out, their presence will become more evident, and tolerant, acceptance, and support will increase (Gates, 2017).

Second-parent adoption: legal procedure that allows individuals to adopt their partner's biological or adoptive child without terminating the first parent's legal status as parent.

SUMMARY

What are problems with identifying and classifying sexual orientation?

To avoid the stigma, prejudice, and discrimination associated with homosexuality, some individuals hide their sexual orientation. Others do not self-identify as gay or bisexual even though they are attracted to those of the same sex or have engaged in same-sex behavior. Still others may change their attitudes, attractions, behaviors, and identity across time.

What are the origins of sexual-orientation diversity?

Although a number of factors have been correlated with sexual orientation, including genetics, gender role behavior in childhood, and fraternal birth order, no single theory can explain diversity in sexual orientation.

Those who believe that gay and lesbian individuals choose their sexual orientation tend to think that members of this community can and should change their orientation. Various forms of conversion therapy are focused on changing one's sexual orientation, but professional associations agree that being gay is not a mental disorder and needs no cure. In spite of treatment programs offering to "cure" a person who is gay, data confirm that conversion therapy is ineffective and misguided and, in some states, illegal.

What are heterosexism, homonegativity, homophobia, biphobia and transphobia?

Heterosexism refers to "the institutional and societal reinforcement of heterosexuality as the privileged and powerful norm." Heterosexism is based on the belief that heterosexuality is superior to homosexuality. The term homophobia, also known as homonegativity, refers to negative attitudes and emotions toward homosexuality and those who engage in it. Biphobia and transphobia are negative attitudes and emotions toward bisexual and trans individuals.

What are the relationships of LGBTQ individuals like?

While LGBTQ relationships tend to be more similar to rather than different from heterosexual couples, LGBTQ relationships tend to involve partners of equal power and control who are emotionally expressive and share decision making. Lesbian couples tend to have the highest levels of relationship quality. A major difference gay couples have from heterosexual relationships is whether, when, and how to disclose their relationship to others.

What is coming out to parents, peers, colleagues, etc., like?

Parental reaction to a child coming out has a major effect on the child's development. Although every family is different, White parents are comparatively more accepting; Black parents often have more difficulty due to the presumed impact of religion on their attitudes and beliefs (Irizarry & Perry, 2018).

Rejection by peers at school can invite harassment and discrimination, bullying, and so forth. Workplace involves risk to promotion and advancement. Being the target of a hate crime permeates the decision to come out.

The result of coming out is more often positive than negative. Individuals feel relieved at no longer having to hide their orientation and are surprised by the unexpected support. Partners who have the most difficult reaction are spouses. Social media is sometimes the mechanism used in the coming out process.

What are the pros and cons of same-sex marriage?

The pros of same-sex marriage are that children benefit from being brought up in a loving, stable, nurturing relationship. The spouses also benefit from the structural, legal support. Arguments against same-sex marriage focus on the "pathology" of homosexuality, the "immorality," and the subversion of traditional marriage. Same-sex marriage is now legal in every state.

What does research on gay and lesbian parenting conclude?

Children raised by gay and lesbian parents adjust positively and their families function well. Lesbian and gay parents are as likely as heterosexual parents to provide supportive and healthy environments for their children, and the children of lesbian and gay parents are as likely as those of heterosexual parents to flourish.

What is the future of LGBTQ relationships?

While heterosexism, homonegativity, biphobia, and transphobia are realities, they, like racism, will unfortunately continue. However, with the legalization of same-sex marriage and more LGBTQ individuals coming out, acceptance and support will increase. A policy change allowing gay individuals to join the Boy Scouts as well as numerous positive portrayals of gay individuals on television and in movies reflect this cultural shift.

WEB LINKS

Advocate (Online Newspaper for LGBT News)
http://www.advocate.com/

American Institute of Bisexuality
www.bi.org

Bisexual Resource Center
http://www.biresource.org

People with a Lesbian, Gay, Transgender or Queer Parent (COLAGE)
http://www.colage.org

Compatible Partners
http://www.compatiblepartners.net/

Gay and Lesbian Support Groups for Parents
http://www.gayparentmag.com/

PFLAG (Parents, Families, and Friends of Lesbians and Gays)
http://www.pflag.org

Get the tools you need to sharpen your study skills. SAGE edge offers a robust online environment featuring an impressive array of free tools and resources.
Access practice quizzes, eFlashcards, video, and multimedia at **edge.sagepub.com/knox13e**

Vladimir Gerdo/TASS/Getty

8 Communication and Technology in Relationships

My wife said I don't listen.
At least, that's what I think she said.

—Lawrence Peter, Humorist

Learning Objectives

8.1.   Define interpersonal communication and effective communication

8.2.   Review how communication varies between genders and across cultures

8.3.   Identify the communication choices individuals make to enhance their relationships

8.4.   Understand how self-disclosure and secrecy can impact relationships

8.5.   Explain the effects of lying and cheating on relationships

8.6.   Describe how technology impacts relationships and review cell phone etiquette

8.7.   Discuss the sources of conflict and six strategies of conflict resolution

8.8.   Review the future for communication in relationships

Master the content at
edge.sagepub.com/knox13e

Whenever marriage and family therapists are asked the "secret" of a "successful" relationship, their standard answer is "communication." Communication is at the core of every relationship and the barometer of a relationship. Notice that someone who says "we can talk all night" or "we never have anything to say to each other" is telling you about how happy they are in their relationship. Indeed, there is an implied association between communication and relationship satisfaction. But a question arises: do satisfying relationships result in good communication or do satisfied couples find it easy to communicate? Lavner et al. (2016) found that it goes in both directions about equally.

What is new about communication in romantic relationships is that it is influenced by the technological explosion of Smartphones, texting, Facebook, sexting, Skype, and so forth. Lovers now "stay connected all day." This chapter acknowledges the effect of technology on romantic relationships today. We begin by looking at the nature of interpersonal communication.

INTERPERSONAL COMMUNICATION

Interpersonal communication is sending and receiving verbal and nonverbal messages between two individuals in a dyad. Whether the communication is effective is another matter.

Effective Communication

Effective communication is the process of exchanging accurate information and feelings in a timely manner: "Accurate" in the sense that what is

conveyed reflects reality and "timely" in the sense that it can benefit the receiver now. An example of effective communication is a partner who said, "I need you to know that I have begun to lose feelings for you." Not only does this communication convey how the individual is feeling but lets the partner know that the relationship is in trouble "now." A partner who says, "I lost feelings for you years ago and I want a divorce" may be giving accurate information, but they're not presenting it in a timely fashion. It is now too late for the recipient to do anything about it. Refer to the Self-Assessment on Effective Communication on page 385.

Verbal and Nonverbal Communication

Communication is conveyed in two parts: verbal and nonverbal. Although most communication is focused on verbal content, most interpersonal communication, which is estimated to be as high as 80%, is nonverbal. **Nonverbal communication** is the "message about the message," the gestures, eye contact, body posture, tone, and rapidity of speech. Even though a person says, "I love you and am faithful to you," crossed arms and lack of eye contact will convey a different meaning than if the same words are accompanied by a tender embrace and sustained eye contact. The greater the congruence between verbal and nonverbal communication, the better. For example, volume of speech can have a significant impact on a relationship. If someone raises his or her voice when speaking to a partner, there are negative

....

Effective communication: the process of exchanging accurate information and feelings in a timely manner.

Nonverbal communication: the "message about the message," using gestures, eye contact, body posture, tone, volume, and rapidity of speech.

The nonverbal behavior of each partner reflects that he or she is discussing a very serious issue over which he or she disagrees.

Each of these emojis can add new meaning to a message. The wink emoji is a commonly used symbol for flirting.
©iStockphoto.com/James Silver

physiological outcomes, such as high blood pressure and a higher heart rate.

Flirting is a good example of both nonverbal and verbal behavior. **Flirting** is showing an interest in someone without serious intent. Smiling, touching, and saying something cute are examples. People

Flirting: to show interest without serious intent.

often use flirtatious pickup lines to approach someone new and indicate romantic interest. Mae West, an actress from the 40s is often credited with the famous pickup line: "Is that a pistol in your pocket or are you glad to see me?" Although pickup lines such as this are still used today, technology has greatly affected how people flirt. Memes, GIFS, and emojis are often used for flirting and may act as a stand-in for nonverbal actions, such as sending wink emoji. Words and emojis are often used together as in saying "Let's hang out" accompanied by a smiley face.

PERSONAL CHOICES

How Close Do You Want to Be?

Individuals differ in their capacity for, and interest in, an emotionally close and disclosing relationship. See Figure 8.1, which represents the alternative levels of closeness. These preferences may vary over time; the partners may want closeness sometimes and distance at other times. Individuals frequently choose partners according to an "emotional fit"—an agreement about the amount of closeness they desire in their relationship.

In addition to emotional closeness, some partners prefer a pattern of physical presence and complete togetherness, which may be labelled codependency, where they depend on each other for all of their leisure and discretionary time together. Others enjoy time alone and time with other friends

and do not want to feel burdened by the demands of a partner with high companionship needs. Su (2016) argues that while texting and digital media allow for a constant connection between romantic lovers, it may push one's personal boundaries as well as cultivate an intolerance for separation. Partners might consider their own needs and choices and those of their partners in regard to emotional, spatial, and digital closeness.

The two circles on the left reflect a distant emotional relationship. The half and half overlapping circles in the middle reflect a moderate level of emotional closeness. The two mostly overlapping circles on the right reflect a very close emotional relationship. Any pattern is acceptable as long as both partners agree. ●

FIGURE 8.1

Variations in Closeness

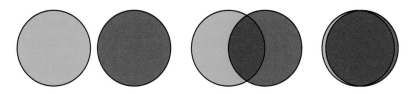

Although flirting is often thought of as a behavior between two new singles, it can also occur between established partners. In fact, flirting between older partners can benefit their relationship. Frisby and Booth-Butterfield (2015) studied 164 spouses and observed that flirting was motivated by a desire for sexual activity and the desire to create a private world with the spouse with women more likely to flirt with their spouses. Flirting was associated with both relationship satisfaction and commitment.

Words Versus Action

A great deal of social discourse depends on saying things that sound good but that have little behavioral impact. Although someone saying "Let's hang out sometime" seems positive—as it implies an interest in spending time together—it doesn't initiate a specific plan. The intent or interest may be there, but the action may not happen. In reality, "Let's hang out sometime" is an intentionally vague statement, which may reflect various motivations. Someone may fear rejection and be too shy to suggest a specific time. Alternatively, someone may not be able to commit to a specific time or won't prioritize spending time with the other person. By suggesting a specific time and place, such as "Let's hang out Thursday night at Chico's," there is a specific intention and plan to spend time together.

Another disconnect between words and action is when one says "I love you" but has his or her arms folded. One must pay attention to both the verbal and nonverbal communication. A similar issue may occur when two partners are communicating their respective desires regarding how close they want to be. We discuss this scenario in the "Personal Choices" section.

GENDER, CULTURE, AND COMMUNICATION

How individuals communicate with each other depends on which gender is talking and listening and the society and culture in which they were socialized and live.

Gender Differences in Communication

Numerous jokes address the differences between how women and men communicate. Take this anonymous quote:

> When a woman says, "I'm sorry," what she means is "You'll be sorry." When a woman says, "I'll be ready in a minute," what she means is "Kick off your shoes and start watching a football game on TV."

Although many factors such as culture, beliefs, and perception can affect one's communication, past research has recognized gender differences in communication. Women and men frequently differ in their view of situations (Busby et al., 2019) and how they communicate. Women are more communicative about relationship issues, view a situation emotionally, and initiate discussions about relationship problems. Deborah Tannen (1990; 2006) is a specialist in communication. She observed that, to women, conversations are negotiations for closeness in which they try "to seek and give confirmations and support, and to reach consensus" (1990, p. 25). To men, conversations are about winning and achieving the upper hand.

The genders tend to differ regarding emotionality. Garfield (2010) reviewed men's difficulty with emotional intimacy. He noted that their emotional detachment stems from the provider role, which requires them to stay in control. Below is an example of the woman trying to make an emotional connection, while her male partner is oblivious.

Mary came home after a long and difficult day at work. She's hoping to spend some quality time together. When she walks in, John has the TV on.

John: "Hey Babe–"

Mary: "Are you watching the Super Bowl rerun again?"

John: grabbed the remote and switched the channel to wrestling.

Mary: "Now you are watching wrestling?" (in disbelief and raising her eyebrows)

John: "Chill, Mary, you told me not to watch football, so I changed channels already. Why are you mad? Okay you win—here is the remote."

In this example, John is clueless about what Mary wants—his attention and interest in her. He doesn't ask her, and instead makes assumptions about what she means. Mary may be nervous to express her emotions, because being emotional can often be seen as a weakness. In the end, they are unable to connect emotionally and walk away frustrated with the situation and each other. What choices could they have made that would've resulted in a more positive interaction? We discuss these choices in the following sections.

Cultural Differences in Communication

While there is a great diversity within each culture, there are also commonly shared characteristics by those in the culture. Research has noted that African

Americans have a more direct conflict communication style than White Americans (Shuter & Turner, 1997; Turner & Shuter, 2004). An example of this direct conflict communication style is choosing to ask someone, "How could you do that?" instead of choosing not to question another person's actions. However, such directness may be perceived as inappropriate for those in the Latino culture. The concept of simpatia—being kind, considerate, focusing on others—emphasizes polite and pleasant exchanges (Rodriguez-Arauz et al., 2018). For example, the direct question, "Can you give me a ride to the new museum this morning?" may be viewed as inconsiderate or lack of simpatia. An indirect statement would be preferable, such as, "I would like to visit the new museum if I can find a ride."

The meaning of certain words varies by country, as well. Xu (2013) emphasized the importance of being aware of cultural differences in communication. An American woman was dating a man from Iceland. When she asked him, "Would you like to go out to dinner?" he responded, "Yes, maybe." She felt confused by this response and was uncertain whether he wanted to eat out. It was not until she visited his home in Iceland and asked his mother, "Would you like me to set the table?"—to which his mother replied, "Yes, maybe"—that she discovered "Yes, maybe" means "Yes, definitely." Individuals reared in France, Germany, Italy, or Greece regard arguing as a sign of closeness—to be blunt and argumentative is to keep the interaction alive and dynamic; to have a tone of agreement is boring. Asian cultures place a high value on avoiding open expression of disagreement and emphasizing harmony. Deborah Tannen (1998) observed the different perceptions of a Japanese woman married to a Frenchman:

> *He frequently started arguments with her, which she found so upsetting that she did her best to agree and be conciliatory. This only led him to seek another point on which to argue. Finally, she lost her self-control and began to yell back. Rather than being angered, he was overjoyed. Provoking arguments was his way of showing interest in her, letting her know how much he respected her intelligence. To him, being able to engage in spirited disagreement was a sign of a good relationship (p. 211).*

MAKING CHOICES FOR EFFECTIVE COMMUNICATION

We continually make choices in how we communicate in our relationships. The following section identifies the various choices we can make to ensure that communication in our relationships has a positive outcome.

1. **Make communication a priority**. Communicating effectively implies that communication is a priority in one's relationship. When communication is a priority, partners make time for it to occur in a setting without interruptions: they are alone; they are not texting or surfing the Internet; they do not answer the phone; and they turn the television off.

2. **Avoid negative and hurtful statements to your partner**. Because intimate partners can hurt each other so intensely, it is important to avoid brutal statements to the partner. Such negativity is associated with vulnerability to divorce (Woszidlo & Segrin, 2013). Indeed, be very careful how you give negative feedback or communicate disapproval to your partner. For example, consider saying "I know you got overwhelmed and busy but please try to call in the future when you get tied up" rather than "you were completely insensitive of my feelings and rude not to call me when you knew you were going to be late." Markman et al. (2010a) noted that spouses in marriage counseling often will report "it was a bad week" based on one negative comment made by the partner.

3. **Say positive things about your partner**. It is not enough to avoid making negative statements—frequent positive statements must be made to one's partner. Hiew et al. (2016) compared communication patterns in Chinese, Western, and intercultural Chinese-Western couples and found that a low frequency of negatives and a high frequency of positives was associated with relationship satisfaction across all the couples.

4. **Establish and maintain eye contact**. Shakespeare noted that a person's eyes are the "windows to the soul." Partners who look at each other when they are talking not only communicate an interest in each other but also are able to gain information about the partner's feelings and responses to what is being said. However, making direct eye contact in some cultures can be considered disrespectful and inappropriate.

5. **Ask open-ended questions**. When your goal is to find out your partner's thoughts and feelings about an issue, using **open-ended questions** is best. Such

Open-ended question: question which elicits a lot of information.

questions like "How do you feel about me?" encourage your partner to give an answer that contains a lot of information. **Closed-ended questions**—for example, "Do you love me?"— which elicit a one-word answer such as *yes* or *no*, do not provide the opportunity for the partner to express a range of thoughts and feelings.

6. **Use reflective listening**. Effective communication requires being a good listener. One of the skills of a good listener is the ability to use the technique of **reflective listening**, which involves paraphrasing or restating what the person has said to you while being sensitive to what the partner is feeling. For example, suppose you ask your partner, "How was your day?" and your partner responds, "I felt exploited today at work because I went in early and stayed late and a memo from my new boss said that future bonuses would be eliminated because of a company takeover." Listening to what your partner is both saying and feeling, a reflective statement would be "You feel frustrated because you really worked hard and felt unappreciated."

Reflective listening serves the following functions: (1) it creates the feeling for speakers that they are being listened to and are being understood; and (2) it increases the accuracy of the listener's understanding of what the speaker is saying. If a reflective statement does not accurately reflect what a speaker

has just said, the speaker can correct the inaccuracy by saying it again.

Another important quality of reflective statements is that they be nonjudgmental. "You always complain" is a judgmental response. Such responses serve to punish or criticize the partner for what they think, feel, or want and often results in an argument or emotional distance. Table 8.1 provides several examples of nonjudgmental reflective statements.

7. **Use "I" statements**. "I" statements focus on the feelings and thoughts of the communicator *without* making a judgment on others. For example, rather than say, "You are so lazy," say "I feel frustrated when wet towels are left on the floor when we have guests coming. Please put them in the laundry room." Because "I" statements are a clear and nonthreatening way of expressing what you want and how you feel, they are likely to result in a positive change in the listener's behavior. Making "I" statements reflects being authentic. Being authentic means speaking and acting in a manner according to what one feels. Being authentic in a relationship means being open with the partner about one's preferences and feelings about the partner's behavior. Being authentic has positive consequences for the relationship in that one's thoughts and feelings are out in the open in contrast to being withdrawn and resentful.

....

Closed-ended question: question that allows for a one-word answer and does not elicit much information.

Reflective listening: paraphrasing or restating what the person has said to you while being sensitive to what the partner is feeling.

"I" statements: statements which focus on the feelings and thoughts of the communicator without making a judgment on others.

TABLE 8.1

Judgmental and Nonjudgmental Responses to a Partner's Saying, "I'd like to go out with my friends one night a week."

NONJUDGMENTAL, REFLECTIVE STATEMENTS	JUDGMENTAL STATEMENTS
You value your friends and want to maintain good relationships with them.	You only think about what you want.
You think it is healthy for us to be with our friends some of the time.	Your friends are more important to you than I am.
You really enjoy your friends and want to spend some time with them.	You just want a night out so that you can meet someone new.
You think it is important that we not abandon our friends just because we are involved.	You just want to get away so you can drink.
You think that our being apart one night each week will be good for us.	You are selfish.

In contrast, **"you" statements** blame or criticize the listener and often result in increasing negative feelings and behavior in the relationship. Suppose you are angry with your partner for being late. Rather than say, "You are always late and irresponsible"—a "you" statement—you might respond with, "I get upset when you are late and ask that you call me when you will be delayed." The latter focuses on your feelings and a desirable future behavior rather than blaming the partner for being late.

8. **Touch**. Touch provides another layer of communication. Holding someone close conveys a sense authenticity to feeling close to another that words alone cannot communicate. Touching norms vary by culture. For example, the French kiss each other on both cheeks when greeting.

9. **Use soft emotions**. Both "hard" emotions like anger or outrage and "soft" emotions such as sadness or being hurt are used when individuals communicate (Sanford & Grace, 2011). Flat emotions such as being bored or indifferent are also used. Hard emotions can escalate negative interactions, whereas soft emotions result in more pleasant communication which increases the couple's willingness to resolve an interpersonal conflict.

10. **Identify specific new behavior you want**. Focus on what you want your partner to do rather than on what you don't want. For example, if your partner routinely drives the car but never puts gas in it, rather than saying, "Stop leaving the gas tank empty," you can ask, "Would you try to keep at least a quarter tank of gas in the car please? I will always do this for you, so you will always have gas in the car." Be careful that the tone used when asking your partner what you want is not demanding. Demanding is associated with a demand and withdraw pattern in which one partner demands and the other withdraws. Couples with this pattern are more likely to be dissatisfied with their relationship (Balderrama-Durbin et al., 2012).

11. **Stay focused on the issue**. In discussing an issue, stay focused on the topic. Branching refers to going out on different limbs of an issue rather than staying focused on the issue. If you are discussing a credit card bill, stay focused on the credit card bill and don't bring up other issues that aren't related. Stay focused.

12. **Make specific resolutions to disagreements**. To prevent the same issues or problems from recurring, partners should agree on what each person will do in similar circumstances in the future. For example, if going to a party together results in one partner's drinking too much and drifting off with someone else, what needs to be done in the future to ensure an enjoyable evening together? In this example, a specific resolution would be to decide how many drinks the partner will have within a given time and an agreement to stay together.

13. **Give congruent messages. Congruent messages** are those in which the verbal and nonverbal behaviors match. A person who says, "Okay, you're right" and smiles while embracing the partner is communicating a congruent message. In contrast, the same words accompanied by leaving the room and slamming the door communicate a very different message.

14. **Share power. Power** is the ability to impose one's will on the partner and to avoid being influenced by the partner. One way to assess power in a relationship is to identify who has the least interest in maintaining the relationship. The **principle of least interest** says that the person who has the least interest in continuing the relationship is in control of the relationship. If you are less involved than your partner, you control the relationship since the partner wants to please you. Communication of power in a relationship occurs in many ways:

Withdrawal: Not speaking to the partner

Guilt induction: "How could you ask me to do this?"

Being pleasant: "Kiss me. I was thinking about you all day."

Negotiation: "We can go to the movie if we study for a couple of hours before we go."

Deception: Running up credit card debts of which the partner is unaware

"You" statement: statement that blames or criticizes the listener and often results in increasing negative feelings and behavior in the relationship.

Branching: in communication, going out on different limbs of an issue rather than staying focused on the issue.

Congruent messages: message in which the verbal and nonverbal behaviors are the same.

Power: the ability to impose one's will on the partner and to avoid being influenced by the partner.

Principle of least interest: the person who has the least interest in the relationship, controls the relationship.

Blackmail: "I'll find someone else if you won't have sex with me."

Physical abuse or verbal threats: "You will be sorry if you try to leave me."

Criticism: "You are stupid and fat."

Dominance: "I make more money than you, so I will decide where we go."

Power may also take the form of love and sex. The person in the relationship who loves less and who needs sex less has enormous power over the partner who is very much in love and who is dependent on the partner for sex. This pattern also reflects the principle of least interest.

One of the greatest sources of dissatisfaction in a relationship is a power imbalance and conflict over power (Knudson-Martin et al., 2015; Kurdek, 1994). Almost two-thirds or 65% of 12,406 undergraduates from two universities reported that they had the same amount of power in the relationship as their partner. Fifteen percent felt that they had less power; 20% felt they had more power, with 24% of men and 19% of women each reporting that they had more power (Hall & Knox, 2019). The happiest of relationships are those in which the partners have equal power so that the partners feel they are communicating with an equal (Hall & Knox, 2017).

15. **Keep the process of communication going.** Communication includes both content—verbal and nonverbal information—and process or interaction. It is important to keep talking in spite of topics which may be difficult. To ensure that the process continues, the partners should focus on the fact that talking is important and reinforce each other for keeping the communication process alive. For example, if your partner tells you something that you do that bothers him or her, it is important to thank your partner for telling you rather than becoming defensive. In this way, your partner's feelings stay out in the open rather than being hidden behind a wall of resentment. If you punish such disclosure because you don't like the content, disclosure will stop. For example, a wife told her husband that she felt his lunches with a woman at work were becoming too frequent and wondered if it were a good idea. Rather than the husband becoming defensive and saying he could have lunch with whomever he wanted he might say, "I appreciate your telling me how you feel about this…"

By making these choices, couples can improve their communication skills and work toward more healthy relationships. These are steps that couples can take on their own, but it can also be beneficial to seek outside help. Some communities and churches offer communication training and workshops. Couples can also seek the help of a counselor.

Communication During First Hangouts and First Dates

Communication choices in a relationship begin the first time a couple meet. The success of a first date or first meeting—and the possibility of a relationship—depend on one's words and actions. On a successful first outing, both parties signal their interest in and attraction to each other. However, it can be difficult to interpret these signals as people express attraction in different ways. Cohen (2016) asked 390 undergraduates to rate the verbal and nonverbal behaviors on the part of their date which signaled that their date was attracted to them. Results revealed that there were differences between females and males. Women viewed the following behaviors as signaling attraction:

- compliments about their physical appearance
- centering the conversation on them with comments like "Tell me about you."
- making references to things in common
- maintaining a lively conversation
- making references to the future like "Maybe we could go to that concert?"
- paying for the meal
- extending the date, such as taking a walk or going to another location
- hugging or kissing goodbye when parting
- texting or calling shortly after the time together

Men also viewed hugging and kissing goodbye at the end of the date as a signal that their partner was attracted to them. But in contrast to women, men viewed women talking about themselves as a sign of attraction, because the man perceived this as the woman letting her guard down and revealing herself. Men also liked it when women steered the conversation to the topic of sex. Men did not want women to initiate contact after the date, just to respond to their texts or calls.

Both genders noted that waving hello and goodbye, talking about past relationships, focusing on differences, and no subsequent contact after they hung out signaled that the person was not attracted to them.

SELF-DISCLOSURE AND SECRETS

Shakespeare noted in *Macbeth* that "the false face must hide what the false heart doth know," suggesting that withholding information and being dishonest may affect the way one feels about oneself and relationships with others. All of us make choices about the degree to which we disclose information about past relationships, are honest, and keep secrets.

Self-Disclosure in Intimate Relationships

One aspect of intimacy in relationships is self-disclosure, which involves revealing personal information and feelings about oneself to another person. Relationships become more stable when individuals disclose themselves to their partners (Tan et al., 2012). Areas of disclosure include one's formative years, previous relationships—positive and negative—experiences of elation and sadness, and goals, achieved and thwarted. We noted in the discussion of love in Chapter 2 that self-disclosure is a psychological condition necessary for the development of love. To the degree that you disclose yourself to another, you invest yourself in and feel closer to that person. People who disclose nothing are investing nothing and remain aloof. One way to encourage disclosure in one's partner is to make disclosures about one's own life and then ask about the partner's life.

Secrets in Romantic Relationships

Most lovers keep one or more secrets from their partners. Some secrets may be harmful and others more innocent, but they all reflect a partner's hesitancy to self-disclose. Oprah Winfrey's biographer alleged that Oprah kept some of her eating habits from her long-term boyfriend Stedman Graham. When the couple was vacationing at a resort and Stedman left for a round of golf, Oprah promptly called room service and ordered two whole pecan pies. She called room service back a short time later to come and remove the empty tin plates (Kelley, 2010). For Oprah, it seems like eating sweets was something that she felt like she should keep from her partner. As someone who has been very open in the past about her struggles with weight loss, she may have felt embarrassed to tell her partner about her eating habits. This is an example of

---

How Much Do I Tell My Partner About My Past?

How much to tell a partner about one's past is not an easy decision since it is not easy to predict a partner's reaction.
Courtesy of Trevor Werb

Because of the fear of HIV infection and other sexually transmitted infections (STIs), some partners want to know the details of each other's previous sex life, including how many partners they have had sex with and in what contexts—for example, hookups or stable relationships. Those who are asked will need to decide whether to disclose the requested information, which may include one's sexual orientation, present or past sexually transmitted infections, and sexual preferences or kinks that one might be hesitant to share. Ample evidence suggests that individuals are sometimes dishonest about their sexual history. The "number of previous sexual partners" is the most frequent lie undergraduates report telling each other. One female undergraduate when asked about her past just smiled and did not answer.

In deciding whether to talk honestly about your past to your partner, you may want to consider the following questions: How important is it to your partner to know about your past? Do you want your partner to tell you, honestly, about her or his past? What impact on your relationship will open disclosure have? What impact will withholding such information have on the level of intimacy you have with your partner? Caughlin and Bassinger (2015) question whether "completely open and honest communication is really what we want." They suggest that the value of openness should be "balanced against other values, such as politeness, respectfulness and discretion." (p. f 2). ●

a secret that may seem innocent to others but could still present a problem for a couple's communication. Meanwhile, other couples may keep secrets that seem less innocent, such as infidelity or debt.

Easterling et al. (2012) studied a group of college students to determine what self-defined secrets they kept from their partners. The researchers found the following:

1. **Most kept secrets**. Over 60% of the respondents reported having kept a secret from a romantic partner, and over one-quarter of respondents reported currently doing so.

2. **Females kept more secrets**. Out of a desire to avoid hurting the partner, females may be more likely than males to keep a secret from a romantic partner.

3. **Spouses kept more secrets**. Spouses have a great deal to lose if there is an indiscretion or if one partner does something the other will disapprove of such as a hookup. Partners who are dating or "seeing each other" have less to lose and are less likely to keep secrets.

4. **Blacks kept more secrets**. Blacks are a minority who are relentlessly victimized by the White majority. One way to avoid such victimization is to keep one's thoughts to oneself—to keep a secret. This skill of deception may generalize to one's romantic relationships.

5. **Gays and lesbians kept more secrets**. People who self-identify as queer may hesitate to share their sexual orientation, as well as other information about their lives. The phrase "in the closet" means "keeping a secret."

Respondents were asked why they kept a personal secret from a romantic partner. "To avoid hurting the partner" was the top reason reported by 39% of the respondents. "It would alter our relationship" and "I feel so ashamed for what I did" were reported by 18% and 11% of the respondents, respectively.

Some secrets, such as communication with an old lover, may involve the use of technology as in secret text messages, e-mails, and cell phone calls. Being deceptive with one's text messaging, e-mails, and cell phone calls is disapproved of by both women and men. In a study of 5,500 never-married individuals, 76% of the women and 53% of the men reported that being secretive with e-mails was a behavior they would not tolerate. Similarly, 69% of the women and 47% of the men said they would not put up with a partner who answered cell phone calls discretely (Walsh, 2013).

DISHONESTY, LYING AND CHEATING

Relationships are compromised by dishonesty, lying, and cheating.

Dishonesty

Dishonesty and deception take various forms. One is a direct lie—saying something that is not true, such as telling your partner that you have had six previous sexual partners when, in fact, you have had 13. Not correcting an assumption is another form of dishonesty—for example, your partner assumes that you do not have genital herpes).

Lying and Cheating in Romantic Relationships

Lying, a deliberate attempt to mislead, is pervasive. Sixty-two percent of 125 Harvard students admitted to cheating on either tests or papers (Webley, 2012). Politicians routinely lie to citizens when they say "Lobbyists can't buy my vote," and citizens lie to the government by cheating on taxes. Teachers lie to students when they announce that "the test will be easy," and students lie to teachers by saying "I studied all night." Parents lie to their children when they utter the words, "It won't hurt," and children lie to their parents by telling them "I was at my friend's house." Partners in a relationship lie to each other by insisting "I'm not mad"; women lie to men when they claim "I had an orgasm," and men lie to women by reassuring them "I'll call." Although the intentions of lying may not be malicious, lying is frequently considered a big problem in intimate relationships.

Lying is pervasive in college student romantic relationships. Easterling et al. (2019) analyzed data on 11,497 undergraduates, 69% of whom reported that they had lied to a romantic partner. Cantarero et al. (2018) found that men lie more than women and that the most acceptable lies don't benefit someone else in terms of protecting them from harm.

Cheating may be defined as having sex with someone else while involved in a relationship with a romantic partner. In the Easterling et al. (2019) study above, 44% reported having cheated. Because the potential to harm an unsuspecting partner is considerable, should we have a national social policy regarding HIV disclosure (see Family Policy feature)?

Disclose HIV and STI Status to New Partner?

An estimated 25% of undergraduates report that they have or have had an STI. Individuals often struggle over whether or how to tell a partner if they have an STI, including HIV infection. If a person in a committed relationship acquires an STI, then that individual, or the partner, may have been unfaithful and have had sex with someone outside the relationship. Thus, disclosure about an STI may also mean confessing one's own infidelity or confronting the partner about his or her possible infidelity. The infection may, however, have occurred prior to the current relationship but gone undetected. Individuals who have an STI and who are beginning a new relationship face a different set of concerns. Will their new partner view them negatively? Will they want to continue the relationship? One Internet ad began, "I have herpes—Now that that is out of the way. . . ."

Although telling a partner about having an STI may be difficult and embarrassing, avoiding disclosure or lying about having an STI represents a serious ethical violation. The responsibility to inform a partner that one has an STI—before having sex with that partner—is a moral one. But there are also legal reasons for disclosing one's sexual health condition to a partner. If you have an STI and you do not tell your partner, you may be liable for damages if you transmit it to your partner.

Reporting HIV infection and acquired immunodeficiency syndrome (AIDS) is mandatory in most states, although partner notification laws vary from state to state. New York has a strong partner notification law that requires health care providers to either notify any partners the infected person names or to forward the information about partners to the Department of Health, where public health officers notify the partners that they have been exposed to an STI and to schedule an appointment for STI testing. The privacy of the infected individual is protected by not revealing names to the partner being notified of potential infection. In cases where the infected person refuses to identify partners, standard partner notification laws require doctors to undertake notification without cooperation if they know of the sexual partner or spouse. ●

TECHNOLOGY MEDIATED COMMUNICATION IN ROMANTIC RELATIONSHIPS

The following scenario from one of our students reflects that technology has an enormous effect on romantic relationships.

"I saw his photo on Tinder and swiped it."

"He swiped my photo too, so we started messaging each other."

"We were long distance, so we began to have long talks on Facetime."

"To keep his interest, I would sext him, saying 'What would you like me to do to you?'"

[or] *"To keep him interested I would send him sexually suggestive Snapchats"*

"After we moved in together, I snooped, checked his cell phone—discovered other women."

"I sent him a text message that it was over and moved out."

Texting, Relationship Formation, and Interpersonal Communication

Use of Smartphones is pervasive. Ninety-five percent of U.S. adults own and use a cell phone (Vaterlaus et al., 2018). **Texting** or text messaging—short typewritten messages on a cell phone—is now the primary mean for initiating, escalating, and maintaining relationships. Some also rely on texting to end relationships. Coyne et al. (2011) examined the use of technology by 1,039 individuals in sending messages to their romantic partner. The respondents were more likely to use their cell phones to send text messages than any other technology. The most common reasons respondents gave for texting were broken down in the following way: Seventy-five percent were to express affection, 25% discussed serious issues, and 12% were to apologize. (In the survey respondents could select more than one reason for texting.) There were no significant differences in use by gender, ethnicity, or religion. Texting has become the preferred form of communication with friends among teenagers. Thirty-five percent of a national sample of 1,141 teens reported this preference

Texting: short typewritten messages sent via a cell phone that are used to "commence, advance, and maintain" interpersonal relationships.

with over 32% choosing face-to face-interaction (Smith & Bravo, 2019). However, Rappleyea et al. (2014) surveyed a sample of college students who revealed that "talking," "hanging out," and "sharing intimate details" were more important than using communication technologies to establish a relationship (p. 269).

The use of technology in relationships has both positive and negative effects. On the positive side, it allows for instant and unabated connection—individuals can text each other throughout the day so that they are "in effect, together all the time." Technology impacts families, particularly transnational families where family members are separated by significant distances in that the individuals can be co-present or emotionally "there" for each other via Skype and "FaceTime" on one's cell phone or computer. Baldassar (2016) noted that Australian migrants use communication technologies to remain together for emotional support even though they are physically apart.

On the negative side is the lack of interpersonal skill development when technology-based communication is used more than face-to-face talking (Nesi et al., 2017). The development of **nomophobia**, where the individual is dependent on virtual environments to the point of having a social phobia, may also be a concern (King et al., 2013). A negative consequence of nomophobia is that social relationships are more difficult to initiate and maintain because

....

Nomophobia: the individual is dependent on virtual environments to the point of having a social phobia.

of the comfort with technology (Seunghee et al., 2017). There is also the fear of missing out (FoMo) and fear of being offline (FoBo) to the point where interacting with technology is necessary for a person's well-being. Routledge (2019) concluded that "A growing body of survey and experimental research indicates that our online lives are harming our real lives, from our relationships to our mental and emotional well-being."

Some individuals feel that they are "addicted" to their cell phone or the Internet. Narges et al. (2017) analyzed data on 141 undergraduates and found that there was a significant negative relationship between over dependence on one's cell phone and psychological well-being. Similarly, Internet addiction has been linked to low levels of self-care among adolescents and high anxiety and high avoidant coping among adults.

There has been a concern that Internet use could negatively impact one's relationships. However, Vilhelmson et al. (2017) studied Internet use to discover where the time is taken from and found that heavy use does not affect time spent for social interaction with family and friends. Rather, time spent on sports or recreational activities is reduced. Finally, while Facebook connections can facilitate relationship development, Carpenter et al. (2018) noted that private rather than public messages are associated with closer relationships. See the Applying Social Research insert which further discusses how technology impacts intimate relationships

Impact of Technology on Intimate Relationships

A random sample of 225 undergraduate and graduate students responded to an open-ended question on an Internet survey regarding the top three ways technology had benefitted and hurt their relationships. The respondents also responded to general questions, such as "how do you feel technology impacts relationships today?" A content analysis of 1,455 units of behavior revealed the following (other content from other research is also identified).

Positive Aspects of Technology

Improved communication was the primary benefit identified by the respondents. The meaning of the term "benefits" included:

1. Meeting each other online via online dating—Tinder, Match.com, and so forth.

2. Keeping in contact—respondents benefitted from regular texting of each other with emotional support and love messages.

3. Learning new information via Google searches and sharing news and information (e.g., new releases on Netflix).

4. Visual technology—being able to see and hear the partner via FaceTime, Skype.

5. Facilitating long distance relationship—texting and Skyping were particularly noted as valuable when partners were separated for long periods of time.

6. Life management and planning—examples included being able to meet up with each other and communicate about errands.

7. Intimacy, sexuality—text messages of love affirmation and sexting to spice up the interaction.

8. Leisure and relaxation—downloading and watching movies, playing video games, enjoying apps, such as Yik Yak and Trivia Crack.

9. Learning about the partner—profiles on dating sites or Facebook provided information about the person and their interests.

10. Connections to social support—staying connected to one's parents, sibling(s), and close friends was a major benefit of technology. Chai and Kalyal (2019) noted the positive association between cell phone use and self-reported happiness, particularly for elderly adults in rural settings.

11. Preserving relationship memories—one's smartphone had become a small computer that stored previous text messages, photographs of the couple, and so forth. These memories enhanced the sense of being a couple and having a history together.

Negative Aspects of Technology on Intimate Relationships

The undergraduates also identified the negative impact of technology on relationships.

1. Impaired, compromised communication and intimacy. Texts can be misunderstood and, without the individuals being together, there can be upset feelings or frustration. Partners may also disagree about how often and how soon they should text each other. Feelings can be hurt without intention or awareness. Texting also does not allow the individuals to get practice with face-to-face talking—they can send a message with their thumbs but they can't carry on a conversation with their mouth.

2. More superficial and inauthentic communication—some respondents felt texting was impersonal and not to be preferred to face-to-face communication. "Talk to me" was the message to the partner.

3. Privacy infringements—snooping into one's Internet history, emails, or text messages can cause feelings of having one's privacy invaded and not feeling trusted.

4. Gossip, drama, and harassment—some felt that their former partners could reach into their current relationship via Facebook and cause trouble by sending text messages to you or the new partner. Technology allowed for the invasion of one by others.

5. Jealousy and trust issues—individuals can keep their email and cell phones private and secure which causes the other to wonder why the secrecy and feel the partner has something to hide.

6. Online pornography and infidelity—either partner can use the Internet to watch porno, to contact previous partners, or to develop new relationships online.

7. Distracts from or infringes on the relationship—feeling that one's partner cares more about texting someone else, spending time online, or playing videos games than spending time together. Not being present for each other.

8. Overuse of technology—Being obsessive about Play Station, video games, or checking one's email or text messages to the point that the person can't function without constant involvement with technology.

9. Pet peeve with partner's use—Answering the phone in the restaurant.

10. Features of technology—the cost of technology, video games, and so forth can cause economic problems and disagreements. Bad connections on programs like Skype can cause frustration. ●

Sources: Abridged and adapted from Murray, C. E. & Campbell, E. C. (2015). The pleasures and perils of technology in intimate relationships. *Journal of Couple & Relationship Therapy, 14*(2), 116-140. Additional research included Hertlein, K. M. & Ancheta, K. (2019). Advantages and disadvantages of technology in relationships: Findings from an open-ended survey. *The Qualitative Report, 19*, 1-11. Vaterlaus, J. M., Tulane, S., & Brown, M. (2018). Interactive technology and marital relationships: A qualitative study. Poster presented at annual meeting, National Council on Family Relations, San Diego, CA. Vilhelmson, B., Thulin, E., & Ellder, E. (2017). Where does time spent on the Internet come from? Tracing the influence of information and communications technology use on daily activities. Information, Communication & Society, *20*(2), 250-263. Carpenter, J., M. Green, & Laflam, J. (2018). Just between us: Exclusive communications in online social networks. *Journal of Social Psychology, 158*(4), 405-420. Chai, X. & Kalyal, H. (2019). Cell phone use and happiness among Chinese older adults: Does rural/urban residence status matter? *Research on Aging, 41*(1), 85-109.

When Texting and Social Media Become a Relationship Problem

Technology comes at a relationship price. Of the 31% of vacationing couples (750 adults) who reported that they disagreed while on vacation 37% reported that they "bickered over the use of technology" (Byrne & Loehrke, 2015). In a study on the effects of technology on romantic relationships, Schade et al. (2013) analyzed data from 276 adults ages 18-25 in committed relationships and found that male texting frequency was negatively associated with relationship satisfaction and stability scores for both partners while female texting frequency was positively associated with their own relationship stability scores. Hence, females thrived on texting, which had a positive relationship effect. Males tolerated it, which had the opposite and negative effect.

While social media may help individuals keep up with each other, it may also have a negative impact on individuals by creating a context for feelings of envy (Verduhn et al., 2015). Norton and Baptist (2012) identified how social networking sites are problematic for some couples—the sites are intrusive: The partner surfs while the lover is talking; they encourage compulsive use with partners always sending or receiving messages; and they make cheating easy to do with partners flirting or cheating online. The researchers also identified how 205 married individuals reduced the negative impact of technology on their relationship. Three strategies included openness—for example, each spouse knew the passwords and online friends and had access to each other's online social networking accounts, e-mail, and so forth; fidelity—flirting and online relationships were off limits; and appropriate people, such as knowing the friends of the partner and no former partners allowed.

> *Smartphones may be a wonderful technological achievement that make our lives easier in many ways, but they also undermine the quality and meaningfulness of time spent with loved ones, including our children, and make even more casual social encounters less pleasant and less likely.*
>
> Clay Routledge, Institute for Family Studies

Cell Phone and Tech Etiquette

Etiquette, norms and guidelines for polite social behavior, is learned from one's society and culture. For example, eye contact is a sign of respect and attentiveness in most Western societies, but may be considered as rude or even offensive in other cultures. Etiquette is not a set of stagnant and rigid rules; it evolves with the society and is transformed by the ways which individuals relate to each other. With the growth of Internet availability and cell phone use, cell phone etiquette, also known as netiquette or techniquette, is the use of one's cell phone which reflects thoughtfulness, empathy, and respect for those around them. This means prioritizing one's partner over technology and not being rude, self-absorbed, and inconsiderate by using technology.

Cell phone use is relentless. In a survey of 1,000 adults, 30% reported that they could not go more than 30 minutes without checking their phone before feeling anxious (Wise & Loehrke, 2017). The presence of a cell phone may undermine the enjoyment at social gatherings (Dwyer et. al., 2018). Hales et al. (2018) noted that cell phone use can sometimes create the feeling of being ostracized. For example, when a friend checks his or her cell phone during a serious conversation, there is the feeling that the person does not value the relationship or interaction. Cell phone use can also be found in public places such as elevators, classrooms, restaurants and parks. Norms for cell phone use vary from being encouraged to being tolerated or from being permitted to being prohibited (Weimer, 2018). In general, being courteous and polite, which is digital etiquette, has not been given a high priority (Hui & Campbell, 2018). Individuals may choose to reverse this norm.

The famous Emily Post Institute, which has been giving etiquette advice since 1946, has included suggestions for cell phone use and text messaging. The four basic choices for cell phone use include turning one's cell phone off at meetings or social gatherings, stepping away when receiving or making a call, avoiding discussing private or personal matters on one's cell phone in public, and keeping the volume low (Emily Post Institute, 2018a).

Texting should be regarded as a conversation and conversations should not occur in various contexts such as a church or a movie. And when talking with a friend, do not pull out your cell phone and text. To do so is to communicate, "I would rather be texting than interacting with you." Finally, text messaging should not be used to end relationships or to deliver sad news (Emily Post Institute, 2018b).

Our society has frequently emphasized the functions of technology—what can it do?— but paid relatively little attention to proper usage like the kinds of choices that can be made so that it can be used properly. Cell phones, smart devices, and new innovations will continue to influence our daily lives. Choosing tech etiquette should be kept in mind. ●

Sexting

Another way in which technology affects communication, particularly in romantic relationships, is **sexting**—sending erotic text, photos or videos via cell phone, Internet, or social media. The goal of sexting for heterosexual males is to get the partner to engage in sexual behavior (Currin & Hubach, 2019).

Sexting often begins in high school and continues into college. The behavior has become common in undergraduate relationships. Weisskirch et al. (2017) surveyed 459 heterosexual unmarried undergraduates: 80% reported sending a sexually suggestive text, 62% proposed a sexual activity, and 55% sent a sexually suggestive photo or video or both. The researchers noted that "sexting may emerge in romantic relationships when one individual feels comfortable in the romantic relationship, perceives the partner as desiring or receptive to sexting, and feels a degree of commitment" (p. 691). Sexting can also be a component of a long-distance relationship to make up for the lack of physical contact. Drouin et al. (2018) found that 79% of 272 U.S. adults, a sample not specific to college students, also reported sexting with romantic partners.

Sexting typically implies a consensual conversation, but in some instances, people may receive unwanted messages or pictures. It has become increasingly common for men to send pictures of their genitals, often referred to as "dick pics." Vogels and Stewart (2018) surveyed 108 people, ranging in age from 9 to 54, of whom 88% were cis-women and 12% were trans and asked about their having received a dick pic. Almost three-quarters (72%) reported having received a dick pic with their predominant reaction being that the photos were "intrusive," "gross," and "harassing." Hence, dick pics were not viewed as fun and sexy but nonconsensual harassment.

Burke-Winkelman et. al. (2014) found that 65% of 1,652 undergraduates reported sending sexually suggestive texts or photos to a current or potential partner and 69% reported receiving them. African Americans reported higher frequencies of sending sex content to a romantic partner. Almost a third (31%) reported sending the text messages to a third party. Regarding how they felt about sending nude photos, less than half were positive, and females were more likely to feel pressure to send nude photos. Van Ouytsel et al. (2017) noted that adolescent females feel pressure to send sexts out of fear of losing their boyfriends.

Klettle et al. (2019) found that a sample of 444 young adults that received unwanted sexts or were sexting under coercion reported higher levels of depression, anxiety, and stress, and lower levels of self-esteem. Additional downsides of sending sexting photos include: (1) they could be used to coerce or blackmail the partner, (2) they could be distributed out of revenge after a breakup, a practice that is commonly known as **revenge porn**, or (3) they could be forwarded to others to boast about having received the photographs. Revenge porn can have catastrophic consequences when employers and parents view these photos. A more accurate term is nonconsensual pornography (NCP), which is the distribution of sexually graphic images of individuals without their consent. While undergraduates are not at risk as long as the parties are age 18 or older, sending erotic photos of individuals younger than 18 can be problematic. Sexting is considered by many countries as child pornography and laws related to child pornography have been applied in cases of sexting. Six high school students in Greensburg, Pennsylvania, were charged with child pornography after three teenage girls allegedly took nude or semi-nude photos of themselves and shared them with male classmates via their cell phones. Former congressman of New York 9th district Anthony Weiner was sentenced to 21 months in prison in 2017 for sexting with a 15-year-old girl.

Video-Mediated Communication (VMC)

Communication via computer between separated lovers, spouses, and family members is becoming more common. Furukawa and Driessnack (2013) assessed the use of VMC (**video-mediated communication**) in a sample of 341 online participants between ages 18 and 70-plus. VMC can occur through several

Skype provides a way for separated partners to see and hear each other.
Courtesy of Trevor Werb

....

Sexting: sending erotic text and photo images via a cell phone.

Revenge porn: ex partner posts nude photos on the Internet, which may be seen by employers and parents with devastating consequences.

Video mediated communication (VMC): individuals are able to see and hear others they are separated from to simulate their presence and enjoyment of "being with" their beloved.

platforms, such as Skype and FaceTime. Ninety-six percent reported that VMC was the most common method they used to communicate with their family and 60% reported doing so at least once a week. VMC allows the person to see and hear what is going on; for example, while the grandparents can't be present Christmas morning, they can see the excitement of their grandchildren opening their gifts.

CONFLICT RESOLUTION

Lexicon for marital fighting:

Amnesia: "Who do you think you ARE?"

Apology: "PARdon me for LIVing!"

Family Tree: "She's YOUR mother, not mine."

Hearing impairment: "Could you speak up a little? They can't hear you in Europe."

Mining: "I hadn't realized we'd descended to that level."

Wildlife: "That's right, use physical violence. That's all an animal like you knows anyway."

Dan Greenburg and Suzanne O'Malley, *How to Avoid Love and Marriage*

Conflict occurs when the expectations or behaviors of one person are in contrast to or interfere with those of the other. Since the meaning of words is largely conveyed by one's tone of voice and other nonverbal cues, face-to-face communication is preferred when managing conflicts. Otherwise, one should choose richer communication mediums such as video conferencing with audio and visual rather than text messaging. Technology can also become the source of conflict. Papp (2018) reported that techno habits such as texting during dinner were among the most frequent sources of conflict among 55 couples whose grown children had left home. Managing conflict so that arguments are avoided is functional for both the couple and their children. Before reading about how to resolve conflict, you may wish to take the Self-Assessment: Communication Danger Signs Scale on page 386 to assess the degree to which you may have a problem in this area.

Resolving conflict is an important skill to ensure that one's relationship continues to be win-win. If either partner feels that he or she is controlled and "always the loser" in a disagreement or conflict, resentment will develop and grow. Basic etiquette is required. Gottman (1994) identified "the four horsemen of the apocalypse"—criticism like direct attacks; defensiveness such as blaming one's partner; contempt,

Trying to resolve an issue over the phone should be avoided. Partners can benefit from discussing issues in person and being attentive to verbal and nonverbal cues.

meaning rolling one's eyes or expressing sarcasm—the most damaging; and stonewalling or withdrawing from the conversation. He also noted that being positive about the partner is essential—partners who said positive things to each other at a ratio of 5:1 positives to negatives were more likely to stay together. We have noted that "avoiding giving your partner a zinger" is also essential to maintaining a good relationship.

Howard Markman is head of the Center for Marital and Family Studies at the University of Denver. He and his colleagues have been studying 150 couples at yearly intervals beginning before marriage to determine those factors most responsible for marital success. They found that "constructive arguing," where decisions are made so that the source of the argument doesn't recur, is the single biggest predictor of marital success over time (Marano, 1992). According to Markman, "Many people believe that the causes of marital problems are the differences between people and problem areas such as money, sex, and children. However, our findings indicate it is not the differences that are important, but how these differences and problems are handled, particularly early in marriage" (Marano, 1992, p. 53). The following sections identify standard steps for resolving interpersonal conflict.

Address Recurring, Disturbing Issues

Addressing issues in a relationship is important. Couples who claim to have never had an argument may seem healthy, but a lack of conflict usually conveys that that one partner controls the other and one is resentful. All partners in all relationships have chronic issues—things their partner does that upset

....

Conflict: the context in which the perceptions or behavior of one person are in contrast to or interfere with the other.

them—and these should be addressed. However, the ways that these issues are addressed are important, such as identifying new desired behaviors instead of focusing on behaviors you don't like. Refer back to the discussion on "Making Choices for Effective Communication."

Identify New Desired Behaviors

Rather than change behavior, changing one's perception of a behavior may be easier and quicker. Rather than expect one's partner to always be on time, it may be easier to drop this expectation and to find ways to distract oneself, such as check text messages, rather than be angry.

Understand Your Partner's Perspective

We often assume that we know what our partner thinks and why they do things. Sometimes we are wrong. Rather than assume how our partner thinks and feels about an issue, we should make a deliberate effort to understand our partner's perspective.

Generate Alternative Win-Win Solutions

Looking for win-win solutions to conflicts is imperative. Solutions in which one person wins means that the other person is not getting needs met. As noted previously, the person who loses may develop feelings of resentment, anger, hurt, and hostility toward the winner and may even look for ways to get even. In this way, the winner is also a loser. In intimate relationships, one winner really means two losers.

Forgive

Forgiveness is one of the most important factors contributing to the healing of a damaged relationship.

Previous researchers have noted that when an offender expresses remorse, there is a greater chance that the offended will be forgiving. Offender remorse positively predicts forgiveness and such forgiveness is associated with helping to resolve the damage (Merolla & Zhang, 2011). Researcher Hill (2010) studied forgiveness and emphasized that it is less helpful to try to "will" oneself to forgive the transgressions of another than to engage in a process of self-reflection—that one has also made mistakes, hurt others, and is guilty—and to empathize with the fact that we are all fallible and need forgiveness.

It takes more energy to hold on to resentment than to move beyond it. One reason some people do not forgive a partner for a transgression is that one can use the fault to control the relationship. "I wasn't

going to let him forget," said one woman of her husband's infidelity. Of course, there are instances where it may be foolish to forgive too quickly. A person who has deliberately hurt his or her partner and who continues to do so without remorse does not deserve forgiveness. Forgiveness ultimately means letting go of one's anger, resentment, and hurt. Its power comes from offering forgiveness as an expression of love to the person who has betrayed them. Forgiveness also has a personal benefit—it reduces hypertension and feelings of stress. To forgive is to restore the relationship—to pump life back into it.

Avoid Recovery Sabotage

What happens after a conflict is resolved is as important as resolving the conflict. Haydon et al. (2017) used the term **recovery sabotage** to refer to the extent to which individuals "actively harped on the prior conflict, dredged up new disagreements, or negated their partner's positive contributions during a post-conflict rebound conversation." Partners who engage in recovery sabotage virtually destroy the gains from having resolved a conflict and further depress relationship satisfaction. Once a conflict is resolved, move on.

Be Alert to Defense Mechanisms

Effective conflict resolution is sometimes blocked by **defense mechanisms**—techniques that function below the level of awareness to protect individuals from anxiety and to minimize emotional hurt. The following paragraphs discuss some common defense mechanisms.

Escapism is the simultaneous denial of and avoidance of dealing with a problem. The usual form of escape is avoidance. The spouse becomes "busy" and "doesn't have time" to think about or deal with the problem, or the partner may escape into recreation, sleep, alcohol, marijuana, or work. Denying and withdrawing from problems in relationships offer no possibility for confronting and resolving the problems.

Rationalization is the cognitive justification for one's own behavior that unconsciously conceals one's true motives. For example, one wife complained that her husband spent too much time at the health club in the evenings. The underlying reason for the husband's

....

Recovery sabotage: actively harping on a prior conflict, dredging up new disagreements, or negating a partner's positive contributions during a post-conflict rebound conversation.

Defense mechanism: techniques that function without awareness to protect individuals from anxiety and to minimize emotional hurt.

Escapism: the simultaneous denial of and avoidance of dealing with a problem.

Rationalization: the cognitive justification for one's own behavior that unconsciously conceals one's true motives.

going to the health club was to escape an unsatisfying home life. However, the idea that he was in a dead marriage was too painful and difficult for the husband to face, so he rationalized to himself and his wife that he spent so much time at the health club because he made a lot of important business contacts there. Thus, the husband avoided confronting his unhappy marriage.

Projection is attributing one's own thoughts, feelings, and desires to someone else while avoiding recognition that these are one's own thoughts, feelings, and desires. For example, the person involved in an affair may accuse the partner of infidelity.

Displacement involves shifting your feelings, thoughts, or behaviors from the person who evokes them onto someone else. The wife who is turned down for a promotion and the husband who is driven to exhaustion by his boss may direct their hostilities—in other words, displace them—onto each other rather than toward their respective employers. Similarly, spouses who are angry at each other may displace this anger onto someone else, such as the children.

FUTURE OF COMMUNICATION

The future of communication will increasingly involve technology in the form of texting, smartphones, Instagram, Snapchat, and so forth. Such technology will be used to initiate, enhance, and maintain individual relationships. Indeed, intimates today may text each other 60 times a day. Over 2,000 messages a month are not unusual. With the spike of communication technology, the likelihood of technological related interruption or distraction—technoference or phubbing—also increases (McDaniel & Drouin, 2019). **Phubbing** is to ignore someone by attending to one's cell phone or other mobile device.

Parental communication with children continues to be altered. Technology has both positive and negative outcomes for the family. A positive effect is that parents will be able to use technology to monitor content as their children surf the Internet, send text messages, and send and receive photos on their cell phone. Parents may also use technology to know where their children are by global tracking systems embedded in their cell phones. Another positive use is that children can communicate directly with their parents without others knowing.

The downside is that children can use this same technology to establish relationships external to the family which may be nefarious, such as with child predators. Family members may also be so compulsive with their use of cell phones, that they are constantly on them texting and surfing to the exclusion of interaction with each other.

Projection: attributing one's own thoughts, feelings, and desires to someone else while avoiding recognition that these are one's own thoughts, feelings, and desires.

Displacement: shifting one's feelings, thoughts, or behaviors from the person who evokes them onto someone else.

Phubbing: to ignore someone by attending to one's cell phone or other mobile device.

SUMMARY

How do communication, gender, and culture enhance relationships?

Communication is the exchange of information and feelings by two individuals. It involves both verbal and nonverbal messages. The nonverbal part of a message often carries more weight than the verbal part. "Good communication" is regarded as the primary factor responsible for a good relationship. Individuals report that communication confirms the quality of their relationship or condemns their relationship. Words have no meaning unless they are backed up by actions.

Men and women tend to focus on different content in their conversations. Men tend to focus on activities and negotiation and "to achieve and maintain the upper hand." To women, communication focuses on emotion, relationships, interaction, and maintaining closeness.

Culture is an important context for communication. While some cultures value direct and candid communication, others avoid confrontation.

It is important that we make deliberate choices about how we communicate with our partner. Choosing to prioritize time to communicate, making positive statements to one's partner, and avoiding criticizing one's partner are essential to relationship enhancement.

How do self-disclosure and secrets impact relationships?

High levels of self-disclosure are associated with increased intimacy. Most individuals keep secrets to avoid hurting the partner and damaging the relationship. STI disclosure can be a difficult and embarrassing task. The ethical, legal, and relational impacts of STI disclosure has generated much discussion.

What is the extent of lying and cheating in relationships?

Lying is epidemic in college student romantic relationship. One study indicated that 69% of 11,497 undergraduates reported that they had lied to their partner and 44% reported having cheated (Easterling et al., 2019).

How is technology used in romantic relationships?

Smartphones are playing an increasingly important role in romantic relationships. Text messages are the primary way many individuals initiate, escalate, and maintain romantic relationships. Text messaging allows individuals to stay connected all day. However, the use of texting or social media may also be a source of distraction, called technoference, in that a partner may surf the Internet or text while the other is talking to him or her. Partners must decide to prioritize their relationship and communicate expectations. In addition to staying connected, smartphones may also be used to flirt and facilitate being unfaithful.

What are the steps involved in conflict resolution?

Knowing how to resolve conflict is important for a good relationship. The sequence of resolving conflict includes deciding to address recurring issues rather than suppressing them, identifying new behaviors to replace negative behaviors, finding out the partner's point of view, and identifying alternative win-win solutions. Defense mechanisms that interfere with conflict resolution include escapism, rationalization, projection, and displacement.

What is the future of communication?

The future of communication will increasingly involve technology to initiate, enhance, and maintain relationships. Parental communication with children will also be altered. Technology will involve both positive and negative effects on communication in relationships.

KEY TERMS

Branching, 167

Closed-ended question, 166

Conflict, 176

Congruent messages, 167

Defense mechanism, 177

Displacement, 178

Effective communication, 162

Escapism, 177

Flirting, 163

"I" statements, 166

Nomophobia, 172

Nonverbal communication, 162

Open-ended question, 165

Phubbing, 178

Power, 167

Principle of least interest, 167

Projection, 178

Rationalization, 177

Recovery sabotage, 177

Reflective listening, 166

Revenge porn, 175

Sexting, 175

Texting, 171

Video mediated communication, 175

"You" statements, 167

WEB LINKS

Better Marriages
http://www.bettermarriages.org/

Episcopal Marriage Encounter
http://www.episcopalme.com/

 SAGE edge™

Get the tools you need to sharpen your study skills. SAGE edge offers a robust online environment featuring an impressive array of free tools and resources.
Access practice quizzes, eFlashcards, video, and multimedia at **edge.sagepub.com/knox13e**

9

Sexuality in Relationships

Sex isn't good unless it means something. It doesn't necessarily need to mean "love" and it doesn't necessarily need to happen in a relationship, but it does need to mean intimacy and connection . . . There exists a very fine line between being sexually liberated and being sexually used . . .

—Laura Sessions Stepp, *Unhooked*

Learning Objectives

9.1. Compare the various sexual values, sources, and choices

9.2. Explain the sexual double standard

9.3. Identify the various sexual behaviors individuals engage in

9.4. Describe the various relationship contexts in which sexual behavior occurs

9.5. Review the importance of practicing safe sex

9.6. Discuss the various prerequisites to sexual fulfillment

9.7. Discuss the future of sexuality in relationships

"Guys now expect sex the first time they meet you" lamented one of our students. This sentiment represents a shift in sexual expectations. Although it's assumed that sex will occur at some point in a romantic relationship—unless an individual is asexual—the range of expectations can vary from a first meeting to after marriage. Most regard sex as an important aspect of a relationship and having a happy family. In fact, 88% of survey respondents reported that good sex = a happy family (Smith & Trapp, 2017).

Love is often a factor which creates a context for sexual behavior. Researchers Lefkowitz and Wesche (2014) noted that the greater the emotional involvement of a couple, the more likely they are to have engaged in all forms of sexual activity—kissing, touching, oral and penetrative sex. Hernandez et al. (2018) also noted that, for females ages 15-19, an important factor associated with their having their first sexual experience was being involved in a dating relationship with an older partner.

The choices we make in sexuality represent a major relationship game changer and are the subject of this chapter. We begin by discussing the sexual values individuals bring to the interaction with a new partner. From there, we discuss what sexual behavior occurs in relationships.

SEXUAL VALUES AND SEXUAL CHOICES

Think about the following situations:

Two people are at a party, drinking and flirting. Although they met only two hours ago, they feel a strong attraction to each other. Each is wondering what will occur when they go back to one of their rooms later that evening. How much sexual involvement is appropriate in a first-time encounter?

* * *

Two students have decided to live together, but they know their respective parents would disapprove. If they tell their parents, the parents may cut off their money and both students will be forced to drop out of school. Should they tell?

* * *

While Maria was away for a weekend visiting her grandmother, her live-in partner hooked up with his ex-girlfriend. He regretted his behavior, asked for forgiveness, and promised never to be unfaithful again. Should Maria take him back?

* * *

Randy has decided to wait until marriage to become sexually involved. The basis for his absolutist value is his religion. But he sometimes feels stigmatized since he is viewed as too prudish in what is often a liberal university context. How does he cope with these negative views in the absence of acceptance and support for his values?

* * *

A woman is married to a man whose career requires that he be away from home for extended periods. Although she loves her husband, she is lonely, bored, and sexually frustrated in his absence. She has been asked out by a colleague at work whose wife also travels. He, too, is in love with his wife but is lonely for emotional and sexual companionship. They are ambivalent about whether to hook up occasionally while their spouses are away. What would you tell them?

TABLE 9.1

Sexual Values of 13,070 Undergraduates

RESPONDENTS	ABSOLUTISM	RELATIVISM	HEDONISM
Male students (N = 2,978)	13%	55%	32%
Female students (N = 9,631)	15%	62%	23%

Source: Hall, S. & Knox, D. (2019). Relationship and sexual behaviors of 13,070 undergraduates. Unpublished data collected for this text. Department of Family, Consumer, and Technology Education Teachers College, Ball State University, and Department of Sociology, East Carolina University

Sexual values are moral guidelines for making sexual choices in nonmarital and marital relationships. Attitudes and values sometimes predict sexual behavior. One's sexual values may be identical to one's sexual choices, but this is not always the case. For example, a person who values abstinence until marriage may choose to remain a virgin until marriage, but another individual with the same values may have intercourse before marriage. One explanation for the discrepancy between values and behavior is that a person may engage in a sexual behavior, then decide the behavior was wrong, and adopt a sexual value against it.

At least three sexual values guide choices in sexual behavior: absolutism, relativism, and hedonism. **Absolutism** is a value system based on unconditional allegiance to tradition or religion. **Relativism** emphasizes that sexual decisions should be made in reference to the emotional, security, and commitment aspects of the relationship. In contrast, **hedonism** is the belief that the ultimate value and motivation for human actions lie in the pursuit of pleasure and the avoidance of pain. See Table 9.1 for the respective sexual values of 13,070 undergraduates. Individuals may have different sexual values at different stages of the family life cycle. For example, elderly individuals are more likely to be absolutist, whereas those in the middle years are more likely to be relativistic. Young unmarried adults are more likely than the elderly to be hedonistic.

Absolutism

Absolutism is a sexual value system which is based on unconditional allegiance to tradition or religion— that is, waiting until marriage to have sexual intercourse. People who are guided by absolutism in their sexual choices have a clear notion of what they

believe is right and wrong. The official creeds of fundamentalist Christian and Islamic religions encourage absolutist sexual values. According to these doctrines, intercourse is solely for procreation, and any sexual acts that do not lead to procreation— masturbation, oral sex, or homosexual acts—are immoral and regarded as sins against God, Allah, self, and community. Absolutist Christian beliefs are reflected in Hebrews 13:4, "Let marriage be held in honor among all, and let the marriage bed be undefiled, for God will judge the sexually immoral and adulterous."

While many parents guide their children's early religious beliefs, parents influence sexual values in

This university senior is an absolutist in her sexual values—she has not had oral or penetrative sex and is waiting until marriage to do so. She is not judgmental of others with different sexual values: She just notes that absolutism works for her.
Courtesy of Breanna Gilbert-Love

....

Sexual values: moral guidelines for making sexual choices in nonmarital, marital, heterosexual, and homosexual relationships.

Absolutism: a sexual value system which is based on unconditional allegiance to tradition or religion: for example, waiting until marriage to have sexual intercourse.

Relativism: value system emphasizing that sexual decisions should be made in the context of a particular relationship.

Hedonism: the belief that the ultimate value and motivation for human actions lie in the pursuit of pleasure and the avoidance of pain.

numerous ways. Adolescents who have high quality relationships with their parents report having fewer sexual partners (Van de Bongardt et al., 2016). There is also a genetic influence when someone first has sexual intercourse. Day et al. (2016) noted that risk-taking behavior is a result of biological wiring and contributes to 25% of the variance in first intercourse timing.

Waiting until marriage to have intercourse is also an absolutist sexual value. When first intercourse occurs, religious individuals report having higher levels of sexual guilt and lower levels of sexual satisfaction than nonreligious unmarried individuals engaging in sexual intercourse (Hackathorn et al., 2016). However, some who espouse traditional religious values such as the Religious Zionist Society may not adhere to absolutist sexual values. These individuals define religion as flawed and restrictive resulting in their compartmentalizing their faith to enjoy singlehood (Engelberg, 2016). The value of waiting until marriage is often promoted in public schools (see Family Policy feature).

"True Love Waits" is an international campaign designed to challenge teenagers and college students to remain sexually abstinent until marriage. Under this program, created and sponsored by the Baptist Sunday School Board, young people are asked to agree to the absolutist position and sign a commitment to the following: "Believing that true love waits, I make a commitment to God, myself, my family, my friends, my future mate, and my future children to sexual purity including abstinence from this day until the day I enter a biblical marriage relationship." Since 1993 over 2.4 million have taken then pledge (True Love Waits, 2018).

How effective are the "True Love Waits" and "virginity pledge" programs in delaying sexual behavior until marriage? Paik et al. (2016) revealed that approximately 12% of girls and young women in the United States pledge abstinence. Yet most break their pledges, engaging in first intercourse before marriage with few differences between pledge breakers and nonpledgers in sexually transmitted infections and nonmarital pregnancies. However, the author suggests that pledgers are at higher risk for human papillomavirus (HPV) and nonmarital pregnancies.

Virginity and Virginity Loss

Individuals conceptualize their virginity in one of three ways—as a process, a gift, or a stigma. The process view regards first intercourse as a mechanism of learning about one's self and one's partner and sexuality. The gift view regards being a virgin as a valuable positive status wherein it is important to find the right person since sharing the gift is special. Some cultures such as those in Jordan and Iran

A Southern California high school teacher leads his health class on a discussion on sexual abstinence.
Marmaduke St. John/Alamy Stock Photo

require that women be virgins until marriage. The stigma view considers virginity as something to be ashamed of, to hide, and to rid oneself of. When 215 undergraduates were asked their view, 54% classified themselves as process oriented, 38% as gift oriented, and 8.4% as stigma oriented at the time of first coitus (Humphreys, 2013).

The stigma toward virginity may be increasing in the United States. Gesselman et al. (2017) reviewed three studies focused on virginity and sexual inexperience. The participants reported that they felt stigmatized due to their inexperience and that they were not highly desired as relationship partners. The result is that the value of virginity "may result in negative interpersonal consequences such as limited opportunities for romantic relationships" (p. 202). Virginity is seen as less desirable by potential romantic partners since these partners have alternative partners who are willing to have sex—and hence, no need to waste time with virgins who won't provide sex.

Although religion and tradition are two of the main reasons for abstinence, there may be other factors. Individuals, primarily females, may engage in oral sex rather than sexual intercourse to avoid getting pregnant, to avoid getting an STI, to keep their partner interested, to avoid a bad reputation, and to avoid feeling guilty over having sexual intercourse (Vazonyi & Jenkins, 2010). Males who are virgins report that "my partner was not willing" as the most frequent reason for their virginity (Sprecher & Treger, 2015). Of 783 Australian adolescents who reported never having had sexual intercourse, the majority of them said the primary reasons they gave for remaining a virgin, in addition to religion, were being proud of being a virgin, not being ready, and fearing negative outcomes like contracting STIs. However, over half of the respondents reported that they had engaged in some form of sexual activity—deep kissing, sexual touching, oral sex (Heywood et al., 2016).

Sex Education in the Public Schools

While comprehensive sex education in the United Kingdom is mandated from primary school through high school, sex education in the United States is required in only 24 states and is a source of conflict between conservatives and liberals (Guttmacher Institute, 2018). Sex education was introduced in the U.S. public school system in the late 19th century with the goal of combating STIs (sexually transmitted infections) and instilling sexual morality, typically understood as abstinence until marriage. Over time, the abstinence agenda became more evident.

Santelli et al. (2017) emphasized that the abstinence-only-until-marriage (AOUM) theme has continued to be promoted and funded for the past 35 years. The Trump Administration has been in favor of abstinence-only teaching in the nation's public schools and sought to defund any federal programs to the contrary. Such movements disregard the scientific evidence that these programs result in higher rates of STIs and unplanned pregnancies, as well as evidence that they are not effective in delaying initiation of sexual intercourse or changing sexual risk behaviors, such as using condoms. Valerie Huber, the Department of Health and Human Services official overseeing this effort, explained, "As public health and policymakers, we must normalize sexual delay."

Hence, programs that discuss contraception and other means of pregnancy protection in addition to abstinence have been targets for defunding. Referred to as **comprehensive sex education programs,** these programs result in lower rates of STIs and unplanned pregnancies. They are in great contrast to AOUM programs, which threaten fundamental human rights to health, information, and life. Indeed, young people need access to accurate and comprehensive sexual health information to protect their health and lives.

Although this information isn't being provided by the federal government, there are other sources which can illuminate the reality of sexual activity for teens. Levin (2016) emphasized that it is sometimes the impact of a particular teacher that is more influential than the content. Sun et al. (2018) noted that peer-led sexual health education was effective in changing knowledge and attitudes about sex protection but not behaviors. It's also notable that the release of MTVs "16 and Pregnant" series resulted in a decreased teen birth rate (Kearney, 2015). Hence, informing teens of the reality of sex, contraception, child care, and sexuality has positive outcomes.

There are 18 topics typically included in sexual health education programs such as reproduction, love and intimacy, sexual values, pleasure, rape, abortion, sexual pleasure, sexual decision making and healthy relationships. A majority of 560 undergraduates noted approval for all 18 topics. (Canan & Jozkowski, 2017). However, existing sex education programs generally exclude content relevant to lesbian, gay, bisexual, transgender, and queer or questioning youth. This deficit disenfranchises these populations by ignoring LGBTQ issues such as STI prevention and healthy relationships (Gowen & Winges-Yanez, 2014).

Sex education is also focused on the negative. In a review of 300 articles sampled from *The Journal of Sex Research* from 2010 to 2015, there was a focus on risk, disease, dysfunction and heteronormativity with a noted absence on pleasure. Hence, a holistic portrait of human sexuality is missing. "Researchers must discuss pleasure . . ." (Jones, 2019). ●

These studies demonstrate how the concept of virginity varies. For queer individuals, engaging in oral and anal sex is typically associated with virginity loss. Some heterosexual people may have similar views, though for many, virginity loss is tied to vaginal intercourse. Of 2,953 undergraduate males, 74% agreed with the statement "If you have oral sex, you are still a virgin," while 71% of 9,751 undergraduate females concurred with that statement (Hall & Knox, 2019).

Rather than a dichotomous "one is or is not a virgin" concept that gets muddled by one's view of "sex," a three-part view of virginity might be adopted—oral sex, vaginal sex, and anal sex. No longer might the term "virgin" be used to reveal sexual behaviors in these three areas. Rather, whether one has engaged in each of the three behaviors must be identified. Hence, an individual would not say "I am a virgin," but "I am an oral virgin" or intercourse virgin or anal virgin as the case may be. There is also the issue that some "virgins" provide manual genital stimulation for their partners. Hence the concept of virginity is complex and varies with the individual.

Sexual and Romantic Avoidance

Some virgins decide not only against having sex but also elect not to become involved in a romantic relationship. Byers et al. (2016) surveyed 411

....

Comprehensive sex education program: learning experience which recommends abstinence but also discusses contraception and other means of pregnancy protection.

adolescents of whom 56% were female, ages 16-21 years old, and found that 27% had engaged in sexual avoidance with more females than males abstaining. Reasons for sexual avoidance for females was often sexual coercion; for males, religion. Other reasons included lack of sexual pleasure and enjoyment, relationship reasons, fear of negative outcomes, disinterest in commitment, wrong time, and negative outcomes from involvement in previous relationships. Almost half or 47% engaged in romantic avoidance with more females than males following this practice.

A subcategory of absolutism is **asceticism**. Ascetics believe that giving in to carnal lust is unnecessary and attempt to rise above the pursuit of sensual pleasure into a life of self-discipline and self-denial. Accordingly, spiritual life is viewed as the highest good, and self-denial helps one to achieve it. Catholic priests, monks, nuns, and some other celibate people have adopted the sexual value of asceticism.

Relativism

Relativism, the value system held by the highest percentage of both female and male undergraduates (see Table 9.1), emphasizes that sexual decisions should be made in reference to the emotional, security, and commitment aspects of the relationship. Indeed, the longer partners see each other and become emotionally involved the more they become comfortable, trust, respect, and enjoy each other.

Whereas absolutists might feel that having intercourse is wrong for unmarried people, relativists might feel that the moral correctness of sex outside marriage depends on the particular situation. For example, a relativist might say that marital sex between two spouses who are emotionally and physically abusive to each other is not to be preferred over intercourse between two unmarried individuals who love each other, are kind to each other, and are committed to the well-being of each other.

A relativist sexual value reflects that sex has both meaning and commitment. Olmstead et al. (2018) found that over half or about 57% of their sample of 803 emerging adults noted the importance of a commitment or "connection" as important for sex. Therefore, establishing emotional connection precedes any sexual intimacy

A disadvantage of relativism as a sexual value is the difficulty of making sexual decisions on a relativistic case-by-case basis. The statement "I don't know what's right anymore" reflects the uncertainty of a

relativistic view. Once a person decides that mutual positive feelings, including love, is the context justifying intercourse, how often and how soon is it appropriate for the person to develop these feelings? Can the "vibe" develop after two glasses of wine and two hours of conversation? The freedom that relativism brings to sexual decision-making requires responsibility, maturity, and judgment. In some cases, individuals may convince themselves that they "have chemistry" so that they will not feel guilty about having intercourse.

Script for Delaying Intercourse in a Relationship

The section below provides a script for the person—more often a female—who wants to pace the partner to ensure that a relationship develops before sexual involvement.

I need to talk about sex in our relationship. I'm not comfortable talking about this and don't know exactly what I want to say so I have written it down to try and help me get the words right. I like you, enjoy the time we spend together, and want us to continue seeing each other. Sex is something I need to feel good about to make it good for you, for me, and for us.

I need for us to slow down sexually. I need to feel an emotional connection that goes both ways— we both have very strong emotional feelings for each other. I also need to feel secure that our relationship is going somewhere—that we have a future and that we are committed to each other. We aren't there yet so I need to wait till we get there to be sexual with you.

How long will this take? I don't know—the general answer is "longer than now." This may not be what you have in mind and you may be ready for us to go further than we already have. I'm glad that you want us to be sexual and I want this too, but I need to feel right about it.

So, for now, can you let me take the lead on this? I know our sex life will be great once I feel that our relationship has a future and that there is an emotional connection.

If this is too slow for you or not what you had in mind, maybe I'm not the right one for you. It is certainly OK for you to tell me you need more and move on. Otherwise, we can still continue to see each other and see where the relationship goes.

How do you feel about this?

....

Asceticism: sexual belief system which emphasizes that giving in to carnal lust is unnecessary and one should attempt to rise above the pursuit of sensual pleasure into a life of self-discipline and self-denial.

The Experience of Casual Sex

Researchers Farvid and Braun (2017) interviewed 30 ethnically diverse heterosexual women and men (ages 18 to 46) in New Zealand about their experiences with casual sex. Various themes emerged.

Thrilling Context to Be or Do Whatever

Aside from casual sex being a new, anxious, thrilling experience, one 25-year-old female reported that she enjoyed the fact that she could be completely uninhibited and do whatever she wanted. She noted that with a boyfriend, she would be scripted but with someone she doesn't know and who doesn't know her "we can do lots of things I don't normally do . . .' cause I don't care what his image is of me."

Newness in Contrast to the Usual and Dull

Casual sex was also described as a departure from the mundane. One 33-year-old male said, ". . . things with the same person would get kinda dull but you can do the same things you like with different people and it never does."

The Value of Flirting

For some, the casual sex was fun due to the flirting beforehand. ". . . it's the talking about it without talking about it" thing, where you hint to each other that you're gonna go home and have sex. For many the act of sex was disappointing in terms of physical pleasure; the fun was the new partner, the context, the flirting.

Forbidden, Naughty, Unusual

Others said that casual sex crossed boundaries such as sex with a friend, sex in public, or sex in a van. It was the perceived deviousness which made the encounter exciting.

Ego Boost

Some men thought of casual sex as an ego boost, that they were able "to take a woman down." One respondent said, ". . . I scored this cheerleader from Alabama University or something."

Some women had a similar ego experience in that they were able to get a "really good looking, really popular guy" to take them home for sex. The meaning was in the conquest.

Awkward and Tricky

Feeling anxious, awkward, and uncomfortable are terms used by some to describe their casual sex experience. "Not awkward, awkward . . . but it becomes better if you know someone over a period of time." The difficulty of negotiating the sex and the morning after were sometimes uncomfortable.

Casual Sex as Deficient

Women respondents often talked of the downside of casual sex—quick, unemotional, drunken. ". . . there's just nothing there." Some men had a similar experience, comparing casual sex to meeting a need like eating to reduce hunger . . . nor fulfilling. "In some ways it's actually nice to even just spend close comfortable time with someone you really care about than to have sex with someone you don't . . ."

Summary

The researchers summarized the reactions to casual sex by saying that the participants identified both positives and negatives but "ultimately claimed a preference for relationship sex as more pleasurable, more meaningful, and better than casual sex" (p. 86). ●

Source: Adapted and abridged from Farvid P., & Braun, V. (2017). Unpacking the "pleasures" and "pains" of heterosexual casual sex: Beyond singular understandings. *The Journal of Sex Research, 54*(1), 73-90.

Refer to the Self-Assessment: The Conservative-Liberal Sexuality Scale on page 387 to identify the degree to which you are conservative or liberal in your attitudes toward sexuality.

Hedonism

Hedonism is the belief that the ultimate value and motivation for human actions lie in the pursuit of pleasure and the avoidance of pain. Of 2,978 undergraduate men, 32% reported being hedonistic; of 9,631 undergraduate women, 23% reported being hedonistic (Hall & Knox, 2019). Men, compared to women, report higher sexual desire (Dosch et al., 2016).

Hedonism is often associated with casual sex or hooking up. As discussed in Chapter 4, hooking up is defined as a sexual encounter that occurs between individuals who have no relationship commitment. Bersamin et al. (2014) analyzed data on single, heterosexual college students (N = 3,907) ages 18 to 25 from 30 institutions across the United States. A greater proportion of men—18.6%—compared to 7.4% of women reported having had casual sex in the month prior to the study.

The researchers also found that casual sex was negatively associated with psychological well-being, which is defined in reference to high self-esteem, life satisfaction, and eudaemonic well-being—having found oneself. Casual sex has also been linked to psychological distress—for examples, anxiety, depression, suicide ideation, and depressive symptoms (Sandberg-Thoma, 2014). Fielder et al. (2014) studied hookups in first-year college women and found an association with experiencing depression, sexual victimization, and STIs. These data reflect that casual sex is negatively associated with one's mental health, physical health like STIs and life satisfaction. The Applying Social Research insert reviews the positive and negative aspects of hedonism.

SEX AND GENDER

Sexual expression is different for both women and men. In the following sections, we discuss which factors contribute to these differences.

Sexual Double Standard

The **sexual double standard** is the view that encourages and accepts sexual expression of men more than women. Men can be promiscuous and have more sexual partners than women (Guo, 2019; Sohn, 2016). Table 9.1 reveals that men are almost two times more hedonistic than women (Hall & Knox, 2018). Acceptance of the double standard is evident in the words used to describe hedonism—hedonistic men are labeled as "studs," but hedonistic women as "sluts."

Indeed, Porter (2014) emphasized the double standard in her presentation on "slut-shaming" which she defined as "the act of making one feel guilty or inferior for engaging in certain sexual behaviors that violate traditional dichotomous gender roles." Porter surveyed 240 undergraduates and found that 81% of the females reported having been slut-shamed in contrast to 7% of the males. Fulle et al. (2016) reported that hedonistic females develop various strategies to mitigate their exposure to disapproval and stigma—detach from religion, withhold information about their sexual behavior from significant others, and reducing their expectations of a future relationship developing from a "hookup" encounter.

....

Sexual double standard: the view that encourages and accepts the sexual expression of men more than women.

The double standard is also reflective of the gendered sexual scripting of female sexual behavior. Fahs (2016) noted that women give the "gift" of virginity and "direct attention away from their own needs and prioritize their partners' resulting in gendered inequalities such as faking orgasm, giving in to unwanted sex, sexual assault, tolerating sexual pain, and prioritization of their partner's pleasure over their own." Jones (2016) also revealed that the double standard is evident in regard to the sexual past of a man or woman, respectively. Whereas a man's sexual promiscuity in the past may be "forgiven" particularly if he decides to commit to monogamy, a woman's sexual past may haunt her in that her "reputation" is damaged.

Themes in Women Making Sexual Decisions

Two researchers (Cooper & Gordon, 2015) studied the sexual decision-making (SDM) of a group of women who had previously participated in casual sex without a condom. In interviews with eleven women, four major themes of sexual decision-making emerged. (No comparable study exploring decision making in men was found to make a comparison).

The first theme was "the importance of being in a relationship."

I have sex with someone to date them . . . and hope they will call again . . . the idea that you're having casual sex with a guy . . . and then it will turn into a relationship . . . a lot of girls see it as a way into a relationship with someone.

Research by Sassler et al. (2016) revealed that 12 months after a sexual relationship began, less than a quarter, about 23%, of the individuals were still with the partner. Hence, the most likely outcome of having sex in a new relationship is that it will not last.

A second theme of sexual decision-making was the influence of alcohol.

. . . it loosens you up, and your inhibitions run wild . . . you're freer . . . more confident and flirt a bit more . . . you sort of think you can do anything when you're drunk, there's no consequences.

Research on threesomes and anal sex reveal that both behaviors were associated with the use of alcohol (Morris et al., 2016; Molinares et al., 2017).

A third theme of decision-making about sex was the need to be seen as normal.

Like when all your friends are having sex you feel like you are missing out 'cause you are not doing it . . . it kind of felt ok to do it because everyone else was doing it.

A final theme of sexual decision-making was a feeling of powerlessness in negotiating condom use.

where if you say no to them they might not like you; or think oh if I say no, that's going to be the end of our night . . . and then they won't call me the next day, or whatever.

Trinh (2016) surveyed the sexual socialization of women by their female friends. Translation: what this means is what their girlfriends tell them about their sexual choices. Examples of what women tell other women includes:

You should enjoy being a female and not feel hindered by stereotypes and really enjoy your sexuality but do it in secret. Don't be outward with sexual promiscuity.

—A 21-year-old student, on what her female friends told her about sex and relationships:

If you aren't having sex within the first month, he is going to dump you. Guys like you based on how much you pleasure them.

PERSONAL CHOICES

Deciding to Have Intercourse With a New Partner

The following are issues to consider in making the decision to have sexual intercourse with a new partner:

1. **Personal consequences**. How do you predict you will feel after you have had intercourse with a new partner? An increasing percentage of college students are relativists and feel that the outcome will be positive if they are in a relationship; they may or may not be in love. The following quote is from a student in our classes:

"I believe intercourse is OK as long as the couple is in a relationship. Even that sounds loose since relationships vary in intimacy. But it's better than hooking up."

The effect intercourse will have on you will be influenced by your sexual values, your religious values, and your emotional involvement with the partner. Some individuals, primarily young and religious, prefer to wait until they are married to have intercourse and feel that this is the best course for future marital stability and happiness. Strong religious values against nonmarital intercourse may result in guilt and regret following an intercourse experience. Kim (2016) reported that a conservative

and religious context lends itself to a negative outcome like depression following first intercourse.

Galperin et al. (2013) confirmed higher sexual regret among women—they lamented that they had not been more selective. In contrast, men regretted that they failed to act on some sexual opportunities.

2. **Timing.** In a sample of over 5,000 unmarried singles, about a third or 28% reported that they had sex by the third date; almost half, about 46%, had done so by the sixth date (Walsh, 2013).

Delaying intercourse with a new partner was associated with achieving a positive outcome and avoiding regret. The table below reveals that a third of 429 undergraduates—regretted having sexual intercourse "too soon" in a relationship (Merrill & Knox, 2010).

Willoughby et al. (2014) confirmed the positive outcomes of delaying sex in a romantic relationship. The researchers analyzed data on a sample of 10,932 individuals in unmarried, romantic relationships and compared relationship outcomes from when sex was initiated—having sex prior to dating, having sex on the first date or shortly after, having sex

Regret for Engaging in Behavior "Too Soon" or "Too Late" (N = 429)

BEHAVIORS	"TOO SOON"	"TOO LATE"	"PERFECT TIMING"	"DID NOT DO"
Sexual Intercourse	33.3%	3.3%	48.4%	15.0%
Spent the night	26.6%	3.7%	58.8%	11.4%
Saying "I love you"	26.1%	3.9%	50.8%	19.2%
Kissing	11.1%	3.1%	82.8%	3.1%

(Continued)

(Continued)

after a few weeks of dating, and sexual abstinence. Results revealed that waiting to initiate sexual intimacy in unmarried relationships was associated with higher relationship satisfaction, more leisure time together, and greater emotional feelings. This effect was strongly moderated by relationship length, with individuals who reported early sexual initiation describing increasingly lower outcomes in relationships of longer than two years. Hence, the positive effects of delaying sex in a relationship continued over time.

3. **Partner consequences.** Because a basic moral principle is to do no harm to others, it is important to consider the effect of intercourse on the partner. Whereas intercourse may be a pleasurable experience with positive consequences for you, your partner may react differently. What is your partner's religious background, and what are your partner's sexual values? A highly religious person with absolutist sexual values will more likely experience guilt and regret, particularly if the relationship is casual, than a person with low religiosity and relativistic or hedonistic sexual values.

4. **Relationship consequences.** What is the effect of intercourse on a couple's relationship? The immediate reaction is positive in that 89% of 209 undergraduates reported "feeling closer" (Vasilenko et al., 2012). However, recall the research by Sassler et al. (2016) that 12 months after having sex in a new relationship less than one quarter or 23% of the couples were still together.

5. **Contraception.** Another potential consequence of intercourse is pregnancy. Discussion and decision on contraception use and unintended

pregnancy needs to take place prior to intercourse. Both partners are equally responsible for contraception usage, not just the woman. Since each contraception method yields different levels of risk, it is still possible to become pregnant while using contraception. Therefore, a separate discussion must be made as to whether intercourse should result in pregnancy. And if pregnancy occurs, what are the respective feelings about the outcome: abortion, have the baby, and so forth?

6. **HIV and other sexually transmissible infections.** Engaging in casual sex has potentially fatal consequences. Avoiding HIV infection and other STIs is an important consideration in deciding whether to have intercourse in a new relationship, as well as what contraception you use. The increase in the number of people having more partners results in the rapid spread of the bacteria and viruses responsible for numerous varieties of STIs. However, in a sample of 12,516 undergraduates, exactly half reported using a condom in their last sexual intercourse experience (Hall & Knox, 2019).

7. **Influence of alcohol and other drugs.** A final consideration with regard to the decision to have intercourse in a new relationship is to be aware of the influence of alcohol and other drugs on such a decision. Bersamin et al. (2014) confirmed that the amount of alcohol consumed by undergraduates was associated with having sex with a stranger. Persons who are impaired by alcohol are not capable of consent and the person who has sex with someone who is impaired is raping that person. In addition, consent is ongoing and needs to be communicated each time. ●

SEXUAL BEHAVIORS

We have been discussing the issues to consider before first intercourse with a new partner. We now focus on what people report that they do sexually which is often different from what is perceived as occurring. Anders et al. (2016) gave examples of **pluralistic ignorance**—overestimating acceptance and prevalence of behaviors. For example, in a sample of 1,622 undergraduates, 57% estimated that their peers engaged in vaginal sex during a hookup, but only

37% had actually done so. Perceiving peers as more accepting of hooking up is associated with being more likely to engage in hookup behaviors oneself.

Similarly, people often have misconceptions about the number of sexual partners a person has had. The reality of someone's sexual experience may be quite different. For example, Rossi et al. (2017) identified the number of sexual partners from ages 16-22 of 332 participants and found four patterns: 9.1% percent fell into the abstainers group, 30.6% were in the low-increasing group, 53.0% in the medium-increasing, and 7.3% were in the multiple-partners group. Only in the latter group did the number of partners exceed five. Hence, they were more likely to abstain from sex than have five or more partners.

Pluralistic ignorance: overestimating acceptance and prevalence of behaviors.

There may be several reasons for people not engaging in sexual activity. Some individuals are **asexual,** which means there is an absence of arousal or interest in having sex with a partner. As noted in Chapter 7, asexuality may be regarded as a sexual orientation. Just as asexuality individuals may be emotionally attracted to the other or same sex, they may be emotionally attracted to neither. Between eight and 10% of individuals self-identify as asexual. Asexuals report that finding a partner is difficult. One woman said of partners she "matched" with on Tinder that "As soon as I tell them I am asexual, they disappear." It's important to note that asexuality is different from celibacy and abstinence. Celibacy and abstinence reflect an individual's deliberate decisions and should not be confused with asexuality, which is a sexual orientation.

What Is Sex?

Definitions of sexual behavior vary with most agreement that vaginal—5.9 on a 6-point scale—and anal—5.6 on a 6-point scale—intercourse constitute "having had sex" but less agreement, 3.8, on whether oral sex is defined as "having sex." These data are from an analysis of three hundred 18- to 30-year-old respondents (Horowitz & Bedford, 2017). Ratings of heterosexual males and females did not differ significantly, but gay individuals were more likely than heterosexuals to rate various forms of genital stimulation as "having sex." These contrasting views of sex are reflected in one's views of virginity and virginity loss, as discussed earlier.

Kissing

Kissing has been the subject of literature and science. The meanings of a kiss are variable—love, approval, hello, goodbye, or as a remedy for a child's hurt knee. There is also a kiss for luck, a stolen kiss, and a kiss to seal one's marriage vows. Kisses have been used to denote hierarchy. In the Middle Ages, only peers kissed on the lips; a person of lower status kissed someone of higher status on the hand, and a person of lower status showed great differential of status by kissing on the foot. Kissing also has had a negative connotation as in the "kiss of death," which reflects the kiss Judas gave Jesus as he was about to betray him. Kissing may be considered an aggressive act as some do not want to be kissed.

Although the origin of kissing is unknown, one theory posits that kissing is associated with parents putting food into their offspring's mouth . . . the bird pushes food down the throat of a chick in the

The meaning of a kiss is variable—a hello, a goodbye, "I love you," and so forth.
Courtesy of Chelsea Curry

nest. Some adult birds also exchange food by mouth during courtship.

The way a person kisses reflects the person's country, culture, and society. French people kiss each other once on each cheek or three times in the same region. Greeks tend to kiss on the mouth, regardless of the sex of the person. Anthropologists note that some cultures, such as Eskimos and Polynesians, promote meeting someone by rubbing noses.

Masturbation

Masturbation involves stimulating one's own body with the goal of experiencing pleasurable sexual sensations. Ninety-seven percent of 2,992 undergraduate males and 72% of 9,830 undergraduate females reported ever having masturbated (Hall & Knox, 2019). These findings reflect how male masturbation is normalized, while female masturbation is not. Until recently, female masturbation has been stigmatized.

There is also a discrepancy in the frequency of male and female masturbation. Based on a survey of American adults ages 18-64 of 7,648 men and 8,090 women, 61% of the men and 35% of the women reported having masturbated in the past two weeks. In addition to being male, not having a partner, being White, and being college educated were associated with higher rates of masturbation. Men tended to masturbate more out of compensation if partner sex was not occurring; women tended to masturbate to ensure clitoral stimulation/orgasm.

Alternative terms for masturbation include *auto-eroticism, self-pleasuring, solo sex,* and *sex without a partner*. An appreciation of the benefits of masturbation has now replaced various myths about it—for example, it causes blindness. Most health care providers and therapists today regard masturbation as a normal and healthy sexual behavior. Masturbation

Asexual: the absence of desire to engage in sexual behavior with another.

Masturbation: stimulating one's own genitals with the goal of experiencing sexual pleasure.

is safe sex in that it involves no risk of transmitting diseases such as HIV or pregnancy.

Masturbation is also associated with orgasm during intercourse. In a study by Thomsen and Chang (2000), 292 university undergraduates reported whether they had ever masturbated and whether they had an orgasm during their first intercourse experience. The researchers found that the strongest single predictor of orgasm and emotional satisfaction with first intercourse was previous masturbation. Suschinsky and Chivers (2018) reported that masturbation continues to be the way most women report experiencing an orgasm. The reason is that the clitoris receives direct stimulation during masturbation, not via sexual intercourse.

Oral Sex

Fellatio is oral stimulation of the man's genitals by his partner. Cunnilingus is oral stimulation of the woman's genitals by her partner. Wood et al. (2016) found that over two-thirds of 899 male and female university students reported that their last sexual encounter included giving or receiving oral sex or both. About 73% of men and about 69% of women reported that receiving oral sex was "very pleasurable." However, men were significantly more likely than women to report that giving oral sex was very pleasurable with 52% of men saying so compared with 28% of women reporting that feeling of enjoyment. Overall, ratings of pleasure for giving oral sex were higher for men, but no gender differences were found for overall pleasure ratings of receiving oral sex.

Vaginal Intercourse

Vaginal intercourse, or **coitus**, refers to the sexual union of a man and woman by insertion of the penis into the vagina. Brenot & Wunsch (2016) assessed the sexual needs of 5,000 heterosexual men and women and found that men reported needing a higher sexual frequency than women and a partner who was more active, erotic, faithful, and understanding. In contrast, women reported needing a partner who was gentle, caring, and attentive to the relationship conditions in which love-making occurs.

Anal Intercourse

Molinares et al. (2016) analyzed data from a survey on anal sex completed by 205 undergraduates, primarily heterosexual females. Analysis revealed that 37% of the respondents had experienced anal sex, with over

three fourths, about 78%, reporting that their partner had brought up the idea. Of the respondents, 32% said the primary reason for having anal sex was "to please the partner" with 26% identifying curiosity as another motive and 11% saying it was "to spice things up."

> *Among men, sex sometimes results in intimacy; among women, intimacy sometimes results in sex.*
>
> Barbara Cartland, English romance novelist

Sexual Readiness and Sexual Competence

Individuals engaging in any sexual activity—whether their first time or not—need to be coherent and able to give consent. In addition, the consent must be clear, ongoing, and voluntary without manipulation or coercion. Consent is tied to the concept of **sexual readiness**, which is also determined by contraception, autonomy of decision that is not influenced by alcohol or peer pressure, and the absence of regret where the individual feels it is the "right" time. Hawes et al. (2010) studied first intercourse experiences in the United Kingdom and emphasized that sexual readiness, not age, was the more meaningful criteria. Using these criteria, the negative consequences of first intercourse are more likely to be minimized.

A related term to sexual readiness is **sexual competence** with four criteria: use of contraception, autonomy of decision, equally willing, and the "right time" (Palmer et al., 2017). Individuals not displaying sexual competence at first heterosexual intercourse were more likely to report having HPV, low sexual function in the last year, an unplanned pregnancy, and nonvolitional sex. Soller et al. (2017) noted that sexual intercourse in adolescence has negative consequences if the relationship context is inauthentic—deceptive, exploitative, abusive—but it can be positive if committed, romantic, and consensual.

What if one or both people has an intellectual disability? Should the consent or decision involve their parents or guardians? People with intellectual disabilities may not be able to comprehend the complexities of sexual decisions and are more vulnerable to mistreatment. Tailored sexuality education has been found to be effective in enhancing an understanding and decision-making for people with intellectual disabilities (Duke & McGuire, 2009).

Fellatio: oral stimulation of the male genitalia.

Coitus: the sexual union of a man and woman by insertion of the penis into the vagina.

Sexual readiness: factors such as autonomy of decision where one is not influenced by alcohol or peers; consensuality where both partners are equally willing; and absence of regret, or figuring out the right time to have first intercourse.

Sexual competence: characterized by contraception, autonomy of decision, equally willing, and the "right time".

Cybersex

Cybersex is any consensual sexual experience mediated by a computer that involves at least two people. In this context, sexual experience includes sending text messages or photographic images that are sexual. Individuals typically send sexts and photos with the goal of arousal or looking at each other naked or masturbating when viewing each other on a web cam.

Cybersex may occur with one's partner, a known non-partner, or a stranger. Courtice and Shaughnessy (2018) studied cybersex among sexual minority women and men, and noted that more women engage in cybersex with a primary partner compared to men, and that more men than women report cybersex outside a committed-partner context and engage in it more frequently. Cybersex is also used by a couple in a long-distance relationship to keep the sexual aspect of their relationship alive.

SEXUALITY IN RELATIONSHIPS

The frequency of sex reported by American adults reached an all-time low in 2018. The percentage of Americans having sex at least once a week declined from 51% in 1996 to 39% (2018). Almost a quarter or 23% of those between the ages of 18 and 29 report having no sex in the past year. Explanations include stress over jobs or lack of one and relentless playing of video games which can consume an entire evening (Ingraham, 2019). Individuals are also staying longer in their parents' home.

Sexuality occurs in a social context that influences its frequency and perceived quality. First, we look at sexual tempo and outcomes.

Sexual Tempo, Relationship Quality, Cohabitation, and Marriage

Sexual tempo is the number of months between the start of a relationship and when the couple first have sex. Bartholomew et al. (2015) examined data on 12,105 adolescents and found that early sex in the relationship was not associated with subsequent relationship quality. However, early sex was related to an increased chance that the couple would live together while delayed sex was related to an increased chance of marriage. Persons most likely to have early sex in a relationship were Black, male, older, from a single parent household, those who had parents with less

than a college education, and those who first had sex at a young age. They also experienced a difference in age between the sex partners and reported having had more sexual partners.

Sexual Relationships Among Never-Married Individuals

Unmarried individuals, when compared with married individuals and cohabitants, reported the lowest level of sexual satisfaction. One-third of a national sample of people who were not married and not living with anyone reported that they were emotionally satisfied with their sexual relationships. In contrast, 85% of the married and pair-bonded individuals reported emotional satisfaction in their sexual relationships. Hence, although never-married individuals have more sexual partners, they are less emotionally satisfied (Michael et al., 1994).

Sexual Relationships Among Married Individuals

Marital sex is distinctive for its social legitimacy, declining frequency, and satisfaction, both physical and emotional.

1. **Social legitimacy**. In our society, marital heterosexual intercourse is the most legitimate form of sexual behavior. Those who engage in homosexual, premarital, and extramarital intercourse do not experience as high a level of social approval as do those who engage in marital heterosexual sex. It is not only okay to have intercourse when married, it is expected. People assume that married couples make love and that something is wrong if they do not.

2. **Declining frequency**. Sexual intercourse between spouses declines across time from five times a week in early marriage to once a year in one's nineties. Pregnancy and childcare also decreases the frequency of sexual intercourse. In addition to biological changes due to aging and pregnancy, satiation also contributes to the declining frequency of intercourse between spouses and partners in long-term relationships. Psychologists use the term **satiation** to mean that repeated exposure to a stimulus results in the loss of its ability to reinforce. For example, the first time you listen to a new song, you derive considerable enjoyment and satisfaction from it. You may listen to it over and over during the first few days. After a week or so, listening to the same

....

Cybersex: consensual, computer-mediated, participatory sexual experience involving two or more individuals.

Sexual tempo: the number of months between the start of a relationship and when the couple first have sex.

Satiation: a stimulus loses its value with repeated exposure (e.g., lovers tire of each other if around each other all the time).

music is no longer new and does not give you the same level of enjoyment that it first did. So, it is with intercourse between spouses or long-term partners. The thousandth time that a person has sex with the same partner is not as new and exciting as the first few times.

However, as we will note below, while frequency decreases, quality increases. Married couples consistently report higher emotional and sexual satisfaction than persons in new sexual relationships. Love, respect, security, practice—learning what each other likes—and comfort with each other are all involved in higher quality sex among long term partners.

Polyamorists use the term **new relationship energy** (NRE) to refer to the euphoria of a new emotional and sexual relationship which dissipates over time. Polyamorists often talk with a long-term partner about the NRE they are feeling and both watch its eventual decline. Hence, polyamorists don't get upset when they see their partner experiencing NRE with a new partner since they view it as having a cycle that will not last forever (Starr, 2018).

3. **Satisfaction (emotional and physical).** Despite declining frequency and less satisfaction over time, marital sex remains a richly satisfying experience. Contrary to the popular belief that unattached singles have the best sex, married and pair-bonded adults enjoy the most satisfying sexual relationships. In the national sample referred to earlier, 88% of married people said they received great physical pleasure from their sexual lives, and almost 85% said they received great emotional satisfaction (Michael et al., 1994). Individuals least likely to report being physically and emotionally pleased in their sexual relationships are those who are not married, not living with anyone, or not in a stable relationship with one person. The higher reported satisfaction is not related to a high frequency of sexual intercourse. Muise et al. (2015) noted that once a week—the norm for most couples in long term relationships—not less or more, is associated with reported satisfaction. Hence, more is not better.

SEXUAL HISTORY AND MARRIAGE SATISFACTION

While marriage satisfaction is influenced by quality and frequency of sexual relationships, it is also linked to one's sexual history. Wolfinger (2018) confirmed

that virgins who marry have the lowest divorce rate. Beyond that finding, having multiple or a few sexual partners does not seem to make a significant difference in the divorce rate. But what about the impact of one's sexual history on marital satisfaction? Analysis of national data revealed that for both women and men the fewer the sexual partners, the more likely the person is to report being very happily married. This finding was true more for men than women. For example, for women who had one sexual partner, 63% reported being very happily married; for men, 71% reported being very happily married. For women reporting having had six to 10 partners, 59% reported being very happily married; men, 63%. One explanation is that having had a lot of sexual partners provides the ability to compare partners, so if there were those with whom sex was particularly good are used as the benchmark for subsequent comparisons, unhappiness may result.

Sexual Relationships Among Divorced Individuals

Of the over 800,000 getting divorced every year, most will have intercourse within one year of being separated from their spouses. Indeed, Morrissey Stahl et al. (2018) interviewed women following their divorce and found divorce empowering for them in both exploration and satisfaction. But the meanings of intercourse for separated or divorced individuals will vary. For many, intercourse is a way to reestablish—indeed, repair—their crippled self-esteem. Questions such as, "Am I a failure?" and "Is there anybody out there who will love me again?" loom in the minds of divorced people. One way to feel loved, at least temporarily, is through sex. Being held by another and being told that it feels good often provides the experience that one feels desirable. Because divorced people may be particularly vulnerable, they may reach for sexual encounters as if for a lifeboat. "I felt that, as long as someone was having sex with me, I wasn't dead and I did matter," said one recently divorced person.

Because divorced individuals are usually in their mid-30s or older, they may not be as sensitized to the danger of contracting HIV as are those in their 20s. Divorced individuals should always use a condom to lessen the risk of an STI, including HIV infection and AIDS.

Friends With Benefits

"Friends with benefits" has become part of the relational sexual landscape. A **friends-with-benefits** relationship is one in which the friends

New relationship energy (NRE): the euphoria of a new emotional/sexual relationship which dissipates over time.

Friends with benefits: platonic friends who engage in some degree of sexual intimacy on multiple occasions.

"Netflix and chill" may be a standard agenda for people in a friends-with-benefits' relationship.
Courtesy of Chelsea Curry

do not have a romantic relationship but who get together regularly for sex. Stein et al. (2019) emphasized that the motivation for involvement in a friends-with-benefits relationship is sex with men focused more on the sex and with women on the relationship aspects. This sexual activity could range from kissing to sexual intercourse and is a repeated part of a friendship, not just a one-night stand. Forty-nine percent of 3,007 undergraduate males reported that they had been in a FWB relationship compared with 43% of 9,902 undergraduate females (Hall & Knox, 2019). Jovanovich and Williams (2018) conducted a focus groups of women and men about involvement in a friends-with-benefits relationship and found several themes: empowerment in which the woman, like the man, was free to have sex, control—for example, the woman could depart from traditional roles and initiate sex with the guy—and safety, such as with a comfortable friend, not a random hookup.

In addition to having a "safe" sexual partner—low STI exposure and partner, not an unpredictable hookup—other advantages of a friends-with-benefits relationship were having a predictably "good" sexual partner who knows one's likes and dislikes and not increasing one's number of sexual partners. Other advantages include having a regular sex partner, not being burdened with having to devote the time that an emotional relationship would require, and being free to date or find one's true love while still having one's sexual needs met.

Disadvantages include developing a bad reputation as someone who does not care about emotional involvement, coping with discrepancy in feelings of emotional attachment, and missing the combination of good sex, emotional intimacy, and secure future.

Concurrent Sexual Partnerships

Concurrent sexual partnerships are those in which the partners have sex with several individuals with whom they have a relationship. These are different from polyamorous relationships in that in the former, the partner may be unaware of other sexual relationships. Jolly et al. (2016) studied African-American relationships and found that men were more likely to engage in concurrent sexual relationships than women. They were also more likely to use a condom with casual than with stable partners.

Consensually Nonmonogamous Relationships

Consensensually nonmonogamous relationships are typically understood to be polyamorous relationships where individuals love/have sex with multiple people with the knowledge and consent of all individuals involved. The percent of adults in the U.S. involved in these relationships ranges from 5% to 20% (Kalata & Bermea, 2019). In a sample of undergraduates, 13% of 2,838 undergraduate males reported that they could be comfortable with their partner being emotionally and sexually involved with someone else; 7% of 9,242 undergraduate females agreed (Hall & Knox, 2019). Refer to the Self-Assessment: Consensual Non-monogamy Attitude Scale on page 388, which follow allows you to identify your attitudes toward these relationships.

Cohen (2016) studied 122 CNM (consensually nonmonogamous) partners in which the partners agreed that each could become involved with others outside the dyad. The greatest advantage was "to experience something new," to be "free," and to not be "tied down." Males were attracted by the opportunity to have sex with others; females were attracted by the notion of not being stuck in a relationship. The greatest disadvantage of CNM relationships was the stigma associated with the lifestyle, followed by problems in communication, jealousy, and trust. Based on a nationally representative sample of 2,003 Canadian adults, 4% of those currently in a relationship reported being in an open relationship. Relationship satisfaction did not differ significantly between monogamous and **open relationships** (Fairbrother et al., 2019).

Some consensually nonmonogamous relationships are polyamorous in which the partners agree

Concurrent sexual partnership: Relationship in which one partner has sex with several individuals concurrently—unbeknownst to the other partners.

Consensually non-monogamous relationships: polyamorous relationships where individuals love or have sex with multiple people with the knowledge and consent of all individuals involved.

Open relationship: relationship in which the partners agree that each may have emotional and sexual relationships with those outside the dyad.

to have emotional and sexual relationships with others (polyamory was discussed in detail in Chapter 2). Other couples have **swinging** relationships which are thought to be increasing (Kimberly, 2016) and where the focus is sex, not love, with others. Each partner may have sex with someone outside the relationship or they may go together and have sex with others at the same event or house. Some swinging individuals and couples often have rules, the following of which were developed by a former student swinging couple:

1. **Honesty**—we tell each other everything we do with someone outside the relationship. If we flirt, we even tell that. Openness about our feelings is a must—if we get uncomfortable or jealous, we must talk about it. [Not all couples are so open. Some agree to outside sex but agree not to talk about the details].

2. **Recreational sex**—sex with the other person will be purely recreational—it is not love and the relationship with the other person is going nowhere. The people we select to have sex with must know that we have a loving committed relationship with someone else.

3. **Condom**—a requirement every time.

4. **Approval**—every person we have sex with must be approved by the partner in advance. Each partner has the right to veto a selection. The person in question must not be into partner snatching, looking for romance, or jealous. Persons off the list are co-workers, family—he can't have sex with her sister or she, with his brother—old lovers, and old friends. [Again, other partners do not discuss other partners with the primary].

5. **Online hunting**—prohibited. Each agrees not to go looking on the Internet for sex partners.

Pornography

The impact of pornography on a relationship is contingent upon an individual's acceptance toward pornography. For example, pornography use is associated with less relationship satisfaction among women who have low acceptance of pornography (Maas et al., 2018).

Religious exposure also impacts the effect of pornography in that pornography use is associated with lower sexual satisfaction, but only among men who regularly attend religious services. For men who rarely attend religious services, the association essentially disappears (Perry & Whithead, 2019).

Perry and Schleifer (2018) found that beginning pornography use during marriage was associated with subsequent divorce. However, it is possible that there was a reverse causation such that a spouse, unhappy, may begin pornography, and it is the unhappiness that drives the pornography, not the pornography that drives the unhappiness associated with divorce. The effect of pornography use on relationships may depend on whether the partners watch together or alone. Kohut et al. (2018) identified pornography use as shared where both partners watch pornography together, concordant where both partners watch pornography independently or alone, or discordant where one watches and the other does not. Partners who shared pornography reported more open sexual communication and relationship closeness whereas partners who had discordant use reported both lower sexual communication and relationship closeness.

Gurevich et al. (2017) emphasized the positive educational and interpersonal functions of pornography. One of their respondents noted:

> *It can give ideas sometimes I guess . . .Stuff like when actual couples have actual sex . . . it can give you ideas for your own relationship . . . Mostly it's my boyfriend's idea because we have, kind of, the same taste and he'll bring it up and we will watch together.*

(Participant 44, 22 years old, Canadian, bisexual)

McKeown et al. (2018) noted the benefits of pornography for women include helping them to fulfill their sexual needs and exploring their sexual selves as well as connecting with sexual partners who may normalize their sexual desires.

BEING SEXUALLY SAFE

Being sexually safe includes having sex with low risk partners and using a condom. This means that a condom is needed for all interpersonal sexual activities—oral, vaginal, and anal. If the condom is used for anal sex, another condom needs to be used if oral or vaginal sex is involved. Anal sex is associated with the highest risk for HIV.

Wright et al. (2012) reviewed the concept of **condom assertiveness**—the clear message that sex without a condom is unacceptable—and identified the characteristics of undergraduate women who are more likely to insist on condom use. These women have more faith in the effectiveness of condoms,

---

Swinging: individuals in a committed relationship agree to have recreational sex with other individuals, independently or as a couple.

Condom assertiveness: the unambiguous messaging that sex without a condom is unacceptable.

believe more in their own condom communication skills, perceive that they are more susceptible to STIs, believe there are more relational benefits to being condom assertive, believe their peers are more condom assertive, and intend to be more condom assertive (Peasant et al., 2014). A problem with condom assertiveness is the false sense of security that insisting on a condom may involve. **Stealthing** is the nonconsensual condom removal during sexual intercourse which exposes victims to physical risks of pregnancy and disease and many considered it to be a form of sexual assault (Brodsky, 2017)

Condom assertiveness is important not only for sexual and anal intercourse but also for oral sex. Not to use a condom or dental dam is to increase the risk of contracting a sexually transmitted infection (STI). Indeed, individuals think "I am on the pill and won't get pregnant" or "No way I am getting pregnant by having oral sex" only to discover HPV or another STI in their mouth or throat.

Also known as sexually transmitted disease, or STD, **STI** refers to the general category of sexually transmitted infections such as chlamydia, genital herpes, gonorrhea, and syphilis. The most lethal of all STIs is that caused by the human immunodeficiency virus (HIV), which attacks the immune system and can lead to autoimmune deficiency syndrome (AIDS). Persons potentially exposed to HIV should use **PEP (post-exposure prophylaxis)** which means taking antiretroviral medicines (ART) within 72 hours after exposure to prevent becoming infected. PEP should be used only in emergency situations and must be started within 72 hours after suspected exposure.

Individuals who have an STI sometimes struggle with how to alert a potential sexual partner to their STI. See the Personal Choices box on disclosing an STI.

Stealthing: nonconsensual condom removal during sexual intercourse which exposes victims to physical risks of pregnancy and disease.

STI (sexually transmitted infection): refers to the general category of sexually transmitted infections such as chlamydia, genital herpes, gonorrhea, and syphilis.

PEP (post-exposure prophylaxis): taking antiretroviral medicines (ART) within 72 hours after suspected exposure to HIV to prevent becoming infected.

Script for Disclosing One's STI

Individuals who have a sexually transmitted infection may choose to disclose this to a potential sexual partner in a developing relationship. A suggested script follows.

I have something to say and I want you to wait and hear all of the information before reacting. This is difficult for me to talk about and I know this is going to sound and feel scary for you. The reason I want to talk to you about this is because I like you, care about you, and want to be honest with you. I have (insert STI). I have spoken to doctors, therapists, nurses (insert desired professionals), and feel confident in my ability to keep it under control and keep you from contracting it. I feel very aware of when I am having a flare or outbreak and know how to stop it. (Insert detailed information about pertinent treatments and safe sex practices pertinent to one's specific STI.) I want us to be able to have a continued open dialogue about concerns as they arise.

The disclosing person might want to include sharing how he or she contracted the STI. In addition, the disclosing person might want to anticipate shock, and initial fear from his or her partner until he or she hears the facts and learns more information from professionals or doing his or her own Internet research. In this regard, the disclosing person should set aside a few hours to reveal having an STI. The script may be short, but it takes a long time to process the emotions and questions. Finally, the disclosing person might want to include an "escape clause" to the disclosure script (see below).

I know my telling you this can be unsettling. It unnerves me at times. I need for you to know that if this is too much for you and you need for us to stop seeing each other, I completely understand. I definitely want us to manage this together so that we can continue, but I want you to be completely free to say this is more than you bargained for.

Appreciation to colleagues Adrienne Alden and Samantha Scuderi, Marriage and Family Therapists, in Raleigh, NC, for this script which they use with their clients who have an STI. ●

The Illusion of Safety in a "Monogamous" Relationship

Most individuals in a serious "monogamous" relationship assume that their partner is faithful and that they are at zero risk for contracting an STI. In a study of 373 heterosexual college students and 282 gay men, over one third of those in self-defined monogamous relationships reported infidelity in their current relationship (Swan & Thompson, 2016). These data suggest that individuals, even in committed monogamous relationships, cannot count on their partner being faithful, that they themselves are not immune to being unfaithful, and that they are always at risk for contracting an STI.

SEXUAL FULFILLMENT: SOME PREREQUISITES

There are several prerequisites for having a good sexual relationship.

Self-Knowledge, Body Image, and Health

Sexual fulfillment involves knowledge about yourself and your body. Such information not only makes it easier for you to experience pleasure but also allows you to give accurate information to a partner about pleasing you. It is not possible to teach a partner what you don't know about yourself. Most sexuality education at public schools, if any, is abstinence based and focuses on the reproductive mechanism and disease prevention. Very little is taught about pleasure, relationships, sexual negotiation, and sexual well-being. One must actively seek and learn about sexuality from reputable and reliable sources such as taking the course in which you are currently enrolled.

Sexual fulfillment also implies having a positive body image. To the degree that you have positive feelings about your body, you will regard yourself as a person someone else would enjoy touching, being close to, and making love with. If you do not like yourself or your body, you might wonder why anyone else would. Woertman and Van den Brink (2012) found sexual arousal, initiating sex, sexual satisfaction, and orgasm related to a positive body image in women.

Effective sexual functioning also requires good physical and mental health. This means regular exercise, good nutrition, adequate sleep, and regular health checkups. Performing well in all areas of life may continue reasonably well into old age, contingent on individuals taking care of themselves physically.

Good health also implies being aware that some drugs may interfere with sexual performance. Alcohol is the drug most frequently used by American adults, including college students. Although a moderate amount of alcohol can help a person become aroused through a lowering of inhibitions, too much alcohol can slow the physiological processes and deaden the senses. Shakespeare may have said it best: "It [alcohol] provokes the desire, but it takes away the performance" (*Macbeth*, act 2, scene 3). The result of an excessive intake of alcohol for women is a reduced chance of orgasm; for men, overindulgence results in a reduced chance of attaining an erection.

Regarding marijuana, also called cannabis, Moser (2019) analyzed data from a survey completed by 811 social media respondents who revealed that cannabis use for them was associated with both enhanced sexual functioning and satisfaction. Age and gender were not found to have significant effects on cannabis use, sexual functioning, and satisfaction. Participants reported increased desire, orgasm intensity, and masturbation pleasure. Results indicated that taste and touch were also enhanced when using cannabis.

> *Remember that sex is not out there, but in here, in the deepest layer of your being. There is not only a morning after—there are lots of days and years afterwards.*
>
> Jacob Heusner, Words of Wisdom

A Committed Loving Relationship

A guideline among therapists who work with couples who have sexual problems is to treat the relationship before focusing on the sexual issue. The sexual relationship is part of the larger relationship between the partners, and what happens outside the bedroom in day-to-day interaction has a tremendous influence on what happens inside the bedroom. Indeed, love and relationship satisfaction are associated with sexual satisfaction (Mark et al., 2016). The statement, "I can't fight with you all day and want to have sex with you at night," illustrates the social context of the sexual experience. And, just as a good relationship is the context for good sex, it is also true that a good sexual relationship is associated with a thriving romantic relationship. Muise et al. (2018) confirmed that good sex was more conducive to romance than adequate income or shared interests.

In the chapter on love, we reviewed the concept of alexithymia or the inability to experience and express emotion. Scimeca et al. (2013) studied a sample of 300 university students who revealed that higher alexithymia scores were associated with lower levels of sexual satisfaction and higher levels of sexual detachment for females, and with sexual shyness and sexual nervousness for both genders. Conversely, being able to experience and express emotion has positive outcomes for one's sexual relationship.

In the interest of sexual equality, sex should be called clitoral stimulation and intercourse should be called afterplay.
Laurie Mintz, sex educator

Approach Rather Than Avoidance Goals for Sex

The motivations or goals one has for sex has an effect on the outcome. Pursuing sex with a partner for one's own sexual pleasure, for the partner's sexual pleasure, or to increase relationship intimacy—known as approach goals—rather than to avoid the partner's disapproval—called an avoidant goal—are associated with greater sexual and relationship quality and higher sexual desire (Muise et al., 2017a).

An Equal Relationship

Carlson and Soller (2019) examined data on 2,018 individuals from 1,009 heterosexual—413 married, 261 cohabiting, and 335 dating—couples and found that women's sexual equality attitudes were positively associated with couples' sexual frequency, suggesting that women who perceive that women should be as active as male partners in scripting sexual behavior have sex more often. Hence, the shared empowerment of both women and men escalate the sex frequency of a couple.

Open Sexual Communication and Feedback

Sexually fulfilled partners are comfortable expressing what they enjoy and do not enjoy in the sexual experience. Unless both partners communicate their needs, preferences, and expectations to each other, neither is ever sure what the other wants. In essence, the Golden Rule—"Do unto others as you would have them do unto you"—is *not* helpful, because what you like may not be the same as what your partner wants.

Sexually fulfilled partners take the guesswork out of their relationship by communicating preferences and giving feedback. Women may be less assertive about what they want sexually than men, particularly when they want oral sex. In a study of 237 sexually active women, the researchers observed that if they perceived that their partners would not be open to giving them oral sex, they were less likely to ask them to do so (Satinsky & Jozkowski, 2015). However, more recent research revealed that women who identify as feminists or endorse feminists' beliefs are more likely to be open about their sexual needs and to be less likely to fake orgasm since their sexual needs are being met (Hilliard et al., 2019). This means that women should be clear that receiving clitoral stimulation is important for their experiencing an orgasm.

Sexual communication training is available online. Rosier and Tyler (2017) analyzed data on 40 couples who participated in an online sexual training program called Love Guru Program and reported a decrease in apprehension in talking about sex, an increase in sexual knowledge and skill, and an increase in sexual and relationship satisfaction.

Communication About Differences in Sexual Interests

For most couples, sex is an important part of their relationship, particularly in new relationships. However, individuals vary in their interest in, capacity for, and preference for sexual behaviors over time. Although some individuals need sex daily, are orgasmic, and enjoy a range of sexual behaviors, others never think of sex, never have an orgasm, and want to get any sexual behavior over with as soon as possible. When two people of widely divergent views on sex end up in the same relationship, clear communication, and choices are necessary. The person who has no interest must decide if developing an interest is a goal and be open to learning about masturbation and sexual fantasy. If becoming interested in sex is not a goal, the partner will decide the degree to which this is an issue. Some will be pleased that the partner has no interest because it means no sexual demands, whereas others will bolt. Openness about one's sexual feelings, preferences, and expectations will help resolve the dilemma.

Hypersexuality may impact a relationship. Hypersexuality, also known as hyperphilia, and compulsive sexual disorder, may become a problem for the partner through its expression of being driven to and feeling a loss of control by spending hours viewing pornography, having cybersex, visiting strip clubs, having affairs, and so forth. Such loss of control suggests the wisdom of consulting a counselor since choices are being made that will be damaging to one's relationship.

Having Realistic Expectations

To achieve sexual fulfillment, expectations must be realistic. A couple's sexual needs, preferences, and expectations may not coincide. It is unrealistic to assume that your partner will want to have sex with the same frequency and in the same way that you do on all occasions. It may also be unrealistic to expect the level of sexual interest and frequency of sexual interaction to remain consistently high in long-term relationships.

Sexual Compliance

Given that partners may differ in sexual interest and desire, Vannier and O'Sullivan (2010) identified the concept of **sexual compliance** whereby an individual willingly agrees to participate in sexual behavior without having the desire to do so. Sexual compliance is similar to consent in that one is agreeing to participate in sexual behavior. Typically, sexual compliance occurs in the context of a relationship, meaning that there is a history of sexual activity with that partner. Quinn-Nilas and Kennett (2018) noted that "upwards of 60% of young women report compliant sexual behaviors when unwanted sexual advances are conceptualized broadly to include unwanted dancing, kissing, petting, oral sex, and vaginal intercourse not involving coercion." In the Vannier and O'Sullivan (2010) research sexual compliance was a strategy these individuals used in their committed relationships to cope with different levels of sexual desire. Sexual desire can fluctuate due to health, stress, and circumstances.

There were no gender differences in sexual desire and no gender differences in providing sexual compliant behavior. The majority of participants reported enjoying the sexual activity despite not wanting to engage in it at first. A technique used by couple and sex therapists to treat discrepant sex desires is the "15-minute rule" whereby the person who is less interested in sex agrees, that for 15 minutes, the partner who is more interested in sex can try to get the less interested partner in the mood. What often happens is that once the partner with less interest begins to participate in low levels of intimacy with sexual behavior such as kissing, the desire for more sex occurs. In effect, one can "act one's self into a new way of feeling quicker than one can think one's self into a new way of acting." Another way of saying this is "begin the behavior and the feelings will follow." Braksmajer (2017) also noted that partners who were unable to have sex because of pain or disability often engaged in "sex care work" for their partners as a way of maintaining intimacy, keeping the sexual relationship going, and so forth.

However, Muise et al. (2017b) emphasized that it is equally important to legitimize one partner not being in the mood as well as the partner who wants sex. Indeed, greater sexual satisfaction and relationship quality were associated, particularly for young mothers, when their partners recognized their need not to have sex.

Impact of Job Satisfaction on Sexual Health

Stulhofer et al. (2013) analyzed data on job satisfaction and sexual health among a sample of over 2,000 males and found that a negative mood resulting from job stress or unhappiness at work was associated with sexual difficulties. Having low job stress, high income, and emotional intimacy with one's partner were also associated with sexual health.

Avoiding Spectatoring

One of the obstacles to sexual functioning is **spectatoring**, which involves mentally observing your sexual performance and that of your partner. When researchers observed how individuals actually behave during sexual intercourse, they reported a tendency for sexually dysfunctional partners to act as spectators by mentally observing their own and their partners' sexual performance. For example, the man would focus on whether he was having an erection, how complete it was, and whether it would last. He might also watch to see whether his partner was having an orgasm (Masters & Johnson, 1970). Just focusing on one's own body can have an effect.

Spectatoring, as Masters and Johnson conceived it, interferes with each partner's sexual enjoyment because it creates anxiety about performance, and anxiety blocks performance. A man who worries about getting an erection reduces his chance of doing so. A woman who is anxious about achieving an orgasm probably will not. The desirable alternative to spectatoring is to relax, focus on and enjoy your own pleasure, and permit yourself to be sexually responsive.

CULTURE AND DIVERSITY

Sexual desire is influenced by various sociocultural factors such as religion, one's view on sexuality, and gender role expectations (Rosenkrantz & Mark, 2018).

Woo et al. (2012) compared Chinese women with European and Canadian women and found that the former reported higher sex guilt and lower sexual desire than the latter. The researchers identified the Confucian philosophy which views sex as positive as long as it is in reference to producing children to carry on the family line. Sex outside of marriage and sex for pleasure are discouraged.

Sexual compliance: an individual willingly agrees to participate in sexual behavior without having the desire to do so.

Spectatoring: involves mentally observing your sexual performance and that of your partner.

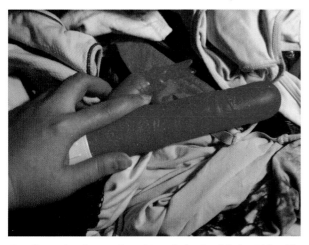

The vibrator has been referred to as being "a girl's best friend."
Courtesy of Chelsea Curry

Female Vibrator Use, Orgasm, and Partner Comfort

It is commonly known that vibrators—also known as sex toys and novelties—are beneficial for increasing the probability of orgasmic behavior in women. During intercourse, women typically report experiencing a climax less than 10% of the time; vibrator use increases orgasmic reports to over 90% (Mintz, 2017). Herbenick et al. (2010) studied women's use of vibrators within sexual partnerships. They analyzed data from 2,056 women aged 18–60 years in the United States. Partnered vibrator use was common among heterosexual-, lesbian-, and bisexual-identified women. Most vibrator users indicated comfort using them with a partner and related using them to positive sexual function. In addition, partner knowledge and perceived liking of vibrator use was a significant predictor of sexual satisfaction for heterosexual women.

Individuals threatened by their partner's use of a vibrator are often informed that the vibrator does not replace them but another aspect of the sexual experience to be enjoyed. In addition, some women do not climax without intense stimulation which the vibrator supplies.

Sexual Growth Beliefs

How important is working on your sexual relationship to make it a good one? Frederick et al. (2017) confirmed that while sexual satisfaction and passion decline over time, couples can choose to do those things associated with keeping passion alive such as focusing on sexual communication, mood setting, sexual variety, oral sex, orgasm, and frequency. **Sexual growth** is the term for sexual satisfaction being the result of work and effort with one's partner for a good sex life.

....

Sexual growth: term for sexual satisfaction resulting from work and effort over time for a good sex life.

Sexual Enhancement Products

Modern technology provides new choices to enhance one's sexual experience. Sexual enhancement products, also known as sexual wellness products, refer to items used to aid one's sexual pleasure during solo or partnered sex. These aids include taking supplements—for example, the "Pink" Viagra pill, Viagra, and Cialis—and using massage oils and sex toys. The newer generation of sex toys is made with more body friendly materials and some are even equipped with Bluetooth and can be programmed by your smartphone. With the availability of online shopping, sales of sexual enhancement products like sex toys is booming (Business Wire, 2018).

Researchers have reported that vibrators and sex toys have potential therapeutic benefits such as predictable orgasms and improving sexual well-being (Döring & Pöschl, 2018; Rullo et al., 2018). These sexual aids can be particularly valuable in helping individuals with disabilities meet their sexual needs and improve their sexual wellness (Morales et al., 2018).

While the good news of sexual enhancement products is their availability, insufficient attention has been given to their use, safety, and regulations. For example, the type of lubrication needed with a particular sex toy will depend on what the sex toy is made of. Water-based lubrication is needed rather than silicone-base for silicone sex toys. In addition, toxic materials like thermoplastic elastomer are still used in production of some sex toys. Choosing the correct lubrication or avoiding some sex toys altogether is important.

With the development of medical grade silicon, cyberskin which is soft, stretchy material resembling human skin, and artificial intelligence, lifelike, responsive sex dolls or sexbots are now available. Indeed, it is possible to create one's own sexbot by looking through a catalog and choosing different body parts such as head, lips, and

(Continued)

(Continued)

breasts. Sexbots are frequently over sexualized and are programmed to be submissive sex slaves. Whether the development of sexbots further objectifies women and children remains unresolved. Attitudes toward the use of sex dolls have been primarily negative. In a study of 345 undergraduates, over two thirds or 68% reported that they "could not understand how anyone could think of having sex with a doll" (Knox et al., 2017). Hence, most undergraduates in this study would not choose to experience sex with a doll.

Technological innovations such as Virtual Reality and Augmented Reality can change one's sexual experience. Virtual Reality can transport an individual to a completely different world—for example, a fancy restaurant on Mars; and Augmented Reality adds animation or sensory experience to enhance the current physical environment

by, for example, turning your partner into a cartoon character. In addition, teledildonics, also known as cyberdildonics, involves the virtual control of sex toys or vibrators remotely. For example, individuals in long distance relationships may choose to continue their sex life together by stimulating each other over the internet using these sex toys (Faustino, 2018; Farivar, 2018). Cybersex is no longer a purely virtual experience; it can also simulate touch and various sensations.

Technologies are embedded in modern life. The link between sexuality and technology is here and the variations will continue as new technologies emerge. This union can enrich and expand human sexuality. At the same time, the merger between sex and technology poses ethical challenges for consideration, debate, and choices. ●

FUTURE OF SEXUAL RELATIONSHIPS

The future of sexual relationships will continue to mirror sexual values, patterns, and behaviors of the past 30 years. Netting and Reynolds (2018) reported on the changes in sexual values among Canadians over a thirty-year period. Contrary to the claims of popular media, casual sex—"hookup culture"—has not replaced romantic relationships as the most common context for student sexual behavior. While individuals may go through a period of hedonism, the superior value of relationship sex continues.

Julian (2018) reviewed data and trends regarding sexual behavior and noted that young people are having less sex than in previous generations. The causes include fewer social skills due to digital engagement, the normalization of masturbation via the media, sex toys, and young adults living longer with their parents.

The future of sexuality also includes changes in technology, both medical and mechanical. Drug companies are forever trying to find a new "sex pill" and sex shops continue to feature the latest vibrator. These technologies are for both solo and couple play.

SUMMARY

How is sex defined and what are three main sexual values?
Sex is defined variably but includes the elements of anatomy and physiology, behaviors, relationship context, and sexual orientation. The definition also includes sexual values, such as absolutism, relativism, and hedonism. Relativism is the most frequent sexual value of undergraduates.

What are the four themes surrounding sexual decision-making?
The impact of the sexual decision on the relationship with the partner, the amount of alcohol one has consumed, wanting to be regarded as "normal," and, for females, feeling powerless over negotiating the use of condoms are all involved in deciding about sex.

What are various sexual behaviors?
Kissing involves various meanings and may also be used as an ointment such as when a parent kisses the hurt knee of a child.

Masturbation involves stimulating one's own body with the goal of experiencing pleasurable sexual sensations. Fellatio is oral stimulation of the man's genitals by his partner. Cunnilingus is oral stimulation of the woman's genitals by her partner. Three fourths of undergraduates believe that one can have oral sex and still be a virgin.

Sexual behavior with a partner is associated with feelings of well-being. Indeed, researchers have found that experiencing affection and sex with a partner on one day predicted lower negative mood, higher positive mood, and lower stress the following day.

Cybersex refers to a computer-mediated sexual experience which may include sending sexual text or photos.

What are the various relationship contexts of sexual behavior?

Never-married and noncohabiting individuals report more sexual partners than those who are married or living with a partner. Marital sex is distinctive for its social legitimacy, declining frequency, and satisfaction, both physical and emotional. Marital sex is also the most emotionally and physically rewarding context for sexual behavior. Divorced individuals have a lot of sexual partners but are the least sexually fulfilled.

What is condom assertiveness and which women are more likely to practice it?

Condom assertiveness is the unambiguous message from one sexual partner to another that sex without a condom is unacceptable. The characteristics of undergraduate women who are most likely to insist on condom use are those who believe that condoms are effective in preventing STIs, have confidence in their own condom communication skills, perceive that they are susceptible to STIs, believe that there are relational benefits to being condom assertive, believe their peers are condom assertive, and have the intention to be more condom assertive.

The person most likely to get an STI has sexual relations with a number of partners or with a partner who has a variety of partners. Even if you are in a mutually monogamous relationship, you may be at risk for acquiring an STI, as 30% of male undergraduate students and 20% of female undergraduate students in monogamous relationships reported having oral, vaginal, or anal sex with another partner outside of the relationship.

What are the prerequisites of sexual fulfillment?

Fulfilling sexual relationships involve self-knowledge, positive body image, self-esteem, health, a good nonsexual relationship, open sexual communication, sexual self-disclosure, safer sex practices, and making love with, not to, one's partner. Other variables include realistic expectations—"my partner will not always want what I want"—and avoiding spectatoring, not being self-conscious and observing one's "performance."

What is the future of sexual relationships?

Individualism will continue to be the driving force in sexual relationships. Numerous casual partners, a common characteristic of hooking up, with predictable negative outcomes—higher frequencies of STIs, unexpected pregnancies, sexual regret, and relationships going nowhere—will continue to characterize individuals in late adolescence and early twenties. As these persons reach their late twenties, the goal of sexuality begins to transition to seeking a partner not just to hook up and have fun with but to provide an emotional connection and relationship over time. This new goal is accompanied by new sexual behaviors such as delayed first intercourse in the new relationship, exclusivity, and movement toward a more permanent union. The future of sexuality will also include changes in reference to technology, both medical and mechanical.

KEY TERMS

Absolutism, 183

Asceticism, 186

Asexual, 191

Coitus, 192

Comprehensive sex education program, 185

Concurrent sexual partnership, 195

Condom assertiveness, 196

Consensually nonmonogamous relationships, 195

Cybersex, 193

Fellatio, 192

Friends with benefits, 194

Hedonism, 183

Masturbation, 191

New relationship energy (NRE), 194

Open relationship, 195

PEP (post-exposure prophylaxis), 197

Pluralistic ignorance, 190

Relativism, 183

Satiation, 193

Sexual competence, 192

Sexual compliance, 200

Sexual double standard, 188

Sexual growth, 201

Sexual readiness, 192

Sexual tempo, 193

Sexual values, 183

Spectatoring, 200

Stealthing, 197

STI (sexually transmitted infection), 197

Swinging, 196

WEB LINKS

Body Health: A Multimedia AIDS and HIV Information Resource
http://www.thebody.com

Centers for Disease Control and Prevention (CDC)
http://www.cdc.gov

Go Ask Alice: Sexuality
http://www.goaskalice.columbia.edu/

National Center for Health Statistics
http://www.cdc.gov/nchs/

Kinsey Institute
http://www.kinseyinstitute.org/

Sexuality Information and Education Council of the United States (SIECUS)
http://www.siecus.org

Get the tools you need to sharpen your study skills. SAGE edge offers a robust online environment featuring an impressive array of free tools and resources.
Access practice quizzes, eFlashcards, video, and multimedia at **edge.sagepub.com/knox13e**

10

Violence and Abuse in Relationships

The one thing that is unforgivable is deliberate cruelty.

—Blanche, *A Streetcar Named Desire*

Learning Objectives

10.1.   Explain the various types of abuse

10.2.   Identify various ways to recognize and resist abuse

10.3.   Summarize the explanations for abuse in intimate relationships

10.4.   Describe four types of sexual coercion

10.5.   Discuss types of abuse that occur in marriages and long-term relationships

10.6.   Review the effects of abuse

10.7.   Illustrate the cycle of abuse

10.8.   Compare parent, sibling, and elder abuse

10.9.   Discuss the future of abuse in intimate relationships

A student of the authors noted her shock at drifting into an abusive relationship. She had fallen in love quickly, regarded her partner as a prince, and, against her parents' advice, married within six months of meeting. "Almost instantly he changed," she said, including putting "a gun to my head." She noted that she was too proud to tell her parents since they had warned her against him. But the thought that she might kill herself to escape led her to call her parents, who came and got her.

The awareness of such abuse in relationships strikes sadness and fear in all of us—that what begins as an intimate love relationship can include emotional, verbal, physical, and sexual abuse, even murder. And such abuse can begin early, such as in teen relationships between 13-19 (Murray et al., 2016). In this chapter, we examine the other side of intimate relationships.

The human failing I would most like to correct is aggression.

The late Steven Hawking, renowned physicist

NATURE OF RELATIONSHIP ABUSE

The various terms and types of abuse are discussed in this section.

Violence and Homicide

Also referred to as physical abuse, **violence** is physical aggression for the purpose of controlling or intimidating and subjugating another person. Examples of physical violence include pushing, throwing something at the partner, slapping, hitting, and forcing the partner to have sex. Eleven percent of 10,004 undergraduate females and 4% of 3,061 undergraduate males reported that they had been in a physically abusive relationship (Hall & Knox, 2019).

Intimate partner violence (IPV) is an all-inclusive term that refers to physical, sexual, or psychological harm by a current or former partner or spouse. IPV is a serious public health problem that affects millions of couples. IPV can be unilateral where one person is an abuser and his or her partner is a victim, or IPV can be mutual. Marcus (2012) assessed the frequency of unilateral or mutual partner violence in a sample of 1,294 young adults. A quarter of the couples reported a mutually violent pattern compared to three-quarters who evidenced a unilateral pattern.

IPV can happen to anyone, though Guadalupe-Diaz and Anthony (2017) noted that transgender individuals are particularly vulnerable. Due to barriers such as stigma and lack of clinical guidelines, transgender IPV survivors are less likely to receive appropriate care and support (Knox, 2018).

One trans partner noted:

I do feel like it [being trans and transitioning] made me more vulnerable. I was in a really sensitive and kind of unstable place and I was trying

Violence: physical aggression with the purpose to control, intimidate, and subjugate another human being.

Intimate partner violence (IPV): an all-inclusive term that refers to crimes committed against current or former spouses, boyfriends, or girlfriends.

to find my footing and I just, it's not good; it's an ideal time for an abuser to strike. They take advantage of your fears or your uncertainty.

There are two types of violence. One type is **situational couple violence** (SCV) where conflict escalates over an issue—for example, money or sex—and one or both partners lose control. The person feels threatened and seeks to defend themselves. Control is lost and the partner strikes out. Both partners may lose control at the same time so it is symmetrical. A second type of violence, referred to as **intimate terrorism** (IT), is designed to control the partner.

Many victims of abuse feel helpless and may see retaliation as their only avenue for survival. In instances where a woman kills her abusive husband, the term battered woman syndrome is used. **Battered woman syndrome**, also referred to as battered woman defense, is a legal term used in court that the person accused of murder was suffering from abuse so as to justify his or her behavior—"I shot him because he raped me." While there is no medical or psychological term, the "syndrome" refers to frequent, severe maltreatment which often requires medical treatment. Therapists define battering as physical aggression that results in injury and is accompanied by fear and terror (Jacobsen & Gottman, 2007).

Klipfel et al. (2014) assessed the occurrence of emotional, physical, and sexual interpersonal aggression reported by 161 individuals within various levels of relationships. The relationship and percent of reported intimate partner violence in the various relationships follow: 69% of committed romantic relationships experience some form of abuse; the figure is 33% for casual dating relationships, and 31% for friends with friends-with-benefits relationships. The take-home message is that, in general, the greater the commitment in the relationship, the greater the reported intimate partner violence.

Alcohol is often a precursor to interpersonal violence (Smith et al., 2014). Alcohol and other drugs affect the cognitive function, reducing self-control which means that individuals are less able to negotiate non-violent outcomes to conflicts. Rather than "talk something through," individuals may resort to force via physical violence to make their point or get their way.

Excessive drinking or drug use can also lead to unemployment, infidelity, or role breakdown as a parent so that relationship tension is increased with

Fear is the emotional reaction to a partner who is being abusive or intimidating.
Courtesy of Trevor Werb

violence as a way of expressing one's anger. Some individuals may also use alcohol or being high on other drugs as an excuse to become violent—"I hit my partner but I didn't mean to. I was out of it and didn't know what I was doing." Finally, alcohol and other drugs can be used to cope with violence individuals are exposed to (Ahmadabadi et al., 2019).

The Self-Assessment: Abusive Behavior Inventory on page 389. allows you to assess the degree of abuse in your current or most recent relationship. There are several types of abuse in relationships.

Emotional and Cyber Abuse

Emotional abuse, also known as psychological abuse, verbal abuse, or symbolic aggression, is nonphysical behavior designed to denigrate and control the partner. Thirty-nine percent of 10,002 undergraduate females and 24% of 3,061 undergraduate males reported that they "had been involved in an emotionally abusive relationship" (Hall & Knox, 2019). Examples of emotionally abusive behaviors of one's partner include refusal to talk to the partner as a way of punishing the partner, often called the silent treatment; making personal decisions for the partner such as what to wear, what to eat, and whether to smoke; throwing a temper tantrum and breaking things to frighten the partner; criticizing or belittling the partner to make him or her feel bad; and acting jealous when the partner is observed talking or texting a potential romantic partner.

Some forms of emotional abuse may be subtle, but they can still have harmful effects, such as opposing or arguing against everything the partner says and challenging his or her opinions, blocking or aborting conversations or switching topics, interrupting, and denying that agreements or promises were made or that a conversation or other events

Situational couple violence (SCV): conflict escalates over an issue and one or both partners lose control.

Intimate terrorism (IT): behavior designed to intimidate, terrorize, and control the partner.

Battered woman syndrome: legal term used in court that the person accused of murder was suffering from to justify his or her behavior. Therapists define battering as physical aggression that results in injury and accompanied by fear and terror.

Emotional abuse: nonphysical behavior designed to denigrate the partner, reduce the partner's status, and make the partner feel vulnerable to being controlled by the partner.

The frequency of female partner abuse is unknown since males are reluctant to admit that they are afraid of their partner.
Courtesy of Chelsea Curry

took place. Denying can lead to gaslighting, where an abuser makes someone question his or her own memory, perceptions, and experiences. Davies (2019) interviewed 25 young Welsh women aged 15-18 and revealed their difficulty in recognizing abuse and being assertive in regard to egalitarian attitudes about what they expected, wanted or desired within a 'healthy relationship'.

Other examples of abuse are easier to discern such as prohibiting the partner from spending time with friends, siblings, and parents; and threatening the partner with abandonment or threats of harm to oneself, family, or partner's pets, and demanding that the partner have sex without his or her consent.

Emotional abuse may also take the form of cyber abuse, such as threatening text messages and posting embarrassing content on social media. Temple et al. (2016) revealed that adolescents who have experienced interpersonal physical abuse were also likely to report cyber abuse. Hence the same person may experience multiple layers of abuse. The internet allows anonymity, which abusers may take advantage of. For example, a woman from Edmonton, Alberta, was harassed by her abusive ex-boyfriend (Snowdon, 2017). He created a series of fake dating profiles in her name, prompting more than 30 men to show up to her house expecting to meet her. Although she wasn't harmed, this example demonstrates how cyber abuse can lead to potential physical abuse or violence.

Female Abuse of Partner

People often assume that men are the main perpetrators of IPV, but women can also be abusive toward their partners. Nybergh et al. (2016)

Intimate partner homicide: murder of a boyfriend, girlfriend, or spouse.

interviewed 20 men who had been subjected to IPV, primarily by female partners. They reported that the violence was not physical but more emotional and psychological. Their partners were described as jealous, disliked their friends, made them pay for things, excluded them from family events or belittled, humiliated or called them names, or some combination of these behaviors. One of our male students wrote of his abusive girlfriend:

I had been dating this girl for three months and was shocked the first time she slapped me. It came out of the blue and I was stunned. I questioned her about it and she said she did not know what had come over her (I later learned that she had been abusive with previous boyfriends).

The abuse happened again. The second time we were arguing in the kitchen and she threw a knife at me. Luckily, it missed but she picked up a jar of peanut butter and threw it at me, hitting me on the arm. I was aghast that she was this violent. Again, she apologized.

The third time, we were discussing ending our relationship and she kicked me in the chest. She literally jumped up and threw her knee out and whammed me in the chest. This was followed by her beating me with both hands in a furious rage. I did the best I could to defend myself and get free of her.

When women are abusive, they are rarely arrested by the police. The issue of under-reporting is more pronounced among male victims than female victims. Some men are afraid to report their abuse because they fear that they may appear unmanly about what happened to them. In addition, women are perceived as less fearful and less likely to be blamed for being abusive in an interpersonal relationship. Using the same scenario, a study manipulated a perpetrator's sex, changing it from male to female and doing the same with gender identity and the victim's sex. Results revealed that female perpetrators are less likely to be blame for IPV than were men who committed the same offense (Russell et al., 2019).

Murder

It is important to keep in mind that a violent partner can become deadly. Battering may lead to murder. **Intimate partner homicide** is the murder of a spouse.

Uxoricide is the murder of a woman by a romantic partner. Other forms of murder in the family are filicide which is the murder of an offspring by a parent, parricide which is the murder of a parent by an offspring, and siblicide, the murder of a sibling. Cunha and Goncalves (2016) compared moderate violent partners with severely violent partners—murderers—and found that the latter were more likely to use weapons, to be involved in a separation or breakup, and to be of high socioeconomic status (SES).

Domestic violence often leads to murder. Worldwide data published by the United Nations revealed that 87,000 women and girls were intentionally killed in 2017, most or 58% by an intimate partner or relative (Hjelmgaard, 2018). Fox (2017) used FBI data from police departments to find that 44.8% of women and 5% of men killed from 2007 to 2016 were killed by an intimate partner. Such data demonstrates how much violence can escalate.

Stalking

Abuse may take the form of stalking. **Stalking** is defined as unwanted following or harassment that

Stalking: also known as unwanted pursuit behavior; unwanted following or harassment of a person that induces fear in the victim.

TECHNOLOGY AND THE FAMILY

Intimate Partner Violence (IPV)

While choosing to use technology for positive outcomes such as using texts and emails to keep individuals connected, nefarious choices can be made to use technology to harass, abuse, and harm. Hence, with basic computer knowledge, abusive partners can use technology to control, stalk, and threaten victims. Technology-based gender or sexual violence against women has increased (Henry & Powell, 2018). Cyberspace is the new context for power, and technology has been used as the abuser's most effective accomplice.

Choices using technology-facilitated abuse consists of a range of behaviors. According to a survey conducted by National Network to End Domestic Violence (2018), the top three were broken down into the following categories: 53% were unwanted and abusive text messages, 39% were intimidation and threats, and 31% were unwanted or abusive social media messages or images. In addition, impersonation—creating false social media accounts of the victim—and revenge porn—sharing or posting the victim's non-consensual intimate photos and videos—have also occurred (Freed et al., 2018). Furthermore, victims and survivors of IPV can be stalked and tracked through the use of a mini camera, GPS tracking device, and even apps. While apps may have been designed for legitimate purposes, such as parental monitoring or finding friends close by, they can be used by an abuser for remote monitoring (Chatterjee et al., 2018).

Spyware also allows unauthorized monitoring of an individual's activities via a smartphone or computer and can be installed remotely by downloading an app, sending an email, photo or instant message. The presence of spyware is usually undetectable. Furthermore, once a survivor's smart devices are installed or configured by their abusers the spyware is difficult to eliminate.

Technology also has positive uses for IPV survivors (Gibson, 2018). Instead of calling a hotline or contacting professionals face-to-face, survivors have found websites useful. Online resources and personal safety apps are available to promote healthy relationship and to assist persons in a crisis. The One Love Foundation launched the *MyPlan* app to enable survivors to access a trained advocate 24/7 through live chat. In addition, this app provides a decision aid for supporters who are concerned about the safety of a friend's relationship (Alvarez et al., 2018).

Caution must be taken by an abuse victim when using the Internet to reach out for help since one's computer records online activity automatically and one's search history may be uncovered by abusers. Therefore, choosing safety measures such as using a public computer or enabling the private browsing mode should be considered. The private browsing mode is available on most web browsers such as Safari (Private Browsing) and Google Chrome (Incognito), which can protect private information from being tracked. The National Network to End Domestic Violence launched the Safety Net Project to address issues surrounding the intersection of technology and IPV. This project offers resources such as "Technology-Facilitated Stalking: What You Need to Know," "Who's Spying on Your Computer?" and "Technology Safety Quick Tips" to enhance safety, privacy, and confidentiality.

Although these technological innovations are helpful to expand services, they cannot rescue people from life-threatening situations. Technological advances have simultaneously encouraged different manifestations of violence, such as obsession and control, while also providing innovative resources and interventions to survivors. Technology does not cause intimate partner violence. Rather, sinister choices result in its misuse. At the same time, technology can also be a great tool for assisting IPV victims and survivors. ●

induces fear in the victim. Twenty-eight percent of 9,942 undergraduate females and 19% of 3,028 undergraduate males reported that they had been stalked or, in other words, followed and harassed (Hall & Knox, 2019). Another term for stalking is **unwanted pursuit behavior** (UPB). Dardis and Gidycz (2017) found that of 1,168 undergraduates approximately 80% of men and women reported engaging in UPBS (unwanted pursuit behaviors) toward former partners. Unwanted pursuit behavior refers to the repeated unsolicited privacy violation and intrusion from prior relation partners (De Smet et al., 2015). Stalkers can be fearsome strangers but some UPB tactics may seem innocuous. Nevertheless, the ongoing and persistent unwanted in-person or cyber UPBs are frequently overlooked (Dardis et al., 2019).

Less physically threatening than stalking is **obsessive relational intrusion** (ORI), the relentless pursuit of intimacy with someone who does not want it. The person becomes a nuisance but does not have the goal of harm as does the stalker. People who cross the line in terms of pursuing an ORI relationship or responding to being rejected engage in a continuum of behavior. Examples of ORI behaviors are hyperintimacy and **cybervictimization**, which includes being sent threatening texts or e-mails, unsolicited obscene e-mails, computer viruses, or junk mail like spamming. Short of cyber victimization is cybercontrol, whereby individuals use communication technology, such as cell phones, e-mail, and social networking sites, to monitor or control romantic partners. Marcum et al. (2017) noted that such cyberstalking may also involve logging into a previous partner's social media accounts. IPV and technology use is discussed in detail in the section on Technology and the Family.

Revenge Porn

Another form of sexual abuse is revenge porn, as discussed in Chapter 8. Revenge porn entails posting explicit photos on the Internet of another individual without his or her consent. Hall and Hearn (2019) noted that men are most likely to engage in revenge porn and they often do so against their ex partners. These men may view themselves as a "victim" for a variety of reasons, such as their partner breaking up with them or being unfaithful. They post these pictures as a way to get "revenge." However, they are not victims in these situations. They are abusers and revenge porn is another form of violence against women.

....

Obsessive relational intrusion (ORI): the relentless pursuit of intimacy with someone who does not want it.

Cybervictimization: harassing behavior which includes being sent threatening e-mail, unsolicited obscene e-mail, computer viruses, or junk mail (spamming); can also include flaming (online verbal abuse) and leaving improper messages on message boards.

It should be noted that there is resistance to the term "revenge porn," as some advocate for using alternative language, such as image-based sexual abuse. The term "image-based sexual abuse" addresses the fact that this behavior does not always occur in the context of revenge. It can encompass images created without consent, such as upskirt images. Additionally, it highlights that these images, by nature of being nonconsensual, are not pornography.

RECOGNIZING AND RESISTING ABUSE

How do you recognize abuse? Is it possible to resist physical abuse? What tactics can you take? We discuss these issues in the following sections. Later in the chapter, we discuss how to leave an abusive relationship.

Recognizing Abuse

It is not always easy to know what constitutes abuse. Is a partner's moodiness, irritability, and criticism considered abuse? Is calling a partner stupid considered abuse? Is shoving a partner an abusive act? In general, any verbal or physical behavior that is designed to denigrate or control a partner is abuse. Based on a sample of 338 university students with 122 males and 216 females, one-third reported at least one type of dating abuse: 33.1% were psychological, 9.5% were physical, 10.4% were sexual, and 9.8% were technological violence (Cho & Huang, 2017).

How much abuse should a person tolerate? The answer is zero because the partner will be reinforced for being abusive and will continue or escalate the abuse. In only a short time, demeaning and pushing or shoving a partner can become routine acts considered normative in a couple's relationship. If you don't like the way your partner is treating you, it is important to register your disapproval quickly so that being abused stops. In Chapter 1, we discussed, "Not to decide is to decide." If you don't make a decision to stop abusive behavior, the abuse will continue. However, leaving an abusive relationship can be challenging. Safely leaving an abusive relationship requires not only the firm intention and decision, but also planning, strategy, support, and resource. Most colleges and universities have police departments and counseling centers with trained personnel to assist persons being abused.

Fighting Back: What Is the Best Strategy?

Once a victim has recognized that he or she is being abused, how might he or she respond to or resist physical abuse? First, the goal is to avoid serious physical injury. Such injury is increased if the attacker is drunk, on drugs, or has a weapon so forceful physical resistance like pushing, striking, and struggling should be avoided. Verbal resistance, such as pleading, crying, or trying to assuage the offender or nonforceful physical resistance—fleeing or hiding—should be used.

However, if the attacker is not on drugs, drunk, or violent, Wong and Balemba (2018) surveyed 25 databases on rape resistance and found that women who physically resisted their attacker were significantly more likely than nonresisters to avoid rape. Hence, don't physically resist a drunk, violent partner; do resist if a partner is not drunk or violent.

Once abused, who do people tell or who do they seek for help? Of the victims of dating abuse in the Cho and Huang (2016) study, abuse victims were more likely to seek informal help from friends and family than formal help from professionals.

Reacting to the Stalker

Being very controlling in an existing relationship is predictive that the partner will become a stalker when the relationship ends. Ending a relationship with a potential stalker in a way that does not spark stalking is important. Some guidelines include:

1. Make a direct statement to the person: "I am not interested in a relationship with you, my feelings about you will not change, and I know that you will respect my decision and direct your attention elsewhere".

2. Seek help from Title IX coordinators on campus.

3. In the meantime, ignore text messages or e-mails, and don't walk with or talk to; hang up if the person calls.

4. Use informal coping methods such as blocking text messages phone calls.

5. Stay away. Do not offer to be friends since the person may misinterpret this as a romantic overture.

Intervention

Trabold et al. (2018) noted IPV victims who experienced trauma-informed brief intervention (TIBI) regarded the treatment as beneficial, safe, and innovative. Positive changes included improved physical health, psychological well-being, quality of life, confidence, hope, and personal control. One of the techniques of TIBI is to help the IPV victim reframe recurring negative thoughts about

having been victimized. Roddy et al. (2018) also found that even couples with low levels of IPV benefitted from face-to-face as well as web-based interventions. These interventions involved recognition of the abuse in its various forms, taking responsibility for the abuse, identifying "triggers," for abusive behavior, and making commitments to change behavior.

CULTURE AND DIVERSITY

It is estimated that every day 36,000 Russian women are beaten by their partners. Yet the penalty for doing so is nothing if it does not cause "substantial bodily harm" and does not occur more than once a year. If the person is found guilty, the penalty is $500 or 15 days in jail. Russia is one of three countries in Europe which does not have laws targeting domestic violence (Stanglin, 2017).

Data on IPV for married women in Kenya is 38% and varies by tribe. There are 40 tribes. Compared with Kikuyu women, Luo and Luhya women were significantly more likely to report having experienced violence all three types—physical, sexual, and emotional (Kimuna et al., 2018).

REASONS FOR VIOLENCE AND ABUSE IN RELATIONSHIPS

Research suggests that numerous factors contribute to violence and abuse in intimate relationships. These factors operate at the cultural, community, individual, and family levels.

Cultural Factors

In many ways, American culture tolerates and even promotes violence. Violence in the family stems from the acceptance of violence in our society as a legitimate means of enforcing compliance and solving conflicts at interpersonal, familial, national, and international levels. An example of national or international violence is the emphasis on militarism, the belief that the country must maintain a strong military capability to protect and advance national interests (Steuter & Martin, 2018). Violence and abuse in the family may also be linked to such cultural factors as violence in the media, acceptance of corporal punishment, gender inequality, and the view of women and children as property.

Honor crime or **honor killing** is the killing of an unmarried woman who has intercourse—even if through rape—because she brings shame on her parents which may be recovered by her death.

In Sindh, the province of southeastern Pakistan, a woman who elopes and marries against the family's consent may also be punished by death (Zia, 2019). Siblings often do the killing.

In cultures where a man's honor is threatened if his wife is unfaithful, the husband's violence toward her is tolerated by the legal system. Unmarried women in countries such as Pakistan, India, Morocco, Jordan, Egypt, and Lebanon who have intercourse are vulnerable to an honor killing. Over 1,000 are annually killed in Pakistan alone and 5,000 worldwide. The legal consequence for the person carrying out the murder is typically minimal to nonexistent. For example, a brother may kill his sister if she has intercourse with a man she is not married to and spend no more than a month or two in jail as the penalty; his parents often forgive the killing so prosecution is limited.

New laws are being passed such as in Pakistan which carry a minimum penalty of 25 years in jail for an honor killing. But there is a loophole—death must be officially ruled as an honor crime to warrant this sentence. Hayes et al. (2016) identified 16 honor crimes in the United States from Jan 1, 1990 until December 31, 2014; most often the murder of a daughter or former wife was committed by the father or husband. In one case, a husband beheaded his wife after she filed for divorce. In addition, the prosecution of an honor crime occurs more often in urban areas. Rural areas in the United States are under less scrutiny and may ignore such honor killing laws with impunity.

Corporal Punishment of Children

Some forms of violence are culturally accepted as a means for disciplining children, although groups like the American Academy of Pediatrics has strongly urged against the use of violence. The use of physical force with the intention causing a child pain, but not injury, for the purposes of correcting or controlling the child's behavior or making the child obedient or both is **corporal punishment**. Lorber and Slep (2018) identified six behaviors which constitute corporal punishment—shaking,

Honor crime/Honor killing: refers to the killing of female family members who are accused of bringing shame to the family. This crime is usually committed by a male relative who kills to reclaim family "honor".

hitting the bottom with an object, spanking, slapping the hand or leg, pinching, and slapping the head or face with spanking. Slapping the head or face were the two most common. These behaviors are legal in all states in the United States as long as they do not rise to the level of the state's definition of child abuse.

Ward et al. (2015) found that parental use of corporal punishment was associated with children's internalizing depression and anxiety and externalizing rule breaking and aggression symptoms. According to a meta-analysis of five decades of research on spanking—defined as an open-handed hit on the behind or extremities—parents should seek alternatives to spanking, such as a time-out. The more children are spanked, the more likely they are to defy their parents, experience mental health issues and cognitive difficulties, and to exhibit a spectrum of problem behaviors such as being antisocial and aggressive (Gershoff & Grogan-Kaylor, 2016).

In 1979, Sweden passed a law that effectively abolished corporal punishment as a legitimate child-rearing practice. Forty-eight other countries, including Italy, Germany, and the Ukraine, have also banned corporal punishment in all settings, including the home.

Similarly, under Africa's Agenda for Children 2040: Fostering an Africa Fit for Children, adopted at the 28th Ordinary Session of the ACERWC in Banjul, Gambia, a small West African country, in 2016, states have again committed to ensuring "Every child is protected against violence, exploitation, neglect, and abuse," including that by 2040, no child is subjected to corporal punishment.

Violence in the Media

Individuals need only to watch a football game or the evening news to see violence. With war, mass shooting, and domestic murder, we are inundated with examples of violence. As a result, it can be difficult to not become desensitized to these events. Wright and Tokunaga (2016) noted that male violence against women is related to men's magazines such as *Maxim* and *Esquire*, reality TV, and pornography which objectify women as sexual targets for men. Similarly, movies and TV may normalize some types of violence. For example, numerous movies and TV shows

Corporal punishment: the use of physical force with the intention of causing a child to experience pain, but not injury, for the purpose of correction or control of the child's behavior.

include scenes where women slap their male partners in order to express anger. These actions are framed in a different way than they would be if a man was slapping his female partner. Examples such as these can lead individuals to believe that certain behaviors are acceptable when they are actually abusive.

Gender Inequality

Domestic violence and abuse may also stem from traditional gender roles. Traditionally, men have been taught that they are superior to women and that they may use their aggression toward women, believing that women need to be "put in their place." The greater the inequality and the more the woman is dependent on the man, the more likely the abuse. Another issue that intersects with gender inequality and abuse is pregnancy and child care. A man can try to trap a woman by impregnating her and he may threaten to get custody of their kids.

Some occupations, such as police officers and military personnel, lend themselves to contexts of gender inequality. In military contexts, some men devalue, denigrate, and sexually harass women. In spite of the rhetoric about gender equality in the military, women in the Army, Navy, and Air Force academies continue to be sexually harassed. Data reveal a 10% increase in reports to almost 7,000 of sexual assaults at over 200 military installations from 2016 to 2017 (Vanden Brook, 2018).

Community Factors

Community violence itself presents in the form of robberies, stabbings, and shootings. Kennedy and Ceballo (2016) found that urban youth become desensitized to such events in their communities over time. One woman remarked that "pop, pop, pop" has almost become commonplace.

Individual Factors

Elmquist et al. (2016) studied motivations for physical dating violence. These included the various categories of power and control, self-defense, and expression of negative emotion. Examples of the latter include anger, communication difficulties retaliation, and jealousy. Communication difficulties and self-defense were the most frequently identified motives by both women and men. Other factors include:

1. **Dependency.** Because the thought of being left by their partners induces panic and abandonment anxiety, batterers use physical aggression and threats of suicide to keep their partners with them.

2. **Jealousy.** Batterers exhibit jealousy, possessiveness, and suspicion.

3. **Need to control.** Abusive partners have an excessive need to exercise power over their partners and to control them. The abusers do not let their partners make independent decisions, including what to wear, and they want to know where their partners are, whom they are with, and what they are doing.

4. **Unhappiness and dissatisfaction.** Abusive partners often report being unhappy and dissatisfied with their lives, both at home and at work. Many abusers have low self-esteem and high levels of anxiety, depression, and hostility. They may take out their frustration with life on their partner.

5. **History of aggressiveness.** Abusers often have a history of interpersonal aggressive behavior. They have poor impulse control and can become instantly enraged and lash out at the partner. Battered women report that episodes of violence are often triggered by minor events, such as a late meal or a shirt that has not been ironed.

6. **Quick involvement.** Because of feelings of insecurity, the potential batterer will rush his partner quickly into a committed relationship. If the woman tries to break off the relationship, the man will often try to make her feel guilty for not giving him and the relationship a chance.

7. **Blaming others for problems.** Abusers take little responsibility for their problems and blame everyone else.

8. **Jekyll-and-Hyde personality.** Abusers have sudden mood changes so that a partner is continually confused. One minute an abuser is nice, and the next minute angry and accusatory. Explosiveness and moodiness are the norm.

9. **Isolation.** An abusive person will try to cut off a partner from all family, friends, and activities. Ties with anyone are prohibited. Isolation may reach the point at which an abuser tries to stop the victim from going to school, church, or work.

10. **Alcohol and other drug use.** Whether alcohol reduces one's inhibitions to display violence, allows one to avoid responsibility for being violent, or increases one's aggression, it is associated with violence and abuse (Foshee et al., 2016).

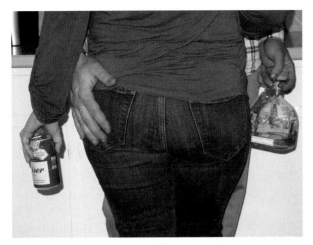

Alcohol gets a party started but may be the precursor to a dangerous or abusive interaction.
Courtesy of Chelsea Curry

11. **Antisocial**. Being antisocial and having no empathy are also associated with violence and abuse (Romero-Martinez et al., 2016).

12. **Criminal and psychiatric background**. Eke et al. (2011) examined the characteristics of 146 men who murdered or attempted to murder their intimate partner. Of these, 42% had prior criminal charges, 15% had a psychiatric history, and 18% had both. Shorey et al. (2012) identified the mental health problems in men arrested for domestic violence and found high rates of PTSD, depression, generalized anxiety disorder (GAD), panic disorder, and social phobia.

13. **Impulsive**. Miller et al. (2012) identified one of the most prominent personality characteristics associated with aggression and abuse. "Impulsive behavior in the context of negative affect" was consistently related to aggression across multiple indices.

14. **Reinforced for violence.** Individuals are often violent because their target becomes more compliant as a result. Hence, the behavior of being violent is reinforced.

Relationship Factors

LaMotte et al. (2018) identified the relationship context in which abuse occurs. A sample of 589 men in treatment for intimate partner violence identified poor communication, difficulties over money, constant bickering, lack of trust between partners, selfishness, and lack of cooperation as common relationship problems. Other problems included substance use and sexual difficulties. Hence, abuse occurs in a relationship context, suggesting that treatment should not only focus on the individual perpetuating the abuse but the context in which it occurs.

Family Factors

Family factors associated with domestic violence and abuse include being abused as a child and having parents who abused each other.

Child Abuse in Family of Origin

Individuals who were abused as children are more likely to be abusive toward their intimate partners as adults. Indeed, they feel that violence in dating relationships is both normative and acceptable (Lee et al., 2016). In addition, children who were abused by their parents are also more likely to abuse their own children (Hellmann et al., 2018).

Family Conflict

Children learn abuse from their family context. Children whose fathers were not affectionate were more likely to be abusive to their own children.

Parents Who Abuse Each Other

Children who had parents who were abusive toward each other are more likely to be abusive in their own relationships. Liu et al. (2018) sampled 610 parents and their dating adolescent children, ages 12–21 years. Children who had parents who were verbally abusive toward each other were more likely to experience similar patterns in their own relationships. In addition, children who had parents who were physically and verbally abusive toward each other were more likely to report psychological, physical, and sexual abusive behaviors in their own relationships.

SEXUAL COERCION, SEXUAL ASSAULT, AND RAPE

Sexual coercion involves using force, actual or threatened, to engage a person in sexual acts against that person's will. While legal definitions vary from state to state, four types of sexual coercion include verbal coercion until the person gives in, someone doing something sexual to a partner without asking for consent, someone doing something sexual to the person while that person is intoxicated or asleep, or using or threatening to use physical force (Mustapha & Muehlenhard, 2014). French et al. (2017) emphasized that sexual coercion can also be a result of manipulation—for example, saying "I love you" and promising marriage—as well as using alcohol or drugs or both and physical force.

Sexual coercion: involves using force, actual or threatened, to engage a person in sexual acts against that person's will.

Sexual assault is any type of sexual contact or behavior that occurs without the consent of the recipient. It is an umbrella term that includes fondling, groping, attempted rape, and rape. **Rape**, also referred to as forced sex, refers to acts of sex or attempted sex in which one party is nonconsenting regardless of the age and sex of the offender and victim and regardless of whether the act meets the criteria for what legally constitutes rape. When "scary sexual situations" (e.g., sexual assault, being held down, anal sex) is the criteria for sexual coercion, 24% of adult women and 10% of adult men in a national sample report such an experience (Herbenick et al., 2019).

Sexual coercion and sexual assault continue to be issues with high cultural visibility, as evidenced by the cases against Jeffrey Epstein, Harvey Weinstein, and Bill Cosby. In recent years, these issues have faced higher visibility in both politics and the entertainment industry. In 2018, Christine Blasey Ford accused Supreme Court nominee Brett Cavanaugh of sexual assault. When testifying before the Senate Judiciary Committee and to a national televised audience, Dr. Ford said, "I believed he was going to rape me." Despite these allegations, Cavanaugh was sworn in to the Supreme Court on October 8, 2018.

Dozens of women in the entertainment industry accused Harvey Weinstein, a film producer, of sexual misconduct, ranging from inappropriate touching to rape. After the story broke, social media was flooded with hundreds of thousands of women sharing their own experiences with sexual harassment, sexual assault, and rape. These women were responding to the hashtag #MeToo, which represents a movement founded in 2006 to help survivors of sexual violence. The Me Too movement went viral, prompting thousands of women to come forward with accusations of sexual violence. Sixty women accused Bill Cosby of a variety of sexual misconduct, with several accusing him of drugging and raping them. He was found guilty on three counts of aggravated indecent assault and was sentenced to three to 10 years in state prison. Finally, the conviction of Lawrence Nassar is the most horrific sexual scandal in the US sport history. Hundreds of victims have come forward with sexual abuse accusations against this former doctor of the American Women's Gymnastics Team.

These examples emphasize that sexual coercion and sexual assault are frequent phenomena in our society.

One in five women in the United States are victims or survivors of rape. The effects of rape include depression, anxiety, substance abuse, suicide ideation, loss of self-esteem, loss of trust, and the inability to be intimate or sexual with a new partner.

Who Commits Rape?

The word *rape* often evokes images of a stranger jumping out of the bushes to attack an unsuspecting victim. However, most rapes are perpetrated not by strangers but by people who have a relationship with the victim. Indeed, emotional, physical, and sexual aggression are more likely to occur in 69% of committed relationships and may also occur in 31%–36% of casual sexual relationships such as friends with benefits or hook ups (Klipfel et al., 2014). In a sample of 10,004 undergraduate females at a large southeastern university, 39% reported being pressured by a partner they were dating to have sex; 21% of 3,065 undergraduate males experienced the same behavior (Hall & Knox, 2019). About 85% of rapes are perpetrated by an acquaintance, someone the woman knows, while 12% of victims have been raped by both an acquaintance and a stranger (Hall & Knox, 2011). We discuss this research further in Applying Social Research.

Rape Myths

The perpetrator of a rape is likely to believe in various rape myths. **Female rape myths** are beliefs about the female that deny that she was raped or cast blame on the woman for her own rape. These beliefs are false, widely held, and justify male aggression. Examples include: "women deserve to be raped" or "she was asking for it," particularly when they drink too much and are provocatively dressed; "women fantasize about and secretly want to be raped" and "women who really don't want to be raped resist more—they could stop a guy if they really wanted to." Moser and Ballard (2017) surveyed 549 students and found that first year students, males, and those in Greek life were more likely to show support for female rape myths. There are also **male rape myths** such as "men can't be raped" and "men who are raped are gay."

Rape myths harm victims in that the focus is on their behavior—for example, were they drinking?—rather than the perpetrator. Victims fear going public with their story of having been raped since they fear that they will become the focus of prosecution by the attorney representing the alleged rapist.

....

Sexual assault: generic term which refers to sexual contact or behavior that occurs without the consent of the other person.

Rape: nonconsensual acts of sex or attempted sex.

Female rape myths: beliefs that deny victim injury or cast blame on the woman for her own rape.

Male rape myths: beliefs that deny victim injury or make assumptions about his sexual orientation.

Double Victims: Dating Partner and a Stranger

This study attempted to identify the characteristics of rape, where victims had been raped by both a dating partner and a stranger. Hence, the person was a victim of both kinds of perpetrators.

Sample and Methods

The sample consisted of 2,747 undergraduates from two relatively large universities. The participants completed a 100-item online survey, "Sexual Attitudes and Behaviors of College Students Questionnaire." The dependent variable was created based on the responses to whether the respondent had been pressured to have sex by a stranger and whether the respondent had been pressured to have sex by a dating partner. Four levels of the *pressure* and *coercion* variable were created to represent 1) those who answered "no" to both questions (n = 1,516; 58.5%) referred to as the "no sexual pressure group," 2) those who answered "yes" to the *stranger* item and "no" to the *dating* item (*n* = 166; 6.4%) referred to as "yes-stranger/no dating pressure," 3) those who answered "no" to the *stranger* item and "yes" to the *dating* item (*n* = 620; 23.9%) referred to as "no-stranger/yes dating pressure," and 4) those who answered "yes" to both items (n = 291; 11.2%) referred to as "double victims."

Findings

The percent of undergraduates experiencing sexual coercion follows in the respective categories: 23.9% were grouped with dates, 6.4% were with strangers, 11.2% with both, and 58.5% with neither. Those who reported pressure to have sex from both a stranger and a date were more likely to be a White female who had been abused as a child, been emotionally abused by a partner, lived with her partner, used alcohol or drugs or both, used the Internet to find a partner, dated interracially, hooked up with a previous partner, been in a friends with benefits relationship, and lied to a partner. What emerged may be an early victimized female who suffered child abuse or possible prior emotional partner abuse, who lowers inhibitions via alcohol or drug use or both, and engages in sex in non-committed relationships, such as with hooking up or with friends with benefit. Lying to one's partner suggests a less than ideal relationship. ●

*Source: Hall, S. S. & Knox, D. (2011). Double victims: Sexual coercion by a dating partner and a stranger. Poster presented at the annual meeting of the National Council on Family Relations, Orlando, FL.

Sexual Abuse in Same-Sex Relationships

Gay, lesbian, and bisexual individuals also experience sexual abuse in their relationships. Rothman et al. (2011) reviewed studies which involved a total sample of 139,635 gay, lesbian, and bisexual women and men and found that the highest estimate reported for lifetime sexual assault was 85% for lesbian and bisexual women.

Transgender people also face an alarming rate of sexual violence. According to the 2015 U.S. Transgender Survey, 47% of transgender people are sexually assaulted at some point in their lifetime (Hames, 2016). Among people of color, 65% of American Indian, 59% of multiracial, 58% of Middle Eastern, and 53% of Black respondents of the 2015 U.S. Transgender Survey were most likely to have been sexually assaulted in their lifetimes.

Male Rape

Compared to research on female rape and sexual assault, male rape has not received equal attention. While male rape is often thought of as a gay issue with men raping men, both men and women can be rapists (Javaid, 2018). Male rape is an underreported issue, which is shaped by many cultural factors. Many men fear coming forward about their abuse, due to outdated ideas that "real" men can't be raped, rape is a homosexual issue, and rape by a woman is not serious. Nevertheless, men are traumatized by the experience and have limited healing venues. O'Brien et al. (2016) studied rape in the military and confirmed that half of military sexual assault survivors are men. A systematic review of 15 empirical studies with more than 5,000 male-on-male sexual assault cases revealed that most offenders and victims were young and heterosexual (Ioannou, Hammond, & Machin, 2017).

Alcohol and Rape

Alcohol is the most common rape drug. A person under the influence cannot give consent. Hence, a person commits rape when they have sex with someone who isn't sober. Alcohol consumption is quite common—especially on college campuses—and women may be encouraged to drink more so they can be taken advantage of.

Results of a study by Buvik and Baklien (2016) revealed that intoxicated females were more likely

Protecting one's drink at a party is a good idea.
Courtesy of Chelsea Curry

to be served alcohol at a bar than intoxicated men. One explanation is that intoxicated women are good for business in that men are more likely to remain in the bar and to spend money. In addition, intoxicated women are viewed as more available to have sex not only with the patrons but with the bar staff. Regardless, it can lead to a dangerous situation where women can be taken advantage of.

However, based on self-reporting from 160 adult bargoers about their own and their friends' alcohol consumption, almost five drinks (4.97) was the average number of drinks each consumed. Few respondents thought they or their friend had diminished cognitive function. Ninety-three percent thought they, themselves, could consent to sex and their friends could do so as well (83%; Drouin et al., 2019).

Rohypnol, GHB, Special K

Rohypnol—also known as the date rape drug, rope, roofies, or the "forget (me) pill"—causes profound, prolonged sedation and short-term memory loss. Similar to Valium but ten times as strong, Rohypnol is a prescription drug used as a potent sedative in Europe. It is sold in the United States for about $5 and

....

Rohypnol: drug that causes profound, prolonged sedation and short-term memory loss; also known as the date rape drug or roofies.

can be dropped in a drink where it is tasteless and odorless and cause victims to lose their memory for eight to 10 hours. During this time, victims may be raped yet be unaware until they notice signs of it, such as blood in their underwear, the next morning. Other drugs such as GHB (gamma hydroxybutyrate) and Special K (ketamine) also render the victim defenseless. Warner et al. (2018) noted that about 5% of rape victims report being drugged with the risk being higher in a fraternity party context.

The Drug-Induced Rape Prevention and Punishment Act of 1996 makes it a crime to give a controlled substance to anyone without his or her knowledge and with the intent of committing a violent crime, such as rape. Violation of this law is punishable by up to 20 years in prison and a fine of $250,000.

Campus Sexual Assault

Evidence suggests that college-age women are at an even greater risk for sexual violence than other female age groups. Sexual violence is more prevalent on college campuses than other crimes as college women are twice as likely to be sexually assaulted as robbed. In a study of how often what form of sexual assault occurs on campus, Fedina et al. (2018) observed that sexual coercion including relentless pressure to "give in," followed by incapacitated rape in which the victim was drugged, and then followed by forcible rape were most common.

Yet, only 20% of female student victims report these crimes. The primary reasons rape victims do not report their experience to the police are not wanting others to know the shame they felt from the assault; not acknowledging that the rape occurred—for example, "It wasn't really rape...I just gave in"; and criminal justice concerns such as "It won't do any good" or "I will be blamed" (Cohn et al., 2013). Those who do report these crimes rarely get justice as less than 5% of alleged rapists are prosecuted. This issue is documented in the *The Hunting Ground,* which focuses on the institutional cover-ups and the devastation faced by victims. The title comes from the fact that males on campus can "hunt" for women and rape them with relative impunity.

Reducing Sexual Violence on Campus

Although anyone can experience sexual violence, sexual violence affects college women disproportionately. Sell et al. (2018) noted that the potential for being raped is reduced when individuals moderate their alcohol use, do not mix types of alcohol, and engage in "protective behavioral strategies" (PBS) such as letting others know one's whereabouts and "having a buddy" to be with.

A passersby writes messages to sexual assault victims during an event held by an organization, 7,000 in Solidarity, on UCLA's campus to pay respect to the 7,000 students nationwide who have or will experience sexual violence over the course of their lifetime.
The Washington Post/Getty

Eggett and Irvin (2016) reviewed 29 research articles on sexual violence prevention programs on campus. While all claimed "success"—for example, reduced rape myths or increased bystander effectiveness—only one reported a reduction of the sexual assaults on campus. The researchers concluded that colleges and universities are focused on reducing parental anxiety about rape by showing that the administration is engaged in keeping campuses safe to keep the money flowing. The reality is that almost none of the programs reduce sexual violence on campus.

Affirmative Consent

Only eight states require that sex education classes in high school include the topic of consent (Maxouris & Ahmed, 2018). This clearly has great implications for consensual sexual activity on college campuses, and recent attention to sexual assault has resulted in new definitions of consent. The new "affirmative consent" or "yes means yes" law adopted in California and New York requires college students in state universities receiving sex to be enthusiastically affirming that they are not just agreeing to sex but want sex to occur with this person. In the absence of such unambiguous consent to any sexual activity, the other person will be guilty of violating campus sexual assault policies. The policy applies only to college students.

Apps have already surfaced to handle the awkward area of agreement in regard to sex. Consent Amour, LegalFling, and YesMeansYes are examples. Another is The Consent App where an individual asserts that he or she is of legal age, understands the laws of legal consent, and declares that the agreement is made of one's own free will. After signing the app electronically, the person gives the phone to the partner who also signs the same app, and the couple take a selfie which goes in the "vault" of the company. However, these apps still cannot guarantee

that consent was given throughout the experience. Just because someone has consented to one activity does not mean that consent has been established for all activity. Additionally, people can change their minds and no longer consent to a certain activity, regardless of whether they originally consented. Consent must be ongoing.

ABUSE IN MARRIAGE AND LONG-TERM RELATIONSHIPS

The chance of abuse in a relationship increases with marriage. Indeed, the longer individuals know each other and the more intimate their relationship, the greater the abuse. Abuse in marriage is both general and sexual.

Abuse in Marriage

Abuse in marriage may differ from unmarried abuse in that the dominant spouse may feel ownership of the other partner and feel the need to control him or her. But the behaviors of abuse are the same—belittling the spouse, controlling the spouse, physically hurting the spouse, and so forth.

Rape in Marriage

Marital rape, now recognized in all states as a crime, is vaginal, oral, or sexual intercourse with one's spouse without that spouse's consent. Until 1979, most states had exceptions for marital rape as part of their rape laws. Some states, such as Washington, still recognize a marital defense exception for third-degree rape in which force is not used even though there is no consent. Over 30 countries—for example, China, Afghanistan, and Pakistan—have no laws against marital rape. These laws are often based on the belief that that a spouse's unconditional sexual consent is part of marriage.

EFFECTS OF ABUSE

Abuse has devastating effects on the physical and psychological well-being of victims. Abuse between parents also affects the children.

Effects of Partner Abuse on Victims

Abuse has devastating consequences. Being a victim of intimate partner violence is associated with symptoms of depression, anxiety, fear, feeling detached from others, inability to sleep, and irritability.

Marital rape: rape by one's spouse: a crime in all states.

Victims may become involved in individual therapy or couple therapy or both (Maharaj, 2017).

Effects of Partner Abuse on Children

The most dramatic effects of abuse occur on pregnant women, which include increased risk of miscarriage, birth defects, low birth weight, preterm delivery, and neonatal death. Earlier we noted that children who observe abuse are more likely to display the behavior in their own adult relationships.

THE CYCLE OF ABUSE

Abusive relationships often follow a predictable pattern, which has become known as the cycle of abuse. The cycle begins when a person is abused and the perpetrator feels regret, asks for forgiveness, and engages in positive behavior, such as an abusive husband bringing flowers or a gift to his wife. In many cases, the victim perceives few options and is fearful of terminating the relationship, especially when there are kids involved. Upon seeing the contriteness of the abuser, the victim may feel renewed hope for the relationship and decide not to call the police or file charges.

After the forgiveness, couples usually experience a period of making up or honeymooning, during which the victim feels good again about the partner and is hopeful for a nonabusive future. However, stress, anxiety, and tension mount again in the relationship, which the abuser relieves by violence toward the victim. Such violence is followed by the familiar sense of regret and pleadings for forgiveness, accompanied by a new round of positive behavior.

As the cycle of abuse reveals, most victims do not prosecute their partners who abuse them. Many feel intimated by their partner, feel that the person will try to get back at them, and that actual legal penalties will be both brief and inadequate. In response to the victim backing out of going to court once an abuse claim has been filed, Los Angeles has adopted a zero-tolerance policy toward domestic violence. Under the law, an arrested person is required to stand trial and the victim required to testify against the perpetrator. The sentence in Los Angeles County for partner abuse is up to six months in jail and a fine of $1,000.

Figure 10.1 illustrates this cycle, which occurs in clockwise fashion. In the rest of this section, we discuss reasons why people stay in abusive relationships and how to get out of them.

Why Victims Stay in Abusive Relationships

One of the most frequently asked questions to people who remain in abusive relationships is, "Why do you stay?" The primary reason female victims of abuse return again and again to an abusive relationship is the emotional attachment to her partner—she is in love. While someone who criticizes, lies to, or physically harms a partner creates a context of interpersonal misery, the victim might still love that person.

People's reasons for staying in an abusive relationship are extremely complex. There may be legal concerns as victims with children may fear that they will lose custody of their children. Victims may also not receive necessary support from police officers and law enforcement. One's ability to leave a relationship may depend on his or her physical abilities. People with disabilities may be physically dependent on their partner and have additional hurdles to leaving. Other reasons individuals give for remaining in an abusive relationship include those identified by Cravens et al. (2015):

- Rationalization: "I felt like it was my fault. . . I should have listened to him more."

- Fear: "I was afraid of him—he'd make leaving an ugly drawn-out nightmare."

- Savior: "I believed I could love the abuse out of him."

- Commitment: "I was determined to make it work."

- Help partner: "He needed me to make his life better."

- Children: "I was afraid if he wasn't beating me, he would beat the children."

FIGURE 10.1

The Cycle of Abuse

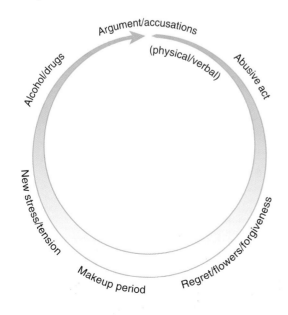

Still other reasons identified by our students included:

- Fear of loneliness: "I'd rather be with someone who abuses me than alone."

- Emotional dependency: "I needed him."

- Hope: "He will stop being abusive—he's just not himself lately."

- A view of violence as legitimate: "All relationships include some abuse."

- Guilt: "I can't leave a sick man."

- Economic dependence: "I have no money and no place to go."

- Isolation: "I don't know anyone who can help me."

- No alternative: "I have nowhere to go and no one else to go to."

- Negative self-concept: "This is the best I can do."

- Deserve abuse: "I deserve to be abused."

Another explanation for why some people remain with abusive partners is that the abuse is only one part of the relationship. When such partners are not being abusive, they may be kind, caring, and loving. It is these positive behaviors which can make the victim stay. The psychological term **aperiodic reinforcement** means that every now and then the abusive person "floods" the partner with strong love and positives which keep the partner in the relationship. In effect, the person who is abused stays in the relationship since it includes positives that entice her or him to stay in the relationship. However, it's important to note that this issue is complex, and there are many factors that prevent a victim from leaving an abusive relationship.

Triggers for Leaving an Abusive Relationship

A study of 123 survivors of past abusive relationships revealed the triggers behind their decision to end an abusive relationship (Murray et al., 2015). These were: (a) facing the threat of severe violence, such as the victim felt her or his life or that of her or his child was in danger, (b) changing their perspective about the relationship, abuse, or their partner or a combination of all of these—for example, concluding that things would never improve but would only get worse, (c) learning about the dynamics of abuse—such as the cycle of abuse (d) experiencing an intervention from external sources—for example, if a friend told

....

Aperiodic reinforcement: random reinforcement for a behavior such as winning the lottery or fishing.

her or him that her or his life was being destroyed and should leave (e) realizing the impact of the violence on children—for example, the children were learning to be aggressive and (f) the relationship was being terminated by the abuser, such as the husband had an affair and left. Some of the respondents could not identify a trigger.

I never had a turning point but always knew I needed to get out of the situation, I just didn't know how without having to move away from my family who was my main support. Therefore I felt 'stuck' in my situation (p. 236)

Cravens et al. (2015) noted that clarity about oneself and believing that "I deserve better," clarity about one's partner and realizing that "It was not up to me to change him," or clarity about the relationship and understanding that "Someone who loves you will make an effort instead of excuses" were related to leaving. In addition, some abused women felt it important that they be a good role model for their children and not stay in an abusive relationship since children might think this was OK.

Finally, Negash et al. (2016) identified exposure to relationship education in a college course for those who had experienced psychological aggression in their exclusive dating relationship as a trigger to leave. Compared to those in the control group, participants receiving relationship education were significantly more likely to end their romantic relationship and to attribute their leaving to participation in the class.

How to Leave an Abusive Relationship

A study of 26 survivors of intimate partner violence revealed the use of various strategies to cope with IPV (Vil et al., 2017). These included internal use of religion and becoming self-reliant, interpersonal like fighting back, and external, such as relying on informal, formal, or both kinds of sources of support, strategies. Some try couple therapy. But couple therapy is hampered by the fact of previous abuse. Being a victim of previous psychological aggression, whether female or male, is related to fear of speaking in front of the partner (O'Leary et al., 2013). Hence, gains may be minimal.

Leaving an abusive partner begins with the person making a plan and acting on the plan—packing clothes and belongings, moving in with a sister, mother, or friend, or going to a homeless shelter. If the new context is better than being in the abusive context, the person will stay away. Otherwise, the person may go back and start the cycle all over. As noted previously, this leaving and returning typically happens seven times.

Sometimes the woman does not leave while the abuser is at work but calls the police and has the man arrested for violence and abuse. While the abuser is in jail, she may move out and leave town. In either case, disengagement from the abusive relationship takes a great deal of courage. Calling the National Domestic Violence Hotline (800-799-7233 [SAFE]), available 24 hours, is a point of beginning.

Involvement with an intimate partner who is violent may be life threatening. Particularly if the individual decides to leave the violent partner, the abuser may react with more violence and murder the person who has left. Indeed, a third of murders that occur in domestic violence cases occur shortly after a breakup. Specific actions that could be precursors to murder of an intimate partner are stalking, strangulation, rape, physical abuse, gun ownership, and drug or alcohol use on the part of the abuser. Moving quickly to a safe context like returning home to parents is important.

Treatment of Abusers

The cycle of abuse can end by getting treatment for abusers. Satyanarayana et al. (2016) confirmed the effectiveness of integrative cognitive behavioral intervention in group therapy contexts designed to reduce subsequent violent acts against one's partner. Relaxation techniques, anger management, and cognitive reframing were skills the previous perpetrators found helpful. However, Armenti and Babcock (2016) emphasized that male-only treatment groups miss at least a third of the perpetrators of violence and abuse: women. Conjoint therapy whereby both partners are involved is more efficacious, particularly when violence tends to be situational.

CHILD, PARENT, SIBLING, AND ELDER ABUSE

In addition to intimate partner abuse, child, parent, sibling, and elder abuse occurs.

Child Abuse

Child abuse is any behavior or lack of behavior by parents or caregivers that results in deliberate harm to a child's physical or psychological well-being. A child is defined as an individual younger than the age of 18. Children are vulnerable to abuse due to their age and maturity. Most children are not able to remove themselves from an abusive situation due to lack of autonomy.

Abusive acts may be acts of commission where the child is deliberately harmed by the parents or acts of omission where the parents fail to look out for the child. There are four types of child abuse and neglect: physical abuse, such as beating and burning; psychological or emotional abuse, such as insulting or demeaning behavior; sexual abuse, such as sexual activity or exploitation; and neglect, such as not providing a child adequate supervision, nutrition and medical care. By this definition, neglect can include failure to vaccinate one's child (Parasidis & Opel, 2017). According to Centers of Disease Control and Prevention, one in seven children experienced child abuse or neglect in 2017. However, not all reported cases are confirmed. Of 204,414 reported cases of child physical abuse, only 13% were confirmed (Ho et al., 2017). Some abuse can remain hidden for years. One notable case discovered in Perris, California, involved 13 children and siblings, ages two to 29, who had been deprived by their parents, David and Louise Turpin, of food—one older child weighed 80 lbs—and had been tied to a bed, not allowed "bathroom breaks," and forbidden to bathe except once a year (Kelman, 2018).

One in four children in the United States is a victim of maltreatment (Ho et al., 2017). Various forms of child psychological maltreatment and neglect were identified by Nash et al. (2012) and included the following: A lack of emotional involvement by parents—for example, the child does not feel loved; terrorizing and spurning, where the child is frightened or made to cry for no reason; isolating, where the child is confined, for example, to a closet or other small place; abandonment where the child is thrown out of the house after an argument; an absence of monitoring—the parents don't require the child to attend school; and medical neglect where the parents, for example, do not feed the child, provide hygiene, or take the child to a doctor. Holmes et al. (2018) estimated that the average lifetime costs resulting from child abuse were over $50,000 per victim due to increased health care costs of about $11,000, increased crime costs totaling about $14,000, and productivity losses of $26,000. For an annual birth cohort of young adults, these costs amount to over $55 billion nationwide. The percentages of various types of child abuse in substantiated victim cases are illustrated in Figure 10.2. Notice that neglect is the largest category of abuse with 3.9 million cases reported annually (Green et al., 2016).

Yang and Maguire-Jack (2018) studied 1,181 low-income families and found that multiple stresses—economic pressures, having a sick child, an absence of parental or extended family support, depression, and substance abuse—predispose the parent to abuse the child. While all states prosecute parents whose children experience severe harm through neglect, in 34 states as well as the District of Columbia, Guam, and Puerto Rico, there are exemptions in the civil child abuse statutes when medical treatment for a

....

Child abuse: any behavior or lack of behavior by parents or caregivers that results in deliberate harm to a child's physical or psychological well-being.

FIGURE 10.2

Child Abuse and Neglect Cases: 2017

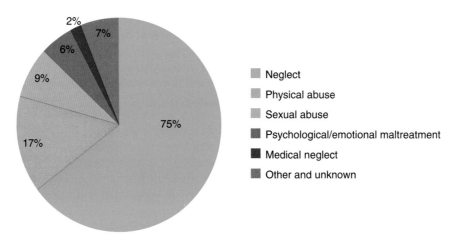

- Neglect
- Physical abuse
- Sexual abuse
- Psychological/emotional maltreatment
- Medical neglect
- Other and unknown

Source: ProQuest Statistical Abstract of the United States, 2019, Online Edition, Table 379.

child conflicts with the religious beliefs of parents. This means that parents may withhold medical treatment from a child for religious reasons; if the child dies, the parents are not prosecuted.

Below is a list of common reasons for why child abuse occurs.

1. **Parental psychopathology.** Symptoms of parental psychopathology that may predispose a parent to abuse or neglect children include low frustration tolerance, inappropriate expression of anger, and alcohol or substance abuse.

2. **Unrealistic expectations.** Abusive parents often have unrealistic expectations of their child's behavior. For example, a parent might view the crying of a baby as a deliberate attempt on the part of the child to irritate the parent so the abusive parent strikes back.

3. **History of abuse.** Individuals who were abused as children are more likely to report abusing their own children. Doing so reflects the principle of modeling. Although parents who were physically or verbally abused or neglected as children are somewhat more likely to repeat that behavior than parents who were not abused, the majority of parents who were abused do *not* abuse their own children. Indeed, many parents who were abused as children are dedicated to ensuring nonviolent parenting of their own children precisely because of their own experience of abuse.

4. **Displacement of aggression.** One cartoon shows several panels consisting of a boss yelling at his employee, the employee yelling at his wife, the wife yelling at their child, and the child kicking the dog, who chases the cat up a tree. Indeed, frustration may spill over from the adults to the children, the latter being less able to defend themselves.

5. **Social isolation.** The saying "it takes a village to raise a child" is relevant to child abuse. Unlike inhabitants of most societies of the world, many Americans rear their children in closed and isolated nuclear units. In extended kinship societies, other relatives are always present to help with the task of child rearing. Isolation means parents have no relief from the parenting role as well as no supervision by others who might interrupt observed child abuse.

6. **Young, poor, and no partner.** Camperio Ciani and Fontanesi (2012) studied 110 mothers who killed 123 of their babies, called **neonaticide**, within the first day of life. All fit the same profile—young, poor, and no partner.

7. **Alcohol and drugs and other factors.** In addition to alcohol and illicit drug use the following factors are also associated with child abuse and neglect: premarital or unplanned pregnancy, the absence of mother-infant attachment, spousal abuse, having adopted or foster children or both, and having a disabled child (Choenni et al., 2017).

The consequences of child maltreatment may be long term. Cecil et al. (2017) noted that the combination of maltreatment behaviors, such as physical or emotional abuse, particularly emotional

....

Neonaticide: killing a baby the first day of life.

abuse, was related to a greater number of psychiatric symptoms of high risk youths. Dorahy et al. (2016) found that child emotional abuse predicted later shame, guilt, relationship anxiety and fear of relationships. Li et al. (2017) studied 276 pregnant women and confirmed that those who reported maltreatment, particularly emotional neglect, as children reported higher levels of depression during their pregnancy and four weeks postpartum.

Aadnanes and Gulbrandsen (2018) emphasized that it is emotional rather than physical abuse that has the most enduring negative impact on children. The following is from a young adult remembering her father:

> *But what has been the worst is not the fear that he was going to hurt me [physically], but the things he said to me. (cries) He would call me stupid, dumb. Question how smart I was. Those sorts of things. Made me feel incompetent. I never felt loved... That he did not really love me.*

Parental emotional abuse has implications for one's romantic relationships later in life. Peterson et al. (2018) found that women who reported emotional abuse in their families of origin were compromised in their current romantic relationships and were less likely to report relationship satisfaction. Emotional neglect predicted relationship anxiety and relationship depression. Lin et al. (2016) also confirmed that children who are emotionally neglected and physically abused have negative interpersonal relationships with parents, teachers, and peers. But there is hope.

While previous research has revealed that abused children tend to become abusing partners in adulthood, Maxwell et al. (2016) provided data on 816 individuals to confirm that those who had been abused as children were significantly less likely to be violent or abusive in their relationships with adults if they had received counseling or therapy; hence, having been abused does not "doom" one to be an abuser. Such micro intervention functions best in the context of broader public health strategies such as reducing poverty and encouraging community support for families (Prinz, 2016). Eckenrode et al. (2017) also noted that family planning and economic factors are central in reducing child maltreatment. Finally, Green et al. (2016) confirmed that the evidence-based intervention (EBI) SafeCare ® (SC) programs significantly reduce child neglect recidivism rates.

Child Sexual Abuse

Child sexual abuse, sexual activity with a child, is a specific type of child abuse. Forms of child sexual abuse include a wide range of inappropriate behavior such as touching, fondling, obscene digital communication, exploitation, sex trafficking, or any other sexual conducts that is harmful to a child's overall well-being. Some forms of child sexual abuse do not require physical contact. Perpetrators may be both inside the family, **intrafamilial**, and outside, **extrafamilial**; females can be perpetrators as well as males. A neighbor is an example of an extra familial perpetrator for whom Megan's Law was passed (see the Family Policy feature).

FAMILY POLICY

Megan's Law and Beyond

In 1994, Jesse Timmendequas lured 7-year-old Megan Kanka into his Hamilton Township house in New Jersey to see a puppy. He then raped and strangled her and left her body in a nearby park. Timmendequas had two prior convictions for sexually assaulting girls. Megan's mother, Maureen Kanka, argued that she would have kept her daughter away from her neighbor if she had known about his past sex offenses. She campaigned for a law, now known as **Megan's Law,** requiring that communities be notified of a neighbor's previous sex convictions. Forty-five other states have enacted laws similar to New Jersey's Megan's Law.

The 1994 Jacob Wetterling Act requires states to register individuals convicted of sex crimes against children. The law requires that convicted sexual offenders register with local police in the communities in which they live. It also requires the police to go out and notify residents and certain institutions, such as schools, that a previously convicted sex offender has moved into

the area. This provision of the law has been challenged on the belief that individuals should not be punished forever for past deeds. Critics of the law argue that convicted child molesters who have been in prison have paid for their crime. To stigmatize them in communities as sex offenders may further alienate them from mainstream society and increase their vulnerability for repeat offenses.

In many states, Megan's Law is not operative because it is on appeal. Parents ask, "Would you want a convicted sex offender, even one who has completed his prison sentence, living next door to your eight-year-old daughter?" However, the reality is that little notification is afforded parents in most states. Rather, the issue is tied up in court and will likely remain so until the Supreme Court decides it. A group of concerned parents, Parents for Megan's Law, are trying to implement the law nationwide. ●

Vaillancourt-Morel (2016) found that 21.5% of 1,033 adults reported child sexual abuse. McElvaney et al. (2014) interviewed 22 young people who experienced child sexual abuse and revealed ambivalence about disclosing. They feared not being believed, being asked questions about their well-being, felt ashamed of what happened, and blamed themselves for the abuse and for not telling. The HBO documentary, *Leaving Neverland*, highlights this issue by telling the story of the child sex abuse of James "Jimmy" Safechuck, at age 10, and Wade Robson, at age 7, by Michael Jackson over several years. The documentary revealed how Michael Jackson manipulated these children into hiding the abuse from the parents. Experiencing abuse can have significant effects later in life. Associations included higher sexual compulsivity—for example, constantly thinking about sex or feeling driven to engage in sexual behavior—in unmarried individuals. Among married individuals, higher sexual avoidance, such as not wanting to engage in sexual behavior, has been observed. Polydrug use (taking multiple drugs) in adolescence has also been associated with sex abuse in childhood (Alvarez-Alonso et al., 2016). Easton and Kong (2017) found in a longitudinal study of older (average age of 62) adult males who reported childhood sexual abuse, higher levels of depression, and somatic complaints were evident. O'Leary et al. (2017) also found negative outcomes of male child sexual abuse and devised a scale— The Male Sexual Abuse Effects Scale. Dorahy et al. (2016) previously noted that child sexual abuse predicted pathological dissociation. Trauma focused cognitive behavioral therapy has been effective in helping the individual to process the abuse and relearn cognitive, emotional, and behavioral ways of moving forward (Zenter, 2017).

Can sex be consensual but illegal? Yes. Individuals under a certain age are not legally able to give consent to sexual activity. **Statutory rape** is nonforcible sexual contact in which one of the individuals is under the age of consent. The legal age of consent varies by state and is usually between ages 16 and 18. Some states consider not only the

minor's age but also the perpetrator's age, the relationship—whether the perpetrator is in an authority position—and the age difference between the adult and minor. Statutory rape is complex and has not received adequate attention (Bierie & Budd, 2016).

CULTURE AND DIVERSITY

Soliman et al. (2018) reported that some parents in Egypt arrange for their children to "marry" tourists to circumvent local laws so that the tourists can have sex with children. In effect the children were being rented out to tourists to escape prosecution since the child was legally their spouse. The motive of the parents is economic.

Boko Haram, a militant group, kidnapped 276 girls at Government Secondary School Chibok, Borno State, Nigeria, in 2014 in an act of sexual and gender-based violence (SGBV) against women. Boko Haram terrorists conducted mass rapes of women, impregnating and kidnapping the offspring of such women. About 200 of the captured school children remain at large (Oriola, 2017). The abuse continues-—in 2018, one hundred teenage girls were seized by Boko Haram in the town of Dapchi in Nigeria's northeastern Yobo tribe.

Sibling Abuse

Sibling abuse is a phenomenon that often goes unnoticed, and studies indicate that sibling violence is the most common form of family violence (Haelle, 2018). Even in "well-adjusted" families, some degree of fighting and name calling among children is expected—and that's part of the problem. Most incidents of sibling violence consist of slaps, pushes, kicks, bites, and punches. What passes for normal, acceptable, or typical behavior between siblings would often be regarded as physical and emotional abuse outside the family. Inside the family, sibling rivalry is the label used for playful abusive acts. . . but when these acts become secret, one sibling is always the aggressor, or when there is a considerable age difference, the label of sibling abuse applies.

Perkins and O'Connor (2016) revealed that 60% of undergraduates report physical abuse from a sibling. In addition, 89% of males and 98% of females report emotional abuse. Sibling abuse may include sexual exploitation, such as an older brother coercing younger female siblings into nudity or sex.

Intrafamilial child abuse: child sexual abuse referring to exploitive sexual contact or attempted sexual contact between relatives before the victim is 18.

Extrafamilial child abuse: child sexual abuse in which the perpetrator is someone outside the family who is not related to the child.

Megan's Law: law requiring that communities be notified of a neighbor's previous child sex convictions.

Statutory rape: nonforcible sexual contact in which one of the individuals is under the age of consent.

In addition to physical and sexual sibling abuse, there is **sibling relationship aggression.** This is behavior of one sibling toward another sibling that is intended to induce social harm or psychic pain in the sibling. Examples include social alienation or exclusion, such as not asking the sibling to go to a movie when a group is going; telling secrets or spreading rumors like revealing a sibling's sexual or drug past; and withholding support or acceptance—not acknowledging a sibling's achievements in school or sports.

Elder Abuse

As increasing numbers of the elderly end up in the care of their children, abuse, though rare, may occur. When it occurs, the elderly are reluctant to report abuse since they may feel self-blame or lack knowledge about the nature of abuse. Examples of elder abuse and the percent of 1,123 older adults surveyed included the following (Gil et al., 2015):

1. **Psychological abuse (6%)** – verbal abuse, deprivation of mental health services, harassment, and deception.

2. **Financial abuse (6%)** – taking over and draining the bank accounts or resources of the elderly.

3. **Neglect (4%)** – failing to buy or give the elderly needed medicine, failing to take them for necessary medical care, or failing to provide adequate food, clean clothes, and a clean bed.

Another type of elder abuse is **granny dumping.** Adult children or grandchildren who feel burdened with the care of their elderly parent or grandparent leave an elder at the emergency entrance of a hospital with no identification. If the hospital cannot identify responsible relatives, it is required by state law to take care of the abandoned elder or transfer the person to a nursing home facility, which is paid for by state funds. Relatives of the dumped elder, hiding from financial responsibility, never visit or see the elder again.

Adult children who are most likely to dump or abuse their parents tend to be under a great deal of stress and to use alcohol or other drugs. In some cases, parent abusers are getting back at their

Sibling relationship aggression: behavior of one sibling toward another sibling that is intended to induce social harm or psychic pain in the sibling.

Granny dumping: refers to adult children or grandchildren, burdened with the care of their elderly parent or grandparent, leaving the elder at the entrance of a hospital with no identification.

parents for mistreating them as children. In other cases, the children are frustrated with the burden of having to care for their elderly parents.

FUTURE OF VIOLENCE AND ABUSE IN RELATIONSHIPS

Prevention of relationship violence or abuse is a daunting task. Singular workshops and training prevention programs might have little impact since the causes are often cultural or gender scripted and abusers may be under the influence of drugs or alcohol.

Progress toward reducing sexual assaults on college and university campuses had been under way. Title IX of the Education Amendments Act of 1972 prohibits sex discrimination in educational programs that receive federal financial assistance. Title IX encompasses discrimination in sports as well as sexual misconduct.

Title IX of the Educational Amendment of 1972 is designed to prevent sex-based discrimination in any institution, program, or activity receiving federal funding. The law empowers students to combat campus violence or rape or both, requiring federally funded colleges and universities to take every complaint of violence, rape, or sexual assault seriously by filing a federal complaint or a civil lawsuit. Schools that do not comply are fined $150,000 per violation and up to 1% of their operating budget for failure to investigate reports of sexual assault on campus. However, these guidelines were rescinded by Betsy DeVos under the Trump administration (Green, 2018). Previously the lowest standard of proof, "preponderance of the evidence," was used in deciding whether a student is responsible for sexual assault, a verdict that could lead to discipline and even expulsion. The new guidelines make colleges free to abandon that standard and raise it to a higher standard known as "clear and convincing evidence."

Reducing family violence through education involves altering aspects of American culture that contribute to such violence. Violence in the media must be curbed. This is not an easy feat, with nightly news clips of random gun shootings and the prevalence of violent films.

Another important cultural change is to reduce violence-provoking stress by reducing poverty and unemployment and by providing adequate housing, nutrition, medical care, and educational opportunities for everyone. Integrating families into networks of community and kin would also enhance family well-being and provide support for families under stress.

SUMMARY

What is the nature of relationship abuse?

There are various types of relationship abuse. Violence or physical abuse is defined as physical aggression with the purpose of controlling, intimidating, and subjugating another human being. Emotional abuse, also known as psychological abuse, verbal abuse, or symbolic aggression, is designed to denigrate the partner, thereby giving the abuser more control.

What are explanations for violence in relationships?

Many factors have been identified to explain violence in relationships. Cultural explanations for violence include violence in the media, corporal punishment in childhood, gender inequality, and stress. Community explanations involve social isolation of individuals and spouses from extended family, poverty, inaccessible community services, and lack of violence prevention programs. Individual factors include psychopathology of the person such as being antisocial, having personality issues like dependency or jealousy problems, and alcohol abuse. Family factors include child abuse by one's parents, observing parents who abuse each other, and not having a father in the home.

How does sexual abuse in undergraduate relationships manifest itself?

About 40% of undergraduate females and 20% of undergraduate males report having been pressured to have sex by a partner they were dating. Acquaintance rape is the most frequent context with the perpetrator believing in male or female sex myths.

Is there abuse in marriage?

The longer individuals know each other and the more intimate the relationship, the greater the abuse. All states have laws prohibiting marital rape though there are exceptions to the law in Washington State. Over 30 countries provide no protection for wives against rape by their husbands.

What are the effects of abuse?

The effects of IPV include physical harm, mental harm—depression, anxiety, low self-esteem, loss of trust in others, and sexual dysfunctions—unintended pregnancy, and multiple abortions. High levels of anxiety and depression often lead to alcohol and drug abuse. Violence toward pregnant women significantly increased the risk for infants of low birth weight, preterm delivery, and neonatal death.

What is the cycle of abuse and why do people stay in an abusive relationship?

The cycle of abuse begins when a person is abused and the perpetrator feels regret, asks for forgiveness, and starts acting nice—for example, gives flowers. The reasons people stay in abusive relationships include love, emotional dependency, commitment to the relationship, hope, view of violence as legitimate, guilt, fear, economic dependency, and isolation. The catalyst for breaking free combines the sustained aversiveness of staying, the perception that victims and their children will be harmed by doing so, and the awareness of an alternative path or of help in seeking one.

What is the nature of child, parent, sibling, and elder abuse?

Child abuse includes physical abuse, such as beating and burning; verbal abuse, such as insulting or demeaning the children; and neglect, such as failing to provide adequate food, hygiene, medical care, or adult supervision for children. Children can also experience emotional neglect by their parents and sexual abuse from both within, intrafamilial, and outside, extrafamilial, the family.

Parent abuse is the deliberate harm, physical or verbal, of parents by their children. Sibling abuse is a frequent form of abuse that occurs with limited detection. The difference between sibling rivalry and sibling abuse is that the latter is secret and there is usually one perpetrator.

Elder abuse is another form of abuse in relationships. Granny dumping occurs by children or grandchildren who feel burdened with the care of their elderly parents or grandparents and leave them at the emergency entrance of a hospital. If the relatives of the elderly patient cannot be identified, the hospital will put the patient in a nursing home at state expense.

What is the future of violence and abuse in relationships?

Various individual, relationship, familial, and cultural factors contribute to relationship violence and abuse. Progress toward reducing sexual assaults on college campuses had been made with the Title IX office but these guidelines were rescinded by Betsy DeVos under the Trump administration (Green, 2018).

Decreasing family violence through education involves altering aspects of American culture that contribute to such violence. For example, reducing poverty and unemployment and by providing adequate housing, nutrition, medical care, and educational opportunities for everyone. Integrating families into networks of community and kin would also enhance family well-being and provide support for families under stress.

WEB LINKS

Childabuse.com
http://www.childabuse.com/

Male Survivor
http://www.malesurvivor.org/

Rape, Abuse & Incest National Network (RAINN)
http://www.rainn.org/

Stop It Now! The Campaign to Prevent Child Sexual Abuse
http://www.stopitnow.com/

V-Day (movement to stop violence against women and girls)
http://www.vday.org/

Get the tools you need to sharpen your study skills. SAGE edge offers a robust online environment featuring an impressive array of free tools and resources.

Access practice quizzes, eFlashcards, video, and multimedia at **edge.sagepub.com/knox13e**

11 Planning for Parenthood

*Pregnancy was the most beautiful
experience of my life.*

—Beyoncé

Learning Objectives

11.1. Discuss the social influences that encourage childbearing and the individual motivations for having children or remaining child-free

11.2. Explain the considerations parents must take into account when deciding how many children to have

11.3. Discuss the phenomenon of teen parenthood

11.4. Know the causes of infertility and technology available to help create a pregnancy

11.5. Summarize the motives for adoption and the demographics of who adopts and who is adopted

11.6. Discuss the types of abortion and the outcome of having an abortion

11.7. Predict the future of planning for children

Master the content at
edge.sagepub.com/knox13e

Becoming a parent is both a personal and societal issue. As has been discussed in other chapters, the concept of a family varies. While many individuals become parents, some decide not to have children. For those who cannot have biological children, they may become parents through adoption or surrogacy. Additionally, some women may become pregnant through unintended pregnancies and must decide whether they want to keep the child. This chapter will discuss some of the trends around parenthood and fertility as well as the motivations for becoming a parent.

DO YOU WANT TO HAVE CHILDREN?

About 3.8 million babies are born each year in the United States (Dvorak, 2018). This number represents a general downturn that started with the Great Recession of 2008. The number of births in the United States dropped by 2% between 2016 and 2017 to 60.2 births per 1,000 women ages 15 to 44. The fertility rate is the lowest it has been in 30 years, and the current rate is below **replacement level,** which is the fertility rate at which a population replaces itself from one generation to the next (Mathews & Hamilton, 2019).

Despite this declining birthrate, most individuals want children. Seventy-two percent of 598 undergraduates reported that they wanted to have children (Bragg et al., 2018). Beyond a biological drive

to reproduce, which not all adults experience, societies socialize their members to have children. This section examines the social influences that motivate individuals to have children, the lifestyle changes that result from such a choice, and the costs of rearing children.

Social Influences That Encourage Childbearing

Our society tends to encourage childbearing, an attitude known as **pronatalism**. Our family, friends, religion, and government encourage positive attitudes toward parenthood. Cultural observances also function to reinforce these attitudes.

Family of Orientation

Our experience of being reared in families encourages us to have families of our own. Our parents are our models. They had children; we have children. We also expect to have a "happy family."

Partner

One's partner has an impact on the decision to have a child. Decisions take place in a social context and do not reflect sole individualistic thinking (Matias & Fontaine, 2017).

Friends

Our friends who have children influence us to do likewise. After sharing an enjoyable weekend with friends who had a little girl, one husband wrote to the host and hostess, "Lucy and I are always affected by Lisa—she is such a good child to have around. We haven't made up our minds yet, but our desire

Replacement level: the average number of children born per woman at which a population exactly replaces itself from one generation to the next, without migration.

Pronatalism: cultural attitude which encourages having children.

to have a child of our own always increases after we leave your home." This couple became parents sixteen months later.

Religion

While religion is in decline in the United States (Brauer, 2018), it remains a strong influence on an individual's decision to have children (Marshall & Shepherd, 2018). Catholics are taught that having children is the basic purpose of marriage and gives meaning to the union. Mormons and Orthodox Jews also have a strong interest in having and rearing children.

Race

Racial minorities have the highest fertility rate, primarily due to the fact that they represent a higher proportion of younger females in the prime

....

Morbidity: chronic illness and disease.

child-bearing ages of 20-34. Hispanics have the highest fertility rate of any racial or ethnic category.

Government

The taxes, or lack of them, that our federal and state governments impose support parenthood. Although individuals have children for more emotional than financial reasons, married couples with children pay lower taxes than married couples without children. The federal tax savings in 2019 from having two dependent children for a family making $80,000 would be a $2,000 tax credit for each of the first two children or a total of $4,000. Hence, by giving a financial incentive for those who have children, our government takes a prontatalist position.

Media

People Magazine and other media outlets provide photos and interviews of the royal family as well as celebrities when there is a new baby.

FAMILY POLICY

How Old Is Too Old to Have a Child?

Mick Jagger was 73 when his girlfriend Melanie Hamrick gave birth to their son. Richard Gere was 69 when he and his wife Alejandra Sila had their first child. An American woman, Aleta St. Hames, gave birth to twins at the age of 56. Such births by an older parent are counter to the notion that parenting is for the young. They raise the question of whether there should be policies which limit the age a parent might have a biological child.

There are advantages and disadvantages of having a child as an older parent. The primary developmental advantage for the child of an older parent is that the parent likely wants the child and is able to provide for that child. The primary disadvantage of having a child in the later years is that the parents are likely to die before, or early in, the child's adult life. Mick Jagger will be 91 when his son graduates from high school.

There are also medical concerns for both the mother and the baby during pregnancy in later life. They include an increased risk of **morbidity,** a term used to describe chronic illness and disease, and mortality—death—for the mother. These risks are typically a function of chronic disorders that go along with aging, such as diabetes, hypertension, and cardiac disease. Stillbirths, miscarriages, ectopic pregnancies, multiple births, congenital malformations, and childhood cancer are also more frequent for women with advancing age (Barclay & Myrskyla, 2016). Prenatal testing can identify some potential problems such as the risk of Down syndrome

and any chromosome abnormality—negative neonatal outcomes are not inevitable. Because an older woman can usually have a healthy baby, government regulations on the age at which a woman can become pregnant are not likely. For example, Tamron Hall of the *Today Show* had her baby at age 48 and Janet Jackson gave birth at 50.

Age of the father may also impact the health of the child with higher risks of autism, schizophrenia, bipolar disorder, and childhood leukemia (Puleo et al., 2012; Sharma et al., 2015). Similarly, Krishnaswamy et al. (2011) found that Malaysian children born to fathers aged 50 or above had an increased risk of having CMD, common mental disorders—for example, bipolar disorder, depression, or anxiety—compared to children who were fathered by young men.

Men and women have several options for ensuring healthy offspring later in life. They may "freeze" their biological clock by freezing eggs or freezing sperm. Brown and Patrick (2018) confirmed that some women freeze their eggs to give them the freedom to choose parenting when they want it rather than responding to their biological clock. Women who are not in a relationship may also freeze their eggs to protect their ability to have a child regardless of if they have a partner. Some women may also give birth via a surrogate, a woman who agrees to become pregnant and give birth to a child for another person. ●

These discussions are always presented with happy smiling faces—the subtext being what a joy parenthood is. Additionally, sitcoms routinely support couples who have children. Can you think of one child-free couple on television?

Cultural Observances

Our society reaffirms its value for having children by identifying special days for parents. Each year on Mother's Day and Father's Day and now Grandparents' Day, parenthood is celebrated across the nation with cards, gifts, and embraces. People choosing not to have children have no nationally recognized "Child-free Day."

In addition to influencing individuals to have children, society and culture also influence when people have children, how they become parents, and how people feel about the age parents should be when they have children. Recently, couples have been having children at later ages. Is this a good idea? The Family Policy feature discusses this issue.

Individual Motivations for Having Children

People become parents for many different reasons. Positive reasons for having children include the desire to love and nurture one's own offspring, to fulfill a personal goal as a loving parent, and companionship. Negative motivations include solving a problem such as "saving" one's marriage or seeking to gain the acceptance or approval of one's partner, parents, and peers.

Unintended Pregnancies

Some women become mothers through an unintended pregnancy. An unintended pregnancy is defined by the CDC as a "pregnancy that is reported to have been either unwanted—that is, the pregnancy

Discovering one is pregnant is a time of delight or fright.
Courtesy of Trevor Werb

occurred when no children, or no more children, were desired—or mistimed and the pregnancy occurred earlier than desired. A survey of women aged 15-44 found that 13.5% of pregnancies were unwanted and 19.5% were mistimed. Of course, an unplanned, unwanted, or mistimed pregnancy does not mean an unwanted child.

Unintended pregnancies typically occur when a couple is not using contraception or is using contraception inconsistently or incorrectly. Twenty-six percent of 9,635 undergraduate females and 30% of 2,933 undergraduate males reported that they have always used a condom before intercourse (Hall & Knox, 2019). Most sexually active high school students use contraceptives. Only 16% of sexually active females and 10% of males reported that they or their partner had not used any method to prevent pregnancy at last intercourse (Witwer et al., 2018). Note that the first study does not speak to other forms of contraception. Even though a couple is careful about contraception use, pregnancy can still occur.

In some cases, reproductive coercion may occur, which is when a partner controls another person's reproductive choices. Such behavior can include **reproductive coercion**, coercion by either partner to affect a pregnancy, or **birth control sabotage**, a partner's interference with contraception—for example, the woman stops taking the pill without her partner's knowledge or a man pokes a hole in a condom. These behaviors are forms of abuse.

There can be consequences for unintended pregnancies. Unintended pregnancies are associated with individual depression, anxiety, and stress as well as increased relationship conflict and decreased satisfaction. Societal consequences for unintended children include higher divorce rates and a drain on social services (Bell et al., 2018). Unintended pregnancies may also pose a risk to the health of both the mom and the baby. These women are not able to modify their behaviors or break habits that can be harmful to a fetus, such as drinking alcohol or smoking cigarettes. Additionally, they can't seek preconception care from a health care practitioner to maximize their chances of having healthy pregnancies and babies.

Lifestyle Changes and Economic Costs of Parenthood

Having a child can drastically change an individual's or a couple's life. One's life changes in countless ways. However, two of the biggest effects are lifestyle

Reproductive coercion: coercion by either partner to result in a pregnancy.

Birth control sabotage: partner interference with contraception.

One motivation for having children is the joy of spending time with one's child.

changes and the financial costs of parenthood. We discuss these below.

Lifestyle Changes

Becoming a parent often involves changes in lifestyle. A major lifestyle change is the loss of freedom of activity and flexibility in one's personal schedule. Daily living routines become focused around the needs of the children. Living arrangements change to provide space for another person in the household. Some parents change their work schedule to allow them to be home more. Food shopping and menus change to accommodate the appetites of children. New parents also discover that it is difficult to maintain outside relationships.

Lifestyle changes are particularly dramatic for women. The time and effort required to be pregnant and rear children often compete with the time and energy needed to finish one's education or build one's career. The absence of mandatory paid parental leave in the United States is also a significant barrier. We discuss this issue further in Chapter 13. Parents learn quickly that being both an involved parent and climbing the career ladder are difficult. The careers of women may suffer most. Shreffler (2017) found that women in professional jobs with greater prestige, autonomy, and supervisory characteristics are more likely to postpone childbearing than women employed in jobs with lower scores on professional characteristics. It is not that women in more professional jobs prefer fewer children but that they experience greater barriers to having children. If they have children and do not have a sufficient support system, their time away from work may translate into less productivity with consequences for lower annual evaluations.

To give our students a simulated exposure to the effect of a baby on their lifestyle we asked them to take care of a "fake baby" for a week. Baby Think It Over (BTIO) is a very realistic-seeming life-sized computerized infant simulation doll that has been used in pregnancy prevention programs with adolescents. The following is part of the write-up of one of our students:

> The whole idea of the electronic baby was to see if I was ready to be a mother. I am sad to say that I failed the test. I am not ready to be a mother. This whole experience was extremely difficult for me because I am a full-time student and I have a job. It was really hard to get the things that I needed to get done. Suddenly, I couldn't just think about myself but I also had a little one to think about.
>
> The baby seemed to cry a lot, even if I had just changed her, she still cried. The experience really hit me when I had to wake up four and five times in the night to feed and to change the baby. I learned that when the baby sleeps, I need to sleep as well. I also learned that if I had to take care of the baby by myself, I just couldn't do it. What is sad is that single moms do it every day. If I had a supportive boyfriend or husband to help, the whole idea of having a baby wouldn't be so bad. But my boyfriend told me to call him when the project was over and I had given the baby back.

One flaw of the fake baby exercise is that it does not expose the potential parent to the joy most women experience in carrying their own baby, birthing their baby, and emotionally bonding with their baby. The fake baby exercise emphasizes the hassle and work of parenting but the baby does not emotionally bond with the parents. However, other students had a very positive experience with the baby and did not want to part with it at the end of the week. Indeed, in one case the "fake baby" became a part of the family. One student said that she awakened early one morning to find her father rocking the baby.

Financial Costs

Meeting the financial obligations of parenthood is difficult for many parents. There may be costs associated with conceiving or adopting. Additionally, delivering a child can cost up to $37,000 (Goo, 2017). After these initial conception and delivery costs, the annual cost of a child less than two years old for a married couple making an average of $81,700 per year is $12,680, with the largest expense being housing at 40% (*ProQuest Statistical Abstract*, 2019, Table 717). According to the U.S. Department of Agriculture, the estimated cost, including projected inflation, to middle class parents for rearing a child born today to age 18 will be $233,061 (Picchi, 2018). These costs do not include the wages lost when a parent drops out of the workforce to provide child care.

Kageyama and Matsuura (2018) noted that when a couple's life satisfaction is tied to their financial satisfaction, an additional child can lower their life satisfaction.

The $233,061 figure does not include college tuition, which many parents cover. Though college tuition varies, in 2019 the total cost for attending four years at a public college in the state of residence was $97,061, including tuition, dorm, meals. In 18 years, tuition is expected to increase to $222,466 for four years.

Such costs demonstrate the importance of family planning. Parents who plan for their children are able to pace the economic needs of their offspring. For example, having children four years apart helps to avoid having more than one child in college at the same time.

Living Child-free

Despite the cultural forces that influence people to have children, many individuals decide not to become parents. In doing so, they exercise their **procreative liberty**, or the freedom to decide whether to have children. Bruna (2018) noted that the narrative has shifted from "when" to have children to "whether." There has been an increase in the number of people electing not to have children. In a national sample of adult women, 16% said that they were not trying to have a child, nor did they want a child (Greil et al., 2016). About one in five of American women ages 40 to 44 with a master's degree do not have children.

Laura Scott (2009), a married woman who is child-free, set up the Childless by Choice Project and surveyed 171 child-free adults, ages 22 to 66, 71% of whom were female and 29% of whom were male, to identify their motivations for not having children. The categories of her respondents and the percentage of each follow:

Early articulators (66%)—these adults knew early that they did not want children

Postponers (22%)—adults who kept delaying when they would have children and remained childless

Acquiescers (8%)—those who made the decision to remain childless because their partner did not want children

Undecided (4%)—those who are childless but still in the decision-making process

The top five reasons her respondents gave for wanting to remain child-free were (Scott, 2009):

1. Current life and relationship satisfaction were great and they feared that parenthood would only detract from it.
2. Freedom and independence were strong values that they feared would be affected by children.
3. Avoidance of the responsibility for rearing a child.
4. No maternal or paternal instinct.
5. Accomplishing career and travel goals would be difficult as a parent.

Some of Scott's interviewees also had an aversion to children, having had a bad childhood or concerns about childbirth. Some child-free individuals enjoy children—and some deliberately choose careers to work with children—but they don't want the full-time emotional and economic responsibility of becoming parents.

Scott's findings represent just a few of the personal reasons why individuals choose not to have children, but there are many other factors at play. Other reasons may be medical, such as fertility issues or fear of passing down mental health issues. The fear of passing on medical issues is discussed further in Personal Choices: Is Genetic Testing For You? Financial reasons are also a huge factor, as many millennials are unsure of their ability to provide for themselves and pay off student loans, much less afford to have a child. Even still, there may be environmental reasons, based on concerns about population growth. In the end, there is no single reason. The decision to live child-free is just as personal as the decision to become a parent.

Despite these reasons, individuals who choose not to have children may find little social acceptance. Their decision may be seen as a "challenge to people who believe procreation is instinctive, intrinsic, biological, or obligatory" (p. 191). Indeed, child-free individuals are often viewed with suspicion, discomfort, and pity. Parents may think of child-free individuals as selfish and wrong not to want to have

These child-free spouses spend time with each other enjoying activities they may not be able to afford if they had children.

Is Genetic Testing for You?

Because each of us may have flawed genes that carry increased risk for diseases such as cancer and Alzheimer's, the question of whether to have a genetic test before becoming a parent becomes relevant. The test involves having a blood sample drawn. About 900 genetic tests are available. The advantage is the knowledge of what defective genes you may have and what diseases you may pass to your biological children.

The disadvantage is stress or anxiety surrounding the question of how you should handle the information as well as discrimination from certain health insurance companies who may deny coverage.. The validity of the test is also problematic as some tests may provide inaccurate information. And, because no treatment may be available if the test results are positive, the knowledge that they might pass diseases to their children can be unsettling to a couple. Genetic testing can be expensive, ranging from $200 to $2,400. ●

children. Their feelings may range from "since they don't have children, they won't like us or support our family values" to "they are wrong not to want children." People with children may even avoid child-free individuals, saying "I don't want to spend time with these people."

Koropeckyi-Cox et al. (2018) assessed the views of 1,266 undergraduates toward childless or child-free adults compared to parents. They found persistent negative stereotypes. Child-free individuals with no plans to have children were viewed as least warm and more emotionally troubled. Stereotypes about couples who deliberately elect not to have children include that they don't like kids, are immature, and are not fulfilled because they don't have a child to make their lives "complete." The Self Assessment: Child-free Lifestyle Scale on page 390 allows you to identify some of your own beliefs regarding child-free lifestyles.

To what degree are child-free individuals less happy than those who have children? It depends on where the individuals live. Those living in pronatalist countries where 70% or more believe motherhood is necessary are more unhappy and report less life satisfaction than those living in countries with weak pronatalist values where 30% or less believe motherhood is necessary. This finding is a result of examining the data from 36 nations (Tanaka & Johnson, 2016).

Although child-free individuals are often told that they will regret not becoming a parent, many individuals are happy with this decision. Stephanie Zacharek (2019) never had children and does not have regrets being child-free:

What I want to say to younger women who believe that a child-free life is an unfilled life is that your future self is a person you haven't met yet. Don't presume to know everything about her in advance. And don't presume that you can

control every element of your life just by making choices. Because sometimes even the choices you make by default can bring great happiness—just not the sort you envisioned (p. 45).

In contrast, some parents express regrets about having children. Moore and Abetz (2019) reported on regrets shared by parents in five countries—the United States, Canada, the United Kingdom, Australia, and Germany—on Reddit, the online global community. Some regrets were circumstantial: they had children too early or too late, had too few or too many, missed their freedom or child-free life, or the partner did not like children. Other regrets were specific to the child as in having a difficult child.

Some respondents felt trapped by the whole experience:

I never wanted kids, ever, and was very clear about this with my (now ex) wife from the day we met. . . . Sometime later, my wife unexpectedly fell pregnant.

She's always said it was a surprise, and that it was the one in a million chance of our birth control failing. I'm not convinced, but I've never been able to prove anything. . . . I tried to stick at it for just under four years, but it was awful.

I felt nothing for the child; it was like an object to me. . . . I couldn't take it anymore and filed for divorce. I happily granted full custody to my wife, and moved away to seek employment elsewhere. That was six years ago and I haven't seen her or the child since (p. 405).

While this example shows that not having children is the right choice for some individuals, it also demonstrates that individuals who choose to be child-free may become parents. Moore (2017) interviewed 32 individuals who, at one point, had told others they did not want to have children, but became parents later on. Three principle reasons for the change were accidental conception, ambiguous desire, and purposeful decision. A couple who had accidently gotten pregnant and had discussed abortion noted their experience to go through with having the baby:

> *It happened when we'd just moved into a new house, there were all these things we wanted to do, and it just felt like being pregnant would derail everything. And we actually got to the point of making an appointment to have an abortion. I remember sitting on the couch, and we were supposed to be putting on our jackets and going out the door, and just sitting there, and sitting there, and sitting there. And, finally, just saying, "I can't do this." He was like, "Yeah."*

HOW MANY CHILDREN DO YOU WANT?

Once an individual or couple decide to become parents, a natural next step is deciding on how many children. The most recent data show that in 2011-2015, among U.S. women ages 40-44, 85% had given birth; 17% had only one child, 34% had two children, 22% had three children, and 13% had given birth to four or more children (Martinez et al., 2018).

It is not unusual that spouses disagree on the number of children they want. Indeed, based on national data in Nigeria, 66% of spouses disagreed (Olawole-Isaac et al., 2018). When deciding how many children to have, parental time and economic resources are major factors. With each subsequent child, the economic resources available for each child are affected. Each additional child can also have a negative effect on the existing children by reducing the amount of parental time available to the other children.

Although individuals may have children with a partner or spouse, they may also have biological children with more than one partner, known as **multiple partner fertility.** U.S. national data reveal that 16% of parents have biological children with one or more partners (Monte et al., 2019). Cultural acceptability is one factor influencing this percentage. For example, in Iceland where marriage and parenthood are not strongly linked, it is not unusual to have several children with several partners. In the following sections, we look at the various options, beginning with ways individuals can control the number of children they have.

Methods of Contraception

To achieve the desired family size and to prevent unwanted pregnancies, various contraception options are available. See the Special Topics II section on page 369 for a list of the methods, rates of effectiveness, STI protection, benefits, disadvantages, and costs. Thomas and Karpilow (2018) emphasized the value on long-acting reversible methods such as the IUD, which does not rely on remembering to take a pill. However, the IUD and other forms of long-acting reversible contraceptives (LARC) do not provide protection against STIs (Hunter et al., 2018)

Emergency contraception (also called **postcoital contraception)** refers to various types of combined estrogen-progesterone morning-after pills or post-coital IUD insertion. These methods are used primarily in three circumstances: when a woman has unprotected intercourse, when a contraceptive method fails, such as condom breakage, which occurs 7% of the time, or slippage, and when a woman is raped. "Better safe than sorry" requires immediate action because the sooner the EC pills are taken, the lower the risk of pregnancy—twelve hours is best, and 72 hours at the latest.

While emergency contraception medication is available over the counter—no prescription is necessary and no pregnancy test is required for women age 17 and above—some parents feel their parental rights are being undermined. For females under age 17, a prescription is required. Although side effects, such as nausea and vomiting, may occur, they are typically over in a couple of days and the risk of being pregnant is minimal.

One Child

Those who have only one child may do so because they want the experience of parenthood without children markedly interfering with their lifestyle and careers. Still others have an only child because of the difficulty in pregnancy or birthing the child. One mother said, "I threw up every day for nine months including on the delivery table. Once is enough for me." There are also those who have only one child because they can't get pregnant a second time. There are also stereotypes of being an only child—they are selfish, lonely, and maladjusted. The data reveal positive outcomes for being only children in regard to having access to more resources, parental attention, and support for their goals.

Multiple partner fertility: having biological children with more than one partner.

Emergency contraception: various types of morning-after pills; also known as **postcoital contraception**.

Only children typically report positive outcomes of being the focus of parental attention, the benefactor of resources, and the exposure to a range of experiences.

CULTURE AND DIVERSITY

In 1979, China implemented a controversial national family planning policy designed to slow population growth by limiting families to one child. Penalties for having more than one child included arrest, jail, fines, termination of employment, and confiscation of property (Oxford, 2017). China's one-child policy was effective in slowing population growth in China, which has the highest rate of modern contraceptive use in the world (tied with the United Kingdom) (Population Reference Bureau, 2018).

The one-child policy created a number of human rights and economic problems. Many women were forced to have abortions or undergo sterilization or implantation of an IUD contraceptive device. Some Chinese women subjected to coercive measures and fled China to seek asylum in the United States (Oxford, 2017). The one-child policy also contributed to female infanticide in cases where parents wanted their only allowed child to be a boy. Furthermore, the cultural preference for a male child led to a shortage of women, and this imbalance in the sex-ratio of the population has made it difficult for men to find Chinese marriage partners.

The one-child policy has also led to a decrease in China's working age population, which means fewer workers to support the nonworking elderly population. The one-child policy was in effect for 35 years before it ended in 2015. Chinese authorities now offer incentives, such as tax breaks and cash bonuses, to couples that have a second child (Kotecki, 2018).

Two Children

Women and men want a similar number of children with two being the most preferred number (Morita et al., 2016). Indeed, the most preferred family size in the United States for non-Hispanic White women is the two-child family—1.9 to be exact! Reasons for this preference include feeling that a family is "not complete" without two children, having a companion for the first child, having a child of each sex, and repeating the positive experience of parenthood enjoyed with their first child.

Three Children

Couples are more likely to have a third child, and do so quickly, if they already have two girls rather than two boys. They are least likely to bear a third child if they already have a boy and a girl. One father said, "I have 12 older sisters...my parents kept having children till they had me."

Having a third child creates a middle child. This child is sometimes neglected because parents of three children may focus more on the baby and the firstborn than on the child in between. However, an advantage to being a middle child is the chance to experience both a younger and an older sibling.

Four Children

More than three children are often born to parents who are immersed in a religion, which encourages procreation. Catholics, Mormons, and Orthodox Jews typically have more children than Protestants. When religion is not a factor, **competitive birthing** may be operative whereby individuals have the same number or more of children as their peers.

The addition of each subsequent child dramatically increases the possible relationships between parents and children. For example, in a one-child family, four interpersonal relationships are possible: mother-father, mother-child, father-child, and father-mother-child. In a family of four, eleven relationships are possible.

Sex Selection

Some couples use sex selection technologies to help ensure a boy or a girl. Among some groups, a bias for male children continues, which is examined further in Applied Social Research: Are Male Children Still Preferred? (Bragg et al., 2018). MicroSort is a preconception sperm-sorting technology, which allows parents to increase the chance of having a girl or a boy baby. The procedure is also called "family balancing" since couples that already have several children of

....

Competitive birthing: having the same number (or more) of children as one's peers.

Are Male Children Still Preferred?

If you could have only one child, does the sex of the child matter to you? This research assesses undergraduates' preference for their child being born a particular sex.

Sample and Methods

Five hundred ninety-eight undergraduate students at a large southeastern university completed a 40-item online survey about their attitude toward children. Of the participants, 77% were women and 23% were men. Sixty-eight percent were White and 18% African American. As for the family context in which they grew up, over 90% had siblings with 34% having younger siblings and 33% having older siblings. Twenty-three percent had both younger and older siblings. Seventeen percent of the respondents had siblings who already had children of their own.

The survey consisted of demographic questions—for example, sex, age, race, religion, relationship status, and number of siblings—and questions regarding attitudes toward children. A 7-point Likert scale was used for attitudinal questions. The current study used a subset of the data. The data were analyzed using SPSS (version 21) statistical software.

Findings

As for wanting children, 72% agreed that "having children is important to me" and 65% reported that they always knew that they wanted to have children. Seventy-one percent also agreed that it was important that the person they married want children, though women reported a stronger desire in this area. Regarding the number and sex of children, 46% reported that they wanted two children with 87% wanting a boy and a girl. If they could have only one child, 35% reported that they wanted a male, 23% wanted a female, and 42% "could care less" about the sex of an only child.

There was a gender difference regarding sex preference of the first child. Two-thirds (66.4%) of the men and approximately a quarter (25.9%) of the women wanted a boy. Regarding preference for a female child, 7.8% of the men reported wanting a girl compared to 27.7% of women as their first child. The sex of the child was not as important to women. Approximately half (46.4%) of the women respondents reported that they could care less about the sex of the child if they were to have only one child. In contrast, only a quarter (25.8%) of the men reported that they could care less. ●

Source: Bragg, B., Chang, I. J., & Knox, D. (2018, Nov. 9). Some traditions die as slow as molasses: Are male children still preferred? Poster presented at the National Council on Family Relations Annual meeting, San Diego, CA.

one sex often use it. The eggs of a woman are fertilized and the sex of the embryos three to eight days old is identified. Only embryos of the desired sex are then implanted in the woman's uterus. The FDA has *not* approved MicroSort as a sex selection technique.

There are ethical considerations in regard to sex selection. One perspective held by sex-selection technology providers argues that sex selection is an expression of reproductive rights and a sign of female empowerment by giving the woman control over her pregnancies. Alternatively, sex selection could be viewed as sexist since female embryos are often destroyed.

TEENAGE PARENTHOOD

Teenage parenthood is a major life event, especially for the mothers. Teenage motherhood can significantly alter one's life course trajectory. It is associated with dropping out of high school. Teenage pregnancy is more prevalent in communities facing poverty with low education and employment opportunities (World Health Organization, 2018). Reasons for teenagers having a child include not using contraception, having limited parental supervision, and perceiving few alternatives to parenthood. Childhood socioeconomic disadvantage has been found to be associated with teen pregnancy (Smith et al., 2018). Unfortunately, having a child may be perceived as one of the only remaining meaningful roles available to adolescents in marginalized communities. Some teenagers may feel lonely and unloved and want a baby to create a sense of being needed and wanted. Teenage moms may also have had a teenager for a mother, thus making having a child as a teenager normative (Margherita et al., 2017).

The rate of teenagers having children has decreased, but the U.S. teen pregnancy rate is still noticeably higher than other industrialized countries such as Canada (U.S. Department of Health & Human Services, 2017). The expansion of youth friendly family planning services into lower income areas is one of the important prevention strategies (Colen et al., 2016). Giving young females more opportunities via education is also important.

Teens in countries such as France and Germany are as sexually active as U.S. teenagers, but the teenage birth rate in these countries is very low. Teens in France and Germany grow up in a society that promotes responsible contraceptive use. In the Netherlands, for example, individuals are taught to use double protection of both the pill and the condom, an approach called **double Dutch**, for prevention of pregnancy and sexually transmitted infections (STIs).

INFERTILITY

Infertility is the inability to achieve a pregnancy after at least one year of regular sexual relations without birth control or the inability to carry a pregnancy to a live birth.

Unfortunately, with infertility, time is not your friend. People are waiting longer to have kids and many experience infertility issues. Nobody ever talks about it.

Bill Rancic

Different types of infertility include the following:

1. **Primary infertility.** The woman has never conceived even though she wants to and has had regular sexual relations for the past twelve months.

2. **Secondary infertility.** The woman has previously conceived but is currently unable to do so even though she wants to and has had regular sexual relations for the past twelve months.

3. **Pregnancy wastage.** The woman has been able to conceive but has been unable to produce a live birth.

Causes of Infertility

Although popular usage does not differentiate between the terms *fertilization* and the *beginning of pregnancy,* fertilization or **conception** refers to the

....

Conception: the fusion of the egg and sperm; also known as fertilization.

Double Dutch: a strategy of using both the pill and condom; also known as dual protection.

Infertility: the inability to achieve a pregnancy after at least one year of regular sexual relations without birth control, or the inability to carry a pregnancy to a live birth.

fusion of the egg and sperm, whereas **pregnancy** is not considered to begin until five to seven days later, when the fertilized egg is implanted, typically in the uterine wall. Hence, not all fertilizations result in a pregnancy. An estimated 30% to 40% of conceptions are lost prior to or during implantation. One's chances of conceiving can also decrease with age, as the chance of conceiving per month in one's thirties is 20% and 10% in one's forties.

Forty percent of infertility problems are attributed to the woman, 40% to the man, and 20% to both of them. Some of the more common causes of infertility in men include low sperm production, poor semen motility, effects of STIs (such as chlamydia, gonorrhea, and syphilis), and interference with passage of sperm through the genital ducts due to an enlarged prostate. Female infertility is related to age, not having been pregnant before, blocked fallopian tubes, endocrine imbalance that prevents ovulation, dysfunctional ovaries, chemically hostile cervical mucus that may kill sperm, and effects of STIs. Obesity in the woman is also related to her infertility. Unexplained infertility is one of the most common diagnoses in fertility care.

Being infertile is a major life crisis for a woman. Bell (2019) conducted interviews with 58 women who were medically infertile and involuntarily childless and noted how they denied their infertility status to maintain their sense of being a woman. For example, a woman would say that she just hasn't gotten pregnant yet as though she would in the next month. There is now a variety of at-home fertility kits, which can allow women to measure the level of their follicle stimulating hormones or for men to measure the concentration of their sperm.

Assisted Reproductive Technology (ART)

A number of technological innovations are available to assist women and couples in becoming pregnant. These include hormonal therapy, artificial insemination, ovum transfer, in vitro fertilization, gamete intrafallopian transfer, and zygote intrafallopian transfer. These options can also help LGBTQ individuals and couples have biological children. ART is expensive and may be a barrier for some. The average cost of one round of IVF is $12,000, but costs of ART will increase if the individual or couple goes through years of different methods and cycles. The first author knows a couple who spent $100,000 on having a baby. However, insurance may defray the cost for the well insured.

....

Pregnancy: when the fertilized egg is implanted, typically in the uterine wall.

Hormone Therapy

Drug therapies are often used to treat hormonal imbalances, induce ovulation, and correct problems in the luteal phase of the menstrual cycle. Frequently used drugs include Clomid, Pergonal, and human chorionic gonadotropin (HCG), a hormone extracted from human placenta. These drugs stimulate the ovary to ripen and release an egg. Although they are fairly effective in stimulating ovulation, hyperstimulation can occur, which may result in permanent damage to the ovaries.

Hormone therapy also increases the likelihood that multiple eggs will be released, resulting in multiple births. The increase in triplets and higher order multiple births over the past decade in the United States is largely attributed to the increased use of ovulation-inducing drugs for treating infertility. Infants of higher order multiple births are at greater risk of having low birth weight and their mortality rates are higher. Mortality rates have improved for these babies, but these low birth weight survivors may need extensive neonatal medical and social services.

Artificial Insemination

When the sperm of the male partner are low in count or motility, sperm from several ejaculations may be pooled and placed directly into the cervix. This procedure is known as *artificial insemination by husband* (AIH). When sperm from someone other than the woman's partner are used to fertilize a woman, the technique is referred to as *artificial insemination by donor* (AID). Wyverkens et al. (2017) interviewed infertile couples who used a sperm donor and found that "Once the family was formed, most couples avoided talking about the donor because it was perceived as disrupting men's growing confidence in their position as father" (p. 203).

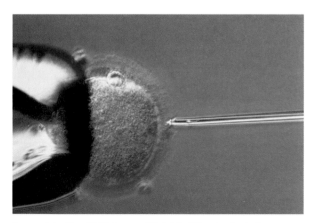

Sperm Injection (ICSI) is an artificial fertilization technique. A single sperm is injected into the cytoplasm of an egg via a microneedle. Used in treatment of severe male infertility.
Mark Harmel/The Image Bank/Getty Images Plus

Regardless of the source of the sperm, it should be screened for genetic abnormalities and STIs, quarantined for 180 days, and retested for human immunodeficiency virus (HIV); the donor should also be younger than 50 to diminish hazards related to aging. However, these precautions are not routinely taken.

Artificial Insemination of a Surrogate Mother

In some instances, artificial insemination does not help a woman get pregnant. Her fallopian tubes may be blocked, or her cervical mucus may be hostile to sperm. The couple that still wants a child and has decided against adoption may consider parenthood through a surrogate mother. There are two types of surrogate mothers. One is the contracted surrogate mother who supplies the egg, is impregnated with the male partner's sperm, carries the child to term, and gives the baby to the man and his partner. Alternatively, donor sperm may also be used to fertilize the surrogate mother. A second type is the surrogate mother who carries to term a baby to whom she is not genetically related. In this instance, a mother and father would provide the egg and sperm and a surrogate mother would carry the embryo. Or a donor egg can be fertilized by donor sperm and the embryo can be implanted in the surrogate mother's uterus.

Although some American women are willing to "rent their wombs," women in India also provide this service. For $5,000, an Indian wife who already has a child will carry a baby to term for an infertile couple for a fraction of the cost of an American surrogate. *Google Baby* is the name of a documentary showing how infertile couples with a credit card can submit an order for a baby—the firm will find the donor egg and the donor sperm, fertilize the egg, and implant it in a surrogate mother in India. The couple need only fly to India, pick up their baby, and return to the states. Nebeling Petersen (2018) noted how gay men plan to become fathers via transnational commercial surrogacy. For heterosexual couples, **transnational commercial surrogacy** is often the last options they seek; for gay males, it may be their first option.

California is one of 12 states in which entering into an arrangement with a surrogate mother is legal. The fee to the surrogate mother is around $30,000. Other fees such as travel, hospital, lawyers, and so on can add another $70,000. Surrogate mothers typically have their own children which may make giving up a child that they carry easier.

Transnational commercial surrogacy: having a baby by means of paying a third party to secure sperm, egg, fertilization, and surrogacy of the pregnancy. The new parents then come to take the baby home. Facilities in India provide this service.

Donor Sperm

A number of questions arise when donor sperm is used. For example, the importance of a father in the life of a child is brought into question. The provision of sperm from an anonymous donor allows the father to walk away with no financial obligations to the child. Countries such as Britain, Sweden, Norway, and Switzerland have banned anonymity in sperm donation, which sends the message that fathers are important.

Another concern is if a donor's sperm has resulted in multiple children. Persaud et al. (2017) revealed the reaction of teenagers to their same donor siblings—their mothers used the same donor to conceive—as one of curiosity and uniqueness. Some established close, long-term relationships. Others were more distant.

In Vitro Fertilization

About 2 million couples cannot have a baby because the woman's fallopian tubes are blocked or damaged, preventing the passage of eggs to the uterus. In some cases, blocked tubes can be opened via laser surgery or by inflating a tiny balloon within the clogged passage. When these procedures are not successful or when the woman decides to avoid invasive tests and exploratory surgery, *in vitro*, meaning "in glass," *fertilization* (IVF), also known as test-tube fertilization, is an alternative.

Using a laparoscope, a narrow, telescope-like instrument inserted through an incision just below the woman's naval to view tubes and ovaries, the physician is able to see a mature egg as it is released from the woman's ovary. The time of release can be predicted accurately within two hours. When the egg emerges, the physician uses an aspirator to remove the egg, placing it in a small tube containing stabilizing fluid. The egg is taken to the laboratory, put in a culture petri dish, kept at a certain temperature and acidity level, and surrounded by sperm from the woman's partner or donor. After one of these sperm fertilizes the egg, the egg divides and is implanted by the physician in the wall of the woman's uterus. Usually, several eggs are implanted in the hope one will

---

TECHNOLOGY AND THE FAMILY

Fertility Enhancement

Pregnancy is not a certainty as most couples assume it to be. Although an overview of the human reproduction process is part of the K-12 curriculum, many adults do not have sufficient knowledge about fertility (Pedro et al., 2018). Many choose to delay having children into their mid to late thirties which results in a lower chance of conception. Faced with infertility, individuals may choose Assisted Reproductive Technology (ART) which attempts to increase one's success rate in getting pregnant.

Calculating the woman's ovulation date is crucial for conception and can be an arduous experience. Every woman is unique and ovulation does not always occur in the middle of the classic 28-day cycle. Stress, nutrition, and daily activities also affect the woman's ovulation cycle. Learning about one's cycle is a grueling process which includes recording basal body temperature every morning, charting menstrual cycles, noting bodily signals during ovulation, and being sensitive to and understanding changes in one's body.

Various technological devices claim to increase one's fertility (Lundberg et al., 2018; Newman, 2018). Although the sperm and egg are both essential elements in conception, over-the-counter devices and apps target women as primary users. For example, Daysy is a fertility monitoring device which is typically used with the Daysy view app; it records the woman's body temperature, tracks her monthly cycle, and calculates her fertility status (Daysy, 2018). The Daysy View app not only displays the optimal window for conception, but also keeps track of sexual activity and can share this information with a significant other. However, the effectiveness of fertility monitors and tracking devices has received mixed reviews (Koch et al., 2018; Polis, 2018).

Since conception normally takes place in the fallopian tube, delivering live semen to the closest deposit point is crucial. One device claims to dispense the sperm at the opening of the cervix to boost conception (Stork OTC, 2018). Artificial insemination can be accomplished in the comfort of one's home with donor's semen. The home artificial insemination kits, containing items such as needleless syringes and collection cups, allow the couple to be actively involved (Matthews, 2018). This home insemination technique is also known as the "turkey baster method."

Although new technological inventions offer consumers a range of choices to improve fertility, consumers should be cautious about product credibility. From supplements and vitamins to devices and apps, many products have not been confirmed by clinical data. Fertility products with FDA approval or with official medical device certification are more reliable. With proper regulation and clinical evidence, advancement in technology and wise choices will bring hope to many infertile couples. ●

survive. Sometimes, several eggs survive as in the case of Nadya Suleman, who ended up giving birth to eight babies.

Occasionally, some fertilized eggs are frozen and implanted at a later time, if necessary. This procedure is known as **cryopreservation**. Separated or divorced couples may disagree over who owns the frozen embryos, and the legal system is still wrestling with the fate of their unused embryos, sperm, or ova after a divorce or death.

Ovum Transfer

In conjunction with in vitro fertilization is **ovum transfer**, also referred to as embryo transfer. In this procedure, an egg is donated, fertilized in vitro with the husband's sperm, and then transferred to his wife. Alternatively, a physician places the sperm of the male partner in a surrogate woman. After about five days, her uterus is flushed out in a process called endometrial lavage, and the contents are analyzed under a microscope to identify the presence of a fertilized ovum.

The fertilized ovum is then inserted into the uterus of the otherwise infertile partner. Although the embryo can also be frozen and implanted at another time, fresh embryos are more likely to result in successful implantation. Infertile couples that opt for ovum transfer do so because the baby will be biologically related to at least one of them—the father—and the partner will have the experience of pregnancy and childbirth.

Success Using Reproductive Technologies

Based on data of 231,936 cycles from fertility clinics throughout the United States, 26% resulted in a live birth (CDC, 2015). Another source (WebMD) reports that 22.4% of infertility treatments and in vitro fertilization result in a live birth (Todd, 2017). The sooner an infertility problem is suspected—and the younger the woman—the more successful the intervention.

ADOPTION

There are various routes to adoption: Public, whereby children are adopted from the child welfare system; private agencies, whereby children are placed with nonrelatives through agencies; independent adoption, whereby children are placed directly by birth parents or through an intermediary such as a physician or attorney; kinship, whereby children are placed in a family member's home; and stepparent, whereby children are adopted by a spouse. Motives

for adopting a child include a desire to give an otherwise unwanted child a permanent loving home, a desire to expand one's family, or a desire to avoid contributing to overpopulation by having more biological children. Some couples with a biological child adopt a child to blend into their existing family (Santos-Nunes et al., 2018). Less than one percent (0.7%) of women aged 18-44 report ever having adopted a child (Ugwu & Nugent, 2018).

Adoption is also an avenue for LGBTQ individuals and couples—for example, Elton John and his partner adopted two male children. These couples may also seek to have a baby themselves like lesbians who choose to have artificial insemination and gay males who opt for surrogate parenthood.

Characteristics of Children Preferred for Adoption

Burge (2016) assessed the child profile preferences of 5,830 adults seeking to adopt a child. Would-be parents preferred babies and young children the most, but they were least often adopted because there were not enough children in that category for them to adopt. However, between 43% and 60% indicated a willingness to consider adopting children with degrees of learning disabilities, emotional behavioral disorders, and physical disabilities. The most preferred, among 20 categories of available children's possible exposures and health diagnoses, were those children who had been abused in the past.

Children Who Are Adopted

Adoption is not an easy experience for children. Soares et al. (2019) interviewed 102 children ages 8-10 who were adopted at different ages. While being part of a family and experiencing family life were their greatest positives, "most adoptees reported facing family and social relationship difficulties in their post-adoption life, such as communicating openly about adoption with the adoptive parents and peers. Findings showed that children's adaptation to adoption is complex, ambivalent, and individually experienced. Adopted children need parents and professionals to help them elaborate and make sense of their life story." "Who are your real parents?", "Why did your mother give you up?", and "Are those your real parents?" are questions children who are adopted must sometimes cope with. These are microaggressions reflecting that adopted children are stigmatized (Baden, 2016). W.I.S.E. UP is a tool provided to adopted children who are aware that they are adopted to help them cope with these intrusive, sometimes uncomfortable questions. W.I.S.E. is an acronym for the following: **W**alk away, **I**gnore or change the subject, **S**hare what you

Cryopreservation: the freezing of fertilized eggs for implantation at a later stage.

Ovum transfer: a fertilized egg is implanted in the uterine wall.

are comfortable sharing, and **E**ducate about adoption in general. The tool emphasizes that adopted children are wiser about adoption than their peers and can educate them or remove themselves from the situation.

Costs of Adoption

The cost of an adoption varies by the type of adoption. The least expensive—no cost—adoption is adoption via being a foster parent but, with various fees, it may cost up to $2,800 (National Infertility and Adoption Nonprofit, 2016). We know of a couple who adopted a child from Moldavia at a cost of $30,000. Private adoptions, through an agency, cost an average of $41,500 (National Fertility and Adoption Nonprofit, 2016).

While being a foster parent is the least expensive route to adopting a child, the foster parents run the risk of the parents resurfacing and claiming the child after the foster parents become emotionally attached. Stepparent and kinship adoptions are also usually without cost and have less risk of the child being withdrawn.

Transracial Adoption

Transracial adoption is defined as the practice of adopting children of a race different from that of the parents—for example, a White couple adopting a Korean or an African American child. Celebrities Sandra Bullock and Angelina Jolie adopted children of another race. Forty percent of all adoptions are transracial (Baden, 2016).

Transracial adoptions are controversial. The motivations of persons wanting to adopt cross racially are sometimes questioned—are they trying to make a political statement? Another controversy is whether it is beneficial for children to be adopted by parents of the same racial background. In regard to the adoption of African-American children by same-race parents, the National Association of Black Social Workers (NABSW) passed a resolution against transracial adoptions, citing that such adoptions prevented Black children from developing a positive sense of themselves.

The counterargument is that healthy self-concepts, an appreciation for one's racial heritage, and coping with racism or prejudice can be learned in a variety of contexts. Legal restrictions on transracial adoptions have disappeared, and social approval for transracial adoptions is increasing.

How transracial adopted children process their being adopted varies. Author Nicole Chung writes

....

Transracial adoption: adopting children of a race different from that of the parents.

An instructor shows a couple in Arlington Heights how to braid hair at Cradle adoption agency in Evanston, Illinois. The class was formed to help transracial families with child hair care.
Chicago Tribune/Tribune News Sevie/Getty

about her experience as a Korean child adopted by a White family:

> I doubted it had ever occurred to my adoptive parents that I might not want to learn anything about Korea. Had they ever suggested a language class, I'm sure I would have complained—it was bad enough that I couldn't change the way I looked; did I really have to emphasize my differences by learning a language no one else I knew could speak?

Another transracial child wanted to know everything about her race and ethnicity. While she appreciated the life her parents provided, she always resented having to be separated from her own race and culture, but never told her parents.

Open Versus Closed Adoptions

Another controversy is whether adopted children should be allowed to obtain information about their biological parents. Some adopted children want to find their birth parents but face policies which prohibit giving them information, such as sealed records. In general, there are considerable benefits for having an open adoption, especially the opportunity for the biological parent to stay involved in the child's life. Adoptees learn early that they are adopted and who their biological parents are. Birth parents are more likely to avoid regret and to be able to stay in contact with their child. Adoptive parents have information about the genetic background of their adopted child.

However, Jones (2016) emphasized that there are difficulties faced by members of the adoption triad that are likely to threaten rather than promote further progress regarding openness in adoption. These difficulties include the management of emotions by each party in regard to who belongs to whom, where the alliances are, and a continual process of redefining an arrangement that is ambiguous.

Regarding the issue of when should a child be told that he or she is adopted, Baden et al. (2019) studied 254 adult adoptees and found that those who learned of their adoptions from age 3 and older reported more distress and lower life satisfaction than those who learned earlier. Adoptees also reported a desire for communicative openness and having support for seeking contact with birth relatives and other adoptees.

Embryo Adoption

The increase of fertility treatment has resulted in the rise of frozen embryos. Instead of disposing of those embryos, donating them for research, or leaving them in a freezer indefinitely, some couples donate their embryos for adoption. **Embryo adoption** refers to the adoption of the frozen embryo which will be implanted in the adoptive mother's uterus. Embryo adoption offers the experience of pregnancy and child birth.

International Adoption

Thousands of children are adopted from other countries and may also be transracial adoptions. Reinoso et al. (2016) reviewed the stressors, coping strategies, and psychological adjustment of internationally adopted children and found that half reported problems concerning adoption. Bailey (2015) interviewed 26 children from Eastern Europe who had been adopted by American parents. Several themes emerged—

Fear –Tatiana, a 15-year-old from Russia explained:

[In the orphanage] people get abused and the food is horrible. You feel like you are a prisoner basically, especially when you're little. They don't show you any love. So most kids who get adopted put up a wall towards their parents because they don't know how to love back. And the parents get frustrated. Lack of trust.

This theme was revealed by Sasha, age 12:

Everybody, I guarantee you, who gets adopted [...] they are scared at least for a year. They're scared of you really. They are not scared that you are going to hurt them or anything; they are just scared. They don't know how to handle the love. They don't know how to love back. They just need to learn.

Desire for independence – revealed by 17-year-old Luba:

My biggest problem with my family that we had is that they didn't understand that for an orphan kid at my age, I already have so much more experience with being on my own than being in a family. They don't understand that I am so independent and so well kept that I want freedom and want to do things.

Lack of acceptance – Mikhail was treated badly by his birth mother, and he transferred his feelings toward her to his new adoptive mother whom he did not trust. He recalled:

Like knowing what my [birth] mom did to me and everything, I just didn't want anything to do with her [adoptive mom]. I pushed her away.

Internet Adoption

Some couples use the Internet to adopt a baby. The use of the Internet to adopt a baby can pose serious problems of potential fraud and exploitation. Couples should proceed with great caution. Policy makers should also be aware of the practice of "re-homing" where parents who have adopted a child use the Internet to place unwanted adopted children in new families. There is no monitoring or regulation of this practice. In effect, a couple can adopt a child internationally and if they are not happy with the child, can "re-home" the child by simply getting another adult to sign a paper that they assume the role of legal guardian for the child. Social Services is not involved, and no social worker interviews the prospective new parents. The potential for abuse, including re-homing children who are then sex trafficked, is horrifying.

Foster Parenting

Some individuals seek the role of parent via foster parenting. A **foster parent**, also known as a family caregiver, is neither a biological nor an adoptive parent but is one who takes care of and fosters a child taken into custody. Foster care may be temporary or long term. A foster parent has made a contract with the state for the service, has judicial status, and is reimbursed by the state. Foster parents are screened for previous arrest records, child abuse, and neglect. They are licensed by the state; some states require a "foster parent orientation" program.

Children placed in foster care have typically been removed from parents who are abusive, who are substance abusers, who are mentally

---

Embryo adoption: the adoption of a frozen embryo which will be implanted in the adoptive mother's uterus.

Foster parent: neither a biological nor an adoptive parent but a person who takes care of and fosters a child taken into custody by social services.

incompetent, or all of these. Although foster parents are paid for taking care of children in their home, they may also be motivated by their love of children. The goal of placing children in foster care is to improve their living conditions and then either return them to their family of origin or find a more permanent adoptive or foster home for them. Some couples become foster parents in the hope of being able to adopt a child who is placed in their custody.

Over 400,000 children are in foster care. While about 5% of youth in the United States are LBGTQ, 15% to 19% of LGBTQ are in foster homes. The rejection LGBTQ youth experienced in their homes often continues in their foster homes. Efforts are now being made, such as with The Connecting Program, to match LGBTQ youth with families knowledgeable about and embracing of LGBTQ youth (Salazar, 2018). Steenbakkers et al. (2018) also noted that foster care children may have unique, unanticipated needs which foster parents should be aware of. For example, one previously sexually abused foster child said that she did not want an emotional relationship with a foster parent. Rather, the youth wanted an instrumental, professional relationship.

STERILIZATION

Sterilization is a permanent surgical procedure that prevents reproduction. Sterilization is the contraceptive of choice when the woman should not have more children for health reasons or when individuals are certain about their desire to have no more children or to remain child-free. Most couples complete their intended childbearing in their late twenties or early thirties, leaving more than fifteen years of continued risk of unwanted pregnancy. Because of the risk of pill use at older ages and the lower reliability of alternative birth control methods, sterilization has become the most popular method of contraception among married women who have completed their families. Four in ten married women ages 15 to 44 rely on sterilization, primarily tubal ligation with more in the later age range; the pill and condom are used more often in their early reproductive life. Tubal ligation is used 1.5 times more often than vasectomy (Eeckhaut, 2019).

Female Sterilization

Although a woman may be sterilized by removal of either her ovaries with a surgical procedure called an **oophorectomy** or her uterus with another surgical procedure known as a **hysterectomy**, these operations are not normally undertaken for the sole purpose of sterilization because the ovaries produce important hormones, as well as eggs, and because both procedures carry the risks of major surgery. Sometimes, however, another medical problem requires hysterectomy.

The usual procedures of female sterilization are the salpingectomy and a variant of it, the laparoscopy. **Salpingectomy,** also known as tubal ligation or tying the tubes (see Figure 11.1), is performed under a general anesthetic, often while the woman is in the hospital just after she has delivered a baby. An incision is made in the lower abdomen, just above the pubic line, and the fallopian tubes are brought into view one at a time. A part of each tube is cut out, and the ends are tied, clamped, or cauterized (burned). The operation takes about 30 minutes. A less expensive and quicker form of salpingectomy, which is performed on an outpatient basis, is **laparoscopy** and it only takes about 15 minutes. Often using local anesthesia, the surgeon inserts a small, lighted viewing instrument called a laparoscope through the woman's abdominal wall just below the navel, through which the uterus and the fallopian tubes can be seen. The surgeon then makes another small incision in the lower abdomen and inserts a special pair of forceps that carry electricity to cauterize the tubes. The laparoscope and the forceps are then withdrawn, the small wounds are closed with a single stitch, and small bandages are placed over the closed incisions. Laparoscopy is also known as "the Band-Aid operation." As an alternative to reaching the fallopian tubes through an opening below the navel, the surgeon may make a small incision in the back of the vaginal barrel, following a procedure called vaginal tubal ligation.

To what degree do women who become sterilized regret their decision? Eeckhaut and Sweeney (2018) noted that about a fourth of sterilized reproductive-aged women in the United States regret their decision. Those who were cohabiting compared to those were married or single but not living together at the time the sterilization decision was made and who later broke up reported the most regret.

Male Sterilization

Vasectomies are the most frequent form of male sterilization. They are usually performed in the physician's office under a local anesthetic.

....

Sterilization: a permanent surgical procedure that prevents reproduction.

Oophorectomy: form of female sterilization whereby the woman's ovaries are removed.

Hysterectomy: form of female sterilization whereby the woman's uterus is removed.

Salpingectomy: type of female sterilization whereby the fallopian tubes are cut and the ends are tied.

Laparoscopy: a form of tubal ligation that involves a small incision through the woman's abdominal wall just below the navel.

Male and Female Sterilization

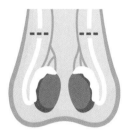
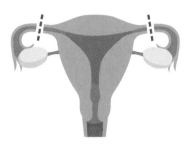

MALE STERILIZATION
VASECTOMY

FEMALE STERILIZATION
TUBAL LIGATION

ElenaBs/Alamy Stock Vector

Vasectomy is a safe and cost-effective intervention for permanent male contraception. Sperm are still produced in the testicles, but because there is no tube to the penis, they remain in the epididymis and eventually dissolve.

The procedure takes about 15 minutes. The patient can leave the physician's office within a short time. Because sperm do not disappear from the ejaculate immediately after a vasectomy—some remain in the vas deferens above the severed portion—a couple should use another method of contraception until the man has had about 20 ejaculations. In about 1% of the cases, the vas deferens grows back and the man becomes fertile again. A vasectomy does not affect the man's desire for sex, ability to have an erection or an orgasm, amount of ejaculate— sperm account for only a minute portion of the seminal fluid—health, or chance of prostate cancer. Although a vasectomy may be reversed with a 30% to 60% success rate, a man should get a vasectomy only if he does not want to have a biological child.

ABORTION

Abortion remains a controversial issue in America. An abortion may be either an **induced abortion**, which is the deliberate termination of a pregnancy through chemical or surgical means, or a **spontaneous abortion (miscarriage)**, which is the unintended termination of a pregnancy.

In this text we will use the term *abortion* to refer to induced abortion. In general, abortion is legal in

the United States but it was challenged under the Bush administration. Specifically, federal funding was withheld if an aid group offered abortion or abortion advice. However, the Obama administration restored governmental approval for abortion. President Obama said that denying such aid undermined "safe and effective voluntary family planning in developing countries." In February 2019, the Trump administration announced that funding will be blocked for programs or agencies that provide abortion referrals.

CULTURE AND DIVERSITY

There are wide variations in the range of cultural responses to the abortion issue. On one end of the continuum is the Kafir tribe in Central Asia, where an abortion is strictly the choice of the woman. There is no taboo or restriction with regard to abortion, and the woman is free to exercise her decision to terminate her pregnancy. One reason for the Kafirs' approval of abortion is that childbirth in the tribe is associated with high rates of maternal mortality. Because birthing children may threaten the life of significant numbers of adult women in the community, women may be encouraged to abort. Such encouragement is particularly strong in the case of women who are viewed as too young, too old, too sick, or too small to bear children.

A tribe or society may also encourage abortion for a number of other reasons, including practicality, economics, lineage, and honor. Abortion is practical for women in migratory societies. Such women must control their pregnancies, because they are limited in the number of children they can nurse and transport. Economic motivations become apparent when resources are scarce—the number of

Vasectomy: form of male sterilization whereby the vas deferens is cut so that sperm cannot continue to travel outside the body via the penis.

Induced abortion: the deliberate termination of a pregnancy through chemical or surgical means.

Spontaneous abortion (miscarriage): the unintended termination of a pregnancy.

children born to a group must be controlled. Abortion for reasons of lineage or honor involves encouragement of an abortion in those cases in which a woman becomes impregnated in an adulterous relationship. To protect the lineage and honor of her family, the woman may have an abortion.

Incidence of Abortion

When the United States was founded, abortion was legal and accepted by the public up until the time of "quickening"—the moment when a woman can feel the fetus inside her. By the time of the Civil War, one in five pregnancies was terminated by an abortion. Opposition to abortion grew in the 1870s, led by the American Medical Association launching a fierce campaign to make abortion illegal unless authorized and performed by a licensed physician. Abortion was made illegal in 1880, which did not stop the practice; a million abortions were performed illegally by the 1950s. In 1973, the Supreme Court upheld in Roe v. Wade the right of a woman to have a legal abortion. However, the law is continually challenged. In May 2019, Alabama outlawed abortion at almost every stage of pregnancy and criminalized the procedure for doctors. The goal was to set up a Supreme Court test with the arrival of conservative Justice Brett Kavanaugh to overturn Roe V. Wade which allows abortion up to the 24th week (Williams & Blinder, 2019). Missouri, Georgia, Kentucky, Mississippi, and Ohio have also passed restrictive abortion laws.

About 1.2 million abortions are performed annually in the United States. Although the number of abortions has been increasing among the poor who have lower access to health care and health education, there has been a decrease among higher income women due to increased acceptability of having a child without a partner and increased use of contraception.

The **abortion ratio** refers to the number of abortions per 1,000 live births. Abortion is affected by the need for parental consent and parental notification. **Parental consent** means that a woman needs permission from a parent to get an abortion if she is under a certain age, usually 18. **Parental notification** means that a woman has to tell a parent she is getting an abortion if she is under a certain age, usually 18, but she doesn't need parental permission. Laws

vary by state. Call the National Abortion Federation Hotline at 1-800-772-9100 to find out the laws in your state.

Reasons for an Abortion

In a survey of 1,209 women who reported having had an abortion, 74% of the women said the most frequently cited reasons for having the procedure were that having a child would interfere with a woman's education, work, or ability to care for dependents; 73% said that she could not afford a baby now; and 48% said that she did not want to be a single mother or was having relationship problems. Nearly four in 10 women said they had completed their childbearing, and almost one-third of the women were not ready to have a child (Finer et al., 2005).

Abortions performed to protect the life or health of the woman are called **therapeutic abortions**. However, there is disagreement over this definition as some physicians may argue that an abortion is therapeutic if it prevents or alleviates a serious physical or mental illness.

Some women who are pregnant with more than one fetus—a common outcome of the use of fertility drugs—may have a procedure called **transabdominal first-trimester selective termination**. In this procedure, the lives of some fetuses are terminated to increase the chance of survival for the others or to minimize the health risks associated with multifetal pregnancy for the woman. For example, a woman carrying five fetuses may elect to abort three of them to minimize the health risks of the other two.

Pro-Life Position

A dichotomy of attitudes toward abortion is reflected in two opposing groups of abortion activists. Pro-life groups favor letting the fetus grow and continue life; these groups favor antiabortion policies or a complete ban on abortion. Of 12,766 undergraduates at two large universities, 22% rejected the idea that abortion was acceptable under certain conditions (Hall & Knox, 2019). Pro-life groups believe the following:

1. The unborn fetus has a right to live and the government should protect that right.
2. Abortion is a violent and immoral solution to unintended pregnancy.

Abortion ratio: refers to the number of abortions per 1,000 live births. Abortion is affected by the need for parental consent and parental notification.

Parental consent: a woman needs permission from a parent to get an abortion if under a certain age, usually 18.

Parental notification: a woman has to tell a parent she is getting an abortion if she is under a certain age, usually 18, but she doesn't need parental permission.

Therapeutic abortion: abortions performed to protect the life or health of the woman.

Transabdominal first-trimester selective termination: a procedure where the lives of some fetuses are terminated to increase the chance of survival for the others or to minimize the health risks associated with multifetal pregnancy for the woman.

3. The life of an unborn fetus is sacred and should be protected, even at the cost of individual difficulties for the pregnant woman.

Venezuela is very pro-life. The population is 70% Catholic. Abortion is forbidden even in the case of incest or if the fetus is deformed. The punishment for abortion is six months to two years in prison. However, women are desperate to control whether or not they have a baby. Some will take Cytotec pills which are available on the black market for $12 and are used to treat stomach ulcers which will induce an abortion (Marillier & Squires, 2018).

Pro-Choice Position

Pro-choice advocates support the legal availability of abortion for all women—they have the right to choose to have an abortion. Of 12,766 undergraduates at two large universities, 65% reported that abortion was acceptable under certain conditions, which is usually interpreted to mean pregnancy by rape or incest (Hall & Knox, 2019). Pro-choice groups believe the following:

1. Freedom of choice is a central value—the woman has a right to determine what happens to her own body.

2. Those who must personally bear the burden of their moral choices ought to have the right to make these choices.

3. Procreation choices must be free of governmental control.

Although many self-proclaimed feminists and women's organizations, such as the National Organization for Women (NOW), have been active in promoting abortion rights, not all feminists are pro-choice.

Confidence in Making an Abortion Decision

To what degree do women considering abortion feel confident of their decision? Foster et al. (2012) studied 5,109 women who sought 5,387 abortions at one U.S. clinic and found that 87% of the women reported having high confidence in their decision before receiving counseling. Variables associated with uncertainty included being younger than 20, being Black, not having a high school diploma, having a history of depression, having a fetus with an anomaly, having general difficulty making decisions, having spiritual concerns, believing that abortion is murder, and fearing not being forgiven by God.

Physical Effects of Abortion

Part of the debate over abortion is related to its presumed effects. In regard to the physical effects, legal abortions, performed under safe medical conditions, are safer than continuing the pregnancy. The earlier in the pregnancy the abortion is performed, the safer it is. Vacuum aspiration, a frequently used method in early pregnancy, does not increase the risks to future childbearing. However, late-term abortions do increase the risks of subsequent miscarriages, premature deliveries, and babies of low birth weight. If abortions are outlawed, women will be forced to have unsafe abortions, jeopardizing their life, health, and safety.

Psychological Effects of Abortion

Of equal concern are the psychological effects of abortion. Steinberg et al. (2016) found that the greatest amount of depression, anxiety, and stress regarding an abortion decision occurred *before* the abortion. The stigma associated with having an abortion was a significant factor associated with these psychological states. The researchers suggested that addressing stigma among women seeking abortions may significantly lower their psychological distress. Wenzel (2017) noted the effectiveness of cognitive behavioral therapy in helping with problems of pregnancy loss.

Regarding the mental health of women after an abortion, the American Psychological Association reviewed all outcome studies on the mental health effects of abortion and concluded the following:

Based on our comprehensive review and evaluation of the empirical literature published in peer-reviewed journals since 1989, this Task Force on Mental Health and Abortion concludes that the most methodologically sound research indicates that among women who have a single, legal, first-trimester abortion of an unplanned pregnancy for nontherapeutic reasons, the relative risks of mental health problems are no greater than the risks among women who deliver an unplanned pregnancy (Major et al., 2008, p. 71).

Effects of Being Denied an Abortion

What difference does it make for later life mental health if a woman experiences an unintended pregnancy and does not have easy access to abortion? Herd et al. (2016) used the Wisconsin Longitudinal

Should You Have an Abortion?

The decision to have an abortion continues to be a complex one. Women who are faced with the issue may benefit by considering the following guidelines:

1. **Consider all the alternatives available to you, realizing that no alternative will have only positive consequences and no negative consequences**. As you consider each alternative, think about both the short-term and the long-term outcomes of each course of action, what you want, and what you can live with.

2. **Obtain information about each alternative course of action**. Inform yourself about the medical, financial, and legal aspects of abortion, childbearing, parenting, and placing the baby up for adoption.

3. **Talk with trusted family members, friends, or unbiased counselors**. Consider talking with the man who participated in the pregnancy. If possible, also talk with women who have had abortions as well as with women who have kept and reared a baby or placed a baby for adoption. If you feel that someone is pressuring you in your decision-making, look for help elsewhere.

4. **Consider your own personal and moral commitments in life**. Understand your own feelings, values, and religious beliefs concerning the fetus and weigh those against the circumstances surrounding your pregnancy. ●

Study, a 60-year ongoing survey, and controlled for such factors as early life socioeconomic conditions, adolescent IQ, and personality. The researchers found that for these mostly married White women who completed their pregnancies before the legalization of abortion, unwanted pregnancies were strongly associated with poorer mental health outcomes in later life.

In addition, what about women who have complicated or risky pregnancies? Suppose a woman with 10 children who is 52 gets pregnant. What happens then? With abortion removed as an option, continuing the pregnancy can be fatal.

What happens to women economically who request but who are denied having an abortion compared to women who receive an abortion? Foster et al. (2018) followed 813 women in both groups for five years and found that those who were denied having an abortion and forced to continue the pregnancy were less likely to be employed full time and more likely to be living in poverty.

FUTURE OF PLANNING FOR CHILDREN

As birthrates in the United States and Western Europe continue to fall, being child-free will continue to lose its stigma. "The reason is choices. For the first time in human history, women truly have them" (Dvorak, 2018). To quote Laura Scott, "Having children will change from an assumption to a decision." Once the personal, social, and economic consequences of having children come under scrutiny

the automatic response to have children will be tempered. The trend for those who have kids is to have no more kids; for those who don't have kids, four in 10 say they will keep it that way (Livingston & Horowitz, 2018).

Individuals who are not married and who want a baby are also able to have a child. Such a cultural option was not available until recently. Cook (2019) reported on interviews with 33 women over the age of 40 who did not have children. An enduring theme of these respondents was sadness in not having a child due to the absence of cultural support to have a child out of wedlock 40 years ago. Today, women are free to have a baby as a single adult; marriage is no longer a prerequisite. LGBTQ individuals, whether single or married, will also benefit from new cultural norms of approval for having children.

What about the male contraceptive pill? Researcher Christina Wang of LABio Med noted that "Safe, reliable hormonal male contraception should be available in about 10 years" (Hafner, 2019). Wilson (2018) assessed male reaction to a future male pill and found rejection by men. A comment in reference to the male pill which would restrict the amount of ejaculate was viewed as affecting the male orgasm—which was regarded as off-limits. One of Wilson's respondents revealed male skepticism:

. . . How about because the idea [is] it seems completely unnatural, and the sensation of ejaculation is part and parcel of the male orgasm experience? (at least in healthy men).

There's a lot of reasons why men would be wary . . .you're talking about taking away not just conception but a key part of the sexual experience.

However, a male contraceptive pill could be key in helping reduce the amount of unintended pregnancies. Additionally, women would no longer bear the burden of contraception.

Babies can now be created with the DNA of three parents. Abrahim Hassan of Jordan is a child born with the DNA from his mother, a surrogate, and sperm from father. Physicians at the New Hope Fertility Center in New York performed a "spindle nuclear transfer" whereby they removed the

nucleus from one of the eggs of the mother, Shaban, and inserted it into a donor egg which had had its nucleus removed. The resulting egg was then fertilized by the father's sperm. An embryo was then implanted in Shaban—and, nine months later, Abrahim was born (Samuelson, 2016). Polyamorous and group marriage couples may want to benefit from this technology.

Finally, for women born without a uterus—that figure is about one in 4,500—uterine transplants can now be performed. At Baylor University Medical Center in Dallas, Texas, healthy babies have now been delivered to women who received such transplants (Sifferlin, 2019).

SUMMARY

What are the social influences and individual motivations for having children?
Having children continues to be a major goal of most individuals, especially for women more than men. Social influences to have a child include family, friends, religion, government, favorable economic conditions, and cultural observances. The reasons people give for having children include love and companionship with one's own offspring, the desire to be personally fulfilled as an adult by having a child, and the desire to recapture one's youth. Having a child, particularly for women, is more likely to reduce one's educational and career advancement. The cost for housing, food, transportation, clothing, health care, and child care for a child from birth to age 18—college is not included—is over $230,000.

How many children do individuals want?
About 20% of women aged 40 to 44 do not have children. Whether these women will remain child-free or eventually have children is unknown. Categories of those who do not have children include early articulators who knew early that they did not want children, postponers who kept delaying when they would have children and remained child-free, acquiescers who made the decision to remain childless because their partner did not want children, and undecided, who are child-free but still in the decision-making process.

The top five reasons individuals give for wanting to remain child-free are a high level of current life satisfaction, being free and independent, avoiding the responsibility of rearing a child, the absence of maternal or paternal instinct, and a desire to accomplish and experience things in life which would be difficult as a parent.

About 3% of individuals have one child. The most preferred family size is two children—a boy and a girl. To get this sex balance, some couples use sex selection as an expression of reproductive rights and a sign of female empowerment. A contrasting view, more likely to be held by primary care

physicians, is that sex selection contributes to gender stereotypes that could result in neglect of children of the lesser-desired sex.

What are the causes of teenage parenthood?
Reasons for teenagers having a child include nonuse of contraception, having limited parental supervision, and perceiving few alternatives to parenthood. Indeed, motherhood may be one of the only remaining meaningful roles available to young females coming from communities facing poverty, limited education, and employment opportunities. In addition, some teenagers feel lonely and unloved and have a baby to create a sense of being needed and wanted.

What are the causes of infertility and the technology available to help?
Infertility is defined as the inability to achieve a pregnancy after at least one year of regular sexual relations without birth control or the inability to carry a pregnancy to a live birth. Forty percent of infertility problems are attributed to the woman, 40% to the man, and 20% to both of them. The causes of infertility in women include blocked fallopian tubes, endocrine imbalance that prevents ovulation, dysfunctional ovaries, chemically hostile cervical mucus that may kill sperm, and the effects of STIs.

A number of technological innovations are available to assist women and couples in becoming pregnant. These include hormonal therapy, artificial insemination, ovum transfer, and in vitro fertilization. Being infertile for the woman may have a negative lifetime effect, both personal and interpersonal. Half the women in one study were separated or reported a negative effect on their sex lives.

What are the motives for adoption?
Motives for adoption include a couple's inability to have a biological child—infertility—the desire to give an otherwise unwanted child a permanent loving home, or the desire

to avoid contributing to overpopulation by having more biological children.

What are the motives and outcomes for an abortion?
In a survey of 1,209 women who reported having had abortions, the most frequently cited reasons for induced abortion were that 74% of women felt that having a child would interfere with a women's education, work, or ability to care for dependents; 73% believed that she could not afford a baby now; and 48% said that she did not want to be a single mother or was having relationship problems. In regard to the psychological effects of abortion, the American Psychological Association reviewed the literature and concluded that "among women who have a single, legal, first-trimester abortion of an unplanned pregnancy for nontherapeutic reasons, the relative risks of mental health problems are no greater than the risks among women who deliver an unplanned pregnancy."

What is the future of planning for children?
As birthrates in the United States and Western Europe continue to fall, being child-free will continue to lose its stigma. There will be more options for different contraceptive methods. Assisted reproductive technology will continue to advance and there will be more viable treatments to assist families for better planning. For example, babies can have three biological parents, and uterine transplants are now possible.

KEY TERMS

Abortion ratio, 247

Birth control sabotage, 232

Competitive birthing, 237

Conception, 239

Cryopreservation, 242

Double Dutch, 239

Embryo adoption, 244

Emergency contraception, 236

Foster parent, 244

Hysterectomy, 245

Induced abortion, 246

Infertility, 239

Laparoscopy, 245

Morbidity, 231

Multiple partner fertility, 236

Oophorectomy, 245

Ovum transfer, 242

Parental consent, 247

Parental notification, 247

Pregnancy, 239

Procreative liberty, 234

Pronatalism, 230

Replacement level, 230

Reproductive coercion, 232

Salpingectomy, 245

Spontaneous abortion (miscarriage), 246

Sterilization, 245

Therapeutic abortion, 247

Transabdominal first-trimester selective termination, 247

Transnational commercial surrogacy, 240

Transracial adoption, 243

Vasectomy, 246

WEB LINKS

Alan Guttmacher Institute
www.guttmacher.org/

Childfree by Choice
http://thechildfreelife.com/

The Childless by Choice Project
http://www.childlessbychoiceproject.com/

College Cost Calculator
http://apps.collegeboard.com/fincalc/college_cost.jsp

Contraception
http://bedsider.org/

Engenderhealth
http://www.engenderhealth.org/

The Evan B. Donaldson Adoption Institute
http://www.adoptioninstitute.org/

Fetal Fotos (bonding with your fetus)
http://www.fetalfotosusa.com/

National Right to Life
http://www.nrlc.org/

No Kidding!
http://www.nokidding.net/

Planned Parenthood Federation of America, Inc.
http://www.plannedparenthood.org

NARAL Pro-Choice America (reproductive freedom and choice)
http://www.naral.org/

$SAGE edge™

Get the tools you need to sharpen your study skills. SAGE edge offers a robust online environment featuring an impressive array of free tools and resources.
Access practice quizzes, eFlashcards, video, and multimedia at **edge.sagepub.com/knox13e**

Barcroft Media/Getty

12 Diversity in Parenting

(24/7) once you sign on to be a mother, that's the only shift they offer.

—Jodi Picoult, *My Sister's Keeper*

Learning Objectives

12.1.   Identify the nature of parenting choices

12.2.   Describe how women, men, and couples transition to parenthood

12.3.   Summarize the facts of parenthood

12.4.   Explain child rearing theories

12.5.   Review the various principles of effective parenting

12.6.   Know the unique challenges of single parents

12.7.   Discuss the future of parenting

Modern Family is an American sitcom on ABC which follows an extended family living in suburban Los Angeles. The series features a couple, Claire and Phil Dunphy, their two daughters, Haley, Alex, and their son Luke. Throughout the series, Claire is a high-intensity stay-at-home mother and helicopter parent. Her husband Phil, however, wants more than anything for his children and their friends to think he's "cool" and often behaves as an overgrown child in attempting to earn their favor. The sitcom also features a White same-sex couple with an adopted daughter from Vietnam, as well as a stepfamily comprised of a White man, his younger Colombian wife, her son, and their mixed race son. *Modern Family* and other sitcoms, such as *Blackish*, emphasize that parents and parenting today are very diverse. *Blackish* is about a successful Black family in the context of a White dominated society. The parents in both sitcoms have the same goal of facilitating happy, economically independent, socially contributing adult offspring. They try to achieve this goal in different ways and through different parenting styles. In this chapter, we discuss diversity in parenting and review how parents go about rearing their children. We begin by examining the various choices that parents make.

Notice how focused these parents are on their children to ensure appropriate eating out behavior. Parents who don't make the choice to teach their children appropriate behavior have children who do not know how to behave in public.
Courtesy of Chelsea Curry

the nature of parental choices and some of the basic choices parents make.

Nature of Parenting Choices

Parents might keep the following points in mind when they make choices about how to rear their children:

1.   **Not making a parental decision is still a decision.** Parents are constantly making choices even when they think they are not doing so. When a child is impolite and the parent does not provide feedback and encourage polite behavior, the parent has chosen to teach the child that being impolite is acceptable. If a child makes a promise—"I'll text you when I get to my friend's house"—and doesn't follow through, a parent who doesn't address the issue is allowing the child to regard commitments casually. Hence,

THE CHOICES PERSPECTIVE OF PARENTING

Although both genetic and environmental factors are at work, the choices parents make have a profound impact on their children. In this section, we review parents cannot choose not to make choices in their parenting, because their inactivity is a choice that has as much impact as a deliberate decision.

2. **All parental choices involve trade-offs.** Parents are also continually making trade-offs in the parenting choices they make. The decision to take on a second job or to work overtime to afford the larger house will come at the price of having less time to spend with one's children and being more exhausted when such time is available. The choice to enroll a younger child in the highest-quality day care will mean less money for an older child's karate lessons. Parents should increase their awareness that no choice is without a trade-off and should evaluate the costs and benefits of making such decisions.

3. **"Regretful" parental decisions can be reframed.** All parents regret a previous parental decision. For example, they believe they should have held their child back a year in school or not done so; they should have intervened in a bad peer relationship; and they should have handled their child's drug use or coming out differently. Whatever the issue, parents chide themselves for their mistakes. Rather than berate themselves as parents, they might emphasize the positive outcome of their choices, such as not holding the child back made the child the first to experience some things among his or her peers; and they made the best decision they could at the time.

4. **Parental choices are influenced by society and culture.** In the United States, parents are continually assaulted by commercial interests to get them to buy products for their children. Corporations regularly market to young parents to get them to buy the latest learning aid for their child, which promises a genius by age five. These products are marketed in a way that makes them seem necessary for a child's well-being. Parents may feel pressured to buy these products, based on the idea that it makes them a better parent.

Similarly, the commercial industry has been successful in getting "good" parents to "buy into" the belief that the more the activity, the better the parent (Vincent & Maxwell, 2016). Hence, parents today, particularly those who are middle class, are focused on enrolling children in numerous after-school extracurricular activities to enhance their skills, qualities, and distinction for the future. These enrichment activities also function as enjoyment, social bonding, and purposeful activity. This phenomenon is known as **concerted cultivation**, the social program where parents are expected to enroll their children in a series of extracurricular activities to maintain their status as "good parents." While these activities may be beneficial for the child, they may put additional stress on the child.

Worldwide, parental choices are influenced by the education of the parents. In a study of 227,431 parents from 90 nations, child independence was more popular in nations with more highly educated populations. In contrast, obedience was more popular in nations with lower percentages of educated and urban populations (Park & Lau, 2016)

Because of the racist and heterosexist society in which we live, parents must customize the socialization of their children. For example, Curenton et al. (2018) noted that African American mothers include in their child rearing, lessons about racism, stereotyping, and discrimination. These mothers felt that their children should be prepared for the racist society they will experience. Parents with biracial children have similar concerns, as Durrant and Gillum (2018) found that White fathers with Black-White biracial sons were concerned about the impact of racism on their sons, how they would provide their sons access to the minority culture, and teacher expectations. Edwards (2017) noted that African American parents emphasize preparing their children to override negative cultural racial messages by teaching about African American history, culture, and heritage and teaching self-respect and dignity. African American parents are also intent on teaching their children correct grammar so that they are not victims of negative stereotyping (Edwards & Few-Demo, 2016). LGBTQ parents must also alert their children of the heterosexist society in which they live and provide them with ways of understanding and reacting to prejudice and discrimination.

5. **Parents can help children avoid ACEs.** All parents have the goal of rearing their children so that they avoid ACEs—Adverse Child Experiences. These include physical, emotional, and sexual abuse, physical and emotional neglect, and dysfunction within the household such as mental illness, violence, and substance abuse (Cassidy, 2017). While few children escape exposure to some trauma, the goal remains an important one and parents are constantly alert to protecting their children.

....

Concerted cultivation: the belief that parents are expected to enroll their children in a series of extracurricular activities to maintain their status as "good parents".

Many factors have been identified to protect or buffer the negative effects of ACEs such as enhancing strengths and ability like promoting positive self-concepts, minimizing family and parental stress, providing quality early care, and having a supporting community. Dr. Kenneth Ginsburg (2014) encouraged parents and adults to help children to develop the seven crucial "C's"—competence, confidence, connection, character, contribution, coping, and control.

The "Good Enough" Parent

Parents have an idea of the standard of performance they hold for themselves in their role as parent. Ishizuka (2019) analyzed data on a national sample of more than 3,600 parents of elementary school-aged children and confirmed that parents (both mothers and fathers) across different social classes express remarkably similar support for intensive child-centered, time-intensive mothering and fathering pointing to "high contemporary standards for parental investments in children." But while the cultural expectation is that parents be outstanding parents to their children, the reality is that being "good enough" is "good enough" and much more realistic. Psychoanalyst Donald Winnicott introduced in 1953 the notion of the "good enough" parent, suggesting that perfect parenting was neither possible nor desirable. In effect, the "good enough" parent provides love, security, and structure but does not become "lost" in the role or obsess about every parental decision.

Nevertheless, parents are continually trying to do what is right and best for their children. There is no shortage of norms. Perron (2018) noted that parenting is a challenge in every culture but that there are four basic Cs of parenting which promote positive development of one's children: care that is both emotional and physical; consistency that enables offspring to know what to expect; choices that give offspring some control over their lives; and consequences that make offspring aware that choices have consequences.

Corkin et al. (2018) examined the various challenges mothers of infants report they face: "Challenges fulfilling maternal role and responsibility"; "Time management and work issues"; "Sleep deprivation"; "Personal change and adjustment"; and "Attributes of the child." Corkin et al. (2018) found that the number of infants the mother had was associated with more challenges. Hence, the more young children a mother had, the greater the number of challenges, and these pressures increased her need to adopt a "good enough" philosophy. Similarly, if both parents have full time jobs, the availability of time to parent will be reduced so that being the "good enough" parent becomes more reasonable and acceptable.

Religion may create a context where parents feel compelled to be more than just "good enough."

Nelson and Uecker (2018) analyzed data from the Baylor Religion Survey and found that, in general, the higher one's religiosity, the greater the reported parenting satisfaction. However, the religiously unaffiliated had higher odds than evangelical Protestants of having high actual parenting satisfaction. The latter finding was explained by the possible presence of parenting pressures within religious communities with a strong emphasis on family life to report high parenting satisfaction. In reality, religious parents may feel pressured to be the ultimate family and report that they are.

Parents interested in improving their child rearing skills may avail themselves of parent training programs. Barlow and Coren (2018) reviewed parenting programs and found that these were effective in improving the emotional and behavioral adjustment of children in addition to enhancing the psychosocial well-being of parents. Corralejo and Domenech Rodriguez (2018) noted the effectiveness of behavioral parent training programs but emphasized that these interventions had been primarily validated with White American families and may lack adaptations that may make the interventions accessible to underserved populations.

Seven Basic Parenting Choices

Parents make decisions every day, ranging from their child's exposure to technology to the vaccinations they should receive. While each decision has an impact, all parents make seven basic choices:

(1) whether or not to have a child

(2) the number of children to have

(3) the interval between children

(4) the method of discipline

Researchers suggest that parents should monitor the amount of screen time of children.
Courtesy of Mary Jane LaNeave

(5) the degree to which they will invest time with their children

(6) whether or not to co-parent, and whether they will cooperate and work together or whether one of them will be the more engaged parent

(7) how much technological exposure they will allow their children at what age

Though all of the above decisions are important, the relative importance one places on parenting as opposed to one's career will have implications for the parents, their children, and their children's children. The issue of technology and its impact on children is also important (see "Technology and the Family").

Toddlers and Media Consumption

With the advent of television into American homes in the late forties, researchers began investigating the effects of media on children. Screen-based media now extends beyond television and includes content from video game consoles, DVD/Blue Ray players, computers, smartphones, tablets, and other mobile devices. Devices and tablets are now made to target infants and toddlers. While technology can be a valuable tool for learning and connection, the potential negative impacts on young children has fostered debate. Vigilant choices in regard to the use of technological devices by their children have become major concerns for parents.

For example, the interactivity of touch screen technology is reinforcing to infants and toddlers—they are entranced by the movement and light on the screen which responds to their touch so they repeat the behavior. A study found that the tablet is the most commonly owned mobile device for young children aged 1 – 60 months with infants as young as 6 months old able to learn how to use a mobile device (Kiliç et al., 2018). Benefits at this young age include improved fine motor development, motivation for learning (Martin et al., 2018), letter recognition (Neumann, 2018) and pro social behavior (Ralph, 2018). However, as parents make their choices about what and how much technology to expose their children to, they are rarely informed by their physicians of potential problems (Kılıç et al., 2018).

Researchers are concerned about the negative effects of using technological devices for young children from birth to two years. Sensory motor experience is essential for brain development during this critical period. Hands-on activities are more developmentally appropriate since young children learn primarily through their senses. For example, digital "painting" is not the same experience as the child dipping his or her finger into a jar of paint and smearing different colors on canvas, paper, window, or his or her own face. Holding, touching, squeezing, smelling, feeling, tasting, and discovering the rich content inside of a kiwi fruit, is not the same as seeing a kiwi image on a flat screen. Young children may be able to touch the screen, press different buttons, be entertained by music, video, and images on the device, but they do not understand, and transferring what they have seen on the screen to real life is difficult (Yadav et al., 2018). Other risks for unregulated use of technology for children this age include sleep disturbances (Nathanson & Beyens, 2018), impaired opportunity for discovery—by focusing on technology, they are not discovering and learning about the world around them— (Günüç & Atli, 2018) and problem behaviors (McDaniel & Radesky, 2018).

Parents also make decisions about the nature and amount of media their children are exposed to (Lee et al., 2018; McDaniel & Radesky, 2018). Parents are becoming cautious about what devices they expose their children to. Aristotle by Mattel is a child-focused artificial intelligence voice assistant. Enabled with a camera and designed to be placed in a child's room, Aristotle can not only answer questions like Siri, but also monitor sleep, read stories, and soothe a crying baby by playing lullabies (Wiederhold, 2018). Aristotle faced strong opposition from scholars and parents, which forced Mattel to scrap the release of Aristotle to the public. What remains is the question about the degree to which technology may be used in rearing children.

Professional and health organizations such as the National Association for the Education of Young Children, the American Heart Association, and the American Academy of Pediatrics have issued policy statements warning parents about media overuse for young children. The most recent policy statement by the American Academy of Pediatrics (AAP) in 2016 claimed that research found limited benefits of media usage under the age of two and emphasized the importance of adult interaction with the child during media usage (American Academy of Pediatrics, 2016; Healthy Children, 2018; Hutton et al., 2018). The American Heart Association also advises parents to limit screen time to one to two hours a day for children and adolescents (LaMotte, 2018). In order to better support families and parents, Gabrielli and colleagues (2018) proposed the TECH parenting framework to restrict and monitor media use of children. The acronym TECH stands for Talk, Educate, Co-use, and House rules. Parents and guardians are advised to make deliberate choices to talk to their children about technology use, monitor exposure, co-use media with children, and establish clear house rules use. Examples of the latter include not allowing these devices at the dining table as well as there being a central charging location for all devices at home controlled by the parents. ●

TRANSITION TO PARENTHOOD

The **transition to parenthood** refers to that period from the beginning of pregnancy through the first few months after the birth of a baby. The family life cycle framework emphasizes that having children is a major life transition—the mother, father, and couple undergo changes and adaptations during this period. Brandel et al. (2018) analyzed data on couples making the transition and found both mothers and fathers reported an enhanced sense of well-being in response to becoming a parent with fathers expressing that sentiment more than mothers. Co-parenting was associated with a positive reaction and fewer episodes of depression as the mother and father adjusted to their new role of parents (Williams et al., 2018).

Sometimes pregnancy is very stressful. In addition to the changes in the woman's body, the couple's sex life, and their spending money in getting the nursery ready, pregnancy can be catastrophic. Cote-Arsenault and Denney-Koelsch (2018) interviewed 16 mothers and their spouses who were confronted with a pregnancy in which there was a lethal fetal diagnosis. Couples in committed relationships who shared decision-making and provided mutual support fared the best in the aftermath of the baby's death.

Transition to Motherhood

Becoming a mother, particularly a biological or adoptive mother in contrast to a stepmother, is a major event for a woman. **Matrescence** is the transition to motherhood in the same sense that adolescence is a shift of body, mind, and hormones (Sack, 2019). The transition is a process.

Sociobiologists suggest that the attachment between a mother and her offspring has a biological basis and is one of survival. The mother alone carries the fetus in her body for 9 months, lactates to provide milk, and, during the expulsive stage of labor, produces **oxytocin,** a hormone from the pituitary gland that has been associated with the onset of maternal behavior in lower animals. Most new mothers bond emotionally with their babies and resist separation.

Because of this resistance, maternity leave, especially paid maternity leave, is a key issue. Working mothers who take off from work a month or more following childbirth report less parental stress

Transition to parenthood: period from the beginning of pregnancy through the first few months after the birth of a baby during which the mother and father undergo changes.

Matrescence: transition to motherhood.

Oxytocin: hormone from the pituitary gland during the expulsive stage of labor that has been associated with the onset of maternal behavior in lower animals.

and depression compared to mothers who take off a month or less (Petts, 2018). Hence, family leave policies, which provide time off from work after childbirth even without pay, are beneficial to both mother and child. The time off gives the mother time to bond, focus on her role as mother, recover from the birthing experience, and get some sleep, while the time off also allows the child to bond with the mother.

The level of support new mothers receive from their parents and extended kin and from their partner can help ease the transition to motherhood. A supportive partner who co-parents can help ease the mother into her role. The situation where there are children from different biological fathers may be particularly challenging. Fomby (2018) noted that these mothers with multi-partner fertility were more likely to experience parenting stress and depression compared with mothers whose children shared the same biological father. Mothers' depression was explained by poor relationship quality with the father of her prior children and by boundary ambiguity in complex families.

Another aspect of the motherhood transition is dealing with pressure from others to be a "good mother." New mothers are victims of a cultural script about what mothers are "supposed" to do. A new term, mom shaming, has emerged to describe the phenomenon of mothers being judged by others for their parenting choices. Mothers are momshamed for a variety of reasons, such as breastfeeding vs. bottle feeding, working vs. staying at home, and even the decision to feed their child organic food. In a *Time* magazine survey, 72% reported some pressure to become pregnant, birth a child, and feed the child a certain way (Howorth, 2017). One issue, which mothers and fathers face, is the decision to co-sleep with their children, which is discussed in the Personal Choices section.

Postpartum Depression, Peripartum Depression, and Maternal Well-being

Not all mothers feel joyous after childbirth. Naomi Wolf uses the term "the conspiracy of silence" to note that motherhood is "a job that sucks 80 percent of the time" (quoted in Haag, 2011, p.83). Some mothers don't bond immediately with their child and feel overworked, exhausted, mildly depressed, and irritable. They cry, suffer loss of appetite, and have difficulty in sleeping. Many new mothers experience **baby blues**—transitory symptoms of depression 24 to 48 hours after the baby is born.

Baby blues: transitory symptoms of depression in a mother 24 to 48 hours after her baby is born.

Co-sleeping With One's Infant?

The term "co-sleeping" refers to the practice of parents sleeping with their infant or toddler. This practice is also referred to as "bed-sharing" although co-sleeping refers more broadly to sleeping on any sleeping surface.

Co-sleeping is considered normal in 70% of the world today and has been the pattern in family life for 5 million years; however, in the United States, co-sleeping is controversial (Barry, 2018). Health care professionals often advise against co-sleeping: The Centers for Disease Control and the American Academy of Pediatrics recommend room-sharing with infants, but not bed-sharing. (Bombard et al., 2018; Centers for Disease Control and Prevention, 2018).

Co-sleeping is not uncommon: In a 2015 survey of new mothers in 14 states, 24.4% reported bed-sharing with their infant "often or always" (Bombard et al., 2018). While some parents make the deliberate choice to co-sleep, other parents describe a process in which they drifted into the pattern of co-sleeping and were not sure how to "transition out" (Stewart, 2017). Although many parents co-sleep when their babies are first born, most transition babies into sleeping in their own room by 6 months of age (Shimuzu & Teti, 2018). Mothers who choose to co-sleep with their infants do so for a variety of reasons, including to make breast-feeding easier, to be close to their infant, or because they do not have another place, such as a crib, for the baby to sleep. Some of the benefits of co-sleeping include the nurturing of close emotional bonds between children and parents. Such emotional attachment is a major source of emotional security for children. Parents who are considering co-sleeping might consider the following:

1. Co-sleeping may increase risk of Sudden Infant Death Syndrome (SIDS), and may involve other safety concerns such as accidental suffocation and the baby falling off the bed. The risks of co-sleeping also apply to napping and falling asleep unintentionally while holding one's infant.

2. Babies who grow accustomed to co-sleeping may have difficulty learning to fall asleep on their own.

3. Co-sleeping can cause loss of sleep for the parents.

4. Co-sleeping is more dangerous for babies when the parent sleeping with the baby is under the influence of some medications, drugs, or alcohol. Co-sleeping deaths have led to criminal charges when the co-sleeping parent was found to be under the influence of drugs or alcohol (Clopton, 2018).

5. Co-sleeping is riskier for babies when it occurs on sofas, chairs, and soft mattresses. Bean bag chairs and waterbeds are not considered safe for infants.

6. Wherever the baby sleeps, it is considered safer for the baby to sleep on her back, rather than side or tummy. Pillows, stuffed animals, and heavy blankets or quilts should be avoided as they increase the risk of infant suffocation.

7. There is an added risk to an infant's safety when parents who co-sleep are obese or heavy.

8. In two-parent families, co-sleeping may interfere with the couples' intimacy.

Whatever the decision, it is desirable for both parents to agree with whatever infant sleeping arrangement the parents choose. In addition, parents should talk with their pediatrician or health care provider about the risks and benefits of co-sleeping. ●

About 10% to 15% of mothers experience **postpartum depression,** a more severe reaction than baby blues which usually occurs within a month of the baby's birth (Brummelte & Galea, 2016). A complicated delivery is also associated with postpartum depression. Although pregnancy and childbirth—the physical factors—are frequently the primary reasons contributing to postpartum depression, other psychological and emotional factors have been identified (National Institute of Mental Health, 2018). Gelabert et al. (2012) looked at various personality traits that were associated with postpartum depression. They found that women who were perfectionistic and overly concerned about mistakes, personal standards, parental expectations, parental criticism, doubt about actions, and organization were more likely to report postpartum depression.

Postpartum depression: a severe reaction following the birth of a baby which occurs in reference to a complicated delivery as well as numerous physiological and psychological changes occurring during pregnancy, labor, and delivery; usually in the first month after birth but can be experienced after a couple of years have passed.

While postpartum depression is well known, little attention has been given to **peripartum depression**, which is similar in symptoms to postpartum depression, yet these feelings begin as early as four months into the pregnancy. Moncada and Natrajan-Tyagi (2018) interviewed 15 women who reported feeling anxious, depressed, and moody during the pregnancy. *The Diagnostic and Statistical Manual of Mental Disorders* (5th edition) was recently updated to include peripartum depression.

To minimize peripartum, baby blues, and postpartum depression, individual and relationship therapy as well as antidepressants, such as Zoloft and Prozac, may be helpful. Regarding antidepressants, these should be used after careful discussion with one's health care provider if the mother is breastfeeding.

The transition to motherhood varies. Hickey et al. (2019) studied mothers with young children whose average age was 10.13 weeks and found that those mothers with more risk factors—single parents, teenage parents, socioeconomic disadvantage, low social support—reported higher levels of depression and lower parental self-efficacy.

Some parents become so despondent they consider killing or abandoning their child. Each state provides an alternative **Safe Haven,** which, according to the **Baby Moses Law**, allows overwhelmed despondent parents to give their baby to someone who will take care of him or her with no criminal prosecution until a permanent home can be found. The intent is that the parent will not return for the child and the child becomes a ward of the state. The rules in Texas which was the first state to enact a Safe Haven law for the parent are below:

- Your baby *must* be 60 days old or younger and unharmed and safe.

- You may take your baby to *any* hospital, fire station, or emergency medical services (EMS) station in Texas.

- You need to give your baby to an employee who works at one of these safe places and tell this person that you want to leave your baby at a Safe Haven.

- You may be asked by an employee for family or medical history to make sure that your baby receives the care he or she needs. If you leave your unharmed infant at a Safe Haven, you will not be prosecuted for abandonment

or neglect. See https://www.nationalsafehavenalliance.org/ for more information.

Postpartum psychosis, a reaction in which a woman wants to harm her baby, is even rarer than postpartum depression. While having misgivings about a new infant is normal, the parent who wants to harm the infant should make these feelings known to the partner, a close friend, and a professional.

Aside from negative feelings sometimes experienced in the early days of parenting by some mothers, how do women, in general, feel about the role of motherhood and how is it related to their sense of personal and parental well-being over time? Luthar and Ciciolla (2016) analyzed Internet survey data of 2,200 mostly well-educated mothers with children ranging from infants to adults. The researchers found a curvilinear pattern across their children's developmental stages, with mothers of middle-schoolers faring the most poorly, and mothers of adult children and infants faring the best in terms of personal and parental well-being.

How does the use of social media influence maternal well-being? Coyne and McDaniel (2014) analyzed data on 721 married or cohabiting mothers, 94% of whom reported use of social media, with Facebook being used the most often. Findings revealed that greater use of social network sites was associated with mothers reporting more maternal stress, depression, and conflict with their partners over use of social networking sites and lack of help with parenting. Hence, there was a detrimental effect of using social media to compare one's self with others. The researchers suggested that mothers need to be aware that many parents on social media sites may not present their true selves. Parenting is difficult and social media posts may only present a happy face of family life.

Transition to Fatherhood

Fatherhood exists in many contexts and is changing (Roopnarine & Yildirim, 2019). Petts et al. (2018) noted that men today are caught between old and new norms regarding masculinity and fatherhood. Older norms suggest that "real" men are minimally involved with their children. Indeed, Shafer et al. (2019) found that males with high masculinity scores were less warm and engaged with their children. Today's new fatherhood ideal promotes active involvement of fathers in the lives of their children both at the instrumental and emotional and nurturing levels.

The increased involvement of today's fathers with their children begins with the fathers giving

....

Peripartum depression: similar to postpartum depression except the symptoms may begin as early as four months into the pregnancy.

Safe Haven (Baby Moses Law): allows the overwhelmed despondent parent to give his or her baby to someone who will take care of him or her with no criminal prosecution.

....

Postpartum psychosis: a reaction in which a woman wants to harm her baby.

Protection is an important role of parents—this father is protecting his child from sunburn.

support to their pregnant partner and may continue with their taking paternity leave (Cubbins et al., 2018). Petts and Knoester (2018) confirmed that paternity leave-taking was associated with fathers being more engaged during the first few years of a child's life, including fathering commitments and attitudes.

Although male post-partum depression is not as widely recognized as female post-partum depression, men may suffer from this, as well. Eddy et al. (2019) found that 5%–10% of new fathers reported symptoms of postpartum depression. These feelings included feeling overwhelmed with the role of father but believing it was unmanly to have these feelings.

While parents delight in their child, their attention shifts from each other to the baby.

The degree to which heterosexual fathers experience their role is also related to their partner's. Puhlman and Pasley (2017) created the Maternal Gatekeeping Scale and emphasized that mothers are the gatekeepers of the father's involvement with his children via encouragement, discouragement, and control. Fathers who perceived mothers as more encouraging and less discouraging and controlling reported higher quality and more frequent involvement with their children. Altenburger et al. (2018) also noted that fathers reported greater regard for their role when they perceived the gate to be "open." The **gatekeeper role** is particularly pronounced after a divorce in which the mother receives custody of the children and the role of the father may be severely limited.

The importance of the father in the lives of his children is enormous and goes beyond his economic contribution. The following is a summary of outcomes for children with an involved father:

Higher grades	Higher income as an adult
Less involved in crime	Higher education level
Good health/self-concept	Higher cognitive functioning
Strong work ethic	More stable job
More durable marriage	Fewer premarital births
Stronger moral conscience	Lower incidence of child sex abuse
Higher life satisfaction	Exhibits healthier and on time physical development

Transition From a Couple to a Family

I think if you ask any couple, straight or gay, what the major changes are, it's adjusting to having a person that's completely dependent on you for absolutely everything and learning to survive with no sleep and getting them into a routine.

A new parent

Parenting can be difficult and exhausting. It can take a while to feel a sense of **parental empowerment**, which refers to feeling in control as a parent and feeling that one's children are flourishing. Examples of feeling empowered as a parent include being able to control the behavior of one's child and feeling a low level of stress in reference to the parental role (Damen et al., 2017). Mikolajczak et al. (2018) focused on parental burnout, which results from an overwhelming sense of exhaustion

Gatekeeper role: term used to refer to the influence of the mother on the father's involvement with his children.

Parental empowerment: term used to refer to feeling in control as a parent and that one's children are flourishing.

related to the parental role, an emotional distancing from one's children, and a sense of ineffectiveness in one's parental role. Gillis and Roskam (2019) confirmed in their research on 157 mothers and 157 fathers the negative impact of exhaustion on the quality of the parent-child relationship and the positive impact of partner support in helping to offset parental exhaustion.

After having children, one's partnered relationship changes. The dyad has expanded to include one or more children, and as a result, the dyad will never be the same again. Even when the children leave home as emerging adults, the parents will have changed in the past 18 or so years. Craft and Perry-Jenkins (2017) surveyed 153 mothers and fathers their first year of parenthood as well as these parents and their children six years later. The researchers found that conflict between the parents increased across the transition to parenthood. In addition to conflict, there was a gradual decline in vaginal intercourse, which began the first trimester of pregnancy and continued throughout the pregnancy. Most couples resume vaginal intercourse eight weeks after the birth but the pre-pregnancy frequency does not return until about a year later (Jawed-Wessel & Sevick, 2017). The result of this decline is lower reported sexual satisfaction for first- time parents (Maas et al., 2018).

The presence of children also impacts a couple's relationship by reducing the amount of time the partners spend together. Some parents are so focused on their children that they live apart from their spouse. Qiu (2017) documented Chinese "study mothers" who move to where the child, adolescent, or young adult is in school. The mothers live with the child, prepare meals, laundry, and monitor studying and social relationships to ensure that the child prioritizes education. Such a living apart arrangement from the husband may be at the expense of the marriage.

Regardless of how children affect relationship satisfaction, spouses report more commitment to their relationship once they have children. A primary reason for this increased commitment is the desire on the part of both parents to provide a stable family context for their children. Of course, couples should not have a child with the hope of "saving their relationship." In addition, parents of dependent children may keep their marriage together to maintain continued access to their children and a higher standard of living for them. Finally, parents, especially mothers, with small children feel more pressure to stay married if the partner provides sufficient economic resources regardless of how unhappy they may be. Hence, though children may decrease marital happiness, they increase marital stability—the greater the number of children, the more difficult one's post-economic divorce survival.

Finally, increasingly, partners are working to parent their children together. In a study of 174 couples who were living together and parenting at least one child ages 5 years or older, both partners reported feeling positively about their daily co-parenting (McDaniel et al., 2017).

PARENTHOOD: SOME FACTS

Parenting is only one stage in an individual's or couple's life. Children typically live with an individual 30% of that person's life and with a couple 40% of their marriage. Parenting involves responding to the varying needs of children across time.

Some additional facts of parenthood follow.

Parental Roles

Parents have six basic roles:

1. **Protector and caregiver**. The first role of parents is to protect their children from harm. The protector role may begin in pregnancy as pregnant mothers cut back or stop smoking. Other expressions of the protective role include insisting that children wear seat belts in cars, protecting them from violence or nudity in the media, and protecting them from strangers. Media coverage of the 3-year-old who slipped into the hands of a gorilla at the Cincinnati, Ohio zoo and the 2-year-old who was snatched into the water by an alligator at a Disney Resort remind parents that 100% vigilance is required.

2. **Emotional resource**. Beyond providing physical care, parents are sensitive to the emotional needs of children in terms of their need to belong, to be loved, and to develop positive self-concepts. In hugging, holding, and kissing an infant, parents not only express their love for the infant but also reflect awareness that such displays of emotion are good for the child's sense of self-worth. Parents also provide "emotion work" for children—listening to their issues, helping them figure out various relationships they are struggling with, and so forth.

3. **Teacher.** All parents think they have a philosophy of life or set of principles their children will benefit from. Parents soon discover that their children may not be interested in their religion or philosophy and, indeed, may rebel against it. This

possibility does not deter parents from their role as teacher.

4. **Economic resource**. New parents are also acutely aware of the costs for medical care, food, and clothes for infants, and seek ways to ensure that such resources are available to their children. Working longer hours, taking second jobs, and cutting back on leisure expenditures are attempts to ensure that money is available to meet the needs of the children.

One of the roles of parents is to provide financial assistance to their children. Henretta et al. (2018) noted that money transfers to children have increased among more recent cohorts. Two trends—declining family size and children's delay in marriage—account for part of the increase across cohorts. However, other trends, such as the increase in the number of stepchildren tend to decrease the observed cohort trend. Most felt it was their obligation as parents to help their children financially, particularly while their children were "emerging adults" between 18 and into their late 20s.

5. **Health promoter**. The family is a major agent for health promotion in promoting healthy food choices, responsible use of alcohol, nonuse of drugs, and safe driving skills. However, governmental policy may affect parents' medical decisions for their children. See Family Policy: Childhood Vaccinations.

6. **Ritual bearer**. To build a sense of family cohesiveness, parents often foster rituals to bind members together in emotion and in memory. Praying together at meals and before bedtime, having birthday and holiday celebrations, and going on vacations at the same place at the beach, mountains, or wherever they gather regularly provide predictable times of togetherness and sharing.

Childhood Vaccinations: Public Policy and Parental Rights

The Centers for Disease Control (CDC) recommends that by age 6, children receive 28 doses of nine vaccines plus a yearly flu shot after 6 months. There is no U.S. federal policy mandating childhood vaccinations. However, all states require specified vaccinations—including those for measles, mumps and rubella; diphtheria, tetanus and pertussis (whooping cough); and varicella (chickenpox)—before children enter school or a childcare center. In 2019, due to an outbreak of measles, unvaccinated children in Rockland County, New York, were banned from attending public school.

More than 90% of U.S. kindergarteners have received their state-required vaccinations (Mellerson et al., 2018). However, a small but growing anti-vaccination movement opposes mandated vaccinations. All states allow exemptions from vaccinations based on medical reasons, such as an impaired immune system or adverse reactions to vaccination. All states except for Mississippi, Virginia, and California grant religious exemptions, and 18 states allow philosophical exemptions for those who oppose immunization due to personal, moral or other beliefs (National Conference of State Legislators, 2017). Public health officials are concerned that in recent years the number of nonmedical exemptions increased in 12 of the 18 states that allow these exemptions (Olive et al., 2018). More exemptions mean lower vaccination coverage, resulting in local outbreaks of a potentially fatal disease, such as the 2018 outbreak of chickenpox at a private school in Asheville, North Carolina, where many parents were granted religious exemption from vaccinating their children.

Opposition to vaccinations is partly due to their success—because vaccinations have greatly reduced the incidence of disease, some parents view vaccinations as unnecessary. Other parents question the safety of vaccinations, fearing they may cause developmental disorders and serious health problems. Some parents oppose the recommended vaccine schedule. They want to wait until their child is older and to space out the vaccinations over a longer period of time. Some parents also believe that vaccines are part of a conspiracy among government, health organizations, and pharmaceutical companies (Weithorn & Reiss, 2018).

In the medical and public health literature, there is general consensus that adverse reactions to vaccinations are rare and any risk is greatly outweighed by the benefits of preventing diseases that can be disabling and potentially fatal. Medical and public health officials suggest that the anti-vaccination movement is partly due to misinformation. After the publication of a 1998 study by researchers who claimed to find a link between the MMR vaccination and the onset of developmental disorders in children, many parents chose not to give their children the MMR vaccination. But the study's methods were flawed and an investigative journalist revealed that the researchers had been "hired to attack the MMR vaccine by a lawyer…for the express purpose of bringing a class

(Continued)

(Continued)

action lawsuit against vaccine manufacturers" (Hendrick, 2018, p. 261).

The National Vaccine Information Center defends parental rights in making informed decisions about vaccinating their children and rejects laws and policies that restrict parents' vaccination choices. But disease outbreaks linked to unvaccinated children have led some states to pass legislation banning nonmedical vaccination exemptions. Other states have instituted policies requiring parents to view educational information about vaccinations or consult with a health care professional before obtaining a nonmedical exemption. Due to a measles outbreak of school age children in Olympia, Washington, the House approved a measure that would remove the ability of the parents to claim a personal or philosophical exemption to vaccinating their school-age children.

The tension between mandating childhood vaccinations and allowing parents to choose to not vaccinate their children is not easily resolved. The best solution may be one that balances respect for parental authority, protection of public health, and the well-being of children (Weithorn & Reiss, 2018). ●

Overparenting

While most parents try to care and provide for their children, some may take their roles too far and risk overparenting. In doing so, they can negatively affect their child. Some parents are identified as **helicopter parents** (HP), or as parents who make important decisions for their children, such as where they live, work, and classes they take, and intervene in settling disputes with landlords, professors, and employers. Rousseau and Scharf (2018) found that helicopter parents are prevention focused. They want their offspring to avoid difficulties, failure, and negative experiences, which the parents see as a sign of incompetence on the part of their offspring rather than an opportunity to learn and develop themselves.

Helicopter parenting may have negative outcomes for offspring. Moilanen and Lynn Manuel (2019) analyzed data on 302 young adults 18-24 and found that high helicopter parenting was linked to low mastery, self-regulation, and social competence, and to high depression. Collectively, the findings suggest that helicopter parenting has comparatively stronger impacts for socio-emotional versus behavioral adjustment. Schiffrin and Liss (2017) also found that children with helicopter parents are likely to have an extrinsic motivation to learn and to feel entitled. The authors concluded: "This study suggests that helicopter parenting is related to maladaptive academic motivations that may have negative implications for academic achievement." Finally, employers do not like helicopter parents discussing benefits or negotiating salaries on behalf of their adult children. An Office Team Survey of 608 senior managers revealed that 69% were annoyed by helicopter parents and would not recommend that they be involved in the job search of their children (Yang & Trap, 2016).

....

Helicopter parents: parents who make decisions for their children, intervene in their disputes, and resolve problems for them.

A variation of the helicopter parent is the parent as concierge. Hamilton et al. (2018) noted that affluent parents often serve as a college concierge to provide their offspring with academic, social, and career support. They can facilitate getting their children into the "right" schools, introduce them to important contacts, and provide financial resources as needed. The academic scandal of 2019 whereby parents bought admission for their children into prestigious schools is an example of the ultimate concierge service provided by parents. Hollywood actresses Lori Loughlin (aged 54) and Felicity Huffman (aged 56) made headlines for college admission scams. Indeed, millennials may be blamed for behavior parents have been engaging in all along.

CULTURE AND DIVERSITY

Parents are diverse. Amish parents rear their children in homes without electricity, which means the households have no televisions or video games. Charismatics and evangelicals—members of the conservative religious denominations—frequently send their children to Christian schools which emphasize a Biblical and spiritual view of life. More secular parents bring up their children with liberal views including cohabitation and pro-choice values.

Parents Are Only One Influence in a Child's Development

Although parents often take the credit and the blame for the way their children turn out, they are only one among many influences on child development. The environment, culture, society, peers, siblings, teachers, technology, social media, and the Internet influence the development of children. Regarding the Internet, although parents may encourage their children to use the Internet for homework, they may fear their children are also looking at material that they deem inappropriate. Parental supervision of teenagers and their privacy rights on the Internet remain potential sources of conflict. Technology use is discussed later in the chapter.

Each Child Is Unique

Children differ in their genetic makeup, physiological wiring, intelligence, tolerance for stress, capacity to learn, comfort in social situations, and interests. Parents soon become aware of the uniqueness of their child—of their differences from every other child they know. Parents of two or more children are often amazed at how children who have the same parents can be so different. Children also differ in their mental and physical health.

Because all children are unique, parents may have to adapt their parenting styles and make different parenting choices depending on the different qualities of their children. For example, children may have varying gender identities and sexual orientations. Parents of trans, gender fluid, or queer children may have to make different choices from parents with cis or heterosexual children. They may not be able to parent one cis and on trans child in the same way. Similarly, children with special intellectual, behavioral, levels, and skills require different needs from their parents.

Parenting Styles Differ

Diana Baumrind (1966) developed a typology of parenting styles that has become classic in the study of parenting. She noted that parenting behavior has two dimensions: responsiveness and demandingness. **Responsiveness** refers to the extent to which parents respond to and meet the emotional needs of their children. In other words, how supportive are the parents? Warmth, reciprocity, person-centered communication, and attachment are all aspects of responsiveness. **Demandingness**, on the other hand, is the manner in which parents place demands on children in regard to expectations and discipline. How much control do they exert over their children? Monitoring and confrontation are also aspects of demandingness. Categorizing parents in terms of their responsiveness and their demandingness creates four categories of parenting styles. They are permissive, which is also known as indulgent, and authoritarian, authoritative, and uninvolved:

Responsiveness: the extent to which parents respond to and meet the emotional needs of their children.

Demandingness: the manner in which parents place demands on children in regard to expectations and discipline.

1. **Permissive parents are high on responsiveness and low on demandingness.** These parents are very lenient and allow their children to largely regulate their own behavior. These parents may specify punishments but do not follow through; they give in to their children. These parents act out of fear that disciplining the child will cause the child to dislike his or her parents. The parents are controlled by the potential disapproval of the child. One parent said, "I want my children to love me."

2. **Authoritarian parents are high on demandingness and low in responsiveness.** They feel that children should obey their parents no matter what. Yaffe (2018) studied 101 children, ages 11-13, and found that children who perceived their parents as authoritarian—highly controlling and strict disciplinarians—were significantly more anxious in regard to separation anxiety, social anxiety, and school anxiety than the children who perceived their parents as authoritative, encouraging independence while maintaining limits and behavioral control. Mowen and Schroeder (2018) confirmed that the authoritarian parenting style was the least effective in deterring delinquency.

3. **Authoritative parents are both demanding and responsive.** They impose appropriate limits on their children's behavior but emphasize reasoning and communication. Authoritative parenting offers a balance of warmth and control and is associated with the most positive outcome for children. As noted above, Yaffe (2018) found that children who perceived their parents as authoritative were significantly less anxious in separation anxiety, social, and school contexts than children of authoritarian parents. Similarly, Olivari et al. (2018) surveyed 816 adolescents and found that an authoritative parenting style was associated with their lower risk-taking behavior and their ability to withstand peer pressure.

4. **Uninvolved parents are low in responsiveness and demandingness.** These parents are not invested in their children's lives. Beato et al. (2016) found that the children of disengaged mothers were more likely to report higher levels of anxiety.

The outcome of a parenting style may also vary by gender. McKinney and Kwan (2018) found that emerging adults preferred parenting styles that granted autonomy but that only males reported lower psychological problems as a result when compared to females.

The combination of parenting style and family relationships has a greater influence on children than the family structure itself (Murry & Lippold, 2018). Hence, an authoritative parenting style characterized by discipline and guidelines in the context of emotional warmth is more predictive of positive child outcomes than whether the child is reared in a two-parent home versus a single parent home.

CHILD REARING THEORIES

Parenting professionals have offered parents conflicting advice across time. For example, in 1914, parents who wanted to know what to do about their child's thumb sucking were told to try to control such a bad impulse by pinning the sleeves of the child to the bed if necessary. Today, parents are told that thumb sucking is a common behavior and it meets an important psychological need for security and they should not be alarmed.

Advice may also be profit driven. Much of what passes for "research-based advice" to provide parents with information about specific toys or learning programs turns out to be child development research funded by corporations who are intent on selling parents merchandise for their children.

There are several theories about rearing children (see Table 12.1). In examining these approaches, it is important to keep in mind that no single approach is superior to another. What works for one child may not work for another. Any given approach may not even work with the same child at two different times.

PRINCIPLES OF EFFECTIVE PARENTING

If we don't shape our kids, they will be shaped by outside forces that don't care what shape our kids are in.
Louise Hart, parent educator

Parenting is a complex and evolving process. Best parenting practices are dependent on factors such as the parent, child, situation, social context, and culture. Numerous principles are involved in being

TABLE 12.1

Theories of Child Rearing

THEORY	KEY CONCEPTS	APPLICATION/CHILD REARING
Psychosocial Developmental Theory **Theorist: Erik Erikson**	Eight stages of psychosocial development from birth through death. Each stage presents specific conflicts and focuses on different significant relationships such as parents and peers. The outcome of each stage will affect later stages and future development.	Development is a life-long process. Identity and identity formation are key concepts.
Behavioral Theories **Theorist: B.F. Skinner**	Focus on observable behaviors and importance of environment. All behaviors are learned through conditioning, operant conditioning, and modeling.	Children's behavior is a result of positive and negative consequences. Behavior modification uses learning principles to alter behavior.
Social Cognitive Theory (Social Learning Theory) **Theorist: Albert Bandura**	Observed behaviors are influenced by not only environmental factors but also personal factors such as attention and personality. Behaviors can be learned by observation and imitation.	Observational learning and modeling. Actions speak louder than words. Effects of media and social learning.
Attachment Theory **Theorist: Mary Ainsworth**	The strong bond between infant and caregivers shapes how individuals form relationships later in life.	Caregivers need to be sensitive and responsive to facilitate secure attachment. The types of attachment can affect later development and relationships.
Cognitive Developmental Theory **Theorist: Piaget**	Individuals play an active role in constructing their own development. Explains intellectual development from birth with four separate stages.	Promotes understanding of children's cognitive development and unique characteristics of each stage, such as preschool children are not able to understand abstract concepts. Parents can provide age appropriate toys, experiences, and guidance to support each stage.

Source: Various sources used in the development of the table, including Green and Piel (2010).

effective parents. We begin with the most important of these principles, which involves giving time and love to your children as well as praising and encouraging them.

Give Time, Love, Praise, Encouragement, and Acceptance

Children need to feel that they are worth spending time with and that they are loved. Because children depend first on their parents for the development of their sense of emotional security, it is critical that parents provide a warm emotional context in which the children develop. Feeling loved as an infant also affects one's capacity to become involved in adult love relationships (Reis et al., 2014).

"Quality time" with one's family is a term often used but rarely defined. Hodge (2018) reviewed the concept and emphasized that it means spending structured time with someone outside of daily routines engaging in meaningful conversations. Of course, "meaningful" is a vague term but is understood to refer to connecting with one's core thoughts. Burns et al. (2018) confirmed the long-term positive outcomes for mental health and absence of depression among older individuals, ages 60-64, reporting high quality emotional bonding with their parents. As might be expected, there is a gender gap in spending time with children. Negraia et al. (2018) noted that women consistently spend more time with children of all ages.

Abundant evidence from children reared in institutions where nurses attended only to their physical needs testify to the negative consequences of early emotional neglect. **Reactive attachment disorder** is common among children who were taught as infants that no one cared about them. Such children have no capacity to bond emotionally with others since they have no learning history of the experience and do not trust adults, caretakers, or parents.

Jaggers et al. (2017) assessed **parental warmth**—interest in child's activities and friends, involvement in a child's activities, enthusiasm and praise for children's accomplishments, and demonstration of affection and love—as experienced by a national sample of African American adolescents and found that warmth from biological fathers decreased across time whereas warmth from biological mothers

remained stable. Warmth from other parental figures such as grandparents, aunts, and siblings increased from 11 to 18.

Parental warmth often includes encouragement but this must be realistic. Sometimes parents "feed their children the loving, well-intentioned lie that there are 'no limits' and they can be 'anything,' which leaves the kids blaming themselves, rather than the market's brutality, when they inevitably come up short" (Schwartz, 2018).

Monitor Teens' Activities

Parents who monitor their teens' behavior and know where their teenagers are, who they are with, and what they are doing are less likely to report that their adolescents are engaged in early sexual activity, which can lead to early pregnancy, STIs, delinquent behavior that can result in entry into the court system, and alcohol or drug use. Indeed, Henchoz et al. (2016) found that lack of parental monitoring in the teen years contributed to teenagers becoming chronic adult marijuana users. Those users began smoking marijuana an average of two years earlier than those with no use or moderate use. "Keep your eye on your children" is the takeaway message for parents. Such monitoring is also associated with higher academic competence (Johnsen et al., 2018).

Parents who drank alcohol under age and who used marijuana or other drugs wonder how to go about encouraging their own children to be responsible alcohol users and drug free. Drugfree.org has some recommendations for parents, including being honest with their children about previous alcohol and drug use, making clear that they do not want their children to use alcohol or drugs, and explaining that although not all alcohol or drug use leads to negative consequences, staying clear of alcohol and drug use is the best course of action.

Monitor Screen Time, Gaming, and Pornography Exposure

In recent years, concerns about children's exposure to technology have increased. However, these concerns are also specific to those of a certain socioeconomic status. Katz et al. (2019) emphasized how parents' socioeconomic status impacts the choices that they are able to provide for their children regarding technology. In low-income families, Internet connectivity is often absent which impacts their children's ability to benefit from digital technology. Those without Internet connectivity are disadvantaged in progressing through the educational system. Similarly, those who are connected to the Internet reflect frequent use of such technology by children, giving them increased equality in competing with already

Reactive attachment disorder: common among children who were taught as infants that no one cared about them; these children have no capacity to bond emotionally with others since they have no learning history of the experience and do not trust adults, caretakers, or parents.

Parental warmth: interest in child's activities and friends, involvement in child's activities, enthusiasm and praise for children's accomplishments, and demonstration of affection and love.

connected higher socioeconomic status children and achieving higher grades.

Parents with the resources to afford Internet connectivity and who have access to computers, tablets, smartphones, or all of these devices must make another decision about use. Dervin (2016) noted the temptation of parents to use technology to entertain their children, which focuses them on solitary interaction with a digital screen rather than social interaction with humans. The researcher also noted that public spaces for children outside such as playgrounds are also disappearing since the electrical outlets are in the house and children often prefer to be indoors.

For these families, screen time is a major concern. New guidelines for screen time from the American Academy of Pediatrics calls for no screen time for babies 18 months and younger except video chatting with parents, grandparents, and loved ones. From ages two to five, one hour of screen time per day watching educational children's programs, like *Sesame Street* or *Daniel Tiger's Neighborhood*, preferably with a parent is sufficient. For example, if the program is about learning colors, the parent should ask the child to identify various colors in the room. For middle and high school children, parents should decide what is appropriate, while trying to minimize their exposure to inappropriate content, such as violence and sex.

Amazon's Fire tablets for children can be monitored via the Parent's Dashboard with Amazon's FreeTime Service, which provides details about what their children watched, books they read, apps, and games they played and websites they visited. Parents may also have a dialogue with their children by sending messages, "What did you like about the book you read?" Some teens spend 8 hours a day playing video games. Some parents view this amount of use as an addiction and point to its interference with both academic performance and social development. These parents may make time playing video games contingent on school performance and spending time with friends. If the teen resists, the equipment is removed from the teen's room. Indeed, "gaming disorder" has been added to the list of mental health diseases.

However, analysis of a SurveyMonkey online survey of a national sample of parents and teenagers revealed benefits of teens playing Fortnite: Battle Royale—making a friend online, bonding with a sibling, and interacting with parents (Baig, 2019). In addition, Eklund and Roman (2019) found in their study of 115 seventeen- to nineteen-year-olds that the amount of game time was not a significant factor in friendship formation, but what was significant was that adolescents did learn time-management strategies. Hence, time spent on gaming as well as the academic and social outcome are variable.

Pornography websites are concerns for most parents. The negative effects of pornography exposure among children include their developing sexist and unhealthy notions of sex and relationships. Pornography teaches unrealistic expectations, such as females are expected to have bodies like porn stars, to enjoy "facials" and anal sex, and are devoid of integrating intimacy in sexual expression (Knox & Milstein, 2021). Using the Internet with one's children (Festl & Gniewosz, 2019) or having a computer in a common area and being able to track site history are ways parents might monitor pornography activity. Of course, at some point, discussions about porn—what it is and isn't—replace trying to keep children from exposure.

Monitor Cell Phone Use, Texting, and Sexting

Cell phone use has positive applications in the family. Adolescents frequently text their parents—mothers more often than fathers—in regard to managerial and structural issues as well as maintaining emotional bonding (Fletcher et al., 2018). But there are also negative outcomes for cell phones. Apple acknowledged the phone addiction of children citing an American Psychological Association survey of 3,500 parents, 58% of whom viewed their child as "attached to their phone" (Hjelmgaard, 2018). This behavior may start fairly young. According to the Department of Health and Human Services, 10 is the average age reported by parents in the United States as the age they gave their child his or her first smartphone (Heid, 2017).

Twenge (2017) has suggested reducing smartphone time since higher exposures are related to sleep deprivation, depression, and suicide. The American Academia of Pediatrics director David Hill recommends keeping smartphones out of teen bedrooms, setting online firewalls, data cutoffs, and limits, such as use only after homework and not at the dinner table (Heid, 2017). Many parents have started to take such measures. Seventy-three percent of 1,565 U. S. parents in a T-Mobile survey reported monitoring their child's cell phone (Smith & Loehrke, 2018).

CULTURE AND DIVERSITY

Citing the potential for phone addiction and disruption in the classroom, France has banned the use of smartphones, tablets, and so forth for children ages three to 15 in the school system. The ban began in September 2018 (Smith, 2018).

New technology called SMS Tracker for Android permits parents to effectively take over their child's mobile phone. This technology can protect children from being contacted by predators and also allows parents to monitor unsafe messages that their children send. A parent can see all incoming and outgoing calls, text messages, and photos. Family Link by Google downloads on both the parent's and the child's phones and allows the parents to monitor all functions of the child's phone including when it will work. Another protective device is MyMobileWatchdog (known as MMWD), which monitors a child's cell phone use and instantly alerts the parents online if their child receives unapproved e-mail, text messages, or phone calls. SecuraFone can reveal how fast the car in which the cell phone of the user is moving and alert parents. If a teen is speeding, the parents will know. One version shuts the texting capability down if the phone is going faster than five miles an hour. Mobiflock for Android allows parents to lock their child's phone for a predetermined time, such as 7 p. m. to 10 p.m. when studying is scheduled. In effect, these smartphones have web filters which can block inappropriate websites, app filters which make sure apps are kid-friendly, and contact filters which can prevent harassing calls or texts by blocking certain numbers. These filters allow parents to monitor their child's location, texts, calls, browsing histories, app downloads, and photos they send and receive.

Parents also monitor their children's computer activity and can track their browsing history. A survey of 3,282 parents of teens, aged 14-17, found that more than 25% monitored their child's online activity (Brett, 2017). This number is in contrast to the 15% of teens who think that their parents track their online activity. Such monitoring is often in the best interest of the child, as a child can engage in many different types of unsafe activity online.

Follow the Rules for Social Media

Being a "friend" of your children on Facebook (FB) will provide you insight into their life experiences. However, many teens and young adults do not want to be FB friends with their parents or older relatives. If your child allows you to be his or her FB friend, consider it a privilege. If you do not "behave," your child may "unfriend" you or block you from certain posts. Similar rules apply to other social media, such as Instagram, Snapchat, or Twitter, where children may block parents from "following" them.

Provide Discipline

While parents want to be good disciplinarians, this is the area in which they least excel. Gleditsch and Pedersen (2017) surveyed 78 mothers and 66 fathers whose children were enrolled in a daycare for preschool-age children on five dimensions of parenting, including discipline, support for spouse, spending time with children, praise and affection, and attentiveness. Both mothers and fathers rated themselves most highly on praise and affection and lowest on discipline and also rated their spouse least favorably in terms of discipline. In a study of 1,000 parents of teenage drivers, almost four in 10 (37%) reported that they did not enforce punishments with their teenagers who broke a rule or law while driving (Smith & Gonzalez, 2018).

Parental discipline involves reinforcing desired behavior and punishing undesirable behavior. Unless parents levy negative consequences for lying, stealing, and hitting, children can grow up to be dishonest, to steal, and to be inappropriately aggressive. A **time-out** is a noncorporal form of punishment that involves removing the child from a context of reinforcement to a place of isolation, usually for a specified amount of time. Time outs are an effective consequence for inappropriate behavior. Withdrawal of privileges—for example, use of cell phone, watching television, or being with friends—pointing out the logical consequences of the misbehavior such as "You were late; we won't go, " and positive language like "I know you meant well but…." are also effective methods of guiding children's behavior.

American Academy of Pediatrics (AAP) issued policy opposing corporal punishment in 2018. Physical punishment is less effective in reducing negative behavior (see the Personal Choices section on spanking)—it teaches the child to be aggressive and encourages negative emotional feelings toward the parents. When using a time-out or the withdrawal of privileges, parents should make clear to the child that they disapprove of the child's behavior, not the child. It is also important to reinforce the child for engaging in positive behavior by such statements as "I appreciate your being honest with us," "Thank you for texting me when you got to the party," and "The kindness you showed your sister is wonderful."

Encourage Responsibility

Giving children increased responsibility encourages the autonomy and independence they need to be assertive and self-governing. Giving children more responsibility as they grow older can take the form of encouraging them to choose healthy snacks and letting them decide what to wear and when to return from playing with a friend; of course, the parents should praise appropriate choices. The curfew rule of the parents of the first author was "be reasonable." Such a rule avoided racing home and getting in an accident as well as engendering a feeling of being trusted.

Children who are not given any control over, and responsibility for, their own lives remain dependent

Time-out: a noncorporal form of punishment that involves removing the child from a context of reinforcement to a place of isolation.

Should Parents Use Corporal Punishment?

Parents differ in the type of punishment they feel is appropriate for children. A team of researchers examined parenting practices from a total of 9,973 respondents in three transnational eastern European countries and found that 27% of the respondents practiced only nonviolent child discipline. Parents from more affluent households were more likely to be against physical punishment of children and more likely to practice nonviolent discipline than those from less affluent households (Petrovic et al., 2016). Toure et al. (2019) found that African American parents were more likely to approve of using physical punishment to correct misbehavior of children (Toure et al., 2019).The decision to choose a corporal or noncorporal method of punishment might be based on the consequences of use. In general, the use of time-out and withholding of privileges is more effective than corporal punishment in stopping undesirable behavior. Though beatings and spanking will temporarily decrease negative verbal and nonverbal behaviors, they may have major side effects. First, punishing children by inflicting violence teaches them that it is acceptable to physically hurt someone you love. Hence, in spite of their belief "spare the rod and spoil the child," parents may be inadvertently teaching their children to use violence toward others. Turns and Sibley (2018) found that spanking a child at age 1 was associated with male children being a bully toward others at age 3.

Second, parents who beat their children should be aware that they are teaching their children to fear and to avoid them. Ansari and Gershoff (2016) confirmed that decreased spanking is associated with gains in children's academic and behavioral skills in Head Start. In recognition of the negative consequences of corporal punishment, the law in Sweden forbids parents to spank their children.

An alternative to corporal punishment is the use of the principles of behavioral family therapy which include the following:

1. **Be a positive role model.** Children learn behaviors by observing their parents' actions, so parents must model the ways in which they want their children to behave. If a parent yells or hits, the child is likely to do the same.

2. **Set rules and consequences.** Make rules that are fair, realistic, and appropriate to a child's level of development. Explain the rules and the consequences of not following them. If children are old enough, they can be included in establishing the rules and consequences for breaking them.

3. **Encourage and reward good behavior.** When children are behaving appropriately, give them verbal praise, touch them, and reward them with tangible objects occasionally, privileges, or increased responsibility.

4. **Use charts.** Parents discover that charts help them keep up with the degree to which they reward their children for the behavior that the parents want. Charts may also be used to identify what chores children are to complete, by what time, and with what consequence.

5. **Use time-outs.** A time-out involves removing children from a situation following a negative behavior. This can help children calm down, end an inappropriate behavior, and reenter the situation in a positive way. Explain what the inappropriate behavior is, why the time-out is needed, when it will begin, and how long it will last. Set an appropriate length of time for the time-out based on age and level of development, usually one minute for each year of the child's age (see the Self-Assessment: Spanking Versus Time-Out on page 391). ●

on others. A dependent child is a vulnerable child. Successful parents can be defined in terms of their ability to rear children who can function as independent adults.

Parents also recognize that there is a balance they must strike between helping their children and impeding their own growth and development. One example is making decisions on how long to provide free room and board for an adult child. See the following Personal Choices section, which details this issue.

Teach Emotional Competence and Empathy

Wilson et al. (2012) emphasized the importance of teaching children **emotional competence**—experiencing, expressing, and regulating emotion. Being able to label when one is happy or sad and experiencing emotion, expressing emotion like

Emotional competence: the ability to experience emotion, express emotion, and regulate emotion.

Boomerang Children

The **boomerang generation** refers to adult children who return to live with their parents.

Sixty-percent of adults ages 18 to 25 live with their parents or other relatives (Davidson, 2017). Some remain in the home, preferring the advantages of living in a well-equipped home with certain amenities such as Wi-Fi, washing machines, and regular meals to living with roommates in a less desirable section of town. Their doing so is associated with an economic cost to parents. Maroto (2017) studied 4,671 parents with adult children living in the home and found that they held 24% less in financial assets and 23% less in savings when compared to the years the adult children did not live with them.

What are negotiations like when children move back into the parental home? Some parents charge no rent while others allow a reduced rent to subsidize their children while they struggle to gain their financial footing. Another issue is who does the housework when adult children return home? It depends on whether the offspring have a job and are in school. ●

"I love you," and regulating emotion, such as reducing anger, assists children in getting in touch with their feelings and being empathetic with others.

Children also need to learn empathy. Borba (2016) identified these benefits in degrees of sensitivity and understanding of others: happier, more cooperative, and engaging. It's a win-win for all.

Provide Sex Education

Parents are important sources in what and when their children learn about sex. Goldfarb et al. (2018) conducted focus groups of 74 first- and second-year undergraduates to identify the sexual communication contexts and content they experienced with their parents prior to their sexual debut—first sexual intercourse. The contexts were mainly with mothers, and many characterized these conversations as awkward. Many also feared their parents' reactions if they told them anything. The content was commonly about "protection" and the message to women was to "wait." Grossman et al. (2018) also reported on interviews with 22 teens, 86% of whom reported talking with both parents and extended family about sex. The teens said that parents were more likely than extended family to convey messages about delaying sex and avoiding teen pregnancy. They also noted that extended kin were easier to talk with about sex.

Overbeek et al. (2018) noted that parents who communicate directly to their children that love should be a part of sexual expression and consent of partners always involved find that their adolescents' have less permissive sexual attitudes, sexual behavior, and sexual risk behavior. Klein et al. (2018) noted the impact on sexual agency—the ability to make decisions and assertions related to one's own sexuality—of the relationship young women have with their parents. The researchers surveyed 320 females and found that having communication with their parents about sexuality predicted sexual agency in the daughters.

> *Each time your child or teenager comes to talk with you about something important or interesting in their lives, you are auditioning to have another conversation down the road.*
>
> Karen Rayne, *Breaking the Hush Factor*

Express Confidence

"One of the greatest mistakes a parent can make," confided one mother, "is to be anxious all the time about your child, because the child interprets this as your lack of confidence in his or her ability to function independently." Rather, this mother noted that it is best to convey to one's child that you know that he or she will be fine because you have confidence in him or her. "The effect on the child," said this mother "is a heightened sense of self-confidence." Another way to conceptualize this parental principle is to think of the self-fulfilling prophecy as a mechanism that may facilitate self-confidence. If parents show their child that they have confidence in him or her, the child may begin to accept these social definitions as real and become more self-confident.

Tell Children the Truth

Simmons (2019) emphasized telling children the truth that hard work does not always pay off.

Boomerang generation: adult children who return to live with their parents.

Teenagers are challenging to parents in that they will test their parents' authority as they establish their own independence.
Courtesy of Vicki Oliver

"The humbling, brutal, messy reality is that you can do everything in your power and still fail." The message is that the world is not fair and that children should not expect it. Simmons advises parents, "We would be wise to remind our kids that life has a way of sucker-punching us when we least expect it. It's often the people who learn 'stuff happens' who get up the fastest."

Respond to the Teen Years Creatively

Parenting teenage children presents challenges that differ from those in parenting infants and young children. Meier et al. (2018) analyzed data on 18,124 parents in regard to how they felt about activities with their children of different ages. Parents noted that their greatest stress and lowest time of happiness with their children was when their children were adolescents.

Teenagers literally have altered brains that have lower amounts of dopamine, which may disrupt their reward function and make them less responsive to social stimuli (Forbes & Dahl, 2012). Teenagers are more likely to engage in a high rate of risky behavior—smoking, alcohol consumption, hazardous driving, drug use, delinquency, dares, sporting risks, rebellious behavior, and sexual intercourse. Seeking novelty, peer influences, genetic factors, and brain function are among the elements accounting for the vulnerability of adolescents.

Managing conflict with adolescents is important. McElwain and Bub (2018) found that high conflict with teenagers predicted adolescent engaging in sexual intercourse behavior by age 15. These conflicts typically revolve around money and independence. The desired cell phone, nicer clothes, and car can outstrip the budgets of many parents. Teens also want increasingly more freedom. The parent-child relationship may be inconsequential. One parent tells his children, "I'm just being the parent, and you're just being who you are; it is okay for us to disagree, but you can't go."

Tokic Milakovic et al. (2018) emphasized creating a context of openness and disclosure with teens—initiating conversation and providing support and respectful guidance. The following suggestions are standard aspects of relating to teens.

1. **Communicate love and warmth.** Adolescents who report that they feel loved by their parents feel open to being around and interacting with them. Killoren et al. (2019) found that adolescent girls disclosed information about their dating and sexuality to their mothers and sisters before doing so to friends. Such disclosure was associated with a positive relationship with both family members.

2. **Catch them doing what you like rather than criticizing them for what you don't like.** Adolescents are like everyone else—they don't like to be criticized, but they do like to be noticed for what they do that is exemplary.

3. **Be direct when necessary.** Certain rules should be explicit, such as wear your seat belt, never drink and drive, and always use a condom.

4. **Provide information rather than answers.** When teens are confronted with a problem, try to avoid making a decision for them. Rather, provide information on which they may base a decision. What courses to take in high school and what college to apply to are decisions that might be made primarily by the adolescent. The role of the parent might best be to listen.

5. **Use technology to encourage safer driving.** GPS devices are now available which can tell a parent where their teenager is, record any sudden stops, and record speed. Teenagers may resent such intrusion. There is a fine line between being respectful of a teen's privacy and monitoring their behavior. In general, when teen behavior has demonstrated to parents that they cannot be trusted—for

example, drug use or police violations—parents can take the position that they are going to monitor their behavior and that there is no option.

All of the above are helpful in rearing teenagers but the factors are beneficial in combination, not alone (Janssen et al., 2016). Teaching children to exercise self-control, monitoring their time and associations with peers, and restricting their access to problematic contexts in combination is associated with low frequencies of delinquent behavior. Just one of these parental behaviors has a limited impact.

Be Aware of Texting Symbols Teens Use

Texting has become a primary means of communication among teenagers. In addition to texts, adolescents are using various symbols and images to communicate, such as emojis and gifs. Parents may not understand the meanings of these messages. Some abbreviations, acronyms, slangs, or emojis may represent sexual content or problematic behaviors, such as drug use. For example, a green tree image may represent marijuana and the word ice can be a code word for methamphetamines.

SINGLE-PARENT ISSUES

Forty percent of births in the United States are to unmarried mothers. Distinguishing between a single-parent "family" and a single-parent "household" is important. A **single-parent family** is one in which there is only one parent—the other parent is completely out of the child's life and no contact is ever made. In contrast, a **single-parent household** is one in which one parent typically has primary custody of the child or children, but the parent living out of the house is still a part of the child's life. This arrangement is also referred to as a binuclear family. In most divorce cases in which the mother has primary physical custody of the child, the child lives in a single-parent household because the child is still connected to the father, who remains part of the child's life. In cases in which one parent has died, the child, or children live with the surviving parent in a single-parent family because there is only one parent.

....

Single-parent family: family in which there is only one parent and the other parent is completely out of the child's life through death, sperm donation, or abandonment and no contact is made with the other parent.

Single-parent household: one parent has primary custody of the child/children with the other parent living outside of the house but still being a part of the child's family; also called binuclear family.

This single mother's life is focused on the well-being of her son.

Single Parent by Choice

Single parents enter their role though divorce or separation, widowhood, adoption, or deliberate choice to rear a child or children alone. An organization for women who want children and who may or may not marry is Single Mothers by Choice. Golombok et al. (2016) compared the well-being of children born to single mothers by choice with children born to two-parent families, all children by donor insemination. There were no differences in child adjustment. However, the researcher did observe lower mother child conflict in single mother-headed families.

Challenges Faced by Single Parents

While many single parent-headed families have great resources and strong supportive network, data on the single-parent lifestyle in general involves numerous challenges. Challenges associated with being a single parent include the following.

1. **Responding to the demands of parenting with limited help.** Perhaps the greatest challenge for single parents is taking care of the physical, emotional, and disciplinary needs of their children alone (McArthur & Winkworth, 2017). Stress is common among single parents and contributes to more negative outcomes, both emotional and behavioral, in children and adolescents when compared to the stress and outcomes of two biological parents and their offspring (Mostafa et al., 2018; Fomby & Osborne, 2017; Daryanani et al., 2016). Berryhill and Durtschi (2017) analyzed data from a national sample of 1,229 single mothers and found that the level of stress experienced was predicted by the infant's negative emotionality. Hence, some children are easier to parent than others. Pollmann-Schult (2018) noted that the stereotype of single mothers being unhappy is more related to the absence of generous family

benefits, extensive child care provision, and high levels of gender equality than the role of single parent.

2. **Coping with lack of money.** Single-parent families, particularly those headed by women, report that money is always lacking. According to the U. S. Census Bureau (2017), 31% of custodial parents report that they do not receive child support from the noncustodial parent.

The median income of a single-woman householder is $36,658 which is much lower than the $51,568 of a single-man householder or a married couple with a median income of $106,082 (*ProQuest Statistical Abstract,* 2019, Table 727).

3. **Ensuring guardianship.** If the other parent is completely out of the child's life, the single parent needs to appoint a guardian to take care of the child in the event of the parent's death or disability.

4. **Obtaining prenatal care.** Single women who decide to have a child have poorer pregnancy outcomes than married women. Their children are likely to be born prematurely and to have low birth weight. The reason for such an association may be the lack of economic funds—no male partner with economic resources available— as well as the lack of social support for the pregnancy or the working conditions of the mothers.

5. **Developmentally delayed child of teen mothers.** In those cases where the single mother is a teen mother, there is an added risk to the child. Lehr et al. (2016) confirmed that a third of the young children of stressed teen mothers were developmentally delayed and had difficulties with fine motor skills and personal-social interaction.

6. **Lower academic achievement.** Nonoyama-Tarumi (2017) compared the educational achievement of children from Japanese single-mother and single father families and found lower educational achievement in both compared to children in two parent families. The reason for lower academic achievement in single-mother homes was lack of finances. The lack of academic achievement was due to a deficit of parenting resources measured by discussions and supervision at home.

Though the risk of negative outcomes is higher for children in single-parent homes, most are happy and well-adjusted. Indeed, the reality is that there are numerous positives associated with being a single parent. These include having a stronger bonding experience with one's children since they "are" the family, a sense of pride and self-esteem for being independent, and being a strong role model for offspring who observe their parent being able to "wear many hats."

EMPTY NEST VIA EMIGRATION OF CHILDREN

Parenting couples enter a new stage in life when there are no more children reside at home. Are those couples depressive empty nesters or happy that they are child free? Most parents adapt to this phase without experiencing a major depressive episode. The couple's marital satisfaction is associated with their belief of raising successful children (Bouchard, 2018). A unique type of empty nest is when a couple's offspring emigrate to another country. Yahirun and Arenas (2018) surveyed 4,718 Mexican parents whose offspring had immigrated to the United States and found that the parents reported more loneliness and sadness than parents whose children were still with them. However, their reaction did not rise to the level of displaying depressive symptoms.

FUTURE OF PARENTING

The future of parenting will involve new contexts for children and new behaviors that children learn and parents adjust to. While parents will continue to be the primary source for childcare, children will increasingly end up in childcare, after-school programs, and day camps during the summer, due to both parents earning an income. There will also be an increasing number of children reared in single-family contexts. These contexts may result in new parental norms where a wider range of behaviors on the part of their children may be accepted. Hence, since parents may be increasingly preoccupied with their job and careers, the norms their children are learning in child care facilities and other contexts may be more readily accepted since parents may have less time and energy to reverse them.

Although parenting is one of the most rewarding and meaningful life experiences, it is also demanding and stressful. Sophisticated innovation such as robots, smart devices, and virtual reality are likely to make parenting easier. For example, sensors can monitor infants' vital signs and inform caretakers about infants' needs, such as feeding; smart bassinets can rock the baby to sleep many different ways; and communication technology is likely to redefine human connection. Digital entertainment will be more enticing and realistic. Many innovations are intrusive and mentally taxing which may interfere with relationship quality. Future parents will need to be cautious about how to use technology wisely without hindering the development of the precious parent-child relationships.

SUMMARY

What are the basic choices parents make?
The seven basic choices parents make include deciding (1) whether to have a child, (2) the number of children, (3) the interval between children, (4) one's method of discipline and guidance, and (5) the degree to which one will be invested in the role of parent, (6) the degree to which the parents will co-parent and (7) how much technological exposure they will allow their children. The choices perspective also emphasizes that not to make a choice is to make a choice, all decisions are trade-offs, reframing regretful decisions is important, and one's society and culture has an impact on choices.

What is the transition to parenthood like for women, men, and couples?
Transition to parenthood refers to that period of time from the beginning of pregnancy through the first few months after the birth of a baby. The mother, father, and couple all undergo changes and adaptations during this period. Most mothers relish their new role; some may experience the transitory feelings of baby blues, peripartum depression, and postpartum depression.

What are several facts about parenthood?
Parental roles include providing physical care for children, loving them, being an economic resource, providing guidance as a teacher or model, protecting them from harm, promoting their health, and providing meaningful family rituals. Parents are only one influence on their children, each child is unique, and parenting styles differ. Research suggests that an authoritative parenting style, characterized as both demanding and warm, is associated with positive outcomes. In addition, being emotionally connected to a child, respecting the child's individuality, and monitoring the child's behavior to encourage positive contexts have positive outcomes.

What are some of the principles of effective parenting?
Giving time, love, praise, and encouragement; monitoring the activities of one's child; setting limits; encouraging responsibility; and providing sexuality education are aspects of effective parenting.

What are the issues of single parenting?
About 40% of all children will spend one fourth of their lives in a female-headed household. The challenges of single parenthood for the parent include taking care of the emotional and physical needs of a child alone, meeting one's own adult emotional and sexual needs, money, and rearing a child without a father, the influence of whom can be positive and beneficial.

What is the future of parenting?
Focused on earning income, parents will depend more on secondary and nonfamily resources to take care of and rear their children. The result will be a wider set of norms that children learn and behaviors they engage in with less parental correction. Technology will play an increasingly important role in future parenting.

KEY TERMS

Baby blues, 258

Boomerang generation, 271

Concerted cultivation, 255

Demandingness, 265

Emotional competence, 270

Gatekeeper role, 261

Helicopter parenting, 264

Matrescence, 258

Oxytocin, 258

Parental warmth, 267

Parental empowerment, 261

Peripartum depression, 260

Postpartum depression, 259

Postpartum psychosis, 260

Reactive attachment disorder, 267

Responsiveness, 265

Safe Haven (Baby Moses Law), 260

Single-parent family, 273

Single-parent household, 273

Time-out, 269

Transition to parenthood, 258

WEB LINKS

Attachment Parenting International
http://www.attachmentparenting.org/

Family Wellness Workshops
http://www.familywellness.com/

The Children's Partnership Online
http://www.childrenspartnership.org/

Saving Mothers
http://www.savingmothers.org/

Single Parenting
http://singleparent.lifetips.com/

Single Parenting—Grants to go back to school
https://www.schoolgrantsblog.com/grants-for-single-mothers/

Un/Hushed—Talking with Adolescents about Sex
http://www.unhushed.net/

Get the tools you need to sharpen your study skills. SAGE edge offers a robust online environment featuring an impressive array of free tools and resources.
Access practice quizzes, eFlashcards, video, and multimedia at **edge.sagepub.com/knox13e**

13 Money, Work, and Relationships

Working women and the double income family are changing how we choose partners and how we love.

—Helen Fisher, Biological Anthropologist

Learning Objectives

13.1.   Discuss how money affects relationships

13.2.   Summarize how employment impacts relationships, marriages, and families

13.3.   Identify the effect of parental employment on children

13.4.   Review the various strategies of balancing work and family life

13.5.   Identify strategies for balancing work and leisure time

13.6.   Discuss the future of the effect of work on family life

Master the content at
edge.sagepub.com/knox13e

Work occupies a major facet of one's life. It can affect families positively in the sense that it allows individuals to provide for themselves and their families. However, one's career can also have a negative impact, affecting the frequency which with one spends time with their family and partner, as well as the quality of that time. Whillans and Dunn (2019) confirmed that persons who value money over time with others have fewer relationships.

In the United States, while there are couples in which neither partner has a strong orientation toward paid work (Miller et al., 2019), there is a trend of people being overworked. Researchers analyzed data on working persons aged 16 to 64 from 2011-2014 from the Center for Economic and Policy Research's Current Population Survey. Results revealed that 29% of legal workers and 30% of management workers worked more than 45 hours a week. They were followed by 21% of workers in farming, fishing, and forestry; 17% in architecture and engineering; and 15% in business and financial services. Long hours such as these, combined with work travel, can significantly affect one's relationships.

It's likely that many individuals who are overworked can also be described by the concept of **everwork**. Introduced by Wynn (2018), everwork is an all-consuming preoccupation on work whereby the individual is either physically at work or mentally focused via video conferencing and emailing about work issues from home. Regardless, the partner is not psychologically available to family members. Workers are often aware of how caught up they are and may even have plans to quit someday. An example is Rodrigo, a 32- year-old father:

Everwork: always working, either physically at work or at home on the computer doing work for one's employer. The individual never unplugs.

My last case was a new client, a huge client here in the Bay Area that is one of our competitors' stronghold. We finally got in there, and it's a priority one client, as they say, globally, so it's important for the company. Yeah. I mean, we agreed to do things that we knew from the beginning were not gonna be sustainable for anyone. It was hell for eight weeks. . . . My peers said that I looked like a vulture for two months because I was sleeping three hours a night, basically, and I was falling asleep on my computer. There was a lot of unhealthy stuff in terms of just drinking ridiculous amounts of coffee and not sleeping and eating poorly (p. 721)

Parents in the "everworker" mode are often aware of the impact on themselves and their children. Keith is a 39-year-old father who lamented:

I don't like not being around during the week, especially times like now when [my son's] probably going to start walking any day. It's tough. You try to adjust by Skyping in the morning and stuff like that, but it's not the same, obviously. . . .. In the past two years it's been a lot more thinking about what's right for the family, what's right for my desire to—what kind of dad do I want to be and those types of things. It makes it a little bit of a different decision process around, okay, I could stay, I could keep killing myself for a while longer. . . . Do I really want to do that? Probably not. I'd rather have something where I'm not traveling 80% to 100%, where I get to see the little guy more than just on the weekends and just have more of a family time presence than I have over the past nine months that the little guy's been around (p. 727).

The lure of money is often one of the culprits, which is why everwork is not unique to any one profession. Sometimes the pursuit of money just for the sake of

This dual-earner couple represent the norm of "Everwork." They are at the beach for their summer vacation but inside on their laptops doing work.

accumulating more is at the expense of one's relationships. In these situations, the real stress that money inflicts on relationships is the result of internalizing the societal expectations of who one is, or should be, in regard to the pursuit of money. However, low wages may also affect one's relationships, as some may be forced to work long hours or multiple jobs in order to provide for themselves and their families. There are many factors involved when it comes to relationships, work, and finances. In the following section, we examine the impact that money and work have on relationships.

Many people who know me call me 'the hardest working man in the news business' because you're never ever going to outwork me.

Don Lemon, American journalist

MONEY AND RELATIONSHIPS

Money affects relationships at every stage, whether two individuals are dating, married, or divorced. Even from the first date, "Who pays?" is a key question. This question and others continue throughout the duration of a relationship, affecting dates, housing situations, and vacations. Even more questions arise when partners have significant differences in income and have different spending habits. Money can even impact the decision to marry, as Ishizuka (2018) noted that cohabiting couples with high and equal incomes were more likely to transition to marriage than those who had low incomes.

Money can also affect who someone chooses as a partner. While some partners may be more appealing because they can afford a certain lifestyle, others might find a person unappealing because of how they handle their money. As Brienza and Grossman

(2017) demonstrated, money can affect one's personality. Their research emphasized that individuals with high incomes are less likely to display "wise reasoning," which was defined as a consideration of another's point of view, an openness to compromise, and recognition of the importance of conflict resolution. Each of these qualities can affect relationships.

While individuals say they marry for love, they have expectations in regard to money. In two national U.S. samples, 97% of women and 74% of men said that it was "essential" that their potential partner had a steady income. Sixty-nine percent of women and 47% of men said it was equally important that the partner made or would make a lot of money (Fales et al., 2016). According to a Merrill Edge report based on 1,034 adults with investable assets ranging from $50,000 to $250,000, 56% said that they wanted financial security and 44% to be head-over-heels in love (Smith & Gelles, 2019).

Financial compatibility is an important part of a relationship. There are several financial deal breakers that can affect a relationship. For example, someone who is careful about saving his or her money may have difficulty being in a relationship with someone who is more focused on spending than saving. Debt is a huge financial deal breaker, which may affect whether a couple decides to marry. In a study by Goldman Sachs of 500 adults, 75% reported that they were concerned about the amount of credit card debt of a romantic partner (Smith & Loehrke, 2018). One undergraduate mused, "She has $150,000 in student loans . . . too much for me to sign on."

Money also impacts marital stability and one's financial satisfaction. Kaplan and Stier (2017) noted that the two-income family is less likely to divorce than the traditional family of one breadwinner. In traditional families with one breadwinner and one homemaker, the division of labor was assumed and understood. With two-income households, the division of labor must be negotiated. Mencarini and Vignoli (2018) found that employed women were less likely to initiate divorce if their partner contributed to domestic work, such as child care.

Being in a committed relationship affects one's view of money. Fulda and Lersch (2018) noted that committed cohabiting couples take the long view—for example, with saving—in regard to their finances. One of the reasons spouses have a stronger economic position is that they are more likely to save.

Money may represent power, resource, and even love to some people. However, money can also be a great source of conflict. It is crucial for couples to converse about finances before marriage. Please refer to the Self-Assessment: Involved Couple's Inventory on page 377, which provides some starting points for couples discussing their finances. The key issue is to reach an agreement on how a couple will manage their finances—for example, regarding priorities, expectations, and goals—and decide on what is "mine," "yours," and "ours." Couples ought to discuss topics such as income, expense, debt, budget, assets, future planning, and other financial responsibilities.

Money as Power in a Couple's Relationship

Money is a central issue in relationships because of its association with power, control, and dominance. Generally, the more money a partner makes, the more power that person has in the relationship. This power may be demonstrated when making larger purchases. For example, if a woman earns more money than her husband, and is therefore contributing more to the purchase, she may have more influence in which home they purchase. Men, in general, make considerably more money than women and generally have more power in relationships. (see Table 13.1)

To some individuals, money means love. While admiring the engagement ring of her friend, a woman said, "What a big diamond! He must really love you." The cultural assumption is that a big diamond equals expense and a lot of sacrifice and love. Similar assumptions are often made when gifts are given or received. People tend to spend more money on presents for the people they love, believing that the value of the gift symbolizes the depth of their love. People receiving gifts may make the same assumption. "She must love me more than I thought," mused one man. "I gave her some winter socks from Walmart, but she bought us concert tickets that must have cost her a fortune. I felt embarrassed." Because of these assumptions, individuals who struggle financially and cannot afford expensive gifts may feel embarrassed about their situation.

Some households live below the poverty line and struggle on a daily basis to have enough food to survive. Table 13.2 lists the poverty guidelines, which are used to determine financial eligibility for certain federal programs, such as Head Start and the Supplemental Nutrition Assistance Program (SNAP).

Effect of Money on Personal Well-being

Lindqvist et al. (2018) studied the long-term effects of winning the lottery on personal happiness and

TABLE 13.1

Median Income and Education

	BACHELOR'S	MASTER'S	DOCTORAL DEGREE
Men	$63,269	$80,083	$101,591
Women	$41,045	$54,571	$72,018

Source: *ProQuest Statistical Abstract of the United States, 2019, Online Edition.* Table 730.

TABLE 13.2

2019 Poverty Guidelines for the 48 Contiguous States and the District of Columbia

PERSONS IN FAMILY/ HOUSEHOLD	POVERTY GUIDELINE
1	$12,490
2	$16,910
3	$21,330
4	$25,750
5	$30,170
6	$34,590
7	$39,010
8	$43,430

Source: https://aspe.hhs.gov/poverty-guidelines

found positive outcomes on one's psychological well-being. Sohn (2016) also found a direct relationship between the husband's income and the wife's happiness. Indeed, a 100% increase in the husband's income was related to a 72% increase in the wife expressing that she was "very happy." The opposite is also true: lower income is associated with more stress and conflict which translates into less satisfaction. We discuss financial struggle and stress in Chapter 14.

WORK, RELATIONSHIPS, AND FAMILIES

A couple's relationship is organized around the job of each partner. Where the couple live is determined by where the partners get jobs. Jobs influence how much time they have to spend with each other and their children; what time they eat; which family members eat with whom, when they go to bed; and when, where, and for how long they vacation. Hwang and Ramadoss (2017) noted that both men and women employees are happiest when they have high levels of job control, support from their supervisor, and support from their coworkers. The degree to which one is satisfied with one's job may be assessed in Self-Assessment: Job Satisfaction Scale on page 392.

Individuals may even base their career decisions on potential flexibility. Indeed, Valentino et al. (2016) surveyed 3,229 college students in 16 North Carolina public universities and found that "a concern for the potential inflexibility of one's future career was associated with a decreased likelihood of majoring in the 'hard' STEM fields (science, technology, engineering, and mathematics)" (p. 273). Of interest, there were no gender differences—both men and women noted a concern about the family flexibility of their future career and were equally likely not to pursue STEM careers. These findings correspond with Hall and Willoughby's (2016) research on 434 graduates and their future role centralities: child centered, marriage centered, child and marriage centered, career centered, and family and career centered. They found that students were less family and career centered and more marriage and child centered.

In this section, we examine some of the various influences of work on a couple's relationship. We begin by looking at the skills identified by dual-earner spouses to manage their work, job, or career so as to provide income for the family but minimal expense to their relationship.

Basic Rules for Managing One's Work Life to Have a Successful Marriage

Ma a tta and Uusiautti (2012) analyzed data from 342 married couples who explained their secrets for maintaining a successful relationship in the face of the demands of work. These secrets included turning a negative into a positive—a job loss can be an opportunity for a better job—being creative and adjusting the division of labor depending on someone's week, tolerating dissimilarity by accepting the partner, and being committed to the relationship.

Johnston (2016) focused on couples with two incomes and two young children. She noted the importance of keeping finances transparent so that neither is blindsided, being flexible about whatever

is needed to make a situation work, and checking in or turning up. Checking in meant spending quality time together, such as getting a babysitter for a date night so that the parents can reconnect.

Sometimes people change jobs to benefit themselves and their relationship. About two percent of white-collar employees annually trade their 24/7 jobs where they are always answering emails and being on call for blue-collar jobs (Davidson, 2017). While the income is about half, the change in life and relationship satisfaction can be worth it.

"We-Talk" and Effect on Work and Marital Satisfaction

Lin et al. (2016) noted that "we-talk" has different meanings when used by a husband or wife in reference to their work-family stress. "We-talk" reflects

Some individuals prefer a blue-collar to a white-collar job.
Courtesy of Trevor Werb

Work or Relationships?

People who consistently choose their work over their relationships either have partners who have also made such choices or partners who are disenchanted. Traditionally, men have chosen their work over their relationships; women have chosen their relationships over work.

Most people try to balance their work and relationship so as to experience a life they enjoy. Some professions or careers inherently provide the opportunity for balance. One example is elementary school teaching, where the person is home relatively early in the day with a couple of months off in the summer. Some individuals may work from home full time, which allows them more flexibility.

Some individuals require very little income and have no interest in material wealth. We, the authors, have a friend who has little to no regard for material wealth. He has been homeless and now runs a homeless shelter where he and his staff feed two meals a day to over 100 individuals, paid for through private funding and donations. At night, he goes back to his $200-a-month loft where he reads and paints. We asked him how his lack of concern for money affects the interest women have in establishing a long-term relationship with him. "It kills it," he noted. "They simply have no interest in being pair-bonded to someone living this vagabond existence." ●

the view that the couple is working together as a unit and they are "in this together." The researchers surveyed 31 dual-earner couples about how they coped with work-family stress. The results showed that we-talk used by wives increased their husbands' work and marital satisfaction. Such we-talk used by wives was about the couple and implied a togetherness that we work on issues together. However, we-talk used by husbands decreased their wives' work satisfaction since the husbands' meaning of we-talk was not "you and me" but "you." Hence, the husbands' statement, "We need to get the groceries before we go home" means "You get the groceries before you go home."

Types of Dual-Career Marriages

A **dual-career marriage** is defined as one in which both spouses pursue careers and may or may not include dependents. A career is different from a job in that the former usually involves advanced education or training, full-time commitment, long hours, night and weekend work "off the clock," and a willingness to relocate. While many couples choose to have dual careers in order to pursue their own goals or live a certain life style, some couples do not have a choice. Based on their financial circumstances, both partners must work in order to make ends meet and to provide for themselves and their families.

Dual-career spouses typically operate without someone to function full time in the role of "a traditional home maker"—someone to prepare meals, take care of the children, and do housework. Increasingly, dual-career spouses share the work themselves after they get home from their respective careers. Indeed, there is a continuing trend toward viewing egalitarian relationships in marriage as the ideal (Pepin & Cotter, 2018). Other couples may seek outside help for child care or housekeeping. Types of dual-career marriages are those in which one partner's career takes precedence (**PRIMARY/secondary career**), both careers are equally important (**PRIMARY/PRIMARY career**) or both spouses share a career or work together (**SAME** career).

Couples with two careers may drift into traditional roles because one partner's income is higher than the other's (PRIMARY/secondary career). When both careers are of equal importance (PRIMARY/PRIMARY career) the partners will try to accommodate both careers, support each career but

Dual-career marriage: a marriage in which both spouses pursue careers.

PRIMARY/secondary career: dual career marriage in which one career takes precedence.

PRIMARY/PRIMARY career: dual career marriage in which both careers are viewed as equal.

SAME career marriage: dual-career marriage in which spouses share a career or work together.

at different times and may, for example, move in reference to each other's career, or have a **commuter marriage** whereby the partners will live apart but stay connected electronically and see each other when they can (Lindemann, 2017). The authors know of an "independent actress" who is away from her husband for five months at a time doing nightly dinner theaters in different cities. Her husband is an academic in a theater department at a university. "Our marriage works for us," she said.

In heterosexual commuter marriages the woman is often able to enjoy a full career without traditional expectations (Lindemann, 2018). Lee (2018) analyzed national data in Korea on commuter couples and found that both spouses reported lower life satisfaction with the husbands observing that their satisfaction was lower than their wives.

Finally, some dual-career marriages are those in which the partners work in the same profession (SAME career). Some news organizations hire both spouses to travel abroad to cover the same story. These career marriages are rare.

Effects of Two Careers in One Relationship

What happens when the partners of a committed couple each have careers they want to pursue? Wong (2017) interviewed 21 heterosexual young adult couples who were deciding whether to move for early career opportunities. Strategies included the men adjusting to the woman's career by waiting till the woman identified her job and then finding one in the area. Another strategy involved the woman relinquishing her career desires in favor of following the partner. Findings revealed that women disproportionately shouldered the burden of geographic relocation to accommodate their partners.

Effects of Both Partners' Employment on the Marriage

Are marriages in which both partners have their own earned income more vulnerable to divorce? Not if the partners are happy. But if a partner is unhappy, the income will provide a mechanism of support if the person leaves. In other words, a partner's employment does not destabilize happy marriages but "increases the risk of disruption in unhappy marriages" (Schoen et al., 2002, p. 643). Hence, employment won't affect a happy marriage but it can affect an unhappy one. Kaplan and Herbst-Debby (2018) also noted that it is the husband's economic instability in combination with the wife's employment that influences the potential for divorce. Inanc (2018) extended this

Commuter marriage: arrangement whereby the spouses live in different places because of their work but use technology to stay connected.

connection to point out that when husbands were temporarily employed—and hence, in an unstable job—in combination with the wife being employed, wives reported higher marital dissatisfaction.

Another factor involved in the association between the wife's employment and divorce is the country in which the couple live. Vignoli et al. (2018) noted that divorce has less impact on an employed woman's decision to divorce in those countries with easier access to divorce and in those countries with more generous financial support for families and single mothers such as Germany and Hungary.

Parents and Work

Work has an even greater effect on individuals who are parents, particularly mothers. Traditional conceptions of the role of mother are that she will work part time, give priority to her child, and be pair-bonded with someone who has an additional source of income. These conceptions are changing. Dow (2016) noted that African American mothers assume that they will be gainfully employed full time, that they will be financially independent, and that they will look to kin and community for help with their child caregiving.

Similarly, in traditional heterosexual marriages, men are often pressured to be the breadwinner, while women focus on child care. However, today's economy typically requires couples to have dual incomes. Seventy-six percent of wives are in the labor force (*Proquest Statistical Abstract, 2019,* Table 624). The time mothers are most likely to be in the labor force is when their children are teenagers between the ages of 14 and 17, which is the time when food and clothing expenses are the highest.

Florian (2018) revealed how motherhood impacts employment. In general, becoming a mother is associated with less involvement in the workforce, as some drop out of the workforce or reduce hours to take care of the baby. But this varies by race and ethnicity, with motherhood reducing full time employment the most for Whites, then Hispanics, and then Blacks, who spend the least amount of time out of the paid workforce due to economic need.

Pregnancy can also affect employment. Mirick and Wladkowski (2018) revealed what pregnant women and mothers face in academia as they pursue higher education. They interviewed 29 pregnant women getting their doctorate who reported that they felt they would be most successful if they maintained a silence about their identity as a mother and made clear to their professors that their family life would not negatively impact their work productivity. Some perceived lost opportunities in graduate school or in the job market or both due to their pregnancies and parenting during graduate school. The majority

of these respondents spoke of wanting to find a position in a family-friendly organization where family was valued and work-life balance was possible.

Glauber and Day (2018) noted that paid work may have an unanticipated positive impact on reducing depression. For women in the caregiving role to a spouse who experience depression, paid employment is associated with attenuating the depression by providing another role to focus on. However, when men were in the spousal caregiving role, paid employment seemed to worsen the depression. The researchers suggested these men may feel distressed, as their work-family experiences conflict with traditional gender norms, where they are expected to be the sole provider.

Parents can benefit from work-family or work-life policies, which allow more flexibility for child care duties. These policies are discussed in Family Policy: Government and Corporate Work-Family Policies and Programs.

Effects of the Mother's Employment on the Mother

How are mothers affected by employment? The short answer is stress. Research by Westrupp et al. (2016) has confirmed the reciprocal relationships between employed mothers' work-family conflict and psychological distress across 8 years of the child's life (0 to age 9). Associations persisted after controlling for family socioeconomic status, maternal age, or job quality.

While some new mothers enjoy their work role and return to work soon after their children are born, others anguish over leaving their baby to return to the workforce. One new mother who went back to work after the birth of her daughter said, "You go through periods of guilt for leaving her, sadness, missing her, worrying to death, and even a slight bit of anger at your spouse. Hey, if you made more money, we could afford for me to stay home."

The new mother discovers that there are now two spheres to manage—work and family—which may result in **role overload**—not having the time or energy to meet the demands of their responsibilities in the roles of partner, parent, and worker. Because women have traditionally been responsible for most of the housework and child care, some employed women come home from work to what Hochschild (1989) calls the second shift, housework and child care to be done after work. According to Hochschild, the **second shift** has the following result:

Role overload: not having the time or energy to meet the demands or responsibilities in the roles of wife, parent, and worker.

Second shift: the housework and childcare that employed women engage when they return home from their jobs.

Government and Corporate Work-Family Policies and Programs

Policies that help adults balance their work and family responsibilities are called *work-family*, *work-life*, and *family-friendly* policies. Work-family policies include policies that allow workers flextime, the option for workers to control when they begin and end their workday; policies and programs that provide private space for pumping breast-milk and breastfeeding at work; child care at or near the work site and paid maternity and paternity leave; and paid sick leave. Compared with many other countries, the United States lags far behind in providing national work-family provisions. For example, the United States is the only industrialized country that does not provide paid leave for employed mothers of infants: 33 of 34 OECD (Organization for Economic Cooperation and Development) countries guarantee paid leave to mothers of infants; 32 countries guarantee paid leave to fathers of infants (Raub et al., 2018).

Canada offers a year of paid leave, Norway offers up to 91 weeks, and in Finland, new mothers are entitled to up to 3 years of paid leave (Ingraham, 2018). Paid parental leave is associated with a number of benefits, including increased breast-feeding, increased parent-infant bonding, better infant and child health, as well as physical and mental health benefits for parents (Raub et al., 2018). Paid leave is not just in countries that are predominantly White. Numerous African countries also provide these benefits.

Work-family policies benefit not only new parents but also every employee who experiences personal or family illness or injury or both, or the aging of a family member who requires caregiving or some combination of these issues. Indeed, as the population ages, there is a growing need for policies that help employed adults take care of their aging family members. There are an estimated 24 million family caregivers taking care of an older family member. Sixty percent of these family caregivers of adults are also employed (Feinberg, 2018).

In 1993, the Clinton Administration passed the Family and Medical Leave Act (FMLA), which requires all U.S. companies with 50 or more employees to provide eligible workers with up to 12 weeks of *unpaid* leave for reasons of family illness, birth, or adoption of a child. While the majority of industrialized countries guarantee paid leave for workers who take time from work to care for family member's health needs, the United States guarantees only *unpaid* leave to only *some* workers. Being eligible for FMLA leave depends on the length of employment, work hours, and the size of the workplace in terms of the number of employees. Fifty-six percent of U.S. workers are eligible for FMLA; 44% are not eligible (Gould, 2018).

Although there are no U.S. national paid leave policies, as of August 2019, eight states* and the District of Columbia have passed legislation providing paid leave days for family caregivers. Aside from government-mandated work-family policies, some corporations and employers have work-family policies and programs for their employees. Google offers parents who give birth up to 24 weeks of paid leave and 12 weeks for parents who did not give birth.

State and employer-provided paid leave policies may be a step in the direction of helping working families, but are not even close to providing universal paid leave coverage. Only a small percentage of U.S. civilian employees—16% in 2018—have access to paid family leave (Bureau of Labor Statistics, 2018). Workers who do have access to paid family leave tend to be higher paid white-collar workers; 94% of low-income employees, who are disproportionately people of color, have no access to paid family leave (Guynn, 2018).

In 2017 the Family and Medical Insurance Leave Act (FAMILY Act) was introduced into Congress. This legislation proposed to provide workers with partial wage replacement for up to 12 weeks of family medical leave for reasons of pregnancy, the birth or adoption of a child, to recover from illness, or to care for an ill family member. Paid parental leave is associated with better job performance, employee retention, and increased economic growth (Gault et al., 2014). It is sobering to consider that even if the FAMILY Act or similar legislation passes—and the likelihood of that happening in the near future is not promising—the United States would still be far behind other industrialized countries that offer much more generous paid leave support for working families. ●

* States with paid family leave as of August 2019: California, New Jersey, Rhode Island, New York, Washington, Massachusetts, Connecticut, and Oregon, and the District of Columbia.

…women tend to talk more intently about being over-tired, sick, and "emotionally drained." Many women could not tear away from the topic of sleep. They talked about how much they could "get by on"…six and a half, seven, seven and a half, less, more….

Some apologized for how much sleep they needed. … They talked about how to avoid fully waking up when a child called them at night, and how to get back to sleep. These women talked about sleep the way a hungry person talks about food (p. 9).

Relationships today are increasingly egalitarian so that both partners work outside the home and come home to prepare dinner, feed, and bathe the children, and so forth.

Another stressful aspect of employment for employed mothers in dual-earner marriages is **role conflict,** being confronted with incompatible role obligations. For example, the role of a career woman is to stay late and prepare a report for the following day. However, the role of a mother is to pick up her child from day care at 5 p. m. When these roles collide, there is role conflict—some give priority to the career role and feel guilty about it.

Role strain, the anxiety that results from being able to fulfill only a limited number of role obligations, occurs for both partners in PRIMARY/PRIMARY career marriages. Neither partner is at home to take care of housework and children while they are working, and they feel strained at not being able to do everything.

Women's careers may suffer when they reduce work hours or take time off to care for their children. Unless a mother has a supportive partner with a flexible schedule, family who live close and who can take care of her children, or money to pay for child care, she will discover that corporations want the work done and don't care about the wanting to spend time in the role of mother. Indeed, women who are promoted in corporate America aren't particularly happy about it. Lup (2018) noted that men, but not women, who are promoted into higher level management report an increase in job satisfaction. In addition, following promotion, the job satisfaction of women promoted to higher-level management starts to decline. One explanation is that women are more socialized to derive their life satisfaction from their relationships rather than from their work. A promotion usually comes with the expectation of increased responsibilities and work.

Alternative or Flexible Work Arrangements

Alternative work arrangements, such as working from home or working in the gig economy, have been on the rise. These arrangements allow greater flexibility and greater access to partners and family members.

Working From Home

Those in dual-career marriages or partnerships may benefit from jobs that allow them to work from home or work remotely. Parents may also benefit from such working arrangements, which allow them the freedom and flexibility to care for children while still earning an income. Working from home is on the rise. Based on a Gallup State of the American workforce study, 42% of American employees work remotely (Wise & Trap, 2017).

Those who work from home may have their own businesses, while others may work remotely for a company. Some companies facilitate working from home, such as www.powertofly.com, which connects women, primarily those with children, to remote tech jobs in the United States. The goal is to provide a way for women to continue to have a job when they have their children without leaving home. The rise of telework is discussed in Technology and Family: Telework.

Gig Economy and Sharing Economy Jobs

As individuals tire of corporate jobs that demand more work and pay less, some are working in the **gig** or **shared economy**. Also referred to as the on-demand, peer, or platform economy, these individuals offer their skills on websites such as TaskRabbit. An example is Seth F who posted that he "was a smart guy with tools," had worked on almost 1,000 tasks and had a 99% approval rating. He charged

Being able to work from home—telework—is, increasingly, an important criteria in agreeing to work for a company.

Role conflict: one role (e.g., parent) conflicts with another (e.g., worker).

Role strain: the anxiety that results from being able to fulfill only a limited number of role obligations.

Gig economy: also known as the shared, on-demand, peer, or platform economy; individuals market their labor directly to the public and choose their own time and context of work.

Telework

Advances in technology impact various aspects of work including when, where, and how work is to be accomplished. **Telework** is an arrangement with an employer that the employee can perform duties and responsibilities from a remote location such as home. Other terms for telework include telecommuting, flexible work, remote work, virtual work, alternative work place, off-site work, and distance work. Some individuals will only work for a firm or corporation that allows some level of telework. These individuals have made the choice that the flexibility of their work life, which telework provides, is a requirement for their personal and relationship functioning and satisfaction.

The prevalence of telework varies depending on the definition and method of sampling. According to research by Global Workplace Analytics (2018), 50% of U.S. workers hold a job with partial telework opportunities. Previous research has addressed the impacts of telework on individuals, relationships, organizations, and the society. Benefits for individual workers include a greater work-life balance, saving commuting time, less stress from interruptions, and greater efficiency (Chung and van der Horst, 2018; Walker, 2018). From the employer's perspective, telework can increase space usage efficiency, reduce overhead cost, boost retention rates, and tap into a larger pool of talent (U.S. Government Accountability Office, 2018; PR Newswire, 2018). Telework can also reduce rush hour traffic and improve the environment by reducing automobile emissions.

Telework is a particularly desirable choice for mothers with young children. Chung and van der Horst (2018) analyzed national data in the United Kingdom and observed that mothers with access to teleworking were less likely to reduce their working hours after childbirth. Indeed, in the absence of such an arrangement, these mothers may have chosen to drop out of the workforce altogether.

Although there are many benefits of telework, hostility and jealousy from non-teleworkers has been noted. Corporate decisions regarding who is allowed to work from home and who is not can be a difficult task which may be perceived as an act of favoritism. Managers are more likely to approve telework for trustworthy employees with a good work ethic (Kaplan et al., 2018). Corporate efforts to build collegial relationships and maintain social connections is important for productivity and retention.

The blurring of physical and emotional boundaries between home and work is a commonly mentioned problem (Jostell & Hemlin, 2018; van der Lippe & Lippényi, 2018). Tips for successful telework in the home include making decisions in regard to having a designated work space, setting clear work schedules and deadlines, managing distractions and interruptions in the home, and maintaining connection with the main office and attending work functions in person (TeleworkVA, 2018). The acceptance of telework by corporations is variable. While some companies are expanding telework, others require workers to be at the physical office with other employees. ●

$55 an hour and was hired to hang a mirror for this particular caller (Heller, 2017). "Gigging is not only about a living, but a life. Many observers see it as something more: the future of American work" (p. 52). Some individuals may participate in this economy by taking on a side gig, which allows them to supplement the income from their full-time position with income from these other positions. These individuals can choose to pick up side gigs when needed. Persons who work for Uber and Lyft or are Airbnb hosts are more in control of their lives. And, while health insurance and retirement with a pension are not benefits, the flexibility to work when one wants and in the context of one's choosing are benefits.

Corporations love the gig economy. It is ideal for their bottom line and investors. They can pay workers low wages and no benefits. In effect, they are

Telework: an arrangement with an employer that the employee can perform duties and responsibilities from a remote location such as home.

This husband and father supports his family doing what he loves—playing nightly gigs at local venues.
Charlene Ginger Johnson

paying them off in "flexibility" which means the corporation makes zero commitment to them.

WORK AND FAMILY: EFFECTS ON CHILDREN

Since two incomes are typically necessary for a family to pay its bills, what is the effect on the children when both partners work outside the home? The answer to this question often comes from studies on the effect of the mother working outside the home. Of course, parenting today includes equal involvement of both partners in child rearing. While this is the egalitarian model, lingering societal expectations result in the mother often taking the primary responsibility.

Effects of the Mother's Employment on Children

Independent of the effect of employment on the wife, husband, and marriage, what is the effect on the children of the mother being employed? The bottom line is that mothers who enjoy their work have high life satisfaction and this means that her children live with a happy mother and benefit accordingly (Mauno et al., 2018).

The mother's work schedule is often a variable impacting the mother's happiness. Prickett (2018) found that mothers who had a nonstandard work schedule—not 8 to 5—reported less involved parenting and lower parenting satisfaction.

The concept of intensive mothering reflects the belief that mothers should prioritize their time to take care of their children, which is incompatible with full-time employment. Those who endorse intensive mothering would argue that one must be unemployed to be a good mother. In their study of over 2,000 full-time employed mothers of infants, Walls et al. (2016) found that the majority of the mothers did *not* endorse the beliefs of intensive mothering. The relationship between women in employment and children at home is clear—the more children at home, the lower employment involvement of the woman. This finding was found in 58 countries (Bongaarts et al., 2019). Preisner et al. (2018) noted that as norms change and allow women to select the lifestyle that they want, including being employed and being a mother or not, life satisfaction increases.

Effects of the Father's Employment on Children

As with employed mothers who take off from work after childbirth, Petts and Knoester (2018) confirmed that employed fathers who take paternity leave report more involvement with their children both as infants and as young children. Children are also aware of how work reduces the time they have with their fathers. Strazdins et al. (2017) analyzed how 10- to 13-year-old Australian children viewed their fathers' employment. A third thought their father worked too much and one eighth wished that their fathers did not work at all.

Latchkey Children

A disadvantage for children of two-earner parents is that they may receive less supervision due to the parents' long hours and inflexible schedules. Forty-two million U.S. children ages 5 to 14—eleven percent of children in this age group—cared for themselves without adult or older sibling supervision on a regular basis during a typical week. The percentage of children who used self-care varied by age, ranging from 2 percent of 5- and 6-year-olds to 29 percent of 14-year-olds. The average time spent in self-care situations was 5 hours a week for children ages 5 to 11 and 7 hours for children ages 12 to 14 (Laughlin, 2013).

Children who are alone at home for long periods of time are vulnerable to an accident. Children who must spend time alone at home should know the following:

1. How to reach their parents at work with relevant contact information, including the phone number, extension number, and name of the person to talk to if the parent is not there

2. Their home address and phone number in case information must be given to the fire department or an ambulance service

3. How to call emergency services, such as the police and fire departments

4. The name and number of a relative or neighbor to call if the parent is unavailable

5. To keep the door locked and not let anyone in

6. How to avoid telling callers their parents are not at home, and instead tell callers that their parents are busy or can't come to the phone

7. How to avoid playing with appliances, matches, or the fireplace

Parents should also consider the relationship of the children they leave alone. If the older one terrorizes or is sexually abusive toward the younger one, the children should not be left alone. In addition, if the younger one is out of control, it is inadvisable to put the older one in the role of being responsible for the child. If something goes wrong, such as a serious accident, the older child may be unnecessarily burdened with guilt.

Quality Time

The term *quality time* has become synonymous with good parenting. The definition is variable from having heart-to-heart talks, to getting ice cream, or to watching TV together. Some parents feel that all the time they are with their children is quality time, whether having dinner together or riding to the post office.

Child Care Considerations

Child care options include a relative or informal care, a home-based child care arrangement, or a child care center. The younger the child, the more likely the child will be placed with a relative. Hispanic and Black children are more likely than White children to be placed with relatives or informal care by employed mothers (Ackert et al., 2018). Craig and Churchill (2018) analyzed data on 6,886 employed fathers and mothers and found that they reported the least amount of parental stress when their children, ages 5 and below, were being taken care of by informal family caregivers.

Quality of Child Care

The best child care provider is a stable, warm, engaging person to not only nurture the child but also provide developmentally appropriate activities to stimulate physical, cognitive, and social emotional growth in a safe and healthy setting. When care by relatives is not feasible, many parents must choose other child care options. Since our country does not subsidize early childhood programs, many child care programs only offer their workers minimum wage, require minimum training, and have high turnover rates. While most child care programs are safe, vigilance can also be a problem. The authors of this text know of a child in a public day care facility who ate a pebble which lodged in the child's windpipe and the child died. While tragic, such events are rare and could happen at the parents' home.

What are the effects of child care programs varies widely and the licensing requirements are determined by each state. Child care licensing only requires the passing of basic safety and health criteria and does not guarantee quality. Each state sets its own licensing rules. In order to help families make better decisions regarding child care programs, the National Association of Education for Young Children (NAEYC) has identified ten quality indicators including curriculum, assessment of child progress, health, and physical environment. (https://www.naeyc.org/our-work/families/10-naeyc-program-standards).

What are the effects of child care on young children? Coontz (2016) noted in her review of this question, "day-care children do as well or better than their at-home counterparts in the areas of sociability,

Some companies, like Google, offer on-site day care to help employees balance work and child care.
Andrei Stanescu/Alamy Stock Photo

social competence, problem solving, achievement, language skills, empathy, and self-confidence" (p. 291). While some research suggests that child care children are less compliant, Coontz suggests that these children may simply have learned to think for themselves. In addition, high-quality child care programs can have long lasting positive effects on children (Ansari & Pianta, 2018).

Cost of Child Care

Although there are federally funded early programs such as Head Start for children from birth to five years old for low-income families, the cost of child care is expensive. Child care costs are a factor in whether low-income parents seek employment, because the cost can absorb their paychecks. Even for dual-earner families, cost is a factor in choosing a child care center. Child care costs vary widely from nothing, where friends trade off taking care of the children, to very expensive institutionalized child care in large cities.

Due to the lower adult-child ratio for infant care, the cost of quality infant care is especially high. In Menlo Park, California, the heart of the tech industry and Silicon Valley, the cost of child care can be over $4,000 a month. One such child care center in Menlo Park provides continuous webcam video for parents and daily reports on the eating, sleeping, and elimination behavior of the infant. The average cost of center-based infant child care in the United States, adjusted for inflation, exceeds 27% of millennial median income (State Fact Sheets, 2018).

BALANCING WORK AND FAMILY LIFE

Balestra et al. (2018) assessed the preferences of almost 88,000 users of the Better Life Index and found that men were more concerned with material issues and women with quality of life issues, including life satisfaction and work-life balance. Brockmann et al. (2018) emphasized that managerial women are generally less happy than managerial men since there is a fertility cost to women. Managerial careers usually take off between the ages of 35 and 45 and women who decide not to have children pay a price in less life satisfaction during this time. The researchers contented that in order to compensate, women need much more income for each hour of spare time given up than men do.

Women who have both careers and a family are more likely to be concerned about the **spillover effect** of work into family life than vice versa. Haines et al. (2019) observed that when women work outside the home, they report higher family to work conflict. Hence, work may spread into family life in the form of doing overtime, taking work home, attending seminars organized by the company, and being "on call" on the weekend and during vacation. The presence of a family makes these intrusions particularly burdensome. Men may also experience the spillover effect but to a lesser degree due to cultural programming.

When there is conflict between work and family, parents (more often mothers) employ various strategies to cope with the stress of role overload and role conflict, including (1) adopting the superperson strategy, (2) reframing, (3) delegating responsibility, (4) using time management, and (5) engaging in role compartmentalization. Lee and Sirgy (2018) emphasized that work-life balance is best achieved when there is a combination of the behavior and cognitive-based strategies.

Adopting a Superperson Strategy

The superperson strategy involves working as hard and as efficiently as possible to meet the demands of work and family. A superperson often skips lunch and cuts back on sleep and leisure to have more time available for work and family. Women are particularly vulnerable because they feel that if they give too much attention to child care concerns, they will be sidelined into lower paying jobs with fewer opportunities. However, women are more likely than men to scale back on work demands when these are in conflict with family (Young & Schieman, 2018).

Hochschild (1989) noted that the terms **superwoman** or **supermom** are cultural labels that allow a woman to regard herself as very efficient, bright, and confident. However, Hochschild noted that this is a

"cultural cover-up" for an overworked or frustrated woman who may also have both of these feelings. Not only does the mother have a job that is often called the "first shift," she comes home to another set of work demands in the form of dinner, house care, and child care that leave her feeling she is tackling a "second shift."

Finally, she has a **third shift** (Hochschild, 1997). The **third shift** is the expense of emotional energy by a spouse or parent in dealing with various issues in family living. Although young children need time and attention, responding to conflicts and problems with teenagers also involves a great deal of emotional energy.

How does equality of housework translate into the frequency of sex? "There is no association" according to Johnson et al. (2016) who examined housework division of labor and sexual frequency. However, the researchers noted that it is the perception of fairness that is the key. If the female partner perceives that she is being treated fairly, which may include housework, sexual frequency and reported sexual satisfaction increases.

Cognitive Restructuring and Reframing

Another strategy used by some experiencing role overload and role conflict is reframing, which involves viewing a situation in positive terms. Exhausted dual-career earners often justify their time away from their children by focusing on the benefits of their work—primarily being able to provide for their family and provide greater economic resources. For example, two parents working full time can reframe their situation by focusing on their ability to move to a bigger apartment in a safe neighborhood. While many couples choose to be dual-earner families to support their personal values or a preferred lifestyle, some couples do not have a choice. Having both parents earning an income may be necessary if the partners have low-paying jobs.

Delegating Responsibility

A third way couples manage the demands of work and family is to delegate responsibility to others for certain tasks. Since women typically perform more housework and child care than men (Horne et al., 2018), a more egalitarian division of labor results in one partner having fewer demands or frustrations. Geiger (2016) noted that sharing household labor is associated with reported marital success.

....

Spillover effect: one's work role impacts one's family life in terms of working overtime, being on call on weekends, and so forth. Rarely does the family role dictate what will happen in the work role.

Superwoman/supermom: a cultural label that allows a woman to regard herself as very efficient, bright, and confident; usually a cultural cover-up for an overworked and frustrated woman.

....

Third shift: the expenditure of emotional energy by a spouse or parent in dealing with various emotional issues in family living.

Another form of delegating responsibility involves the decision to reduce one's current responsibilities or not take on additional ones. For example, women and men may give up or limit committing to volunteer responsibilities. One woman noted that her life was being consumed by the responsibilities of her church; she had to change churches because the demands were relentless. In the realm of paid work, women and men can choose not to become involved in professional activities beyond those that are required.

Finally, grandparents, siblings, and extended kin are resources one may call on, particularly in times where there is sickness on the part of a family member. A final alternative is to hire someone to take on specific roles, such as a nanny, housecleaner, or yard service.

Using Time Management

By working full time, a parent may be able to afford high-quality child care that allows her or him to focus on the child when at home. In managing her or his time and seeking child care, the parent may be more "emotionally ready" for dinner, bath, and reading time with her or his children at night.

Other parents use time management by prioritizing and making lists of what needs to be done each day. This method involves trying to anticipate stressful periods, planning ahead for them, and dividing responsibilities with the spouse. Such division of labor allows each spouse to focus on an activity that needs to be done, such as grocery shopping, and results in a smoothly functioning unit.

Some professions or companies allow employees to have flexible work schedules, which are particularly beneficial for two-earner couples with children. Ruppanner et al. (2018) analyzed data on 19,134 workers in 32 nations to confirm that flexible work hours are associated with higher job satisfaction. Being self-employed, telecommuting, or working

in academia permit flexibility of schedule. Alternatively, some dual-earner couples solve the problem of child care by having one parent work during the day and the other parent work at night so that one of them can always be with the children. However, shift workers often experience sleep deprivation and fatigue, which may make fulfilling the roles of parent or spouse challenging. Shift work may also have a negative effect on a couple's relationship because of their limited time together.

Engaging in Role Compartmentalization

Some couples use **role compartmentalization** separating the roles of work and home so that they do not think about or dwell on the problems of one when they are at the other. Partners unable to compartmentalize their work and home lives feel role strain, role conflict, and role overload, with the result that their efficiency drops in both spheres. Some families look to the government and their employers for help in balancing the demands of family and work with paid maternity and paternity leave, flextime, telecommuting, and health benefits.

BALANCING WORK AND LEISURE TIME

Leisure refers to the use of time to engage in freely chosen activities perceived as enjoyable and satisfying. Leisure may include exercise or even time to sleep. Leisure varies by social class. Working class families may enjoy low cost, at-home activities, such as playing board games, while middle class families may spend money on outings like going to the movies.

Being able to "get off the clock" both structurally and psychologically is important. Rodríguez-Muñoz et al. (2018) found that the degree to which spouses were able to detach from work and relax was positively associated with individual, partner, and relationship satisfaction. Nonpartnered individuals also benefit from leisure. Pepin et al. (2018) analyzed data from the American Time Use Surveys and found that leisure time of never married and cohabiting mothers was more than for married mothers, which may be due to the third shift.

Research by Kamp Dush et al. (2018) revealed that fathers were more likely to enjoy their own

---

Role compartmentalization: strategy used to separate the roles of work and home so that an individual does not think about or dwell on the problems of one when he or she is at the physical place of the other.

Leisure: the use of time to engage in freely chosen activities perceived as enjoyable and satisfying

---

CULTURE AND DIVERSITY

France, Denmark, and Germany have experimented with fewer required work hours per week. France tried the 35-hour workweek with eight weeks of vacation. The goal was to increase employment. However, over the ten years during which the 35-hour workweek was in place, the desired gains did not occur. In 2008, France moved to increase its workweek, with the result that the French now work an average of 41 hours a week; in America, the average is 41.7 hours. The Fair Labor Standards Act in 1938 established the 40-hour week and overtime payment laws. This law was a way to allow companies to get employees to work more rather than hire new employees.

Anger Over Romantic Partner's Video Game Playing

Playing video games provides a major source of enjoyment for gamers, particularly among adolescents and college age males. Mobile gaming is now available on smartphones, but a couple's relationship may pay a price—the focus of this study.

Sample and Methods

The data consisted of a nonrandom sample of 148 undergraduate volunteers at a large southeastern university who responded to a 45-item questionnaire which was a "Video Game Survey" approved by the university's Institutional Review Board. The objective of the study was to identify current uses and interpersonal consequences of playing video games.

General Findings

Of the respondents, 98% of the men and 93% of the women reported having played a video game. These respondents would not be classified as having a "gaming disorder" as they rarely skipped class or played relentlessly for days. Indeed, only two males and one female—less than 3% of the respondents—used the term *obsessive* to describe their video game playing. The average GPA of these students was 2.96, suggesting that their academic performance was standard for their year in school. Although Ingram and Cangemi (2019) found positive consequences of game playing on the individual's self-esteem, Lee and Kim (2017) found that extensive game playing had a negative impact on relationships with parents, peers, and teachers.

Significant Gender Differences

In addition to the previous general findings, three significant sex differences emerged.

1. **Women viewed video games as more experimental than recreational.** Women and men differed in why they played video games. Female respondents were significantly more likely than male respondents—34% versus 8%—to report that playing video games was experimental in the sense of curiosity—just seeing what it was like. In contrast, 65% of male respondents were significantly more likely to report that playing video games was recreational compared with 41% of females (p < .000).

2. **Male partners of females were more likely to play video games.** Females were much more likely to have a partner who played video games than vice versa. Of the undergraduate females in this study, 76% reported having been involved in a relationship with a partner who played video games in contrast to 42% of male undergraduates involved with a female who played video games (p < .001).

3. **Females were more likely to be angry over a partner playing video games.** Of the female respondents, 33% reported that they had become upset with their partners' relentless video game playing. Of the males, only 5% reported having told his partner that she spent too much time playing video games. The difference was statistically significant (p < .005). We asked an undergraduate female who reported that her partner's game playing was a problem in their relationship to explain the source of her frustration:

   Not only are video games expensive (not to speak of the equipment) but he hogs the TV for an entire evening and acts like I don't exist. Quality time— what is that?

   . . .

   He will play video games for five hours at a time on Friday and Saturday night, the very time I want to be with him. I feel like he cares more about playing those games than playing with me. . . .

We asked a male gamer to respond to the above reactions. One noted:

   I totally get why women feel this way about a guy playing video games. I have played Call of Duty 15 hours straight and love every minute of it. But what's the big deal. Women like to shop and can do that for hours. . . .to each his own. ●

Updated in 2019 and abridged from Knox, D., Zusman, M., White, A., & Haskins, G. (2009). "Coed anger over romantic part- ner's video game playing." *Psychology Journal* 6(1), 10–16.

leisure time while mothers performed child care and routine housework labor. For optimum men- tal and physical health, 38 employed hours per week for women and 44 for men. These hours are based on data from 4,062 women, and from 3,828 men (Dinh et al., 2017). The lower number of work hours for women is no doubt due to the "second shift."

Functions of Leisure

Leisure fulfills important functions in our individual and interpersonal lives. Leisure activities may relieve work-related stress and pressure; facilitate social interaction and family togetherness; foster self-expression, personal growth, and skill development; and enhance overall social, physical, and emotional well-being. Hickman-Evans et al. (2018) studied couple leisure in newlywed couples and found that it created the context for improving communication and conflict management skills.

The relationship between family leisure and family satisfaction has been confirmed by previous research. Two types of family leisure patterns, core and balance, have been identified. The **core family leisure pattern involving** regular, predictable leisure activities, such as a game or movie night, facilitates family stability and cohesiveness. In addition, the **family balance leisure pattern** provides novel experiences, are usually more memorable—for example, there are vacations, trips, or special events—and enhance family adaptability. The balance activities typically occur less frequently and require more resources and planning (Hudge et al., 2018; Zabriskie & McCormick, 2001).

Leisure may also represent an area of stress and conflict. Some couples function best when they are busy with work and child care so that they have limited time to interact with each other. Indeed, some prefer not to have a lot of time alone together.

Individual and Relationship Problems Related to Leisure

Individual problems may occur in reference to leisure. Passias et al. (2017) found that being a single mother, particularly a Black single mother, is often associated with the highest amount of socially isolated leisure, such as watching TV alone. Excessive drinking or drug consumption may also occur in leisure contexts as well as dangerous activities, such as zip lining or bungee jumping.

There may also be a cost associated with leisure activities, which can cause additional stress on individuals and couples. Some couples or families may travel in their leisure time, but cost is a barrier for many. Vacations are expensive. The average one-week vacation, including air, hotel, food, and activities, costs $1,145 per person or $4,580 for a family of four (P, 2018). Many couples and families may view this amount as excessive and seek enjoyable, less expensive alternatives such as camping.

Core family leisure pattern: regular predictable family leisure activities (e.g., movie night).

Family balance leisure pattern: occasional memorable family leisure activities (e.g., beach vacation).

Relationship problems may also occur in reference to leisure. A partner who is a "gamer" may create a context of relationship stress, particularly among young couples. (see the "Applying Social Research" feature)

Intrusive Technology

The use of technology can be an intrusion on a relationship. Because of the technology used to conduct one's work—laptops, iPads, and phones or smartphones—it is easy for spouses to work all the time, wherever they are. One dual-career couple noted that they are forever sending text messages or working on their iPads when they are at home so that the time they are not working and are communicating directly with each other is becoming less frequent. Even on vacation, some spouses insist that their vacation place have "wireless Internet access" so that they can continue to work. McDaniel and Collins (2018) found that greater use of technology during leisure time reflects lower commitment to the relationship.

Sharaievska and Stodolska (2017) interviewed 22 individuals from seven families who identified the positives and negatives of the use of social network sites—namely, Facebook or Twitter—on family satisfaction as related to leisure. Positives included being able to find out valuable information about family vacations friends had taken and staying connected to extended family members while on vacation. Negatives included the potential for negative comparisons about the vacations of others, such as "they stayed in a nicer place than we could afford," and there was a decrease in person-to-person time while on vacation which meant that individuals were on their cell phones or computers rather than talking with each other.

FUTURE OF WORK AND FAMILY LIFE

Families will continue to be stressed by work. Employers will, increasingly, ask employees to work longer and do more without the commensurate increases in salary or benefits. Businesses are struggling to stay solvent and workers will take the brunt of the instability.

The number of women who work outside the home will increase—the economic needs of the family will demand that they do so. Men will adapt, most willingly, some reluctantly. Children will become aware that budgets are tight, tempers are strained, and leisure with the family in the summer may not be as expansive as previously.

While the percent of all women in the workforce will increase, the percent of young mothers who do not work outside the home will also increase. Difficulty finding part time employment and concerns about the employment effects on children are explanations.

Greater gender equality in the home has also changed gender role at work. As more women increase in the workforce, fewer men will seek employment (Eberstadt, 2016). The number of "house-husbands and stay-at-home dads" has increased. Not only are there fewer jobs with the decline in manufacturing, the rise of outsourcing, and automation, and slower economic growth, the cultural imperative that men work outside the home is weakening. One woman noted that when her husband lost his $600,000 annual salary job, he quickly morphed into the role of stay-at-home dad and never returned to the paid labor force, even after the child was in day care.

SUMMARY

What is the effect of money on relationships?
Having adequate income impacts the probability that a couple will decide to get married and their relationships will be more stable if they do. The reason money is such a profound issue in marriage is its symbolic significance as well as the fact that individuals do something daily in reference to money—work, spend, save, or worry about money.

What is the effect of work on a couple's relationship?
Money is a central issue in relationships because of its association with power, control, and dominance. Generally, the more money a partner makes, the more power that person has in the relationship. Men make considerably more money than women and generally have more power in relationships. When a married woman earns an income, her power increases in the relationship. Money also provides an employed woman the power to be independent and have more options when confronted with an unhappy marriage.

Spouses report how to ensure that one's job has a positive impact on one's marriage: Turn a negative into a positive by, for example, recognizing that a job loss can be an opportunity for a better job; be creative and acknowledge that while the division of labor on chores is usually functional, sometimes it's better to assess who is having a tough week and the other takes up the slack; tolerate dissimilarity and accept the partner; and be committed to the relationship and stay out of trouble.

Whether a wife is satisfied with her job is related to the degree to which the job takes a toll on her family life. When the wife's employment interferes with her family life, she reports less job satisfaction. Husbands also report benefits from their wives' employment. These include being relieved of the sole responsibility for the financial support of the family and having more freedom to quit jobs, change jobs, or go to school.

What is the effect of parents' work decisions on the children?
Children do not appear to suffer cognitively or emotionally from their parents working outside the home as long as positive, consistent child care alternatives are in place. In addition, less supervision of children by parents is an outcome of having dual-earner parents. And lower parental monitoring is associated with increased adolescent problem behaviors.

What are the various strategies for balancing the demands of work and family?
Strategies used for balancing the demands of work and family include the superperson strategy, cognitive restructuring and reframing, delegation of responsibility, planning and time management, and role compartmentalization. Government and corporations have begun to respond to the family concerns of employees by implementing work-family policies and programs. These policies are typically inadequate and cosmetic.

What is the importance of leisure and what are its functions?
Corporations are learning that the new millennials value leisure and will not forego it for their work life. Leisure helps to relieve stress, facilitate social interaction and family togetherness, and foster personal growth and skill development. However, leisure time may also create conflict over how to use it.

What is the future of work and the family?
Families will continue to be impacted by the outside paid employment of its members. Employers will, increasingly, ask employees to work longer and to take on more responsibilities. Businesses are struggling to stay solvent and the workers will take the brunt of the instability. Telework will increase and benefit both employers and workers. Greater gender role flexibility is also likely to contribute to an increasing number of stay-home husbands and dads.

KEY TERMS

Commuter marriage, 282

Core family leisure pattern, 292

Dual-career marriage, 282

Everwork, 278

Family balance leisure
pattern, 292

Gig economy, 285

Leisure, 290

PRIMARY/PRIMARY career, 282

PRIMARY/secondary career, 282

Role compartmentalization, 290

Role conflict, 285

Role overload, 283

Role strain, 285

SAME career marriage, 282

Second shift, 283

Spillover effect, 289

Superwoman/supermom, 289

Telework, 286

Third shift, 289

WEB LINKS

Ms. Money (budgeting documents)
http://www.msmoney.com

Dual Career Couples
https://www.apa.org/gradpsych/2006/01/couples

Get the tools you need to sharpen your study skills. SAGE edge offers a robust online environment featuring an impressive array of free tools and resources.
Access practice quizzes, eFlashcards, video, and multimedia at **edge.sagepub.com/knox13e**

14

Stress and Crisis in Relationships

Turn your wounds into wisdom.

—Oprah

Learning Objectives

14.1.   Review the definition of stress, resilience, and the family stress model

14.2.   Identify positive and negative stress management strategies

14.3.   Discuss various types of family crises

14.4.   Review the effectiveness of marriage and family therapy

14.5.   Predict the future of stress and crisis in the family

Master the content at
edge.sagepub.com/knox13e

Stress is part of life. No one lives without it. Even the wealthy are plagued by something. This chapter focus on personal stress and relationship crisis events with a focus on how we react to these situations. We begin with defining stress and crisis.

PERSONAL STRESS AND CRISIS EVENTS

In this section, we review the definitions of stress and crisis events, the characteristics of resilient families, and how individuals and couples can choose to view and respond to stress and crisis events.

Definitions of Stress and Crisis Events

Stress is a reaction of the body to substantial or unusual demands. The effects can be emotional, such as feeling irritable; physical, such as high blood pressure; and psychological, such as depression. Stress may occur because of physical, environmental, or interpersonal demands or circumstances. On average, people are moderately stressed. Lee et al. (2016) assessed the stress level of a national sample of adults ages 25 to 64. On a scale of 0 to 6, with 6 being very much, the respondents averaged a 4.5.

Psychological factors associated with an extreme form of stress—post-traumatic stress disorder (PTSD)—have been identified as depression, anxiety, borderline personality disorder, dissociation, destructive behaviors, suicidal ideation, and self-harm (Hyland et al., 2018). While our discussion will focus primarily on stress reactions to negative causes, stress may have positive causes such as stress

before a wedding or stress associated with going into labor and the anticipation of birthing a baby.

Holmes and Rahle (1967) identified events that trigger stress. They asked respondents to rank stressful events from one to 100. The top stressful event was "death of a spouse" and the least stressful event was a "minor violation of the law." Stressful events or circumstances may happen at the same time and stress may be cumulative. When a person experiences a specific stressor—the death of a parent—which is added to the person already experiencing psychological issues, such as substance abuse, there can be a cascade effect with other disorders like depression beginning to emerge. Hilpert et al. (2018) confirmed that the more stress individuals experience, the greater their reported marital dissatisfaction. Even the diet of children is affected by the stress experienced by one's parents. Webb et al. (2018) found that higher levels of family stress were predictive of a negative change in the child's diet—namely, lower fruit and vegetable intake.

Stress is a process rather than a state. For example, a person will experience different levels of stress in reference to a romantic breakup—acknowledging that the relationship is over, telling one's friends and family of the breakup and coping with the absence of the partner and memories all result in varying levels of stress. Stress varies by occupation and sexual orientation. Tuttle et al. (2018) emphasized that police officers work in high stress contexts which may spill over into their marital relationship. They analyzed data from 1,180 married law enforcement officers, which revealed that stressful career demands and the accompanying emotional spillover were predictors of variance in marital functioning. Regarding sexual orientation, Totenhagen et al. (2018) revealed that same-sex couples routinely cope with added stress due to living in a heterosexist society. Eighty-one same-sex couples revealed that having high levels of internalized homophobia and low levels of "outness" created stress which spilled over into their relationship.

....

Stress: reaction of the body to substantial or unusual demands whether they are physical, environmental, or interpersonal.

Stress may also vary by race and socioeconomic status with persons of color and those of lower socioeconomic status evidencing more stress. Persons of color often experience prejudice and discrimination, which can lead to increased stress. For those of lower socioeconomic status, financial struggle causes stress.

Finally, stress may be direct and personal or indirect and secondary. Whitt-Woosley and Sprang (2018) studied the phenomenon of secondary traumatic stress which is stress derived from being exposed to those experiencing stress. An example would be as an advocate of child sex abuse victims and hearing the stories of anguish all day only to feel their stress at night. Benuto et al. (2018) noted that the prevalence rates of secondary traumatic stress among 135 child sexual abuse advocates is approximately 50% and risk factors included number of hours worked per week and number of direct service hours.

In contrast to stress, a **crisis** is a situation that requires changes in normal patterns of response behavior. A family crisis is a situation that upsets the normal functioning of the family and requires a new set of responses to the stressor. Sources of stress and crises can be external, such as the hurricanes that annually hit our coasts or devastating tornadoes in the spring. Other examples of an external crisis are economic recession, downsizing, or military deployment. Still another source of stress and crisis events may be internal, such as alcoholism or an extramarital affair.

Stressors or crises may also be categorized as expected or unexpected. Examples of expected family stressors include the need to care for aging parents and the death of one's parents. Unexpected stressors may include contracting an infection, such as human immunodeficiency virus (HIV) or having a miscarriage.

Both stress and crisis events are normal aspects of family life and sometimes reflect a developmental sequence. Pregnancy, childbirth, job change or loss, children leaving home, retirement, and widowhood are predictable stress and crisis events for most individuals. Crisis events may have a cumulative effect: the greater the number in rapid succession, the greater the stress. "I'm all out of being able to cope," said one spouse who was just confronted with another crisis.

Resilient Families

Just as the types of stress and crisis events vary, individuals and families vary in their abilities to respond successfully to crisis events. **Resilience** refers to a family's strengths and ability to respond to a crisis in a positive way. Hence, resiliency is both about bouncing back and the factors associated with doing so (Rodriguez-Rey et al., 2016). Various factors associated with **family resilience** include framing a crisis positively, working together, and being flexible. Donnelly et al. (2018) noted that one's capacity to handle stress in adulthood is influenced by the degree of childhood adversity—the greater the adversity, the more compromised the ability to handle stress. A family's ability to bounce back from a crisis such as a negative health diagnosis, the loss of one's job, or the death of a family member reflects a family's level of resiliency.

A Family Stress-Coping Model

Various theorists have explained how individuals and families experience and respond to stressors. The ABCX model of family stress was developed by Reuben Hill in the 1950s. The model can be explained as follows:

A = stressor event

B = family's management strategies and resources, coping skills

C = family's perception, definition of the situation

X = family's adaptation to the event

A is the stressor event, which interacts with B, the family's coping ability or crisis-meeting resources. Both A and B interact with C, the family's appraisal or perception of the stressor event. X is the family's adaptation to the crisis. Thus, a family that experiences a major stressor—for example, a spouse with a spinal cord injury—but has great coping skills, such as a belief in religion or spirituality, and perceives

A crisis can have an internal source as in a physical disability of one partner.

Crisis: a crucial situation that requires change in one's normal pattern of behavior.

Resilience: a family's strength and ability to respond to a crisis in a positive way.

Family resilience: the successful coping of family members under adversity that enables them to flourish with warmth, support, and cohesion.

FIGURE 14.1

Diagram of Family Stress Model

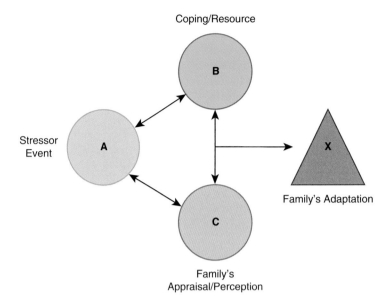

the event to be manageable will experience a moderate crisis. However, a family that experiences a less critical stressor event— their child makes Cs and Ds in school—but has minimal coping skills where, for example, everyone blames everyone else, and perceives the event to be catastrophic will experience an extreme crisis.

STRESS MANAGEMENT STRATEGIES

Positive stress management strategies are crucial. Several of these are discussed in this section. In addition to utilizing various positive stress management strategies, coping flexibility—the ability to modify and adapt coping strategies depending on the circumstances—is also valuable. Based on 1,132 participants, Heffer and Willoughby (2017) found that those with a higher number of coping strategies reported less stress over time.

Choosing a Positive Perspective

The importance of how an event is perceived is crucial. In response to a financial setback, Adolf Merckle threw himself in front of a train. He was a billionaire who had lost hundreds of millions of Euros on Volkswagen shares. How does one who has billions feel life is over after losing a few million? One's perception of an event dictates the outcome.

Indeed, the strategy that most respondents reported as being helpful in coping with a crisis was choosing a positive view of the crisis situation. Survivors of hurricanes, tornadoes, and earthquakes routinely focus on the fact that they and their loved ones are alive rather than the loss of their home or material possessions. Buddhists have the saying, "Pain is inevitable; suffering is not." This view is another way of emphasizing that how one views a situation, not the situation itself, determines its impact on you. One Chicago woman said after a pipe burst and caused $30,000 worth of damage to her home, "If it's not about your health, it's irrelevant."

Regardless of the crisis event, one can view the crisis positively. A betrayal can be seen as an opportunity for forgiveness, unemployment as a time to spend time with one's family or to change careers, and ill health a context to focus on one's inner life. While the crisis does not disappear, it provides a way of moving forward. Although it may be difficult to reframe certain crises, managing one's reaction to a crisis is a critical skill. Some circumstances may be out of one's control, but one always has control over the perception.

> If we don't change the direction we are headed, we will end up where we are going.
>
> Chinese Proverb

Following Through With Behavior

Equally important in having a positive view is following through with new behavior. Backes et al. (2017) confirmed that an action to do something about the stress on the part of one or both partners is associated with relationship benefits. Similarly, Brisini et al. (2018) studied transitions in marriage focusing on crisis events and noted that spouses' explicit attempts to increase interaction, feel connected to each other, and increase confidence in their relationship were negatively associated with perceptions of relational uncertainty and relational turbulence. Doing the things that enhanced the relationship helped couples get through a crisis.

Dyadic Coping

Similarly, dyadic coping is related to marital satisfaction. **Dyadic coping** is defined as the partners working on their crisis and stress events together, as well as supporting each other through each partner's own personal stresses. Breitenstein et al. (2018) found that stress emerging outside the relationship, called extradyadic stress, which spills over into the relationship evoking conflict between the partners, known as intradyadic stress, can be mitigated by dyadic coping to reduce the negative effect on marital satisfaction.

In addition, being emotionally involved with another and sharing the experience with that person helps to insulate individuals from being devastated

Walking is a convenient exercise, which is associated with reducing stress.
Courtesy of Chelsea Curry

....

Dyadic coping: both partners contribute to resolving the issues they face.

by a crisis event. Over 85% of 12,716 undergraduates agreed—with more females than males concurring—with the statement, "A deep love can get a couple through any difficulty or difference" (Hall & Knox, 2019).

Exercise

The Centers for Disease Control and Prevention (CDC) and the American College of Sports Medicine (ACSM) recommend that people ages 6 years and older engage regularly, preferably daily, in light to moderate physical activity for at least 30 minutes at a time. These recommendations are based on research that has shown the physical, emotional, and cognitive benefits of exercise. Exercise is the most important of all behaviors for good physical and mental health. Theisen et al. (2016) confirmed in a sample of 144 couples, that in conditions of high stress, those highest on exercise had the highest levels of reported satisfaction.

Family Cohesion, Friends, and Relatives

A network of friendships and relatives is associated with coping with various life transitions. Such relationships provide both structural and emotional support. Coppola and Wadsworth (2017) also confirmed that positive family functioning is associated with coping with PTSD stress for veterans exposed to combat stress.

What about social media? Does greater engagement or taking a break help with coping with stress? Vanman et al. (2018) noted that people sometimes cut themselves off from their online social contacts by taking extended breaks from Facebook. This study investigated whether abstaining from Facebook would reduce stress. Results found that Facebook users who took a vacation from Facebook noted a reduction in **stress.**

Religion and Spirituality

A strong religious belief is associated with coping with stress and loss. Stanko et al. (2018) assessed the role of religion in coping with an external crisis—for example, loss of home due to fire, tornado, or flood. Results revealed that higher scores on religiosity were related to a greater coping ability with the crisis.

Mindfulness-based stress reduction (MBSH) has its origin in Buddhist spiritual practices with the aim of restoring wholeness and well-being. Hazlett-Stevens (2018) analyzed data on 30 participants seeking psychological services and found significant reductions in stress along with increases in personal growth, life satisfaction, and improved quality of life.

Humor

Humor has been used in treating anxiety and depression (Consoli et al., 2018) and adjusting to divorce (Frisby et al., 2016). Humor functions to provide a reframing of a situation, not to take oneself or a situation too seriously. Humor and witty conversation can draw people closer to the others around them.

Sleep

Adequate sleep is necessary for optimum health. Mrug et al. (2016) confirmed that sleep problems—getting to sleep, staying asleep, not enough sleep—were related to higher stress and academic, behavioral, and health problems in a sample of adolescents. Maume et al. (2018) found that women's sleep was more troubled when they had children in the house and when their partner was unemployed. Men's sleep was troubled by their own unemployment and worry about household finances.

Pets

Jorolmen and Patel (2018) found that interacting with a therapy dog before and after taking a final exam was associated with lowing one's anxiety and stress. Similarly, Jau and Hodgson (2018) confirmed the benefits to mental well-being, including reducing depression, from regular interaction with animals. Finally, pets have demonstrated their value in promoting empathy and healthy relationships (Thomas & Matusitz, 2016). Some hotels are aware that pets are

regarded as family members and alert travelers that they are "pet friendly."

Harmful Stress Management Strategies

Some coping strategies not only are ineffective for resolving family problems but also add to the family's stress by making the problems worse—keeping feelings inside, taking out frustrations on or blaming others, and denying or avoiding the problem.

Burr and Klein's (1994) classic research also suggested that women and men differ in their perceptions of the usefulness of various coping strategies. Women were more likely than men to talk with relatives and friends, to embrace religion, and to express emotions. Men were more likely than women to use alcohol, keep feelings inside, or keep others from knowing how bad the situation was.

FAMILY CRISIS EXAMPLES

Some of the more common crisis events that spouses and families face include physical illness, mental illness, infidelity, substance abuse, and death. (Separation and divorce, a major crisis, is discussed in detail in Chapter 15.)

Physical Illness

Most individuals are healthy most of the time, but when one partner has a debilitating illness, there are profound changes in the roles of the respective partners and their relationship. Stroke is the leading cause of disability in the United States. Changes include practical challenges—for example, helping the partner to the bathroom—and relationship changes such as a becoming the provider if the partner was the sole provider. London-Johnson et al. (2017) noted that some physical illnesses have a greater negative impact on the couples' relationship quality than others, for example, a gastrointestinal condition over hypertension.

West and Haynes-Lawrence (2017) analyzed open-ended survey data on 181 parents who had been diagnosed with multiple sclerosis. Physical and cognitive fatigue occurred together resulting in the respondents feeling guilty

Pets are an enormous source of joy and stress reduction for their owners.
LA TIMES OUT/MediaNews Group/Orange County Register via Getty Images

about not being the parent they wanted to be. While respondents used naps and resting, medications and prioritizing, no one management technique worked for all in coping with MS. Finding the combination of techniques that worked for them and using community resources were recommended.

Individuals often have disabilities that are not visible. These include chronic back pain, rheumatoid arthritis, and chronic fatigue syndrome. These illnesses are particularly invasive in that conventional medicine has little to offer besides pain medication. For example, spouses with chronic fatigue syndrome may experience financial consequences, such as "I could no longer meet the demands of my job so I quit," or changed perceptions by their children which one parent reported as, "They have seen me sick for so long they no longer ask me to do anything."

In those cases in which the illness is fatal, **palliative care** is helpful. This term describes the health care for the individual who has a life-threatening illness by focusing on relief of pain and suffering, as well as support for the individual and his or her loved ones. Such care may involve the person's physician or a palliative care specialist who works with the nurse, social worker, and chaplain. Pharmacists or rehabilitation specialists may also be involved. The goals of palliative care are to approach the end of life with planning—considering questions like how long life should be sustained on machines—and with forethought given to the kinds of medication that relieve pain and provide closure.

We have been discussing stress and reacting to the crisis of a spouse with a physical illness or disability. Children may also have a chronic illness which will be a continuing crisis event for the parents. Nabors et al. (2018) interviewed parents of children with a chronic illness who were hospitalized for procedures related to his or her illness. Coping strategies were used to view the hospital stay as positive for the child or to accept what had to occur as having the possibility of improving the child's life or to learn to be able to handle both circumstances.

Kish et al. (2018) emphasized that being employed was an added stress for parents already dealing with

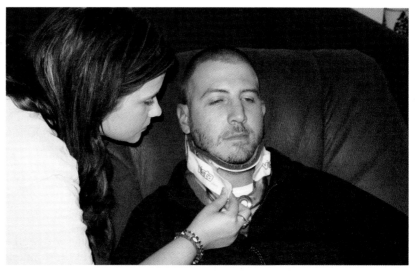

One week after an ocean cruise to celebrate his and his wife's one-year wedding anniversary, this husband fell off a ladder and seriously injured his neck. His wife is adjusting his neck brace.
Courtesy of Chelsea Curry

a chronically ill child. The need to work with the concomitant physical exhaustion of doing so combined with the emotional toil of having a chronically ill child were challenging. However, some parents may need to work in order to afford medical treatments.

Mental Illness

Mental illness is defined as a state in which one's thoughts or behavior result in distress and impair functioning. Mental illness affects a person's perceptions, thoughts, feelings, moods, or behaviors (American Psychiatric Association, 2018; World Health Organization, 2018). Some of the common mental illnesses include depression, anxiety disorders, psychotic disorders, and post-traumatic stress disorder (Center for Disease Control and Prevention, 2018). It is estimated that one of every five American adults has some form of mental illness (National Institute of Mental Health, 2018). Factors typically associated with mental illness include low physical activity, poor diet, smoking, and alcohol abuse (Moon & Han, 2019). Despite the prevalence of mental illness, it is frequently overlooked, untreated, and stigmatized.

One of our students noted how mental illness impacts romantic relationships.

Dealing with mental illness in romantic relationships is exhausting—physically, mentally, and emotionally. Whether it is you or your partner who suffers from a mental illness, the strain of trying to cope with the symptoms can be overwhelming. My boyfriend and I are in a similar struggle at the moment, as we both have extensive histories of mental illness. I have suffered from panic attacks, debilitating anxiety, clinical depression,

Palliative care: health care for the individual who has a life-threatening illness which focuses on relief of pain or suffering and support for the individual.

suicidal thoughts, and anorexia. While it seems like my worst days are behind me, there are times when I wrestle with destructive thoughts and detrimental behaviors. My boyfriend is also no stranger to mental issues, as he has had severe depression, suicidal thoughts, generalized anxiety disorder, obsessive compulsive disorder, and recent episodes of prolonged mania. He is as tough as nails and fights his demons on a daily basis, but there have been times when these struggles affect our relationship together.

The toll of adult mental illness on individuals, their relationships, and their children is immense.

UP CLOSE: BLACK HOLE—A SPOUSE TALKS ABOUT BEING DEPRESSED

If you have experienced life in the Black Hole, then you don't need an explanation of it.

If you have never experienced life in the Black Hole, it is impossible for anyone to explain it to you, and even if someone could explain it to you, you still wouldn't understand it.

The Black Hole is, by definition, an irrational state. The only thing you can comprehend about it is that you cannot comprehend it. Offering ANY advice, judgmental comments, suggestions like—"If you would only . . . ," "You've got to want to help yourself . . . ," "I know you are depressed, BUT . . . ," "You are not being rational . . ."—to someone who is in the Black Hole is not helpful. On the contrary, it is very destructive. It may temporarily relieve YOUR frustration with the person, but all it does for them is to give them a serving of guilt to deal with as they wait for the Black Hole to pass.

If you really want to help somebody who is in the Black Hole, there IS one thing you can do—and that one thing is NOTHING. After living in the Black Hole for a lifetime, a person has pretty much heard everything that you plan to tell them about it. Eventually, people who visit the Black Hole learn that it is a Monster, which comes without warning or invitation, it stays for a while, and it leaves when it is ready. The Monster doesn't time its visits to avoid holidays, vacations, or rainy days. It just barges in.

A person also knows what works for them while they are in the Black Hole. For some it may be exercise, or fishing, or sex (if they are still physically able), or music, or going to the beach, or talking about it, or employing logic to deal with it, or prayer, or reciting positive affirmations.

For others, like me, there are only two things that help—complete solitude and sleep.

Those two things do not provide a cure, but they do help you cope with the Monster until he leaves. Nobody asks why you wear glasses. They just assume that you wear glasses because you need to, they don't ask questions about it, they don't offer suggestions, and they don't try to fix it. And they don't assume that you wear glasses because of something they did. What a blessing it would be if people treated those who struggle with clinical depression with the same respect.

Source: Name withheld by request

• •

Mitchell and Abraham (2018) explicated how undergraduate transition to college is impacted by the mental illness of a parent. In their study of 196 undergraduates, the researchers found that participants with a parent with a mental illness experienced higher levels of depression and anxiety when compared to emerging adults without a parent with mental illness. Such depression and anxiety may be a function of reaction to the parents' mental illness or a biological connection to the parents' same mental health issues.

The mentally ill are stigmatized. Young (2018) noted the stigma associated with mental illness and identified cognitive behavioral therapy as effective in providing the mentally ill alternative cognitions about others who stigmatize them. For example, rather than buying into the belief that the mentally ill are a burden to themselves and others, the person would reject these ideas and replace them with "everyone deals with various levels of anxiety and depression . . . I can successfully cope with them too and enjoy life with myself and others."

Midlife Crises

There is the cultural belief that some people go crazy during their middle years or experience what's often called a "midlife crisis." A midlife crisis is defined as an emotional crisis of identity and self-confidence that can occur in early middle age. The stereotype is that people become depressed about getting older and often act out in different ways. However, some people embrace middle age. The Red Hat Society is a group of women who have decided to "greet middle age with verve, humor, and élan. We believe silliness is the comedy relief of life [and] share a bond of affection, forged by common life experiences and a genuine enthusiasm for wherever life takes us next." The society traces its beginning to when Sue Ellen Cooper bought a bright red hat because of a poem Jenny Joseph wrote in 1961, titled the "Warning Poem." The poem says the following:

Mental Health Issues

The availability, accessibility, and affordability of new technology has brought about new choices for improving one's mental health. Innovations such as smartphone apps, wearable devices, and virtual reality have therapeutic mental health uses (Bakker et al., 2018; Bush et al., 2018). For instance, virtual reality has been used to help individuals with post-traumatic stress disorder (Digital Health Today, 2018). In the virtual world, individuals can be brought back to re-experience the traumatic event and to learn to cope with anxiety in a controlled therapeutic context. Smartphone applications such as Calm and Pacifica can improve mental health functioning by providing meditation, relaxation, and breathing exercises. These apps can also aid in self-awareness and mood regulation (Nichols, 2018).

Virtual appointments with health care professionals can also be arranged. Remote geographic location, lack of transportation, or mobility issues are no longer obstacles to receiving mental health services. In addition, the anonymity of technology can ease stigma concerns. Individuals can choose to access new resources, assessments, and treatment options—all at the user's fingertips—without being seen, labeled, or discriminated against. Smartphone-based mental health support can also be cost effective and easy to use. Simply pressing one button or sending a text message can connect the individual to immediate help (Meyer et al., 2018). There are many health applications targeting different mental illnesses such as mood, stress, and anxiety (Digital Health Today, 2018). Some apps can also save lives. Apps such as BRITE prompt users to be aware of their daily distress level and provide personalized safety planning

and coping strategies. Suicide intervention programs including personalized apps like BRITE have reduced the rate of attempted teen suicide after hospitalization (Beltran, 2018; Kennard et al., 2018).

While new innovations have the potential to improve mental health, technology may also hinder one's mental well-being (Rue, 2018). Excessive use of smartphones has been linked to poor self-regulation and increased behavioral problems for adolescents (George et al., 2018). Currently, there is no national standard to evaluate the degree to which mobile app use has negative outcomes for one's mental health (Bertoncello et al., 2018). Patients must also make choices and take ownership of their treatment plan (Rootes-Murdy et al., 2018). Ensuring patient's safety, verifying identity, protecting privacy, and guarding digital records are also involved (Hollis et al., 2018; Lustgarten & Elhai, 2018). In order to gain a better understanding of the impact of technology on mental health, the National Institute of Mental Health (2018) encourages researchers to investigate the effects of utilizing technology to prevent, assess, treat, and deliver services.

While the development of mental health technology has made mental health support more affordable, accessible, and available, guidelines for optimal use are needed to maximize benefits and minimize risks. It is up to the individual to make informed decisions and decide the best way to heighten one's mental health. Parents may also be sensitive to the mental health needs of their children since they are constantly confronted with the process of growing up, hormonal changes, and school and interpersonal stress, and so forth. ●

When I am an old woman I shall wear purple

With a red hat which doesn't go and doesn't suit me.

Cooper then gave red hats to friends as they turned 50. The group then wore their red hats and purple dresses out to tea, and that's how it got started. Now there are over 1 million members worldwide.

In the rest of this chapter, we examine how partners cope with the crisis events of infidelity, drug abuse, and death of a child. Each of these events can be viewed either as devastating and the end of meaning in one's life or as an opportunity and challenge to rise above.

Infidelity

Infidelity is another source of stress. **Infidelity** refers to any type of sexual or emotional behavior outside the current relationship that violates the understanding of monogamy between the partners, and both forms of behavior may be regarded as equally egregious (Ellis & Kleinplatz, 2018). Moreno and Kahumoku-Fessler (2018) analyzed data from 83 undergraduates who identified sexual and emotional behaviors they regarded as being unfaithful. Persons who had previously cheated or been

....

Infidelity: any type of sexual or emotional behavior outside the current relationship that violates the understanding of sexual/emotional monogamy between the partners that results in feelings of betrayal.

cheated on rated more sexual behaviors as being unfaithful. Females, in contrast to males, were also more likely to rate more behaviors, both sexual and emotional, as expressive of infidelity. Adams et al. (2018) reported that "loyalty and faithfulness" was the most common definition of fidelity by a sample of undergraduates.

Another term for infidelity is **extradyadic involvement** or extrarelational involvement defined as the sexual involvement of a pair-bonded individual with someone other than the partner. The partners may be married but not necessarily. Extradyadic involvements are not uncommon among undergraduates. Of 3,024 undergraduate males, 26% agreed with the statement, "I have cheated on a partner I was involved with" compared with 27% of 9,943 undergraduate females. When the statement was "A partner I was involved with cheated on me," 49% of the males and 55% of the females agreed (Hall & Knox, 2019). One third of 655 both heterosexual and homosexual individuals reported that they had been unfaithful in their current monogamous relationship (Swan & Thompson, 2016).

Altgelt et al. (2018) examined personality traits associated with being unfaithful and found that extraversion and narcissism were predictive. High income and absence of religiosity were also predictive of infidelity among the 702,309 members of AshleyMadison.com, a website for spouses interested in having an affair (Chohaney & Panozzo, 2018). Isanejad and Bagheri (2018) found that low marital quality was associated with feeling lonely and both were associated with online infidelity. Finally, power is also associated with infidelity. Lammers and Maner (2016) found that power "releases people from the inhibiting effects of social norms and thus increases their appetite for counter normative forms of sexuality." A recent example is billionaire, founder, and CEO of Amazon, Jeff Bezos, and his alleged affair with Lauren Sanchez.

Twenty-four Mexican American adolescent females, ages 14-18, were interviewed and noted greater fear if their romantic partner had a competing love interest as opposed to another sexual interest. Most accepted that men were players and became skilled at identifying "red flags" of their infidelity such as acting like they were "putting in the time," "seeming less interested," and "being secretive" (Lopez, 2017).

When spouses are unfaithful, the term is **extramarital affair**. Of spouses in the United States,

20% of husbands and 13% of wives reported having cheated on their partner, which was defined as having had intercourse with someone other than their spouse during the marriage. Being middle age, Black, and not religious were associated with higher rates of infidelity (Wang, 2018).

Types of Infidelity

Types of infidelity include the following:

1. **Brief encounter**. One partner meets and hooks up with a stranger. In this case, the partner is usually out of town, and alcohol is often involved.

2. **Paid sex**. A partner pays a sex worker for sexual activity. The encounter usually goes undetected unless there is an STI, the person confesses, or the sex worker exposes the client.

3. **Instrumental or utilitarian infidelity**. This is sex to get back at the partner, to evoke jealousy, or to transition out of a relationship.

4. **Coping mechanism**. Partners who have been rejected sexually may seek another to rebuild their self-concept or feelings of sexual inadequacy.

5. **Paraphiliac affairs**. The partner seeks sexual practices that their partner considers bizarre or abnormal, such as BDSM (Bondage and Discipline, Sadism and Masochism).

6. **Cybersex**. **Cybersex** is the use of technology to become sexually aroused. Examples of cybersex include masturbation in reference to interaction with another person via a webcam or sexual dialogue. Arousal to the point of orgasm may or may not be involved. Partners who discover their partner is engaged in cybersex or romantically involved feel angry, betrayed, and depressed. Carter (2016) emphasized that spouses who communicate with the other sex on Facebook are doing so at a risk to their marriage relationship. The Self-Assessment Attitudes: Toward Infidelity Scale on page 393 allows you to measure your attitude toward infidelity.

Table 14.1 identifies the alternative lifestyles of monogamy, cheating within monogamy, swinging, and polyamory.

Reasons for Infidelity

Common reasons spouses give for being unfaithful include:

Extradyadic involvement: refers to sexual involvement of a pair-bonded individual with someone other than the partner; also called extrarelational involvement.

Extramarital affair: refers to a spouse's sexual involvement with someone outside the marriage.

TABLE 14.1

Monogamy	Spouse or partner is only sex partner
Cheating	Spouse or partner has sex outside of the monogamous relationship and it is a secret from the partner
Swinging	Spouses or partners agree that they will have sex with others, often at the same venue
Polyamory	Partners agree that they will have multiple romantic/sexual relationships with others.

1. **Reaction to relationship dissatisfaction.** An unhappy, unfulfilling relationship creates a context for infidelity. Spouses who feel misunderstood, unloved, and ignored sometimes turn to another who offers understanding, love, and attention. Indeed, a relationship is like a plant—it will thrive with proper care and will wither if neglected. It is easy for spouses to drift apart if they do not make emotional and physical intimacy a priority. Research by Norona et al. (2018) revealed that "unmet needs" in the existing relationship was the number one reason respondents gave for infidelity.

2. **Variety, novelty, and excitement.** Most spouses enter marriage having had other sexual partners. Infidelity may be motivated by the desire for continued variety, novelty, and excitement. One of the characteristics of sex in long-term committed relationships is the tendency for it to become routine. Early in a relationship, the partners cannot seem to have sex often enough. However, with constant availability, partners achieve a level of satiation, and the attractiveness and excitement of sex with the primary partner decreases.

The **Coolidge effect** is a term used to describe this waning of sexual excitement and the effect of novelty and variety on sexual arousal:

One day President and Mrs. Coolidge were visiting a government farm. Soon after their arrival, they were taken off on separate tours. When Mrs. Coolidge passed the chicken pens, she paused to ask the man in charge if the rooster copulated more than once each day. "Dozens of times," *was the reply. "Please tell that to the President," Mrs. Coolidge requested. When the President passed the pens and was told about the rooster, he asked, "Same hen every time?" "Oh no, Mr. President, a different one each time." The President nodded slowly and then said, "Tell that to Mrs. Coolidge." (Bermant, 1976, 76–77)*

Whether or not individuals are biologically wired for monogamy continues to be debated. Monogamy among mammals is rare with only 3% to 10% of mammals adhering to the practice, and it tends to be the exception more often than the rule (Morell, 1998). In spite of a biological wiring for a plurality of partners, individuals, particularly those in long-term relationships, are responsible for their decisions and most choose to remain monogamous.

Jeanfreau and Michael (2019) emphasized that spouses who remain faithful to each other reported intense love for their partner, similar religious values and commitment, and ongoing communication as factors operative in their fidelity. Regarding communication, one respondent said, "I tell my husband everything—we're honest with each other," Similarly, another commented, "I don't keep anything from him."

3. **Sex as an extension of workplace friendship.** Drifting from being friends to lovers is not uncommon in the workplace. About 60% of persons in the workforce report having become involved with someone at work. Not only might the at-home partner be stressed when the office affair is discovered but the individuals involved in the affair may be stressed over trying to keep their affair secret or coping with an office breakup.

4. **Coping with sexual dissatisfaction.** Some spouses engage in extramarital sex because their partner is not interested in sex. Others may go outside the relationship because their partners will not engage in the sexual behaviors they want and enjoy. The unwillingness of the spouse to engage in oral sex, anal intercourse, or a variety of sexual positions sometimes results in the other spouse's looking elsewhere for a more cooperative and willing sexual partner.

5. **Seeking revenge.** When partners find out that their mate has had or is having an affair, they are often hurt and angry. One response to this hurt and anger is to have an affair to get even with the unfaithful partner.

6. **Getting same-sex relationship needs met.** Some married individuals are bisexual or use heterosexuality as a cover for their

Coolidge effect: term used to describe waning of sexual excitement and the effect of novelty and variety on increasing sexual arousal.

homosexuality. Songwriter Cole Porter, known for "I've Got You Under My Skin," was a gay man who feared that no one would buy his music if his sexual orientation was known. He married Linda Lee Porter, who was alleged to be a lesbian, and their marriage lasted until Porter's death 30 years later. Individuals in these situations may have extramarital affairs that allow them to act on their same sex desires. Other gay or queer individuals marry as a way of denying their sexual orientation— "If they marry, they can't really be gay" is the thinking. These individuals are likely to feel unfulfilled in their marriage and may seek involvement in an extramarital homosexual relationship.

Other individuals may marry and then discover later in life that they desire a same-sex relationship. Such individuals may feel that (1) they have been homosexual or bisexual all along, (2) their sexual orientation has changed from heterosexual to homosexual, bisexual, or queer (3) they are unsure of their sexual orientation and want to explore a homosexual relationship, or (4) they are predominantly heterosexual but wish to experience a homosexual relationship for variety.

7. **Reacting to aging.** Another motive for intercourse outside marriage is the desire to return to the feeling of youth. Ageism, which is discrimination against the elderly, promotes the idea that being young is good and being old is bad. Sexual attractiveness is equated with youth, and having an affair may confirm to older partners that they are still sexually desirable. Aging individuals may also try to recapture the love, excitement, adventure, and romance associated with youth by having an affair.

8. **Coping with being separated from partner.** Separation may predispose one to involvement with another. Some military wives whose husbands are deployed report that the loneliness can become unbearable. Some deployed husbands say that remaining faithful is difficult. Partners in long-distance relationships may also be vulnerable to infidelity.

9. **Commitment issue.** Some individuals note that they are unable to be committed to one person. More often, these individuals have a history of being unfaithful and have rarely experienced a negative consequence for being so.

APPLYING SOCIAL RESEARCH

Reactions to Discovery of a Partner's Cheating

"How could you?" asked an angry wife who had discovered her husband in a secluded parked car with a woman from his office. The scene was on *Cheaters*, a television program which features partners caught in the act of cheating on their mates. Individuals may have extreme reactions to discovering their partner's infidelity. The purpose of this research was to identify how undergraduates react to the knowledge that one's romantic partner has cheated, which this study defined as having sexual intercourse with someone other than one's primary partner.

The Survey

A 47-item questionnaire was posted on the Internet and completed by 244 undergraduates of whom 83% were female, 69% were White, and 52% were in their first year. Over 60% were emotionally involved with one person.

Results—Gender Differences in Reactions

Over half (51%) reported they had been cheated on by a partner with whom they were in a romantic relationship. Seventeen percent of the sample reported that they had cheated on a romantic partner. Significantly more women than men—55% versus 31%—reported that a romantic partner had cheated on them.

In addition to a significant gender difference with men cheating more than women, there were significant gender differences in the reactions to a partner's cheating. Women were more likely to cry, put their partner under surveillance, confront their partner, and get tested for STIs. Shrout and Weigel (2018) also studied the reaction to a partner's infidelity and found that the greater the partner blame, self-blame, and causal attribution of the infidelity, the greater the depression, anxiety, and distress symptoms, which in turn were associated with more health-compromising behaviors, such as greater alcohol use.

Results—Differences in "Unhealthy" and "Healthy" Reactions by Gender

A subset of 19 "Unhealthy" and 9 "Healthy" reactions to a partner's cheating were identified to ascertain if there were gender differences. For example, increasing one's alcohol consumption, becoming suicidal, and having an affair out of revenge were identified as "unhealthy" reactions, while confronting the partner, forgiving the partner, and seeing a therapist were regarded as more "healthy" reactions. For each item, participants were assigned a score of 1 point if they agreed (somewhat agree, agree, strongly agree) with the reaction—for example, "I drank more alcohol" or "I forgave my partner." Scores on the unhealthy and healthy reactions were summed to create an overall count of demonstrated unhealthy and healthy reactions.

When unhealthy reactions were considered, there were no significant gender differences. Women and men were just as likely to have unhealthy reactions to a partner's infidelity. However, in regard to healthy reactions, females reported a significantly higher percentage of healthy reactions and behaviors than males. Females averaged 3.71 healthy behaviors (SD = 1.46) compared to males who averaged 2.44 healthy behaviors (SD = 1.58).

Theoretical Framework and Discussion

Symbolic interaction theory and social exchange theory provided frameworks for understanding reactions to the knowledge that one's partner had cheated. Symbolic interaction posits that a couple's relationship is created and maintained on agreed upon meanings of various behaviors. A major concept inherent in this theoretical framework is definition of the situation. In reference to cheating, partners in a relationship will have definitions about the meaning of one partner having sexual intercourse with someone outside the dyad. Among the undergraduates in the current study, most of whom expected fidelity, the definition of the situation was a monogamous relationship with the expectation of fidelity. As such, a feeling of betrayal occurred when fidelity was breeched.

The social exchange framework views the interaction between partners in a romantic relationship in terms of reward and cost. Both partners enter the relationship with promised love and fidelity and expect the same in return. When one partner does not exchange fidelity for fidelity, there is a significant "cost" to the faithful partner for remaining in a relationship where the partner has been unfaithful. Indeed, a common reaction among the sample of undergraduates in this study to the knowledge that their partner had cheated was to terminate the relationship. Almost half (47%) ended the relationship with the partner who cheated. Not explored in this study was the physiological effect of compromising one's heart. ●

Source: Abridged and adapted from Barnes, H., Knox, D. & and Brinkley, J. (2012, March). *CHEATING: Gender differences in reactions to discovery of a partner's cheating.* Paper presented to the Southern Sociology annual meeting. New Orleans, LA. Updated in 2018.

Alienation of Affection Lawsuits

Seven states—North Carolina, Illinois, Mississippi, New Hampshire, New Mexico, South Dakota and Utah—recognize **alienation of affection** lawsuits, which give a spouse the right to sue a third party for "criminal conversation" or for taking the affections of a spouse away. The former means that the plaintiff may recover damages from a third party who engages in sexual intercourse with the plaintiff's spouse. The plaintiff must prove that the plaintiff and spouse were married, that the third party had sex with the plaintiff's spouse without consent, and that the plaintiff and spouse were not legally separated at the time the sex occurred.

Sex need not be involved between the third party and the spouse whose affections have been alienated (Gardner, 2017). Alienation of affection claims evolved from common law, which considered women property of their husbands. The reasoning was if another man was accused of stealing his "property," a husband could sue him for damages. The law applies to both women and men, so a third-party woman who steals another woman's husband's affections can be sued for taking her "property" away. About 200 Alienation of Affection lawsuits are filed annually each year in North Carolina. In 2018, a North Carolina judge awarded $8.8 million to a husband to be paid by the man whom he said seduced his wife and wrecked his marriage (Shaffer, 2018).

Children's Reactions to Parents' Infidelity

Thorson (2017) interviewed 38 children who had a parent who was unfaithful and identified how they behaved toward the parent. While some changed how they referred to the parent by saying "I no longer called him dad but by his first name," others withheld terms of endearment like "I stopped telling my mom I loved her," and still others stop talking to their parent altogether. Acting out also occurred in that one of the respondents ran off a letter written by her mother to the lover and gave it to their pastor. In another case,

Alienation of affection: law which gives a spouse the right to sue a third party for taking the affections of a spouse away.

the respondent announced that he never wanted to see the person her parent had an affair with and would leave if confronted with the person. The point of the research was to reveal the difficulty with which offspring may have processing the infidelity of their parents.

CULTURE AND DIVERSITY

In China, an escalating divorce rate and adultery with a mistress has spawned a new career path to help the frustrated and concerned wife—the mistress dispeller (Fan, 2017). Such a professional is hired to dissuade the mistress and remove her from her husband's life. The cost begins at $15,000 but can cost as much as $75,000 if the mistress has a child with her husband. Tactics include buying off the mistress, embarrassing the mistress by alerting her parents and friends of her behavior, or alienating the husband from her. In the latter, the dispeller gets photos of the mistress with someone else which may enrage the husband, prompting him to end the relationship.

A Comparison of Those Who Divorce and Those Who Stay Married Post Affair

Yuan and Weiser (2019) analyzed data on 325 spouses whose partner had cheated on them to identify the characteristics of those who divorced and those who remained married. Those who divorced were more likely to be men, those who perceived a greater number of alternatives, those who were less committed to their marriage, those who perceived that divorce was less stigmatizing, and those who were White. In contrast, those who remain married if their spouse cheated were more likely to be women, those who perceived few alternatives, those who were more committed to their marriage, those who felt divorce would be a stigma, and those who were Asian Americans.

Successful Recovery From Infidelity

Infidelity changes one's relationship and often makes it worse. While an affair is a frequent cause of a couple deciding to divorce, keeping the relationship together with forgiveness and time is the most frequent outcome. Abrahamson et al. (2012) interviewed seven individuals who had experienced an affair in their relationship and who were still together two years later. The factors involved in rebuilding their relationship included:

1. **Be motivated to stay together**. Having been together several years, having children, having property jointly, not wanting to "fail," and fearing life alone were factors which motivated the partners to stay together. The basic feeling was that the partners had a lot to gain by working through the issue and staying together.

2. **Taking joint responsibility for the affair**. The betrayed partner found a way to acknowledge she or he had contributed to the affair.

3. **Forgive and don't refer to the affair again**. Forgiveness involved letting go of one's resentment, anger, and hurt; accepting that everyone needs forgiveness; and moving forward. Aalgaard et al. (2016) emphasized the value of forgiveness for getting over an affair, for marital satisfaction, and for one's own health and well-being.

4. **Learn vicariously from others who divorced over an affair**. Some partners noted that others who ended their relationship over an affair were not necessarily happier or better off. Perhaps they might have been better off working it out and staying together?

5. **Developing a sense of pride at being resilient over a major crisis**. The partners felt a sense of pride in coming through a difficult experience.

Ester Perel (2017) is a therapist who helps couples cope with an affair. She emphasizes the importance of being realistic about love, life, and relationships—that to expect one's partner to never cross the line with another in a lifetime relationship may be an idea attached to an unnecessary outcome, such as ending one's relationship. Rather, couples can become closer as a result of an affair by communicating about their relationship and how they can meet each other's needs.

One wife whose husband had had an affair was told by their counselor . . . "you're going to need to resolve this in a way that it does not wreck your life whether or not you stay married . . . one option is to resolve it AND stay married . . . to keep your family together." The couple worked it out, improved their relationship, and are still together. Positive outcomes of having experienced and worked through infidelity include a closer marital relationship, placing a higher value on each other, and realizing the importance of good marital communication.

What is the effect of having an affair for the spouse who has the affair? Walker (2019) surveyed 1,070 spouses who had an extramarital encounter and identified their perceptions of life satisfaction before, during, and after the affair. Findings included that having an affair was necessary in order to remain in the marriage and a desire to remain in the marriage was important for overall life satisfaction. Hence, these respondents indicated the positive function of an affair and the condition under which one's life satisfaction was enhanced during the affair.

Spouses who remain faithful to their partners have decided to do so. Lee and O'Sullivan (2018) surveyed 741 adults in intimate relationships who identified the 24 strategies of affair avoidance or monogamy maintenance. These could be categorized as proactive avoidance such as deciding not to drink alone with a potential partner, relationship enhancement involving insuring one's own relationship was both emotionally and physically enriching, and derogation, conceptualizing a potential partner as not very attractive. All of these strategies were endorsed but were largely unsuccessful.

UP CLOSE: WE BOTH HAD AFFAIRS AND DECIDED TO REMAIN MARRIED

We were like all couples who begin their lives together—in love, happy, and looking forward to a wonderful life together. We had a rocky beginning with an unplanned pregnancy, unsupportive parents for our wedding, unemployment, debt, and so forth. After twelve years of marriage, I, Jan—the wife—became involved with someone at work. What began as a harmless friendship at work escalated into emotions and sex. It blew up two months later when my lover's wife found out.

When I told Eric, my husband, he was in shock. Feeling devastated and betrayed, my husband had a stern, pained reaction of "let's get through it" which was more difficult than we imagined.

I changed jobs, we went to counseling, things were better . . . but we were both very busy with our two young children, working long hours, and had little time together.

Two years later, Eric drifted into a relationship that was both emotional and sexual. His lover's husband found out and exposed the affair of six months. After months of coping with the fallout, I had a mental breakdown and was admitted to the hospital. Our younger daughter also became depressed, grades began to drop, and so forth.

It is now four years later. We are out of danger. We are both dreadfully sorry for the pain we inflicted on ourselves, our partner, and our children. We have become involved in counseling, learned to prioritize each other, spend time together, and talk openly about our relationship and our family. Not a day goes

by that we don't think about the mess we caused. But we celebrate that we made it through this most difficult time and feel improved by our struggle. We think affairs are devastating but glad that we were able to keep our marriage and our family together. While I wrote the above, my husband Eric acknowledges his agreement with every word.

Courtesy of Jan Molinares (published with her permission)

Poverty and Unemployment

Poverty and unemployment can be profoundly stressful on individuals and families. Chronic poverty-related stress has negative outcomes for one's mental, physical, and relationship health (Perzow et al., 2018). Poverty and low income are linked to family problems such as domestic violence, child abuse and neglect, substance abuse, teen pregnancy, and behavioral problems in children and teens (Kaiser et al., 2017). Families with the highest poverty rates are most likely to experience the stress of material and economic hardship.

Because the federal poverty line is set so low (see Table 13.2-previous chapter), many individuals and families who experience economic-related stress are not considered officially poor. Families need, on average, an income of twice the official poverty level to meet basic needs (NCCP, 2019). Hence, while more than one in ten persons in the United States is officially "poor" with statistics showing a rate of 12.3% in 2017, more like twice that number—about one in four—of Americans live in a household that struggles to pay for basic needs such as housing, food, transportation, and medical care. U.S. poverty rates are highest among Blacks and Hispanics and among female-headed single families, a quarter of which live under the official poverty line (Fontenot, 2018). Therefore, research on families living in poverty may include families living on an income that is up to twice the official poverty level.

Unemployment sometimes results in poverty and family stress. Reasons why a parent or spouse or both may be unemployed include ill health or disability, child care or other family care-giving responsibilities, lack of available jobs, and discriminatory hiring practices. Unemployment rates are higher among Blacks than other populations (Emeka, 2018).

When spouses lose their jobs as a result of physical illness or disability, the family experiences a double blow—loss of income combined with higher medical bills. Unless an unemployed spouse is covered by the partner's medical insurance, unemployment can result in loss of health insurance for the family. As might be expected, becoming reemployed in a full-time job was associated with a decrease in depressive symptoms (Schauss et al., 2019).

However, employment does not necessarily protect a family from the stresses of economic survival. In general, the U.S. federal minimum wage does not provide a "living wage" that is sufficient to meet basic needs. Hence, some parents and spouses work at full-time jobs that do not pay enough to provide a comfortable and secure economic base for a family. In other cases, employees may not be given enough hours so that they work part time not out of choice. Individuals who are employed, but who are still struggling to meet basic economic needs, are known as the "working poor." In 2017, 5.3% of U.S. employed adults ages 18 to 64 were considered "poor" by the official U.S. Census criteria (Fontenot et al., 2018). The working poor endure not only the stresses of poverty but also the stresses of employment. The working poor are at greater risk for work-related injuries and are more likely to have inadequate health care (Topete et al., 2018). Since the working poor are employed, their needs are more likely to be overlooked. For example, federal supplemental nutritional assistance programs frequently underserve the working poor (Smith et al., 2017).

Substance Abuse

Substance abuse is another crisis that can significantly impact a family. A person has a problem with a substance if it interferes with his or her health, job, or relationships. Alcohol is the most frequently used drug in colleges and universities (see family policy on alcohol use on campus). If your partner is an alcoholic, it is important to recognize that you can do nothing to stop your partner from drinking. Your partner must "hit bottom" or have an epiphany and make a personal decision to stop. In the meantime, you can join Al-Anon to help you cope with your partner's alcoholism, regard the alcoholism as a disease, and decide to stay with your partner or end the relationship. Most individuals stay with their partner because there is an enormous emotional cost of leaving. However, some pay the price. Only you can decide.

FAMILY POLICY

Alcohol Abuse on Campus

Drinking alcohol is common among college students. Patrick and Terry-McElrath (2017) found in a national survey of 1,657 college age students that 24% reported binge drinking or drinking more than five drinks on one occasion; 10% reported high-intensity drinking or more than 10 drinks on one occasion; and 4% reported upwards of 15 drinks on one occasion. Four-year college students and those who did not live with their parents were more likely to engage in high-intensity drinking than their peers. Riordan et al. (2018) surveyed 569 New Zealand undergraduates in regard to their drinking alcohol prior to attending a concert. Eighty-nine percent reported drinking a median of six drinks before the concert. While most college students who drink alcohol do not have a problem with alcohol, some do. Thirteen percent of 2,935 male undergraduates and 8% of 9,749 female undergraduates reported that "I have a problem with alcohol" (Hall & Knox, 2019).

Tyler et al. (2017) noted that "widespread" alcohol-focused reduction efforts should be undertaken since peer influence was so powerful. Indeed, one moderate drinking college student could be an important model for peers. Campus policies throughout the United States include alcohol-free dorms; alcohol bans, enforcement, and sanctions; peer support; alerting parents and education; and alcohol-free events.

An example of the latter is Western State Colorado University which offers late night movies, $1 breakfasts, dances, and a safe spring break alternative. The University of Albany also has a year-round campaign that addresses making healthy choices, not just flyers distributed during freshmen orientation. Wilson et al. (2016) identified specific evidenced-based therapies that address individual student problem drinking behaviors. Two of these are known as BASICS (Brief Alcohol Screening and Intervention for College Students) and BMI (Brief Motivational Interventions). Eaton et al. (2018) found that peer-implemented, minimal interventions by peers of an undergraduate who had a campus alcohol violation were associated with positive behavior change.

Most colleges and universities do not ban alcohol or its possession on campus. Administrators fear that students will attend other colleges where they are allowed to drink. Alumni may want to drink at football games and view such university banning as intrusive. Some attorneys think colleges and universities can be held liable for not stopping dangerous drinking patterns, but others argue that college is a place for students to learn how to behave responsibly. If policies are too restrictive, drinking may go underground where detecting use may be more difficult. ●

TABLE 14.2

Use in Last Month by Type of Drug and Age Group

TYPE OF DRUG USED	AGE 12 TO 17	AGE 18 TO 25	AGE 26 AND OLDER
Marijuana and hashish	7.0%	20.8%	7.2%
Cocaine	.1%	1.6%	.6%
Alcohol	9.2%	57.1%	54.6%
Cigarettes	3.4%	23.5%	20.2%

Source: Adapted from *ProQuest Statistical Abstract of the United States*. (2019). Online Edition. Bethesda, MD. Table 215

Alcohol is not alone as being a problematic drug or substance. Table 14.2 reflects substance use in various age categories.

Opioid addiction has become a U. S. epidemic. Hendy et al. (2018) analyzed Internet data on 1,047 adults and found that opioid use among the 11% of the respondents was associated with low self-esteem as well as problems with health, money, family and romance. Research on successful treatment to end opioid use has been limited (Peisch et al., 2018). Brown (2018) reviewed 14 studies and noted that psychosocial interventions have not been successful in preventing relapses. Opioid drug overdoses continue to increase (Kertesz & Gordon, 2019).

Death of Family Member

Another family crisis, the death of a family member, is especially devastating. The crisis is particularly acute when the death is a suicide. Reactions to the death of a loved one is not something one "gets over." Burke et al. (1999) noted that grief is not a one-time experience that people adjust to and move on. She identified the concept of **"chronic sorrow,"** where grief-related feelings occur periodically throughout the lives of those left behind. Grief feelings may be particularly acute on the anniversary of the death or when the bereaved individual thinks of what might have been had the person lived. Burke et al. (1999) noted that 97% of the individuals in one study who had experienced the death of a loved one 2 to 20 years earlier met the criteria for chronic sorrow. Celebrity Liam Neeson noted three years after the death of his wife that he still experienced

Chronic sorrow: grief-related feelings that occur periodically throughout the lives of those left behind.

Part of getting over it is knowing you will never get over it.

Anne Finger, novelist

waves of grief. Particularly difficult are those cases of ambiguous loss where the definitions of death become muddled—the loved one disappeared or the person had Alzheimer's.

Moore et al. (2019) revealed how grieving individuals use social media during bereavement—to share information with family or friends, to discuss death with others who are also mourning, to connect with a broader mourning community, to commemorate the deceased, and to continue a connection with the deceased. Regarding the latter, mourners sent messages to the deceased whom they felt were capable of listening but were not capable of responding.

Death of One's Child

A parent's worst fear is the death of a child. Most people expect the death of their parents but not the death of their children. Albuquerque et al. (2016) examined the effect of a child's death on the couple's marriage and found it can cause cohesive as well as detrimental effects. Pre-death characteristics of the relationship, communication, incongruent grieving, social support, and religious affiliation were factors involved in each parent's adjustment. Finnas et al. (2018) noted that the primary effect of the death of a child on the parent's relationship is not divorce but no subsequent children. The death of a child is compounded when the cause is suicide, which we discuss in "Suicide of a Family Member."

Death of One's Parent

Terminally ill parents may be taken care of by their children. Such care over a period of years can be emotionally stressful, financially draining, and exhausting. Hence, by the time the parent dies, a crisis has already occurred.

Suicide of Family Member

Suicide is a devastating crisis event for families and is not that unusual. Annually there are 40,000 suicides and 750,000 attempts, and these are more often by 15-to-19-year-olds, males, sexual minorities, substance abusers, and victims of child sexual abuse. Each suicide immediately affects at least six other people in that person's life. O'Hare et al. (2018) analyzed data on individuals who were mentally ill and who were age 50 or older and found that all had experienced at least one traumatic event, more than half had attempted suicide at least once, and one third had attempted multiple times. Examples of traumatic events included physical abuse, witnessed severe violence, or having been homeless. Coping with the death of a loved one's suicide is ongoing. Pritchard and Buckle (2018) examined the 117 posts of 50 users of a public online group support forum.

I don't know what to say.

Kate Basile on what people should say to her about the suicide of her son Ryan.

They found sustained psychological distress, an ongoing struggle to make meaning of their partners' suicide, focusing on memories, and longing for the deceased. There is also depression and social stigma to deal with.

Adjustment to the suicide of a family member takes time. Part of the recovery process is accepting that one cannot stop the suicide of those who are adamant about taking their own life and that one is not responsible for the suicide of another. Indeed, family members often harbor the belief that they could have done something to prevent the suicide.

APPLYING SOCIAL RESEARCH

What to Say to a Person Who Has Attempted Suicide

When a family member or close friend experiences a nonfatal suicide attempt, what do you say? A team of researchers attempted to answer this question and to find out the most helpful response to the person who had previously attempted to end his or her life.

Sample and Methods

Forty interviews were conducted with suicide attempt survivors, 70% of whom were women and 90% Caucasian between the ages of 28 and 62, who had disclosed their suicide behavior to another person. The average number of previous attempts was four, and the average length of time since the last attempt was 11 years. Taking pills or cutting and stabbing were the most frequent methods used in their attempts to end their lives. Respondents reported most commonly disclosing their suicide attempt to a friend or spouse or romantic partner.

Findings

The respondents revealed three themes of how those they told about their suicide attempt reacted: The first theme included reactions that perpetuated the belief of "I do not belong and I am a burden." All attempt survivors reported at least one negative reaction from someone they told. These negative reactions included criticizing the person as being selfish and worthless. The result was for the attempt survivor to feel worse, to feel stigmatized, and to feel awful.

A second theme included reactions that led attempt survivors to believe "I can belong and not be a burden or hurt if I hide my suicidal behavior." These reactions resulted in attempt survivors concealing

their suicide behavior in order to maintain their relationships with family and friends. For example, some family members used excessive monitoring in an attempt to be helpful, but this behavior often led attempt survivors to believe they could not be open about how they were feeling.

A third theme involved helpful reactions that resulted in attempt survivors believing "I belong and I am not a burden." These reactions by family members or friends included (1) empathetic questions such as "tell me about your feelings," (2) remaining present and available to hear the answers, and (3) projecting stability and strength to the attempt survivor. This latter theme mirrors a structured counseling context where the therapist seeks to understand the individual, is not put off by the answers, and is there for the person. Not stigmatizing suicide was also therapeutic for the person who had attempted suicide (Frey & Cerel, 2015).

Implications

Friends and family members can provide a needed reaction to persons who attempt suicide by remaining nonjudgmental and empathetic while also being an attentive listener who is available to the attempt survivor. Such a reaction might also be in conjunction with encouraging the person to see a therapist who has learned these skills and who may recommend medication as necessary. Individuals feeling suicidal should seek help via a hotline or mental health professional. ●

Source: Frey, L. M., Cerel, J., & Hans., J. D. (2014, November). *A phenomenological exploration of family reaction after suicide.* Paper presented at the National Council on Family Relations Annual Conference, Baltimore, MD. Used by permission.

MARRIAGE AND FAMILY THERAPY

Papp (2018) identified the conflicts of 55 couples involved in marriage therapy. Communication, chores, and habits were the most frequent sources of disagreements reported by spouses. The conflicts varied by length of time the issue had been a problem, how often it occurred, who initiated the conflict, and how important the partners regarded the topic. Resolution strategies also varied by being constructive, angry, or depressive. Spouses also rated money and habits as recurring topics and conflicts concerning money and children as holding high levels of importance to the relationship.

Signs to look for in your own relationship which suggest that you might consider seeing a marriage and relationship therapist include feeling distant and not wanting or being unable to communicate with your partner, avoiding each other, feeling depressed, drifting into a relationship with someone else, increased drinking, and privately contemplating separation or breaking up. If you are experiencing one or more of these symptoms, it may be wise to intervene early so as to stop the spiral toward an estranged relationship before there is no motivation to improve it. Marriage therapy may serve to reverse relationship issues early by helping the partners to sort out values, make decisions, and begin new behaviors so that spouses can start feeling better about each other. Williamson et al. (2018) noted that having experienced premarital education earlier predisposes one to seek marriage therapy later.

There are various "types" of marital and family therapy: emotion-focused couple therapy, integrative behavioral couple therapy, cognitive behavioral couple therapy, family therapy, multidimensional family therapy, multisystemic therapy, brief strategic family therapy, attachment-based family therapy, family-focused therapy, and a new general systems theory (Lebow, 2017; Gottman & Gottman, 2018). While several sessions are usually indicated, even brief therapy can help. Kanter and Schramm (2018) confirmed that even brief interventions and therapy focusing on such issues as managing conflict and expressing gratitude promoted healthy relationship functioning. Cook-Darzens et al. (2018) also noted that marriage and family therapy is a helpful adjunct when individual family members are being treated for other psychiatric problems.

If you don't have time to work on your marriage, you will need to take time to work through your divorce.

A spouse who ignored the partner and waited too late.

Availability of Marriage and Family Therapists

There are more than 50,000 marriage and family therapists in the United States. Their professional roles include college and university professors, psychologists, social workers, professional counselors, and those who focus exclusively on marriage and family therapy. The American Association for Marriage and Family Therapy (AAMFT) is the professional organization for marriage and family therapists. All fifty states plus the District of Columbia have regulations regarding marriage and family therapy.

Licensing for marriage and family therapists varies from state to state and each state may have therapists with different levels of training. Licensing requirements usually include graduate training in marriage and family therapy, a national exam, and a minimum of a thousand clinical hours with a portion of these under supervision of an AAMFT approved supervisor.

Whatever marriage therapy costs, it can be worth it in terms of an improved relationship. If divorce can be averted, both spouses and children can avoid the trauma and thousands of dollars that would be saved. Managed care has resulted in some private therapists making marriage therapy affordable. Effective marriage therapy usually involves seeing the spouses together and is called conjoint therapy. However, there are occasions where individual therapy is necessary and helpful. Issues of depression, alcoholism and substance abuse, chronic infidelity, and PTSD may best be dealt with in individual sessions.

Even for couples who do seek therapy, they still might do well to heed a bit of wisdom from Supreme Court Justice Ruth Bader Ginsburg about how to have a happy marriage. She gave this advice in a meeting she had with singer-actress Jennifer Lopez and her fiancé, former professional baseball player Alex Rodriguez. J-Lo sought the meeting with Ginsburg to ask her about the secrets to a happy marriage. The justice recalled the words her mother-in-law told her when she married her own husband, Martin Ginsburg, "It helps, sometimes, to be a little deaf." And she added, "And that good advice I have followed in every workplace, including the good job I now have" (Schmidt & Barnes, 2019).

Effectiveness of Relationship and Marriage Therapy

The public perception of the scientific validity of marriage counseling is suspect. Only 7% of a nationally representative sample regarded marriage counseling as "very scientific"; 40% rated it as "not scientific at all" (Platt & Scheitle, 2017). If the definition of *scientific* is the systematic use of established principles of learning applied to the relationship dyad, marriage counseling is very scientific.

What is the outcome for those who become involved in relationship and marriage therapy? The answer is complex. In large randomized studies, most couples report improved couple adjustment. But in smaller clinical studies, the gains are more modest. One consideration is the goal of therapy: Is it to clarify commitment to the relationship—for example, "do we want to stay together?"—or work on the relationship (Kim et al., 2016)? A couple may decide to divorce, but this does not mean that therapy failed since the goal of therapy was to help the couple decide if they wanted to split or work on their marriage.

Thirty-one percent of therapists report that they use either a behavioral or "cognitive-behavioral" approach. A behavioral approach, also referred to as **behavioral couple therapy**, means that the therapist focuses on behaviors the respective spouses want increased or decreased, initiated or terminated, and negotiate behavioral exchanges between the partners (Knox & Crisp, 2019).

Behavior therapists use behavior contracts which are agreements that partners make of new behaviors to engage in between sessions. The following is an example and assumes that the partners argue frequently, never compliment each other, no longer touch each other, and do not spend time together. The contract calls for each partner to make no negative statements to the other, give two compliments per day to the other, hug or hold each other at least once a day, and allocate Saturday night to go out to dinner alone with each other. On the contract, under each day of the week, the partners would check that they did what they agreed and return to the therapist. Partners who change their behavior toward each other often discover that the partner changes also and there is a new basis for each to feel better about each other and their relationship.

Sometimes clients do not like behavior contracts and say to the behavior therapist, "I want my partner to compliment me and hug me because my partner wants to, not because you wrote it down on one of these silly contracts." The behavior therapist acknowledges the desire for the behavior to come from the heart of the partner and points out that the partner is making a choice to engage in new behavior to please the partner.

Research on the effectiveness of various approaches to couple therapy shows that no one approach is superior (Kim et al., 2016). Indeed, the problem of the couple, their age, their motivation, and the skill and personality of the therapist are all involved in whether a couple report improvement. Two moderately motivated partners with numerous conflicts over several years are less likely to work out their problems than a highly motivated couple with minor conflicts of short duration. Severe depression, alcoholism on the part of either spouse, or an affair are factors that will limit positive marital and family gains. In general, these issues must be resolved individually before the spouses can profit from marital therapy. Johnson and Bradbury (2015) emphasized that effective therapy must address the contextual issues of the couple—job loss, financial strain, health issues, in-laws, and so forth.

Owen et al. (2019) reported on 87 couples who began therapy as part of a longitudinal study in the military. The couples were assessed six times over the course of three years, including time points before and after starting couple therapy. Results demonstrated that the couples' negative communication was increasing, their relationship satisfaction was decreasing, and they were prone to divorce prior to entering couple therapy. After the couples began therapy, these three factors leveled off but did not show further change. When this and other research studies are examined in regard to the success of relationship therapy, the pattern emerges that "typically demonstrates a significant increase in relational functioning from pre- to post-therapy with mixed evidence of the maintenance of such gains over longer periods of time (i.e., 3–4 years). That is, there is typically a return to pre-therapy levels of relationship adjustment."

Even clients who involuntarily experience family therapy—that is, they are ordered by the courts to undergo therapy—report just as much improvement as couples who voluntarily seek therapy (Sotero et al., 2018). Regarding emotionally focused couple therapy, Wiebe et al. (2017) found that positive relationship improvement, defined as relationship satisfaction, was maintained in 32 couples at a two-year follow-up.

Tele-relationship Therapy

Increasingly couples are seeking tele-relationship couple therapy (Roddy et al., 2029). When compared with couples who seek face-to-face therapeutic contexts, online couples are younger and more likely to have issues of trust, time together, and child and parenting problems. They are similar to other couples in that presenting problems tend to be those of communication and emotional intimacy.

Behavioral couple therapy (BCT): therapeutic focus on behaviors the respective spouses want increased or decreased, initiated or terminated.

BEHAVIOR CONTRACT FOR PARTNERS							
NAME OF PARTNERS _____				DATE: WEEK OF *JUNE 8–14*			
BEHAVIORS EACH PARTNER AGREES TO ENGAGE IN AND DAYS OF WEEK							
	Mon.	Tues.	Wed.	Thurs.	Fri.	Sat.	Sun.
1. *No negative statements to partner*	❏	❏	❏	❏	❏	❏	❏
2. *Compliment partner twice each day*	❏	❏	❏	❏	❏	❏	❏
3. *Hug or hold partner once a day*	❏	❏	❏	❏	❏	❏	❏
4. *Out to dinner with each other Saturday night*	❏	❏	❏	❏	❏	❏	❏

From B. Crisp, & Knox, D. (2009). *Behavioral family therapy.* Durham, NC: Carolina Academic Press.

Tele-relationship therapy, commonly known as Skype therapy, is an alternative to face-to-face therapy. Both therapist and couple log on to Skype, where each can see and hear the other so that the session is conducted online. Terms related to tele-relationship therapy are *tele-health, tele-psychology, tele-psychiatry, tele-counseling, virtual therapy,* and *video interaction guidance (VIG).*

Tele-relationship therapy allows couples to become involved in marriage and family therapy independent of several key factors: where they live—for example, in isolated rural areas; the availability of transportation; and time—that is, sessions can be scheduled outside the 9 to 5 block. Problems of

Dr. Katie O'Hara conducts tele-relationship therapy sessions, which research shows can be as effective as face-to-face sessions.

Tele-relationship therapy: therapy sessions conducted online, often through Skype, where both therapist and couple can see and hear each other.

tele-relationshp therapy include that the Internet therapist does not know local resources if a suicide referral is needed.

OurRelationship program is another example of relationship help available over the Internet. It is an eight-hour program whereby couples complete online activities and have four 15-min calls with the project staff. Doss et al. (2016) reported on 300 heterosexual couples (N = 600 participants) throughout the United States who participated in a study involving couples who were randomly assigned to begin the program immediately or who were put on a two-month wait-list control group.

Compared to the wait-list group, intervention couples reported significant improvements in relationship satisfaction, relationship confidence, and relationship quality. Gains were also noted including a decrease in depressive and anxious symptoms and an increase in perceived health, work functioning, and quality of life. Hence, distressed couples can benefit significantly from online couple therapy, specifically the low cost, web-based OurRelationship program.

FUTURE OF STRESS AND CRISIS IN RELATIONSHIPS

Stress and crisis will continue to be a part of life and relationships. No individual, spouse, partner, marriage, or family is immune. A major source of stress will be economic—the difficulty in securing and maintaining employment and sufficient income to take care of one's needs and the needs of the family.

One's perception of an event, not the event itself, will continue to determine the severity of a crisis and the capacity to cope with it. Cognitive behavior therapy has emerged as helpful in bringing perspective, humor, and resilience to whatever event an individual is confronted with. As noted earlier, advances in technology may provide ways to reduce stress and provide support to family with the help of robots. However, technology may also increase stress levels and open another door for problems such as addiction and cyber affairs.

SUMMARY

What is stress and what is a crisis event?
Stress is a reaction of the body to substantial or unusual demands whether they are physical, environmental, or interpersonal. Stress is associated with irritability, high blood pressure, and depression. Stress may be both negative and positive. An example of the latter is wedding stress, which may be mixed with excitement and joy.

A crisis is a situation that requires changes in normal patterns of behavior. A family crisis is a situation that upsets the normal functioning of the family and requires a new set of responses to the stressor. Sources of stress and crises can be external—for example, hurricane, tornado, downsizing, or military separation—or internal, such as alcoholism, extramarital affair, Alzheimer's disease, or inherited wealth.

Family resilience is when family members successfully cope under adversity, which enables them to flourish with warmth, support, and cohesion. Key factors include positive outlook, spirituality, flexibility, communication, financial management, family shared recreation, routines or rituals, and support networks.

What are positive and negative stress management strategies?
Changing one's view is the most helpful strategy in reacting to a crisis. Viewing ill health as a challenge, bankruptcy as an opportunity to spend time with one's family, and infidelity as an opportunity to improve communication with one's partner are examples. Other positive coping strategies are exercise, adequate sleep, love, religion, friends, or relatives, and humor. Some harmful strategies include keeping feelings inside, taking out frustrations on one's partner, and denying or avoiding the problem.

What are several of the major family crisis examples?
Some of the more common crisis events discussed in this chapter include physical illness, mental illness, an extramarital affair, unemployment, substance abuse, and the death of one's spouse or children. Surviving an affair involves forgiveness on the part of the offended spouse and to relinquish the right to retaliate against the offending spouse. In exchange, the offending spouse must take responsibility for the affair, agree not to repeat the behavior, and grant the partner the right to check up on the offending partner to regain trust.

Individuals may use technology to help avert crisis events. For example, a first alert necklace can call 911 if the person falls. In addition, virtual reality can be used to assist in resolving post-traumatic stress disorder. A spouse may be brought back to the traumatic event and learn to cope with anxiety in a therapeutic context. Smartphones may be used to assist in meditation, relaxation, and breathing exercises.

What help is available from marriage and family therapists?
Marriage and family therapists are highly trained mental health professionals assisting individuals, couples, and families with various issues. There are various "types" of marital and family therapy: emotion-focused couple

therapy, behavioral couple therapy, cognitive behavioral couple therapy, family therapy, multidimensional family therapy, multisystemic therapy, brief strategic family therapy, attachment-based family therapy, and family-focused therapy. While several sessions are usually indicated, brief therapy can help to assist couples in managing conflict. Online, tele-relationship (Skype) therapy is convenient and just as effective as-face-to-face therapy.

What is the future of coping with crisis events?
Stress and crisis are embedded into the fabric of life. They will never cease to present themselves. Nevertheless, one's perception of an event, not the event itself, will continue to determine the severity of a crisis and the capacity to cope with it. Cognitive behavior therapy has emerged as helpful in bringing perspective, humor, and resilience to whatever event an individual is confronted with.

KEY TERMS

Alienation of affection, 307

Behavioral couple therapy (BCT), 314

Chronic sorrow, 311

Coolidge effect, 305

Crisis, 297

Dyadic coping, 299

Extradyadic involvement, 304

Extramarital affair, 304

Family resilience, 297

Infidelity, 303

Palliative care, 301

Resilience, 297

Stress, 296

Tele-relationship therapy, 315

WEB LINKS

American Association for Marriage and Family Therapy
http://www.aamft.org

Association for Applied and Therapeutic Humor
http://www.aath.org

Better Marriages
http://www.bettermarriages.org/

Center for Disease Control and Prevention
https://www.cdc.gov/features/copingwithstress/index.html

Center for Disease Control and Prevention
https://www.cdc.gov/features/copingwithstress/index.html

OurRelationship
https://www.ourrelationship.com/

US National Library of Medicine
https://medlineplus.gov/stress.html

Get the tools you need to sharpen your study skills. SAGE edge offers a robust online environment featuring an impressive array of free tools and resources.
Access practice quizzes, eFlashcards, video, and multimedia at **edge.sagepub.com/knox13e**

15

Divorce, Remarriage, and Stepfamilies

Mutual parenting is the one thing parents who are divorcing should do for their children.

—*Penelope Leach*, British Parenting Guru

Learning Objectives

15.1.   Define divorce

15.2.   Review the deal breakers in relationships and the factors involved in ending a relationship

15.3.   Identify macro factors associated with divorce

15.4.   Identify micro factors associated with divorce

15.5.   Understand the consequences of divorce for spouses

15.6.   Understand the consequences of divorce for children

15.7.   Describe the conditions under which one can have a successful divorce

15.8.   Discuss the differences between first marriages and remarriages

15.9.   Predict what the future holds for divorce and remarriage

Master the content at
edge.sagepub.com/knox13e

Although many believe that divorce is rampant, the divorce rate has dropped in recent years. In 2017, the rate was 2.9 per 1,000 population; in 2010, the rate was 3.6; 2,000, 4.0. Many factors have led to this decrease in divorce, including the individuals in the marriage and the choices they make.

Divorce is a choice. Spouses who call lawyers to initiate litigation might first consider calling a counselor to explore if managing their differences or recovering their love for each other is possible. Neither choice is easy, but a knee-jerk response to divorce when difficult issues, hard times, and unhappiness occur should be avoided. Undergraduates have seen divorce up close. In a sample of 12,744 undergraduates, 32% reported that their biological parents were divorced (Hall & Knox, 2019). This chapter looks not only at the deal breakers partners report on whether they want to continue a relationship but the societal and cultural context in which divorce occurs. As we will note, individualistic societies such as the United States have much higher divorce rates than familistic societies, which represent about 40% of the world's population, such as India.

Similarly, most undergraduates have had experience with the breakup of a romantic relationship. Eighty-seven percent of 353 university students reported that they had experienced at least one such breakup. Of these, 39% said that they initiated the break, 30% had a partner initiate the break, and 23% had mutual breakups

(Brenner & Knox, 2018). We begin by examining the deal breakers of a dating relationship and whether to end a relationship.

DEFINITION AND PREVALENCE OF DIVORCE

Divorce is the legal ending of a valid marriage contract. The often-quoted statistic that half of *all* marriages end in divorce is not true. Some marriages such as those by teenagers who drop out of high school, end at the 50% plus rate. But for college graduates married at age 26 or later, 82% were still married 20 years later; hence, less than 20% divorce. Nationally, about 40 to 50% of first marriages will end in divorce; 60% of second marriages will do so as well (Hawkins et al., 2016). Being White and religious are also associated with a lower divorce rate (Coontz, 2016). Regarding religion, Bell et al. (2018) conducted 30 interviews to assess the impact of religion and spirituality on the decision to divorce. About half reported that staying married was "morally right."

As noted earlier, divorce rates have been stable or dropping in recent years. The principal reason for divorce rates stabilizing is that individuals are delaying marriage so that they are older at the time of marriage. Indeed, the older a person at the time of marriage, the less likely the person is to divorce. Reasons for divorce can be conceptualized as both macro and micro. Some couples seek an **annulment**, which

....

Divorce: the legal ending of a valid marriage contract.

Annulment: the legal erasing of a valid marriage contract. Unlike divorce, the annulment conveys that the marriage never took place since it was illegal.

erases the fact that they were once legally married. Persons who have had an annulment never think of themselves as ever having been married. Reasons for an annulment include the fact that one of the persons was already married, the partners were related by blood, or one of the parties was under age. Celebrity Nicolas Cage sought an annulment after four days of marriage because he said he was drunk and "lacked understanding of his actions" during his Las Vegas wedding to Erika Koike. His annulment request was denied so he divorced.

DECIDING WHETHER TO END A RELATIONSHIP

Relationships end when deal breakers surface. Although there are a number of factors to consider before ending a relationship, we discuss some of the key deal breakers.

Deal Breakers

In a survey of almost 5,000 singles, men and women identified the following characteristics of a partner as deal breakers: poor hygiene (68%), unclean appearance (45%), laziness (43%), lack of humor (41%) and emotionally needy (39%) (Fisher & Garcia, 2019). Notice the focus on personal cleanliness and personality as primary early deal breakers in a relationship.

The deal breakers for a marriage or a long-term relationship may be quite different. Hansson and Ahborg (2016) identified the reasons 39 parents gave for their separation including: strains from parenthood, lack of intimacy, insufficient communication, differing interests, no commitment, and negative effects of addiction. We will discuss other reasons for ending a marriage or long-term relationship in the section on "Micro Factors Contributing to Divorce."

Being secretive in regard to texting is also a deal breaker in some relationships.
Courtesy of Bobby Davis

Choices to Make Before Ending a Relationship

Whether ending a short-term relationship, a long-term relationship, or a marriage, there are a variety of factors to consider. However, some relationships are better off ending in divorce. Specifically, we do not recommend giving an abusive relationship more time, as abuse, once started, tends to increase in frequency and intensity.

1. **Consider improving your relationship rather than ending it.** In some cases, individuals end relationships and later regret having done so. Particularly in our individualistic society with the focus on relationships as a primary source of fun, love, and sexual satisfaction, anything that deviates may be considered justification for divorce. Doherty et al. (2016) surveyed 624 parents who had filed for divorce. One quarter reported that they were ambivalent about going through with the divorce; 8% did not want the divorce.

Given the uncertainty of over a million and a half spouses contemplating divorce every year, it may be wise to contact a marriage therapist before an attorney. Many relationships cannot just be salvaged but can flourish. Harris and Crabtree (2016) reported the outcome of 100 couples involved in **discernment counseling** designed for couples who are on the brink of divorce but who have not pulled the trigger. Almost half (47%) were able to reconcile their differences and stayed married, 41% divorced, and 12% returned to the status quo. The research on deciding to divorce is clear: Don't end a relationship without a great deal of thought and consideration. About half of spouses on the brink of divorce are able to reconcile.

2. **Be creative.** If someone's needs are not being met in a relationship, there is more than one solution. Be creative. For example, a woman whose husband was clinically depressed avoided divorce by focusing on other aspects of her life. Her husband had little interest in doing fun things, but he was a good provider, a good father, a faithful partner with no bad habits, such as alcoholism. Instead of divorcing him, she focused on making herself happy by enjoying her children and spending time with friends. The husband was relieved that she found other ways of meeting her social needs. The result was that the marriage continued and the three children were spared

Discernment counseling: spouses on the brink of divorce examine their options to DIVORCE, accept status quo, or reconcile/make changes.

Getting one's wedding ring back elicits feelings of fear, anger, and anxiety as it reveals the end of the relationship for both partners.
Courtesy of Brittany Bolen

a divorce. Instead of expecting a partner to meet all of your needs, you can find ways to meet some of your needs that do not involve your partner, still enjoy those aspects of your marriage that your spouse can accommodate, and avoid divorce.

3. **Acknowledge and accept that terminating your relationship will be a difficult and painful process.** Divorce is the termination of a major source of intimacy.

The uncoupling process can be brutal and your emotional, mental, and physical health will be challenged. Divorce is the number two crisis in life. Unhappiness, depression, anxiety, and loss of self-esteem are just some of the noted outcomes of divorce. We discuss these outcomes later in "Consequences of Divorce for Spouses and Parents." Applying Social Research identifies those for whom a breakup is more difficult.

4. **Take responsibility for ending the relationship.** It is important to blame yourself for the reason you want to break up, such as "I am no longer interested in staying together." If you blame your partner, you may feel obligated to continue the relationship if your partner agrees to change. For example, if you say, "You drink too much," your partner can reply "I have stopped drinking and joined AA."

5. **Unless there are children, cut off the relationship with your former partner completely.** While you may wish to continue spending time with or talking to your ex-partner, doing so will have different consequences depending on whether you are the "dumper" or "dumpee." If you are

---

Romantic Breakup—Difficult Loss or Not?

This research focused on identifying the profiles of those who adjust with relative ease to a romantic loss and breakup and those who do not.

Sample and Methods

A convenience sample of 286 from a large southeastern university completed a voluntary, anonymous 36-item online survey on romantic breakups. The sample was 80% female, 76% White, and 90% heterosexual. Results from multivariate analyses follow.

Findings–Who Broke the Relationship?

About 48% of the broken romances were ended by the respondent, 29% by the partner, and 22% by mutual agreement. Person to person was the means by which the highest percent—46%—reported that their relationship ended. Other means by which the relationships were terminated included 32% by text

message and 20% by phone. Virtually no respondent—less than 1%—reported that their relationship ended via an email or a post on a social network site.

Findings–Positive and Negative Reactions

The most frequent positive outcomes for a romantic breakup and the percent experiencing them included a range of emotions: Sixty percent felt a sense of relief; 53%, a sense of freedom; 42%, no longer anxious; and 42%, happy.

The most frequent negative outcomes and the percent experiencing them included 68% who felt sadness, 34%, jealousy, 30%, loss of self-esteem, and 30%, anxiety. The mean number of the five positive outcomes tallied was 1.85 (*SD* = 1.37) and the mean number of 16 negative outcomes tallied was 3.4 (*SD* = 3.15), suggesting relatively low variety in the number of breakup outcomes identified by respondents.

Profile of Respondents Who Have an Easier Adjustment to a Romantic Breakup

Respondents who were female, Black, the initiator of the breakup, and heterosexual were more likely to report having had an easier adjustment to the romantic breakup. Multivariate analyses suggested that being the initiator of the breakup was a key predictor associated with more favorable breakup outcomes.

Symbolic Interaction Theoretical Framework

Symbolic interaction is an overarching theory which may be helpful in conceptualizing the process of adjusting to a romantic breakup. This theory posits that the participants in a broken romance are actors in a symbolic world who give meaning to each other's behavior. Human behavior can be understood only by the meaning attributed to behavior. The term *symbolic interaction* refers to the process of interpersonal interaction and includes two major concepts—the definition of the situation and the looking-glass self.

In regard to the definition of the situation, partners going through a romantic breakup transition from a definition of being lovers to being each others' ex. About half of the respondents initiated the breakup so they defined the relationship as ending and socialized the partner to adopt this new definition. In one third of the cases, the partner socialized the respondent that the relationship was breaking and in a fourth of the cases, the partners shared the same definition that the relationship was soon to break.

A second concept of symbolic interaction theory is the looking-glass self whereby the individuals in the relationship see an image of themselves reflected by those in a relationship with them. For the person who initiates the romantic breakup, this means replacing the message to the partner from "I love you and our relationship" to "Our relationship isn't working out and I want us to stop seeing each other." Hence, the partner sees a new reflected image which morphs from being together to being apart.

Summary

The overall results emphasize that breaking up is hard to do—over two thirds of the respondents reported that they felt sad that their romantic relationship was over. But reaction to one's romantic breakup and loss was variable—there were no "one-size-fits-all" patterns. While some were devastated by a romantic loss, over half felt relief and freedom. The perceived impact of a breakup differed based on demographic variables, but the evidence generally suggested the potential for high commonality. Participants suggested that being patient and giving oneself time to heal were important aids to recovery from the loss. Being selective in their thoughts such as focusing on the partner's negatives and reminding oneself why the relationship ended, involvement with a new partner, and being open to support from one's friends were valuable to heartbreak healing.

Source: Based on Hilliard, T., Carter, K. R., D. Knox, and S. Hall. 2019. *Romantic breakup: Difficult loss for some but not for others.* Poster, Southern Sociological Society annual meeting, Atlanta, April 10-14.

the person who ended the relationship—that is, the dumper—it will be easier for you to transition into a friendship without difficulty. However, the other person, the dumpee, will heal faster if he or she does not see you again. This will also limit any hope he or she might have for reconciliation. In the end, it's usually better for both parties to stop all communication. Of course, if you are parents, continuing the relationship with your partner is necessary and important for the sake of your child.

6. **Learn from the terminated relationship.** Among the reasons for ending a relationship are those of being too controlling; being oversensitive, jealous, or too picky; cheating; fearing commitment; or being unable to compromise and negotiate conflict. Since few

breakups are completely one person's fault, you might consider acknowledging your own contribution to the breakup and working on your own behaviors. For example, did you criticize your partner on a frequent basis or rarely compromise? These issues might be a source of problems in future relationships, if you do not address them.

7. **Allow time to heal.** Ending a love relationship is painful and will take time to heal. Recovering from a breakup or divorce often takes 12 to 18 months. Focusing on the negative qualities of the former partner and relationship and becoming involved with a new partner will help speed the recovery.

8. **Use social media wisely.** Be cautious about not only how you use social media, but what you've previously posted online. Exes may

post nasty things about their former partner on social media, which can complicate the breakup. These posts may be viewed by an ex's lawyer. Additionally, it may be wise to remove any incriminating photos that could be used in court.

It may also be best to avoid a former partner's social media accounts. Facebook has a feature called "take a break" which helps the individual to stop looking at a former partner's posts. Similarly, you can unfollow an ex on Instagram or Twitter.

MACRO FACTORS CONTRIBUTING TO DIVORCE

Sociologists emphasize that social context creates outcome. This concept is best illustrated by the fact that from 1639 to 1760, the Puritans in Massachusetts averaged only one divorce per year (Morgan, 1944). The social context of that era involved strong pro-family values and strict divorce laws, with the result that divorce was almost nonexistent for over 100 years. In contrast, divorce occurs more frequently today as a result of various structural and cultural factors, also known as macro factors.

Economic Factors Associated With Divorce

Marriages and families exist in an economic context. The pursuit of money creates exhaustion and irritability; the lack of money creates frustration and conflict. Arguing over who spends how much on what can become a drumbeat when economic resources are low. Unemployment exacerbates an already strained relationship and is associated with decreased marital satisfaction and divorce (Killewald, 2016).

How does the wife being economically independent impact the chance of her ending the marriage? For the happily married woman, there is no effect. But if she is unhappy and economically independent, she is more likely to file for divorce (Kesselring & Bremmer, 2006). Amount of education is also associated with divorce. Brons and Harkonen (2018) analyzed the association between parental education and family dissolution in 17 European countries. In most countries, with the exception of the United Kingdom, having highly educated parents was either not related to the risk of family dissolution or predicted higher dissolution risk. Two explanations are that higher educated individuals are often more liberal—and therefore, are more open to divorce— and they can afford more of the costs associated with divorce.

Changing Family Functions and Structure

Many of the protective, religious, educational, and recreational functions of the family have been largely taken over by outside agencies. Family members may now look to the police for protection; places of worship for meaning; the school for education; and commercial recreational facilities for fun. The result is that, although meeting emotional needs remains an important and primary function of the family, fewer reasons exist to keep a family together.

The structure of the family has also changed. The historical family structure has shifted from that of a larger extended family in a rural community to a smaller nuclear family in an urban community. In the former, individuals could turn to a lot of people in times of stress; today, more stress necessarily falls on fewer shoulders. This change in family structure is partially caused by increased mobility among individuals.

When individuals are highly mobile, they have fewer roots in a community and greater anonymity. Spouses who move away from their respective families and friends, often for employment, may discover that they are surrounded by strangers who don't care if they stay married or not. Their kin may not live close enough to provide support or express their disapproval for the breakup of a marriage. With fewer social consequences for divorce, Americans are more willing to escape unhappy unions.

Liberal Divorce Laws

Until the late sixties, divorce could only be permitted if one spouse was to be found "at fault." California became the first state granting no-fault divorce in 1969. Family courts now grant a divorce for reasons including "irreconcilable differences," which is code for any reason the spouses dream up, without proving any fault on the part of the other spouse. All states recognize some form of **no-fault divorce** in which neither party is identified as the guilty party or the cause of the divorce—for example, adultery.

Divorce is typically granted after a period of separation. In most states this is between six and 12 months during which the spouses are no longer living in the same place. However, Alaska, South Dakota, and Washington allow spouses to file for divorce immediately with no period of separation. The goal of no-fault divorce is to make divorce less acrimonious. However, this objective has not been achieved as spouses who divorce may still fight over custody of the children, child support, spouse support, and division of property.

....

No-fault divorce: neither party is identified as the guilty party or the cause of the divorce.

Where there is strict social control of divorce, the rates are low. In Saudi Arabia, divorce is low since unhappy wives experience social, economic, psychological, and legal challenges to divorce (Saleh & Luppicini, 2017). "In fact . . . in a society like Saudi Arabia it [divorce] means death [for women]. I hate to say that, but our society is male-oriented, where men have the power in everything," noted one of the respondents who was interviewed.

Compared with other countries, the United States has one of the highest divorce rates in the world. Canada also has a high divorce rate, but Belarus of Eastern Europe has the highest divorce rate in the world. Whether a person gets a divorce has more to do with the society in which the person lives than the "personality" of the person. Prior to 1997, there were no divorces in Ireland; Ireland is predominately Catholic and has historically been staunchly against divorce.

Fewer Religious Sanctions

While previously some churches denied membership to the divorced, today many priests and clergy recognize that divorce may be the best alternative. Churches increasingly embrace single and divorced or separated individuals, as evidenced by divorce adjustment groups which they offer.

Beginning in 2015 Pope Francis recommended annulments via the Catholic Church be expedited from 18 months to 45 days. About half of all annulments sought by Catholics are sought by citizens of the United States. These annulments impact the perception of church law, so a Catholic who gets an annulment is free to remarry, remain in good standing with the Catholic Church, and is for example still able to take communion. Annulments granted by the Catholic Church have no effect on the legal marital status of a couple.

More Divorce Models

The prevalence of divorce today means that most individuals know someone who is divorced. The more divorced people a person knows, the more normative divorce will seem to that person. The less deviant the person perceives divorce to be, the greater the probability the person will divorce if that person's own marriage becomes strained.

Students sometimes fear that because their parents are divorced, that they are doomed to have a divorce themselves. Earlier we noted that about a third of undergraduates experience the divorce of their parents (Hall & Knox, 2019). Of course, one is not doomed to repeat the divorce behavior of one's parents. Rather, the offspring of divorced parents can "reverse model" which means a focused dedication to learn from parental mistakes and commit oneself not to repeat the pattern. The classic example of reverse modeling is that if one's parents are alcoholics, one can focus on controlling one's own alcohol behavior.

Ethnicity and Culture

Asian Americans and Mexican Americans have lower divorce rates than other Americans because the former consider the family unit to be of greater value—familism—than their individual interests—individualism. Unlike familistic values in Asian cultures, individualistic values in American culture emphasize the goal of personal happiness in marriage. When individualistic goals are no longer met, spouses sometimes feel no reason to stay married. Of 12,756 undergraduates, only 9% agreed that "I would not divorce my spouse for any reason" (Hall & Knox, 2019).

MICRO FACTORS CONTRIBUTING TO DIVORCE

Macro factors create the social context for divorce which results in greater acceptance of divorce. Micro factors are the behaviors spouses engage in which result in the partners wanting to end the relationship. First, we discuss the top 20 factors associated with divorce. We then discuss some of these factors in greater detail.

Growing Apart

A reason spouses often give for deciding to divorce is "growing apart." The individuals report that they no longer had anything in common. Spouses cease to view each other as sources of fun, life enhancement, sex, and no longer enjoy being together. One of the respondents in a study on reasons for divorce described the apathy of her husband:

> I asked him if he wanted to go to the seaside together. We hadn't been for 2 years already. He simply looked at me weirdly, closed the door and left (Klobucar & Simonic, 2017).

Depression

While depression may follow the decision to divorce, it may also be a precursor to divorce.

Fowler and Gasiorek (2017) found that for both men and women, depression was a negative predictor of self-reported relationship maintenance. Duncan et al. (2018) also found that spouses experiencing depressive symptoms were more inclined to have negative views of their marriage. When a partner is depressed, he or she is less communicative, less affirming, and less engaging with the partner. The effect on the partner is often to withdraw and no longer feel valued by the other. The negative cycle spins the couple toward further emotional distance.

Limited Time Together

This further emotional distance expresses itself in spouses not making time to be together or nurture their relationship. Time devoted to children and career interferes with couple time. Partners who spend little time together doing things they mutually enjoy often feel estranged from each other and have little motivation to stay together. However, how much time spouses need or prefer to be together to define their relationship as nurturing and fulfilling varies. Actors and musicians are constantly on the road making movies or giving concerts. Individuals and their partners negotiate what works for them.

Low Frequency of Positive Behavior

People marry because they anticipate greater rewards from being married than from being single. During courtship, each partner engages in a high frequency of positive verbal and nonverbal behavior such as compliments and physical affection toward the other. The good feelings the partners experience as a result of these positive behaviors encourage them to marry to "lock in" these feelings across time. Just as love feelings are based on partners making the choice to engage in a high frequency of positive behavior toward each other, negative feelings result when these positive behaviors stop and negative behaviors begin.

To ensure that one's relationship continues to be positive, the "magic ratio" 5:1 has received national attention. This magic ratio was proposed by the well-known scholar Dr. John Gottman after decades of research. The 5 to 1 ratio means for every one criticism to one's partner, there must be five compliments. Gottman has advised couples to stay in the 5:1 ratio in order to keep their relationship on the positive side.

Extramarital Relationships

Of U.S. adults who are divorced, 40% reported that they had cheated on their spouse (Wang, 2018). When unhappy spouses compare the joy of being with a new partner, divorce becomes an option. Alternatively, some spouses are not unhappy in their marriage but surprised by the comparative bump in excitement or joy they feel with a new partner. One man who divorced said, "I traded something good for something new."

Poor Communication and Conflict Resolution Skills

Managing differences and conflict in a relationship helps to reduce the negative feelings that develop in a relationship. Some partners respond to conflict by withdrawing emotionally from their relationship; others respond by attacking, blaming, and failing to listen to their partner's point of view. We discussed conflict resolution in detail in Chapter 8.

Changing Values

Both spouses change throughout the marriage. "He's not the same person I married" is a frequent observation of people contemplating divorce. One minister married and decided seven years later that he did not like the confines of his religious or marital role. He left the ministry, earned a PhD, and began to drink and have affairs. His wife now found that she was married to a man who spent his evenings at bars with other women. The couple divorced.

Because people change throughout their lives, the person selected at one point in life may not be the same partner one would select at another point. Margaret Mead, the famous anthropologist, noted that her first marriage was a student marriage; her second, a professional partnership; and her third, an intellectual marriage to her soul mate, with whom she had her only child. At each of several stages in her life, she experienced a different set of needs and selected a mate who fulfilled those needs.

Onset of Satiation

Satiation, also referred to as habituation, refers to the state in which a stimulus loses its value with repeated exposure. Spouses may tire of each other. Their stories are no longer new, their sex is repetitive, and their presence for each other is no longer exciting as it was at the beginning of the relationship. Some people who feel trapped by the boredom of constancy

....

Satiation: a stimulus loses its value with repeated exposure (e.g., lovers tire of each other if around each other all the time).

decide to divorce and seek what they believe to be more excitement by returning to singlehood and new partners.

A **developmental task** of marriage is for couples to enjoy being together and not demand a constant state of excitement, which is not possible over a 50-year period. If spouses did not expect so much of marriage, maybe they would not be disappointed.

Unequal Housework

Ruppanner et al. (2018) examined unequal housework among 1,057 Swedish couples and found that women who reported performing more housework were less satisfied with their relationships and were more likely to divorce. Similarly, when the woman's housework contribution was discredited, there was an association with less relationship satisfaction and higher divorce.

In-Laws

Respondents in the study on reasons for divorce by Klobucar and Simonic (2017) also mentioned in-laws, specifically their control and intrusiveness, as factors in divorce. One wife noted:

> He was under the influence of his parents, and they interfered in everything. He didn't have his own opinion. He kept on going home, he'd first visit his mom and converse with her, not with me. I never felt accepted or included and the strain just increased among us all.

Having Positive Perceptions About Divorce

One of the reasons for divorce is that spouses feel they will be happier if they dump their partners. Women may feel that they will achieve greater power over their own life—they will have their own money in the form of child support or alimony or both without having a man they don't want in the house. In addition, they will have greater control over their children since women are more often awarded custody. Men may feel that they will be happier by escaping a house in chaos and will be free to have sex with new partners.

CONSEQUENCES OF DIVORCE FOR SPOUSES

Regardless of the various factors associated with divorce, there is debate about the character of people who divorce. Are they selfish, amoral people who

Developmental task: a skill that, if mastered, allows an individual to grow and complete other tasks.

Divorce is a mess. One feels as though he or she is underwater, drowning, and wondering if he or she will ever recover.

are incapable of following through on their wedding vows to each other and who wreck the lives of their children? Or are they individuals who care a great deal about marriage and won't settle for a bad one? Indeed, these individuals may divorce precisely because they value marriage and want to rescue their children from being reared in an unhappy home wrought with conflict.

Divorce can be devastating. Love et al. (2018) revealed that thoughts of suicide are sometimes associated with marital dissolution. Data from 66 in-depth interviews of spouses age 50 and older (**gray divorce**), revealed a mixed reaction to divorce. Negative reactions included financial worries and loneliness. Positive reactions included higher overall levels of happiness, joy at being liberated from the ex-spouse, and enjoying enhanced independence and freedom (Crowley, 2019a).

Divorce is also associated with a decrease in psychological and physical well-being for both women and men (Zella, 2016). However, most adjust to a divorce. In a study of adjustment to divorce from long-term marriages, those over 25 years, the researchers found that about 80% of the 306 respondents were satisfactorily adjusted with a new spouse or cohabiting partner. Those individuals who had resilient and adaptive personalities were the most likely to rebound (Perrig-Chiello et al., 2015).

Lawson and Satti (2016) noted that there is a stereotype of the divorced heterosexual female as "passive, inactive, and despairing victims waiting to be rescued by Prince Charming." However, their research on divorced Black and White women in the United States revealed that they are resilient as they used the coping strategies of keeping busy, relying on family support, and being involved in religious and spiritual activities.

Other gender differences have been noted. Compared to women, men are more likely to be remarry or repartner or, for example, cohabit, and this is especially true among people who are 50 or older (Crowley, 2019). Based on a longitudinal study investigating the economic consequences of divorce in six countries—the United States, the United Kingdom, Switzerland, Germany, Australia, and Korea—men's economic well-being is less negatively affected after divorce (Vaus et. al., 2017). Since same-sex marriages only became legal in 2015, data on same-sex divorces is limited. Hoy (2018) noted that same-sex divorces are less visible than heterosexual divorces resulting in gays and lesbians feeling misunderstood.

Dwelling on a Previous Relationship

Sometimes it is difficult to get over a partner. Even if someone feels that he or she is over the divorce, he or she may still be emotionally tied to his or her former partner. Brenner and Vogel (2014) emphasized that successful recovery from a terminated romantic relationship is related to being selective about one's thoughts—not dwelling on positive memories of the former relationship, such as "we were such good friends and loved each other" but focusing on negative aspects of the relationship like "cheating, drug abuse, and disrespect." The Self-Assessment on page 394 provides a way to assess the degree to which one is selective in reviewing one's past relationship.

Individuals who define themselves solely in reference to their former partner experience more difficulty in getting over the relationship and moving on. These individuals may also use social media to find out current information about the former partner's involvement in a new relationship, which is often an unhealthy behavior (Tong, 2013).

Financial Consequences

Both women and men experience a drop in income following divorce but women typically suffer more. Leopold (2018) examined gender differences for divorce reported by 1,222 respondents and found that the major difference was economic, specifically women's disproportionate losses in household income and associated increases in their risk of poverty and single parenting.

Because men usually have greater financial resources, they may take all they can with them when they leave the marriage. The only money they may continue to give to an ex-wife is court-ordered child support or spousal support, also called alimony. But payments may not be forthcoming. Only about 40% of court-ordered child support is paid and collected (Cuzzolino & Williams, 2017). Beginning January 1, 2019, the party paying alimony may no longer take these payments as a deduction on their taxes (Gregg, 2018). However, the partner receiving the money is to pay taxes on the money received. Regardless of who pays taxes on the alimony, increasingly the ex-husband may receive alimony though women most often receive alimony.

Most states permit some type of alimony. There are five types of alimony. One is called pendente lite alimony, also referred to as **temporary alimony**, which is the support paid to a former spouse from the time of separation until the time the divorce agreement is settled in the court.

A second type of alimony is **rehabilitative alimony**, which is designed to provide funds for the former spouses while they pursue increased education or training, presumably to be able to obtain a job or source of income. Rehabilitative alimony is most often granted to the former wife who took care of the children rather than pursue education or a career. Most types of alimony are of the temporary or rehabilitative alimony. **Reimbursement alimony** is related to rehabilitative alimony, which means former spouses are compensated for giving up their own careers to help the occupational advancement of their spouses.

A third type of alimony is **lump sum alimony** with the spouse getting money at the time of the divorce to promote resource equality. Finally, in

Temporary alimony: money one spouse is to pay the other until the divorce is finalized.

Rehabilitative alimony: money the dependent spouse is to receive to fund education or training to increase one's capacity to earn an income.

Reimbursement alimony: the former wife is compensated since she gave up her own career to help the occupational advancement of her husband.

Lump sum alimony: a onetime amount provided at the time of the divorce to promote resource equality.

some states, judges can order **permanent alimony** for spouses who were married a very long time (e.g., 25 years) and who gave up their earning capacity to support their spouses. This amount is typically due until the spouse receiving support remarries or the spouse giving support retires. Alimony may terminate when the ex-spouse remarries or cohabits or the ex-spouse paying the alimony retires and, therefore, has more limited income.

How money is divided at divorce depends on whether the couple had a prenuptial agreement or a **postnuptial agreement.** Such agreements are most likely to be upheld if an attorney insists on four conditions—full disclosure of assets by both parties, independent representation by separate counsel, absence of coercion or duress, and terms that are fair and equitable.

Fathers' Separation From Children

Obama noted, "I know what it is to grow up without a father." Some divorcing fathers also lament the loss of their children. Mercadante et al. (2014) studied fathers going through divorce in Western Australia and found that they were "at an emotional disadvantage during separation, not only grieving the loss of their former marital relationship, but also their simultaneous loss of contact with their children, their fathering role, and their former family routine."

While fathers in the United States are also disadvantaged, they have a choice of how involved they want to be with their children postdivorce. Most judges today recognize the value of the father for children and provide joint or full custody if warranted. But fathers must be aggressive and insist on a legal contract which gives them equal legal and physical custody. Otherwise, they may be cut out of the lives of their children. Carlson et al. (2017) found that nonresidential fathers who provided more economic resources for their children also spent more time with them. The reverse was also true—less economic support was associated with less time with their children.

What about fathers who are actively involved in the lives of their children predivorce and who get joint custody following divorce? Andresson and Johansson (2019) noted that Swedish fathers with this situation lament that they end up being in the role of parent less than they want. Often it is the structural barriers such as the need to work rather than being legally restricted from access to their children that is the culprit for these divorced fathers.

....

Permanent alimony: for the wife who was married a very long time and who gave up her earning capacity to support her husband.

Postnuptial agreement: an agreement about how money is to be divided should a couple later divorce, which is made after the couple marry.

Parental Alienation

More involvement on the part of the father reduces the opportunity for parental alienation syndrome to manifest itself. **Parental alienation syndrome** (PAS) is an alleged disturbance in which children are obsessively preoccupied with deprecation, criticism, or both kinds of disparaging remarks of a parent, a denigration that is unjustified and can also be exaggerated (Gardner, 1998). While **parental alienation** is not a medical psychosis with specific criteria, it can be defined as an alliance between a parent—either the mother or the father—and a child that isolates the other parent (Godbout & Parent, 2012). In some cases, one parent may accuse the other of child abuse, often sexual abuse, as a means of getting custody.

Examples of behaviors that either parent may engage in to alienate a child from the other parent include talking negatively to the child about the other parent, being unable to tolerate the physical presence of the other parent, and showing no interest in the child's activities when the child is with the other parent. Children are often oblivious to the fact that they have been brainwashed and think it is "normal" that they have negative feelings toward one or both of their parents. Indeed, while they are aware that one parent hates the other, they can't make the connection to their own negative feelings. Such children are similar to those who have been brainwashed by cult leaders to view outsiders negatively.

How the "other spouse" responds when the victim of having one's children alienated from them has been the subject of research. Hartman (2019) noted the costs for men of "taking the high road," which means not "involving the children" when the former wife turned the children against him. The dilemma involves such issues as: (1) Not telling the true story of the divorce is often perceived by children and the men themselves as telling a lie, (2) Fear of inappropriately burdening children with divorce details may stifle communication with the children, (3) In never blaming Mom, a man may become emotionally unknowable to his children, (4) A narrative of the divorce will emerge for the children, but without the father's perspective it will be a distorted narrative, and (5) Not speaking truthfully with the kids when they are young may severely limit subsequent discussions of the divorce when they are adults. These are difficult issues for which there are no easy answers.

....

Parental alienation syndrome: an alleged disturbance in which children are obsessively preoccupied with deprecation or criticism or both of a parent; denigration that is unjustified or exaggerated or both.

Parental alienation: estrangement of a child from a parent due to one parent turning the child against the other.

Reversing parental alienation has been addressed by professionals with little agreement. Mercer (2019) reviewed some of the treatments for PAS which included court-ordered separation of the child from the preferred parent and noted a negative impact on the child. What is often not considered is that the child may independently want limited contact with a parent for legitimate reasons such as abuse. Coping with and reversing PA remains a personal and professional challenge. The best antidote to parental alienation syndrome is spending time with one's children and allowing children to discover for themselves who their parents are and how their parents feel about them. Regardless of what a former spouse says to their children about their parent, the reality of how parents treat their children will determine how children feel about them.

Being Friends With a Former Partner

What about staying friends with one's former partner? Mogilski and Welling (2016) examined the nature of the relationship with one's former partner in two studies of 348 and 513 participants respectively. The primary reasons for staying friends were that the former partner was regarded as reliable and trustworthy. Reasons of less importance were pragmatism and sex, with men more often maintaining the relationship for these reasons. The researchers concluded that maintaining connections with a former partner provides an opportunity for former partners to exchange desirable resources after the romance has gone, such as love, sex, information, and money.

Name Change

Although it is not mandatory for the bride or the groom, many American women and some men as well choose to take their spouse's last name after marriage. What should one do after divorce? Hoffnung and Williams (2016) observed that of 185 divorced women who had changed to their husband's name when they married, 51% changed their name back after the divorce. Those who were younger, had more education, had been married fewer years, and who had fewer children were more likely to change their name back after divorce.

Sexual Values

Emotional heartbreak is associated with changes in sexual values. Analysis of data on 286 never married undergraduates who reported having experienced one or more romantic breakups revealed significant changes in regard to becoming more liberal in their sexual values. Specifically, respondents who were absolutist became more relativistic and those who were relativistic became more hedonistic (Hilliard et al., 2019). While a romantic breakup may be less traumatic than a divorce, these findings are suggestive for the impact of divorce on subsequent sexual values.

CONSEQUENCES OF DIVORCE FOR CHILDREN

The act of separation and divorce of one's parents is a major adverse childhood experience (ACE; Soares et al., 2016). In a study of 3,951 adolescents, when seven types of ACEs were identified—physical abuse, sexual abuse, physical neglect, emotional neglect, domestic violence, parental separation, and parental death—the most common, registering 42% in the study, was parental separation. Most of the research on divorce outcomes for children have been conducted on young children. An exception is research by Watkins and Waldron (2017) who surveyed 577 male and female youth over the age of 26. They found that parental divorce during the time children are emerging adults increases the risk for depression at age 26. Shimkowski et al. (2018) surveyed 401 undergraduates and noted that those with divorced parents were less close with their parents than those whose parents were still married.

Did the Children See the Divorce Coming?

Abetz and Wang (2017) asked adult children whose parents had divorced how they viewed their parents' marriage before they became aware of the divorce. Most had very positive views of their parents' marriage and were surprised that about the divorce. One respondent noted:

> I would have considered them pretty solid—not somebody you would have thought who would have gotten divorced. I mean they had arguments and you know what I would have considered the normal course of a relationship, but nothing that was ever in my opinion to that level that would have led to that [divorce].

Estrangement and Other Negative Outcomes

Above we discussed parental alienation from one's children as a potential consequence of divorce. Not only is the parent deprived of the relationship with

TABLE 15.1

Positive Outcomes of Divorce: Percentage of Undergraduate Agreement

	%
Since my parents' divorce, I am more compassionate for people who are going through a difficult time.	65.63%
I have greater tolerance for people with different viewpoints since my parents' divorce.	63.16%
Since my parents' divorce, I have been exposed to different family values, traditions, and lifestyles.	60.01%
I have liked spending time alone with my mother since my parents' divorce.	57.71%
My mother is happier since the divorce.	57.20%
I rely less on my parents for making decisions since my parents' divorce.	53.51%
I have liked spending time alone with my father since my parents' divorce.	45.61%
My mother has made a greater effort to spend quality time with me since the divorce.	45.61%
I can spend more time with the parent I prefer since my parents' divorce.	45.37%
Since my parents' divorce, I have felt closer to my mother.	44.98%
My relationship with my mother has improved since my parents' divorce.	44.74%
My father is happier since the divorce.	43.85%

Source: Halligan, C., I. J. Chang, and D. Knox. 2014. Positive effects of parental divorce on undergraduates. *Journal of Divorce and Remarriage,* 55: 557-567.

their child, children are also cut off from the relationship with a parent. Beebe and Sailor (2017) found that children were typically alienated from their noncustodial parent by the custodial parent and reported feelings of anger, disappointment, and isolation.

Estrangement may also happen after a divorce. **Estrangement** is defined as one or more relatives intentionally choosing to end contact because of an ongoing negative relationship. About 8% of adults in a British study reported that they had ended a relationship with a family member, such as a child ending a relationship with parent or vice versa (Louis, 2017). But estrangement may happen later in life—for example, parents may disapprove of the mate choice of their son or daughter, cut them out of the will, and never see them again. Adult children can also grow weary of parental control and end the relationship with their parents.

Jackson and Fife (2018) noted that parental divorce may strain the relationships with children and lead to other negative consequences for their child, such as reducing their confidence in their own romantic relationships. Saether (2019) noted that grade performance of children drops not when their parents divorce but from the deterioration of family

....

Estrangement: one or more relatives intentionally choosing to end contact with each other because of an ongoing negative relationship.

relations before the break. College students whose parents divorce are also less likely to graduate (Soria et al., 2018). The explanation may be that divorce is associated with fewer economic resources for the education of the children. In addition, the emotional and structural needs of the parents may also serve as a distraction to children and their educational trajectory.

Positive Outcomes

Based on an analysis of data from 336 undergraduates who were asked to identify positive outcomes they experienced from the divorce of their parents, Table 15.1 provides the percentages "agreeing" or "strongly agreeing" with various positive outcomes (Halligan et al., 2014).

Table 15.1 also reflects that children of divorce may choose to notice the positive aspects of divorce rather than buy into the cultural script that their lives are ruined by their parents' divorce. Given that divorce may have positive consequences for children, spouses in a highly conflictual, loveless marriages should NOT stay married for the children (Gager et al., 2016).

Although the degree to which divorcing parents are civil is a major factor that determines the effect of divorce on children, legal and physical custody are important issues. The following section details how judges go about making this decision.

Child Custody

Judges assigned to hear child custody cases make a judicial determination regarding whether one or both parents will have decisional authority on major issues affecting the children—called **legal custody**—and the distribution of parenting time, called visitation or **physical custody**.

Most people are familiar with sole custody, which means one parent has both the physical and legal custody of the child. But there are two different types of joint custody. In joint legal custody, both parents can make major decisions, such as about medical treatment. The joint legal custody does not require the child to reside with both parents. In joint physical custody, the child will live with both parents with the time split between the two of them. Many fathers do not know that join legal custody is a possibility.

As men have become more involved in the role of father, the courts no longer assume that "parent" means "mother." Indeed, a new **family relations doctrine** has emerged which suggests that even nonbiological parents, such as stepparents, may be awarded custody or visitation rights if they have been economically and emotionally involved in the life of the child. While most parents can make the decision about custody, Waller and Dwyer Emory (2018) noted that high-conflict parents involve the court to work out custody and visitation orders.

Toward this end, judges in all states are guided by the statutory dictum called "best interests of the child." Factors involved in deciding custody include the child's age, sex, and relationship with both parents. What is each parent's capacity to care for the child . . . and what previous parenting behavior demonstrates this? If the child is age 6 or older, the judge may interview the child about his or her preference. The judge may also assign a custody evaluator to interview the child, assess the child's situation and write a recommendation. This recommendation, along with the factors of the child's age, sex, and relationship with the parents, will become the basis for the judge's custody determination. In some cases, joint custody may be awarded.

....

Legal custody: judicial decision regarding whether one or both parents will have decisional authority on major issues affecting the children.

Physical custody: the distribution of parenting time between divorced spouses.

Family relations doctrine: belief that even nonbiological parents may be awarded custody or visitation rights if they have been economically and emotionally involved in the life of the child.

Shared Parenting

New terminology is making its way into the lives of divorcing spouses and in the courts. The term *joint custody*, which implies ownership, is being replaced with *shared parenting*, which implies cooperation in taking care of children. Indeed, when fathers get custody or there is a shared residence agreement where the children spend equal amounts of time in each parent's residence, the children get much greater access to both parents. One of the respondents from the Sigurdardottier et al. (2018) interviews about his or her experience with ETSA (equal time-sharing arrangements) as a child noted:

> *The advantages are mainly to spend equal time with both. I think about children who stay only during the weekend and do not feel a sense of belonging, like a part of the home, but when you stay for a week it is like being home, you have your own room and your own space.*

There are several advantages to shared parenting. First, ex-spouses may fight less because there is no inequity in their involvement in their children's lives and the stress of parenting doesn't fall on one parent. As a result, their children may benefit from the decrease in hostility between parents. Through shared parenting, children might also have greater financial resources available to them than children in sole-custody homes. Finally, Xu et al. (2016) emphasized the importance of the father staying involved in the lives of his children when divorce ensues.

Unlike sole-parent custody, in which one parent, usually the mother, "wins" and the other parent "loses," joint custody allows children to continue to benefit from the love and attention of both parents. Marschall (2017) interviewed children whose parents had divorced and who had joint custody. The researcher concluded "in most cases, post-divorced family life is quite a peaceful matter and children's time-shared everyday lives seem to be something they mostly manage." In a review of 60 outcome studies, children tended to benefit from joint over single-parent custody following a divorce (Nielsen, 2018). Braver and Votruba (2018) confirmed the positive outcomes of joint parental sharing.

A disadvantage of joint custody is that it tends to put hostile ex-spouses in more frequent contact with each other, and the marital war continues. Mahrer et al. (2018) reviewed the studies on high-conflict shared parenting for divorcing parents and concluded that poorer child adjustment results. However, at least one less combative and less hostile parent can mitigate the effect.

Depending on the level of hostility between the ex-partners, their motivations for seeking sole or joint custody, and their relationship with their children, any arrangement can have positive or negative consequences for the ex-spouses as well as for the children. In those cases in which the spouses exhibit minimal hostility toward each other, have strong emotional attachments to their children, and want to remain an active influence in their children's lives, joint custody is the best of all possible choices. The worst choice is the one that cuts a parent from the child's life.

Minimizing Negative Effects of Divorce on Children

Most spouses going through divorce experience a range of emotions which dissipate after a couple of years. About 20% of divorces are **high-conflict divorces** which last longer than two years and are characterized by a "high degree of anger, hostility, and distrust, intensive custody litigation, ongoing difficulty in communicating about the care of their children, and higher than usual rates of nonpayment of child support" (Haddad et al., 2016). A team of researchers (DeAnda et al., 2017) analyzed data of 319 mothers and their children over 24 months and found that continued negative emotional attachment with the former spouse, such as anger, was associated with their children's behavior problems.

Other research has confirmed that a high-conflict divorce is considered an adverse childhood event and the outcome for children is similar to other types of child abuse— psychological distress, poorer health, more medications for anxiety and depression, and so forth. Gager et al. (2016) confirmed that it is the conflict between parents that has the devastating effect on children, including teaching them to be conflictual in their own relationships, which sets them up for their own divorce as adults. Researchers have also found that former spouses are likely to have hostile attribution bias toward each other, which is a tendency to interpret each other's behavior and intention as hostile (Reinstein, 2018). This bias may affect how former partners talk about each other to their children.

Divorcing spouses should endeavor to avoid a high-conflict divorce and a hostile attribution bias. Researchers have identified the following conditions under which a divorce has the fewest negative consequences for children:

1. **Healthy parental psychological functioning.** Children of divorced parents benefit to the degree that their parents remain

psychologically fit and positive, and socialize their children to view the divorce as a "challenge to learn from."

2. **A cooperative relationship between the parents and consistent "house rules."** The most important factor in a child's positive adjustment to divorce is the parents' commitment to be friendly and civil with each other throughout the separation, divorce, and postdivorce period. It is not divorce, but an acrimonious post-divorce relationship between the parents that has a negative effect on children. Bitter parental conflict places the children in the middle. One daughter of divorced parents said, "My father told me, 'If you love me, you would come visit me,' but my mom told me, 'If you love me, you won't visit him.'" When, how, what, and why co-parents communicate with each other are influenced by factors such as relationship with the former partner, the child, custody arrangement, and the new partners (Markham et al., 2017). Note that new partners of the former spouses may shoulder different levels of parenting responsibilities and their involvement can further complicate the divorcing couple's relationship and their co-parenting dynamics.

Co-parenting relationships can benefit from consistent house rules or rules that both parents follow. A cooperative co-parenting postdivorce pattern assumes not demonizing or talking negatively about the other parent. Kang and Ganong (2018) studied how divorced parents go about deciding what to tell their children. Their own parenting philosophy and knowledge of professional thinking were major determinants of deciding what to disclose. One parent of two children said, "Another thing that we sort of did was just no negative talk about the other parent, ever." Rules like this can create a more positive environment for one's children.

Co-parenting involves facing new challenges. Numerous states mandate parenting classes as part of the divorce process. While there is 100% agreement among professionals in regard to the importance of divorcing parents developing and maintaining a positive relationship, training programs for ex-spouses to be effective co-parents are difficult to find and obtain in one's area. One alternative is an online course such as Successful Co-Parenting After Divorce (https://coparenting.fsu.edu/; Ferraro et al., 2016).

3. **Parental attention to the children and allowing them to express their displeasure over the divorce.** Children benefit when

High conflict divorce: divorce which lasts longer than two years and is characterized by continued anger, hostility, litigation, and higher rates of nonpayment of child support.

both parents continue to spend time with them and to communicate to them that they love them and are interested in them. Parents also need to be aware that their children may not want the divorce and should allow them to say so. "I know that you wish we were all still together as a family" is a reflective statement that acknowledges the child's feelings.

4. **Encouragement to see noncustodial parent.** Children benefit when custodial parents, usually the mothers, encourage their children to maintain regular and consistent contact with the other parent. To the degree that children of divorcing parents are allowed to continue uninterrupted access to each parent, the children flourish and the negative effects of divorce are mitigated (Lamb, 2018). Fabricius et al. (2018) confirmed the positive outcome of Arizona's child custody statute which assumes that 50/50 access to both parents is good for children.

5. **Attention from the noncustodial parent.** Children benefit when they receive frequent and consistent attention from noncustodial parents, usually the father. Poortman (2018) noted that to the degree that the father was involved with the child prior to the divorce, that same level of continued involvement is associated with the child's well-being. Frequent court-ordered visitation for parents who were not involved with the child before the divorce is not advisable.

6. **Assertion of parental authority.** Children benefit when both parents continue to assert their parental authority and continue to support the discipline practices of each other.

7. **Regular and consistent child support payments.** Support payments, usually from the father to the mother, are associated with economic stability for the child.

8. **Stability.** Not moving and keeping children in the same school system is beneficial to children. Some parents—called **latchkey parents**—spend every other week with the children in the family home so the children do not have to alternate between residences.

Moving to a new location causes children to be cut off from their friends, neighbors, and teachers. It is important to keep their life as stable as possible during a divorce. Thomas et al. (2018) noted that a major effect of divorce for children is that their

parents may no longer live close to each other so that they are without one of the parents for significant periods time. A typical scenario is that one of the parents, usually the father, gets involved with a new partner, moves away, and has children with the new partner, often leaving their other children to feel "left behind."

9. **Age of children of divorce.** There is no simple answer for the "best age" for parents to divorce. The effect of parental divorce is determined by many factors such as level of conflict between the parents, family dynamics, the child's vulnerability, and postdivorce distress. Early adolescence is often a vulnerable time due to the physical, cognitive, and psychosocial changes of adolescents. Although very young children are not aware of the negative cultural meanings of divorce, the early loss of one parent may affect their attachment and later relationship with the nonresidential parent. Adult children may be less vulnerable to parental divorce because they are better able to understand divorce and they are moving into lives of their own.

10. **Parenting Education Program.** Divorcing parents may also benefit from involvement in a formal education program. Galovan and Schramm (2017) analyzed data on divorced 1,540 participants in a PEP (Parenting Education Program) and identified four groups: Thirty-five percent were Angry Associates; 28%, Fiery Foes; 21%, Cooperative Colleagues; and 16%, Perfect Pals. The more difficult and conflictual the relationships before the PEP classes, the greater the gains. Spencer et al. (2018) also found positive gains reported by parents going through divorce who participated in a divorce education program.

Schramm et al. (2018) noted that divorce education programs that focus on stress-reduction adjustment are the most effective for divorcing parents. The researchers reviewed 103 published articles and identified this model as the most effective.

How Late-Life Divorce Impacts Adult Children

Mikucki-Enyart et al. (2017) interviewed 25 adult children of whom 18 were females and seven were males; their parents divorced when they were age 18 or older. Their parents had been married for an average of 27 years. Four themes of reaction to their parents' late-life divorces emerged. One was "parent-adult child

....

Latchkey parents: divorcing parents who spend every other week with the children in the family home so the children do not have to alternate between residences.

uncertainty" in that daughters wondered how their relationship with their father would change. One observed:

> Yeah, now that I think back, I thought that, well, I probably won't ever talk to him [father] or see him much.

Another theme was "parent as individual uncertainty" such as wondering how their individual parents would adjust to their new divorce status. One respondent said:

> I think I was worried about my dad, to be honest, because he was so emotional. I was kind of, I mean, because it's, he was depressed. I was kind of scared that, you know, something might happen, that he might take it to the next level . . .

A third theme was "divorce-related uncertainty," which focused on questions of why their parents were getting divorced and why now? Regarding the latter, one respondent asked:

> Why it took so long? I mean, why didn't you do that earlier, I mean that was my main question I had through the whole thing, why didn't you do this when we were younger? You know, when I was sixteen for crying out loud!!

A final theme was "being a family uncertainty" in terms of who was now included as "family."

> I was a little bit afraid of what does this mean for our family? Are we still gonna, this is November, you know, Christmas is in a month. Like, what does that mean for Christmas?

what does that mean for, all of a sudden, I started to think about the things that were gonna change and it really, I was gonna have to let go of a lot of things I really liked about my life and my relationships. It was depressing.

Some respondents also expressed that the divorce of their parents shattered their perfect image.

> The hardest thing for me is, was, you know, and I'm ashamed to say it, I wasn't more concerned for the welfare of my mother and father. I just didn't like that my perfect family wasn't perfect anymore.

Another insight regarding late-life divorce is that when parents divorce when their children are young, the parents help their children though the divorce. When parents are older and go through divorce, it is the children who help the parents through the divorce (Kutner, 2015).

PREREQUISITES FOR HAVING A "SUCCESSFUL" DIVORCE

Before identifying the various factors involved in a "successful" divorce, we review how technology impacts postdivorce co-parenting.

In addition to using technology to enhance postdivorce co-parenting, the following are some of the behaviors spouses can engage in to achieve a "successful" divorce by minimizing the negative consequences of divorce for their children:

TECHNOLOGY AND THE FAMILY

Postdivorce Co-Parenting

Technology may make divorce more difficult in that people must go through their divorce online. They have to take down their happy family memories from their social media accounts, unfriend former partner's friends, and see new posts of their former partner's new partner and children (Miller, 2019).

However, technology can be helpful in regard to parenting. Even though divorce ends a couple's legal marriage, it does not end the spouse's role as parent. Many ex-spouses co-parent. Whether former spouses live next door, in another city, or in another country, coordinating

their respective schedules requires organization, cooperation, and patience. Researchers have suggested that smartphones and other communication technology can be helpful in co-parenting.

In general, increased communication between individuals typically results in better relationships (Nichols, 2018; Saini & Polak, 2018). Texting, video chat, social media, email, and so forth provide alternatives ways for remote communication. Once a child has a cell phone, the nonresidential parent, often with the approval of the residential parent, can be reached with

(Continued)

(Continued)

a press of a button anywhere anytime. In addition to increasing the ability of the children to be connected to the noncustodial parent, technology may reduce co-parenting conflicts. For example, if the former spouses tend to quarrel and fight in face-to-face or phone conversations, the use of e-mail or text messaging may be helpful. The sender's message cannot be interrupted and the couple may be more civil since the electronic footprint could be used in court.

Mobile apps are also available to enhance co-parenting. Examples include a child-focused communication platform, a shared calendar for coordinating events/visitation schedule, and mechanism to keep a record of expenses (Amelia, 2018; McKinley Irvin Family Law, 2018; Stephens, 2018). OurFamilyWizard is a commonly used court-ordered app which provides a mechanism for tracking communication between parents and coordinating schedules regarding when the children are with which parent.

Effective use of technology is contingent upon the relationship between the former spouses. Shared

parenting for high-conflict divorced families can still be problematic (Mahrer et al., 2018). Contested connectedness involving mobile phone usage has also been observed, especially among high-conflicts couples (Sjöblom et al., 2018). For example, if the residential parent is setting rules for a child's smartphone usage, the nonresidential parent may perceive the action as a gate-keeping behavior and as forbidding the child to connect with the nonresidential parent. If the parents are hostile and not able to co-parent effectively in person, the use of information and communication technology can become another battleground for conflicts.

While divorce terminates a couple's legal relationship as spouses, their role as parent continues. Use of technology can relieve co-parenting tension and give children more autonomy in staying connected with noncustodial parent and families. On the other hand, these new ways for communication may amplify dispute in high-conflict divorce families. ●

1. **Mediate rather than litigate the divorce.** Divorce mediators encourage a civil, cooperative, compromising relationship while moving the couple toward an agreement on the division of property, custody, and child/spousal support. In contrast, attorneys make their money by encouraging hostility so that spouses will prolong the conflict, thus running up higher legal bills. The couple cannot divide money spent on divorce attorneys. The average amount spent is $30,000 for *each* side so a litigated divorce cost will start at $60,000. Spouses who hire an expensive attorney to "destroy" the former partner end up in a protracted court fight where no one wins—the result is less money to split, the ex-spouses develop an intense hatred for each other, and the children must cope with the acrimonious relationship between their parents for years.

Divorce mediation results in a quicker, less expensive divorce with children who are more likely to benefit from an amicable relationship between their parents. Some states require divorce mediation

to encourage parental civility and to clear the court calendar of protracted legal battles. If one of the parties does not "require their day in court" due to revenge or punishment (Sullivan, 2016), divorce mediation should be considered. However, Morris et al. (2018) confirmed the reluctance of divorcing parents to mediate their divorce. Of 524 parents who called about mediation, only a third ended up completing mediation.

The following Family Policy section focuses on divorce mediation.

Divorce mediation is not for every couple. It does not work where there is a history of spouse abuse, where the parties hide their financial information, where one party is controlled by someone else, such as a parent, or where there is the desire for revenge. Mediation should be differentiated from **negotiation** where spouses discuss and resolve the issues themselves; **arbitration** where a third party, an arbitrator, listens to both spouses and decides about custody, division of property, and so on; and **litigation** where

....

Divorce mediation: divorcing spouses meet together with a neutral professional who negotiates child custody, division of property, child support, and alimony.

Negotiation: spouses discuss and resolve the issues of custody, child support, and division of property themselves.

Arbitration: third party listens to both spouses and decides about custody, division of property, child support, and alimony.

Litigation: a judge hears arguments from lawyers representing the respective spouses and decides issues of custody, child support, division of property, and so forth.

Should Divorce Mediation Be Required Before Litigation?

Most states do not require mediation before a divorce is granted. But should they? Divorce mediation is a process in which spouses who have decided to separate or divorce meet with a neutral third party called a mediator to negotiate four issues: (1) how they will parent their children, which is referred to as child custody and visitation; (2) how they are going to financially support their children, referred to as child support; (3) how they are going to divide their property, known as property settlement; and (4) how each one is going to meet his or her financial obligations, referred to as spousal support.

Benefits of Mediation

There are enormous benefits from avoiding litigation and mediating one's divorce:

1. **Better relationship.** Spouses who choose to mediate their divorce have a better chance for a more civil relationship because they cooperate in specifying the conditions of their separation or divorce. Mediation emphasizes negotiation and cooperation between the divorcing partners.

2. **Economic benefits.** Mediation costs about $8,000 in contrast to $60,000 if attorneys are retained who benefit by dragging out the litigation process for years.

3. **Less time-consuming process.** Whereas a litigated divorce can take two to three years, a mediated divorce takes two to three months. For highly motivated individuals, a mediated settlement can take place in one session.

4. **Avoidance of public exposure.** Some spouses do not want to discuss their private lives and finances in open court. Mediation occurs in a private and confidential setting.

5. **Greater overall satisfaction.** Mediation results in an agreement developed by the spouses, not one imposed by a judge or the court system. A comparison of couples who chose mediation with couples who chose litigation found that those who mediated their own settlement were more satisfied with the conditions of their agreement. In addition, children of mediated divorces were exposed to less marital conflict, which facilitates their long-term adjustment to divorce.

Basic Mediation Guidelines

Divorce mediators conduct mediation sessions with certain principles in mind:

1. **Children.** What is best for a couple's children should be the major concern of the divorcing parents. Children of divorced parents adjust best when: (1) both parents have regular and frequent access to the children; (2) children see the parents relating respectfully to each other; and (3) each parent talks positively about the other parent to the children.

    Sometimes children are included in the mediation. They may be interviewed without the parents present to provide information to the mediator about their perceptions and preferences. Wong et al,. (2019) confirmed that children involved in divorce mediation often feel powerless and ignored. The researchers encouraged divorce mediators to pay particular attention to the children.

2. **Fairness.** It is important that the agreement between the soon-to-be ex-spouses be fair with neither party being exploited or punished. It is fair for both parents to contribute financially to the children and to have regular access to their children.

3. **Open disclosure.** The spouses will be asked to disclose all facts, records, and documents to ensure an informed and fair agreement regarding property, assets, and debts.

4. **Other professionals.** During mediation, spouses may be asked to consult an accountant regarding tax laws. In addition, each spouse is encouraged to consult an attorney throughout the mediation and to have the attorney review the written mediation agreements before signing. During the mediation sessions, all forms of legal action by the spouses against each other should be stopped.

5. **Confidentiality.** The mediator will not divulge anything spouses say during the mediation sessions without their permission. The spouses are asked to sign a document stating that, should they not complete mediation, they agree not to empower any attorney to subpoena the mediator or any records resulting from the mediation for use in any legal action. Such an agreement is necessary for spouses to feel free to talk about all aspects of their relationship without fear of legal action against them for such disclosures. ●

TABLE 15.2

MEDIATION	LITIGATION
Cooperative	Competitive
Low Cost	High Cost
Private	Public
Protects Relationships	Damages Relationships
Focus on the Future	Focus on the Past
Parties in Control	Parties Lose Control
Children Benefit	Children Lose

a judge hears arguments from lawyers representing the respective spouses and decides issues of custody, child support, division of property, and spousal support. Another option is collaborative divorce. **Collaborative practice** is a process that brings a team of professionals—lawyer, psychologist, mediator, social worker, and financial counselor—together to help a couple separate and divorce in a humane and cost-effective way (Alba-Fisch, 2016).

Table 15.2 identifies a continuum of consequences from negotiation to litigation.

2. **Co-parent with your former spouse.** Setting aside negative feelings about your ex-spouse so as to cooperatively co-parent not only facilitates parental adjustment but also takes children out of the line of fire. Such co-parenting translates into being cooperative when one parent needs to change a child care schedule, sitting together during a school performance by the children, and showing appreciation for the other parent's skill in parenting.

Anger is an acid that can do more harm to the vessel in which it is stored than to anything on which it is poured.
Mark Twain, author

3. **Take some responsibility for the divorce.** Because marriage is an interaction between spouses, one person is seldom totally to blame for a divorce. Rather, both spouses share responsibility for the demise of the relationship. What did *you* do wrong that you could correct in a subsequent relationship? Ferraro et al. (2017) emphasized that one's own mental health, which includes

....

Collaborative practice: process involving a team of professionals: lawyer, psychologist, mediator, social worker, and financial counselor; helping a couple separate and divorce in a humane and cost-effective way.

not placing the blame on someone else, is associated with reducing postdivorce stress.

4. **Create positive thoughts.** Divorced people are susceptible to feeling as though they are failures—they see themselves as Divorced with a capital D, a situation sometimes referred to as "hardening of the categories" disease. Improving self-esteem is important for individuals going through divorce. They can do this by systematically thinking positive thoughts about themselves.

One technique for improving one's self-concept, called the stop-think technique, is to write down 21 positive statements about yourself, such as "I am honest" and "I am a good parent," and transfer these statements to three-by-five cards, each containing three statements. Take one of the cards with you each day and read the thoughts at three regularly spaced intervals. This ensures that you are thinking positive thoughts about yourself throughout the day and are not allowing yourself to drift into a negative state by thinking things such as "no one wants to be with me."

5. **Avoid alcohol and other drugs.** The stress and despair that some people feel during and following the divorce process sometimes make them vulnerable to the use of alcohol or other drugs. These should be avoided because they produce an endless negative cycle. For example, alcohol may be used to relieve stress, but it may also result in a hangover and negative feelings, which in turn may be relieved by alcohol and then result in more negative feelings, and so forth.

6. **Engage in aerobic exercise.** Exercise helps one to not only counteract stress but also avoid it. Jogging, swimming, riding an exercise bike, or engaging in other similar exercise for 30 minutes every day increases oxygen to the brain and helps facilitate clear thinking. In addition, aerobic exercise produces endorphins in the brain, which create a sense of euphoria, also known as runner's high.

7. **Continue interpersonal connections.** Adjustment to divorce is facilitated by continuing relationships with friends and family. These individuals provide emotional support and help buffer the feeling of isolation and aloneness.

8. **Let go of the anger for your former partner.** Former spouses who stay negatively attached to a former partner by harboring resentment and trying to get back at the former partner prolong their adjustment to divorce. The old adage that

"you can't get ahead by getting even" is relevant to divorce adjustment.

9. **Allow time to heal.** Because self-esteem usually drops after divorce, a person is often vulnerable to making commitments in a new relationship before working through feelings about the divorce. Although the amount of time to heal depends on many factors such as how long the spouses were married and the reasons for the divorce, most individuals need between 12 and 18 months to adjust to the end of a marriage. Although being available to others may help to repair one's self-esteem, getting remarried during this time should be considered cautiously. A minimum of two years between marriages is recommended.

REMARRIAGE

Divorced spouses are not sour on marriage. Although they may want to escape from the current spouse, they are open to having a new spouse. Forty percent of all new marriages are remarriages. Half of these involve one spouse who has been married before; 20%, both spouses have been married before. Men are more likely to remarry than women with figures showing a rate of 64% vs. 52% (Geiger & Livingston, 2019). The probability of remarriage varies by racial identity. According to Livingston's study (2014), of those who had previously been married, 60% of Whites, 51% of Hispanics, 46% of Blacks, and 42% of Asians remarried.

Watkins and Waldron (2017) analyzed data on the timing of remarriage and found that divorced individuals, particularly fathers, are more likely to remarry than widowed individuals. Remarriage for fathers was particularly more likely if they had a child under the age of 6. In general, for every year the first marriage lasted, parents were slower to remarry. The advantages of remarrying declined with age. One divorced man said in his sixties said that he enjoyed living alone and did not need a spouse or kids around to interrupt his life. Divorced women of similar age may also have a low interest in remarriage, because they have had their children and don't want more, have their own house, and are economically self-sufficient.

Most of the divorced remarry and do so for many of the same reasons as those in their first marriage—love, companionship, emotional security, and a regular sex partner. Other reasons are unique to remarriage and include financial security, particularly for a woman with children; help in rearing one's children; the desire to provide a "social" father or mother for one's children; escape from the stigma associated with being divorced; and legal threats regarding the custody of one's children. With regard to the latter, the courts view a parent seeking custody of a child more favorably if the parent is remarried.

Issues of Remarriage for the Divorced

Several issues challenge people who remarry (Goetting, 1982; Martin-Uzzi & Duval-Tsioles, 2013)

Boundary Maintenance

Ghosts of the first marriage, in terms of the ex-spouse, must be dealt with. A parent must decide how to relate to an ex-spouse to maintain a good parenting relationship for the biological children at the same time as creating the necessary emotional distance with the former spouse to prevent problems from developing with the new partner.

Some spouses continue to be emotionally attached to and have difficulty breaking away from an ex-spouse due to anger or resentment. These former spouses have what Masheter (1999) terms a **negative attachment** whereby such individuals "have decided

Remarriages are a second chance and often begin with a very small private event focused on the couple.
Courtesy of Chelsea Curry

Negative attachment: spouses who continue to be emotionally attached to and have difficulty breaking away from ex-spouses.

to remain [emotionally] in this relationship and to invest considerable amounts of time, money, and effort in it . . . [T]hese individuals do not take responsibility for their own feelings and actions, and often remain 'stuck,' unable to move forward in their lives" (p. 297).

Emotional Remarriage

Remarriage involves beginning to trust and love another person in a new relationship. Such feelings may come slowly as a result of negative experiences in a previous marriage.

Psychological Remarriage

Divorced individuals considering remarriage may find it difficult to give up the freedom and autonomy of being single and reluctant to develop a mental set conducive to pairing. This transition may be particularly difficult for people who sought a divorce as a means to personal growth and autonomy. These individuals may fear that getting remarried will put unwanted constraints on them.

Community Remarriage

This aspect involves a change in focus from single friends to a new mate and other couples with whom the new pair will interact. The bonds of friendship established during the divorce period may be particularly valuable because these friends have given support at a time of personal crisis. Care should be taken not to drop these friendships. Individuals who remarry must also introduce their parents to the new partner who may be approving or rejecting.

Parental Remarriage

Divorced individuals with children often pair bond or remarry someone who also has children (Di Nallo, 2019; Potarca et al., 2017). Hence, most remarriages involve the parents working out the nuances of living with someone else's children. Mothers are usually awarded primary physical custody, and this circumstance translates into a new stepfather adjusting to the mother's children and vice versa. The children are also adjusting to a new stepparent, often a great challenge.

Economic and Legal Remarriage

A second marriage may begin with economic responsibilities to a first marriage. Alimony and child support often threaten the harmony and sometimes even the economic survival of second marriages. Although the income of a new wife is not used legally to decide the amount her new husband is required to pay in child support for his children of a former marriage, his ex-wife may petition the court for more child support. The ex-wife may do so, however, on the premise that his living expenses are reduced with a new wife and that, therefore, he should be able to afford to pay more child support. Although an ex-wife is not likely to win, she can force the new wife to go to court and to disclose her income. This can result in considerable investment of time and legal fees for a newly remarried couple.

Economic issues in a remarriage may become evident in another way. For example, a remarried woman may not have sufficient independent income from her job and may receive inadequate child support from her ex-spouse. When her child needs braces and she is unable to afford them on her own, she might wrestle with how much money to ask her new husband for.

Remarriage for Widowed Individuals

Only 10% of remarriages involve widows or widowers. Unlike divorced individuals, widowed individuals are usually much older and their children are grown. There may be additional barriers to remarriage in that the widow or widower has to work through the death of his or her spouse. For those who do remarry, their former spouse may affect the relationship with their new partner. In addition, the perception of remarriage can vary. Remarriage can be interpreted as a betrayal to the deceased spouse. Compared to divorced individuals, widowed individuals may encounter more barriers to remarriage (Oamani et al., 2018).

Brimhall and Engblom-Deglmann (2011) interviewed 24 remarried individuals about the death of a previous spouse, either theirs or their partner's, and how this previous marriage was affecting the new marriage. Participants were interviewed individually and as a couple. Several themes emerged including putting the past spouse on a pedestal, comparing the current and past spouses, insecurity of the current spouse, curiosity about the past spouse and relationship, the new partner's response to this curiosity, and its impact on the current relationship. The best new relationship outcomes seemed to happen when the spouse of a deceased partner talked openly about the past relationship and reassured the current partner of his or her love for the new partner and the new relationship.

A widow or widower may marry someone of similar age or someone who is considerably older or younger. Marriages in which one spouse is considerably older than the other are referred to as May-December marriages (discussed in Chapter 7, Marriage Relationships). Here we will discuss only December marriages, in which both spouses are elderly.

A study of 24 elderly couples found that the primary motivation for remarriage was the need to escape loneliness or the need for companionship (Vinick, 1978). Men reported a greater need to remarry than did the women. Seventy-five percent of

Osmani et al. (2018) noted the social barriers to remarriage for widows in Iran. One widowed mother noted how her son would react if she were to remarry:

> In front of my children, I can't talk about remarriage at all. My son always says, "Mother, what is remarriage? You can live with your daughter."

> On the other hand, I cannot leave my daughter at home alone, and I also cannot bring a young girl into the husband's home. (p. 61)

the spouses met through a mutual friend or relative and 63% married less than a year after their partner's death. Increasingly, elderly individuals are meeting online. Some sites cater to older individuals seeking partners, including www.seniorfriendfinder.com and www.ourtime.com.

The children of the couples in Vinick's study had mixed reactions to their parent's remarriage. Most of the children were happy that their parent was happy and felt relieved that someone would now meet the companionship needs of their elderly parent on a more regular basis. However, some children disapproved of the marriage out of concern for their inheritance. "If that woman marries Dad," said a woman with two children, "she'll get everything when he dies. I love him and hope he lives forever, but when he's gone, I want the house I grew up in."

Stability of Remarriages

Jensen et al. (2017) found that 40% of second marriages compared to 32% of first marriages ended within the first ten years of marriage. They compared 410 individuals in second marriages with 1,679 individuals in first marriages and concluded that "it appears that the preexisting characteristics of individuals in our sample who selected themselves into divorce and remarriage are more strongly associated with relationship stability than the order of the marriage itself." Hence, it is not the fact that divorce occurs more often in second marriages per se, but that the individuals who divorce once have the characteristics associated with divorce propensity in the second marriage.

Though remarried people are more vulnerable to divorce in the early years of their subsequent marriage, they are less likely to divorce after 15 years of staying in the second marriage than those in first marriages (Clarke & Wilson, 1994). Hence, these spouses are likely to remain married because they want to, not because they fear divorce.

STEPFAMILIES

The ways in which stepfamilies are different from nuclear families are identified in Table 15.3.

Among the differences are that stepchildren are often uncertain how to name and relate to stepparents (Ganong et al., 2018). Papernow (2018) also

Stepfamily: a family in which adults bring biological or adopted children with other partners into the unit.

TABLE 15.3

Differences Between Nuclear Families and Stepfamilies

NUCLEAR FAMILIES	STEPFAMILIES
1. Children are (usually) biologically related to both parents.	1. Children are biologically related to only one parent.
2. Both biological parents live together with children.	2. As a result of divorce or death, one biological parent does not live with the children. In the case of joint physical custody, children may live with both parents, alternating between them.
3. Beliefs and values of members tend to be similar.	3. Beliefs and values of members are more likely to be different because of different backgrounds.
4. The relationship between adults has existed longer than relationship between children and parents.	4. The relationship between children and parents has existed longer than the relationship between adults.
5. Children have one home they regard as theirs.	5. Children may have two homes they regard as theirs.

(Continued)

TABLE 15.3   (Continued)

NUCLEAR FAMILIES	STEPFAMILIES
6. The family's economic resources come from within the family unit.	6. Some economic resources may come from an ex-spouse.
7. All money generated stays in the family.	7. Some money generated may leave the family in the form of alimony or child support.
8. Relationships are relatively stable.	8. Relationships are in flux: new adults adjusting to each other; children adjusting to a stepparent; a stepparent adjusting to stepchildren; stepchildren adjusting to each other.
9. No stigma is attached to nuclear family.	9. Stepfamilies are stigmatized.
10. Spouses had a child-free period.	10. Spouses had no child-free period.
11. Inheritance rights are automatic.	11. Stepchildren do not automatically inherit from stepparents.
12. Rights to custody of children are assumed if divorce occurs.	12. Rights to custody of stepchildren are usually not considered.
13. Extended family networks are smooth and comfortable.	13. Extended family networks become complex and strained.
14. Nuclear family may not have experienced loss.	14. Stepfamily has experienced loss.
15. Families experience a range of problems.	15. Stepchildren tend to be a major problem.
16. Biological parents obligated to provide support to children.	16. Stepparents not obligated to provide support to stepchildren.

Involved stepfathers are one of the unforeseen positive outcomes of the divorce of one's parents.

noted that, unaware of the various differences, family therapists are often ill equipped in working with stepfamilies.

In regard to how children experience stepfamily living, Jensen et al. (2018) studied 191 stepchildren an average of 11.3 years old and found that a good parent-child relationship was associated with lower levels of stepchildren being depressed, anxious, and rebellious toward involvement in the new family.

FUTURE OF DIVORCE AND REMARRIAGE

Divorce marks the end of a legal marital union according to the federal and state laws in which the couple married. Scholars have noticed a decline in number of legal marriages and have suggested that family scholars study the broader union instability instead of using the term divorce (Amato & Patterson, 2017). But perceptions of divorce are not fading away entirely. Divorce will continue to be associated with lower life satisfaction (Roberson et al., 2018) and to be stigmatized in our society as evidenced by the term **divorcism**—the belief that divorce is a disaster. The culture perpetuates the idea that individuals should stay married and that divorce ruins children. Despite the negative connotation associated with divorce, however, it will also be experienced privately with some ambivalence. Winchester et al. (2018) captured the nuance of divorce and how it may be viewed in retrospect. Below are a couple of clips:

> ... [T]his is hard for me because one of the positive things in our relationship was the shopping. We always went shopping and had lunch.

Divorcism: the belief that divorce is a disaster.

Frequently we'd go to Indy. That was one of the few good parts of our life. So here it is, even though I have fun [shopping] with my friend Elizabeth, it brings back memories. (p. 204)

Another respondent looked back on her divorce and lamented:

Because from what I had been through it was a relief. It was wonderful! Now, the long term when you're dealing with life alone and life financially and life with all the teen problems and you're by yourself. I mean, when you look at that big picture it's like, I don't wish this on anybody. Nobody!

SUMMARY

What are deal beakers for women and for men and how prevalent is divorce?
Deal breakers for single men and women were poor hygiene, unclean appearance, laziness, lack of humor, and being emotionally needy. Between 40% and 50% of individuals divorce; the percent is lower for college-educated individuals and those with higher incomes. Discernment counseling is one last attempt to salvage a relationship. In one study of 100 couples, about half were able to reconcile their differences and stay married.

What are macro factors contributing to divorce?
Macro factors contributing to divorce include economic factors such as hardship and increased financial independence, changing family functions where companionship is the only remaining function, increased life expectancy, liberal divorce laws, prenuptial agreements, the Internet, fewer moral and religious sanctions with churches embracing single individuals, more divorce models, mobility and anonymity, and ethnicity and culture with Asian and Mexican Americans having lower divorce rates. Individualism values what is best for the individual rather than familism, what is best for the family.

What are micro factors contributing to divorce?
Micro factors include having numerous differences, growing apart, falling out of love, depression, limited time together, low frequency of positive behavior, extramarital relationships, poor communication and conflict resolution skills, value changes, satiation, loss of income from husband, unequal housework, in-laws, and perception of a happier life after divorce,

What are the consequences of divorce for spouses and parents?
Women tend to fare better emotionally after separation and divorce than do men. Women are more likely than men not only to have a stronger network of supportive relationships but also to profit from divorce by developing a new sense of self-esteem and confidence, because they are thrust into a more independent role.

Both women and men experience a drop in income following divorce, but women suffer more. Although custodial mothers are often awarded child support, the amount is usually inadequate, infrequent, and not dependable, and women are forced to work sometimes at more than one job to take financial care of their children.

What are the effects of divorce on children?
A civil, cooperative, co-parenting relationship between former spouses is the greatest predictor of a positive outcome for children whose parents divorce. Other factors associated with minimizing the negative effects of divorce for children include healthy parental psychological functioning, parental attention to the children, allowing children to grieve, each parent encouraging his or her children to see the noncustodial parent, assertion of parental authority, regular and consistent child support payments, stability—for example, with housing and the neighborhood—and parents not having a new baby with a new partner. The effects of parental divorce are not all negative. Positive effects of divorce were identified.

What is the nature of remarriage in the United States?
When comparing divorced individuals who have remarried with divorced individuals who have not remarried, the remarried who stay together for 15 years are less likely to divorce than those in first marriages. Issues relevant to the remarried are: boundary maintenance, such as not getting entangled with one's former partner; emotional remarriage or being able to love and trust again; psychic remarriage—giving up the freedom of singlehood; community remarriage involving shifting from single friends to a new mate; parental remarriage and adjusting to a stepfamily; and economic and legal remarriage involving responsibilities to the previous and current family.

How do stepfamilies differ from nuclear families?
Stepfamilies differ from nuclear families in numerous ways including the fact that the children in nuclear families are biologically related to both parents, whereas the children in stepfamilies are biologically related to only one parent. Stepfamilies also bring together two families who may have different value systems.

What is the future of divorce and remarriage?
Divorce will continue as will the stigma associated with it. Divorcism is the belief that it is better to be married than divorced. No consideration is given to how bad a marriage may be.

KEY TERMS

Annulment, 320

Arbitration, 336

Collaborative practice, 338

Developmental task, 327

Discernment counseling, 321

Divorce, 320

Divorce mediation, 336

Divorcism, 342

Estrangement, 331

Family relations doctrine, 332

High-conflict divorce, 333

Latchkey parents, 334

Legal custody, 332

Litigation, 336

Lump sum alimony, 328

Negative attachment, 339

Negotiation, 336

No-fault divorce, 324

Parental alienation, 329

Parental alienation syndrome, 329

Permanent alimony, 329

Physical custody, 332

Postnuptial agreement, 329

Rehabilitative alimony, 328

Reimbursement alimony, 328

Satiation, 326

Stepfamily, 341

Temporary alimony, 328

WEB LINKS

Association for Conflict Resolution
http://www.acrnet.org

Center for Divorce Education
http://www.divorce-education.com/

Divorce Source (a legal resource for divorce, custody, alimony, and support)
http://www.divorcesource.com/

DivorceBusting (solve marriage problems)
http://divorcebusting.com/

The New Face of Divorce: First Wives World
www.firstwivesworld.com

Our Family Wizard
https://www.ourfamilywizard.com/

A Guide to the Parental Alienation Syndrome
http://www.coeffic.demon.co.uk/pas.htm

Positive Parenting Through Divorce Online Course
http://www.positiveparentingthroughdivorce.com/

Get the tools you need to sharpen your study skills. SAGE edge offers a robust online environment featuring an impressive array of free tools and resources.
Access practice quizzes, eFlashcards, video, and multimedia at **edge.sagepub.com/knox13e**

16

The Later Years

It's not how old you are, it's how you are old.

—Jules Renard, French Author

Learning Objectives

16.1.   Specify the meanings of age and ageism

16.2.   Describe the caregiving process for the frail

16.3.   Discuss the primary issues confronting the elderly

16.4.   Review relationships of the elderly

16.5.   Summarize the role of grandparents for the elderly

16.6.   Describe the end of life stage

16.7.   Review the future of the elderly in the United States

Master the content at
edge.sagepub.com/knox13e

As a person passes through the various stages of the family life cycle, an awareness eventually comes that one is closer to the end than to the beginning. The world one was born into and grew up in has been replaced with new technological advances. There are over fifty million adults in the United States age 65 and older (*ProQuest Statistical Abstract, 2019,* Table 6). The youngest people in this demographic were born in the 50s and have seen a tremendous amount of change throughout their lives.

The title of this chapter is "The Later Years," which, for youth, often suggests that life is over. The reality is different. When Pablo Picasso was 88, he produced 165 paintings. Explaining his energy as he neared 90, Picasso said "Everyone is the age they have decided on, and I have decided to remain 30."

Bertrand Russell, the famous philosopher, noted that he had three goals for his life—to find love, to search for knowledge, and to develop empathy for the suffering of others. He acknowledged that he was successful in only one of his pursuits: He found love but only when he was 80 and married his fourth wife, Edith Finch. In 2020, Supreme Court Justice, Ruth Ginsburg is 87. The message for our chapter is that the later years are often not the end of life but the beginning.

In this chapter, we focus on the factors that confront individuals and couples as they age. We begin by looking at the concept of age.

AGE AND AGEISM

All societies have a way to categorize their members by age. Societies also provide social definitions for particular ages.

The Concept of Age

A person's **age** may be defined chronologically, physiologically, psychologically, sociologically, and culturally. Chronologically, an "old" person is defined as one who has lived a certain number of years. The concept has obvious practical significance in everyday life. Bureaucratic organizations and social programs identify chronological age as a criterion of certain social rights and responsibilities. One's age determines the right to drive, vote, buy alcohol or cigarettes, and receive Social Security and Medicare benefits.

Age only has meaning in reference to the society and culture in which the individual lives. In ancient Greece and Rome (800–500 BC), where the average life expectancy was 20 years, an individual was old at 18; similarly, one was old at 30 in medieval Europe and at 40 in the United States in 1850. In the United States today, however, people are usually not considered old until they reach age 65. However, our society is moving toward new chronological definitions of "old." Three groups of the elderly have emerged—the "young-old," the "middle-old," and the "old-old." The young-old are typically between the ages of 65 and 74; the middle-old, 75 to 84, and the old-old, 85 and beyond. Gilleard and Higgs (2017) noted that while age, retirement, and income

Age: term which may be defined chronologically in the number of years; physiologically, meaning physical decline; psychologically, in terms of one's self-concept; sociologically, viewed as the roles for the elderly and retired; and culturally, meaning of age in one's society.

This man at 94 qualifies for the category of "old-old." He notes, "It's amazing that I made it this far."

TABLE 16.1

Life Expectancy by Sex, Age, and Race

WHITE, NON-HISPANIC		BLACK, NON-HISPANIC		HISPANIC	
Male	Female	Male	Female	Male	Female
76.1	81	71.5	77.9	79.1	84.2

Source: *ProQuest Statistical Abstract of the United States*, 2019. Table 110. Life Expectancy by Sex, Age, and Race and Hispanic Origin: 2016.

have been markers for who is defined as old in our society, the "new salient line of fracture" is frailty, which distinguishes those who are merely older from those who are old. Current life expectancy in the United States is shown in Table 16.1.

In regard to aging throughout the world: "Between 2015 and 2030, the number of people in the world aged 60 years or over is projected to grow by 56%, from 901 million to 1.4 billion, and by 2050, the global population of older persons is projected to more than double its size in 2015, reaching nearly 2.1 billion. Globally, the number of people aged 80 years or over, the 'oldest-old' persons, is growing even faster than the number of older persons overall. Projections indicate that in 2050 the oldest-old will number 434 million, having more than tripled in number since 2015, when there were 125 million people over age 80. Over the next 15 years, the number of older persons is expected to grow fastest in Latin America and the Caribbean with a projected 71% increase in the population aged 60 years or over, followed by 66% in Asia, 64% in Africa, 47% in Oceania, 41% in Northern America, and 23% in Europe." (United Nations, Department of Economic and Social Affairs, Population Division, 2015, p. 2).

Research is being conducted with the hope of adding hundreds of years to one's life. While adding 30 years in the foreseeable future is more realistic (Friend, 2017), the Cryonics Institute (http://www.cryonics.org/) offers to freeze your body and wake you up, hopefully, in the future when technology is available to replace human body parts indefinitely and to stop the aging process. The promise of never growing old and living forever is here. This thought certainly gives a new slant on "till death do us part."

Physiologically, people are old when their auditory, visual, respiratory, and cognitive capabilities decline significantly. Disease and disability are an inevitable part of aging. Sleep changes also occur for the elderly, including going to bed earlier, waking up during the night, and waking up earlier in the morning, as well as disorders such as obstructive sleep apnea.

People who need full-time nursing care for eating, bathing, and taking medication properly and who are placed in nursing homes are thought of as being old. Indeed, successful aging is culturally defined as maintaining one's health, independence, and cognitive ability. It is not death but the slow deterioration from aging that brings the most fear.

People who have certain diseases are also regarded as old. Although younger individuals may suffer from Alzheimer's, arthritis, and heart problems, these ailments are more often associated with aging. As medical science conquers more diseases, the physiological definition of aging changes so that it takes longer for people to be defined as old.

Psychologically, a person's self-concept is important in defining how old that person is. As individuals begin to fulfill the roles associated with the elderly—retiree, grandparent, nursing home resident—they begin to see themselves as aging. Sociologically, once they occupy these roles, others begin to see them as old.

Culturally, the society in which an individual lives may have different stages of aging. In U.S. society, the periods from age 18 through 64 are generally subdivided into young adulthood, adulthood, and middle age. Cultures also differ in terms of how they view and take care of their elderly. Spain is particularly noteworthy in terms of care for the elderly, with most elderly people receiving care from family members as older parents often live with their children. As we will discuss later, elderly people in the United States may be treated with less care and deference.

Ageism

Gerontology is the study of aging. Every society has some form of **ageism**—the stereotyping, prejudice, and discrimination against people on the basis of their age. Ageism is reflected in negative stereotypes of the elderly being forgetful, lonely, and impoverished. The following Senior Texting Code pokes fun at the elderly which is a cover for being prejudiced against them by viewing them as a group to be laughed at (Berk, 2015):

> ATD: At The Doctor's
>
> BFF: Best Friend Fell
>
> BYOT: Bring Your Own Teeth
>
> DWI: Driving While Incontinent
>
> GGPBL: Gotta Go, Pacemaker Battery Low!
>
> ROTFLCGU: Rolling on the Floor Laughing and Can't Get Up
>
> TTYL: Talk To You Louder

Ageism also occurs when individuals in older age groups are treated differently. Some examples include when they are spoken to loudly in simple language when it is assumed they cannot understand normal speech or when they are denied employment due to their age. Another form of ageism—ageism by invisibility—occurs when older adults are not included in advertising and educational materials. Ageism is similar to sexism, racism, and heterosexism. The elderly are shunned, discriminated against in employment, and sometimes victims of abuse.

Negative stereotypes and media images of the elderly engender **gerontophobia**—a shared fear or dread of the elderly. Such negative stereotypes may create a self-fulfilling prophecy. For example, an elderly person forgets something and attributes forgetting to his or her getting older. A younger person, however, is unlikely to attribute forgetfulness to age, given cultural definitions surrounding the age of the onset of senility.

The negative meanings associated with aging underlie the obsession of many Americans to conceal their age by altering their appearance. Chonody and Teater (2016) noted that the stigma associated with aging is related to the outward appearance, which stems from fears about social identity and death. A wrinkled, slow-moving person occupies social roles, which younger individuals want to delay, and the associations with death bring further retreat.

With the hope of holding on to youth a little bit longer, aging Americans spend billions of dollars each year on plastic surgery, exercise equipment, hair products, facial creams, and Botox injections.

CAREGIVING FOR THE FRAIL

An elderly individual is defined as **frail** if he or she has difficulty with at least one personal care activity or other activity related to independent living; individuals with a severe disability are unable to complete three or more personal care activities. These activities are referred to as activities of daily living (ADL). Six basic ADLs are eating, bathing, getting dressed, toileting, transferring, and continence. Another set of skills include being able to perform instrumental activities such as shopping for groceries, managing money, including paying bills, and driving to the doctor. Assessment of these criteria is important in determining what type of long-term care and health insurance coverage are needed. Over 90% of frail elderly do not have long-term health care insurance. Many slide into poverty because of medical debt or become a burden to their children.

The Sandwich Generation

Most children choose to take care of their elderly parents. Generally, female adult children, who are usually employed, take care of their mothers, while fathers often have a spouse or are deceased. These children provide **family care giving** and are known as the **sandwich generation** because they take care of their parents and their own children simultaneously. Although more women are associated with the sandwich generation, the concept includes both men and women. Thirty percent of men and women ages 35 to 75 provide time and money to their children and elderly, often frail parents. However, the number of women in this role will increase as a result of the increase in life expectancy.

The number of individuals in the sandwich generation will increase for the following reasons:

1. **Longevity.** The over-85 age group, the segment of the population most in need of care, is the fastest-growing segment of our population.

2. **Chronic disease.** In the past, diseases took the elderly quickly. Today, diseases such as

....

Gerontology: the study of aging.

Ageism: stereotyping, prejudice, and discrimination against people on the basis of their age.

Gerontophobia: fear or dread of the elderly, which may create a self-fulfilling prophecy.

Frail: term used to define elderly people if they have difficulty with at least one personal care activity, such as feeding, bathing, or toileting.

Family care giving: adult children providing care for their elderly parents.

Sandwich generation: generation of adults who are "sandwiched" between caring for their elderly parents and their own children.

arthritis and Alzheimer's are associated not with an immediate death sentence but with years of managing the illness and being cared for by others.

3. **Fewer siblings to help.** The current generation of elderly have fewer children than the elderly in previous generations. Hence, the number of siblings available to help look after parents is more limited. Children without siblings are more likely to feel the weight of caring for elderly parents alone.

4. **Commitment to parental care.** Contrary to the myth that adult children in the United States abrogate responsibility for taking care of their elderly parents, most children institutionalize their parents only as a last resort. Many do so since they can't care for an elderly parent by themselves. Caring for a dependent, aging parent requires a great deal of effort, sacrifice, and decision-making on the part of more than twenty million adults in the United States who are challenged with this situation. The emotional toll on the caregiver may be heavy. Guilt over not doing enough, resentment over feeling burdened, and exhaustion over the relentless care demands are common feelings.

Decisions About Long-Term Care

Many Americans wrestle with the decision to put their parents in a nursing home or other long-term care facility. However, there is little variation in regard to health outcomes and cost. Blackburn et al. (2016) analyzed data on 1,291 pairs living in the respective contexts. After one year, 77.7% of home

health beneficiaries were alive compared with 76.2% of nursing home beneficiaries (p < .001). Overall the annual costs were not statistically different with home health costs averaging $31,423 and nursing home, $32,239. We note in the Personal Choices insert that prices in 2020 have escalated to close to $100,000 annually.

China is known for its norms regarding filial piety in terms of taking care of one's parents. However, changes are taking place on the part of both offspring and their parents. Not only are some children busy with their careers and less invested in parental care, some Chinese elderly recognize the benefits of being attended to in a nursing home. One 69-year-old father in a nursing home reported his feeling about being in a nursing home (Zhang, 2019):

> The idea that putting your parents in a nursing home is unfilial is an out-dated concept. We should advance with the times. I was unattended at home, but I am good here. The dinner is cooked for me and someone does the cleaning work. My son and daughter will see me at least once every week, and they are filial. (p. 259),

While the above is a modern perspective of an older Chinese man, he may be the exception. Most elderly individuals prefer to remain in their own home and most children attempt to accommodate the wishes of their parents. While often a strain on everyone, the family members work together to make the situation doable.

PERSONAL CHOICES

Should I Put My Aging Parents in a Long-Term Care Facility?

Emerging adults, ages 17-28, vary in regard to attitudes toward taking care of elderly parents. The Self-Assessment: Attitudes Toward Taking Care of Elderly Parents Scale on page 395 provides a way to assess your views.

Over 1.4 million residents are in a nursing home (*ProQuest Statistical Abstract, 2019,* Table 176). We discuss factors relevant in deciding whether to care for an elderly parent at home, arrange for nursing

home care, or provide another form of long-term care. Note that these factors are in flux and involve a constant reassessment of the elder care decision.

1. **Level of care needed.** As parents age, the level of care that they need increases.

   An elderly parent who cannot bathe, dress, prepare meals, or be depended on to take medication responsibly—for example, the

(Continued)

(Continued)

ADLs referred to earlier—needs either full-time in-home care or a skilled nursing facility that provides 24-hour nursing supervision by registered or licensed vocational nurses. Commonly referred to as "nursing homes" or "convalescent hospitals," these facilities provide medical, nursing, dietary, pharmacy, and activity services. Depending on the condition of the elderly individual, it may be beneficial for them to stay in a nursing home instead of receiving care at home.

An intermediate-care facility provides eight hours of nursing supervision per day. Intermediate care is less extensive and less expensive and generally serves patients who are ambulatory and who do not need care throughout the night.

A skilled nursing facility for special disabilities provides a protective or security environment to people with mental disabilities. Many of these facilities have locked areas where patients reside for their own protection.

An assisted living facility is for individuals who are no longer able to live independently but who do not need the level of care that a nursing home provides. Although nurses and other health care providers are available, assistance is more typically in the form of meals and housekeeping.

Housing involves a range of options, from apartments where residents live independently to skilled nursing care. These housing alternatives allow older adults to remain in one place and still receive the care they need as they age. In addition, adult children may relocate to be near their aging parents.

2. **Temperament of aging parent.** Some elderly parents become paranoid, accusatory, and angry with their caregivers. For example, some individuals with Alzheimer's become abusive and violent and can no longer be taken care of at home. Family members no longer capable of coping with the abuse may arrange for their parents to be taken care of in a nursing home or other facility. However, this may add even more strain to the relationship. One mother screamed at her son, "You wish I were dead so you would not have to mess with me."

3. **Philosophy of adult child and marital considerations.** Most children feel a sense of filial responsibility—a sense of personal obligation for the well-being of their aging parents. The role of taking care of an elderly parent is typically taken up by the daughter. The decision to care for aging parents or put them in a nursing home is relevant to

This daughter has lunch with her 96-year-old mother in the nursing home every day. She told her mother in response to her mother's statement "I don't want to be a burden". . . "I am going to love you to death." Two other daughters live out of town but visit frequently.

one's own marriage. Polenick et al. (2017) found that men are more likely than women to report a drop in marital satisfaction when their partner took care of their aging parents. The probability of divorce also increases if a woman takes on the full-time care of an aging parent (Penning & Wu, 2019).

4. **Length of time for providing care.** Time in dependent care can be extensive. Ten or more years are not unusual. The mother of the first author was dependent on professional care for 15 years until her death at 90.

5. **Cost.** Professional full-time care in a nursing home is expensive at around $100,000 in 2020. Costs vary depending on where the adult care facility is and the range of options.

    Medicare, a federal health insurance program for people 65 and older, was developed for short-term acute hospital care. Medicare generally does not pay for long-term nursing care. In practice, adult children who arrange for their aging parent to be cared for in a nursing home end up paying for it out of the elder's own funds. After all of these economic resources are depleted, **Medicaid**, a state welfare program for low-income individuals, will pay for the cost of care. A federal law prohibits offspring from shifting the assets of an elderly parent so as to become eligible for Medicaid.

    Some adult children may consider buying long-term care insurance (LTCI) to cover what Medicare does not. Many private health care plans do not cover "nonmedical" day-to-day care such as bathing or meals for an Alzheimer's parent, as well as nursing home costs. Costs of LTCI begin at about $1,000 a year but vary a great deal, including costing over $1,000 a month, depending on the age and health of the insured individual.

6. **Availability of care giver.** A societal crisis in care for the elderly is looming. In the past, women have taken care of their elderly parents. However, these were women who lived in traditional families where one paycheck took care of a family's economic needs. Women today work out of economic necessity, and quitting work to take care of an elderly parent is becoming less of an option. As more women enter the labor force, less free labor is available to take care of the elderly. Government programs are not in place to take care of the legions of elderly Americans. Who will care for them when both spouses are working full time?

7. **Other issues.** Alltucker (2018) revealed that family members may fight in court regarding end-of-life decisions. For example, Casey Kasem's widow, Jean Kasem, battled his children in court over his medical care as he struggled with dementia. Family members may also disagree over whether to put a family member in a nursing home. ●

Advance Directives and End-of-Life Decisions

In addition to deciding where their parents will receive care, children of elderly parents may also have to make important end-of-life decisions on their parents' behalf. In order to make these decisions, children may need to be granted certain legal rights. A **durable power of attorney**, which gives adult children complete authority to act on behalf of their elderly parent is advised. These documents also save countless legal hours, time, and money for those responsible for the elderly. The spouse or partner may also benefit since the less anxiety about care-taking responsibilities, the better for the relationship with the partner.

It is also helpful if they know one's parents' wishes regarding key issues, such as if they want to be sustained on a respirator. The elderly person, or those with power of attorney, should complete a document called an **advance directive,** which is also known as a **living will,** detailing the conditions under which life support measures should be used. These decisions, made ahead of time, spare the adult children the responsibility of making them in crisis contexts, and give clear directives to the medical staff in charge of the elderly person. For example, elderly people can direct that a feeding tube should not be used if they become unable to feed themselves. In doing so, children are spared from making the decision on their own.

ISSUES CONFRONTING THE ELDERLY

Numerous issues become concerns as people age. In middle age, the issues are early retirement, which may be forced; job layoffs; age discrimination, specifically with applying for jobs; separation or divorce from a spouse; and adjustment to children leaving home. For some in middle age, grandparenting is an issue if they become the primary caregiver for their grandchildren. As couples move from the middle to the later years, the issues become more focused on income, health, retirement, and sexuality.

Income

The median annual income of men aged 65 and older is $31,618; women, $18,380 (*ProQuest Statistical Abstract,* 2019, Table 730). According to Clarence Kehoe, executive director of accounting firm Anchin, Block, and Anchin, the number one regret of retirees is that they did not save enough money for retirement—that they spent more than they should have during their peak earning years (Brown, 2014). Indeed, for most elderly, the end of life is characterized by reduced income. Social Security and pension benefits, when they exist, are rarely equal to the income a retired person formerly earned. Many elderly continue working since they can't afford to quit. Individuals sometimes ask, "When should I start

---

Medicare: a federal health insurance program for people 65 and older.

Medicaid: a state welfare program for low-income individuals.

Durable power of attorney: gives the identified person complete authority to act on behalf of the elderly.

Advance directive (living will): details for medical care personnel and the conditions under which life support measures should be used for the individual.

saving for retirement?" The best answer is "As soon as you can … and the sooner the better." Elderly women are particularly disadvantaged because their out-of-home employment has often been discontinuous, part time, and low-paying. Social Security and private pension plans favor those with continuous, full-time work histories. In addition, the interrupted employment pattern can also negatively impact later-life employment. Hence, the retirement income of elderly females is considerably lower than the retirement income of elderly males. Either may be financially dependent on their children.

CULTURE AND DIVERSITY

Over half of a sample of 1,402 Swiss women ages 65-84 reported that they were satisfied with their lives. Factors associated with life satisfaction included high education, satisfaction with income, social support, living with a partner, and good self-perceived health (Burton-Jeangros & Zimmermann-Sloutskis, 2016). Countries where the elderly report being the happiest are Norway, Sweden, the United States, the Netherlands, and Japan.

Physical Health

While good physical health is the single most important determinant of an elderly person's reported happiness, there is the inevitable deterioration in physical well-being as one ages. Sometimes there is an acute physical problem such as chronic low back pain (CLBP). Stensland and Sanders (2018) interviewed 23 elderly, aged 66-83, with CLBP who revealed that "It has changed my whole life." Six themes were identified: (a) Pain damages my sense of self; (b) I am trapped in a body that doesn't work anymore; (c) The pain affects me and my partner; (d) Pain complicates my family relationships; (e) I can barely get through the day at my job; and (f) I feel socially and recreationally repressed.

Couples in long-term marriages are challenged to help each other as physical health declines.

Chronic health problems such as heart disease, cancer, and obstructive pulmonary disease threaten the individual's autonomy and independence—two highly regarded values in U. S. society. Some elderly individuals also feel that their "life is completed and no longer worth living." Satorres et al. (2018) confirmed that hopelessness is a key element in suicidal intent. Such hopelessness may be associated with a decrease in one's will to live (Carmel et al., 2018) and result in further depression. Some elderly individuals who feel this way may seek out physician-assisted suicide. We discuss this topic further in "Family Policy."

Mental Health

An individual's cognitive abilities may decline with age. But such a decline is not inevitable and specific activities are associated with mental alertness. Lee and Chi (2016) studied 704 individuals age 70 or older and found that those who engaged in cognitive leisure activities, such as reading newspapers, magazines, or books, or visual spatial activities like crossword puzzles, cards, or board games were more likely to have no cognitive impairment or dementia compared to those who did not evidence such activities.

Aside from possible cognitive changes, depression is more common among the elderly. Bereavement over the death of a spouse, loneliness, physical illness, and institutionalization may be the culprits. Diegelmann et al. (2018) confirmed the positive effects of physical exercise on stabilizing depression among a sample of patients in a nursing home. Nguyen et al. (2016) studied the well-being of 837 elderly and found an association with subjective closeness with family and friends. Actual frequency of contact was less important than subjective feelings of closeness about the relationships.

> *Everything that has a beginning has an ending. Make your peace with that and all will be well.*
>
> Buddha

Dementia, which includes Alzheimer's disease, is the mental disorder most associated with aging. Examples of dementia include asking the same question 5 minutes apart, telling the same story within 10 minutes, and forgetting what day of the week it is. Azman et al. (2019) noted the economic, emotional, social and psychological impact of caring for a mentally ill family member and emphasized the need for seeking a support group.

....

Dementia: a generic term to describe cognitive, physical and psychological impairment in some elderly individuals.

Physician-Assisted Suicide for the Terminally Ill?

Declining health, loss of autonomy and independence, a sense of hopelessness, and depression are all factors that influence a person feeling immense emotional despair. Those who feel this emotional despair may seek measures to end their lives, and thus, end their suffering. The psychological principle of negative reinforcement is to stop the pain: An aversive stimulus leading to activity to end the aversiveness helps to explain how a person decides to commit suicide. Balasubramaniam (2018) noted that the topic of "rational suicide" by those not terminally ill has entered the national debate.

Euthanasia and physician-assisted suicide are two medical methods for ending one's life. Euthanasia is the practice of intentionally ending a life to relieve pain or suffering. The term comes from the Greek words meaning "good death," or dying without suffering. Euthanasia may be passive or active. In passive situations, medical treatment is withdrawn and nothing is done to prolong the life of the patient. In active situations deliberate actions are taken to end a person's life. Unlike euthanasia, physician assisted suicide (PAS) involves providing individuals with the means to end their own life, such as prescription medication. The individuals decide if, when, and where to end their own life.

Adult children or spouses are often asked their recommendations by medical professionals about withdrawing life support, such as food, water, or mechanical ventilation; starting medications like intravenous vasopressors to end life; or withholding certain procedures that would prolong life like cardiopulmonary resuscitation. Family members are usually ambivalent about life-prolonging treatments.

The official position of the American Medical Association (AMA) is that physicians must respect the patient's decision to forgo life-sustaining treatment but that they should not participate in patient-assisted suicide: "PAS is fundamentally incompatible with the physician's role as healer." Rather, the AMA affirms physicians who support life. Arguments against PAS emphasize that people who want to end the life of those they feel burdened by can abuse the practice.

In extreme situations, they may resort to such measures because they want to inherit the elder's money. Another argument is that what is diagnosed as "terminal" may not in fact be terminal, because physicians make mistakes. However, some physicians find that slow euthanasia is more psychologically acceptable than active voluntary euthanasia by injection. This position is based on the fact that sedatives and analgesics such as morphine may hasten death.

In spite of the AMA position, all fifty states now have laws for living wills, permitting individuals or family members to decide to withhold artificial nutrition and hydration from a patient who is wasting away. In practice, this means not putting in a feeding tube. For elderly, frail patients who may have a stroke or heart attack, do-not-resuscitate (DNR) orders may also be put in place.

In the past, advance directives were used to inform the medical personnel about how to handle end-of-life treatment. More effective is the Physicians Orders for Life Sustaining Treatment (POLST) document, which specifies the treatments that the elderly and frail want or do not want so that their wishes may be honored. This document is completed in collaboration with a physician and specifies such issues as "comfort measures only" or "no future hospitalization" for those who wish to die at home.

In 1997, the Death with Dignity act was passed and Oregon became the first state legalizing physician assisted suicide (PAS). Under the Bush administration, the U.S. attorney general John Ashcroft attempted to prosecute Oregon doctors who participated in PAS with violation of the federal Controlled Substances Act of 1970. In January 2006, the Supreme Court ruled that Oregon has a right to physician-assisted suicide. Its Death with Dignity Act requires that two physicians must agree that the patient is terminally ill and is expected to die within six months; the patient must ask three times for death both orally and in writing; and the patient must swallow the barbiturates themselves rather than be injected with a drug by the physician. In addition to Oregon, many states such as Colorado, Washington, Vermont, Maine, Hawaii, California, and District of Columbia, also have Death with Dignity laws. Individuals must meet the residency requirements of each state in order for the Death with Dignity laws of the state to apply to them. More states are considering Death with Dignity Act. ●

Sometimes placing a parent into a nursing home is an agonizing decision. Hogsnes et al. (2014) interviewed 11 spouses of persons with dementia before and after relocating them to a nursing home. Feelings of shame, guilt, and isolation on the part of the partner preceded relocating the spouse to a nursing home. The event which triggered the decision to move the spouse to a nursing home was physical violence—some with a knife—directed toward the

Euthanasia: from the Greek meaning "good death" or dying without suffering; either passively or actively ending the life of a patient.

caring partner. After relocating the spouse to a nursing home, partners described feelings of guilt, freedom, grief, loneliness in the spousal relationship, and striving for acceptance despite a lack of completion.

Insomnia

The elderly often complain of having problems with getting to sleep and staying asleep. However, Miner et al. (2018) found that only 43% of 379 elderly with an average age of 84 could be classified as "mild" insomniacs. Hence, while insomnia is prevalent among the elderly, when it is evident, it is most often mild.

Divorce

While divorce rates in general are dropping, they are rising steeply for couples over 50 (Papernow, 2018). In response to this "gray divorced population," Crowley and DePalma Brand (2019) interviewed 40 men and 40 women who had experienced divorce at or later than age 50—the average age was 59—regarding their attitudes toward divorce. Some felt that divorce should be more difficult to obtain:

> I just think that we live in a time where everything is automatic gratification and that people don't take the time to figure things out. . . . You know, so [you re] unhappy, so what do you do? . . . Let's say there was no Internet or Facebook or anything, and my ex-husband had said, "I'm unhappy [and I am not sure that] I really want to make this work." The options [that] he'd have are looking outside for sexual stuff, [but that] would have been limited, not nonexistent, [but limited]. I think the use of technology allows people who are, you know, quiet, shy, reserved, maybe not good looking . . . to go do something that no one has to know about. So I think now all this stuff is just at your fingertips, really. So, it's not like, I really want to try hard (p. 55).

Others felt divorce at midlife should be easier:

> [Divorce should be easier] because why beat a dead horse? If it's done, it's done. Why prolong people's misery? Give them an out (p.56).

Indeed, middle-aged and older adults don't always stay married and live "happily ever after" (Crowley & DePalma Brand, 2019). Blacks, formerly married, those without college educations, and those married less than ten years were most likely to divorce. Reasons for more divorces in middle age include: 1) older people are more likely to be remarried and persons who have been married before are more likely to divorce; 2) greater acceptance of divorce among one's cohort and friends; and 3) women are more likely to be economically independent, meaning that they can afford to leave the marriage. Other factors that affect later life divorce are the children's age, as there is less concern about how a divorce will affect older children; physical health, since good physical health means that one has time to start a "second life"; prenuptial agreements, which limit people's economic liability to their spouses; and dating sites, which make it easier to find a new partner quickly (Crowley & DePalma Brand, 2019).

Retirement

Retirement represents a rite of passage. Silver and Williams (2018) compared the retirements of older academics in medicine who had little work-life balance with younger academics in medicine who found the transition easier—the older cohort had no life outside of work. Reasons for retirement included wanting to enjoy life without the constraints of employment, the availability of income from sources of other than employment—for example, Social Security and pension—and job satisfaction or lack of it. Steinert and Haesner (2019) found that while retired individuals reported having fewer stresses as older individuals who continued being employed, the stress level for the two groups remained the same.

The retirement age in the United States for those born after 1960 is 67. Individuals can take early retirement at age 62, with reduced benefits. Retirement affects an individual's status, income, privileges, power, and prestige. One retiree noted that he was being waited on by a clerk who looked at his name on his check, thought she recognized him, and said, "Didn't you use to be somebody?" Hence, the retired struggle with an identity. When they worked, they were recognized as having value. Once retired they were "just an old person at Walmart."

People least likely to retire are unmarried, widowed, single-parent women who need to continue working because they have no pension or Social Security benefits. If they don't work or continue to work, they will have no income, so retirement is not an option. Some workers experience what is called **blurred retirement** rather than a clear-cut one. A blurred retirement means the individual works part time before completely retiring or takes a "bridge job" that provides a transition between a lifelong career and full retirement. Others may plan

....

Blurred retirement: an individual working part-time before completely retiring or taking a "bridge job" that provides a transition between a lifelong career and full retirement.

a **phased retirement** whereby an employee agrees to a reduced work load in exchange for reduced income. This arrangement is beneficial to both the employee and employer.

Smeaton et al. (2018) discussed **reverse retirement** as returning to the workforce after retiring. Factors related to doing so included low retirement income, having children under 30, and mortgage debt. Being able to return to work was also related to higher education, good health, and younger age.

To find meaning in retirement, some retired individuals volunteer—give back their time and money to attack poverty, illiteracy, oppression, crime, and so on. Examples of volunteer organizations are the Service Corps of Retired Executives, known as SCORE (www.score.org), Experience Works (www.experienceworks.org), and Generations United (www.gu.org).The retired also report having more time to sleep and to exercise—health promoting behaviors.

Sexuality

Of 1,656 married adults 57 to 85, 22% reported having sex two to three times a month, 29%, once a month or less, and 28% not at all in the last year (Stroope et al., 2015). Sexual frequency typically declines across time for both straight and gay couples. Given this decline, there is the assumption that couples are less satisfied (Muruthi et al., 2018). Schafer et al. (2018) did find an association between higher sexual interest and higher marital quality. However, some midlife spouses reject the idea that a diminished sex life reflects less marital satisfaction or not having a "successful marriage" (Paine et al., 2019).

The media sometimes reflects continued sexual interest in the later years. A content analysis of the sexual scripts depicted of older women via the television program "Hot in Cleveland" over four seasons revealed that these over-50 women viewed sex as desirable. Thus, the cultural scripts for the elderly, particularly older women, sometimes reinforce the idea of lifelong sexual desire (Montemurro & Chewning, 2018).

There are numerous changes in the sexuality of men and women as they age. For men, erectile dysfunction is the most common problem with erections taking longer to achieve, less rigidity, and a longer time to recover so that he can have another erection. "It now takes me all night to do what I used to do all night" is the adage aging men become familiar with.

Levitra, Cialis, and Viagra—prescription drugs that help a man obtain and maintain an erection—are helpful for about 50% of men. Others with erectile dysfunction may benefit from a pump that inflates two small banana-shaped tubes that have been surgically implanted into the penis.

CULTURE AND DIVERSITY

Rutagumirwa and Bailey (2018) conducted interviews with 15 older Tanzanian men and ten focus groups with 60 men, aged 60-82, who reported difficulty with living the male sexual script of their youth as they aged. Jando, also known as male initiation rites, served as a script for male sexuality which the aging males were unable to continue as they aged—declines in their bodies led to an inability to perform sexually and resulted in their feeling diminished masculinity.

Granville and Pregler (2018) reviewed sexuality of older women. While most noted a decline in sexual desire with age, the majority rated sex as important in their lives with emotional intimacy a paramount reason for sexual engagement. Primary sexual problems of older women were the absence of a partner and the partners who were available had difficulty maintaining erections. Regarding the aging female body, a woman's vaginal walls become thinner and less lubricating which is associated with pain during intercourse. Hormones prescribed by a physician knowledgeable of female sexuality typically eliminate the discomfort.

Interviews with 39 single women ages 35–91 revealed the major impact that they felt in their lives as they aged was the small dating pool and caregiving responsibilities. However, these women also highlighted "improvements in their sex lives as they aged in the areas of comfort with sex, sexual assertiveness, and sexual satisfaction". Such sexual advantages in the later years are often not given sufficient emphasis (Miller, 2019).

We discuss the psychosocial sources of sexual interest in couples in "Applying Social Research."

Lack of sex education for older adults also leaves them at risk for STI infection due to unprotected sexual encounters and incorrect condom use. While pregnancy is no longer a concern, STI exposure continues. Older adults account for 17% of new HIV diagnoses in the United States and are more likely to be diagnosed with HIV later in the course of the disease compared to younger people. However, an estimated 83.7% of sexually active older adults are never tested for HIV (Oraka et al., 2018).

Phased retirement: an employee agreeing to a reduced work load in exchange for reduced income.

Reverse retirement: returning to the workforce after retiring.

Sources of Sexual Interest in Older Couples

What is the profile of the elderly person who has an interest in sex?

Sample and Methods

Nine hundred and fifty-three couples, both cohabiting and married, participated in the National Social Life, Health, and Aging Project survey, which provided the data. Sexual interest was assessed by asking questions including (1) "About how often do you think about sex?" with five levels ranging from "less than once a month" to "several times a day;" (2) "For some people, sex is a very important part of their lives and for others it is not very important at all. How important a part of your life would you say that sex is?" with five levels ranging from "extremely important" to "not at all important;" and (3) "When your partner wants to have sex with you, how often do you agree?" with five responses ranging from "always" to "never."

Psychosocial factors assessed included social support from family and friends, properties of social networks, psychological well-being, personality traits, and relationship characteristics.

Social support was assessed by asking how often respondents felt they could rely on their friends and family, and how often they felt they could open up to them. The number of friends in one's network and the number of kin in the network were measured by asking respondents to list up to five individuals with whom they discuss important matters. Depression was measured using both an 11-item questionnaire called the Centers for Epidemiological Studies Depression Scale and by asking about taking antidepressants. Anxiety was measured by the Hospital Anxiety Scale. Personality traits were measured using a six-factor personality model: positivity, openness, conscientiousness, extroversion, agreeableness, and neuroticism. Positive relationship quality was assessed via a scale composed of self-rated overall relationship happiness, whether respondents felt the relationship was going well, how close they felt to their partner, how often they felt they could rely on them, and how often they felt

they could open up to them. Negative relationship quality was measured using a scale composed of how often the respondent's partner made too many demands, criticized them, or got on their nerves. Marital status was measured using self-reporting about being married versus having a non-spousal romantic or sexual partner. Relationship length was also measured by self-reporting and physical health was self-rated as well.

Findings

Results included that positivity, openness to experience, positive relationship quality, and the number of kin in one's social network were all associated with greater interest in sex. The researchers noted that positivity may dispose one more favorably toward sexual encounters, as one more aspect of gratifying social interaction. Furthermore, openness to experience may also include openness to sexual variety. Relationship quality may be explained since one may be more interested in sex with one's partner if the overall relationship is enjoyable. Number of kin may provide an overall emotional and personal lift which may spill over into one's personal and sexual relationship.

A partner's extroversion was negatively associated with interest in sex, possibly because this factor represents an individual tendency toward impulsiveness and is not amenable to the compromise and negotiation that accompanies discovering another's sexual preferences.

Other findings included that sexual interest was significantly lower for females and race was not a discriminating variable. Finally, poor physical health of the partner was associated with lower sexual interest in the respondent, and length of the relationship, which is confounded with age, was negatively associated with sexual interest. ●

Source: Iveniuk, J., & Waite, L. J. (2018). The psychosocial sources of sexual interest in older couples. *Journal of Social and Personal Relationships, 35*, 615-631.

Successful Aging

The World Health Organization defines healthy aging as developing and maintaining functional ability in the later years, including physical, mental, and psychosocial abilities. It is recognized that these abilities interact in environments which facilitate these abilities (Sadana et al., 2016). For example, if one is healthy but lives in poverty, it is more difficult to age successfully.

Aging

Advanced technology has helped to slow the aging process and to empower older adults. The aging process is generally associated with a decline in health, which may lead to impairment, social isolation, and loss of autonomy. Modern technologies have been used to address the health, functional limitations, chronic illnesses, and social relations of aging adults. Innovations, such as ambient assisted living, robotic technologies, and information and communication technologies have increased the **quality of life** for older adults.

Ambient intelligence is an electronic system which utilizes various innovations, such as smart sensor and surveillance cameras to detect and respond to an individual's movement (Navarro et al., 2018). For example, to fall as an elderly person can result in broken bones, extended hospital time and decreased life span. The potential risk is acute for the elderly who live alone. Ambient assisted living technologies can detect accidental falls of the elderly by incorporating sensors in the person's environment, providing a device the elderly can wear, or having surveillance cameras installed, or using all of these methods. With the aging of baby boomers and increasing life expectancy, this technology can provide health and safety monitoring for older adults and support elderly care (Koimizu et al., 2018). However, the use of the ambient assistive technology may be viewed as intrusive and the privacy of older adults may be compromised. Hence, caregiver children might discuss with their elderly parents whether the parents want such devices installed.

Robotic technology is becoming increasingly evident in our lives. Although individuals may have reservations about bringing robots into their homes, robot use for elder care was regarded as highly acceptable by a sample of college students (Chang et al., 2019). In fact, robot care may be an important contribution to meet the needs of an increasing geriatric population (Lehoux & Grimard, 2018).

Robots have been used to serve various functions in health settings including diagnosis, rehabilitation, assistance in surgery and patient comfort (Sniderman, 2018) and have been well received by patients and healthcare professionals. Robots are not only amiable companions with funny jokes and ability to dance (Sarabia et al., 2018), they may also help detect health problems (Costa et al., 2018).

One's culture may influence the acceptance of human-robot relationships. A cross-culture study investigating attitudes toward robot use in elder care revealed that Japanese care personnel have a more positive attitude than those in Finland (Coco et al., 2018). Designing and creating robots that are culturally relevant and acceptable for human users remains a challenge for future robotic technologies (Vandemeulebroucke et al., 2018). An interdisciplinary approach will ensure gerontechnology as an opportunity for older adults (Pilotto et al., 2018).

Another technological advancement that can benefit older adults is information and community technology (ICT), which has broadened the ways in which the elderly can stay connected with others and can stay informed. ICT use is associated with increased independence as well as decreased depression and loneliness. Silva et al. (2018) studied Internet use in a sample of 1,906 adults ages 50 and older and found a positive association with their quality of life via the relationship connection benefit. Research indicated social media such as Facebook can empower and provide a sense of connectedness for older adults (Aarts, 2018; Francis, 2018). Quan-Haase et al. (2017) interviewed 42 adults ages 65 and older and confirmed the use of technology such as email and Skype to stay connected, coordinate plans, and so forth. However, even though technology can impact the aging process positively, it cannot replace face-to-face interaction, physical presence, and touch. ●

Paramount in the definition of successful aging is health. Indeed, Ferdows et al. (2018) noted that "successful" aging is often referred to as "healthy" aging which results from exercising, proper weight, and not smoking. The researchers also noted that "successful" aging is rooted in favorable conditions set in the earlier years, such as education, income, and wealth. Rubio et al. (2018) identified the characteristics of those who are coping well with aging to include a high activity level, ability to express emotions, social engagement, and cognitive restructuring—the ability to frame events positively.

One's personal spirituality is also associated with positive outcomes as one ages. Lifshitz et al. (2019) found in a sample of 306 respondents age 50 and older, those reporting personal spirituality, in contrast to transcendental spirituality, reported lower levels of depression and higher levels of life satisfaction.

Technology also influences how a person ages. In the Technology and Aging section, we examine technology that can help with the aging process.

Quality of life: one's physical functioning, independence, economic resources, social relationships, and spirituality.

RELATIONSHIPS ACROSS TIME

Relationships in the later years vary. Some elderly men and women are lonely while others date or are in relationships.

> Young love is a flame; very pretty, often very hot and fierce . . . the love of the older and disciplined heart is as coals, deep burning, unquenchable.
>
> Henry Ward Beecher, American Congregationalist clergyman

Midlife to Later Life

Bell and Harsin (2018) interviewed couples at midlife in regard to their emotional connection and individuation—nurturing one's personal autonomy—and 25 years later. The researchers found a continuation of the qualities over time confirming evidence for "enhanced marital functioning in later life, more warmth and support, clearer interpersonal boundaries, more comfort with differences, and less overt conflict." Hence, if these qualities are present in midlife, they are predictive of positive outcomes in later life.

Loneliness

Dahlberg et al. (2018) surveyed 823 elderly beginning when they were 62 and again when they were 82 and found that patterns of social engagement in old age are established at least 20 years earlier. Close relationships at 62 predicted the same close relationships 20 years later. Hence, loneliness in old age may often be prevented by developing the skills of making and nurturing friendships earlier in life.

Elderly spouses in long-term marriages who are unhappy may also feel lonely. Stokes studied 1,114 spouses age 60 or older and found the perception of low marital quality was associated with loneliness. The more unhappy the spouses in their marriage, the more lonely they felt (Stokes, 2017).

Two researchers interviewed ten elderly adults who reported feeling lonely, often or all the time. Sources for their loneliness included lost and unfulfilled relationships, loss or lack of a partner, and the absence of a meaningful relationship (Tiilikainen & Seppanen, 2017). For older adults in residential care, Barbosa Neves et al. (2019) confirmed that communication technology can be used to enhance social connectedness. The technology was more likely to be used for those with geographically distant relatives.

Not all elderly are lonely. An 83-year-old known to the authors said:

I am living the life I always wanted. I enjoy each day. . .walking, having a quiet lunch, listening to my music and reading. I have no family or close friends but these are nonissues for me. Some people think I am a lonely old guy and feel sorry for me. . . .they have no idea that I am joyous inside and love my life.

Loneliness may also be dangerous. The New England Center for Investigative Reporting (Singer, 2018) revealed 235,000 elderly victims of abuse, including self-neglect cases. These involve the elderly who live alone who cannot take care of themselves and meet their daily needs like preparing food, ensuring bodily cleanliness, wearing clean clothes, or taking medications regularly, so they simply go without. They are off the radar and in danger.

Looking for Love

McCann and Allen (2018) noted that some women in later life were looking for a romantic partner if they were not intimately integrated into an extended family network. Those who reported that their emotional and social needs for connectedness were met via their family of origin and extended family networks had little interest in finding a romantic partner.

Wada et al. (2019) examined 320 online profiles of heterosexual individuals over 60 who were seeking a partner on dating sites. The individuals characterized themselves as active, adventurous, healthy, and intellectually engaged. They were also involved in volunteer work, had a positive approach to life and presented themselves as happy, fun-loving, and humorous. References to sex were nonexistent. In general, the elderly are more isolated, so the Internet provides a way to connect. Their primary goal is usually companionship.

Living Apart Together

As noted in the chapter on singlehood, the elderly who are single by death of spouse or divorce are increasingly opting to live apart together in a new relationship. Marriage or cohabitation are less attractive than keeping their own place and seeing their partner whenever (Connidis et al., 2017).

Relationships Between Elderly Spouses

Elderly spouses who enjoy their relationship report little conflict, considerable companionship, and mutual supportiveness. Rauer (2013) reported on 64 older couples who were married an average of 42 years and emphasized that being married in late life was the best of all contexts in terms of social,

Among the elderly, those who are married are the most healthy and happy.
Courtesy of Trevor Werb

People in long, happy marriages have won the lottery of life.
David Brooks, *The Second Mountain*

emotional, economic, and behavioral resources, such as taking care of each other. She noted that taking care of a spouse actually benefits the caregiver with feelings of self-esteem. However, the outcome for the spouse being cared for may be negative since he or she may feel dependent.

Koren et al. (2016) noted that when widowed individuals repartner in late life they may talk of caregiving issues. One woman in the Koren et al. (2016) study told the interviewer:

> *I went through radiation, but I told my partner: "Listen, I don't think you need such a punishment, to deal twice with such a story, you had your share, keep your distance, you don't have to," and he said: "There's no such thing, it's for better or for worse." So, there is also beauty in late-life repartnering, it's not shallow, and you know, in the course of time, if he'll need it, I'll be there.... When he had to have a catheterization, I was with him; when he goes to the doctor, I go with him. I don't believe in withdrawal of responsibility in late-life repartnering. I'm there with his children.*

Only a small percentage, about 8%, of individuals older than 100 are married. Most married centenarians are men in their second or third marriage. Many have outlived some of their children. Marital satisfaction in these elderly marriages is related to a high frequency of expressing love feelings to one's partner. Though it is assumed that spouses who have been married for a long time should know how their partners feel, this is often not the case. Telling each other "I love you" is very important to these elderly spouses.

Relationships Among Elderly Siblings After Parents Die

Kalmijn and Leopol (2019) studied the relationship between siblings over time and found that parents were important connecting contexts. When both parents died, the frequency of contact between siblings decreased. The researcher concluded "sibling relations among adult orphans faded in the long run" (p. 99).

GRANDPARENTHOOD

Another significant role for the elderly is that of grandparent, though this is more true for grandmothers than grandfathers (MaloneBeach et al., 2018). Sheppard and Monden (2019) analyzed data from 15 countries in Europe and confirmed that becoming a first-time grandmother was associated with fewer depressive symptoms among women (no association for men).

Among adults aged 40 and older who had children, close to 95% are grandparents and most have, on average, five or six grandchildren. Some grandparents literally live in the backyard of their children in what has become known as a granny pod. This is a small, 12-foot-by-24-foot prefabricated house that is also referred to as a MEDcottage and is hooked up to the water and electricity of the main house. Grandparents not only live on the premises to be close to their children and grandchildren, but the adult children have them close by to take care of them as they age.

Grandfamilies—families in which children reside with and are being raised by grandparents—include multigenerational families where grandparents care for grandchildren so the parent(s) can work or go to school. Grandfamilies also form in response to the parent(s) experiencing job loss, out-of-state employment, military deployment, divorce, deportation, illness, death, substance abuse, incarceration, or mental illness.

Margolis (2016) studied the amount of time grandparents in Canada spend in the role. They found that due to increased childlessness and fertility postponement, the time spent in grandparenting was 24.3 years for women and 18.9 years for men. In general, the older the child, the more likely grandparents spend time with the grandchildren. About 50% of young children, 35% of elementary school-age

Grandfamilies: families in which the grandparents or other relatives step forward to take care of children when their parents are not able to do so.

children, and 20% of teens spent at least some time with their grandparents in a typical week (Dunifon et al., 2018). Wade and Wild (2017) noted the positive impact of grandparent involvement on the prosocial behavior of children. Malone Beach et al. (2018) found that grandsons want support and advice from grandparents; granddaughters want support and friendship.

Some grandparents take care of their grandchildren full time. Almost three million grandparents are rearing their grandchildren (Cancino, 2016). Seven percent of children live with their grandparents (Dunifon et al., 2018). These grandparents often function in the role since the child's parents are incarcerated, substance abusers, or mentally ill. Most grandparents have limited financial resources—48% are below poverty level—and three quarters receive public assistance (Wilmoth, 2016). Hence, raising grandchildren can be a significant financial burden. Other grandparents provide supplemental help in a multi-generational family, assist on an occasional part-time basis, or occasionally visit their grandchildren.

Grandparents see themselves as caretakers, either emotional or economic resource providers or both, teachers, and historical connections on the family tree. While it is assumed that grandmothers are retired and have plenty of time to devote to their grandchildren, Chen et al. (2018) noted that Filipino women are often double burdened in mid and late life due to the demands of both employment and child care. While being a grandparent can be a rewarding experience, it can take an emotional toll. There are additional concerns depending on the grandparents' and grandchildren's races. Chancler and colleagues (2017) interviewed African American grandmothers, who were providing care for their biracial grandchildren, about the racial socialization of their grandchildren. The study revealed that while these grandmothers were actively involved in the daily care of their grandchildren, they unanimously agreed on rearing their grandchildren as African Americans. Since many parents and grandparents in the United States are monoracial, they do not have firsthand experience of being a biracial individual. These families may need support and resources to better prepare their biracial children to successfully cope with issues related to being biracial and minority individuals as they confront racism (Rollins, 2019).

Effects of Divorce on the Grandparent-Child Relationship

While grandparents can be important sources of support for their grandchildren during periods of separation and divorce (Jappens, 2018), divorce may have a negative effect on grandparents seeing their grandchildren, particularly in the case of the grandmother on the father's side. The situation most likely to produce this outcome is when a woman with young children has an adversarial relationship with her ex-husband and she is granted primary custody. Thus, the paternal grandparents may have limited access to their grandchildren.

Some grandparents are not allowed to see their grandchildren. In all 50 states, the role of the grandparent has limited legal and political support. In 2000, by a vote of six to three, the Supreme Court in *Troxel v. Granville* sided with the parents and virtually denied 60 million grandparents the right to see their grandchildren. The court viewed parents as having a fundamental right to make decisions about those with whom their children could spend time—including keeping them from grandparents. However, some courts have ruled in favor of grandparents. Step grandparents have no legal rights to their step grandchildren.

Benefits to Grandchildren

Grandchildren report enormous benefits from having a close relationship with grandparents, including

Grandchildren may benefit from being read to by their grandparents via Skype.

development of a sense of family ideals, moral beliefs, and a work ethic. Feeling loved is also a major benefit.

THE END OF LIFE

Smith et al. (2017) noted the importance of talking about end of life issues with one's parents and partners. Part of this conversation includes talking about death. **Thanatology** is the examination of the social dimensions of death, dying, and bereavement. In the next section, we discuss the death of one's spouse.

Death of One's Spouse

While the death of one's parents is often one's first encounter with death, the death of one's spouse happens later in life and is one of the most devastating adult life events a person experiences. The death of one's wife is often compounded if the family has young children, because the mother often provides more child care. An exception is if the couple are equal co-parents. (McClatchey, 2018). Although individual reactions and coping mechanisms for dealing with the death of a loved one vary, several reactions to death are common. These include shock, disbelief and denial, confusion and disorientation, grief and sadness, anger, numbness, physiological symptoms such as insomnia or lack of appetite, withdrawal from activities, immersion in activities, depression, and guilt. Eventually, surviving the death of a loved one involves the recognition that life must go on, the need to make sense out of the loss, and the establishment of a new identity.

Silverman and Thomson (2018) explicated how grieving varies by gender. The researchers rejected the stereotypical masculine norms of the grieving, stoic male and revealed a broader response of men being emotional. Isherwood et al. (2017) examined widowhood among 20 men and women age 85 and older. While males were more likely to experience social isolation and loneliness, many of the oldest widowed adults were able to continue to live socially engaged and meaningful lives. Because women tend to live longer than men—81.2 versus 76.4 years—they are more likely to experience the role of widow longer.

UP CLOSE: WIDOWHOOD: A PERSONAL STORY

"That which does not kill us, makes us stronger" is a phrase my children and I have proven to be true. I became a widow nine years ago, after having been married for 18 years. My husband and I were blessed

Thanatology: the examination of the social dimensions of death, dying, and bereavement.

with three incredible daughters, Pamela, Hannah, and Rachael. Since Mike's death, the girls and I are incredibly close to and rely on each other and somehow seem to have overcome obstacles in our lives.

Being a widow has changed our lives. Some of the changes follow:

- **Money problems:** While there can be money problems in a two-parent family, when there is just one parent, the economic responsibility is all on that one parent. Mike was able to work overtime and received yearly bonuses. My job does not allow overtime. I have considered getting an additional job at night and on the weekend, but then who would be available to get Rachael to her activities during that time? I am fortunate that Mike was a hard worker and I receive his Social Security, which helps to pay the bills.

- **Honey do:** Mike was a handyman. He could fix appliances, lawn mowers, cars, and other items. Now, when I need a repairman, I have to ask around for a reputable person that does not charge an arm and a leg to repair things.

- **Decision-making:** Mike and I would discuss decisions about discipline for our children, spending money, and other issues. I am now alone and responsible for making decisions.

- **Daily help.** Having someone to help with transporting our children to activities, picking up from after school day care, and chores around the house. If I was running late from work, Mike would pick the girls up and deliver them to where they needed to be. Mike's main job around the house was the yard. I hated yard work then and still do. He would spend all day cutting and trimming, so I did not have to worry about that chore. The girls now help around the yard, but if they are unable to do it, I am responsible.

- **Sharing the joys of life:** Our children have accomplished a lot in their lives—they've been in graduations and school competitions. I returned to school in my forties—Mike missed my graduation. He will not be able to walk our girls down the aisle at their weddings.

- **Companionship:** Mike and I would occasionally go out on dates. I would get so excited. A few hours without children, adult time. I miss those times. I also miss lying in bed or sitting on the couch, cuddling, and watching TV. I miss hugging, kissing, and making love to someone that I loved.

- **Growing old:** I always thought I would grow old with the man that I married. Raising our children together, retiring, enjoying our grandchildren, traveling, and enjoying each other's company in our old ages was what I expected, not burying my husband at 42.

I've heard someone say, "A divorce is like a death." I say, it is not. At least with a divorce your children can call their father if they choose to; my children will never speak to their father again and I know they wish they had one more chance to do so. I too wish I had that opportunity.

The only positive thing that I can say about his death is that we know that he is no longer suffering. I cannot imagine how much more difficult it would be to have your partner die suddenly. Everyone will go through difficult things in life—what matters though is how each person responds to those difficulties. I was determined to show my children that life goes on, no matter how difficult life gets.

I may decide to join the dating circuit someday, but it will not be until Rachael has graduated from high school. I do want to grow old with someone—he just better not try to change me, because I am set in my ways.

Used with the permission of Kim Morris.

• •

Repartnering in Late Life

Rapp (2018) noted that repartnering becomes increasingly unlikely after the fourth decade of life onward, particularly for women. The absence of economic resources accelerates partnership formation particularly in midlife, whereas good health accelerates partnership formation only in the later years. For those who are widowed after the age of 45, 5% of women and 24% of men will remarry. Women are less interested in remarrying and have lower opportunity to do so, because they typically outlive men (Schimmele & Wu, 2016). Bildtgard and Oberg (2017) interviewed 28 individuals, ages 63 to 91 years, who were either widowed or divorced and who repartnered after the age of 60 years. Results showed "that children were generally supportive of their older parents' unions and older individuals were often integrated into the new partner's network." However, Simhi-Meidani and Koren (2018) observed that children of an elder parent were challenged by loyalty conflicts when their parent became involved with a new partner. Coping with the death of a parent combined with accepting a new partner was particularly difficult. Nevertheless, the elderly parent who repartnered preferred to be dependent on partners rather than children and others.

Moore and Sailor (2018) interviewed 14 previously divorced and widowed women between the ages of 65 and 84 who talked of their new romantic partner. Various themes of their experience included being open to new experiences, feeling attracted to a partner, being committed, adjournment—dealing with romantic endings of the previous relationship—and generativity—nurturing new relationships and leaving a legacy.

Thoughts in the Last Year of Life

Johnson and Barer (1997) interviewed 48 individuals with an average age of 93 to find out their per-

> I'd rather have 30 minutes of wonderful than a lifetime of nothing special.
>
> Shelby, *Steel Magnolias*

spectives on death. About 77% of interviewees were women; of those, 56% lived alone, but 73% had some sort of support from their children or from one or more social support services. The following findings are specific to those who died within a year after the interview.

Most of the respondents had thought about death and saw their life as one that would soon end. Most did so without remorse or anxiety. With their spouses and friends dead and their health failing, they accepted death as the next stage in life. They felt like the last leaf on the tree. Some comments follow:

This widow (not the one who wrote the personal story) lives in her own home with three of her seven children living within a half mile. The other four live out of state but visit often.

If I die tomorrow, it would be all right. I've had a beautiful life, but I'm ready to go.

My husband is gone, my children are gone, and my friends are gone.

That's what is so wonderful about living to be so old. You know death is near and you don't even care.

I've just been diagnosed with cancer, but it's no big deal. At my age, I have to die of something. (Johnson and Barer, 1997, p. 205)

The major fear these respondents expressed was not the fear of death but of the dying process. Dying in a nursing home after a long illness is a dreaded fear. Sadly, almost 60% of the respondents died after a long, progressive illness. They had become frail, fatigued, and burdened by living. They identified dying in their sleep as the ideal way to die. Some hastened their death by no longer taking their medications; others wished they could terminate their own life. Competent adults have the legal right to refuse or discontinue medical interventions.

Dying Alone

There is a long-standing cultural belief that dying alone is to be avoided. Family members and institutional staff often try to predict when a parent will die and "be there—so the person will not die alone." But Caswell and O'Connor (2019) interviewed 11 older people living alone and seven hospice nurses. Results revealed that while the nurses were trained to feel it was their duty that no one die alone, the elderly were much less adamant. Rather, dying alone was viewed by some as the way to go. One of the elderly respondents reported:

The way my husband went is the way I'd like to go, suddenly, yeah . . . when you hear tales of people not being found for months on end . . . It's like nobody cared to look . . . that would be a bit distressing . . . if it was just like three days, that would be, yeah, I wouldn't mind that (p. 24).

FUTURE OF THE ELDERLY IN THE UNITED STATES

In the future, life expectancy will increase and advancement in technology will likely enhance the quality of life for the elderly. As the aging population increases in size, greater acceptance of aging will occur. New norms will develop about what the elderly can and should or should not do. For example, having children in later life will become more acceptable.

Living apart together, discussed in Chapter 4, will increasingly become a lifestyle option for the elderly who are single, widowed, or divorced. LAT provides the balance of autonomy and companionship that the elderly desire should they no longer want to give up their home or bring someone into their home.

Finally, men will become more involved taking care of their elderly parents. This phenomenon is already reflected among men in Spain (Comas-d'-Argemir & Soronellas, 2019).

SUMMARY

What is meant by the terms age and ageism?
Age is defined chronologically by time, physiologically by the capacity to see, hear, and so forth, psychologically by self-concept, sociologically by social roles, and culturally by the value placed on the elderly. Ageism is the denigration of the elderly, and gerontophobia is the dreaded fear of being elderly.

What is the "sandwich generation"?
Eldercare combined with child care is becoming common among the sandwich generation—adult children responsible for the needs of both their parents and their children. Two levels of eldercare include help with personal needs such as feeding, bathing, and toileting as well as instrumental care such as going to the grocery store, managing bank records, and so on. Members of the sandwich generation report feelings of exhaustion over the relentless demands, guilt over not doing enough, and resentment over feeling burdened.

Deciding whether to arrange for an elderly parent's care in a nursing home requires attention to a number of factors, including the level of care the parent needs, the philosophy and time availability of the adult child, and the resources of the adult children. Full-time professional nursing care costs can average around $100,000 annually.

Some elderly wish to end their life with the help of a physician. Many states such as Oregon, California, Colorado, Hawaii, Vermont, Washington, and District of Columbia support the Death with Dignity Act, which permits physicians to prescribe lethal medication for their patients under specific circumstances—for example, two physicians must confirm the diagnosis, the prognosis, and the patient's mental competence. More states are considering Death with Dignity legislation.

What issues confront the elderly?
Issues of concern to the elderly include income, mental health, physical health, retirement, insomnia, divorce, and sexuality. One's health becomes a primary focus for the elderly. Good health is the single most important factor associated with an elderly person's perceived life satisfaction. Mental problems may also occur with mood disorders; depression is the most common.

Regarding the sexuality of older couples, those who report a higher interest in sex also report being in good health, having a positive and open personality, and reporting higher marital quality. Inability to have an erection and the absence of a sexual partner are the primary sexual problems of elderly men and women, respectively. "Successful aging" is often referred to as "healthy" aging which includes physical, mental, and psychosocial health.

Exercising, proper weight, and not smoking are also important factors contributing to "healthy" aging.

What are relationships between elderly spouses like?
Elderly spouses who enjoy their relationship report little conflict, considerable companionship, and mutual supportiveness. Taking care of a spouse actually benefits the caregiver with feelings of self-esteem, but the outcome for the spouse being cared for may be negative since he or she may feel dependent.

What is grandparenthood like?
Grandparenthood is important to many elderly. Generally speaking, the grandmother is the more significant grandparent. Some grandparents take care of their grandchildren full time. Other grandparents provide supplemental help in a multigenerational family, assist on an occasional part-time basis, or occasionally visit their grandchildren. Grandparents see themselves as caretakers, either emotional or economic resource providers or both, teachers, and historical connections on the family tree.

What are some end-of-life issues?
While the death of one's parents is often one's first encounter with death, the death of one's spouse happens later in life and is one of the most devastating adult life events a person experiences. Repartnering in late life becomes increasingly unlikely, particularly for women.

What is the future of the elderly in the United States?
As the population continues to age in number, greater acceptance and new norms will be developed. Life expectancy will also increase and advancement in technology will likely enhance the quality of life for the elderly.

KEY TERMS

Advance directive
    (living will), 351

Age, 346

Ageism, 348

Blurred retirement, 354

Dementia, 352

Durable power of attorney, 351

Euthanasia, 353

Family care giving, 348

Frail, 348

Gerontology, 348

Gerontophobia, 348

Grandfamilies, 359

Medicaid, 350

Medicare, 350

Phased retirement, 355

Quality of life, 357

Reverse retirement, 355

Sandwich generation, 348

Thanatology, 361

WEB LINKS

AARP (American Association of Retired Persons)
http://www.aarp.org

Calculate Your Life Expectancy
www.livingto100.com

Channing House Retirement
http://www.channinghouse.org/

ElderWeb
http://www.elderweb.com

Grandfamilies
http://www.gu.org

Life Care Services
http://www.lifecareservices-seniorliving.com/

Senior Crops
http://www.seniorcorps.gov/

Senior Sex
http://www.holisticwisdom.com/senior-sex.htm

Get the tools you need to sharpen your study skills. SAGE edge offers a robust online environment featuring an impressive array of free tools and resources.
Access practice quizzes, eFlashcards, video, and multimedia at **edge.sagepub.com/knox13e**

SPECIAL TOPIC I
Careers in Marriage and the Family

Pleasure in the job puts perfection in the work.
Aristotle, philosopher

Students who take courses in marriage and family sometimes express an interest in working with people and ask what careers are available if they major in family science. In this Special Topics section, we review the primary domains of family practice including family life education, marriage and family therapy, child and family services, and family mediation. These careers often overlap, so you might engage in more than one of these roles within the same job. For example, you may work primarily in family services but participate in family life education as part of your job responsibilities.

For all the careers discussed in this section, having a bachelor's degree in a family-related field such as family science, sociology, or social work is helpful. Family science programs are the only academic programs that focus specifically on families and approach working with people from a family systems perspective. These programs have many different names, including child and family studies, human development and family studies, child development and family relations, and family and consumer sciences. Marriage and family programs are also offered through sociology departments, and social work provides opportunities to focus on family casework or other child and family services. Whereas some jobs are available at the bachelor's level, others require a master's or a PhD degree. More details on the various careers available to you that are related to marriage and family follow.

Family Life Education

Family life education (FLE) is an educational process that focuses on prevention, strengthening, and enriching individuals and families. Family life educators empower family members by providing them with information that will help prevent problems and enrich their family well-being. This education may be offered to families in different ways: a newsletter, one on one, online, or through a class or workshop. Examples of family life education programs include parent education for parents of toddlers through a child care center, a brown bag lunch series on balancing work and family in a local business, a premarital or marriage enrichment program at a local church, a

class on sexuality education in a high school classroom, or a workshop on family finance and budgeting at a local community center. The role of family life educator involves making presentations in a variety of settings, including schools, churches, and even prisons. Family life educators may also work with military families on military bases, within the business world with human resources or employee assistance programs, and within social service agencies or cooperative extension programs. Some family life educators develop their own business providing family life education workshops and presentations.

To become a family life educator, you need a minimum of a bachelor's degree in a family-related field such as family science, sociology, or social work. You can become a certified family life educator (CFLE) through the National Council on Family Relations (NCFR). The CFLE credential offers you credibility in the field and shows that you have competence in conducting programs in all areas of family life education. These areas are individuals and families in societal contexts, internal dynamics of the family, human growth and development, interpersonal relationships, human sexuality, parent education and guidance, family resource management, family law and public policy, and ethics. In addition, you must show competence in planning, developing, and implementing family life education programs.

Your academic program at your college or university may be approved for provisional certification. If you follow a specified program of study at your school, you may be eligible for a provisional CFLE certification. Once you gain work experience, you can then apply for full certification. Visit the NCFR website for more information.

Marriage and Family Therapy

Whereas family life educators help prevent the development of problems, marriage and family therapists help spouses, parents, and family members resolve existing interpersonal conflicts and problems. They treat a range of problems including communication, emotional and physical abuse, substance abuse, and sexual dysfunctions. Marriage and family therapists work in a variety of contexts, including mental health clinics, social service agencies, schools, and private practice.

Currently, all 50 states and the District of Columbia license or certify marriage and family therapists. Although an undergraduate degree in sociology, family studies, or social work is a good basis for becoming a marriage and family therapist, a master's degree and two years of post-graduate supervised clinical work are required to become a licensed marriage and family therapist. Some universities offer accredited master's degree programs specific to marriage and family therapy; these involve courses in marriage and family relationships, family systems, and human sexuality, as well as numerous hours of clinical contact with couples and families under supervision.

Full certification involves clinical experience with 1,000 hours of direct client, couple, and family contact; 200 of these hours must be under the direction of a supervisor approved by the American Association of Marriage and Family Therapists (AAMFT). In addition, most states require a licensure examination. The AAMFT is the organization that certifies marriage and family therapists and you can visit their website for more information.

Child and Family Services

In addition to family life educators and marriage and family therapists, careers are available in agencies and organizations that work with families, often referred to as social service agencies. The job titles within these agencies include family interventionist, family specialist, and family services coordinator. Your job responsibilities in these roles might involve helping your clients over the telephone, coordinating services for families, conducting intake evaluations, performing home visits, facilitating a support group, or participating in grant writing activities. In addition, family life education is often a large component of child and family services. You may develop a monthly newsletter, conduct workshops or seminars on particular topics, or facilitate regular educational groups.

Some agencies or organizations focus on helping a particular group of people. If you are interested in working with children, youth, or adolescents, you might find a position with Head Start, youth development programs such as the Boys and Girls Club, after-school programs (for example, pregnant or parenting teens), child care resource or referral agencies, or early intervention services. Child care resource and referral agencies assist parents in finding child care, provide training for child care workers, and serve as a general resource for parents and for child care providers. Early intervention services focus on children with special needs. If you work in this area, you might work directly with children or

you might work with the families and help to coordinate services for them.

Other agencies focus more on specific issues that confront adults or families as a whole. Domestic violence shelters, family crisis centers, and employee assistance programs are examples of employment opportunities. In many of these positions, you will function in multiple roles. For example, at a family crisis center, you might take calls on a crisis hotline, work one-on-one with clients to help them find resources and services, and offer classes on sexual assault or dating violence to high school students.

Another focus area in which jobs are available is gerontology. Opportunities include those within residential facilities such as assisted-living facilities or nursing homes, senior centers, organizations such as the Alzheimer's Association, or agencies such as National Association of Area Agencies on Aging. There is also a need for eldercare resource and referral, as more and more families find that they have caregiving responsibilities for an aging family member. These families have a need for resources, support, and assistance in finding residential facilities or other services for their aging family member. Many of the available positions with these types of agencies are open to individuals with a bachelor's degree. However, if you get your master's degree in a program emphasizing the elderly, you might have increased opportunity and will be in a position to compete for various administrative positions.

Family Mediation

In Chapter 15 on Divorce, Remarriage, and Stepfamilies, we emphasized the value of divorce mediation. This service is also known as family mediation and involves a neutral third party who negotiates with divorcing spouses on the issues of child custody, child support, spousal support, and division of property. The purpose of mediation is not to reconcile the partners but to help the couple make decisions about children, money, and property as amicably as possible. A mediator does not make decisions for the couple but supervises communication between the partners, offering possible solutions.

Although some family and divorce mediators are attorneys, family life professionals are becoming more common. Specific training is required that may include numerous workshops or a master's degree offered at some universities. Most practitioners conduct mediation in conjunction with their role as a family life educator, marriage and family therapist, or other professional. In effect, you would be in business for yourself as a family or divorce mediator.

Students interested in any of these career paths can profit from obtaining initial experience in working with people through volunteer or internship agencies. Most communities have crisis centers, mediation centers, and domestic abuse centers that permit students to work for them and gain experience. Not only can you provide a service, but you can also assess your suitability for the "helping professions," as well as discover new interests. Talking with people already in the profession is also a good way to gain new insights. Your instructor may already be in the marriage and family profession you would like to pursue or be able to refer you to someone who is.

Note: Appreciation is expressed to Sharon Ballard, PhD, CFLE, for the development of this Special Topic section. Dr. Ballard is Chair of Human Development and Family Science at East Carolina University. She is also a certified family life educator through the National Council on Family Relations.

SPECIAL TOPIC II
Contraception and STI Protection

I am pro responsible choice. You know, there is choice to abstain, choice to use contraception. There are all kinds of good choices.

Sharron Angle, American politician

Once individuals have decided on whether and when they want children, they need to make a choice about contraception. All contraceptive practices have one of two purposes: To prevent the male sperm from fertilizing the female egg or to keep the fertilized egg from implanting itself in the uterus. About five to seven days after fertilization, pregnancy begins.

Although the fertilized egg will not develop into a human unless it implants on the uterine wall, pro-life supporters believe that conception has already occurred.

In selecting a method of contraception, the important issues to consider are pregnancy prevention, STI prevention, opinion of the partner, ease of use, and cost. Often sexual partners use no contraception and live in denial that "this one time won't end in a pregnancy." In a study of 13,119 undergraduates 25% reported that "I have always used a condom before intercourse" (Hall & Knox, 2019).

Contraceptive Effectiveness, STI Protection, Benefits, And Disadvantages

METHOD	RATES[1,2]	STI PROTECTION	BENEFITS	DISADVANTAGES	COST[3]
Oral contraceptive (the pill)	91%	No	High effectiveness rate, 24-hour protection, and menstrual regulation	Daily administration, side effects possible, medication interactions	$0-50 per month
Nexplanon/Implanon NXT or Implanon (3-year implant)	99.95%	No	High effectiveness rate, long-term protection	Side effects possible, menstrual changes	$0-1,300 per month
Depo-Provera (3-month injection) or Depo-subQ Provera 104	94%	No	High effectiveness rate, long-term protection	Decreases body calcium, not recommended for use longer than 2 years for most users, side effects likely	$0-150 per month
Transdermal patch	91%	No	Same as oral contraceptives except use is weekly, not daily	Patch changed weekly, side effects possible	$15–32 per month
NuvaRing (vaginal ring)	91%	No	Same as oral contraceptives except use is monthly, not daily	Must be comfortable with body for insertion	$15–48 per month
Male condom	82%	Yes	Few or no side effects, easy to purchase and use	Can interrupt spontaneity	$2–10 a box
Female condom	79%	Yes	Few or no side effects, easy to purchase	Decreased sensation and insertion takes practice	$4–10 a box
Spermicide	72%	No	Many forms to choose, easy to purchase and use	Can cause irritation, can be messy	$8–18 per box/tube/can
Today Sponge[3]	76–88%	No	Few side effects, effective for 24 hours after insertion	Spermicide irritation possible	$3–5 per sponge

(Continued)

(Continued)

METHOD	RATES[1,2]	STI PROTECTION	BENEFITS	DISADVANTAGES	COST[3]
Diaphragm and Cervical cap	88% diaphragm	No	Few side effects, can be inserted within two hours before intercourse	Can be messy, increased risk of vaginal/UTI infections	$50–200 plus spermicide
Intrauterine device (IUD): Paraguard or Mirena	99.2%	No	Little maintenance, longer term protection	Risk of Pelvic Inflammatory Disease (PID) increased, chance of expulsion	$150–300
Withdrawal	78%	No	Requires little planning, always available	Pre-ejaculatory fluid can contain sperm	$0
Periodic abstinence	76%	No	No side effects, accepted in all religions/cultures	Requires a lot of planning, need ability to interpret fertility signs	$0
Emergency contraception	85%	No	Provides an option after intercourse has occurred	Must be taken within 72 hours, side effects likely	$10–32
Abstinence	100%	Yes	No risk of pregnancy or STIs	Partners both have to agree to abstain	$0

[1]Effectiveness rates are listed as percentages of women not experiencing an unintended pregnancy during the first year of typical use. Typical use refers to use under real-life conditions. Perfect use effectiveness rates are higher.

[2]Lower percentages apply to parous women—those who have given birth. Higher rates apply to nulliparous women—those who have never given birth.

[3]Costs may vary.

REFERENCES

Hall, S. & Knox, D. (2019). College Student Attitudes and Behaviors Survey of 13,119 undergraduates. Unpublished data collected for this text. Department of Family, Consumer, and Technology Education Teachers College, Ball State University and Department of Sociology, East Carolina University, Greenville, NC.

CHAPTER 1

Attitudes Toward Marriage Scale

The purpose of this survey is to assess the degree to which you view marriage positively. Read each item carefully and consider what you believe. There are no right or wrong answers. After reading each statement, select the number that best reflects your level of agreement, using the following scale:

1	2	3	4	5	6	7
Strongly Disagree						Strongly Agree

——— 1. I am married or plan to get married.

——— 2. Being single and free is not as good as people think it is.

——— 3. Marriage is NOT another word for being trapped.

——— 4. Single people are more lonely than married people.

——— 5. Married people are happier than single people.

——— 6. Most of the married people I know are happy.

——— 7. Most of the single people I know think marriage is better than singlehood.

——— 8. The statement that singles are lonelier and less happy than spouses is mostly true.

——— 9. It is better to be married than to be single.

——— 10. Spouses enjoy their lifestyle more than single people.

——— 11. Spouses have a more intimate relationship than singles do in their relationships.

——— 12. Spouses have a greater sense of joy than singles.

——— 13. Being married is a more satisfying lifestyle than being single.

——— 14. People who think that married people are happier than single people are correct.

——— 15. Single people struggle with avoiding loneliness.

——— 16. Married people are not as lonely as single people.

——— 17. The companionship of marriage is a major advantage of the lifestyle.

——— 18. Married people have better sex than singles.

——— 19. The idea that singlehood is a happier lifestyle than being married is nonsense.

——— 20. Singlehood as a lifestyle is overrated.

Scoring

After assigning a number from 1 (strongly disagree) to 7 (strongly agree), add the numbers. The higher your score—140 is the highest possible score—the more positive your view of marriage. The lower your score—20 is the lowest possible score—the more negatively you view marriage. The midpoint is 60. Scores lower than 60 suggest more a negative view of marriage; scores higher than 60 suggest a more positive view of marriage.

Norms

The norming sample of this self-assessment was based on 53 undergraduate men and 155 undergraduate women in 2018. The average score of the males was 87 and the average score of the females was 92, suggesting a predominantly positive view of marriage with females more positive than males. ●

Source: "Attitudes Toward Marriage Scale" was developed for this text by David Knox. It is to be used for general assessment and is not designed to be a clinical diagnostic tool or as a research instrument.

CHAPTER 2

The Love Attitudes Scale

The Love Attitudes Scale provides a way for you to assess the degree to which you tend to be romantic or realistic (conjugal) in your view of love. When you determine your score from the Love Attitudes Scale, be aware that your tendency to be a romantic or a realist is neither good nor bad. Both romantics and realists can be happy individuals and successful relationship partners. Love also conveys enormous benefits, including positive mental health. There are no right or wrong answers.

Directions

After reading each sentence carefully, write the number that best represents the degree to which you agree or disagree with the sentence.

1	2	3	4	5
Strongly agree	Mildly agree	Undecided	Mildly disagree	Strongly disagree

——1. Love doesn't make sense. It just is.

——2. When you fall "head over heels" in love, it's sure to be the real thing.

——3. To be in love with someone you would like to marry but can't is a tragedy.

——4. When love hits, you know it.

——5. Common interests are really unimportant; as long as each of you is truly in love, you will adjust.

——6. It doesn't matter if you marry after you have known your partner for only a short time as long as you know you are in love.

——7. If you are going to love a person, you will "know" after a short time.

——8. As long as two people love each other, the educational differences they have really do not matter.

——9. You can love someone even though you do not like any of that person's friends.

——10. When you are in love, you are usually in a daze.

——11. Love "at first sight" is often the deepest and most enduring type of love.

——12. When you are in love, it really does not matter what your partner does because you will love him or her anyway.

——13. As long as you really love a person, you will be able to solve the problems you have with the person.

——14. Usually you can really love and be happy with only one or two people in the world.

——15. Regardless of other factors, if you truly love another person, that is a good enough reason to marry that person.

——16. It is necessary to be in love with the one you marry to be happy.

——17. Love is more of a feeling than a relationship.

——18. People should not get married unless they are in love.

——19. Most people truly love only once during their lives.

——20. Somewhere there is an ideal mate for most people.

——21. In most cases, you will "know it" when you meet the right partner.

——22. Jealousy usually varies directly with love; that is, the more you are in love, the greater your tendency to become jealous will be.

——23. When you are in love, you are motivated by what you feel rather than by what you think.

——24. Love is best described as an exciting thing rather than a calm thing.

——25. Most divorces probably result from falling out of love rather than failing to adjust.

——26. When you are in love, your judgment is usually not too clear.

——27. Love comes only once in a lifetime.

——28. Love is often a violent and uncontrollable emotion.

——29. When selecting a marriage partner, differences in social class and religion are of small importance compared with love.

——30. No matter what anyone says, love cannot be understood.

Scoring

Add the numbers you wrote to the left of each item. 1 (strongly agree) is the most romantic response and 5 (strongly disagree) is the most realistic response. The lower your total score—30 is the lowest possible score—the more romantic your attitudes toward love. The higher your total score—150 is the highest possible score—the more realistic your attitudes toward love. A score of 90 places you at the midpoint between being an extreme romantic and an extreme realist. Of 52 undergraduate males, 82 was the average score; of 154 undergraduate females, 86 was the average score. Hence, these undergraduates tended to be romantic with men slightly more romantic than women. ●

Source: Knox, D. "Conceptions of Love at Three Developmental Levels." Dissertation, Florida State University, Tallahassee, FL.

CHAPTER 3

Gender Role Attitudes—Family Life Index

Read each item and, using the scale below, select the number that reflects your belief/attitude.

1	2	3	4
Strongly agree	Agree	Disagree	Strongly disagree

——1. The husband should be the head of the family.

——2. Babies and young children need to have their mothers around most of the day.

——3. It is much better for everyone involved if the man is the achiever outside the home and the woman takes care of the home and family.

——4. A woman's most important task in life is being a mother.

——5. By nature, women are better than men at making a home and caring for children.

——6. A preschool child is likely to suffer if his or her mother works outside the home.

——7. A husband should earn a larger salary than his wife.

——8. A woman should not be employed if her husband can support her.

——9. All in all, family life suffers when the wife has a full-time job.

Scoring

Add the numbers you selected for each item. 1 (strongly agree) is the most traditional response and 4 (strongly disagree) is the most egalitarian response. The lower your total score—9 is the lowest possible score—the more traditional you are in respect to gender role attitudes. The higher your total score—36 is the highest possible score—the more egalitarian you are in respect to gender role attitudes. A score of 22.5 places you at the midpoint between being very traditional and very egalitarian.

Norms

The norming sample of this self-assessment was based on 37 males and 172 females. The average score of the males was 23 and the average score of the females was 25, suggesting a lean toward being egalitarian by both males and females with females being more egalitarian. ●

Source: Erarslan, A. B., & Rankin, B. (2013). Gender role attitudes of female students in single-sex and coeducational high schools in Istanbul. *Sex Roles 69*, 455-469. Used by permission of Ayse Burcin Baskurt. Email is aerarslan@ku.edu.tr

CHAPTER 4

Attitudes Toward Singlehood Scale

The purpose of this survey is to assess the degree to which students view remaining single (never getting married) positively. Read each item carefully and consider what you believe. There are no right or wrong answers, so please give your honest reaction and opinion. After reading each statement, select the number that best reflects your level of agreement, using the following scale:

1	2	3	4	5	6	7

Strongly Disagree   Strongly Agree

——1. I plan to remain single.

——2. Getting married is not as advantageous as it used to be.

——3. Marriage is another word for being trapped.

——4. Singlehood is another word for being free.

——5. Single people are happier than married people.

——6. Most of the married people I know are unhappy.

——7. Most of the single people I know enjoy their lifestyle.

——8. The statement that singles are lonely and unhappy is not true.

——9. It is better to be single than to be married.

——10. Of the two lifestyle choices, single or married, single is better.

——11. Singles have more friendships and social connections than spouses.

——12. Singles have a greater sense of independence than spouses.

——13. Being single is a more satisfying lifestyle than being married.

——14. People who think you must be married to be happy are wrong.

——15. You can be alone and not be lonely.

——16. The freedom of singlehood outweighs any advantage of marriage.

——17. The companionship of marriage is overrated.

——18. Singles have better sex than spouses.

——19. The idea that only spouses are fulfilled is nonsense.

——20. Marriage as a lifestyle is overrated.

——21. Most people who are married have envy for those who are single.

——22. Spouses lose control of their lives while singles maintain control.

——23. There is entirely too much social pressure to get married.

——24. People are finding out that being single is a better deal than being married.

——25. The singles I know are happier than the spouses I know.

Scoring

After assigning a number from 1 (strongly disagree) to 7 (strongly agree), add the numbers. The higher your score—175 is the highest possible score—the more positively you view remaining single. The lower your score—25 is the lowest possible score—the more negatively you view singlehood. A score of 75 is the midpoint. Scores below 75 tend to reflect a negative view of singlehood while scores above 75 reflect a positive view of singlehood.

Norms

The norming sample of this self-assessment was based on the responses of 187 undergraduates comprising 24 men and 163 women at a large southeastern university. The mean score for the total sample was 86. The mean for the men was 95; for the women, 85. Hence, the total sample tended to regard singlehood positively with men having more positive attitudes toward singlehood than women. ●

Source: "Attitudes Toward Singlehood Scale," 2014, by Mark Whatley, PhD, Department of Psychology, Valdosta State University, Valdosta, GA 31698-0100. Used by permission. Other uses of this scale only by written permission of Dr. Whatley (mwhatley@valdosta.edu). This scale is intended to provide basic feedback about one's view of singlehood. It is not designed to be a sophisticated research instrument.

Living Apart Together (LAT) Scale

The purpose of this scale is to assess the degree to which you are suited for a Living Apart Together arrangement whereby you live in a separate residence from your partner with whom you have a long-term committed relationship.

Directions

After reading each sentence carefully, circle the number that best represents the degree to which you disagree or agree with the sentence. There are no right or wrong answers.

1	2	3	4	5
Strongly disagree (SD)	Mildly disagree (MD)	Undecided (U)	Mildly agree (MA)	Strongly agree (SA)

——1. I prefer to have my own place—apart from my partner—to live.

    1   2   3   4   5

——2. Living apart from my partner feels "right" to me.

    1   2   3   4   5

——3. Too much togetherness can kill a relationship.

    1   2   3   4   5

——4. Living apart can enhance your relationship.

    1   2   3   4   5

——5. By living apart you can love your partner more.

    1   2   3   4   5

——6. Living apart protects your relationship from staleness.

    1   2   3   4   5

——7. Couples who live apart are happier than those who don't.

    1   2   3   4   5

——8. Couples who LAT are just as much in love as those who live together in the same place.

    1   2   3   4   5

——9. People who LAT probably have less relationship stress than couples who live together in the same place.

    1   2   3   4   5

——10. LAT couples are just as committed as couples who live together in the same residence.

    1   2   3   4   5

Scoring

Add the numbers you circled. The lower your total score—10 is the lowest possible score—the less suited you are to the Living Apart Together lifestyle. The higher your total score—50 is the highest possible score—the more suited you are to the Living Apart Together lifestyle. A score of 30 places you at the midpoint between being the extremes. Of 46 males, the average score was 27.7. Of 185 females, the average score was 27.9. Of 229 students, the average was 27.9. Hence most students are less than enthusiastic about Living Apart Together, with no gender differences. ●

Source: "Living Apart Together Scale" was developed for this text. It is to be used for general assessment and is not designed to be a clinical diagnostic tool or as a research instrument.

CHAPTER 5

The Relationship Involvement Scale

This scale is designed to assess the level of your involvement in a current relationship. Please read each statement carefully, and write the number next to the statement that reflects your level of disagreement or agreement, using the following scale:

1	2	3	4	5	6
Strongly disagree	Disagree	Mildly disagree	Mildly agree	Agree	Strongly agree

—— 1. I have told my friends that I love my partner.

—— 2. My partner and I have discussed our future together.

—— 3. I have told my partner that I want to marry him or her.

—— 4. I feel happier when I am with my partner.

—— 5. Being together is very important to me.

—— 6. I cannot imagine a future with anyone other than my partner.

—— 7. I feel that no one else can meet my needs as well as my partner.

—— 8. When talking about my partner and me, I tend to use the words "us," "we," and "our."

—— 9. I depend on my partner to help me with many things in life.

—— 10. I want to stay in this relationship no matter how hard times become in the future.

Scoring

Add the numbers you assigned to each item. A 1 reflects the least involvement and a 7 reflects the most involvement. The lower your total score—10 is the lowest possible score—the lower your level of involvement; the higher your total score—70 is the highest possible score—the greater your level of involvement. A score of 40 places you at the midpoint between a very uninvolved and a very involved relationship.

Other Students Who Completed the Scale

Students from two universities completed the scale—31 male and 86 female undergraduate psychology students came from Valdosta State University, while 60 male and 129 female undergraduate students from the courtship and marriage courses at East Carolina University participated in the survey.

Scores of Participants

When students' scores from both universities were combined, the men's average score was 50.06 (SD = 14.07) and the women's average score was 52.93 (SD = 15.53), reflecting moderate involvement for both sexes. There was no significant difference between men and women in level of involvement. However, there was a significant difference ($p < .05$) between Whites and non-Whites, with Whites reporting greater relationship involvement (M = 53.37; SD = 14.97) than non-Whites (M = 48.33; SD = 15.14). ●

Source: "The Relationship Involvement Scale" 2004 by Mark Whatley, PhD, Department of Psychology, Valdosta State University, Valdosta, GA 31698-0100. Used by permission. Other uses of this scale by written permission of Dr. Whatley (mwhatley@valdosta.edu). Information on the reliability and validity of this scale is available from Dr. Whatley.

Involved Couple's Inventory

The following questions are designed to increase your knowledge of how you and your partner think and feel about a variety of issues. Assume that you and your partner are considering marriage. Each partner should **ask each other** the following questions:

Partner Feelings and Issues

1. If you could change one thing about me, what would it be?

2. On a scale of 0 to 10, how well do you feel I respond to criticism or suggestions for improvement?

3. What would you like me to say or not say that would make you happier?

4. What do you think of yourself? Describe yourself with three adjectives.

5. What do you think of me? Describe me with three adjectives.

6. What do you like best about me?

7. On a scale of 0 to 10, how jealous do you think I am? How do you feel about my level of jealousy?

8. How do you feel about me?

9. To what degree do you feel we each need to develop and maintain outside relationships so as not to focus all of our interpersonal expectations on each other? Does this include individuals of the other sex?

10. Do you have any history of abuse or violence, either as an abused child or adult or as the abuser in an adult relationship?

11. If we could not get along, would you be willing to see a marriage counselor? Would you see a sex therapist if we were having sexual problems?

12. What is your feeling about prenuptial agreements?

13. Suppose I insisted on you signing a prenuptial agreement?

14. To what degree do you enjoy getting and giving a massage?

15. How important is it to you that we massage each other regularly?

16. On a scale of 0 to 10, how emotionally close do you want us to be?

17. How many intense love relationships have you had, and to what degree are these individuals still a part of your life in terms of seeing them or sending text messages?

18. Have you lived with anyone before? Are you open to our living together? What would be your understanding of the meaning of our living together—would we be finding out more about each other or would we be committed to marriage?

19. What do you want for the future of our relationship? Do you want us to marry? When?

20. On a ten-point scale (0 = very unhappy; 10 = very happy), how happy are you in general? How happy are you about us?

21. How depressed have you been? What made you feel depressed?

22. What behaviors do I engage in that upset you and you would like me to stop?

23. What new behaviors do you want me to develop or begin that would make you happier?

24. What quality for a future partner would be a requirement for you?

25. What quality for a future partner would be a deal breaker—you would not marry this person?

26. Why did your last relationship end?

27. What would your last partner say was your worst characteristic?

28. How many past sexual partners is too many for a person you would be interested in?

29. How much time do you spend playing video games? How do you feel about me playing video games? How much time a day playing video games is "too much"?

30. How often do you post on social media? How do you feel about me posting on social media about our relationship?

(Continued)

(Continued)

Parents and Family

1. How do you feel about your mother? Your father? Your siblings?

2. On a 10-point scale, how close are you to your mom, dad, and each of your siblings?

3. How close were your family members to one another? On a 10-point scale, what value do you place on the opinions or values of your parents?

4. How often do you have contact with your father or mother? How often do you want to visit your parents and/or siblings? How often would you want them to visit us? Do you want to spend holidays alone or with your parents or mine?

5. What do you like and dislike most about each of your parents?

6. What do you like and dislike about my parents?

7. What is your feeling about living near our parents? How would you feel about my parents living with us? How do you feel about our parents living with us when they are old and cannot take care of themselves?

8. How do your parents get along? Rate their marriage on a scale of 0 to 10 (0 = unhappy; 10 = happy).

9. To what degree do your parents take vacations together? What are your expectations of our taking vacations alone or with others?

10. To what degree did members of your family consult one another on their decisions? To what degree do you expect me to consult you on the decisions that I make?

11. Who was the dominant person in your family? Who had more power? Who do you regard as the dominant partner in our relationship? How do you feel about this power distribution?

12. What problems has your family experienced? Is there any history of mental illness, alcoholism, drug abuse, suicide, or other such problems?

13. What did your mother and father do to earn an income? How were their role responsibilities divided in terms of having income, taking care of the children, and managing the household? To what degree do you want a job and role similar to that of the same-sex parent?

Social Issues, Religion, and Children

1. How do you feel about the President? Who did you vote for in the last election?

2. What are your feelings about women's rights, racial equality, and homosexuality?

3. To what degree do you regard yourself as a religious or spiritual person? What do you think about religion, a Supreme Being, prayer, and life after death?

4. Do you go to religious services? Where? How often? Do you pray? How often? How important is prayer to you? How important is it to you that we pray together? What do you pray about? When we are married, how often would you want to go to religious services? In what religion would you want our children to be reared? What responsibility would you take to ensure that our children had the religious training you wanted them to have?

5. How do you feel about abortion? Under what conditions, if any, do you feel abortion is justified?

6. How do you feel about children? How many do you want? When do you want the first child? At what intervals would you want to have additional children? What do you see as your responsibility in caring for the children—changing diapers, feeding, bathing, playing with them, and taking them to lessons and activities? To what degree do you regard these responsibilities as mine?

7. Suppose I did not want to have children or couldn't have them. How would you feel? How do you feel about artificial insemination, surrogate motherhood, in vitro fertilization, and adoption?

8. To your knowledge, can you have children? Are there any genetic problems in your family history that would prevent us from having normal children? How healthy (physically) are you? What health problems do you have? What health problems have you had? What operations have you had? How often have you seen a physician in the last three years? What medications have you taken or do you currently take? What are these medications for? Have you seen a therapist, psychologist, or psychiatrist? What for?

9. How should children be disciplined? Do you want our children to go to public or private schools?

10. How often do you think we should go out alone without our children? If we had to decide between the two of us going on a cruise to the Bahamas alone or taking the children camping for a week, what would you choose?

11. What are your expectations of me regarding religious participation with you and our children?

Sex

1. How much sexual intimacy of what kind do you feel is appropriate how soon in a relationship?

2. What does "having sex" mean to you? If a couple has experienced oral sex only, have they had sex?

3. What sexual behaviors do you most and least enjoy? How often do you need to have an orgasm, oral sex, intercourse? How do you feel about anal sex? Threesomes? How do you want me to turn you down when I don't want to have sex? How do you want me to approach you for sex? How do you feel about nonorgasmic-focused intimacy—cuddling, massaging, holding?

4. By what method of stimulation do you experience an orgasm most easily?

5. What do you think about masturbation, homosexuality, sadism and masochism (S&M)?

6. What type of contraception do you suggest? Why? If that method does not prove satisfactory, what method would you suggest next?

7. What are your values regarding extramarital sex? An open relationship?

8. How often do you look at pornography? How do you feel about my doing so? How do you feel about our watching porn together? How do you feel about my going to a strip club without you? Our going together?

9. How important is our using a condom to you?

10. When is the last time you were tested for sexually transmitted infections (STIs)? What were the results? If you have not been tested what are your feelings about being tested? Do you want me to be tested for STIs?

11. What sexually transmitted infections have you had?

12. How much do you want to know about my sexual behavior with previous partners?

13. How many friends with benefits relationships have you been in? What is your interest in our having such a relationship?

14. How much do you trust me in terms of my being faithful or monogamous with you?

15. How open do you want our relationship to be in terms of having emotional or sexual involvement with others, while keeping our relationship primary?

16. What things have you done that you are ashamed of?

17. What emotional, psychological, or physical health problems do you have? What issues do you struggle with?

18. What are your feelings about your sexual adequacy? What sexual problems do you or have you had?

19. What is your ultimate sexual fantasy?

20. To what degree have you cheated or been unfaithful in a relationship?

21. To what degree has a previous partner cheated or been unfaithful to you?

22. How important is monogamy to you?

Careers and Money

1. What kind of job or career will you have? What are your feelings about working in the evening versus being home with the family? Where will your work require that we live? How often do you feel we will be moving? How much travel will your job require?

2. To what degree did your parents agree on how to deal with money? Who was in charge of spending, and who was in charge of saving? Did working or earning the bigger portion of the income connect to control over money?

3. What are your feelings about a joint versus a separate checking account? Which of us do you want to pay the bills? How much money do you think we will have left over each month? How much of this do you think we should save?

4. When we disagree over whether to buy something, how do you suggest we resolve our conflict?

5. What jobs or work experience have you had? If we end up having careers in different cities, how do you feel about being involved in a commuter marriage?

6. What is your preference for where we live? Do you want to live in an apartment or a house? What are your needs for a car, television, cable service, phone plan, entertainment devices, and so on? What are your feelings about us living in two separate places, the living apart together idea whereby we can have a better relationship if we give each other some space and have plenty of room?

7. How do you feel about my having a career? Do you expect me to earn an income? If so, how much annually? To what degree do you feel it is your responsibility to cook, clean, and take care of the children? How do you feel about putting young children or infants in day-care centers?

(Continued)

(Continued)

When the children are sick and one of us has to stay home, who will that be?

8. To what degree do you want me to account to you for the money I spend? How much money, if any, do you feel each of us should have to spend each week as we wish without first checking with the other partner? What percentage of income, if any, do you think we should give to charity each year?

9. What assets or debts will you bring into the marriage; for example, how much do you owe on student loans? How do you feel about debt? How rich do you want to be?

10. If you have been married before, how much child support or alimony do you get or pay each month? Tell me about your divorce.

11. In your will, what percentage of your assets, holdings, and retirement will you leave to me versus anybody else such as siblings, children of a previous relationship, and so on?

Recreation and Leisure

1. What is your idea of the kinds of parties or social gatherings you would like for us to go to together?

2. What is your preference in terms of us hanging out with others in a group versus being alone?

3. What is your favorite recreational interest? How much time do you spend enjoying this interest? How important is it for you that I share this recreational interest with you?

4. What do you like to watch on television? How often do you watch television and for what periods of time?

5. What are the amounts and frequency of your current use of alcohol and other drugs; for example, beer and/or wine, hard liquor, marijuana, cocaine, crack, meth, or heroin? What, if any, have been your previous alcohol and other drug behaviors and frequencies? What are your expectations of me regarding the use of alcohol and other drugs?

6. Where did you vacation with your parents? Where will you want us to go? How will we travel? How much money do you feel we should spend on vacations each year?

7. What pets do you own and what pets do you want to live with us? To what degree is it a requirement that we have one or more pets? To what degree can you adapt to my pets so that they live with us?

Relationships with Friends and Coworkers

1. How do you feel about my three closest same-sex friends?

2. How do you feel about my spending time with my friends or coworkers, such as one evening a week?

3. How do you feel about my spending time with friends of the opposite sex?

4. What do you regard as appropriate and inappropriate affection behaviors with opposite-sex friends?

Technology

1. What are your expectations in terms of our having complete access to each other's cell phone, email, computer passwords, and so forth?

2. What are your expectations of me texting others during meals together, riding in the car, and so forth?

3. What are your texting expectations—how often do you expect a text message from me? How soon after you text me do you expect a response?

4. When we are separated, how often do you want us to text each other—throughout the day or just now and then? How often should we Skype?

5. How do you feel about me texting a previous partner even though we are just friends? How do you want me to feel about your texting a previous partner?

Note

This self-assessment is intended to be a guide to finding out about each other. It is not intended to be used as a clinical or diagnostic instrument. ●

CHAPTER 6

Satisfaction in Couple Relationship Scale*

This scale is designed to assess the degree to which you are satisfied in your current relationship.

Directions

After reading each sentence, write the number that best represents the degree to which you disagree or agree with each item.

1	2	3	4
Total Disagreement	Disagreement	Agreement	Total Agreement

——1. I feel like I am capable of responding to the expectations my partner has of me.

——2. I feel like my partner is concerned about my welfare.

——3. I am satisfied with the attention I receive from my partner.

——4. I feel like my partner listens to what I have to say.

——5. I feel like my partner understands me.

——6. My partner demonstrates the affection and kindness that I need.

——7. I feel valued by my partner.

——8. My partner expresses what she thinks and how she feels.

——9. My partner is available when I need my partner.

——10. When I am sad or worried, my partner is interested in finding out what is wrong.

——11. I feel like my partner likes me as much as I like my partner.

——12. My partner is interested in what I do day after day.

——13. I feel excited about my relationship with my partner.

——14. I am satisfied with my relationship with my partner.

——15. I worry about what other people think about my relationship with my partner.

——16. I am attracted to my partner sexually.

——17. I attend to the sexual needs and demands of my partner.

——18. I feel satisfied in the sexual relationship with my partner.

——19. My interest in having sex with my partner has decline since the beginning of the relationship.

——20. My partner and I have sex less often than I want.

——21. Sex is important to me in my relationship with my partner.

Scoring

Reverse score items 15, 19, 20. If you wrote down a 1, change it to a 4: if you wrote down a 4, change it to a 1, and so forth. Add the numbers you wrote to the left of each item. 1 (total disagreement) reflects the least satisfaction with your relationship/partner and 4 (total agreement) reflects the most satisfaction with your relationship. The lower your total score—21 is the lowest possible score—the lower your satisfaction in your relationship. The higher your total score—84 is the highest possible score—the higher your satisfaction in your relationship. A score of 52.5 places you at the midpoint between being extremely dissatisfied and extremely satisfied with your relationship. ●

***Source:** Adapted from Urbano-Contreras, A., Iglesias-Garcia, M. T., & Martinez-Gonzalez, R. A. (2017). Development and validation of the Satisfaction in Couple Relationship Scale (SCR). *Contemporary Family Therapy, 39*, 54-61. urbanocontreras@gmail.com is the email of Dr. Antonio Urbano-Contreras who gave permission to use the scale.

CHAPTER 7

Sexual Prejudice Scale

Directions

The items below provide a way to assess one's level of prejudice toward gay men and lesbians. For each item identify a number from one to six which reflects your level of agreement and write the number in the space provided.

1	2	3	4	5	6
Strongly disagree	Disagree	Mildly disagree	Mildly agree	Agree	Strongly agree

Prejudice Toward Gay Men Scale

——1.　You can tell a man is gay by the way he walks.

——2.　I think it's gross when I see two men who are clearly "together."

——3.　Retirement benefits should include the partners of gay men.

——4.　Most gay men are flamboyant.

——5.　It's wrong for men to have sex with men.

——6.　Family medical leave rules should include the domestic partners of gay men.

——7.　Most gay men are promiscuous.

——8.　Marriage between two men should be kept illegal.

——9.　Health care benefits should include partners of gay male employees.

——10.　Most gay men have HIV/AIDS.

——11.　Gay men are immoral.

——12.　Hospitals should allow gay men to be involved in their partners' medical care.

——13.　A sexual relationship between two men is unnatural.

——14.　Most gay men like to have anonymous sex with men in public places.

——15.　There's nothing wrong with being a gay man.

Scoring

Reverse score items 3, 6, 9, 12, and 15. For example, if you selected a 6, replace the 6 with a 1. If you selected a 1, replace it with a 6, and so forth. Add each of the 15 items from 1 to 6. The lowest possible score is 15, suggesting a very low level of prejudice against gay men; the highest possible score is 90, suggesting a very high level of prejudice against gay men. The midpoint between 15 and 90 is 52. Scores lower than this would reflect less prejudice against gay men; scores higher than this would reflect more prejudice against gay men.

Participants

Both undergraduate and graduate students enrolled in social work courses comprised a convenience sample ($N = 851$). The sample was predominantly women with 83.1% of the survey; White, 65.9%; heterosexual, 89.8%; single, 81.3%; non-parenting, 81.1%; 25 years of age or under, 69.3%; and majoring in social work, 80.8%.

Results

The range of scores for the gay men scale was 15 to 84. The M = 31.53, SD = 15.30. The sample had relatively low levels of prejudice against gay men.

Prejudice Toward Lesbians Scale

——1.　Most lesbians don't wear makeup.

——2.　Lesbians are harming the traditional family.

——3.　Lesbians should have the same civil rights as straight women.

——4.　Most lesbians prefer to dress like men.

——5.　Being a lesbian is a normal expression of sexuality.

——6.　Lesbians want too many rights.

——7. Most lesbians are more masculine than straight women.

——8. It's morally wrong to be a lesbian.

——9. Employers should provide retirement benefits for lesbian partners.

——10. Most lesbians look like men.

——11. I disapprove of lesbians.

——12. Marriage between two women should be legal.

——13. Lesbians are confused about their sexuality.

——14. Most lesbians don't like men.

——15. Employers should provide health care benefits to the partners of their lesbian employees.

Scoring

Reverse score items 3, 5, 9, 12, and 15. For example, if you selected a 6, replace the 6 with a 1. If you selected a 1, replace it with a 6, and so forth. Add each of the 15 items from 1 to 6. The lowest possible score is 15, suggesting a very low level of prejudice against lesbians; the highest possible score is 90, suggesting a very high level of prejudice against lesbians. The midpoint between 15 and 90 is 52. Scores lower than this would reflect less prejudice against lesbians; scores higher than this would reflect more prejudice against lesbians.

Results

The range of the scores for the lesbian scale was 15 to 86. M = 30.41, SD = 15.60. The sample had relatively low levels of prejudice against lesbians.

Validity and Reliability

Details are provided in the 2013 reference below.

*Scale is used with the permission of Jill Chonody, School of Psychology, Social Work and Public Policy. University of South Australia, Magill, South Australia. Dr. Chonody's email is *jill.chonody@unisa.edu.au.* The scale is used with the permission of the *Journal of Homosexuality.*

Reference

Chonody, J. M. (2013). Measuring sexual prejudice against gay men and lesbian women: Development of the Sexual Prejudice Scale (SPS). *Journal of Homosexuality, 60,* 895-926. ●

Scale for Assessing Same-Gender Couples

Directions

Couples often have good and not-so-good moments in their relationship. This measure was developed to get an objective view of your relationship. Thinking about your relationship with your partner, put a number between 0 and 6 in the blank space before each item to indicate your level of agreement with the item.

0	1	2	3	4	5	6
Strongly Disagree	Disagree	Somewhat Disagree	Neutral	Somewhat Agree	Agree	Strongly Agree

——*1. There are some things about my partner that I do not like.

——*2. I wish my partner enjoyed more of the activities that I do.

——3. My mate has the qualities I want in a partner.

——4. My partner and I share the same values and goals in life.

——5. My partner and I have an active social life.

——6. My partner's sociability adds a positive aspect to our relationship.

——7. If there is one thing that my partner and I are good at, it's talking about our feelings with each other.

——*8. Our differences of opinion lead to shouting matches.

——*9. I would lie to my partner if I thought it would "keep the peace."

——10. During our arguments, I never put down my partner's point of view.

——11. When there is a difference of opinion, we try to talk it out rather than fight.

——12. We always do something to mark a special day in our relationship, like our anniversary.

——13. I often tell my partner than I love him or her.

——*14. Sometimes sex with my partner seems more like work than play to me.

——15. I always seem to be in the mood for sex when my partner is.

——*16. My partner sometimes turns away from my sexual advances.

——17. My family accepts my relationship with my partner.

——18. My partner's family accepts our relationship.

——19. My family would support our decision to adopt or have children.

——20. My partner's family would support our decision to adopt or have children.

——21. I feel as though my relationship is generally accepted by my friends.

——22. I have a strong support system that accepts me as I am.

——23. I have told my co-workers about my sexual orientation or attraction.

——24. Most of my family members know about my sexual orientation/attraction.

Scoring

Reverse score items 1, 2, 8, 9, 14, and 16. For example, if you wrote down a 0 for item one, replace it with a 6. If you wrote a 1, replace it with a 5, and so forth. After reverse scoring the items, add them. Scores range from 0 to 144 with lower scores reflecting less contentment and more public disapproval and higher scores reflecting greater contentment and higher public approval.

Norms

107 was the average score of individuals who took the scale. ●

Source: Developed by Christopher K. Belous, PhD, and used with his permission. Dr. Belous is Assistant Professor and Clinic Director, Marriage and Family Therapy Program, Mercer Family Therapy Center, Mercer University-Atlanta, 1938 Peachtree Road, Suite 107, Atlanta, GA 30309. For additional use of this scale, contact Dr. Belous at Belous_ck@mercer.edu.

CHAPTER 8

Effective Communication Scale

Any relationship can benefit from partners who are engaged listeners. This scale is designed to assess the degree to which you and your partner experience effective communication in your relationship. After reading each item, circle the number that best approximates your answer.

0	1	2	3	4
Strongly disagree (SD)	Disagree (D)	Undecided (UN)	Agree (A)	Strongly agree (SA)

If you are not involved in a current relationship, respond to the items in reference to your last partner.

	SD	D	UN	A	SA
My partner is open with me about feelings.	0	1	2	3	4
I am open with my partner about my feelings.	0	1	2	3	4
My partner understands where I am coming from.	0	1	2	3	4
I do not understand where my partner is coming from. (reverse scored)	0	1	2	3	4
I am not willing to negotiate or compromise with my partner when we disagree. (reverse scored)	0	1	2	3	4
My partner is not willing to negotiate or compromise with me when we disagree. (reverse scored)	0	1	2	3	4
My partner is attentive when we are having a conversation.	0	1	2	3	4
I find it easy to talk with my partner.	0	1	2	3	4

Scoring

Look at the numbers you circled. Reverse-score the numbers for questions 4, 5, and 6. For example, if you circled a 0, give yourself a 4; if you circled a 3, give yourself a 1, and so on. Add the numbers and divide by 8, the total number of items. The lowest possible score would be 0, reflecting the complete absence of effective communication; the highest score would be 4, reflecting the highest level of effective communication. A score of 2 reflects the midpoint or average communication effectiveness. Of 199 undergraduate respondents, 2.9 was the score with females scoring higher achieving a value of 3.0 compared with males who obtained a value of 2.7. ●

Source: Knox, D. "Effective Communication Scale" was developed for this text. The scale is intended to be thought provoking and fun. It is not intended to be used as a clinical or diagnostic instrument.

Communication Danger Signs Scale

This scale is designed to assess the degree to which there is communication trouble in your relationship.

Directions

After reading each sentence carefully, circle the number that best represents how often this happens in your relationship.

1	2	3
Never/almost never	Occasionally	Frequently

		N	O	F
1.	Little arguments escalate into ugly fights with accusations, criticisms, name calling, or bringing up past hurts.	1	2	3
2.	My partner criticizes or belittles my opinions, feelings, or desires.	1	2	3
3.	My partner seems to view my words or actions more negatively than I mean them to be.	1	2	3
4.	When we have a problem to solve, it is like we are on opposite teams.	1	2	3
5.	I hold back from telling my partner what I really think and feel.	1	2	3
6.	I feel lonely in this relationship.	1	2	3
7.	When we argue, one of us withdraws, that is, doesn't want to talk about it anymore; or leaves the scene.	1	2	3

Scoring

Add the numbers you circled. 1 (never) is the response reflecting the ultimate safe context in which you communicate with your partner and a 3 (frequently) is the most toxic of communication contexts. The lower your total score—7 is the lowest possible score—the greater your communication context comfort. The higher your total score—21 is the highest possible score—the more you are likely to feel anxious when around or communicating with your partner. A score of 14 places you at the midpoint between being extremely comfortable communicating with your partner (a score of 7) and being extremely uncomfortable (a score of 21). ●

Source: Dr. Howard Markman, Director, Center for Marital and Family Studies at the University of Denver. Used by permission. hmarkman@du.edu Contact Dr. Markman at http://loveyourrelationship.com/ for information about Communication/Relationship Retreats. Also see Markman, H. J., Stanley, S. M., & S. L. (2010b). *Fighting for your marriage* (3rd ed.) San Francisco, CA: Jossey-Bass.

CHAPTER 9

The Conservative—Liberal Sexuality Scale

This scale is designed to assess the degree to which you are conservative or liberal in your attitudes toward sex. There are no right or wrong answers.

Directions

After reading each sentence carefully, circle the number that best represents the degree to which you agree or disagree with the sentence.

1	2	3	4	5
Strongly agree	Mildly agree	Undecided	Mildly disagree	Strongly disagree

——1. Abortion is wrong.

——2. Homosexuality is immoral.

——3. Couples should wait to have sexual intercourse until after they are married.

——4. Couples who are virgins at marriage have more successful marriages.

——5. Watching pornography is harmful.

——6. Kinky sex is something to be avoided.

——7. Having an extramarital affair is never justified.

——8. Masturbation is something an individual should try to avoid doing.

——9. ...ne should always be in love when having sex with a person.

——10. Transgender people are screwed up and "not right."

——11. Sex is for youth, not for the elderly.

——12. There is entirely too much sex on TV today.

——13. The best use of sex is for procreation.

——14. Any form of sex that is not vaginal intercourse is wrong.

——15. Our society is entirely too liberal when it comes to sex.

——16. Sex education gives youth ideas about sex they shouldn't have.

——17. Promiscuity is the cause of the downfall of an individual.

——18. Too much sexual freedom is promoted in our country today.

——19. The handicapped probably should not try to get involved in sex.

——20. The movies in America are too sexually explicit.

Scoring

Add the numbers you circled. 1 (strongly agree) is the most conservative response and 5 (strongly disagree) is the most liberal response. The lower your total score—20 is the lowest possible score—the more sexually conservative your attitudes toward sex. The higher your total score—100 is the highest possible score—the more liberal your attitudes toward sex. A score of 60 places you at the midpoint between being the ultimate conservative and the ultimate liberal about sex. Of 191 undergraduate females, the average score was 69.85. Of 39 undergraduate males the average score was 72.89. Hence, both women and men tended to be more sexually liberal than conservative with men more liberal than women. ●

Source: Knox, D. "The Conservative-Liberal Sexuality Scale" was developed for this text. The scale is intended to be thought provoking and fun. It is not intended to be used as a clinical or diagnostic instrument.

Consensual Non-Monogamy Attitude Scale

Please rate the extent to which you agree with the following statements.

1	2	3	4	5	6	7
Strongly disagree	Disagree	Mildly disagree	Neutral	Mildly agree	Agree	Strongly agree

——1.   You must be in a monogamous relationship to be in love.

——2.   I can see myself entering into a non-monogamous relationship.

——3.   A monogamous relationship is the most satisfying type of relationship.

——4.   Intimate relationships with more than one person are too complicated.

——5.   It is possible to have several satisfying intimate relationships at the same time.

——6.   It is possible to date other people while in a loving relationship with your partner.

——7.   It is possible to have sexual relationships with other people while in a loving relationship with your partner.

——8.   It is possible for one partner in a relationship to be monogamous while the other partner is not monogamous.

Total score: _____

Scoring

Reverse score items 1, 3, and 4. For example, if you wrote a 7 for item 1, change this to a 1; if you wrote a 1, change it to a 7. Add the numbers you wrote to the right of each item. The higher your total score—56 is the highest possible score—the more favorable your view of non-monogamy. The lower your score—8 is the lowest possible score—the less favorable your view of non-monogamy. A score of 32 places you at the midpoint between disavowing non-monogamy and embracing it. In a survey of 106 undergraduates, respondents more favorable toward non-monogamy were nonheterosexual, males, and those in a non-monogamous relationship. ●

Source: Cohen, M. T., &Wilson, K. (2017). Development of the Consensual Non-Monogamy Attitude Scale (CNAS) *Sexuality and Culture, 21,* 1-14.

CHAPTER 10

Abusive Behavior Inventory

Write the number that best represents your closest estimate of how often each of the behaviors have happened in the relationship with your current or former partner during the previous six months.

1	2	3	4	5
Never	Rarely	Occasionally	Frequently	Very frequently

_____1. Called you a name and/or criticized you

_____2. Tried to keep you from doing something you wanted to do (for example, going out with friends or going to meetings)

_____3. Gave you angry stares or looks

_____4. Prevented you from having money for your own use

_____5. Ended a discussion and made a decision without you

_____6. Threatened to hit or throw something at you

_____7. Pushed, grabbed, or shoved you

_____8. Put down your family and friends

_____9. Accused you of paying too much attention to someone or something else

_____10. Used your children to threaten you (for example, told you that you would lose custody or threatened to leave town with the children)

_____11. Became very upset with you because dinner, housework, or laundry was not done when or how it was wanted

_____12. Said things to scare you (for example, told you something "bad" would happen or threatened to commit suicide)

_____13. Slapped, hit, kicked, or punched you

_____14. Made you do something humiliating or degrading (for example, begging for forgiveness or having to ask permission to use the car or do something)

_____15. Monitored your behavior or activities (for example, listened to your phone calls, checked the mileage on your car, or called you repeatedly at work)

_____16. Drove recklessly when you were in the car

_____17. Pressured you to have sex in a way you didn't like or want

_____18. Refused to do housework or child care

_____19. Threatened you with a weapon or used a weapon against you

_____20. Told you that you were a bad parent

_____21. Stopped you or tried to stop you from going to work or school

_____22. Threw, hit, kicked, or smashed something

_____23. Physically forced you to have sex

_____24. Physically attacked the sexual parts of your body

_____25. Choked or strangled you

Scoring

Add the numbers you wrote down and divide the total by 25 in determining your score. The higher your score—five is the highest score—the more abusive your relationship.

The above inventory is an abridged version of a questionnaire that was given to 100 men and 78 women. These individuals were equally divided into groups of abusers or abused and nonabusers or nonabused. The men were members of a chemical dependency treatment program in a veterans' hospital and the women were partners of these men. Abusing or abused men earned an average score of 1.8; abusing or abused women earned an average score of 2.3. Nonabusing abused men and women earned scores of 1.3 and 1.6, respectively. ●

Source: Shepard, M. F., & Campbell, J. A. (1992) The Abusive Behavior Inventory: A measure of psychological and physical abuse. _Journal of Interpersonal Violence, 7_(3). 291-305. © 1992 by Sage Publications Inc. Journals. Reproduced with permission of Sage Publications Inc. Journals in the format Other book via Copyright Clearance Center.

CHAPTER 11

Child-free Lifestyle Scale

The purpose of this scale is to assess your attitudes toward having a child-free lifestyle. After reading each statement, select the number that best reflects your answer, using the following scale:

1	2	3	4	5	6	7
Strongly disagree	Disagree	Mildly disagree	Neutral	Mildly agree	Agree	Strongly agree

——1. I do not like children.

——2. I would resent having to spend all my money on kids.

——3. I would rather enjoy my personal freedom than have it taken away by having children.

——4. I would rather focus on my career than have children.

——5. Children are a burden.

——6. I have no desire to be a parent.

——7. I am too "into me" to become a parent.

——8. I lack the nurturing skills to be a parent.

——9. I have no patience for children.

——10. Raising a child is too much work.

——11. A marriage without children is empty.

——12. Children are vital to a good marriage.

——13. You can't really be fulfilled as a couple unless you have children.

——14. Having children gives meaning to a couple's marriage.

——15. The happiest couples that I know have children.

——16. The biggest mistake couples make is deciding not to have children.

——17. Child-free couples are sad couples.

——18. Becoming a parent enhances the intimacy between spouses.

——19. A house without the "pitter patter" of little feet is not a home.

——20. Having a child means your marriage is successful.

Scoring

Reverse score items 11 through 20. For example, if you wrote a 1 for item 20, change this to a 7. If you wrote a 2, change it to a 6, and so forth. Add the numbers. The higher the score—140 is the highest possible score—the greater the value for a child-free lifestyle. The lower the score—20 is the lowest possible score—the less the desire to have a child-free lifestyle. The midpoint between the extremes is 80. Scores below 80 suggest a preference for having children; scores above 80 suggest a desire for a child-free lifestyle. The average score of 52 male and 138 female undergraduates at Valdosta State University was below the midpoint (M = 68.78, SD = 17.06), suggesting a desire for a lifestyle with children. A significant difference was found between males, who scored 72.94 (SD = 16.82), and females, who scored 67.21 (SD = 16.95), suggesting that males are more approving of a child-free lifestyle. There were no significant differences between Whites and Blacks or between students in different ranks such as freshmen, sophomore, junior, or senior. ●

Source: "The Childfree Lifestyle Scale" 2010 by Mark A. Whatley, PhD, Department of Psychology, Valdosta State University, Valdosta, GA 31698-0100. Used by permission. Other uses of this scale only by written permission of Dr. Whatley (mwhatley@valdosta.edu). Information on the reliability and validity of this scale is available from Dr. Whatley.

CHAPTER 12

Spanking Versus Time-Out Scale

Parents discipline their children to help them develop self-control and correct misbehavior. Some parents spank their children; others use time-out. The purpose of this survey is to assess the degree to which you prefer spanking versus time-out as a method of discipline. Please read each item carefully and select a number from 1 to 7, which represents your belief. There are no right or wrong answers.

1	2	3	4	5	6	7
Strongly disagree	Disagree	Mildly disagree	Neutral	Mildly agree	Agree	Strongly agree

——1. Spanking is a better form of discipline than time-out.

——2. Time-out does not have any effect on children.

——3. When I have children, I will more likely spank them than use a time-out.

——4. A threat of a time-out does not stop a child from misbehaving.

——5. Lessons are learned better with spanking.

——6. Time-out does not give a child an understanding of what the child has done wrong.

——7. Spanking teaches a child to respect authority.

——8. Giving children time-outs is a waste of time.

——9. Spanking has more of an impact on changing the behavior of children than time-out.

——10. I do not believe "time-out" is a form of punishment.

——11. Getting spanked as a child helps you become a responsible citizen.

——12. Time-out is used only because parents are afraid to spank their kids.

——13. Spanking can be an effective tool in disciplining a child.

——14. Time-out is watered-down discipline.

Scoring

If you want to know the degree to which you approve of spanking, reverse the number you selected for all odd-numbered items (1, 3, 5, 7, 9, 11, and 13). For example, if you selected a 1 for item 1, change this

number to a 7 (1 = 7; 2 = 6; 3 = 5; 4 = 4; 5 = 3; 6 = 2; 7 = 1). Now add these seven numbers. The lower your score—7 is the lowest possible score—the lower your approval of spanking; the higher your score—49 is the highest possible score—the greater your approval of spanking. A score of 21 places you at the midpoint between being very disapproving of or very accepting of spanking as a discipline strategy.

If you want to know the degree to which you approve of using time-out as a method of discipline, reverse the number you selected for all even-numbered items (2, 4, 6, 8, 10, 12, and 14). For example, if you selected a 1 for item 2, change this number to a seven; that is, 1 = 7; 2 = 6; 3 = 5; 4 = 4; 5 = 3; 6 = 2; 7 = 1. Now add these seven numbers. The lower your score—7 is the lowest possible score—the lower your approval of time-out; the higher your score—49 is the highest possible score—the greater your approval of time-out. A score of 21 places you at the midpoint between being very disapproving of or very accepting of time-out as a discipline strategy.

Scores of Other Students Who Completed the Scale

The scale was completed by 48 male and 168 female student volunteers at East Carolina University. All of the volunteers had an average age of 19. The average score on the spanking dimension was 29.73, and the time-out dimension was 22.93, suggesting greater acceptance of spanking than time-out. ●

Source: "The Spanking vs. Time-Out Scale," 2004 by Mark Whatley, PhD, Department of Psychology, Valdosta State University, Valdosta, GA 31698-0100. Used by permission. Other uses of this scale only by written permission of Dr. Whatley (mwhatley@valdosta.edu). Information on the reliability and validity of this scale is available from Dr. Whatley.

CHAPTER 13

Job Satisfaction Scale

This scale is designed to assess the degree to which you are satisfied with your current or most recent job.

After reading each item, circle the number that best approximates your answer.

0	1	2	3	4
Strongly disagree (SD)	Disagree (D)	Undecided (UN)	Agree (A)	Strongly agree (SA)

	SD	D	UN	A	SA
I enjoy my job.	0	1	2	3	4
I am paid fairly for my work.	0	1	2	3	4
I feel respected at my workplace.	0	1	2	3	4
I feel my employer does not like me. (reverse scored)	0	1	2	3	4
I have thought of quitting my job. (reverse scored)	0	1	2	3	4
I don't like the people I work with. (reverse scored)	0	1	2	3	4
I am fortunate to have my job.	0	1	2	3	4
My employer is flexible with my work hours when I need it.	0	1	2	3	4

Scoring

Look at the numbers you circled. Reverse score the numbers for questions 4, 5, and 6. For example, if you circled a 0, give yourself a 4; if you circled a 3, give yourself a 1, and so on. Add the numbers and divide by 8, the total number of items. The lowest possible score would be 0, reflecting the lowest possible job satisfaction; the highest score would be 4, reflecting the highest job satisfaction. A score of 2 reflects the midpoint or average job satisfaction. Of 201 undergraduate respondents, 2.8 was the average score with women scoring a higher value of 2.9 compared with men who obtained 2.7. ●

Source: The "Job Satisfaction Scale" was developed for this text. The scale is intended to be thought provoking and fun. It is not intended to be used as a clinical or diagnostic instrument.

CHAPTER 14

Attitudes Toward Infidelity Scale

Infidelity can be defined as unfaithfulness in a committed monogamous relationship. Infidelity can affect anyone, regardless of race, color, or creed; it does not matter whether you are rich or attractive, where you live, or how old you are. The purpose of this survey is to gain a better understanding of what people think and feel about issues associated with infidelity. There are no right or wrong answers to any of these statements. Please read each statement carefully, and respond by using the following scale:

1	2	3	4	5	6	7
Strongly disagree	Disagree	Mildly disagree	Neutral	Mildly agree	Agree	Strongly agree

——1.   Being unfaithful never hurt anyone.

——2.   Infidelity in a marital relationship is grounds for divorce.

——3.   Infidelity is acceptable for retaliation of infidelity.

——4.   It is natural for people to be unfaithful.

——5.   Online/Internet behavior (for example, visiting sex chat rooms, porn sites) is an act of infidelity.

——6.   Infidelity is morally wrong in all circumstances, regardless of the situation.

——7.   Being unfaithful in a relationship is one of the most dishonorable things a person can do.

——8.   Infidelity is unacceptable under any circumstances if the couple is married.

——9.   I would not mind if my significant other had an affair as long as I did not know about it.

——10. It would be acceptable for me to have an affair, but not my significant other.

——11. I would have an affair if I knew my significant other would never find out.

——12. If I knew my significant other was guilty of infidelity, I would confront Him or her.

Scoring

Selecting a 1 reflects the least acceptance of infidelity; selecting a 7 reflects the greatest acceptance of infidelity. Before adding the numbers you selected, reverse the scores for item numbers 2, 5, 6, 7, 8, and 12. For example, if you responded to item 2 with a "6," change this number to a "2"; if you responded with a "3," change this number to "5," and so on. After making these changes, add the numbers. The lower your total score—12 is the lowest possible—the less accepting you are of infidelity; the higher your total score—84 is the highest possible—the greater your acceptance of infidelity. A score of 48 places you at the midpoint between being very disapproving and very accepting of infidelity.

Scores of Other Students Who Completed the Scale

The scale was completed by 150 male and 136 female student volunteers at Valdosta State University. The average score on the scale was 27.85. Their ages ranged from 18 to 49, with a mean age of 23.36. Male participants reported more positive attitudes toward infidelity (mean = 31.53) than did female participants (mean = 23.78; $p < .05$). White participants had more negative attitudes toward infidelity (mean = 25.36) than did non-White participants (mean = 31.71; $p < .05$). There were no significant differences in regard to year in college. ●

Source: "Attitudes toward Infidelity Scale" 2006 by Mark Whatley, PhD, Department of Psychology, Valdosta State University, Valdosta, Georgia 31698-0100. Used by permission. Other uses of this scale by written permission of Dr. Whatley only (mwhatley@valdosta.edu). Information on the reliability and validity of this scale is available from Dr. Whatley.

CHAPTER 15

Positive and Negative Ex-Relationship Thoughts Scale (PARERT SCALE)*

Directions

After a breakup, it is common for people to think about or replay events regarding the relationship for a period afterwards. These thoughts may be voluntary or involuntary.

Thinking about the person from your most recent break-up, rate how often you do the following, ranging from *(1) Never* to *(5) Always:*

1	2	3	4	5
Never	Rarely	Sometimes	Often	Always

1. I think of ways to get back together with _____.
2. I think about the happy memories I had with _____.
3. I think about all the things that bothered me about _____.
4. I think about my most romantic moments with ____.
5. I think of what my life would be like if we were together _____.
6. I think about how much it hurt me _____.
7. I think about their negative qualities _____.
8. I think about how hurt, angry, upset, or sad they made me _____.
9. I think about the special connection I shared with _____.
10. I think about the reasons that we should not be together _____.
11. I remember times when they were not a good partner _____.
12. I think about the things from our relationship that I miss. _____

Scoring

Sum the items for each subscale.

Positive Ex-Relationship Thoughts: 1, 2, 4, 5, 8, and 10. Scores range from 6 to 30 with higher scores related to more difficult adjustment. In a college sample: Positive Content Valence mean was 2.48 (SD = 1.03) and Negative Content Valence mean was 2.50 (SD = .86).

Negative Ex-Relationship Thoughts: 3, 6, 7, 8, 10, and 11. Scores range from 6 to 30 with lower scores related to more difficult adjustment. In a college sample: Negative Content Valence mean was 2.50 (SD = .86). ●

* Brenner, R. E., & Vogel, D. L. (2014, November). Measuring thought content valence after a breakup: Development of the positive and negative ex-relationship thoughts scale. Poster presented at the American Psychological Association annual meeting, Washington, DC. Used by permission of Rachel E. Brenner, Department of Education and Counseling Psychology, University at Albany SUNY; and David L. Vogel, Department of Psychology, Iowa State University.

CHAPTER 16

Attitudes Toward Taking Care of Elderly Parents Scale

This scale is designed to assess your attitudes toward taking care of your parents as they age.

After reading each item, circle the number that best approximates your answer.

0	1	2	3	4
Strongly disagree (SD)	Disagree (D)	Undecided (UN)	Agree (A)	Strongly agree (SA)

Answer the scale in reference to the living parent with whom you have the closest relationship.

	SD	D	UN	A	SA
I feel it is my responsibility to take care of my parent as they age.	0	1	2	3	4
I am happy to look after the needs of my elderly parent.	0	1	2	3	4
I accept taking care of my aging parent as my rightful role as their child.	0	1	2	3	4
Parents should not burden their children with having to take care of them as they age. (reverse scored)	0	1	2	3	4
I feel that the government should look after old people and not expect their children to take care of them. (reverse scored)	0	1	2	3	4
I would feel no regret by leaving my parents to fend for themselves as they get older. (reverse scored)	0	1	2	3	4
It is the right thing to do to take care of your parent when they are old.	0	1	2	3	4
The young taking care of the old is the way it should be.	0	1	2	3	4

Scoring

Look at the numbers you circled. Reverse-score the numbers for questions 4, 5, and 6. For example, if you circled a 0, give yourself a 4; if you circled a 3, give yourself a 1, and so on. Add the numbers and divide by 8, the total number of items. The lowest possible score would be 0, reflecting the attitude of taking no responsibility for aging parents; the highest score would be 4, reflecting the most positive attitude toward taking care of elderly parents. Of 203 undergraduate respondents, 3.06 was the average score with women scoring higher (3.1) than men (2.9). ●

Source: Knox, D. "Attitudes Toward Taking Care of Elderly Parents Scale" was developed for this text. The scale is intended to be thought provoking and fun. It is not intended to be used as a clinical or diagnostic instrument.

GLOSSARY

Abortion ratio: refers to the number of abortions per 1,000 live births. Abortion is affected by the need for parental consent and parental notification.

Absolutism: a sexual value system which is based on unconditional allegiance to tradition or religion: for example, waiting until marriage to have sexual intercourse.

Advance directive (living will): details for medical care personnel and the conditions under which life support measures should be used for the individual.

Agape love style: also known as compassionate love, characterized by a focus on the well-being of the love object, with little regard for reciprocation.

Age: term which may be defined chronologically in the number of years; physiologically, meaning physical decline; psychologically, in terms of one's self-concept; sociologically, viewed as the roles for the elderly and retired; and culturally, meaning of age in one's society.

Ageism: stereotyping, prejudice, and discrimination against people on the basis of their age.

Agender: not identifying as having a gender identity.

Alienation of affection: law which gives a spouse the right to sue a third party for taking the affections of a spouse away.

Ally development model: emphasizes those who are supportive of the LGBTQIA movement.

Androgyny: a blend of traits that are stereotypically associated with masculinity and femininity.

Annulment: the legal erasing of a valid marriage contract. Unlike divorce, the annulment conveys that the marriage never took place since it was illegal.

Antigay bias: being biased against lesbians, gays, and bisexuals.

Anxious jealousy: obsessive ruminations about the partner's alleged infidelity that can make one's life a miserable emotional torment.

Aperiodic reinforcement: random reinforcement for a behavior such as winning the lottery or fishing.

Arbitration: third party listens to both spouses and decides about custody, division of property, child support, and alimony.

Arranged marriage: mate selection pattern whereby parents select the spouse of their offspring. A matchmaker may be used but the selection is someone of whom the parents approve.

Asceticism: sexual belief system which emphasizes that giving in to carnal lust is unnecessary and one should attempt to rise above the pursuit of sensual pleasure into a life of self-discipline and self-denial.

Asexual: the absence of desire to engage in sexual behavior with another.

Attachment theory of mate selection: developed early in reference to one's parents, the drive toward an intimate, social/emotional connection.

Baby blues: transitory symptoms of depression in a mother 24 to 48 hours after her baby is born.

Battered woman syndrome: legal term used in court that the person accused of murder was suffering from to justify his or her behavior. Therapists define battering as physical aggression that results in injury and accompanied by fear and terror.

Behavioral couple therapy (BCT): therapeutic focus on behaviors the respective spouses want increased or decreased, initiated or terminated.

Benevolent sexism: the belief that women are innocent creatures who should be protected and supported.

Binuclear family: a family in which the members live in two households.

Biosocial theory: also referred to as sociobiology; social behaviors (for example, mate selection) are biologically based and have an evolutionary survival function.

Biphobia: parallel set of negative attitudes toward bisexuality and those identified as bisexual.

Birth control sabotage: partner interference with contraception.

Bisexuality: cognitive, emotional, and sexual attraction to members of both sexes.

Blended family: a family created when two individuals marry and at least one of them brings a child or children from a previous relationship or marriage. Also referred to as a stepfamily.

Blurred retirement: an individual working part-time before completely retiring or taking a "bridge job" that provides a transition between a lifelong career and full retirement.

Boomerang generation: adult children who return to live with their parents.

Branching: in communication, going out on different limbs of an issue rather than staying focused on the issue.

Bride wealth: also known as bride price or bride payment, the amount of money or goods paid by the groom or his family to the bride's family for losing her as a labor source.

Catfishing: the process of creating a fake social media account to lure victims into a romantic relationship with stolen pictures and false identities.

Child abuse: any behavior or lack of behavior by parents or caregivers that results in deliberate harm to a child's physical or psychological well-being.

Childlessness concerns: the idea that holidays and family gatherings may be difficult because of not having children or feeling left out or sad that others have children.

Chronic sorrow: grief-related feelings that occur periodically throughout the lives of those left behind.

Cisgender: one's gender identity matches his or her biological sex.

Civil union: a pair-bonded relationship given legal significance in terms of rights and privileges.

Closed-ended question: question that allows for a one-word answer and does not elicit much information.

Cohabitation effect: those who have multiple cohabitation experiences prior to marriage are more likely to end up in marriages characterized by lower levels of happiness.

Cohabitation: two adults, unrelated by blood or by law, involved in an emotional and sexual relationship, who sleep in the same residence at least four nights a week for three months.

Coitus: the sexual union of a man and woman by insertion of the penis into the vagina.

Collaborative practice: process involving a team of professionals: lawyer, psychologist, mediator, social worker, and financial counselor, helping a couple separate and divorce in a humane and cost-effective way.

Collectivism: pattern in which one regards group values and goals as more important than one's own values and goals.

Coming out: being open about one's sexual orientation and identity.

Commuter marriage: arrangement whereby the spouses live in different places because of their work but use technology to stay connected.

Common-law marriage: a heterosexual cohabiting couple presenting themselves as married.

Compersion: the opposite of jealousy; the approval of a partner's emotional and sexual involvement with someone else.

Competitive birthing: having the same number (or more) of children as one's peers.

Complementary-needs theory: selecting a mate whose needs are opposite and complementary to one's own needs.

Comprehensive sex education program: learning experience which recommends abstinence but also discusses contraception and other means of pregnancy protection.

Conception: the fusion of the egg and sperm; also known as fertilization.

Concerted cultivation: the belief that parents are expected to enroll their children in a series of extracurricular activities to maintain their status as "good parents."

Concurrent sexual partnership: Relationship in which one partner has sex with several individuals concurrently—unbeknownst to the other partners.

Condom assertiveness: the unambiguous messaging that sex without a condom is unacceptable.

Conflict framework: the view that individuals in relationships compete for valuable resources.

Conflict: the context in which the perceptions or behavior of one person are in contrast to or interfere with the other.

Congruent messages: message in which the verbal and nonverbal behaviors are the same.

Conjugal love: the love between married people characterized by companionship, calmness, comfort, and security.

Connection rituals: behaviors couples engage in to share their time and attention.

Consensually non-monogamous relationships: polyamorous relationships where individuals love or have sex with multiple people with the knowledge and consent of all individuals involved.

Conversion therapy: also called reparative therapy, designed on using techniques to change one's sexual orientation. Recognized as ineffective and harmful.

Coolidge effect: term used to describe waning of sexual excitement and the effect of novelty and variety on increasing sexual arousal.

Core family leisure pattern: regular predictable family leisure activities (e.g., movie night).

Corporal punishment: the use of physical force with the intention of causing a child to experience pain, but not injury, for the purpose of correction or control of the child's behavior.

Cougar: an older affluent woman who enjoys the company of or relationships with younger men.

Crisis: a crucial situation that requires change in one's normal pattern of behavior.

Cross-sectional: analysis of data representing one point in time. For example, infidelity the first year of marriage in contrast to longitudinal data which would look at infidelity throughout the marriage.

Cryopreservation: the freezing of fertilized eggs for implantation at a later stage.

Cybersex: consensual, computer-mediated, participatory sexual experience involving two or more individuals.

Cybervictimization: harassing behavior which includes being sent threatening e-mail, unsolicited obscene e-mail, computer viruses, or junk mail (spamming); can also include flaming (online verbal abuse) and leaving improper messages on message boards.

Dark triad personality: term for inter-correlated traits of narcissism, a sense of entitlement and grandiose self-view; Machiavellianism, being deceptive and insincere; and psychopathy, being callous and having no empathy.

Defense mechanism: techniques that function without awareness to protect individuals from anxiety and to minimize emotional hurt.

Defense of Marriage Act: legislation which says that marriage is a "legal union between one man and one woman" and denies federal recognition of same-sex marriage.

Demandingness: the manner in which parents place demands on children in regard to expectations and discipline.

Dementia: a generic term to describe cognitive, physical, and psychological impairment in some elderly individuals.

Developmental task: a skill that, if mastered, allows an individual to grow and complete other tasks.

Discernment counseling: spouses on the brink of divorce examine their options to divorce, accept status quo, or reconcile/make changes.

Disenchantment: the transition from a state of newness and high expectation to a state of mundaneness tempered by reality.

Displacement: shifting one's feelings, thoughts, or behaviors from the person who evokes them onto someone else.

Divorce mediation: divorcing spouses meet together with a neutral professional who negotiates child custody, division of property, child support, and alimony.

Divorce: the legal ending of a valid marriage contract.

Divorcism: the belief that divorce is a disaster.

Domestic partnership: two adults who have chosen to share each other's lives in an intimate and committed relationship of mutual caring. These relationships are given some kind of official recognition by a city or corporation so as to receive partner benefits: for example, health insurance.

Double Dutch: a strategy of using both the pill and condom; also known as dual protection.

Down low: non-gay-identifying men who have sex with men and women.

Dual-career marriage: a marriage in which both spouses pursue careers.

Durable power of attorney: gives the identified person complete authority to act on behalf of the elderly.

Dyadic coping: both partners contribute to resolving the issues they face.

Educational homogamy: selecting a partner who has a similar level of education.

Effective communication: the process of exchanging accurate information and feelings in a timely manner.

Embryo adoption: the adoption of a frozen embryo which will be implanted in the adoptive mother's uterus.

Emergency contraception: various types of morning-after pills; also known as postcoital contraception.

Emotional abuse: nonphysical behavior designed to denigrate the partner, reduce the partner's status, and make the partner feel vulnerable to being controlled by the partner.

Emotional competence: the ability to experience emotion, express emotion, and regulate emotion.

Endogamous pressures: cultural pressure to marry someone with similar demographic characteristics (e.g., race, religion, education).

Endogamy: cultural expectation to select a marriage partner within one's own social group (e.g., race).

Engagement: time in which the romantic partners are sexually monogamous, committed to marry, and focused on wedding preparations.

Eros love style: also known as romantic love, the love of passion and sexual desire.

Escapism: the simultaneous denial of and avoidance of dealing with a problem.

Estrangement: one or more relatives intentionally choosing to end contact with each other because of an ongoing negative relationship.

Euthanasia: from the Greek meaning "good death" or dying without suffering; either passively or actively ending the life of a patient.

Everwork: always working, either physically at work or at home on the computer doing work for one's employer. The individual never unplugs.

Exchange theory: theory that emphasizes that relationships are formed and maintained based on who offers the greatest rewards at the lowest costs.

Exogamy: the cultural pressure to marry outside the family group.

Extended family: the nuclear family or parts of it plus other relatives such as grandparents, aunts, uncles, and cousins.

Extradyadic involvement: refers to sexual involvement of a pair-bonded individual with someone other than the partner; also called extrarelational involvement.

Extrafamilial child abuse: child sexual abuse in which the perpetrator is someone outside the family who is not related to the child.

Extramarital affair: refers to a spouse's sexual involvement with someone outside the marriage.

Familism: value that decisions are made in reference to what is best for the family.

Family balance leisure pattern: occasional memorable family leisure activities (e.g., beach vacation).

Family care giving: adult children providing care for their elderly parents.

Family life course development: the stages and process of how families change over time.

Family life cycle: stages that identify the various developmental tasks family members face across time.

Family of orientation: also known as the family of origin, the family into which a person is born.

Family of procreation: the family a person begins typically by getting married and having children.

Family relations doctrine: belief that even nonbiological parents may be awarded custody or visitation rights if they have been economically and emotionally involved in the life of the child.

Family resilience: the successful coping of family members under adversity that enables them to flourish with warmth, support, and cohesion.

Family systems framework: views each member of the family as part of a system and the family as a unit that develops norms of interaction.

Family: a group of two or more people related by blood, marriage, or adoption.

Fellatio: oral stimulation of the male genitalia.

Female genital alteration: cutting off the clitoris or excising (partially or totally) the labia minora.

Female rape myths: beliefs that deny victim injury or cast blame on the woman for her own rape.

Feminist framework: views marriage and family as contexts of inequality and oppression for women.

Feminization of poverty: the idea that women, particularly those who live alone or with their children, disproportionately experience poverty.

Fictive kin: nonbiological and nonlegal relationships that are close, meaningful and supportive.

Five love languages: concept made popular by Gary Chapman, these languages are gifts, quality time, words of affirmation, acts of service, and physical touch.

Flirting: to show interest without serious intent.

Forced marriage: at least one of the spouses has no choice in the decision to marry.

Foster parent: neither a biological nor an adoptive parent but a person who takes care of and fosters a child taken into custody by social services.

Frail: term used to define elderly people if they have difficulty with at least one personal care activity, such as feeding, bathing, or toileting.

Friends with benefits: platonic friends who engage in some degree of sexual intimacy on multiple occasions.

Gatekeeper role: term used to refer to the influence of the mother on the father's involvement with his children.

Gay: term which refers to women or men who prefer same-sex individuals as emotional and sexual partners.

Gender binary: a binary that presents gender as either feminine or masculine.

Gender fluid: the capacity to feel and present as a male sometimes, as a female at other times, and as androgyne at still other times.

Gender identity: the psychological state of viewing oneself as male, female, a blend of both, or neither.

Gender nonbinary: gender is viewed on a continuum and a spectrum of gender identities.

Gender role ideology: the proper role of relationships between women and men in a society.

Gender roles: social norms which specify the socially appropriate behavior for females and males in a society.

Gender: social construct which refers to the social and psychological characteristics associated with being female, male, or neither.

Genderqueer: individuals can consider themselves as non-binary—not feminine or masculine—but a blend of both.

Gerontology: the study of aging.

Gerontophobia: fear or dread of the elderly, which may create a self-fulfilling prophecy.

Ghost marriage: A marriage between two deceased parties or one deceased party with a living person. The Chinese ghost marriage is a folk tradition which does not involve a legal bond between the parties.

Ghosting: a situation when a partner breaks off the relationship suddenly without explanation.

Gig economy: also known as the shared, on-demand, peer, or platform economy; individuals market their labor directly to the public and choose their own time and context of work.

Grandfamilies: families in which the grandparents or other relatives step forward to take care of children when their parents are not able to do so.

Granny dumping: refers to adult children or grandchildren, burdened with the care of their elderly parent or grandparent, leaving the elder at the entrance of a hospital with no identification.

Hanging out: refers to going out in groups where the agenda is to meet others and have fun.

Hate crime: violence motivated by prejudice including verbal harassment, vandalism, sexual assault/rape, physical assault, and murder.

Hedonism: the belief that the ultimate value and motivation for human actions lie in the pursuit of pleasure and the avoidance of pain.

Helicopter parents: parents who make decisions for their children, intervene in their disputes, and resolve problems for them.

Heterosexism: the institutional and societal reinforcement of heterosexuality as the privileged and powerful norm. Assumes that homosexuality is "bad."

Heterosexuality: emotional and sexual attraction to individuals of the other sex.

High conflict divorce: divorce which lasts longer than two years and is characterized by continued anger, hostility, litigation, and higher rates of nonpayment of child support.

Homogamy: the tendency for an individual to seek a mate who has similar characteristics.

Homonegativity: attaching negative connotations to homosexuality.

Homophobia: negative attitudes and emotions toward people who are gay or lesbian.

Homosexuality: older prejudicial term which refers to the predominance of cognitive, emotional, and sexual attraction to individuals of the same sex.

Honeymoon: the time following the wedding whereby the couple becomes isolated to recover from the wedding and to solidify their new status change from lovers to spouses.

Honor crime/Honor killing: refers to the killing of female family members who are accused of bringing shame to the family. This crime is usually committed by a male relative who kills to reclaim family "honor".

Hooking up: a sexual encounter that occurs between individuals who have no relationship commitment.

Human ecology framework: views the family and the environment as an ecosystem.

Hypothesis: a suggested explanation for a phenomenon.

Hysterectomy: form of female sterilization whereby the woman's uterus is removed.

"I" statements: statements which focus on the feelings and thoughts of the communicator without making a judgment on others.

Individualism: making decisions that serve the individual's interests rather than the family's.

Individualized marriage: blending of two cultural forces in America; the individualistic need to be autonomous and the need to be grounded in traditional family structure such as the marriage.

Induced abortion: the deliberate termination of a pregnancy through chemical or surgical means.

Infatuation: intense emotional feelings based on little actual exposure to the love object.

Infertility: the inability to achieve a pregnancy after at least one year of regular sexual relations without birth control, or the inability to carry a pregnancy to a live birth.

Infidelity: any type of sexual or emotional behavior outside the current relationship that violates the understanding of sexual/emotional monogamy between the partners that results in feelings of betrayal.

Institution: established and enduring patterns of social relationships (e.g., the family).

Integrative emotion work: the management of one's partner's emotions.

Internalized homophobia: a sense of personal failure and self-hatred among lesbians and gay men resulting from social rejection and stigmatization of being gay.

Intersex: having many of the characteristics (hormonal, physical) of both sexes.

Intersex individuals: those with mixed or ambiguous genitals.

Intimate partner homicide: murder of a boyfriend, girlfriend, or spouse.

Intimate partner violence (IPV): an all-inclusive term that refers to crimes committed against current or former spouses, boyfriends, or girlfriends.

Intimate terrorism (IT): behavior designed to intimidate, terrorize, and control the partner.

Intrafamilial child abuse: child sexual abuse referring to exploitive sexual contact or attempted sexual contact between relatives before the victim is 18.

Jealousy: an emotional response to a perceived or real threat to an important or valued relationship.

Laparoscopy: a form of tubal ligation that involves a small incision through the woman's abdominal wall just below the navel.

Latchkey parents: divorcing parents who spend every other week with the children in the family home so the children do not have to alternate between residences.

Legal custody: judicial decision regarding whether one or both parents will have decisional authority on major issues affecting the children.

Leisure: the use of time to engage in freely chosen activities perceived as enjoyable and satisfying

Lesbian: a woman who prefers same-sex partners.

LGBTQIA (also LGBTQQIA): general term which refers to lesbian, gay, bisexual, queer, transgender individuals, those who question their sexual identity, those who are intersex, and those who are asexual or support the sexual minority movement.

Litigation: a judge hears arguments from lawyers representing the respective spouses and decides issues of custody, child support, division of property, and so forth.

Living apart together (LAT): a living arrangement where partners in a committed relationship live in separate households.

Long-distance relationship: separated from a romantic partner by 500 or more miles, which precludes regular weekly face-to-face contact.

Longitudinal: analysis of data on a phenomenon over time. For example, infidelity over the years of a marriage in contrast to cross-sectional data which would look at infidelity at one point in time.

Ludic love style: views love as a game where the player has no intention of getting involved.

Lump sum alimony: a onetime amount provided at the time of the divorce to promote resource equality.

Lust: sexual desire.

Male rape myths: beliefs that deny victim injury or make assumptions about his sexual orientation.

Mania love style: the out-of-control love whereby the person "must have" the love object. Obsessive jealousy and controlling behavior are symptoms of manic love.

Marital generosity: small acts of service, forgiving the spouse, displaying affection/respect.

Marital rape: rape by one's spouse: a crime in all states.

Marital success: refers to the quality of the marriage relationship measured in terms of marital stability and marital happiness.

Marriage benefit: the advantages of marriage over singlehood, including married persons being healthier and happier.

Marriage rituals: repeated social interactions that reflect emotional meaning to the couple.

Marriage: a legal relationship that binds a couple together for the reproduction, physical care, and socialization of children.

Masturbation: stimulating one's own genitals with the goal of experiencing sexual pleasure.

Mating gradient: norm which gives social approval to men who seek out younger, less educated, less financially secure women and vice versa.

Matrescence: transition to motherhood.

May-December marriage: age dissimilar marriage (ADM) in which the woman is typically in the spring of her life (May) and her husband is in the later years (December).

Medicaid: a state welfare program for low-income individuals.

Medicare: a federal health insurance program for people 65 and older.

Megan's Law: law requiring that communities be notified of a neighbor's previous child sex convictions.

Military contract marriage: a military person will marry a civilian to get more money and benefits from the government.

Millennials: persons born between 1980 and 1996.

Modern family: the dual-earner family, in which both spouses work outside the home.

Morbidity: chronic illness and disease.

Multiple partner fertility: having biological children with more than one partner.

Negative attachment: spouses who continue to be emotionally attached to and have difficulty breaking away from ex-spouses.

Negotiation: spouses discuss and resolve the issues of custody, child support, and division of property themselves.

Neonaticide: killing a baby the first day of life.

New relationship energy (NRE): the euphoria of a new emotional/sexual relationship which dissipates over time.

No-fault divorce: neither party is identified as the guilty party or the cause of the divorce.

Nomophobia: the individual is dependent on virtual environments to the point of having a social phobia.

Nonverbal communication: the "message about the message," using gestures, eye contact, body posture, tone, volume, and rapidity of speech.

Nuclear family: consists of you, your parents, and your siblings or you, your spouse, and your children.

Obsessive relational intrusion (ORI): the relentless pursuit of intimacy with someone who does not want it.

Occupational sex segregation: the concentration of women and men in different occupations.

Oophorectomy: form of female sterilization whereby the woman's ovaries are removed.

Open relationship: relationship in which the partners agree that each may have emotional and sexual relationships with those outside the dyad.

Open-ended question: question which elicits a lot of information.

Ovum transfer: a fertilized egg is implanted in the uterine wall.

Oxytocin: hormone from the pituitary gland during the expulsive stage of labor that has been associated with the onset of maternal behavior in lower animals.

Palimony: refers to the amount of money one "pal" who lives with another "pal" may have to pay if the partners end their relationship.

Palliative care: health care for the individual who has a life-threatening illness which focuses on relief of pain or suffering and support for the individual.

Pansexuality: sexual attraction to other people regardless of their biological sex, gender, or gender identity.

Pantagamy: a group marriage in which each member of the group is "married" to the others.

Parental alienation syndrome: an alleged disturbance in which children are obsessively preoccupied with deprecation or criticism or both of a parent; denigration that is unjustified or exaggerated or both.

Parental alienation: estrangement of a child from a parent due to one parent turning the child against the other.

Parental consent: a woman needs permission from a parent to get an abortion if under a certain age, usually 18.

Parental empowerment: term used to refer to feeling in control as a parent and that one's children are flourishing.

Parental investment: any investment by a parent that increases the offspring's chance of surviving and thus increases reproductive success.

Parental notification: a woman has to tell a parent she is getting an abortion if she is under a certain age, usually 18, but she doesn't need parental permission.

Parental warmth: interest in child's activities and friends, involvement in child's activities, enthusiasm and praise for children's accomplishments, and demonstration of affection and love.

PEP (post-exposure prophylaxis): taking antiretroviral medicines (ART) within 72 hours after suspected exposure to HIV to prevent becoming infected.

Peripartum depression: similar to postpartum depression except the symptoms may begin as early as four months into the pregnancy.

Permanent alimony: payments to the wife who was married a very long time and who gave up her earning capacity to support her husband.

Phased retirement: an employee agreeing to a reduced work load in exchange for reduced income.

Phubbing: to ignore someone by attending to one's cell phone or other mobile device.

Physical custody: the distribution of parenting time between divorced spouses.

Pluralistic ignorance: overestimating acceptance and prevalence of behaviors.

Polyamory: a lifestyle in which two lovers embrace the idea of having multiple lovers. By agreement, each partner may have numerous emotional and sexual relationships.

Polyandry: type of marriage in which one wife has two or more husbands.

Poly families: parents in multiple families who regard each other as also parents of their own and the other children in an emotional and functional sense.

Polygamy: a generic term for marriage involving more than two spouses.

Polygyny: type of marriage involving one husband and two or more wives.

Pool of eligibles: the population from which a person selects a marriage partner.

Possessive jealousy: involves attacking the partner or the alleged person to whom the partner is showing attention.

Postmodern family: lesbian or gay male couples or parents and mothers who are single by choice, which emphasizes that a healthy family need not be the traditional heterosexual, two-parent family.

Postnuptial agreement: an agreement about how money is to be divided should a couple later divorce, which is made after the couple marry.

Postpartum depression: a severe reaction following the birth of a baby which occurs in reference to a complicated delivery as well as numerous physiological and psychological changes occurring during pregnancy, labor, and delivery; usually in the first month after birth but can be experienced after a couple of years have passed.

Postpartum psychosis: a reaction in which a woman wants to harm her baby.

Power: the ability to impose one's will on the partner and to avoid being influenced by the partner.

Pragma love style: love style that is logical and rational. The love partner is evaluated in terms of pluses and minuses and is regarded as a good or bad "deal."

Pregnancy: when the fertilized egg is implanted, typically in the uterine wall.

Prenuptial agreement: a contract between intended spouses specifying which assets will belong to whom and who will be responsible for paying for what in the event of a divorce or when the marriage ends by the death of one spouse.

Primary groups: small numbers of individuals among whom interaction is intimate and informal.

Primary mate ejection: evolutionary device which allows one to transfer and focus resources from one mate to another.

PRIMARY/PRIMARY career: dual career marriage in which both careers are viewed as equal.

PRIMARY/secondary career: dual career marriage in which one career takes precedence.

Principle of least interest: the person who has the least interest in the relationship, controls the relationship.

Procreative liberty: the freedom to decide to have children or not.

Projection: attributing one's own thoughts, feelings, and desires to someone else while avoiding recognition that these are one's own thoughts, feelings, and desires.

Pronatalism: cultural attitude which encourages having children.

Quality of life: one's physical functioning, independence, economic resources, social relationships, and spirituality.

Queer: inclusive term used by individuals desiring to avoid labels. People who labels themselves as "queer" could be gay, lesbian, bisexual, pansexual, trans, intersex, non-conforming heterosexual.

Rape: nonconsensual acts of sex or attempted sex.

Rationalization: the cognitive justification for one's own behavior that unconsciously conceals one's true motives.

Reactive attachment disorder: common among children who were taught as infants that no one cared about them; these children have no capacity to bond emotionally with others since they have no learning history of the experience and do not trust adults, caretakers, or parents.

Reactive jealousy: jealous feelings that are a reaction to something the partner is doing.

Recovery sabotage: actively harping on a prior conflict, dredging up new disagreements, or negating a partner's positive contributions during a post-conflict rebound conversation.

Reflective listening: paraphrasing or restating what the person has said to you while being sensitive to what the partner is feeling.

Rehabilitative alimony: money the dependent spouse is to receive to fund education or training to increase one's capacity to earn an income.

Reimbursement alimony: the former wife is compensated since she gave up her own career to help the occupational advancement of her husband.

Relativism: value system emphasizing that sexual decisions should be made in the context of a particular relationship.

Religious and spiritual homogamy: selecting a partner who has similar religious and spiritual views.

Replacement level: the average number of children born per woman at which a population exactly replaces itself from one generation to the next, without migration.

Reproductive coercion: coercion by either partner to result in a pregnancy.

Resilience: a family's strength and ability to respond to a crisis in a positive way.

Responsiveness: the extent to which parents respond to and meet the emotional needs of their children.

Revenge porn: ex partner posts nude photos on the Internet, which may be seen by employers and parents with devastating consequences.

Reverse retirement: returning to the workforce after retiring.

Rite of passage: an event that marks the transition from one social status to another.

Rohypnol: drug that causes profound, prolonged sedation and short-term memory loss; also known as the date rape drug or roofies.

Role compartmentalization: strategy used to separate the roles of work and home so that an individual does not think about or dwell on the problems of one when he or she is at the physical place of the other.

Role conflict: one role (e.g., parent) conflicts with another (e.g., worker).

Role overload: not having the time or energy to meet the demands or responsibilities in the roles of wife, parent, and worker.

Role strain: the anxiety that results from being able to fulfill only a limited number of role obligations.

Role theory of mate selection: theory which focuses on the social learning of roles. A son or daughter models after the parent of the same sex by selecting a partner similar to the one the parent selected.

Romantic love: an intense love whereby the lover believes in love at first sight, only one true love, and love conquers all.

Safe Haven (Baby Moses Law): allows the overwhelmed despondent parent to give his or her baby to someone who will take care of him or her with no criminal prosecution.

Salpingectomy: type of female sterilization whereby the fallopian tubes are cut and the ends are tied.

SAME career marriage: dual-career marriage in which spouses share a career or work together.

Sandwich generation: generation of adults who are "sandwiched" between caring for their elderly parents and their own children.

Satiation: a stimulus loses its value with repeated exposure (e.g., lovers tire of each other if around each other all the time).

Second shift: the housework and childcare that employed women engage when they return home from their jobs.

Secondary groups: groups in which the interaction is impersonal and formal.

Second-parent adoption: legal procedure that allows individuals to adopt their partner's biological or adoptive child without terminating the first parent's legal status as parent.

Settling: remaining in a relationship that provides a reasonable level of satisfaction with the knowledge that one is fearful of taking the chance to find someone better.

Sex roles: roles defined by biological constraints and enacted by members of one biological sex only: for example, wet nurse, sperm donor, child-bearer.

Sex: the biological distinction between females and males.

Sexism: an attitude, action, or institutional structure that subordinates or discriminates against individuals or groups because of their biological sex.

Sexting: sending erotic text and photo images via a cell phone.

Sexual assault: generic term which refers to sexual contact or behavior that occurs without the consent of the other person.

Sexual coercion: involves using force—actual or threatened—to engage a person in sexual acts against that person's will.

Sexual competence: characterized by contraception, autonomy of decision, equally willing, and the "right time."

Sexual compliance: an individual willingly agrees to participate in sexual behavior without having the desire to do so.

Sexual double standard: the view that encourages and accepts the sexual expression of men more than women.

Sexual growth: term for sexual satisfaction resulting from work and effort over time for a good sex life.

Sexual identity: Individual's self-identification or label an individual chooses.

Sexual orientation fluidity: The capacity to change on a continuum from being more or less one sexual orientation to another.

Sexual orientation: an emotional, cognitive, and sexual attraction or non-attraction (asexuality) to other people.

Sexual readiness: factors such as autonomy of decision where one is not influenced by alcohol or peers; consensuality where both partners are equally willing; and absence of regret, or figuring out the right time to have first intercourse.

Sexual tempo: the number of months between the start of a relationship and when the couple first have sex.

Sexual values: moral guidelines for making sexual choices in nonmarital, marital, heterosexual, and homosexual relationships.

Sibling relationship aggression: behavior of one sibling toward another sibling that is intended to induce social harm or psychic pain in the sibling.

Singlehood: the relationship status of not being married.

Single-parent family: family in which there is only one parent and the other parent is completely out of the child's life through death, sperm donation, or abandonment and no contact is made with the other parent.

Single-parent household: one parent has primary custody of the child/children with the other parent living outside of the house but still being a part of the child's family; also called binuclear family.

Singlism: refers to stereotyping, stigmatizing, and discriminating against people who are single.

Situational couple violence (SCV): conflict escalates over an issue and one or both partners lose control.

Social anhedonia: people who have no interest in social contact or interactions with others.

Social exchange framework: views interaction and choices in terms of profit and loss.

Socialization: the process through which we learn attitudes, values, beliefs, and behaviors appropriate to the social positions we occupy.

Sociobiology: theory which emphasizes the biological basis for all social behavior, including mate selection.

Sociological imagination: the influence of social structure and culture on interpersonal decisions.

Sologamy: marrying onself.

Spectatoring: involves mentally observing your sexual performance and that of your partner.

Spillover effect: one's work role impacts one's family life in terms of working overtime, being on call on weekends, and so forth. Rarely does the family role dictate what will happen in the work role.

Spontaneous abortion (miscarriage): the unintended termination of a pregnancy.

Stalking: also known as unwanted pursuit behavior; unwanted following or harassment of a person that induces fear in the victim.

Statutory rape: nonforcible sexual contact in which one of the individuals is under the age of consent.

Stealthing: nonconsensual condom removal during sexual intercourse which exposes victims to physical risks of pregnancy and disease.

Stepfamily: a family in which adults bring biological or adopted children with other partners into the unit.

Sterilization: a permanent surgical procedure that prevents reproduction.

STI (sexually transmitted infection): refers to the general category of sexually transmitted infections such as chlamydia, genital herpes, gonorrhea, and syphilis.

Storge love style: also known as companionate love, a calm, soothing, nonsexual love devoid of intense passion.

Stress: reaction of the body to substantial or unusual demands whether they are physical, environmental, or interpersonal.

Structure-function framework: emphasizes how marriage and family contribute to society.

Superwoman/supermom: a cultural label that allows a woman to regard herself as very efficient, bright, and confident; usually a cultural cover-up for an overworked and frustrated woman.

Swinging: individuals in a committed relationship agree to have recreational sex with other individuals, independently or as a couple.

Symbolic interaction framework: views marriages and families as symbolic worlds in which the various members give meaning to each other's behavior.

Technoference: the interference of technology on the interaction of two people.

Tele-relationship therapy: therapy sessions conducted online, often through Skype, where both therapist and couple can see and hear each other.

Telework: an arrangement with an employer that the employee can perform duties and responsibilities from a remote location such as home.

Temporary alimony: money one spouse is to pay the other until the divorce is finalized.

Texting: short typewritten messages sent via a cell phone that are used to "commence, advance, and maintain" interpersonal relationships.

Thanatology: the examination of the social dimensions of death, dying, and bereavement.

Theoretical frameworks: a set of interrelated principles designed to explain a particular phenomenon.

Therapeutic abortion: abortions performed to protect the life or health of the woman.

Third shift: the expenditure of emotional energy by a spouse or parent in dealing with various emotional issues in family living.

Time-out: a noncorporal form of punishment that involves removing the child from a context of reinforcement to a place of isolation.

Traditional family: the two-parent nuclear family, with the husband as breadwinner and the wife as homemaker.

Transabdominal first-trimester selective termination: a procedure where the lives of some fetuses are terminated to increase the chance of survival for the others or to minimize the health risks associated with multifetal pregnancy for the woman.

Transgender: abbreviated as "trans," describes a person whose gender identity does not match the biological sex they were assigned at birth.

Transition to parenthood: period from the beginning of pregnancy through the first few months after the birth of a baby during which the mother and father undergo changes.

Transnational commercial surrogacy: having a baby by means of paying a third party to secure sperm, egg, fertilization, and surrogacy of the pregnancy. The new parents then come to take the baby home. Facilities in India provide this service.

Transnational families: families in which the migrant parents are separated from their children.

Transnational family: family in which the mother and child live in another country from the father.

Transphobia: a set of negative attitudes toward transgenderism or those who self identify as transgender.

Transracial adoption: adopting children of a race different from that of the parents.

Transsexual: older term for the person who has had hormonal or surgical intervention to change his or her body to align with his or her gender identity.

Unrequited love: love that is not returned.

Utilitarianism: individuals rationally weigh the rewards and costs associated with behavioral choices.

Vasectomy: form of male sterilization whereby the vas deferens is cut so that sperm cannot continue to travel outside the body via the penis.

Video mediated communication (VMC): individuals are able to see and hear others they are separated from to simulate their presence and enjoyment of "being with" their beloved.

Violence: physical aggression with the purpose to control, intimidate, and subjugate another human being.

"You" statement: statement that blames or criticizes the listener and often results in increasing negative feelings and behavior in the relationship.

REFERENCES

CHAPTER 1

Abbasi, I. S., & Alghamdi, N.G. (2018). The pursuit of romantic alternatives online: Social media friends as potential alternatives. *Journal of Sex & Marital Therapy, 44*(1), 16–28.

ABI research. (2012). Consumer and Personal Robotics. Retrieved from https://www.abiresearch.com/research/product/1014856-consumer-and-personal-robotics/

Andersen, S. H., Andersen, L. S., & Skov, P. E. (2015). Effect of marriage and spousal criminality on recidivism. *Journal of Marriage and the Family, 77*(2), 496–509.

Anderson, J., Rainie., L. & Luchsinger, A. (2018, December 10). Artificial intelligence and the future of humans. *Pew Research Center.* Retrieved from https://www.pewinternet.org/2018/12/10/artificial-intelligence-and-the-future-of-humans/

Animosa, L. H., Lindstrom Johnson, S., & T. L. Cheng, T. L. (2018). "I used to be wild": Adolescent perspectives on the influence of family, peers, school, and neighborhood on positive behavioral transition. *Youth & Society, 50*(1), 49–74.

Ansion, M., & Merali, N. 2018. Latino immigrant parents' experiences raising young children in the absence of extended family networks in Canada: Implications for counseling. *Counselling Psychology Quarterly, 31*(4), 408–427.

Arocho, R. 2019. Do expectations of divorce predict union formation in the transition to adulthood? *Journal of Marriage and Family, 81,* 979–990

Ball, C., Huang, K. T., Rikard, R. V., & Cotton, S. R. (2019). The emotional costs of computers: an expectancy-value analysis of predominantly low-socioeconomic status minority students' STEM attitudes. *Information, Communication and Society, 22,* 105–128.

Barr, A. B., & R. L. Simons, R. L. (2018). Marital beliefs among African American emerging adults: The roles of community context, family background, and relationship experiences. *Journal of Family Issues, 39*(2), 352–382.

Batuman, E. (2018, April 30) A theory of relativity: Japan's rent-a-family industry. *The New Yorker,* 50–61. Retrieved from https://www.newyorker.com/magazine/2018/04/30/japans-rent-a-family-industry

Bay-Chen, L. Y. (2017). Seeing how far you've come: The impact of the Digital Sexual Life History Calendar on young adult research participants. *Journal of Sex Research, 54*(3), 284–295.

Behler, R. L. (2017). You can't always get what you want: Network determinants of relationship inactualization in adolescence. *Social Science Research, 61,* 181–194.

Boccio, C. M., & Beaver., K. M. (2019). The influence of family structure on delinquent behavior. *Youth Violence and Juvenile Justice, 17*(1), 88–106.

Cardoso, J. B., Scott, J. L., Faulkner, M., & Lane, L. B. (2018). Parenting in the context of deportation risk. *Journal of Marriage and the Family, 80,* 301–316.

Cediel, A. (2018, June 26). From slavery to mass incarceration, America has separated families for centuries. *USA Today.* Retrieved from https://www.usatoday.com/story/opinion/2018/06/19/separating-families-border-illegal-immigrant-undocumented-column/711086002/

Chang, I. J., Bragg, B., & Knox, D. (2018, November 9). Some traditions die as slow as molasses: Are male children still preferred? Poster presented at National Council on Family Relations annual meeting, San Diego, CA.

Chang, I. J., Huff, S., & D. Knox, D. (2019). Humanoid robots: Acceptance for personal and family use. *College Student Journal, 53,* 1942–46.

Chapman, B., & Guven, C. (2016). Revisiting the relationship between marriage and well-being: Does marriage quality matter? *Journal of Happiness Studies, 17,* 533–551.

Chemuturi, R., Amirabdollahian, F., & Dautenhahn, K. (2013). Adaptive training algorithm for robot-assisted upper-arm rehabilitation, applicable to individualized and therapeutic human-robot interaction. *Journal of NeuroEngineering and Rehabilitation, 10*(102), 118.

Cherlin, A. J. (2019, January 30). Family policy today. *Journal of Family Theory and Review.* https://doi.org/10.1111/jftr.12315

Cimpian, J. R., Timmer, J. D., Birkett, M. A., Marro, R. L., Turner, B. C., & Phillips II, G. L. (2018). Bias from potentially mischievous responders on large-scale estimates of lesbian, gay, bisexual, or questioning (LGBQ)-Heterosexual youth health disparities. *American Journal of Public Health. 108*(S4), s258-s265.

Clyde, T. L., & Hawkins, A. J. (2019, April 29). Do premarital education promotion policies work? Institute for Family Studies. Retrieved from https://ifstudies.org/blog/do-premarital-education-promotion-policies-work

Cohen, M. (2016). An exploratory study of individuals in non-traditional, alternative relationships: How 'open' are we? *Sexuality and Culture, 20*(2), 295–315.

Cohn, D. (2013.) Love and marriage. *Pew Research Center.* Retrieved from http://www.pewsocialtrends.org/2013/02/13/love-and-marriage

Coontz, S. (2016). *The way we never were: American families and the nostalgia trap* (2nd ed). New York: Basic Books.

Cottle, N. R., Burr, B. K., Hubler, D. S., Payne, P. B., & Kern, B. (2015, November 13). *Assessing unique perceptions of couple relationship education programs.* Presented at the National Council on Family Relations Annual Meeting, Vancouver, BC.

Cottle, N.R., Thompson, A. K., Burr, B. K., & Hubler. D. S. (2014). The effectiveness of relationship education in the college classroom. *Journal of Couple & Relationship Therapy, 13*(4), 267–283.

Cravens, J. D. (2015, Summer). Couples' communication of rules and boundaries for technology and the Internet. *Family Focus, 60*(2), F17.

Dimock, M. (2019, January 17). Defining generations: Where millennials end and generation Z begins. *Pew Research Center.* Retrieved from http://www.pewresearch.org/fact-tank/2019/01/17/where-millennials-end-and-generation-z-begins/? utm_source=Pew+Research+Center&utm_campaign=de1bfe4cf9-EMAIL_CAMPAIGN_2019_01_18_01_43&utm_medium=email&utm_term=0_3e953b9b70-de1bfe4cf9-399499933

Dragojlovic, A. (2016). 'Playing family': unruly relationality and transnational motherhood. *Gender, Place & Culture: A Journal of Feminist Geography, 23*(2), 243–256.

Duncan, J., Bryant, V. Armes, S., & Futris, T. (2016, November). *Changes in marital communication patterns after premarital education.* Paper presented at the National Council on Family Relations annual meeting, Minneapolis, MN.

Dworkin, J., Rudi, J. H., & Hessel, H. (2018, August 22). The state of family research and social media. *Journal of Family Theory and Review.* https://doi.org/10.1111/jftr.12295

Edwards, A. L., & Martinez, G. E. (2018, November 8). *Living out our family histories in the family science classroom: Engaging critical family history through collaborative autoethnography.* Poster presented at the Annual Meeting of the National Council on Family Relations. San Diego, CA.

Erichsen, K. & Dignam. P. (2016, April). *From hookup to husband: Transitioning a casual to a committed relationship.* Paper presented at the Southern Sociological Society, Atlanta, GA.

Finkel, E. J. (2019). *The all or nothing marriage: How the best marriages work.* New York: Penguin.

Gassman-Pines, A., Gibson-Davis, C. M., Vernot, C., Butler, M., Hall, N., Taylor, L., Eastwood, K., & Zhang, X. (2017). They should say "I don't": Norms about midpregnancy marriage and job loss. *Journal of Marriage and the Family, 79*(2), 405–48.

Geiger, A., & Livingston., G. (2019, February 13). 8 facts about love and marriage in America. *Pew Research Center.* http://www.pewresearch.org/fact-tank/2019/02/13/8-facts-about-love-and-marriage/?utm_source=Pew+Research+Center&utm_campaign=ef0f933202-EMAIL_CAMPAIGN_2019_02_14_07_19&utm_medium=email&utm_term=0_3e953b9b70-ef0f933202-399499933

Grandstaff, M. (2016, August 23). This is how much it costs to own a dog. *USA Today*, pp. 4B.

Güttler, J., Georgoulas, C., Linner, T. & Bock, T. (2015). Towards a future robotic home environment: A survey. *Gerontology, 61*(3), 268–280.

Hall, S., & Knox, D. (2019). College Student Attitudes and Behaviors Survey of 13,119 undergraduates. Unpublished data collected for this text. Department of Family, Consumer, and Technology Education Teachers College, Ball State University and Department of Sociology, East Carolina University.

Harknett, K., & Cranney, S. (2017). Majority rules: Gender composition and sexual norms and behavior in high schools. *Population Research & Policy Review, 36*(4), 469–500.

Helliwell, J. F., Layard, R., & Sachs, J. (2016). *The World Happiness Report.* Retrieved from http://worldhappiness.report/wp-content/uploads/sites/2/2016/03/HR-V1_web.pdf

Hertlein, K. M., Blumer, M. L. C. (2013). *The couple and family technology framework: Intimate relationships in a digital age.* New York: Routledge.

Hodges, L. M. (2019, April 13). *Power, pets, and family: A look into the role of pets in the American family structure.* Poster presented at the Southern Sociological Society Annual meeting, Atlanta, GA.

Hughes, R., Young, E., & Baymon, B. (2018, November 8). *What's missing in introductory family science textbooks? A critical analysis.* Poster presented at the Annual Meeting, National Council on Family Relations, San Diego, CA.

Incerti, L., Henderson-Wilson, C., & Dunn, M. (2015). Challenges in the family. *Family Matters, 96*, 29–38.

James-Kangal, N., Weitbrecht, E. M., Francis, T. E., & Whitton, S. W. (2018). Hooking up and emerging adults' relationship attitudes and expectations. *Sexuality & Culture, 22*(3), 706–723.

Jervis, R., & A. Gomez. (2019, May 3). Child separations persist at border. *USA Today*, pp. A1.

Job, A., Baucom, D.H., & Hahlweg, K. (2017). Who benefits from couple relationship education? Findings from the largest German CRE study. *Journal of Couple & Relationship Therapy, 16*(2), 79–101.

Kanat-Maymon, Y., Antebi, A., & Zilcha-Mano, S. (2016). Basic psychological need fulfillment in human-pet relationships and well-being. *Personality and Individual Differences, 92*, 69–73.

Kanter, J. B., & Schramm, D. G. (2018). Brief interventions for couples: An integrative review. *Family Relations, 67*, 211–116.

Kennedy, H. R., Dalla, R. L., & Dreesman, S. (2018). "We are two of the lucky ones": Experiences with marriage and well-being for same sex couples. *Journal of Homosexuality, 65*(9), 1207–1231.

Killoren, S. E., Campione-Barr, N., Streit, C., Giron, S., Kline, G. C. & Youngblade, L. M. (2019). Content and correlates of sisters' messages about dating and sexuality. *Journal of Social & Personal Relationships, 36*(7), 2134–2155.

Klinenberg, E. (2012). *Going solo: The extraordinary rise and surprising appeal of living alone.* New York: Penguin.

Knopfli, B., Cullati, S., Courvoisier, D. S., Burton-Jeangros, C., & Perrig-Chiello, P. (2016, January 5). Marital breakup in later adulthood and self-rated health: A cross-sectional survey in Switzerland. *International Journal of Public Health, 61*(3), 357–366. Retrieved from doi: 10.1007/s00038-015-0776-6

Levesque, C., Lafontaine, M.,Caron, A.,Flesch J. L., & Bjornson, S. (2014, August 7–10). *Dyadic empathy, dyadic coping, and relationship satisfaction: A dyadic model.* Poster presented at American Psychological Association annual meeting, Washington, DC.

Leviton, M. (2016, September, 4–13). Stephanie Coontz on the past, present, and future of marriage. *Sun Magazine*, Issue 489. Retrieved from https://www.thesunmagazine.org/issues/489

Levy, D. (2017). *Love and sex with robot: The evolution of human-robot relationships.* New York: Harper Collins.

Lindemann, D. J. (2017). Going the distance: Individualism and interdependence in the commuter marriage. *Journal of Marriage and Family, 79*, 1419–1434. Retrieved from https://doi.org/10.1111/jomf.12408

Lorber, J. (1998). *Gender inequality: Feminist theories and politics.* Los Angeles, CA: Roxbury.

Luscombe, B. (2017, May 29). Growing up in public. *Time Magazine*, 42–45.

Marx, P. (2018, November 26). Roomba nation: The emergence of the domestic robot. The technology issue. *The New Yorker*, pp. 30–36.

McElwain, A., McGill, J., & Savasuk, R. (2016, November). *A meta-analysis of youth focused relationship education.* Paper presented at the National Council on Family Relations Annual Meeting. Minneapolis, MN.

McGinnis, A. & Burr, B. (2018, November 9). *The Couple and Relationship Education Attitudes Index: Diverse sample fit?* Poster presented at the Annual meeting, National Council on Family Relations. San Diego, CA.

Mekki, M., Delgado, A., Fry, A., Putrino, D., & Huang, V. (2018). Robotic rehabilitation and spinal cord injury: A narrative review. *Neurotherapeutics, 15*, 604–617.

Misselhorn, C. (2018.) Artificial morality: Concepts, issues and challenges. *Society, 55*, 161–169.

Murdock, G. P. (1949). *Social structure.* New York: Free Press.

National Center for Health Statistics, Marriage and Divorce. Retrieved from https://www.cdc.gov/nchs/fastats/marriage-divorce.htm .

Nugent, C. (2018, October 22). #BringBackOurGirls crusader shakes up Nigeria's presidential race. *Time*, pp. 14.

Ogolsky, B. G., Surra, C. A., & Monk, J.K. (2016). Pathways of commitment to wed: The development and dissolution of romantic relationships. *Journal of Marriage and Family, 78*(2), 293–310.

Oriola, T. B. (2017). "Unwilling Cocoons": Boko Haram's war against women. *Studies in Conflict & Terrorism, 40*(2), 99–121.

Ornstein, C. & Thomas, K. (2018, December 8). What these medical journals don't reveal: Top doctors' ties to industry. *The New York Times.* Retrieved from https://www.nytimes.com/2018/12/08/health/medical-journals-conflicts-of-interest.html

Park, S. Y., Bae, H., & Huh, C.A. (2017, Winter). Differences abound: Understanding the generational divides in attitudes on marriage in South Korea. *Family Focus, 74,* F14–F15.

Parker, S., & P. Mayock. (2019). "They're always complicated but that's the meaning of family in my eyes": Homeless youth making sense of "family" and family relationships. *Journal of Family Studies, 40*(4), 540–570.

Pearce, L. D., Hayward, G.M., Chassin, L., & Curran, P. J. (2018). The increasing diversity and complexity of family structures. *Journal of Research on Adolescence, 28*(3), 591–608.

Purina survey shows dogs are more than man's best friend. (2018, July 19). Retrieved from https://kmox.radio.com/articles/purina-survey-shows-dogs-are-more-mans-best-friend

Radford, J. and A. Budiman. (2018, September 14). *Facts on U.S. immigrants, 2016: Statistical portrait of the foreign-born population in the United States.* Pew Research Center. Retrieved from http://www.pewhispanic.org/2018/09/14/facts-on-u-s-immigrants/

Randall, B. (2008). *Songman: The story of an Aboriginal elder of Uluru.* Sydney, Australia: ABC Books.

Rauer, A. (2013, February). *From golden bands to the golden years: The critical role of marriage in older adulthood.* Presented at the annual meeting of the Southeastern Council on Family Relations, Birmingham, AL.

Rinehart, J. K., Nason, E. E., Yeater, E. A., & Miller, G. F. (2017). Do some students need special protection from research on sex and trauma? New evidence for young adult resilience in "sensitive topics" research. *Journal of Sex Research, 54*(3), 273–283.

Routledge, C. (2019). *What are the social and psychological costs of our computer-mediated lives?* Institute for Family Studies. August 15. https://ifstudies.org/blog/what-are-the-social-and-psychological-costs-of-our-computer-mediated-lives

Schneider, D. (2017). The effects of the Great Recession on American families. *Sociology Compass, 11*(4), 1–2.

Schneider, D., Harknett, K., & M. Stimpson, M. (2018). What explains the decline in first marriage in the United States? Evidence from the Panel Study of Income Dynamics, 1969–2013. *Journal of Marriage and the Family, 80*(4), 791–811.

Smith, M. B., & Bravo, V. (2016, December 15). Wellness National Pet Food Survey. *USA Today,* pp. A1.

Smith, M. B., & Loehrke., J. (2017, July 9–11). Finn Partner' Survey of 1000 adults. *USA Today,* pp. A1.

Smith, M. B., & Loehrke, J. (2018, March 20). Data from Prudential study. *USA Today,* pp. A1.

Spitznagel, M. B., Jacobson, D.M., Cox, M. D., & Carlson, M.D. (2017). Caregiver burden in owners of a sick companion animal: a cross-sectional observational study. *Veterinary Record, 181*(12). doi: 10.1136/vr.104295

Taiwan dentist must repay mother for training fees. (2018, January 2). Retrieved from https://www.bbc.com/news/world-asia-42542260.

Tumin, D., & Zheng, H. (2018, June). Do the health benefits of marriage depend on the likelihood of marriage? *Journal of Marriage & Family, 80,* 622–636.

Veterlaus, J. M. and S. Tulane. 2019. The perceived influence of interactive technology on marital relationships. *Contemporary Family Therapy, 41,* 247–257.

Voorpostel, M. (2018). Fictive kin and families of choice in the European context. *Family Focus, 63*(1), 1–3F.

Wang, W. (2018, February 12). The state of our unions: Marriage up among older Americans, down among the younger. *Institute for Family Studies.* Charlottesville, VA. Retrieved from https://ifstudies.org/blog/the-state-of-our-unions-marriage-up-among-older-americans-down-among-the-younger

Wang, Y. (2016). Ghost marriage in twentieth-century Chinese literature: Between the past and the future. *Frontiers of Literary Studies in China, 10*(1), 86–102.

Why human-like robots? Retrieved from http://www.hansonrobotics.com

Wilmoth, J. D., & Blaney, A. D. (2016). African American clergy involvement in marriage preparation. *Journal of Family Issues, 37*(6), 855–876.

Zeitzen, M. K. (2008). *Polygamy: A cross-cultural analysis.* Oxford, UK: Berg.

Zemanek, L. J. (2014, November). *The impact of animals on prosocial behaviors in children with autism spectrum disorders: A critical literature review.* Paper presented at the National Council on Family Relations annual meeting, Baltimore, MD.

Zusman, M. (2019, March 8). Personal interview with Dr. Zusman on social control of choices. Unpublished. Dr. Zusman is retired from Indiana University Northwest.

Zusman, M. E., Knox, D., & Gardner, T. (2009). *The social context view of sociology.* Durham, NC: Carolina Academic Press.

CHAPTER 2

Allendorf, K. (2013). Schemas of marital change: From arranged marriages to eloping for love. *Journal of Marriage and the Family, 75*(2), 453–469.

Balzarini, R. N., Dharma, C., Kohut, T., Holmes, B. M., Campbell, L., Lehmiller, J. J., & Harman, J. J. (2019). Demographic comparison of American individuals in polyamorous and monogamous relationships. *The Journal of Sex Research, 56,* 681–694.

Barelds, D. P., & Barelds-Dijkstra, P. (2007). Love at first sight or friends first? Ties among partner personality trait similarity, relationship onset, relationship quality, and love. *Journal of Social and Personal Relationships, 24,* 479–496.

Barelds-Dijkstra, D. P. H., & Barelds, P. (2007). Relations between different types of jealousy and self and partner perceptions of relationship quality. *Clinical Psychology & Psychotherapy, 14*(3), 176–188.

Beckmeyer, J. (2016, November). *Romantic relationship status and emerging adults' alcohol use.* Paper presented at the National Council on Family Relations, annual meeting, Phoenix, AZ.

Berscheid, E. (2010). Love in the fourth dimension. *Annual Review of Psychology, 61*(1),1–25.

Bland, A. M, & McQueen., K. S. (2018, June). The distribution of Chapman's love languages in couples: An exploratory cluster analysis. *Couple and Family Psychology: Research and Practice, 7*(2), 103–126. http://dx.doi.org/10.1037/cfp0000102

Blomquist, B. A., & Giuliano, T. A. (2012). Do you love me, too? Perceptions of responses to "I love you." *North American Journal of Psychology, 14*(2), 407–418.

Boutwell, B. B., Barnes, J. C., & Beaver, K. M. (2015). When love dies: Further elucidating the existence of a mate ejection module. Review of General Psychology, 19(1), 30–38.

Brown, P. J., & Sweeney, J. (2009). The anthropology of overweight, obesity and the body. *AnthroNotes,* 30(1), 6–12.

Brody, N., & Pena, J. (2015). Equity, relational maintenance, and linguistic features of text messaging. *Computers in Human Behavior, 49*, 499e506. https://doi.org/10.1016/j.chb.2015.03.037

Bunt, S., & Z. J. Hazelwood, Z. J. 2017). Walking the walk, talking the talk: Love languages, self-regulation, and relationship satisfaction. *Personal Relationships, 24*(2), 280–290.

Campbell, K., & Kaufman, J. (2017). Do you pursue your heart or your art? Creativity, personality and love. *Journal of Family Issues, 38*(3), 287–311.

Conley, T. D., Piemonte, J. L., Gusakova, S., & Rubin, J. D. (2018). Sexual satisfaction among individuals in monogamous and consensually non-monogamous relationships. *Journal of Social and Personal Relationships, 35*(4), 509–532.

Carter, C. S., & Porges, S. W. (2013). The biochemistry of love: an oxytocin hypothesis. *Science & Society, 14*(1),12–16.

Chapman, G. (2010). *The five love languages: The secret to love that lasts*. Chicago, IL: Northfield Publishing.

Deepak, S., Bhatia, H., & Chadha, N. K.(2019). A psychological study on the positive impacts of experiencing love. *International Journal of Social Sciences Review, 7*, 513–518.

Diamond, L. M. (2003). What does sexual orientation orient? A biobehavioral model distinguishing romantic love and sexual desire. *Psychological Review, 110*(1), 173–192.

Elliott, L., Easterling, B., & Knox, D. (2016). Taking chances in romantic relationships. *College Student Journal, 50*(2), 241–245.

Fisher, H. E., Brown, L. L., Aron, A., G. Strong, G., & Mashek, D. (2010). Reward, addiction, and emotion regulation systems associated with rejection in love. *Journal of Neurophysiology, 104*(1), 51–60.

Freud, S. (1905/1938). Three contributions to the theory of sex. In A. A. Brill. (Ed.) *The basic writings of Sigmund Freud*. New York: Random House, 1905; republished 1938.

Freeman, D. (1999). *The fateful hoaxing of Margaret Mead: A historical analysis of her Samoan research*. New York: Westview Press.

Frye-Cox, N. (2012, November). *Alexithymia and marital quality: The mediating role of loneliness*. Paper presented at meeting of National Council on Family Relations, Phoenix, AZ.

Goodman-Deane, J., Mieczakowski, A., Johnson, D., Goldhaber, P., & Clarkson, J. (2016). The impact of communication technologies on life and relationship satisfaction. *Computers in Human Behavior, 57*, 219–229.

Hall, S., & Knox, D. (2019). College Student Attitudes and Behaviors Survey of 12,785 undergraduates. Unpublished data collected for this text. Department of Family, Consumer, and Technology Education Teachers College, Ball State University and Department of Sociology, East Carolina University, Greenville, NC.

Halpern, C. T., King, R. B., Oslak, S. G., & Udry, J. R.(2005). Body mass index, dieting, romance, and sexual activity in adolescent girls. Relationships over time. *Journal of Research on Adolescence, 15*(4), 535–559.

Harris, V. W., Bedard, K., Moen, D., & Alvarez-Perez, P. (2016). The role of friendship: Trust and love in happy German marriages. *Marriage and Family Review, 52*(3), 262–304.

Hatfield, E., Bensman, L., & Rapson, R. L. (2012). A brief history of social scientists' attempts to measure passionate love. *Journal of Social and Personal Relationships, 29*(2), 143–164.

Heshmati, S., Oravecz, Z., Pessman, S., Batchelder, W. H., Muth, C., & Vandekerckhove, J. (2019). What does it mean to feel loved: Cultural consensus and individual differences in felt love. *Journal of Social and Personal Relationships, 36*(1), 214–243.

Hsieh, S. H., & Tseng, T. H. (2017). Playfulness in mobile instant messaging: Examining the influence of emoticons and text messaging on social interaction. *Computers in Human Behavior, 69*, 405–414. http://dx.doi.org/10.1016/j.chb.2016.12.052.

Huston, T. L., Caughlin, J. P., Houts, R. M., Smith, S. E., & and George, L. J. (2001). The connubial crucible: Newlywed years as predictors of marital delight, distress, and divorce. *Journal of Personality and Social Psychology, 80*, 237–252.

Johnson, M. D., Home, R. M., & Neyer, F. J. (2019). The development of willingness to sacrifice and unmitigated communion in intimate partnerships. *Journal of Marriage and the Family, 81*(1), 264–79.

Kelly, H. (2012). *OMG, the text message turns 20. But has SMS peaked?* Retrieved from http://www.cnn.com/2012/12/03/tech/mobile/sms-text-message-20/

Kennedy, D. P., Tucker, J. S., Pollard, M. S., Go, M., & Green, H. D. (2011). Adolescent romantic relationships and change in smoking status. *Addictive Behaviors, 36*(4), 320–326.

Knapp, D. J., Norton, A. M., & Sandberg, J. G. (2014, November 19). *Family of origin, relationship self-regulation and attachment in marital relationships*. Paper presented at the National Council on Family Relations annual meeting, Baltimore, MD.

Koontz, A., S. Okorie, & L. Norman. (2019). Realistic love: Contemporary college women's negotiations of princess culture and the "reality" of romantic relationships. *Journal of Social & Personal Relationships, 36*(2), 535–555.

Knox, D., Zusman, M. E., Mabon, L., & Shivar, L. (1999). Jealousy in college student relationships. *College Student Journal, 33*(3), 328–329.

Langeslag, S. J. E., Muris, P., & Fraken, I. H. A. (2013). Measuring romantic love: Psychometric properties of the infatuation and attachment scales. *Journal of Sex Research, 50*(8), 739–774.

Lee, J. A. (1973). *The colors of love: An exploration of the ways of loving*. Don Mills, Ontario, Canada: New Press.

Lee, J.A. (1988). Love-styles. In R. Sternberg & M. Barnes (Eds.), *The psychology of love* (pp. 38–67). New Haven, CT: Yale University Press.

Lomas, T. (2018). The flavours of love: A cross-cultural lexical analysis. *Journal for the Theory of Social Behavior, 48*(1), 134–152

Mar, A. (2017). Love in the time of robots: Are we ready for intimacy with robots? https://www.wired.com/2017/10/hiroshi-ishiguro-when-robots-act-just-like-humans/

Match.com (2017). 2016 Singles in America Study. Retrieved from www.singlesinAmerica.com

Milhausen, R. R., McKay, A., Graham, C. A., Sanders, S. A., Crosby, R. A., Yarber, W. L., & Wood, J. (2018). Do associations between pleasure ratings and condom use during penile-vaginal intercourse vary by relationship type? A study of Canadian university students. *Journal of Sex Research, 55*(1), 21–30.

Miller, J. G., Kahle, S., Lopez, M., & Hastings, P. D. (2015). Compassionate love buffers stress-active mothers from fight or flight parenting. *Developmental Psychology, 51*(1), 36–43.

Milne, C. (2015). *Texting etiquette explained*. Retrieved from http://www.match.com/magazine/article/6802/Texting-Etiquette-Explained

Moore, A. C. (2017). Has the American public's interest in information related to relationships beyond "The Couple" increased over time? *Journal of Sex Research, 54*(6), 677–684.

Morrison, T. G., Beaulieu, D., Brockman, M., & Beaglaoich, C. O. (2013). A comparison of polyamorous and monoamorous persons: are there differences in indices of relationship well-being and sociosexuality? *Psychology and Sexuality, 4*, 75–91.

Neto, F. (2012). Perceptions of love and sex across the adult life span. *Journal of Social and Personal Relationships, 29*(6), 760–775.

Northrup, J., & Smith, J. (2016). Effects of Facebook maintenance behaviors on partners' experience of love. *Contemporary Family Therapy: An International Journal, 38*(2) 245–253.

Ohadi, J., Brown, B., Trub, L., & Rosenthal, L. (2017). I just text to say I love you: Partner similarity in texting and relationship satisfaction. *Computers in Human Behavior, 78*, 126–132.

Ogolsky, B. G., Surra, C. A., & Monk, J. K. (2016). Pathways of commitment to wed: The development and dissolution of romantic relationships. *Journal of Marriage and the Family, 78*(2), 293–310.

Olcay, I. M. What is the impact of choosing one's spouse on marital satisfaction of wives and husbands? The case of arranged and self-choice Turkish marriages. *Journal of Family Issues, 40*, 1270–1298

Pew Research Center. (2018, September 20). *Mobile fact sheet.* Retrieved from Pew Research Center http://www .pewinternet.org/fact-sheet/mobile/

Pew Research Center. (2019). *Mobile fact sheet.* https://www .pewinternet.org/fact-sheet/mobile/

Pines, A. M. (1992). *Romantic jealousy: Understanding and conquering the shadow of love.* New York: St. Martin's Press.

Pombo, S., Felix da Costa, N., Ismail, F., Cardoso, J. M. N., & Figueira, M. L. (2015). Alexithymia and alcohol dependence: Do different subtypes manifest different emotion regulations?. *Addiction Research & Theory, 23*(3), 187–195.

Rauer, A. J., Sabey, A., & Jensen, J. F. (2014). Growing old together: Compassionate love and health in older adulthood. *Journal of Social and Personal Relationships, 31*(5), 677–696.

Reis, H. T., Maniaci, M. R., & Rogge, R. D. (2014). The expression of compassionate love in everyday compassionate acts. *Journal of Social and Personal* Relationships, *31*(5), 651–676.

Reiss, I. L. (1960). Toward a sociology of the heterosexual love relationship. *Journal of Marriage and Family Living, 22*(2), 139–45.

Reynaud, M., Blecha, L., & Benyamina, A.(2011). Is love passion an addictive disorder? *American Journal of Drug & Alcohol Abuse, 36*, 261–267.

Riela, S., Rodriguez, G., Aron, A., Xu, X., & Acevedo, B. P. (2010). Experiences of falling in love: Investigating culture, ethnicity, gender, and speed. *Journal of Social and Personal Relationships, 27*(4), 473–493.

Ross, C. B. (2006, March 24). *An exploration of eight dimensions of self-disclosure on relationship.* Paper presented at the Southern Sociological Society, New Orleans, LA.

Rusu, M. S. (2018). Theorising love in sociological thought: Classical contributions to a sociology of love. *Journal of Classical Sociology, 18*(1), 3–20.

Sandberg, J. G., Novak, J. R., Davis, S. Y., & Busby, D. M. (2016). The Brief Accessibility, Responsiveness, and Engagement (BARE) Scale: A tool for measuring attachment behaviors in clinical couples. *Journal of Marital & Family Therapy, 42*(1), 106–122.

Sato, H., Chan, T., & Mulholland, T. (2018, December 29). Beyond dimensions: The man who married a hologram. *CNN.* Retrieved from https://www.cnn.com/2018/12/28/health/ rise-of-digisexuals-intl/index.html

Scheff, E. (2014). *The polyamorists next door.* Lanham, MD: Rowman & Littlefield.

Seguin, L., Blais, M., Goyer, M. F., Rodrique, C., Magontier, C., Adam, B. D., & Lavoie, F. (2017). Examining relationship quality across three types of relationship agreements. *Sexualities, 20*(1–2), 86–104.

Seguin, L. (2019). The good, the bad, and the ugly: Lay attitudes and perceptions of polyamory. *Sexualities, 22,* 669–690

Sizemore, K. M., & Olmstead, S. B. (2016, November 4). *Willingness to engage in consensual non-monogamy: A mixed-methods study.* Poster presented at the Annual Meeting of National Council on Family Relations, Minneapolis, MN.

Skoyen, J. A., Rentscher, K. E., & Butler, E. A. (2018). Relationship quality and couple's unhealthy behaviors predict body mass index in women. *Journal of Social & Personal Relationships, 35*(2), 224–245.

Smith, M. A., & J. Loehrke. (2018, April 30). Report on Capital Survey of 2000 adults. *USA Today,* pp. A1.

Soller, B. (2014). Caught in a bad romance: Adolescent romantic relationships and mental health. *Journal of Health and Social Behavior, 55*(1), 56–72.

Sprecher, S., & Hatfield, E. (2017). The importance of love as a basis of marriage: Revisiting Kephart (1967). *Journal of Family Issues, 38*(30), 312–335.

Stanik, C. E., McHale, S. M., & Couter. A. C. (2013). Gender dynamics predict changes in marital love among African-American couples. *Journal of Marriage & Family, 75*(4) 795–798.

Stanton, S.C.E., & Campbell, L. (2014). Psychological and physiological predictors of health in romantic relationships: An attachment perspective." *Journal of Personality, 82*, 528–538.

Sternberg, R. J. (1986). A triangular theory of love. *Psychological Review, 93*(2), 119–135.

Stinehart, M. A., Scott, D. A., & Barfield, H. G. (2012). Reactive attachment disorder in adopted and foster care children: Implications for mental health professionals. *The Family Journal: Counseling and Therapy for Couples and Families, 20*(4), 355–360.

Toufexis, A. (1993, February 15). The right chemistry. *Time,* (49), pp. 51.

Tzeng, O. C. S., Wooldridge, K., & and Campbell, K. (2003). Faith love: A psychological construct in intimate relations. *Journal of the Indiana Academy of the Social Sciences, 7,* 11–20.

Vaillancourt, K. T., & Few-Demo, A. L. (2014). The relational dynamics of swinging relationships: An exploratory study. *Family Journal, 22*(3), 311–320.

Vault Careers, (2019). Vault.com Office Romance Survey 2019. http://www.vault.com/blog/workplace-issues/2019-vault- office-romance-survey-results/

Vedes, A., Hilpert, P., Nussbeck, F. W., Randall, A. K., Bodenmann, G., & Lind, W. R. (2016). Love styles, coping and relationship satisfaction: A dyadic approach. *Personal Relationships, 23*(1), 84–97.

Watkins, N. K., & J. Beckmeyer, J. (2018, November 8). *Relationship importance, romantic involvement, and emerging adult well-being.* Poster presented at the annual meeting of the National Council on Family Relations, San Diego, CA.

Watkins, S. & Boon, S. D. (2016). Expectations regarding fidelity in dating relationships. *Journal of Social & Personal Relationships, 33*(2), 237–256.

Weisskirch, R. S. (2017). Abilities in romantic relationships and well-being among emerging adults. *Marriage and Family Review, 53*(1), 36–47.

Zengel, B., Edlund, J. E., & Sagarin. B. J. (2013). Sex differences in jealousy in response to infidelity: Evaluation of demographic moderators in a national random sample. *Personality and Individual Differences, 54*(1), 47–51.

Zsok, F., Haucke, M., DeWit, C. Y., & Barelds, D. P. H. (2017). What kind of love is love at first sight? An empirical investigation. *Personal Relationships, 24*(4), 869–885.

CHAPTER 3

Abboud, P. (2019). Meet the third gender: *Samoa's Fa'afafine people*. Retrieved from http://www.pedestrian.tv/features/arts-and-culture/meet-the-third-gender-samoas-faafafine-people/70b3c7c8–66fc-4453–9f06–1de911d249ee.htm

Abdulcadir, J., Botsikas, D., Bolmont, M., Bilancioni, A., Djema, D. A., Demicheli, F. B., & Yaron. M. (2016). Sexual anatomy and function in women with and without genital mutilation: A cross-sectional study. *Journal of Sexual Medicine, 13*(2), 226–237.

Anderson, H., & Daniels, M. (2017). Film dialogue from 2,000 screenplays, broken down by gender and age. *The Pudding*. https://pudding.cool/2017/03/film-dialogue/

Arvanitake, E. (2019). Postmillennial femininities in the popular romance novel. *Journal of Gender Studies, 28*(1), 18–28.

Azad, A., GinnerHau, H., & Karlsson, M. (2018). Adolescent female offenders' subjective experiences of how peers influence norm-breaking behavior. *Child & Adolescent Social Work Journal, 35*(3), 257–270.

Baldas, T. (2017, April 25). Genital mutilation victims break their silence: "This is Demonic" *USA Today*. 1A.

Barth, J. M., Dunlap, S., & K. Chappetta, K. (2016, February 29). The influence of romantic partners on women in STEM majors. *Sex Roles*, DOI: 10.1007/s11199–016-0596-z

Bay-Cheng, L. Y., Maguin, E., & Bruns, A. E. (2018). Who wears the pants: The implications of gender and power for youth heterosexual relationships. *Journal of Sex Research, 55*(1), 7–20.

Bem, S. L. (1993). *The lenses of gender: Transforming the debate on sexual inequality*. New Haven, CT: Yale University Press.

Bensidoun, I., & D. Trancart, D. (2018). Career choices and gender pay gap: The role of work preferences and attitudes. *Population, 73*, 35–60.

Bhardwaj, P., & Gal, S. (2018). Siri owns 46% of the mobile voice assistant market. *Business Insider*. Retrieved from https://www.businessinsider.com/siri-google-assistant-voice-market-share-charts-2018-6.

Blair, K. L., & Hoskin, R. A. (2019). Transgender exclusion from the world of dating: Patterns of acceptance and rejection of hypothetical trans dating partners as a function of sexual and gender identity. *Journal of Social & Personal Relationships, 36*, 2074–2095.

Brizendine, L. (2006). *The female brain*. New York: Broadway Books.

Buckley, T. R. (2018). Black adolescent males: Intersections among their gender role identity and racial identity and associations with self-concept. *Child Development, 89*, e311–e322. doi: 10.1111/cdev.12950

Bulanda, J. R. (2011). Gender, marital power, and marital quality in later life. *Journal of Women and Aging, 23*(1), 3–22.

Burchardt, M. (2018). Saved from hegemonic masculinity? Charismatic Christianity and men's responsibilization in South Africa. *Current Sociology, 66*, 110–127.

Cass, C. (2014). Associated Press-WE TV poll. Americans say it's OK for woman to propose, but few marriages start that way. http://ap-gfkpoll.com/uncategorized/our-latest-poll-3

Catalyst, (2018). Women in science, technology, engineering and mathematics (STEM). *Knowledge Center*. https://www.catalyst.org/research/women-in-science-technology-engineering-and-mathematics-stem/. Retrieved September 20, 2018.

Chang, I. J., & Ward, R. (2017, November 17). *Disney princess going to college: Using Disney princess films as catalyst for discussion*. Poster presented at the Annual Meeting of National Council on Family Relations.

Clemans, K. H., & Graber, J. A. (2016). Young adolescents' gender, ethnicity, and popularity based social schemas of aggressive behavior. *Youth and Society, 48*(3) 303–317.

Connor, J. J., Hunt, S., Finsaas, M., Ciesinski, A., Ahmed, A., & Robinson, B. B. E. (2016). Sexual health care, sexual behaviors and functioning, and female genital cutting: Perspectives from Somali women living in the United States. *Journal of Sex Research, 53*(3), 346–359.

Cordero-Coma, J. & Esping-Andersen, G. (2018). The intergenerational transmission of gender roles: Children's contribution to housework in Germany. *Journal of Marriage & Family, 80*(4), 1005–1019.

Diop, M. K., & Stewart, P. (2015, November 12–14). *Female genital mutilation in the U.S.: Scope and prevention methods*. National Council on Family Relations Annual Meeting, Vancouver, British Columbia, CN.

Dolan, K. (2019, January 22). *Gender fluidity and gender identity*. Presentation to Sociology of Human Sexuality class, East Carolina University, Greenville, NC.

Erarslan, A. B., & Rankin, B. (2013). Gender role attitudes of female students in single-sex and coeducational high schools in Istanbul. *Sex Roles, 69*, 455–469.

Elder, K., & Griffith, D. M. (2016). Men's health and masculinity. *American Journal of Public Health, 106*(7), 1157.

Fahmy, D. (2018). Americans are far more religious than adults in other wealthy nations. *Pew Research Center*. http://www.pewresearch.org/fact-tank/2018/07/31/americans-are-far-more-religious-than-adults-in-other-wealthy-nations/ Accessed July 31, 2018.

Fernandez-Cornejo, J. A., Escot, L., Kabubo-Mariara, J., Kinyanjui Kinuthia, B., Eydal, G. B., & Bjarnason. T. (2016). Gender differences in young adults' inclination to sacrifice career opportunities in the future for family reasons: comparative study with university students from Nairobi, Madrid, and Reykjavik. *Journal of Youth Studies, 19*(4), 457–482.

Floro, M., Chang, H., Anderson, B., & Alder, N. (2014, August). *Internalization of stereotypes and interracial dating in African American women*. Poster presented at the American Psychological Association annual meeting, Washington, DC.

Flynn, M. A., Craig, C. M., Anderson, C. N., & Holody, K. J. (2016). Objectification in popular music lyrics: An examination of gender and genre differences. *Sex Roles: A Journal of Research 75*(3–4), 164–176. http://dx.doi.org/10.1007/s11199–016-0592-3

Geiger, A., & G. Livingston. (2019, February 13). 8 facts about love and marriage in America. *Pew Research Center*. Retrieved from http://www.pewresearch.org/fact-tank/2019/02/13/8-facts-about-love-andmarriage/

Griggs, B., (2011). Why computer voices are mostly female? Retrieved on August 20, 2015 from http://www.cnn.com/2011/10/21/tech/innovation/female-computer-voices/

Hall, S., & Knox, D. (2019). College Student Attitudes and Behaviors Survey of 13,061 undergraduates. Unpublished data collected for this text. Department of Family, Consumer, and Technology Education Teachers College, Ball State University and Department of Sociology, East Carolina University, Greenville, NC.

Hall, S. S., & Willoughby, B. J. (2019). Relative work and family role centralities: Predicting marriage and family beliefs. *Marriage & Family Review, 55*(7), 667–685.

Hilliard, T., Brenner, R., & Knox, D. (2019, April 10–13). "*What's for dinner?*" – "*Who's Asking?*": Demographics of feminist attitudes. Poster presented at the Southern Sociological Society annual meeting, Atlanta, GA.

Horne, R. M., & Johnson, M. D. (2018). Gender role attitudes, relationship efficiency, and self-disclosure in intimate relationships. *Journal of Social Psychology, 58*(1), 37–50.

Hoy, M. B. (2018). Alexa, Siri, Cortana, and More: An Introduction to Voice Assistants. *Medical Reference Services Quarterly, 37*(1), 81–88.

Hussain, N. H., Wook, T. S., Noor, S. F., & Mohamed, H. (2018). Speech input as an alternative mode to perform multi-touch gestures. *Telkomnika, 16,* 1367–1375.

Joel, D., Berman, Z., Tavor, I., Wexler, N., Gaber, O., Stein, Y., Shefi, N., Pool, J., Urchs, S., Margulies, D. S., Liem, F., Hänggi, J., Jäncke, L., & Assaf, Y. (2015). *Sex beyond the genitalia: The human brain mosaic.* Proceedings of the National Academy of Sciences of the United States of America (PNAS) 112:50. Retrieved from http://www.pnas.org/content/112/50/15468

Jordan-Young, R., & Rumiati, R. (2012). Hardwired for sexism: Approaches to sex/gender in neuroscience. *Neuroethics 5*(3), 305–315. Retrieved from http://link.springer.com/article/10.1007%2Fs12152–011-9134-4.

Kakoudaki, D. (2014). *Anatomy of a Robot.* New Brunswick, NJ: Rutgers University Press.

Keener, E., & Mehta, C. (2017). Sandra Bem: revolutionary and generative feminist psychologist. *Sex Roles, 76*(9–10), 525–528.

Kohlberg, L. (1966). A cognitive-developmental analysis of children's sex-role concepts and attitudes. In E. E. Macoby (Ed.) *The development of sex differences.* Stanford, CA: Stanford University Press.

Kohlberg, L. (1969). Stage and sequence: The cognitive developmental approach to socialization. In D. A. Goslin (Ed.) *Handbook of socialization theory and research,* (pp. 347–480). Chicago: Rand McNally.

Kollmayer, M., Schultes, M. T., Schober, B., Hodosi, T., & Spiel, C. (2018). Parents' judgments about the desirability of toys for their children: Associations with gender role attitudes, gender-typing of toys, and demographics. *Sex Roles, 79*(5–6), 329–341.

Korn Ferry Survey (2018, August 7). *Children and impact on career.* Retrieved from https://www.kornferry.com/press/nearly-half-of-female-professionals-said-theyve-missed-a-promotion-or-opportunity-because-of-their-gender.

Lam, C. B., Stanik, C., & McHale, S. M. (2017). The development and correlates of gender role attitudes in African American youth. *British Journal of Developmental Psychology, 35*(3), 406–419.

Lamm, E. M. (2019). Bye, bye, binary: Updating birth certificates to transcend the binary of sex. *Law & Sexualtiy: A Review of Lesbian, Gay, Bisexual & Transgender Legal Services, 28,* 1–23.

Lien, I. L. (2017). The perspectives of Gambian men on the sexuality of cut and uncut women. *Sexualities, 20*(5–6), 521–534.

Life Expectancy. (2019). http://www.geoba.se/country.php?cc=US&year=2019

Luscombe, B. (2018, March 19). Jordan Peterson: Seven questions. *Time Magazine*, page 76.

Martin, C. L., Cook, R. E., & Andrews, N.C.Z. (2016, March). Reviving androgyny: A modern day perspective on flexibility of gender identity and behavior. *Sex Roles,* 1–12. https://doi.org/10.1007/s11199-016-0602-5

Match.com 2017. 2016 Singles in America Study. Retrieved from www.singlesinAmerica.com

Mead, M. (1935). *Sex and temperament in three primitive societies.* New York: William Morrow.

Mercer, N., Crocetti, E., Meeus, W., & Branje, S. (2018). An experimental investigation of the influence of deviant peers on own deviancy: A replication study. *Journal of Experimental Criminology, 14*(3), 429–438.

Mitchell, K. R., Mercer, C. H., Prah, P., Clifton, S., Tanton, C., Wellings, K., & Copas. A. (2019). Why do men report more opposite-sex partners than women? Analysis of the gender discrepancy in a British national probability survey. *The Journal of Sex Research, 56*(1), 1–8.

Myers, J. (2016). *The future of men: Masculinity in the twenty-first century.* Inkshares Publisher.

Montemurro, B., Bartasavich, J., & Wintermute, L. (2015). Let's (not) talk about sex: The gender of sexual discourse. *Sexuality & Culture, 19*(1), 139–156.

Nakku, M. E. (2019, February 25). *Effects of female genital mutilation on the lives of women and girls in the district of Amudati, Uganda.* Poster presented at the American Association of Behavioral and Social Sciences annual meeting, Las Vegas, NV.

Nelms, B. J., Knox, D., & Easterling, B. (2012). The relationship talk: Assessing partner commitment. *College Student Journal 46*(1), 178–182.

Nowakowski, K. (2017a). Who's the fairest of them all? *National Geographic, 231,* p. 22.

Nowakowski, K. (2017b). Where in the world are women and men most equal? *National Geographic, 231,* 26–27.

Ouahidi, M. (2018). Gender imbalance in Moroccan broadcast news. *Culture & Society: Journal of Social Research, 9*(1), 99–113.

Owens, J. (2016). Early childhood behavior problems and the gender gap in educational attainment in the United States. *Sociology of Education, 89*(3) 236–258.

Pepin, J. R., & Cotter, D. A. (2018). Separating spheres? Diverging trends in youth's gender attitudes about work and family. *Journal of Marriage & Family, 80*(1), 7–24.

Petts, R. J., Shafer, K. M., & Essig, L. (2018). Does adherence to masculine norms shape fathering behavior. *Journal of Marriage and the Family, 80*(3), 704–720.

Pew Research Center. (2018). When American say they believe in God, what do they mean?

Religion and Public Life. Available at http://www.pewforum.org/2018/04/25/when-americans-say-they-believe-in-god-what-do-they-mean/Accessed July 31, 2018.

Picheta, B., & Mirchandani, K. (2019, March 2). Only six countries have equal rights for men and women. CNN. https://www.cnn.com/2019/03/02/europe/world-bank-gender-equality- report-intl/index.html

Prickett, K., Martin-Storey, A., & Crosnoe, R. (2015). A research not on time with children in different and same sex two parent families. *Demography, 52*(3), 905–918.

ProQuest Statistical Abstract of the United States. (2019). Online Edition. Bethesda, MD. Retrieved from https://www.proquest.com/products-services/statabstract.html

Reich, S. M., Black, R. W., & Foliaki, T. (2018). Constructing difference: Lego® Set narratives promote stereotypic gender roles and play. *Sex Roles, 79*(5–6), 285–298.

Rincon, J. A., Costa, A., Novais, P., Julian, V., & Carrascosa. C. (2018). A new emotional robot assistant that facilitate human interaction and persuasion. *Knowledge and Information System*, 1–21. DOI:10.1007/s10115-018-1231-9.

Roberson, P. N. E., Lenger, K. A., Norona, J. C., & Olmstead, S. B. (2018). A longitudinal examination of the directional effects between relationship quality and well-being for a national sample of U.S. men and women. *Sex Roles, 78*(1–2), 67–80.

Saguy, A. C., & Williams, J. A. (2019). Reimagining gender: Gender neutrality in the news. *Signs: Journal of Women in Culture & Society, 43*(2), 465–489.

Salie, F. (2018, January 1). How to raise a sweet son in an era of angry men. *Time Magazine*, p. 27.

Sells, T. G. C., & L. Ganong. (2017). Emerging adults' expectations and preferences for gender role arrangements in long-term heterosexual relationships. *Sex Roles, 76*(3–4), 125–137.

Sharp, E., & Keyton, K. (2016). Caught in a bad romance? The negative effect of normative dating and marital ideologies on women's bodies. *Sex Roles, 75*(1), 15–27.

Soltanpanah, J., Parks-Stamm, E. J., Martiny, S. E., & Rudmin F. W. (2018). A cross-cultural examination of the relationship between egalitarian gender role attitudes and life satisfaction. *Sex Roles, 79*(1–2), 50–58.

Spinner, L., Cameron, L., & Calogero. R. (2018). Peer toy play as a gateway to children's gender flexibility: The effect of (counter) stereotypic portrayals of peers in children's magazines. *Sex Roles, 79*(5), 314–328.

Steele, C. (2018). The real reason voice assistants are female (and why it matters). *PC Magazine.* Retrieved on September 19, 2018. https://www.pcmag.com/newsletter_manage.

Swanbrow Becker, M. A., Nemeth Roberts, S. F., Ritts, S. M., Branagan, W. T., Warner, A. R., & Clark, S. L. (2017). Supporting transgender college students: Implications for clinical intervention and campus prevention. *Journal of College Student Psychotherapy, 31*, 155–176.

Teitel, E. (2017, January 15). Why Siri should sound like an old man. *Toronto Star* (Canada).

Turbitt, U. (2017). Female genital mutilation. *Child Care in Practice, 23*, 237–238.

Urbano-contreras, A., Iglesias-Garcia, M. T., & Martinez-Gonzalez, R. A. (2019, January-March). General and sexual satisfaction with the couple relationship according to the gender. *Revista Espanola de Investigaciones Sociologica, 165*, 143–157.

Weymouth, B. B., & Buehler, C. (2018). Early adolescents' relationships with parents, teachers, and peers and increases in social anxiety symptoms. *Journal of Family Psychology, 32*(4), 496–506.

Woods, H. S. (2018). Asking more of Siri and Alexa: feminine persona in service of surveillance capitalism. *Critical Studies in Media Communication, 35*(4), 334–349.

Young, M., & Schieman, S.(2018). Scaling back and finding flexibility: Gender differences in parents' strategies to manage work-family conflict. *Journal of Marriage & Family, 80*(1), 99–118.

CHAPTER 4

Alaminos, E., & Ayuso, M. (2019). Marital status, gender, mortality and pensions: The disadvantages of being single in old age. *Revista Espanola de Investigagiones Sociologiacas, 165*, 3–23.

Allison, R., & Ralston, M. (2018). Opportune romance: How college campuses shape students' hookups, dates, and relationships. *Sociological Quarterly, 59*(3), 495–518.

Allison, R., & Risman, B. J. (2017). Marriage delay, time to play? Marital horizons and hooking up in college. *Sociological Inquiry 87*(3), 472–500.

Anders, K. M., Goodcase, E., Yazedjian, A., & Toews, M. (2018, Nov. 8). "*Sex is easier to get and love is harder to find": Costs and rewards of hooking up for college students.* Poster presented at the annual meeting of the National Council on Family Relations, San Diego, CA

Aubrey, J. S., & Smith, S. E. (2013). Development and validation of the endorsement of the Hookup Culture Index. *Journal of Sex Research, 50*(5), 435–448.

Arnold, L., & Campbell, C. (2013, January 14). The high price of being single in America. *The Atlantic.* Retrieved from www.theatlantic.com

Ashwin, S., & Isupova, O. (2014). "Behind every great man. . . .": The male marriage wage premium examined qualitatively. *Journal of Marriage and Family, 76*(1), 37–55.

Ayuso, L. (2019). What future awaits couples Living Apart Together (LAT)? *Sociological Review, 67*(1), 226–244.

Benson, J. J., & Coleman, M. (2016). Older adults developing a preference for living apart together. *Journal of Marriage & Family, 78*(3), 797–812.

Birger, J. (2015). *Date Onomics: How dating became a lopsided numbers game.* New York: Workman Publishing Co.

Bivens, R., & Hoque, A. S. (2018). Programming sex, gender, and sexuality: Infrastructural failures in the "feminist" dating app bumble. *Canadian Journal of Communication, 43*(3), 441–459. doi: http://dx.doi.org.cyrano.ucmo.edu:2048/10.22230/cjc.2018v43n3a3375

Booth, A., Rustenbach, E., & McHale, S. (2008). Early family transitions and depressive symptom changes from adolescence to early adulthood. *Journal of Marriage and Family 70*(1), 3–14.

Broese van Groenou, M., te Riele, S. & de Jong Gierveld, J. (2019). Receiving support and care in older age: Comparing LAT relationships with first marriages, remarriages, and cohabitation. *Journal of Family Issues, 40*(13), 1786–1807.

Brown, S. L., Manning, W. D., & Payne, K. K. (2017). Relationship quality among cohabiting versus married couples. *Journal of Family Issues, 38*(12), 1730–1753.

Brown, S. L., Manning, W. D., Payne, K.K., & Wu, H. (2016). *Living apart together (LAT) relationships in the U.S.* Poster presented at the PAA.

Budgeon, S. (2016). The 'problem' with single women: Choice, accountability and social change. *Journal of Social and Personal Relationships, 33*(3), 401–418.

Chang, J., Ward, R., Padgett, D., & Smith, M. F. (2012, November 1). *Do feminists hook up more? Examining pro-feminism attitude in the context of hooking-up.* Paper presented at National Council on Family Relations, Phoenix, AZ.

Cherlin, A. J. (2010). Demographic trends in the United States: A review of research in the 2000s. *Journal of Marriage and Family, 72*(3), 403–419.

Cho, S. B., M. Cui, M., & Claridge, A. M. (2018). Cohabiting parent's marriage plans and marriage realization. *Journal of Social and Personal Relationships, 35*, 137–158.

Coontz, S. (2015). Revolution in intimate life and relationships. *Journal of Family Theory & Review, 7*(1), 5–12.

Coontz, S. (2016). *The way we never were: American families and the nostalgia trap (2nd ed.).* New York: Basic Books.

Connidis, I. A., Borell, K., & Karlsson, S. G. (2017). Ambivalence and living apart together in later life: A critical research proposal. *Journal of Marriage and the Family, 79*, 1404–1418.

Conrad, K. A., & Olmstead, S. B.(2014, November 19). *The meaning and process of dating among gay and lesbian emerging adults.* Paper presented at the National Council on Family Relations annual meeting, Baltimore, MD.

Coulter, R., & Hu, Y. (2017). Living apart together and cohabitation intentions in Great Britain. *Journal of Family Issues, 38*(12), 1701–1729.

De Jong, D. C., Adams, K. N., & Reiss, H. T. (2018). Predicting women's emotional responses to hooking up. Do motives matter? *Journal of Social and Personal Relationships, 35*(4), 532–556.

DePaulo, B. (2018, September 9). Singlism: How serious is it, really? *Psychology Today.* Available at www.psychologytoday.com

DeRose, L., Lyons-Amos, M., Wilcox, W. B., & Huarcaya, G. (2017). *The cohabitation-go-round: Cohabitation and family instability across the globe.* New York: Social Trends Institute.

Du Bois, S. N., Sher, T. G., Grotkowski, K., Aizenman, T., Slesinger, N., & Cohen, M. (2016). Going the distance. *Family Journal 24*,(1), 5–14.

Eickmeyer, K. J., & Manning, W. D. (2018). Serial cohabitation in young adulthood: Baby boomers to Millennials. *Journal of Marriage and the Family, 80*(4), 826–840.

Eliot, M. (2013, April). *Nickolson: A biography*. New York: Crown.

Finkel, E. (2015, February). In defense of Tinder. *New York Times*. http://www.nytimes.com/2015/02/08/opinion/sunday/in-defense-of-tinder.html

Fisher, H. (2015, August 22). *Panel on modern romance: Dating, mating, and more*. Paper presented at American Sociological Association annual meeting, Chicago, IL.

Fisher, H., & Garcia, J. R. (2016). Singles in America. http://www.singlesinamerica.com/

Fokkema, T., Gierveld, J. D., & Dykstra, P. A. (2012). Cross-national differences in older adult loneliness. *The Journal of Psychology, 146*(1–2), 201–228.

Fulle, A., Chang, J., & Knox, D. (2016, Spring). Female sexual hedonism: Navigating stigma. *College Student Journal, 50*, 29–34.

Gadaua, S. P., & Larson, V. (2014). *The New "I Do": Reshaping marriage for skeptics, realists and rebels*. Berkeley, California: Seal Press.

Goldsmith, K. M., & Byers, E. S. (2018). Perceived and reported romantic and sexual outcomes in long distance and geographically close relationships. *The Canadian Journal of Human Sexuality, 27*(2), 144–156.

Gottman, Julie. (2013, June 27). The conversation—a discussion of living apart together relationships. NPR radio.

Guzzo, K. B. (2018). Marriage and dissolution among women's cohabitations: Variations by stepfamily status and shared childbearing. *Journal of Family Issues, 39*(4), 1108–1136.

Hall, S. S., & Knox, D. (2017a). "I Have," "I Would," "I Won't": Hooking up among sexually diverse groups of college students. *Psychology of Sexual Orientation and Gender Diversity, 4*, 233–240,

Hall, S. S., & Adams, R. (2011). Newlyweds' unexpected adjustments to marriage. *Family and Consumer Sciences Research Journal, 39*(4), 375–387.

Hall, S., & Knox, D. (2019). College Student Attitudes and Behaviors Survey of 13,070 undergraduates. Unpublished data collected for this text. Department of Family, Consumer, and Technology Education Teachers College, Ball State University and Department of Sociology, East Carolina University. Sciences, Ball State University and Department of Sociology, East Carolina University, Greenville, NC.

Hall, S. S., & Willoughby, B. J. (2019). Relative work and family role centralities: Predicting marriage and family beliefs. *Marriage & Family Review, 55*(7), 667–685

Halligan, C., Knox, D., Freysteinsdóttir, F. J., & Skulason, S. (2014, April 4). *U.S. and Icelandic college student attitudes toward relationships/sexuality*. Poster presented at Southern Sociological Society, Charlotte, NC.

Hansan, M., & Clark, E. M. (2017). I get so lonely, baby? The effects of loneliness and social isolation on romantic dependency. *Journal of Social Psychology, 157*(4), 429–444.

Hatch, A. (2017). Saying "I Don't" to matrimony: An investigation of why long-term heterosexual cohabitors choose not to marry. *Journal of Family Issues, 38*(12), 1651–1674.

Hess, J. (2012, March 23). Living apart together. *Today Show*. NBC.

Hognas, R. S., & Thomas, J. R. (2016). Birds of a feather have babies together? Family structure homogamy and union stability among cohabiting parents. *Journal of Family Issues 37*(1), 29–52.

Ishizuka, P. (2018). The economic foundations of cohabiting couples' union transitions. *Demography, 55*(2), 535–557

Jacinto, E., & Ahrend, J. (2012). Living apart together. Unpublished data provided by Jacinto and Ahrend.

Jackson, J. B. (2018). The ambiguous loss of singlehood: Conceptualizing and treating singlehood ambiguous loss among never-married adults. *Contemporary Family Therapy: An International Journal, 40*, 210–222.

Jayson, S. (2014, January 21). Could a date get any more confusing? *USA Today*, 4B.

James-Kangal, N., Weitbrecht, E.M., Francis, T. E., & Whitton, S.W. (2018). Hooking up and emerging adults' relationship attitudes and expectations. *Sexuality & Culture 22*(3), 706–723.

Jones, M. M. (2015, March 29). *Living apart together (LAT) as a sign of the second demographic transition*. Paper presented at the Southern Sociological Society annual meeting, New Orleans, LA.

Jones, T. (2014, Winter). Single and childfree! Reassessing parental and marital status discrimination. *Arizona State Law*, 4, 1254–1346.

Jose, A., O'Leary, K. D., & Moyer, A. (2010). Does premarital cohabitation predict subsequent marital stability and marital quality? A meta-analysis. *Journal of Marriage and Family 72*(1), 105–116.

Jurkane-Hobein, I. (2015). When less is more: On time work in long distance relationships. *Qualitative Sociology, 38*(2), 185–203.

Kiernan, K. (2000). European perspectives on union formation. In L.J. Waite (ed.). *The ties that bind*, (pp. 40–58). New York: Aldine de Gruyter.

Kilpi, F., Konttinen, H., Silventoinen, K., & Martikainen. P. (2015). Living arrangements as determinants of myocardial infarction incidence and survival: A prospective register study of over 300,000 Finnish men and women. *Social Science & Medicine, 133*, 93–100.

Krapf, S. (2018). Moving in or breaking up? The role of distance in the development of romantic relationships. *European Journal of Population, 34*(3), 313–336.

Kristen, E., & Dignam, P. (2016). *From hookup to husband: Transitioning to a committed relationship*. Paper presented at Southern Sociological Society, Atlanta, GA.

Kuperberg, A., & Padgett, J.E. (2017). Partner meeting contexts and risky behavior in college students' other-sex and same-sex hookups. *Journal of Sex Research, 54*(1), 55–72.

Kuperberg, A. (2019) Premarital cohabitation and direct marriage in the United States 1956–2015. *Marriage & Family Review, 55*(5), 447–475

Lee, K. S., & Ono, H. (2012). Marriage, cohabitation, and happiness: A cross-national analysis of 27 countries. *Journal of Marriage and Family, 74*(5), 953–972.

LeFebvre, L. E. (2018). Swiping me off my feet: Explicating relationship initiation on Tinder. *Journal of Social and Personal Relationships, 35*(9), 1205–1229.

Lehmann, V., Tuinman, M., Braeken, J., Vingerhoets, A., Saderman, R., & Hagedoorn, M. (2015). Satisfaction with relationship status: Development of a new scale and the role in predicting well-being. *Journal of Happiness Studies, 16*(1), 169–184.

Lewin, A. C. (2017). Health and relationship quality later in life: A comparison of living apart together (LAT), first marriages, and cohabitation. *Journal of Family Issues, 38*(12), 1754–1774.

Lydon, J., Pierce, T., & O'Regan, S. (1997). Coping with moral commitment to long-distance dating relationships. *Journal of Personality and Social Psychology, 73*, 104–13.

Manning, W. D., & Cohen, J. A. (2012). Premarital cohabitation and marital dissolution: An examination of recent marriages. *Journal of Marriage and the Family, 74*(2), 377–387.

Match.com 2017. (2016). Singles in America Study. Retrieved from www.singlesinAmerica.com

McCann, B. R., & Allen, K. R. (2018). Romantic forecasts in later life: Older single women's perspectives on family and kin relationships. *Journal of Family Issues, 39*, 747–770.

Miss Your Mate, Loving from a Distance, IVillage. (2015). Retrieved from http://www.statisticbrain.com/long-distance-relationship-statistics

Montemurro, B. (2014). *Deserving desire: Women's stories of sexual evolution.* New Brunswick, NJ: Rutgers University Press.

Mosuo. (2010). http://en.wikipedia.org/wiki/Mosuo#General_Practice

Munsch, C. (2015, August). *Stigma, status, and singles: The effect of marital status on perceptions of the unmarried.* Paper presented at the American Sociological Association annual meeting, Chicago, IL.

Muraco, J. A., & Curran, M. A. (2012). Associations between marital meaning and reasons to delay marriage for young adults in romantic relationships. *Marriage and Family Review 48*(3), 227–247.

Murray, C. (2012). *Coming apart: The state of white America, 1960–2010.* New York: Crown Forum.

Musick, K., & Michelmore, K. (2018). Cross-national comparisons of union stability in cohabiting and married families with children. *Demography, 55*(4), 1389–1421.

Musick, K., & Bumpass, L. (2012). Reexamining the case for marriage: Union formation and changes in well-being. *Journal of Marriage and Family, 74*(1), 1–18.

Ortyl, T. A. (2013). Long-term heterosexual cohabiters and attitudes toward marriage. *Sociological Quarterly, 54*(4), 584–609.

Perelli-Harris, B., Hoberz, S., Lappegard, T., & Evans, A. (2019). Mind the "Happiness" Gap: The relationship between cohabitation, marriage, and subjective well-being in the United Kingdom, Australia, Germany, and Norway. *Demography, 56*(4), 1219–1246.

Perelli-Harris, B., & Styrc, M. (2018). Mental well-being differences in cohabitation and marriage: The role of childhood selection. *Journal of Marriage and the Family, 80*(1), 239–255.

Pew Research Center. (2010). *Social & demographic Trends: The decline of marriage and rise of new families.* Published and retrieved from http://pewresearch.org/pubs/1802/decline-marriage-rise-new-families

ProQuest Statistical Abstract of the United States. (2019). Table 56. Online Edition, Bethesda, MD. Retrieved from https://www.proquest.com/products-services/statabstract.html

ProQuest Statistical Abstract of the United States. (2019). Table 57. Online Edition, Bethesda, MD. Retrieved from https://www.proquest.com/products-services/statabstract.html

ProQuest Statistical Abstract of the United States. (2019). Table 727. Online Edition, Bethesda, MD. Retrieved from https://www.proquest.com/products-services/statabstract.html

Pope, A. L., & Cashwell, C. S. (2013). Moral commitment in intimate committed relationships: A conceptualization from cohabiting same-sex and opposite sex partners. *Family Journal, 21*(1), 5–14.

Rhoades, G. K., Stanley, S. M., & Markman, H. J. (2012). A longitudinal investigation of commitment dynamics in cohabiting relationships. *Journal of Family Issues, 33*(3), 369–390.

Rinelli, L., & Brown, S. L. (2010). Race differences in union transitions among cohabiters: The role of relationship features. *Marriage & Family Review, 46*(1–2), 22–40.

Rosenfeld, M. J., & Roesler, K. (2019). Cohabitation experience and cohabitation's association with marital dissolution. *Journal of Marriage and the Family, 81*, 42–58.

Root, A., Troilo, J., Legg, B., & Britten, B. (2014). *Social capital and relationship maintenance: The benefits of Facebook.* Poster presented at the National Council on Family Relations annual meeting, Baltimore, MD.

Sarkisian, N., & Gerstel, N. (2016). Does singlehood isolate or integrate? Examining the link between marital status and ties to kin, friends and neighbors. *Journal of Social and Personal Relationship, 33*(3), 361–384.

Sassler, S., Michelmore, K., & Qian, Z. (2018). Transitions from sexual relationships into cohabitation and beyond. *Demography, 55*(2), 511–534.

Sassler, S., & Miller, A. J. (2011). Class differences in cohabitation processes. *Family Relations, 60*(2), 163–177.

Sawyer, A. N., Smith, E. R., & Benotsch, E. G. (2018). Dating application use and sexual risk behavior among young adults. *Sexuality Research & Social Policy, 15*(2), 183–191. doi: http://dx.doi.org.cyrano.ucmo.edu:2048/10.1007/s13178-017-0297-6

Smith, C. (2018, September 28). 50 Interesting Tinder statistics and facts. *Business Statistics* Retrieved from https://expandedramblings.com/index.php/tinder-statistics/

Sobal, J., & Hanson, K. L. (2011). Marital status, marital history, body weight, and obesity. *Marriage & Family Review, 47*, 474–504.

Stovall, K., & Blair, K. (2016). *A comparison of same-sex and mixed sex couples' reasons for cohabiting.* Poster presented at the annual meeting of the Society for the Scientific Study of Sex, Phoenix, AZ.

Thorsen, M. L. (2017). The adolescent family environment and cohabitation across the transition to adulthood. *Social Science Research, 64*, 249–262.

Thorsen, M. L. (2019). Shifting influences of pregnancy on union formation across age and union stability across cohabitation duration. *Journal of Family Issues, 40*(2) 190–214.

Timmermans, E., & Caluwé, E. D. (2017). Development and validation of the Tinder motives scale (TMS). *Computers in Human Behavior, 70*, 3341–350. https://doi.org/10.1016/j.chb.2017.01.028

Trost, J. (2016). Marriage, cohabitation and LAT relationships *Journal of Comparative Family Studies, 47*(1), 17–26.

Uecker, J., Pearce, L. D., & Andercheck, B. (2015, March 28). *The four U's: Latent classes of hooking up motivations among college students.* Paper presented at the Southern Sociological Society Annual Meeting, New Orleans, LA.

Upton-Davis, K. (2015). Subverting gendered norms of cohabitation: Living Apart Together for women over 45. *Journal of Gender Studies, 24*, 104–116.

Valle, G., & Tillman, K. H. (2014). Childhood family structure and romantic relationships during the transition to adulthood. *Journal of Family Issues, 35*(1), 97–124.

Vencill, J., & Christopher, S. (2014, November 7). *"It doesn't matter what I'm wearing:" Four perspectives on a qualitative research project examining slutwalk.* Paper presented at the Society for the Scientific Study of Sex Annual Meeting. Omaha, NE.

Wang, W., & Parker, K. (2014, September 24). *Record share of Americans have never married.* Pew Research

Center. Retrieved from. http://www.pewsocialtrends
.org/2014/09/24/chapter-4-never-married-young-adults-
on-the-marriage-market

Westfall, S. S. (2014, October 20). Jimmy and Rosalynn Carter: A love story. *People Magazine*, 70–75.

Willoughby, B. J., & Belt, D. (2016). Marital orientation and relationship well-being among cohabiting couples. *Journal of Family Psychology*, 30(2), 181–192.

Willoughby, B. J., Carroll, J.S., & Busby, D. M. (2012). The different effects of "living together": Determining and comparing types of cohabiting couples. *Journal of Social and Personal Relationships*, 29(3), 397–419.

Wright, L. (2019). Union transitions and fertility within first premarital cohabitations in Canada: Diverging patterns by education? *Demography*, 56(1), 151–167.

Zurndorfer, H. (2018). Escape from the country: the gender politics of Chinese women in pursuit of transnational romance. *Gender, Place & Culture: A Journal of Feminist Geography*, 25(4), 489–506.

CHAPTER 5

Allan, P. (2018). *How to protect yourself from online dating scams.* Retrieved from https://lifehacker.com/how-to-protect-yourself-from-online-dating-scams-1827106759

Arnocky, S. (2018). Self-perceived mate value, facial attractiveness, and mate preferences: Do desirable men want it all? *Evolutionary Psychology*, 16(1), 1. DOI: 10.1177/1474704918763271

Afrasiabi, H., & Dehaghani Daramroud, R. (2018). Constructions of mate selection mistakes among divorce applicant women. *Journal of Divorce & Remarriage*, 59(2), 92–107.

Aditi, P. (2014). Is online better than offline for meeting partners? Depends: Are you looking to marry or to date? *Cyberpsychology, Behavior, and Social Networking*. Not available-ahead of print. doi:10.1089/cyber.2014.0302.

Alford, J. J., Hatemi, P. K., Hibbing, J. R., Martin, N.G., & Eaves, L. J. (2011). The politics of mate choice. *The Journal of Politics*, 73(2) 362–379.

Assaad, L., & Lemay, E. P. Jr. (2018) Social anhedonia and romantic relationship processes. *Journal of Personality*, 86(2), 147–157.

Barber, L. L., & Cooper, M. L. (2014). Rebound sex: Sexual motives and behaviors following a relationship breakup. *Archives of Sexual Behavior*, 43(2), 251–265.

Bauman, Z. 2003. *Liquid love: On the frailty of human bonds.* Cambridge, UK: Polity.

Boxer, C. F., Noonan, M. C., & Whelan, C. B. (2015). Measuring mate preferences: A replication and extension. *Journal of Family Issues*, 36(2), 163–187.

Baird, M. (2018). *eHarmony Review.* Dating Sites Reviews. Retrieved on October 6, 2018 from http://lovenet-jp.com/eharmony-review

Bruch, Elizabeth E., & Newman, M. E. J. (2018). Aspirational pursuit of mates in online dating markets. *Science Advances*, 4(8), 1–6. doi:10.1126/sciadv.aap9815

Brumbaugh, C. C., & Fraley, R. C. (2015). Too fast, too soon? An empirical investigation into rebound relationships. *Journal of Social & Personal Relationships*, 32(1), 99–118.

Brooks, J. E., & Neville, H. A. (2017). Interracial attraction among college men: The influence of ideologies, familiarity, and similarity. *Journal of Social and Personal Relationships*, 34(2), 166–183.

Burr, B. K, Viera, J. Dial, B., Fields, H., Davis, K., & Hubler. (2011, November 18). *Influences of personality on relationship satisfaction through stress.* Poster presented at the annual meeting of National Council on Family Relations, Orlando, FL.

Bushkin, H. (2013). *Johnny Carson.* New York: Houghton Mifflin Harcourt Publishing.

Carter, G. L., Campbell, A. C., & Muncer, S. (2014). The dark triad personality: Attractiveness to women. *Personality and Individual Differences*, 56, 57–61.

Childs, G. R., & Duncan, S. F. (2012). Marriage preparation education programs: An assessment of their components. *Marriage & Family Review*, 48(1), 59–81.

Dailey, R. M., McCracken, A. A., Jin, B., Rossetto, K. R., & Green, E. W. (2013). Negotiating breakups and renewals: Types of on-again/off-again dating relationships. *Western Journal of Communication*, 77(4), 382–410.

Dijkstra, P., Barelds, D. P. H., Groothof, H. A. K., Ronner, S., & and Nautal, A. P. (2012). Partner preferences of the intellectually gifted. *Marriage & Family Review* 48(1), 96–108.

Eastwick, P. W., Harden, K. P., Shukusky, J. A., Morgan, T. A., & Joel, S. (2017). Consistency and inconsistency among romantic partners over time. *Journal of Personality & Social Psychology*, 112(6), 838–859.

Feng, J. (2018). The Shanghai Marriage Market, Visualized. *SupChina*. Dated 8/21 18. Retrieved on October 6, 2018 from https://supchina.com/2018/08/21/the-shanghai-marriage-market-visualized/

Fisher, H. (2015, August 22). *Panel on Modern romance: Dating, mating, and more.* Paper presented at the American Sociological Association annual meeting, Chicago, IL.

Fisher, H. (2019). "Slow love: Courtship in the Digital Age" in R. J. Sternberg and K. Sternberg's *The New Psychology of Love* (paperback ed). New York: Cambridge University Press, pp. 208–222.

Fisher, H., & Garcia, J. R. (2019). *Singles in America.* Retrieved from https://www.singlesinamerica.com/#DATING2

Fisher, M. L., & Salmon, C. (2013). Mom, dad, meet my mate: An evolutionary perspective on the introduction of parents and mates. *Journal of Family Studies*, 19, 99–107.

Flynn, E. (2018). Who's behind the screen? *The Sun*. Retrieved from https://www.thesun.co.uk/fabulous/1754916/catfishing-meaning-identity-steal-online-dating-law/

Gardner, T. E. (2017, Fall). *Legal aspects of marriage and divorce*, Presentation to Marriage and Family class, East Carolina University, Greenville, NC.

Giebel, G., Moran, J., Schawohl, A., & Weierstall, R. (2015). The thrill of loving a dominant partner: Relationships between preference for a dominant mate, sensation seeking, and trait anxiety. *Personal Relationships*, 22, 275–284.

Haandrikman, K. (2011). Spatial homogamy: The geographical dimensions of partner choice. *Journal of Economic and Social Geography*, 102(1), 100–110.

Hall, J. A., Park, N., Cody, M. J., & Song, H. (2010). Strategic misrepresentation in online dating: The effects of gender, self-monitoring, and personality traits. *Journal of Social and Personal Relationships*, 27(1), 117–135.

Hall, S., & Knox, D. (2019). College Student Attitudes and Behaviors Survey of 12,785 undergraduates. Unpublished data collected for this text. Department of Family, Consumer, and Technology Education Teachers College, Ball State University and Department of Sociology, East Carolina University, Greenville, NC.

Hance, M. A., Blackhart, G., & Dew, M. (2018). Free to be me: The relationship between the true self, rejection sensitivity, and use of online dating sites. *Journal of Social Psychology*, 158(4), 421–429.

Hardy, N., & A. Vennum, A. (2014). *Patterns of stability and marital satisfaction in newlywed couples.* Paper presented at the National Council on Family Relations, annual meeting, Baltimore, MD.

Henderson, A. K., Ellison, C. G., & Glenn, N. D. (2018). Religion and relationship quality among cohabiting and dating couples. *Journal of Family Issues, 39*(7), 1904–1932.

Hobbs, M., Owen, S., & Gerbe, L. (2017). Liquid love? Dating apps, sex, relationships and the digital transformation of intimacy. *Journal of Sociology, 53*(2), 271–284.

Hout, M. (2017). Religious ambivalence, liminality, and the increase of no religious preference in the United States, 2006–2014. *Journal for the Scientific Study of Religion, 56*(1), 52–63.

Huston, T. L., Caughlin, J. P., Houts, R. M., Smith, S. E., & George, L. J. (2001). The connubial crucible: Newlywed years as predictors of marital delight, distress, and divorce. *Journal of Personality and Social Psychology, 80*(2), 237–252.

Jackson, J. (2011, November). *Premarital Counseling: An evidence-informed treatment protocol.* Paper presented at the annual meeting of the National Council on Family Relations, Orlando, FL.

Jones, D. (2016). The 'Chasing Amy' bias in past sexual experiences: Men can change, women cannot. *Sexuality & Culture, 20*(1), 24–37.

Kalinka, C. J., Fincham, F., & Hirsch, A. H. (2012). A randomized clinical trial of online-biblio relationship education for expectant couples. *Journal of Family Psychology, 26*(1), 159–164.

Kotlyar, I., & Ariely., D. (2013). The effect of nonverbal cues on relationship formation. *Computers in Human Behavior, 29*(3), 544–551.

Kreager, D. A., Cavanagh, S. E., Yen, J., & Yu, M. (2014). "Where Have All the Good Men Gone?" Gendered interactions in online dating. *Journal of Marriage and Family, 76*(2) 387–410.

Lindstrom, R., Monk, K., & Vennum, A. (2014, Winter). Together again: The emerging trend of on-again/off-again relationships. *NCFR Report, Family Focus,* St. Paul, MN: National Council on Family Relations.

Livingston, G., & Brown., A. (2017). Intermarriage in the U.S. 50 years after Loving v. Virginia. *Pew Research Center.* May 18. http://www.pewsocialtrends.org/2017/05/18/intermarriage-in-the-u-s-50-years-after- loving-v-virginia/

Lo, S. K., Hsieh, A. Y., & Chiu, Y. P. (2013). Contradictory deceptive behavior in online dating. *Computers in Human Behavior, 29*(4), 1755–1762.

Lucier-Greer, M., Adler-Baeder, F., Ketring, S. A., Harcourt, K. T., & and Smith, T. (2012). Comparing the experiences of couples in first marriages and remarriages in couple and relationship education. *Journal of Divorce and Remarriage, 53*(1), 55–75.

Markman, H. J., Rhoades, G. K., Stanley, S.M., Ragan, E. P., & Whitton, S. W. (2010). The premarital communication roots of marital distress and divorce: The first five years of marriage. *Journal of Family Psychology, 24*(3), 289–298.

Match.com 2017. (2016) Singles in America Study. Retrieved from www.singlesinAmerica.com

Maybruch, C., Weissman, S., & Pirutinsky, S. (2017, March 21). Marital outcomes and consideration of divorce among Orthodox Jews after signing a religious prenuptial agreement to facilitate future divorce. *Journal of Divorce and Remarriage, 58*(4), 276–287.

McClendon, D. (2018) Crossing boundaries: "Some college," schools, and educational assortative mating. *Journal of Marriage and the Family, 80*(4), 812–825.5

McGloin, R., & Denes, A. (2018). Too hot to trust: Examining the relationship between attractiveness, trustworthiness, and

desire to date in online dating. *New Media & Society, 20*(3), 919–936.

Nelms, B. J., Knox, D., & Easterling, B. (2012). The Relationship Talk: Assessing partner commitment. *College Student Journal, 46,* 178–182.

Olcay, I. E., Ads, M. & Weisfeld, C. C. (2019). What is the impact of choosing one's spouse on marital satisfaction of wives and husbands? The case of arranged and self-choice Turkish marriages. *Journal of Family Issues, 40*(10), 1270–1298.

O'Connor, K. M., & Gladstone, E. (2018). Beauty and social capital: Being attractive shapes social networks. *Social Networks, 52,* 42–47.

Olson, J., Marshall, J., Goddard, W., & D. Schramm, D. (2014, November). *Shared religious beliefs, prayer, and forgiveness as predictors of marital satisfaction.* Paper presented at the National Council on Family Relations annual meeting, Baltimore, MD.

Pande, R. (2016). Becoming modern: British-Indian discourses of arranged marriages. *Social & Cultural Geography, 17*(3), 380–400.

Parise, M., Manzi, C., Donato, S., & Lafrate, R. (2017). Free to love? The role of intrusive parenting for young adult children's romantic relationship quality. *Journal of Prevention & Intervention in the Community, 45*(3), 187–201.

Perry, S. L., & Whitehead, A. L. (2016). For better or worse? Gender ideology, religious commitment, and relationship quality. *Journal for the Scientific Study of Religion, 55*(4), 737–755.

Pew Research Center. (2011). *The burden of student debt.* Retrieved from http://pewresearch.org/databank/dailynumber/?NumberID=1257

Potarca, G. (2017). Does the Internet affect assortative mating? Evidence from the U.S. and Germany. *Social Science Research, 61,* 278–297.

Prichard, I., Polivy, J., Provencher, V., Herman, C. P., Tiggemann, M., & Cloutier, K. (2015). Brides and young couples: Partners' weight, weight change, and perceptions of attractiveness. *Journal of Social & Personal Relationships, 32*(2), 263–278.

ProQuest Statistical Abstract of the United States. (2019). Online Edition. Bethesda, MD. Retrieved from https://www.proquest.com/products-services/statabstract.html

Qian, Y. (2017). Gender asymmetry in educational and income assortative marriage. *Journal of Marriage & Family, 79*(2), 318–336.

Saggino, A., Martino, M., Balsamo, M., Carlucci, L., Ebisch, S., Innamorati, M., Picconi, L., Romanelli, R., Sergi, M. R., & Tommasi. M. (2016). Compatibility quotient, and its relationship with marital satisfaction and personality traits in Italian married couples. *Sexual and Relationship Therapy, 31,* 83–94.

Sels, L., Ceulemans, E., & Pe, M. 2019. The impact of emotions on romantic judgements: Sequential effects in a speed-dating study. *Personal Relationships, 36*(8), 2437-2454.

Shambora, J. (2010). eHarmony's algorithm of love. *Fortune.* Retrieved from http://fortune.com/2010/09/23/eharmonys-algorithm-of-love/

Smith, A., & Duggan, M. (2013). Dating, social networking, mobile online dating & relationships. *Pew Research Center.* Oct 21. http://pewinternet.org/Reports/2013/Online-Dating.aspx

Smith, A., & M. Duggan. (2013b). Online dating & relationships. *Pew Research Center.* Retrieved from http://www.pewinternet.org/2013/10/21/online-dating-relationships

Stanley, S. M., Ragan, E. P., Rhoades, G. K., & Markman, H. J. (2012). Examining changes in relationship adjustment and life satisfaction in marriage. *Journal of Family Psychology, 26*(1), 165–170.

Steensland, B., Schmidt, L. C., & Wang, X. (2018). Spirituality: What does it mean to whom. *Journal for the Scientific Study of Religion, 37,* 450–472.

Vanman, E. (2018). *We asked catfish why they trick people online— it's not about money.* Retrieved from https://phys.org/news/2018-07-catfish-people-onlineit-money.html

Vellucci, K., Jackson, J. B., & Willoughby, B. (2014, November). *Perceived relationship approval and inclusion by parents-in-law as predictors of marital satisfaction and stability.* Poster presented at the National Council on Family Relations annual meeting, Baltimore, MD.

Wang, S., Kim, K., & Boerner, K. (2017). *Personality similarity and marital quality in life.* Poster presented at the annual meeting of the National Council on Family Relations, Orlando, FL .

Watkins, N., & J. Beckmeyer, J. (2018, November 8). *Development of the Brief Measure of Romantic Importance.* Poster presented at the annual meeting National Council on Family Relations, San Diego, CA.

Weiser, D. T., Hilliard, T., & Knox, D. (2018, November 9). *"I Thought You Loved Me?": Correlates/outcomes of discrepant involvement among undergraduates.* Poster presented at the annual meeting of the National Council on Family Relations, San Diego, CA.

Whyte, S., Chan, H. F., & Torgler. B. (2018). Do men and women know what they want? Sex differences in online daters' educational references. *Psychological Science, 29*(8), 1370–1375.

Wu, K., Chen, C., & Greenberger, E. (2019). Nice guys and gals finish first: Personality and speed-dating success among Asian Americans. *Journal of Social & Personal Relationships, 36*(8), 2507–2527.

Ybarra, M. L., & Mitchell, K. J. (2016). A national study of lesbian, gay, bisexual (LGB), and Non-GLB youth sexual behavior online and in-person. *Archives of Sexual Behavior, 45*(6) 1357–1372.

Yancey, G., & Emerson, M. O. (2016). Does height matter? An examination of height preferences in romantic coupling. *Journal of Family Issues, 37,* 53–73

CHAPTER 6

Aalgaard, R. A., Bolen, R. M., & Nugent, W. R. (2016). A literature review of forgiveness as a beneficial intervention to increase relationship satisfaction in couples's therapy. *Journal Of Human Behavior in the Social Environment, 26*(1), 46–55.

Aarskaug Wiik, K., & Bernhardt, E. (2017). Cohabiting and married individuals' relations with their partner's parents. *Journal of Marriage and the Family, 79*(4), 1111–1124.

Abrams, J. A., Maxwell, M. L., & Belgrave, F. Z. (2018). Circumstances beyond their control: Black women's perceptions of Black manhood. *Sex Roles, 79*(3–4), 151–162.

Alanen, J. (2016). Custom or crime? (Part I of IV): Catalysts and consequences of forced marriage. *American Journal of Family Law, 29*(4), 227–242.

Alarie, M. (2019). "They're the ones chasing the cougar": Relationship formation in the context of age-hypogamous intimate relationships. *Gender & Society. 33*(3), 463–485.

Alder, M. C., Yorgason, J. B., Sandberg, J. G., & Davis, S. (2018). Perceptions of parents' marriage predicting marital satisfaction: The moderating role of attachment behaviors. *Journal of Couple & Relationship Therapy, 17*(2), 146–164.

Alhassan, A. A., Alqadhib, E. M., Taha, N. W., Alahmari, R. A., Salam, M., & Almutairi, A. F. (2018). The relationship between

addiction to smartphone usage and depression among adults: a cross sectional study. *BMC Psychiatry, 18*(1), 148. doi: 10.1186/s12888-018-1745-4

Amato, P. R. (2015b, November 12–14). *Revisiting the intergenerational transmission of divorce (ITD).* National Council on Family Relations Annual Meeting, Vancouver, British Columbia, CN.

Anderson, J. R., Van Ryzin, M. J., & Doherty, W. J. (2010). Developmental trajectories of marital happiness in continuously married individuals: A group-based modeling approach. *Journal of Family Psychology, 24*(5), 587–596.

Arnold, A. L., O'Neal, C. W., Bryant, C., Wickrama, K. A. S., & and Cutrona, C. (2011, November). *Influences of intra and interpersonal factors in marital success.* Paper presented at National Council on Family Relations, Orlando, FL.

Balderrama-Durbin, C., Stanton, K., Snyder, D. K., Cigrang, J. A., Talcott, G. W., Smith Slep, A. M., Heyman, R. E., & Cassidy, D. G. (2017). The risk for marital infidelity across a year-long deployment. *Journal of Family Psychology, 32,* 629–634.

Bakhtiari, F., Benner, A. D., & Plunkett, S. W. (2018). Life quality of university students from immigrant families in the United States. *Family & Consumer Sciences Research Journal, 46*(4), 331–346.

Barin, E. N., McLaughlin, C. M., Farag, M. W., Jensen, A. R., Upperman, J. S., & Arbogast, H. (2018). Heads up, phones down: A pedestrian safety intervention on distracted crosswalk behavior. *Journal of Community Health 43*(4), 810–815.

Barzoki, M. H., Seyedroghani, N., & Azadarmaki, T. (2012). Sexual dissatisfaction in a sample of married Iranian women. *Sexuality and Culture, 17*(2) DOI: 10.1007/s12119-012-9149

Bryant, C. M. (2018). African American fictive kin: Historical and contemporary notions. *Family Focus, 63*(1), F10-F11.

Bratter, J. L., & Whitehead, E. M. (2018). Ties that bind? Comparing kin support availability for mothers of mixed-race and monoracial infants. *Journal of Marriage and the Family, 80*(4), 951–962.

Briggs, D., & A. Ellis. (2017). The last night of freedom: Consumerism, deviance and the "stag party." *Deviant Behavior, 38*(7), 756–767.

Bugatti, A. (2018). *Competing attachment.* (Doctoral Dissertations). Retrieved from https://login.cyrano.ucmo.edu/login? url=https://search-proquest com.cyrano.ucmo.edu/docview/2061083766? accountid=6143

Buri, J. R., Cromett, C. E., Pappas, S. J., Lucas, H. L., & Arola, N. T. (2014, August). *Soul mates, love, and prospects for marital success.* Poster presented at the American Psychological Association annual meeting, Washington, DC.

Bushatz, A. (2018). Troop divorce unchanged: Marriage rate continues to fall. *Military.com.* https://www.military.com/daily-news/2018/03/21/troop-divorce-rate-unchanged-marriage-rate-continues-fall.html

Campbell, K., Kaufman, J. C., Ogden, T. D., Pumaccahua, T. T., & Hammond, H. (2011a, November). *Wedding rituals: How cost and elaborateness relate to marital outcomes.* Poster presented at the National Council on Family Relations annual meeting, Orlando, FL.

Campbell, K., Silva, L. C., & Wright, D. W. (2011b). Rituals in unmarried couple relationships: An exploratory study. *Family and Consumer Sciences Research Journal, 40*(1), 45–57.

Chaney, C., Shirisia, L., & Skogrand. L. (2017). "Whatever God has yoked together, let no man put apart:" The effect of religion on Black marriages. *Western Journal of Black Studies, 40*(1), 24–41.

Chang, J., Bragg, B., & Knox, D. (2018, November 9). *Some traditions die as slow as molasses: Are male children still preferred?* Poster presented at the National Council on Family Relations Annual meeting, San Diego, CA.

Chapman, B., & C. Guven, C. (2016). Revisiting the relationship between marriage and wellbeing: Does marriage quality matter? *Journal of Happiness Studies, 17,* 533–551.

Chen, H. M., & Lewis, D. C. (2018). *Working with Asian American individuals, couples and friends.* National Resource Center for Healthy Marriages and Families. Washington, DC.

Chen, E. Y., Enright, R. D., & Tung, E. Y. L. (2016). The influence of family unions and parenthood transitions on self-development. *Journal of Family Psychology, 30,* 341–352.

Choi, K. H., & Goldberg, R. E. (2018). Fertility behavior of interracial couples. *Journal of Marriage and the Family, 80*(4), 871–887.

Choi, K. H., & Tienda, M. (2017). Marriage-market constraints and mate-selection behavior: Racial, ethnic, and gender differences in intermarriage. *Journal of Marriage & Family, 79*(2), 301–317.

Coontz, S. (2016). *The way we never were: American families and the nostalgia trap.* (2nd ed). New York: Basic Books.

Cortes, K., Leith, S., & Wilson, A. E. (2018) Relationship satisfaction and the subjective distance of past relational events. *Journal of Social and Personal Relationships, 35*(8), 1092–1117.

Cottle, N. R., Hammond, R., Yorgason, K., Stookey, K., & Mallet, B. (2013, November 5–9). *Marital quality among current and former college students.* Poster presented at the National Council on Family Relations annual meeting. San Antonio, TX.

Covin, T. (2013 Febuary 21–23). *Personal communication.* Southeastern Council on Family Relations annual meeting, Birmingham, AL.

Csizmadia, A., & Nazarian, R. (2014). *Racial identification and social adjustment among young biracial children.* Paper presented at the National Council on Family Relations, annual meeting, Baltimore, MD.

Debnam, K. J., Howard, D. E., Garza, M. A., & Green, K. M. (2017). African American girls' ideal dating relationship now and in the future. *Youth & Society, 49*(3), 271–294.

DeMaris, A. (2018). Marriage advantage in subjective well-being: Causal effect or unmeasured heterogeneity? *Marriage & Family Review, 54,* 335–350.

Dijkstra, P., Barelds, D. P. H., Ronner, S., & Nauta, A. P. (2017). Intimate relationships of the intellectually gifted: Attachment style, conflict style, and relationship satisfaction among members of the mensa society. *Marriage & Family Review, 53*(3), 262–280.

Dilmaghani, M. (2018). Exploring the relationship between secularity and marital behavior. *Marriage & Family Review, 54,* 438–458.

Dixon, P. (2017). *African American Relationships, Marriages, and Families: An Introduction.* (2nd ed.) New York: Routledge.

Drefahl, S. (2010). How does the age gap between partners affect their survival? *Demography, 47*(2), 313–326.

Durrant, L., & Gillum, N. L. (2018). White fathers and their black-white biracial sons. *Marriage and Family Review, 54,* 374–392.

Durtschi, J., & Kimmes, J. (2014, November). *Expressed appreciation and classes of trajectories in relationship quality.* Paper presented at the National Council on Family Relations annual meeting, Baltimore, MD.

Easterling, B. A., & Knox, D. (2010, July 20). Left behind: How military wives experience the deployment of their husbands. *Journal of Family Life.* http://www.journaloffamilylife.org/militarywives

Finkel, E. J. (2015, August 22). *Panel on Modern romance: Dating, mating, and more.* Paper presented at the American Sociological Association annual meeting, Chicago, IL.

Fisher, H. (2015, August 22). *Panel on modern romance: Dating, mating, and more.* Paper presented at the American Sociological Association annual meeting, Chicago, IL.

Flood, S. M., & Genadek, K. R. (2016). Time for each other: Work and family constraints among couples. *Journal of Marriage and Family, 78*(1), 142–164.

Frias, S. M. (2017). Family and partner violence against women: Forced marriage in Mexican indigenous communities. *International Journal of Law, Policy & the Family, 31*(1), 60–78.

Gibson, V. (2002). *Cougar: A guide for older women dating younger men.* Boston, MA: Firefly Books.

Gill, A. K., & Harvey, H. (2017). Examining the impact of gender on young people's views of forced marriage in Britain. *Feminist Criminology, 12*(1), 72–100.

Goldsborough, R. (2018). Is your smartphone killing you? *Teacher Librarian 45*(5), 62.

Gomillion, S., Gabriel, S., Kawakami, K., & Young, A. F. (2017). Let's stay home and watch TV: The benefits of shared media use for close relationships. *Journal of Social and Personal Relationships, 34*(6), 855–874.

Gorman, L., Blow, A., Bowles, R., Farero, A., & Kees, M. (2015, November 13). *Soldier and spouse mental well-being and family health.* Poster presented at the National Council on Family Relations Annual Meeting, Vancouver, British Columbia, CN.

Gottman, J., & Carrere, S. (2000, September/October). Welcome to the love lab. *Psychology Today,* 42.

Grief, G. L., & Deal, K. H. (2012). *Two plus two: Couples and their couple friendships.* New York: Routledge.

Gustafson, P. (2017). Spousal age differences and synchronized retirement. *Ageing & Society, 37*(4), 777–803.

Gustavson, K., Roysamb, E., Borren, I., Torvik, F., & Karevold, E. (2016). Life satisfaction in close relationships: Findings from a longitudinal study. *Journal of Happiness Studies, 17*(3), 1293–1311.

Hall, J. A. (2017). Humor in romantic relationships: A meta-analysis. *Personal Relationships, 24*(3) 306–322.

Hall, S. S., & Knox, D. (2019). College Student Attitudes and Behaviors Survey of 12,780 undergraduates. Unpublished data collected for this text. Department of Family, Consumer, and Technology Education Teachers College, Ball State University and Department of Sociology, East Carolina University, Greenville, NC

Hall, S. S., & Knox, D. (2017). Perceived relationship power in emerging adults' romantic relationships. *Journal of Family Studies.* Retrieved from http://dx.doi.org/10.1080/13229400.2016.1269660

Harasymchuk, C., Cloutier, A., Peetz, J., & Lbreton J. (2017). Spicing up the relationship? The effects of relational boredom on shared activities. *Journal of Social and Personal Relationships, 34*(6), 833–854.

Harris, V., Bedard, K., Moen, D., & Alvarez-Perez, P. (2016). The role of friendship, trust, and love in happy German marriages. *Marriage & Family Review, 52,* 262–304.

Hatch, T., & Marks, L. (2014). *"Light the Shabbath candles": Mining meanings of Jewish home-centric traditions.* Paper presented at the National Council on Family Relations annual meeting, Baltimore, MD.

Huyck, M. H., & Gutmann, D. L. (1992). Thirty something years of marriage: Understanding experiences of women and men in enduring family relationships. *Family Perspective, 26,* 249–265.

Jackson, G., Krull, J. L., Bradbury, T. N., & Karney, B. R. (2017, January 31). Household income and trajectories of marital satisfaction in early marriage. *Journal of Marriage and the Family,* DOI: 10.1111/jomf.12394

Johnson, H. A., Zabriskie, R. B., & Hill, B. (2006). The contribution of couple leisure involvement, leisure time, and leisure satisfaction to marital satisfaction. *Marriage and Family Review, 40*(1), 69–91.

Johnson, K. R., & Loscocco, K. (2014). Black marriage through the prism of gender, race and class. *Journal of Black Studies, 46*(2), 1–30.

James, S. L. (2015). Variation in trajectories of women's marital quality. *Social Science Research, 49,* 16–30.

Januário, D., Narciso, I., Vieira-Santos, S., Fonseca, G., & Relvas, A. P. (2018). First journey by a descriptive review of empirical research on African marital relationships—Scientific dissemination, thematic focus, and methodology. *Marriage & Family Review, 54,* 259–281.

Jiang, J. (2018a). Millennials stand out for their technology use, but older generations also embrace digital life. *Pew Research Center.* Retrieved from http://www.pewresearch.org/fact-tank/2018/05/02/millennials-stand-out-for-their-technology-use-but-older-generations-also-embrace-digital-life/

Jiang, J. (2018b). How teens and parents navigate screen time and device distractions. *Pew Research Center.* Retrieved from http://www.pewinternet.org/2018/08/22/how-teens-and-parents-navigate-screen-time-and-device-distractions/

Karney, B. R., & Trail, T. E. (2017). Associations between prior deployments and marital satisfaction among Army couples. *Journal of Marriage and the Family, 79*(1), 147–160.

Kitchener, C. (2018, July 25). Why don't more men take their wives' last names? *The Atlantic.* Retrieved from www.theatlantic.com

Khoo, I. (2017, November 2). More grooms are taking their wives' surnames, study says. *Huffington Post.* Retrieved from www.huffingtonpost.ca

Knobloch, L. K., Knobloch-Fedders, L. M., Yorgason, J. B., Ebata, A. T., & McGlaughlin, P. C. (2017). Military children's difficulty with reintegration after deployment: A relational turbulence model perspective. *Journal of Family Psychology, 31*(5), 542–552.

Koski, A. (2018). Child marriage in the United States: How common is the practice, and which children are at greatest risk? *Perspectives on Sexual and Reproductive Health, 50*(3). Retrieved from https://onlinelibrary.wiley.com/doi/abs/10.1363/psrh.12055

Lampis, J., Cataudella, S., Busonera, A., & Carta, S. (2018). Personality similarity and romantic relationship adjustment during the couple life cycle. *Family Journal, 26*(1), 31–39.

Langley, C. (2016). Father knows best: Paternal presence and sexual debut in African- American adolescents living in poverty. *Family Process, 55*(1), 155–170.

Leavitt, C. E., Dew, J. P., Alsop, D. P., Runyan, S. D., & Hill, E. J. (2018, November 8). *Relational and sexual costs of materialism in couple relationships: An actor-partner longitudinal study.* Poster presented at the annual meeting of the National Council on Family Relations, San Diego, CA. November 8.

Lee, W. W., & McKinnish, T. (2018). The marital satisfaction of differently aged couples. *Journal of Population Economics, 31*(2), 337–362.

Liew, H. (2016). Is there something unique about marriage? The relative impact of marital status on alcohol consumption among military personnel. *Journal of Divorce & Remarriage, 57*(1), 76–85.

Lissak, G. (2018). Adverse physiological and psychological effects of screen time on children and adolescents: Literature review and case study. *Environmental Research, 164,* 149–157.

Livingston, G., & Brown, A. (2017, May 18). Intermarriage in the U.S. 50 years after Loving v. Virginia. *Pew Research Center.* Retrieved from http://www.pewsocialtrends.org/2017/05/18/intermarriage-in-the-u-s-50-years-after-loving-v-virginia/

Luu, S. (2014, November). *Reciprocal relationships between attitudes, time together, and satisfaction.* Poster presented at the National Council on Family Relations annual meeting, Baltimore, MD.

McDaniel, B. T., Galovan, A. M., Cravens, J. D., & Drouin, M. (2018). "Technoference" and implications for mothers' and fathers' couple and coparenting relationship quality. *Computers in Human Behavior, 80,* 303–313.

McDaniel, B. T., & Coyne, S. M. (2014). "Technoference": The interference of technology in couple relationships and implications for women's personal and relational well-being. *Psychology of Popular Media Culture, 5,* 85–98. Retrieved from http://dx.doi.org/10.1037/ppm0000065

McDonald, J. E., Olson,, J. R., Lanning, A. H., Goddard, H. W., & Marshall, J. P. (2018). Effects of religiosity, forgiveness, and spousal empathy on marital adjustment. *Marriage & Family Review, 54*(4), 393–416.

McNulty, J. K. (2016). Should spouses be demanding less from marriage? A contextual perspective on implications of interpersonal standards. *Personality and Social Psychology Bulletin, 42,* 444–457.

Meier, A., Musick, K., Fischer, J., & Flood, S. (2018). Mothers' and fathers' well-being in parenting across the arch of child development. *Journal of Marriage and the Family, 80*(4), 992–1004.

Michael, R. T., Gagnon, J. H., Laumann, E. O., & Kolata, G. (1994). *Sex in America: A definitive survey.* Boston, MA: Little, Brown.

Miller, R., Canlas, J., & Jackson, J. (2014, November). *Marital quality and physical health.* Paper presented at the National Council on Family Relations annual meeting, Baltimore, MD.

Minnotte, K. L. (2017). Integrative and masking emotion work: Marital outcomes among dual- earner couples. *Marriage & Family Review, 53,* 88–104.

Misra, S., Cheng, L., Genevie, J., & and Yuan, M. (2014, July 1). The iPhone effect: The quality of in person social interactions in the presence of mobile devices. *Environment and Behavior.* Retrieved from DOI:10.1177/0013916514539755

Monin, J. K., Goktas, S. O., Kershaw, T., & Dewan, A. (2019). Associations between spouses' oxytocin receptor gene polymorphism, attachment security, and marital satisfaction. *PLOS.* https://doi.org/10.1371/journal.pone.0213083

Moors, A. C. (2017). Has the American public's interest in formation related to relationships beyond "the couple" increased over time? *The Journal of Sex Research, 54*(6), 677–684.

Mazzucato, V., Dito, B. B., Grassi, M., & Vivet, J. (2017). Transnational parenting and the well-being of Angolan migrant parents in Europe. *Global Networks, 17*(1), 89–110.

Niehuis, S., Reifman, A., & Lee, K.H. (2015). Disillusionment in cohabiting and marrried couples: A national study. *Journal of Family Issues, 36,* 951–973.

Okhotnikov, I., Kisnan, A., & Hans, J. D. (2016, November 4). *Effect of religiousness on marital quality as mediated by commitment and equality.* Poster presented at the annual meeting of the National Council on Family Relations, Minneapolis, MN.

Ortiz, C., Ortiz-Peregrina, S., Castro, J. J., Casares-López, M., & Salas, C. (2018). Driver distraction by smartphone use (WhatsApp) in different age groups. *Accident Analysis & Prevention, 117*, 239–249.

Oviedo-Trespalacios, O., Haque, Md. M., King, M., & S. Demmel, S. (2018). Driving behaviour while self-regulating mobile phone interactions: A human-machine system approach. *Accident Analysis & Prevention, 118*, 253–262.

Perel, E. (2017). *The state of affairs: Rethinking infidelity.* New York: Harper.

Perrin, A. (2017). 10 facts about smartphones as the iPhone turns 10. *Pew Research Center.* Retrieved from http://www.pewresearch.org/fact-tank/2017/06/28/10-facts-about-smartphones/

Petts, A. L., & Petts, R. J. (2019, May 9). Gender matters: Racial variation and marital stability among intraracial couples. *Journal of Family Issues, 40*(13), 1808–1831.

Pew Research Center. (2019). *Internet report on mobile facts.* Retrieved from https://www.pewinternet.org/fact-sheet/mobile/

Porter, S. C., Epstein, N. B., & Smith-Bynum, M. A. (2017, November). *Black women's beliefs and emotions about marital prospects to black men.* Poster presented at the annual meeting of the National Council on Family Relations, Orlando, Florida.

Prabu, D., & L. Stafford. (2015). A relational approach to religion and spirituality in marriage: The role of couples' religious communication in marital satisfaction. *Journal of Family Issues, 36*, 232–249.

ProQuest Statistical Abstract of the United States. (2019), Online Edition. Bethesda, MD. Retrieved from https://www.proquest.com/products-services/statabstract.html

Qian, Z., Lichter, D. T., & Tumin, D. (2018). Divergent pathways to assimilation? Local marriage markets and intermarriage among U.S. Hispanics. *Journal of Marriage & Family, 80*(1), 271–288.

Radford, J., & Budiman, A. (2018, September 14). Facts on U.S. immigrants, 2016: Statistical portrait of the foreign-born population in the United States. *Pew Research Center.* Retrieved from http://www.pewhispanic.org/2018/09/14/facts-on-u-s-immigrants/

Rapacon, S. (2013). 5 choices for changing your name after marriage. *Kiplinger.* Retrieved from www.kiplinger.com

Robinson, M. C. (2017). Black and white biracial marriage in the United States. *Family Journal, 25*, 278–282.

Sayi, T. S., & Sibanda, A. (2018). Correlates of child marriage in Zimbabwe. *Journal of Family Issues, 39*, 2366–2388.

Schroder, J., & Schmiedeberg, C. (2015). Effects of relationship duration, cohabitation, and marriage on the frequency of intercourse in couples. Findings from German panel data. *Social Science Research, 52*, 72–82.

Scott, A. L., & Stafford, L. (2018). An investigation of relational turbulence and depressive symptoms in newly married women. *Personal Relationships, 25*, 22–37.

Sewell, B., Harris, V., & Sengupta, P. (2017, March 17–18). *Hurricanes and happiness: Relationship quality and concensus among Florida's coastal couples.* Paper presented at the annual meeting of the Southeastern Council on Family Relations, Charlotte, NC.

Shafer, E. F. (2017). Hillary Rodham versus Hillary Clinton: Consequences of surname choice in marriage. *Gender Issues, 34*, 316–332.

Sheff, E. (2014). *The polyamorists next door.* Lanham, MD: Rowman & Littlefield Publishers.

Simpson, J. A., Farrell, A. K., Orina, M. M., & Rothman, A. J. (2015). Power and social influence in relationships. In M. Mikulincer & P. R. Shaver (Eds.), *APA Handbook of Personality and Social Psychology,* (pp. 393–420) Vol 3. Interpersonal Relations. American Psychological Association.

Smith, S. M., & Landor, A. M. (2018). Toward a better understanding of African American families: Development of the sociocultural family stress model. *Journal of Family Theory and Review, 10*, 434–450.

Soulsby, L. K., & Bennett, K. M. (2017). When two become one: Exploring identity in marriage and cohabitation. *Journal of Family Issues, 38*, 358–380.

Spears, A., Wang, M., Nyutu, P., & Harcrow, A. (2014, August). *Positive and negative affect, social support and psychological well-being among military spouses.* Poster presented at the American Psychological Association annual meeting, Washington, DC.

Spencer, J., & Amato, P. (2011, November). *Marital quality across the life course: Evidence from latent growth curves.* Poster presented at the annual meeting of the National Council on Family Relations, Orlando, FL.

Stafford, L. (2016). Marital sanctity, relationship maintenance, and marital quality. *Journal of Family Issues, 37*, 119–131.

Stoner, M., Aamlid, C., Hilliard, T., & Knox, D. (2019). What parents don't know: International students' romantic relationships in the United States. *College Student Journal, 53*, 42–46.

Teachman, J. (2016). Body weight, marital status, and changes in marital status. *Journal of Family Issues, 37*(1), 74–96.

Tsui, A., Nolan, D., & Amico, C. (2017). Child marriage in America by the numbers. *PBS.* http://apps.frontline.org/child-marriage-by-the-numbers/

Twenge, J. M., Martin, G. N., & Campbell, W. K. (2018). Decreases in psychological well-being among American adolescents after 2012 and links to screen time during the rise of smartphone technology. *Emotion, 18*, 765–780.

Ulloa, E. C., Hammett, J. F., Meda, N. A., & Rubalcaba, S. J. (2017). Empathy and romantic relationship quality among cohabiting couples. *Family Journal, 25*, 208–214.

Unchained at Last. (2018). *Child marriage—Legal in the United States.* Retrieved from www.unchainedatlast.org

UNICEF. (2018a). Child marriage: Latest trends and future prospects. Retrieved from www.data.unicef.org

UNICEF. (2018b). *Child marriage.* Retrieved from www.data.unicef.org

Urbano-Contreras, A., Iglesias-Garcia, M. T., & Martinez-Gonzalez, R. A. (2017). Development and validation of the Satisfaction in Couple Relationship Scale (SCR). *Contemporary Family Therapy, 39*, 54–61.

Vasilinda, M. (2018, July 17). Florida woman continues to push to end child marriage nationwide. *News4JAX.* Retrieved from www.news4jax.com.

Vernon, L., Modecki, K. L., & Barber, B. L. (2018). Mobile phones in the bedroom: Trajectories of sleep habits and subsequent adolescent psychosocial development. *Child Development, 89*(1), 66–77.

Vesely, C. K., Bravo, D. Y., & Guzzardo, M. T. (2019, July 9). Immigrant families across the life course: Policy Impacts on physical and mental health. *Policy Brief.* Retrieved from https://www.ncfr.org/

Vesely, C. K., Letiecq, B. L., & Goodman, R. D. (2018). Immigrant family resilience in context: Using a community-based approach to build a new conceptual model. *Journal of Family Theory & Review, 9*(1), 93–110.

Vil, N. M. S., McDonald, K. B., & Cross-Barnet, C. (2018). A qualitative study of black married couples' relationships with their extended family networks. *Families in Society: Journal of Contemporary Social Services, 99*(1), 56–66.

Wadsworth, T. (2016). Marriage and subjective well-being: How and why context matters. *Social Indicators Research, 126*(3), 1025–1048.

Wedding costs for 2019. https://www.theknotww.com

Wheeler, L., Updegraff, K., Umana-Taylor, A., & McHale, S. (2014). *Marital and parent-child relationships in Mexican American families: Bidirectional associations across adolescence.* Paper presented at the National Council on Family Relations annual meeting, Baltimore, MD.

Wilcox, W. B., & Dew, J. (2016). The social and cultural predictors of generosity in marriage. *Journal of Family Issues, 37*(1), 97–118.

Wildeman, C., & Wang, E.A. (2017). Mass incarceration, public health, and widening inequality in the USA. *Lancet, 389,* 1464–1474.

Williams, N. D., Foye, A., & Lewis, F. (2016). Applying structural family therapy in the changing context of the modern African American single mother. *Journal of Feminist Family Therapy, 28,* 30–47.

Woldarsky, M., & Greenberg, L. S. (2014). Interpersonal forgiveness in emotion-focused couples' therapy: Relating process to outcome. *Journal of Marital and Family Therapy, 40*(1), 49–67.

Wright, R. G., LeBlanc, A. J., & Badgett, L. (2013). Same-sex legal marriage and psychological well-being: Findings from the California health interview survey. *American Journal of Public Health, 103, 339–346.*

Yang, Z., Asbury, K., & Griffiths, M. D. (2018). An exploration of problematic smartphone use among Chinese University students: Associations with academic anxiety, academic procrastination, self-regulation and subjective wellbeing. *International Journal of Mental Health and Addiction.* Retrieved from http://doi.org/10.1007/s11469–018-9961–1

Yi, B. L. (2018, June 24). World risks missing goal of ending child marriage by 2030. *Reuters.* Retrieved from www.reuters.com

Zella, S. (2017). Marital status transitions and self-reported health among Canadians: A life course perspective. *Applied Research in Quality of Life,* 12 (2), 303–325.

CHAPTER 7

Adler, A., & Ben-Ari, A. (2017). The myth of openness and secrecy in intimate relationships: The case of spouses of mixed-orientation marriage. *Journal of Homosexuality, 64,* 804–824

Adler, A., & Ben-Ari, A. (2018). "How we stay together without going crazy:" Reconstruction of reality among women of mixed-orientation relationships. *Journal of Homosexuality, 65,* 640–658.

American Psychiatric Association. (2018). *What is gender dysphoria?* Retrieved from https://www.psychiatry.org/patients-families/gender-dysphoria/what-is-gender-dysphoria.

American Psychological Association. (2012). *Lesbian and gay parenting.* Retrieved from https://www.apa.org/pi/LGBT/resources/parenting

Aristegui, I., Castro Solano, A., & Buunk, A. P. (2018). Mate preferences of Argentine antransgender people: An evolutionary perspective. *Personal Relationships, 25*(3), 330–350.

Averett, K. H. (2016). The gender buffet. *Gender & Society, 30*(2), 189–212.

Blair, K. L., & Hoskin, R. A. (2019). Transgender exclusion from the world of dating: Patterns of acceptance and rejection of hypothetical trans dating partners as a function of sexual and gender identity. *Journal of Social and Personal Relationships, 36*(7), 2074–2095.

Brumbaugh-Johnson, S. M., & Hull, K. E. (2019) Coming out as Transgender: Navigating the social implications of a transgender identity. *Journal of Homosexuality, 66*(8), 1148–1177.

Becker, A. B., & Todd, M. E. (2013). A new American Family? Public opinion toward family studies and perceptions of the challenges faced by children of same-sex parents. *Journal of GLBT Family Studies, 9,* 425–448.

Blosnich, J. R., Marsiglio, M. C., Gao, S., Gordon, A. J., Shipherd, J. C., Kauth, M., Brown, G. R., & Fine, M. J. (2016). Mental health of transgender veterans in US states with and without discrimination and hate crime protection. *American Journal of Public Health, 106*(3), 534–540.

Bos, H. M., Kuyper, L., & Gartrell, N. K. (2018). A population based comparison of female and male same-sex parent and different-sex parent household. *Family Process 57*(1), 148–164.

Brewer, G., & Lyons, M. (2017). Is Gaydar affected by attitudes toward homosexuality? Confidence, labeling bias, and accuracy. *Journal of Homosexuality, 64,* 1241–1252.

Byrne, T., & Bravo, V. (2016, June 26). The Knot LGBTQQ Weddings Survey, 2016. *USA Today,* 11T.

Canner, J. K.,. Harfouch, O., Kodadek, L. M., Pelaez, D., Coon, D. Offodile, A. C., Haider, A. H., & Lau, B. D. (2018). Temporal Trends in Gender-Affirming Surgery Among Transgender Patients in the United States. *JAMA Surgery, 153*(7), 609–616.

Cao, H., Zhou, N., Fine, M., Liang, Y., & Li, J. (2017). Meta-analysis of research prior to the U.S. nationwide legalization of same-sex marriage. *Journal of Marriage and the Family, 79,* 1258–1277.

Cenegy, L. F., Denney, J. T., & Kimbro, R. T. (2018). Family diversity and child health: Where do same-sex couples fit? *Journal of Marriage & Family, 80,* 198–281.

Chonody, J. M. (2013). Measuring sexual prejudice against gay men and lesbian women: Development of the Sexual Prejudice Scale (SPS). *Journal of Homosexuality, 60*(6), 895–926.

Clunis, D. M., & Dorsey Green, G. (2003). *The lesbian parenting book,* 2nd ed. Emeryville, CA: Seal Press.

Couric, Katie, (2015, July 29). Digital stars make YouTube the 'In' place to come out. *Yahoo! News.* Retrieved from https://www.yahoo.com/katiecouric/shane-dawson-come-out-youtube-its-one-stop-125399663913.html

D'Amico, E., & Julien, D. (2012). Disclosure of sexual orientation and gay, lesbian, and bisexual youth's adjustment: Associations with past and current parental acceptance and rejection. *Journal of GLBT Family Studies, 8*(3), 215–242.

Daboin, I., Peterson J. L., & Parrott, D. J. (2015). Racial differences in sexual prejudice and its correlates among heterosexual men. *Cultural Diversity and Ethnic Minority Psychology, 21*(2), 258–267.

Day, J. K., Perez-Brumer, A., &. Russell, S. T. (2018). Safe schools? Transgender youth's school experiences and perceptions of school climate. *Journal of Youth & Adolescence, 47*(8), 1731–1742.

De Groot, K. (2017, October 1). Psychiatrist, gay rights trailblazer honored in Philadelphia. *The Washington Post.*

Diamond, L. M. (2003). What does sexual orientation orient? A biobehavioral model distinguishing romantic love and sexual desire. *Psychological Review 110,* 173–92.

Doyle, D. M., & Molix, L. (2016). Disparities in social health by sexual orientation and the etiologic role of self-reported discrimination. *Archives of Sexual Behavior, 45*(6), 1317–1327.

Duncan, D., Prestage, G., & Grierson, J. (2015). Trust, commitment, love and sex: HIV, monogamy, and gay men. *Journal of Sex & Marital Therapy, 41*(4), 345–360.

Easterling, B., D., Knox, D., & Brackett, A. (2012). Secrets in romantic relationships: Does sexual orientation matter? *Journal of GLBT Family Studies, 8*(2), 198–210.

Edwards, W. J. (2016). Measuring relationship satisfaction: Is it possible for black gay male couples to be satisfied in a relationship? *Deviant Behavior, 37*, 931–951.

Erez, V., & Shenkman, G. (2016). Gay dads are happier: Subjective well-being among gay and heterosexual fathers. *Journal of GLBT Family Studies, 12*(5), 451–467.

Farr, R. H., Salomon, I., Brown-Iannuzzi, J. L., & Brown C. S. (2019). Elementary school-age children's attitudes toward children in same-sex parent families. *Journal of GLBT Family Studies 15*, 127–150.

Fein, L. A., Salgado, C. J., Sputova, K. Estes, C. M., & Medina C. A. (2018). Sexual preferences and partnerships of transgender persons mid- or post-transition. *Journal of Homosexuality, 65*, 659–671.

Flanders, C. E., Legge, M. M., Plante, I., Goldberg, A. E., & Ross, L. E. (2019). Gender socialization practices among bisexual and other nonmonosexual mothers: A longitudinal qualitative examination. *Journal of GLBT Family Studies, 15*(2), 105–126,

Flanders, C. E., Tarasoff, L. A., Legge, M. M., Robinson, M., & Gos, G. (2017). Positive experiences of young bisexual and other nonmonosexual people: A qualitative inquiry. *Journal of Homosexuality, 64*, 1014–1032.

Flores, A. R., Herman, J. L., Gates, G. J., & Brown, T. N. T. (2016). *How many adults identify as transgender in the United States?* Los Angeles, CA: The Williams Institute.

Fox, K., Knox, D., Hall, S., & Kuck, D. (2019, April 10–14). *Religiosity: Impact on love, relationships and sexual values/behaviors.* Poster presented at the Southern Sociological Society annual meeting, Atlanta, GA.

Gahan, L. (2018). Separated same-sex parents: Troubling the same-sex parented family. *Sociological Research Online, 23*(1), 245–261.

Galupo, M. P., Davis, K. S., Grynkiewicz, A. L., & Mitchell, R. C. (2017). Conceptualization of sexual orientation identity among sexual minorities: Patterns across sexual and gender identity. *Journal of Bisexuality, 14*(3–4) 433–456.

Ganna, A., Verweij, K. H., Nivard, M. G., Maier, R., Wedow, R., Busch, A. S., Abdellaoui, A., Guo, S., Sathirapongsasuti, J. F., 23andMe Research Team, Lichtenstein, P., Lundström, S., Långström, N., Auton, A., Harris, K. M., Beecham, G. W., Martin, E. R., Sanders, A. R., Perry, J. B., Neale, B. M., & Zietsch, B. P. (2019, August 30). Large-scale GWAS reveals insights into the genetic architecture of same-sex sexual behavior. *Science, 365*(6456). Retrieved from DOI: 10.1126/science.aat7693

Gates, G. J. (2011). *How many people are lesbian, gay, bisexual and transgender?* The Williams Institute, UCLA School of Law. Retrieved from https://williamsinstitute.law.ucla.edu/wp-content/uploads/Gates-How-Many-People-LGBT-Apr-2011.pdf

Gates, G. J. (2017). In US, more adults identifying as LGBTQ. *Gallup Poll.* Retrieved from https://news.gallup.com/poll/201731/lgbt-identification-rises.aspx

Gato, J., & Fontaine, A. M. (2016). Attitudes toward adoption by same-sex couples: Effects of gender of the participant, sexual orientation of the couple, and gender of the child. *Journal of GLBT Family Studies, 12*, 46–67.

Gato, J., Santos, S., & Fontaine, A. (2017). To have or not to have children? That is the question. Factors influencing decisions among lesbians and gay men. *Sexuality Research & Social Policy: Journal of NSRC, 14*(3),310–323.

Giunti, D., & G. Fioravanti, G. (2017). Gay men and lesbian women who became parents in the context of a former heterosexual relationship: An explorative study in Italy. *Journal of Homosexuality, 64*, 523–537.

Glass, V. Q. (2014). "We are with family": Black lesbian couples negotiate rituals with extended families. *Journal of GLBT Family Studies, 10*(1–2), 79–100.

Global Market Insight. (2018). *Sex reassignment surgery market size by gender transition.* Retrieved from https://www.gminsights.com/industry-analysis/sex-reassignment-surgery-market

Goldberg, A. E., Allen, K. R., Black, K. A., Frost, R. L., & Manley, M. H. (2018). "There is no perfect school": The complexity of school decision-making among lesbian and gay adoptive parents. *Journal of Marriage & Family, 80*(3), 684–703.

Golombok, S., Blake, L., Slutsky, J., Raffanello, E., Roman, G. D., & Ehrhardt, A. (2018). Parenting and the adjustment of children born to gay fathers through surrogacy. *Child Development, 89*(4), 1223–1233.

Gonzalez, S. (2018, October 25). There are more LGBTQ characters on broadcast TV than ever. *CNN Entertainment.* Retrieved from https://www.cnn.com/2018/10/25/entertainment/lgbtq-television-glaad-report/index.html

Gorman, B. K., & Oyarvide, Z. (2018). Sexual orientation, socioeconomic status, and healthy aging. *Generations, 42*, 56–60.

Gotta, G., Green, R. J., Rothblum, E., Solomon, S., Balsam, K., & Schwartz P. (2011). Heterosexual, lesbian, and gay male relationships: A comparison of couples in 1975 and 2000. *Family Process, 50*, 353–376.

Gray, S. A. O., Sweeney, K. K., Randazzo, R., & Levitt, H. M. (2016). 'Am I Doing the Right Thing?': Pathways to parenting a gender variant child. *Family Process, 55*, 123–138.

Green, E. L., Benner, K., & Pear, R. (2018, October 21). 'Transgender' could be defined out of existence under Trump administration. *New York Times.* Retrieved from https://www.nytimes.com/2018/10/21/us/politics/transgender-trump-administration-sex-definition.html

Gupta, K. (2017). "And now I'm just different, but there's nothing actually wrong with me": Asexual marginalization and resistance. *Journal of Homosexuality, 64*, 991–1013.

Haines, K. M., Boyer, C. R., Giovanazzi, C., &. Galupo, M. P. (2018). "Not a real family": Microaggressions directed toward LGBTQ families. *Journal of Homosexuality, 65*, 1138–1151.

Hall, S., & D. Knox. (2019). College Student Attitudes and Behaviors Survey of 12,816 undergraduates. Unpublished data collected for this text. Department of Family, Consumer, and Technology Education Teachers College, Ball State University and Department of Sociology, East Carolina University, Greenville, NC.

Hart-Brinson, P. (2018). *The Gay Marriage Generation: How the LGBT movement transformed American Culture.* New York: New York University Press.

Hoyt, C. L., Morgenroth, T., & Burnette, J. L. (2019). Understanding sexual prejudice: The role of political ideology and strategic essentialism. *Journal of Applied Social Psychology, 49*, 3–14.

Hu, J., Hu, J., Huang, G., & Zheng, X. (2016). Life satisfaction, self-esteem, and loneliness among LGB adults and heterosexual adults in China. *Journal of Homosexuality, 63*, 72–86.

Irizarry, Y. A., & Perry, R. K. (2018). Challenging the Black church narrative: Race, class, and homosexual attitudes. *Journal of Homosexuality, 65*, 884–911.

Jhang, J. (2018). Scaffolding in family relationships: A grounded theory of coming out to family. *Family Relations, 67*, 161–175.

Johnson, C. W., Singh, A. A., & M. Gonzalez, M. (2014). "It's complicated": Collective memories of transgender, queer, and questioning youth in high school. *Journal of Homosexuality, 61*, 419–434.

Kelly, M., & Hauck, E. (2015). Doing housework, redoing gender: Queer couples negotiate the household division of labor. *Journal of GLBT Family Studies, 11*, 438–464

Kinsey, A. C., Pomeroy, W. B., Martin, C. E., & Gebhard, P. H. (1953). *Sexual behavior in the human female.* Philadelphia, PA: Saunders.

Kirby, B. J., & Michaelson, C. (2015). Comparative morality judgments about lesbians and gay men teaching and adopting children. *Journal of Homosexuality, 62*, 33–50.

Kuper, L. E., Nussbaum, R., & Mustanski, B. (2012). Exploring the diversity of gender and sexual orientation identities in an online sample of transgender individuals. *Journal of Sex Research, 49*, 244–254.

Kurdek, L. A. (1994). Conflict resolution styles in gay, lesbian, heterosexual nonparent, and heterosexual parent couples. *Journal of Marriage and the Family, 56*, 705–22.

Kurdek, L. A. (2008). Change in relationship quality for partners from lesbian, gay male, and heterosexual couples. *Journal of Family Psychology, 22*, 701–11.

Kuyper, L., & Bos, H. (2016). Mostly heterosexual and lesbian/gay young adults: Differences in mental health and substance use and the role of minority stress. *The Journal of Sex Research, 53*, 731–741.

Lannutti, P. (2018). GLBTQ people who decided to marry after the 2016 U.S. election: Reasons for and meanings of marriage. *Journal of GLBT Family Studies, 14*, 85–100.

LeBlanc, A. J., Frost, D.M. & Bowen, K. (2018). Legal marriage, unequal recognition, and mental health among same-sex couples. *Journal of Marriage and the Family, 80*, 397–408.

Leyerzapf, H., Visse, M., DeBeer, A., & T. A. (2018). Gay-friendly elderly care: Creating space for sexual diversity in residential care by challenging the hetero norm. *Ageing and Society. 38*, 352–377.

Macapagal, K., Greene, G. J., Rivera, Z., & Mustanski, B. (2015). "The Best Is Always Yet to Come": Relationship stages and processes among young LGBT couples. *Journal of Family Psychology, 29*, 309–320.

Masci, D., Brown, A. & Kiley, J. (2017, June 26). 5 facts about same-sex marriage. *Pew Research Center.* Retrieved from http://www.pewresearch.org/fact-tank/2017/06/26/same-sex-marriage/

McKie, R. M., Milhausen, R. R., & Llachowsky, N. J. (2017). "Hedge Your Bets": Technology's role in young gay men's relationship challenges. *Journal of Homosexuality, 64*, 75–94.

McLaren, S. (2016). The interrelations between internalized homophobia, depressive symptoms and suicidal ideation among Australian gay men, lesbians, and bisexual women. *Journal of Homosexuality, 63*, 156–168.

Mena, J. A., & Vaccaro, A. (2013). Tell me you love me no matter what: Relationships and self- esteem among GLBQ young adults. *Journal of GLBT Family Studies, 9*, 3–23.

Miller, S. (2018, April 18). Record number of states banning conversion therapy. *USA Today*, p. 3a.

Mitchell, H., & Hunnicutt, G. (2019). Challenging accepted scripts of sexual "normality": Asexual narratives of non-normative identity and experience. *Sexuality & Culture, 23*, 507–524.

Mock, S. E., & Eibach, R. P. (2012). Stability and change in sexual orientation identity over a ten-year period in adulthood. *Archives of Sexual Behavior, 41*, 641–648.

Moran, T. E., Cliff, C. Y., & Tryon, G. S. (2018). Bully victimization, depression, and the role of protective factors among college LGBTQ students. *Journal of Community Psychology, 46*, 871–884.

Moser, C. (2016). Defining sexual orientation. *Archives of Sexual Behavior, 45*, 505–508.

Nadal, K. L. (2018). A decade of microaggression research and LGBTQ communities: An introduction to the special issue. *Journal of Homosexuality.* Retrieved from https://doi.org/10.1080/00918369.2018.1539582

Newcomb, M. E., Birkett, M., Corliss, H. L., & Mustanski, B. (2014). Sexual orientation, gender, and racial differences in illicit drug use in a sample of US high school students. *American Journal of Public Health, 104*, 304–310.

Okutan, N., Buyuksahin, A., & Sakalli Ugurlu, N. (2017). Comparing heterosexuals' and gay men/lesbians' responses to relationship problems and the effects of internalized homophobia on gay men/lesbians' responses to relationship problems in Turkey. *Journal of Homosexuality, 64*, 218–238.

Overby, L. Marvin. (2014). Etiology and attitudes: Beliefs about the origins of homosexuality and their implications for public policy. *Journal of Homosexuality, 61*, 568–587.

Owens, Z. D. (2017). Is it Facebook official? Coming out and passing strategies of young adult gay men on social media. *Journal of Homosexuality, 64*, 431–449.

Özata Yildizhan, B., Yüksel, Ş., Avayu, M., Noyan, H. & Yildizhan, E. (2018). Effects of gender reassignment on quality of life and mental health in people with gender dysphoria. *Türk Psikiyatri Dergisi, 29*(1), 1–10. Retrieved from https://login.cyrano.ucmo.edu/login? url=http://search.ebscohost.com.cyrano.ucmo.edu:2048/login.aspx?direct=true&db=psyh&AN=2018-14571-002&site=ehost-live

Paine, E. A., Umberson, D., & Reczek, C. (2019). Sex in midlife: Women's sexual experiences in lesbian and straight marriages. *Journal of Marriage and the Family, 81*, 7–23.

Pepping, C. A., Cronin, T. J., Halford, W. K., & Lyons, A. (2019). Minority stress and same-sex relationship satisfaction: The role of concealment motivation. *Family Process, 58*(2), 496–508.

Perales, F., & J. Baxter, J. (2018). Sexual identity and relationship quality in Australia and the United Kingdom. *Family Relations, 67*, 55–69.

Persson, T. J., & Pfaus, J. G. (2015). Bisexuality and mental health: Future research directions. *Journal of Bisexuality, 15*, 82–98.

Peterson, F. R., Gantz, T., Hartenstein, J., Likcani, A., & Chang, J. (2017, November). *Coming out: Sibling impact on disclosure of sexual identity.* Paper presented at the annual meeting of the National Council on Family Relations, Orlando, FL

Platt, L. F., & Bolland, K. S. (2017). Trans partner relationships: A qualitative exploration. *Journal of GLBT Family Studies, 13*, 163–185.

Platt, L. F., Wolf, J. K., & Scheitle, C. P. (2018). Patterns of mental health utilization among sexual orientation minority groups. *Journal of Homosexuality, 65*, 135–153.

Potarca, G., Mills, M., & Neberich, W. (2015). Relationship preferences among gay and lesbian online daters: Individual and contextual influences. *Journal of Marriage and the Family, 77*, 523–541.

Power, J. J., Perlesz, A., Brown, R., Schofield, M. J., Pitts, M. K., McNair, R., & Bickerdike, A. (2013). Bisexual parents and family diversity: Findings from the work, love, play study. *Journal of Bisexuality, 12*, 519–538.

Puckett, J. A., Horne, S. G., Surace, F., Carter, A., Noffsinger-Frazier, N. Shulman, J., Detrie, P., Ervin, A., & Mosher, C. (2017). Predictors of sexual minority youth's reported suicide attempts and mental health. *Journal of Homosexuality, 64*, 697–715.

Pyne, J. (2016). "Parenting is not a job. . . It's a relationship": Recognition and relational knowledge among parents of gender non-conforming children. *Journal of Progressive Human Services, 27*, 21–28.

Quidley-Rodriguez, N., & De Santis, J. P. (2019). A concept analysis of bear identity. *Journal of Homosexuality*, 66, 60–76.

Riggle, E., Wickham, R., Rostosky, S., Rothblum, E., & Balsam, K. (2017). Impact of civil marriage recognition for long-term same-sex couples. *Sexuality Research & Social Policy: Journal of NSRC*, 14, 223–232.

Ritter, L., Morris, H., & Knox, D. (2018). Who's getting the best sex?: A comparison by sexual dentity. *Sexuality & Culture*, 22, 1466–1489.

Rockenbach, A. N., Lo, M. A., & Mayhew, M. J. (2017). How LGBT college students perceived and engage the campus religious and spiritual climate. *Journal of Homosexuality*, 64, 488–508.

Rodriguez, E. M., Etengoff, C., & Vaughan, M. D. (2019). A quantitative examination of identity integration in gay, lesbian, and bisexual people. *Journal of Homosexuality*, 66. 77–99.

Rosario, M., Schrimshaw, E. W., Hunter, J., & Braun, L. (2006). Sexual identity development among lesbian, gay, and bisexual youth: Consistency and change over time. *Journal of Sex Research*, 43, 46–58.

Rosenberger, J., Herbenick, D., Novak, D., & Reece, M. (2014). What's love got to do with it? Examinations of emotional perception and sexual behaviors among gay and bisexual men in the United States. *Archives of Sexual Behavior*, 43, 119–128.

Ross, M. W., Daneback, K., & Mansson, S. (2013). Fluid versus fixed: A new perspective on bisexuality as a fluid sexual orientation beyond gender. *Journal of Bisexuality*, 12, 449–460.

Rothman, E. F., Sullivan, M., Keyes, S., & Boehmer, U. (2012). Parents supportive reactions to sexual orientation disclosure associated with better health: Results from a population-based survey of LGB adults in Massachusetts. *Journal of Homosexuality*, 59, 186–200.

Russell, S. T. (2013). *LGBTQ youth well-being: The role of parents and policy.* Paper presented at the National Council on Family Relations annual meeting, San Antonio, TX.

Russell, S. T., Ryan, C., Toomey, R. B., Diaz, R. M., & Sanchez, J. (2011). Lesbian, gay, bisexual and transgender adolescent school victimization: Implications for young adult health and adjustment. *Journal of School Health*, 81, 223–230.

Scherrer, K. S., Kazyak, E., & Schmitz, R. (2015). Getting "Bi" in the family: Bisexual people's disclosure experiences. *Journal of Marriage & Family*, 77, 680–696.

Scherrer, K. S. (2016). Gay, lesbian, bisexual, and queer grandchildren's disclosure process with grandparents. *Journal of Family Issues*, 37, 739–764.

Schoephoerster, E., & Aamlid, C. (2016). College students' attitude toward same sex parenting. *College Student Journal*, 50, 102–106.

Sevecke, J. R., Rhymer, K. N., Almazan, E. P. & Jacob, S. (2015). Effects of interaction experiences and undergraduate coursework on attitudes toward gay and lesbian issues. *Journal of Homosexuality*, 62, 821–840.

Shangani, S., Gamarel, K. E., Ogunbajo, A., Cai, J., & Operario, D. (2019). Intersectional minority stress disparities among sexual minority adults in the USA: The role of race/ethnicity and socioeconomic status. *Culture, Health & Sexuality*. Retrieved from https://doi.org/10.1080/13691058.2019.1604994

Shenkman, G., & D. Shmotkin, D. (2016, April 28). The association between self-perceived parental role and meaning in life among gay and heterosexual fathers. *Journal of Family Psychology*, published online.

Starks, T., & Parsons, J. (2014). Adult attachment among partnered gay men: Patterns and associations with sexual relationship quality. *Archives of Sexual Behavior*, 43, 107–117.

Svab, A., & Kuhar, R. (2014). The transparent and family closets: Gay men and lesbians and their families of origin. *Journal of GLBT Family Studies*, 10, 15–35.

Swann, G., Minshew, R., Newcomb, M. E., & Mustanski, B. (2016). Validation of The Sexual Orientation Microaggression Inventory in two diverse samples of LGBTQ youth. *Archives of Sexual Behavior*, 45, 1289–1298.

Todd, M., Rogers, L. H., & Boyer, C. R. (2013, November 5–9). *Sexual vs. spiritual?* Poster presented at the National Council on Family Relations annual meeting. San Antonio, TX.

Tornello, S. L., & Patterson, C. J. (2018). Adult children of gay fathers: Parent-child relationship quality and mental health. *Journal of Homosexuality*, 65, 1152–1166.

Totenhagen, C. J., Randall, A. K., Lloyd, K. (2018). Stress and relationship functioning in same-sex couples: The vulnerabilities of internalized homophobia and outness. *Family Relations*, 67, 399–413.

Trahan, D. P., & Goodrich, K. M. (2015). "You think you know me, but you have no idea": Dynamics in African-American families following a son's or daughter's disclosure as LGBT. *Family Journal*, 23, 147–157.

Van Bergen, D. D., Bos, H. M. W., van Lisdonk, J., Keuzenkamp, S., & Sandfort, T. G. M. (2013). Victimization and suicidality among Dutch lesbian, gay, and bisexual youths. *American Journal of Public Health*, 103, 70–72.

Van de Grift, T. C., Elaut, E., Cerwenka, S. C., Cohen-Kettenis, P. T., & Kreukels, B. P. C. (2018). Surgical Satisfaction, Quality of Life, and Their Association After Gender-Affirming Surgery: A Follow-up Study. *Journal of Sex & Marital Therapy*, 44(2), 138–148.

Van Eeden-Moorefield, B., Malloy, K., & Benson, K. (2015). *Gay men's (non) monogamy ideals and lived experiences.* Poster presented at the National Council on Family Relations annual meeting, Vancouver, British Columbia, CN.

Williams Institute. (2019). LGBT Demographic Data Interactive. Retrieved from https://williamsinstitute.law.ucla.edu/visualization/lgbt-stats/? topic=LGBT#density

Woodford, M. R., Chonody, J. M., Kulick, A., Brennan, D. J., & Renn, K. (2015). The LGBQ microaggressions on campus scale: A scale development and validation study. *Journal of Homosexuality*, 62, 1660–1687.

Worth, M. A. (2018). *Gender affirmation surgery and post-operative regret: A systematic review of the literature between 2009 and 2017* (Doctoral dissertation, Order No. 10812749). Retrieved from ProQuest Dissertations & Theses Global. (2042918983).

Zammitt, K. A., Pepperell, J., & Coe, M. (2015). Implementing an ally development model to promote safer schools for LGBT youth: A trans-disciplinary approach. *Journal of Homosexuality*, 62, 687–700.

CHAPTER 8

Baldassar, L. (2016). De-demonizing distance in mobile family lives: co-presence, care circulation and polymedia as vibrant matter. *Global Networks*, 16, 145–163.

Balderrama-Durbin, C. M., Allen, E. S., & Rhoades, G. K. (2012). Demand and withdraw behaviors in couples with a history of infidelity. *Journal of Family Psychology*, 26, 11–17.

Burke-Winkelman, S., K., Brinkley, J., & Knox, D. (2014, February 3). Sexting on the college campus. *Electronic Journal of Human Sexuality*, 17.

Busby, D. M., Day, R. D., & Olsen, J. (2019). Understanding couple shared reality: The case of combined couple versus discrepancy assessments in understanding couple forgiveness. *Journal of Child & Family Studies*, 28, 42–51.

Byrne, T., & Loehrke, J. (2015, July 24). Out of sync on vacation. *USA Today*, D1.

Cantarero, K., Szarota, P., Stamkou, E., Navas, M., & Espinosa, A. D. C. (2018). When is a lie acceptable? Work and private life lying acceptance depends on its beneficiary. *Journal of Social Psychology, 158*, 220–235.

Carpenter, J., Green, M., & Laflam, J. (2018). Just between us: Exclusive communications in online social networks. *Journal of Social Psychology, 158*, 405–420.

Caughlin, J. P., & Bassinger, E. D. (2015). Completely open and honest communication: Is this really what we want? *Family Focus*. Issue FF64. Minneapolis, MN: National Council on Family Relations.

Cohen, M. (2016). It's not you, It's me. . . .no, actually it's you: Perceptions of what makes a first date successful or not. *Sexuality & Culture, 20*, 173–191.

Coyne, S. M., L. Stockdale, Busby, D., Iverson, B., & Grant, D. M. (2011). "I luv u:)!": A descriptive study of the media use of individuals in romantic relationships. *Family Relations, 60*, 150–162.

Currin, J. M., & Hubach, R. D. (2019). Motivations for non-university-based adults who sext their relationship partners. *Journal of Sex & Marital Therapy, 45*(4), 317–327.

Drouin, M., Hernandez, E. & Wehle, S. M. J. (2018). "Tell me lies, Tell me sweet lies:" Sexting deception among adults. *Sexuality & Culture, 22*, 865–880.

Dwyer, R. J., Kushlev, K., & Dunn, E. W. (2018). Smartphone use undermines enjoyment of face-to-face social interactions. *Journal of Experimental Social Psychology, 78*, 233–239.

Easterling, B., Kahn, S., Knox, D., & Hall, S. (2019, April 13). Deception in emerging adult romantic relationships: Who's lying and cheating? Poster presented at the Southern Sociological Society annual meeting, Atlanta, GA. Also published in *College Student Journal* (in press).

Easterling, B., D., Knox, D., & Brackett, A. (2012). Secrets in romantic relationships: Does sexual orientation matter? *Journal of GLBT Family Studies, 8*, 198–210.

Emily Post Institute. (2018a). *Four essential cellphone rules*. Retrieved from http://emilypost.com/advice/four-essential-cell-phone-rules

Emily Post Institute. (2018b). Texting Manners. Retrieved from http://emilypost.com/advice/texting-manners

Falconier, M. K. (2015). TOGETHER- A couples' program to improve communication, coping, and financial management skills: Development and initial pilot testing. *Journal of Marital and Family Therapy, 41*, 236–250.

Forgays, D. K., Hyman, I., & J. Shreiber, J. (2014). Texting everywhere for everything: gender and the age differences in cell phone etiquette and use. *Computers in Human Behavior, 31*, 314–321.

Frisby, B. N., & Booth-Butterfield, M. (2015). The "how" and "why" of flirtatious communication between marital partners. *Communication* Quarterly, 60, 465–480.

Furukawa, R., & Driessnack, M. (2013). Video-mediated communication to support distant family connectedness. *Clinical Nursing Research, 22*, 82–94.

Garfield, R. (2010). Male emotional intimacy: How therapeutic men's groups can enhance couples therapy. *Family Process* 49, 109–122.

Gottman, J. (1994). *Why marriages succeed or fail*. New York: Simon & Schuster.

Hales, A. H., M. Dvir, M., Wesselmann, E. D., Kruger, D. J., & Finkenauer, C. (2018). Cell-phone-induced ostracism threatens fundamental needs. *Journal of Social Psychology* 158, 460–473.

Hall, S. S., & Knox, D. (2017). Perceived relationship power in emerging adults' romantic relationships. *Journal of Family Studies,* Retrieved from http://dx.doi.org/10.1080/13229400.2016.1269660

Hall, S. S., & Knox, D. (2019). College Student Attitudes and Behaviors Survey of 12,406 undergraduates. Unpublished data collected for this text. Department of Family, Consumer, and Technology Education Teachers College, Ball State University and Department of Sociology, East Carolina University, Greenville, NC.

Haydon, K. C., Jonestrask, C., Guhn-Knight, H., & Salvatore, J. E. (2017). The dyadic construction of romantic conflict recovery sabotage. *Journal of Social and Personal Relationships, 34*, 915–935.

Hiew, D. N., Halford, W. K., & van de Vijver, F. J. R. (2016). Communication and relationship satisfaction in Chinese, Western and intercultural Chinese-Western couples. *Journal of Family Psychology, 30*, 193–202.

Hill, E. W. (2010). Discovering forgiveness through empathy: implications for couple and family therapy. *Journal of Family Therapy, 32*, 169–185.

Hui, B., & Campbell, R. (2018). Discrepancy between Learning and Practicing Digital Citizenship. *Journal of Academic Ethics, 16*, 117–131.

Iannone, N. E., M. K. McCarty, M. K., Branch, S. E., & Kelly, J. R. (2018). Connecting in the Twitterverse: Using Twitter to satisfy unmet belonging needs. *Journal of Social Psychology, 158*, 491–495.

Jolly, J. (2018, August 10). The ultimate guide to deciphering teen slang. *USA Today*, 2B.

Kelley, K. (2010). *Oprah: A biography*. New York: Crown Publishers.

King, A. L. S., Valenca, A. M., Silva, A. C. O., Baczynski, T., Carvalho, M. R., & Nardi, A. E. (2013). Nomophobia: dependency on virtual environments or social phobia? *Computers in Human Behavior, 29*, 140–144.

Klettke, B., Hallford, D. J., Hallford, Clancy, E., Mellor, D., & Toumbourou, J. W. (2019, April). Sexting and psychological distress: The role of unwanted and coerced sexts. *Cyberpsychology, Behavior, and Social Networking, 22*, online. Retrieved from https://doi.org/10.1089/cyber.2018.0291

Knudson-Martin, C., Huenergardt, D., Lafontant, K., Bishop, L., Schaepper, J. & Wells, M. (2015). Competencies for addressing gender and power in couple therapy: A socio emotional approach. *Journal of Marital & Family Therapy, 41*, 205–220.

Kurdek, L. A. (1994). Areas of conflict for gay, lesbian, and heterosexual couples: What couples argue about influences relationship satisfaction. *Journal of Marriage and the Family, 56*, 923–34.

Lavner, J. A., Karney, B. R., & Bradbury, T. N. (2016). Does couples' communication predict marital satisfaction, or does marital satisfaction predict communication? *Journal of Marriage and Family, 78*, 680–694.

Lenhart, A., Anderson, M., & Smith, A. (2015). Teens, technology and romantic relationships. *Pew Research Center*, Oct 1. http://www.pewinternet.org/2015/10/01/teens-technology-and-romantic-relationships/

Marano, H. E. (1992, January/February). The reinvention of marriage. *Psychology Today*, 49.

Markman, H. J., Rhoades, G. K., Stanley, S. M., Ragan, E. P., & Whitton, S. W. (2010a). The premarital communication roots of marital distress and divorce: The first five years of marriage. *Journal of Family Psychology, 24*, 289–298.

Markman, H. J., S. M. Stanley, S. M., & Blumberg, S. L. (2010b). *Fighting for your marriage* (3rd ed.). San Francisco, CA: Jossey-Bass.

McDaniel, B. T., & Drouin, M. (2015). Sexting among married couples: Who is doing it and are they more satisfied? *Cyberpsychology, Behavior, and Social Networking, 18*, 628–634.

McDaniel, B. T., & Drouin, M. (2019). Daily technology interruptions and emotional and relational well-being. *Computers in Human Behavior, 99*, 1.

McNicol, M. L., & Thorsteinsson, E. B. (2017, April). Internet addiction, psychological distress, and coping responses among adolescents and adults. *Cyberpsychology, Behavior, and Social Networking.* Retrieved from doi:10.1089/cyber.2016.0669.

Merolla, A. J., & Zhang, S. (2011). In the wake of transgressions: Examining forgiveness communication in personal relationships. *Personal Relationships, 18*, 79–95.

Murray, C. E., & Campbell, E. C. (2015). The pleasures and perils of technology in intimate relationships. *Journal of Couple & Relationship Therapy, 14*, 116–140.

Narges, A., Asghari, B., & Manie, F. M. (2017). Relationship between dependence on modern communication tools and psychological well-being in students. *Journal of Research & Health, 7*, 637–646.

Nesi, J., Widman, L., Chokas-Bradley, S., & Pristein, M. J. (2017). Technology-based communication and the development of interpersonal competencies within adolescent romantic relationships: A preliminary investigation. *Journal of Research on Adolescence, 27*, 471–477.

Norton, A. M., & J. Baptist, J. (2012, November). *Couple boundaries for social networking: Impact of Trust and Satisfaction.* Paper presented at the National Council on Family Relations annual meeting, Phoenix, AZ.

Papp, L. M. (2018). Topics of marital conflict in everyday lives of empty next couples and their Implications for conflict resolution. *Journal of Couple & Relationship Therapy, 17*, 1–7.

Rappleyea, D., Taylor, A. C., & Fang, X. (2014). Gender differences in communication technology among emerging adults in the initiation of dating relationships. *Marriage and Family Review, 50*, 269–284.

Rodriguez-Arauz, G., Ramirez-Esparza, N., García-Sierra, A., Ikizer, E. G., & and Fernández-Gómez, M. J. (2018). You go before me, please: Behavioral politeness and interdependent self as markers of simpatia in Latinas. *Cultural Diversity and Ethnic Minority Psychology.* Retrieved from http://dx.doi.org/10.1037/cdp0000232

Rosenthal, S. R., C., Yoojin, C., & Clark, M. A. (2018, October 16). The Internet Addiction Test in a Young Adult U. S. Population. *Cyberpsychology, Behavior, and Social Networking, 21*(10), 16. Retrieved from https://doi-org.jproxy.lib.ecu.edu/10.1089/cyber.2018.0143

Routledge, C. (2019, August 15). What are the social and psychological costs of our computer-mediated lives? *Institute for Family Studies.* Retrieved from https://ifstudies.org/blog/what-are-the-social-and-psychological-costs-of-our-computer-mediated-lives

Sanford, K., & Grace, A. J. (2011). Emotion and underlying concerns during couples' conflict: An investigation of within-person change. *Personal Relationships, 18*, 96–109.

Schade, L. C., Sandberg, J., Bean, R., Busby, D., & and S. Coyne, S. (2013). Using technology to connect in romantic relationships: Effects on attachment, relationship satisfaction, and stability in emerging adults. *Journal of Couple & Relationship Therapy: Innovations in Clinical and Educational Interventions, 12*, 314–338.

Seunghee, H., Joon, K. K., & Hyun, K. J. (2017). Understanding nomophobia: Structural equation modeling and semantic network analysis of smartphone separation anxiety. *Cyberpsychology, Behavior, and Social Networking, 20*, 419–427. Retrieved from https://doi.org/10.1089/cyber.2017.0113

Shuter, R., & Turner, L. H. (1997). African American and European American women in the workplace: Perceptions of conflict communication. *Management Communication Quarterly, 11*, 74–96.

Smith, M. B., & Bravo, V. (2019, January 2). Commensense.org survey, teens and texting. *USA Today*, 1A.

Sprecher, S., Metts, S., Burelson, B., Hatfield, E., & Thompson, A. (1995). Domains of expressive interaction in intimate relationships: Associations with satisfaction and commitment. *Family Relations, 44*, 203–10.

Su, H. (2016). Constant connection as the media condition of love: where bonds become bondage. *Media, Culture & Society, 38*, 232–247.

Tan, R., Overall, N. C., & Taylor, J. K. (2012). Let's talk about us: Attachment, relationship-focused disclosure, and relationship quality. *Personal Relationships, 19*, 521–534.

Tannen, D. (1990). *You just don't understand: Women and men in conversation.* London, UK: Virago.

Tannen, D. (1998). *The argument culture.* New York: Random House.

Tannen, D. (2006). *You're wearing that? Understanding mothers and daughters in conversation.* New York: Random House.

Taylor, A. C., Rappelea, D. L., Fang, X., & Cannon, D. (2013). Emerging adults' perceptions of acceptable behaviors prior to forming a committed, dating relationship. *Journal of Adult Development, 20*, 173–184.

Turner, L. H., & Shuter, R. (2004). African American and European American women's visions of workplace conflict: A metaphorical analysis. *Howard Journal of Communications, 15*, 169–183.

Van Ouytsel, J., Van Gool, E., Wolrave, M., Ponnet, K., & Peeters, E. (2017). Sexting: adolescents' perceptions of the applications for, motivations for, and consequences of sexting. *Journal of Youth Studies, 20*, 446–470.

Vaterlaus, J. M., Tulane, S., & Brown, M. (2018, November 8). *Interactive technology and marital relationships: A qualitative study.* Annual meeting of the National Council on Family Relations, San Diego, CA.

Verduhn, P., Lee, D. S., Park, J., Shablack, H., Orvell, A., Bayer, J., Ybarra, O., Jonides, J., & Koss. (2015). Passive Facebook usage undermines affective well-being: Experimental and longitudinal evidence. *Journal of Experimental Psychology: General, 144*, 480–488.

Vilhelmson, B., Thulin, E., & Ellder, E. (2017). Where does time spent on the Internet come from? Tracing the influence of information and communications technology use on daily activities. *Information, Communication & Society, 20*, 250–263.

Vogels, E., & Stewart, H. (2018). *Sexy messages or sexual harassment: Experience of individuals who have received "dick pics."* Poster presented at the annual meeting of the Society for the Scientific Study of Sexuality, Montreal, CN.

Walsh, S. (2013). Match's 2012 singles in America survey. America-survey

Webley, K. (2012, September 17). Cheating Harvard. *Time*, p. 22.

Weimer, M. (2018). Cell phone policies: A review of where faculty stand. *Faculty Focus.* Retrieved from https://www.facultyfocus.com/articles/effective-classroom-management/cell-phone-policies-review-faculty-stand/

Weisskrirch, R. S., Drouin M., & Delevi, R. (2017). Relational anxiety and sexting. *The Journal of Sex Research, 54*, 685–693.

Wise, S., Loehrke. J. (2017, April 14). Murad EyesUp survey of 1000 adults. *USA Today*, 1A.

Woszidlo, A, & Segrin, C. (2013). Negative affectivity and educational attainment as predictors of newlyweds' problem-solving communication and marital quality. *Journal of Psychology, 147*, 49–73.

Xu, K. (2013). Theorizing difference in intercultural communication: A critical dialogic perspective. *Communication Monographs, 80*, 379–397.

CHAPTER 9

Anders, K. M., Olmstead, S. B., & E. W. (2016, November). *College student's [mis]perceptions of peer hook up behaviors: Investigating changes in injunctive and descriptive norms based on sexual identity development.* Poster presented at the annual meeting for National Council on Family Relations, Minneapolis, MN.

Bartholomew, K., Camp Dush, C. M., & Sassler, S. (2015, November). *Sexual tempo: Is it the pathway to relationship progression or regression?* Poster presented at the National Council on Family Relations annual meeting, Vancouver, British Columbia, CN.

Bersamin, M. M., Zamboanga, B. L., Schwartz, S. J., Donnellan, M. B., Hudson, M., Weisskirch, R. S., Kim, S. Y., Agocha, V. B., Whitborne, S. K., & Caraway, S. J. (2014). Risky business: Is there an association between casual sex and mental health among emerging adults? *The Journal of Sex Research, 51*, 43–51.

Braksmajer, A. (2017). "That's kind of one of our jobs": Sexual activity as a form of care work among women with sexual difficulties. *Archives of Sexual Behavior, 46*, 2085–2095.

Brenot, P. S., & Wunsch, S. (2016). Sexual needs of women in response to the needs of their partners. *Sexologies: European Journal of Sexology and Sexual Health, 25*:20–23.

Brodsky, A. (2017). 'Rape-Adjacent': Imagining legal responses to nonconsensual condom removal. *Columbia Journal of Gender and Law, 32*(2). *Business Wire* (2018). Global Online Sex Toys Market 2018–2022. Retrieved, from https://www.businesswire.com/news/home/20180822005299/en/Global-Online-Sex-Toys-Market-2018–2022-Adult

Byers, E. S., O'Sullivan, L. F., & Brotto, L. A. (2016). Time out from sex or romance: Sexually experienced adolescents' decisions to purposefully avoid sexual activity or romantic relationships. *Journal of Youth and Adolescence, 45*, 831–845.

Carlson, D. L., & Soller, B. (2019). Sharing's more fun for everyone? Gender attitudes, sexual self-efficacy and sexual frequency. *Journal of Marriage and the Family, 80*, 21–41.

Canan, S., & Jozkowski, K. (2017). Sexual health education topics in schools: Inclusion and timing preferences of a sample of southern U.S. college students. *Sexuality Research & Social Policy: Journal of NSRC, 14*, 143–156.

Cohen, M. (2016). An exploratory study of individuals in non-traditional, alternative relationships: How 'open' are we? *Sexuality and Culture, 20*, 295–315.

Cohen, M., & Wilson, K. (2017). Development of the Consensual Non-monogamy Attitude Scale (CNAS). *Sexuality and Culture, 21*, 1–14.

Cooper, A., & Gordon, B. (2015). Young New Zealand woman's sexual decision-making in casual sex situations: A qualitative study. *Canadian Journal of Human Sexuality, 24*, 69–76.

Courtice, E. L., & Shaughnessy, K. (2018). The partner context of sexual minority women's and men's cybersex experiences: Implications for traditional sexual script. *Sex Roles, 78*, 722–285.

Davies, C. T. (2019). This is abuse? Young women's perspectives of what's 'OK' and 'Not OK' in their intimate relationships. *Journal of Family Violence, 34*(5), 479–491.

Day, F. R., Helgason, H., Chasman, D. I., Rose, L. M., Loh, P. R., Scott, R. A., Helgason, A., Kong, A., Masson, G., Magnusson, O. T., Gudjartsson, D., Thorsteinsdottir, U., Buring, J. E., Ridker, P. M., Sulem, P., Stefansson, K., Ong, K. K., & Perry, J. R. B. (2016, April 18). Physical and neurobehavioral determinants of reproductive onset and success. *Nature Genetics*. Retrieved from doi:10.1038/ng.3551

Döring, N., & Pöschl, S. (2018). Sex toys, sex dolls, sex robots: Our under-researched bed-fellows. *Sexologies: European Journal of Sexology and Sexual Health, 27*(3), e51–e55.

Dosch, A., Belayachi, S., & Van der Linden, M. (2016). Implicit and explicit sexual attitudes: How are they related to sexual desire and sexual satisfaction? *Journal of Sex Research, 53*, 251–264.

Drouin, M., Jozkowski, K. N., Davis, J., & Newsham, G. (2019). How does alcohol consumption affect perceptions of one's own and a drinking partner's ability to consent to sexual activity. *The Journal of Sex Research, 56*, 740–753.

Dukes, E., & McGuire, B. E. (2009). Enhancing capacity to make sexuality-related decisions in people with an intellectual disability. *Journal of Intellectual Disability Research, 53*, 727–734.

Engelberg, A. (2016). Religious Zionist singles: Caught between "family values" and "young adulthood." *Journal for the Scientific Study of Religion, 55*, 349–364.

Fahs, B. (2016, May 30). Methodological mishaps and slippery subjects: Stories of first sex, oral sex, and sexual trauma in qualitative sex research. *Qualitative Psychology, 3*(2). Retrieved from http://dx.doi.org/10.1037/qup0000057

Fairbrother, N., Hart, T. A., & Fairbrother, M. (2019). Open relationship prevalence, characteristics, and correlates in a nationally representative sample of Canadian adults. *The Journal of Sex Research, 56*, 695–704.

Farivar, C. (2018). *Cybersex toy industry heats up as infamous "teledildonics" patent climaxes.* Retrieved from https://arstechnica.com/tech-policy/2018/08/cybersex-toy-industry-heats-up-as-infamous-teledildonics-patent-climaxes/

Farvid, P., & Braun V. (2017). Unpacking the "pleasures" and "pains" of heterosexual casual sex: Beyond singular understandings. *The Journal of Sex Research, 54*(1) 73–90.

Faustino, M. J. (2018). Rebooting an old script by new means: Teledildonics—The technological return to the 'Coital imperative'. *Sexuality & Culture, 22*(1), 243–257. Retrieved from doi: http://dx.doi.org.cyrano.ucmo.edu:2048/10.1007/s12119-017-9463-5

Fielder, R. L., Walsh, J. L., Carey, K. B., & Carey, M. P. (2014). Sexual hookups and adverse health outcomes: A longitudinal study of first-year college women. *The Journal of Sex Research, 51*, 131–144.

Frederick, D. A., Lever, J., Gillespie, B. J., & Garcia, J. R. (2017). What keeps passion alive? Sexual satisfaction is associated with sexual communication, mood setting, sexual variety, oral sex, orgasm, and sex frequency in a national U.S. study. *The Journal of Sex Research, 54*, 186–201.

Fulle, A., Chang, I. J., & Knox, D. (2016, Spring). Female sexual hedonism: Navigating stigma. *College Student Journal, 50*, 29–34. Previously presented as a research poster at the Southern Sociological Society. Updated 2019.

Galperin, A., Haselton, M. G., Frederick, D. A., Poore, J., Von Hippel, W., Buss, D. M., & Gonzaga, G. C. (2013). Sexual regret:

Evidence for evolved sex differences. *Archives of Sexual Behavior, 42*, 1145–1161.

Gesselman, A. N., Webster, G. D., & Garcia, J. R. (2017). Has virginity lost its virtue? Relationship stigma associated with being a sexually inexperienced adult. *The Journal of Sex Research, 54*, 202–213.

Goldstein, I., Kim, N., Clayton, A. H., DeRogatis, L. R., Giraldi, A., Parish, S. J., Pfaus, J., Simon, J. A., Kingsberg, S. A., Meston, C., Stahl, S. M., Wallen, K., & Worsley, R. (2017). Hypoactive sexual desire disorder. *Mayo Clinic Proceedings, 92*, 114–128. Retrieved from https://doi.org/10.1016/j.mayocp.2016.09.018

Gowen, K. L., & Winges-Yanez, N. (2014). Lesbian, gay, bisexual, transgender, queer and questioning youths' perspectives of inclusive school-based sexuality education. *Journal of Sex Research, 51*, 788–800.

Guo, Y. (2019). Sexual double standards in White and Asian Americans: Ethnicity, gender, and acculturation. *Sexuality and Culture, 23*, 57–95.

Gurevich, M., Brown-Bowers, A., Cosma, S., Vasilovsky, A. T., Leedham, U., & Cormier, N. (2017). Sexually progressive and proficient: pornographic syntax and postfeminist fantasies. *Sexualities, 20*, 558–584.

Guttmacher Institute. Sex and HIV Education (2018, May 1). State Laws and Policies.

Hackathorn, J., Ashdown, B., & Rife, S. (2016). The Sacred Bed: Sex guilt mediates religiosity and satisfaction for unmarried people. *Sexuality and Culture, 20*, 153–172.

Hall, S., & Knox, D. (2019). College Student Attitudes and Behaviors Survey of 13,070 undergraduates. Unpublished data collected for this text. Department of Family, Consumer, and Technology Education Teachers College, Ball State University and Department of Sociology, East Carolina University, Greenville, NC.

Hartley, H. (2006). *The 'Pinking' of Viagra culture: Repackage sex drugs for women*. Retrieved from https://doi.org/10.1177/1363460706065058

Hawes, Z. C., Wellings, K., & Stephenson, J. (2010). First heterosexual intercourse in the United Kingdom: A review of the literature. *Journal of Sex Research, 47*, 137–152.

Herbenick, D., Bartelt, E., Fu, T. C., Paul, B., Gradus, R., Bauer, J., & Jones, R. (2019). Feeling scared during sex: Findings from a U.S. probability sample of women and men ages 14 to 60. *Journal of Sex & Marital Therapy, 45*, 424–439.

Herbenick, D., Reece, M., Sanders, S. A., Dodge, B., Ghassemi, A., & Fortenberry, J. D. (2010). Women's vibrator use in sexual partnerships: Results from a nationally representative survey in the United States. *Journal of Sex & Marital Therapy, 36*, 49–65.

Hernandez, B. F., Peskin, M. F., Markham, C. M., Burr, J., Roberts, T., & Emery, S. T. (2018). The context of sexual decisions and intrapersonal factors related to sexual initiation among female military-dependent youth. *Journal of Sex Research, 55*, 73–83.

Heywood, W., Patrick, K., Pitts, M., & Mitchell, A. (2016). "Dude. . . I'm seventeen. . . It's okay not to have sex by this age": Adolescents who had not had sexual intercourse. *The Journal of Sex Research, 53*, 1207–1214.

Hill, C. A. (2016). Implicit and explicit sexual motives as related, but distinct characteristics. *Basic & Applied Social Psychology, 38*, 59–88.

Hilliard, T., Knox, D., & Brenner, R. (2019, March 12–17). *"This is how I like it": Association of feminist attitudes with sexual satisfaction*. Annual meeting of Eastern Sociological Society.

Horowitz, A. D., & Bedford, E. (2017). Graded structure in sexual definitions: Categorizations of having "had sex" and virginity

loss among homosexual and heterosexual men and women. *Archives of Sexual Behavior, 46*, 1653–1665.

Humphreys, T. P. (2013). Cognitive frameworks of virginity and first intercourse. *Journal of Sex Research, 50*, 664–675.

Ingraham, C. (2019). The share of Americans not having sex has reached a record high. *The Washington Post*. Retrieved from https://www.washingtonpost.com/business/2019/03/29/share-americans-not-having-sex-has-reached-record-high/?utm_term=.2115aeb8950d

Jolly, D. H., Mueller, M. P., Chen, M., Alston, L., Hawley, M., Okumu, E., Eley, T., Stancil, T., & MacQueen K. M. (2016). Concurrency and other sexual risk behaviors among black young adults in a southeastern city. *AIDS Education and Prevention, 28*, 59–76 https://doi.org/10.1521/aeap.2016.28.1.59

Jones, A. (2019). Sex is not a problem: The erasure of pleasure in sexual science research. *Sexualitie, 22*(4), 643–668.

Jones, D. N. (2016). The 'Chasing Amy' bias in past sexual experiences: Men can change, women cannot. *Sexuality & Culture, 20*, 24–37.

Jovanovic, J., & Williams, J. C. (2018). Gender, sexual agency and friends with benefits. *Sexuality & Culture, 22*, 555–576.

Julian, K. (2018, December). Why are young people having so little sex? *Atlantic Monthly*.

Kalata, D. & Bermea, A. M. (2019, Summer). Centering the experiences and needs of individuals in consensually nonmonogamous relationships in family science. *Family Focus*, F12-F13.

Kearney, M. S., & Levine, P. B. (2015). *Media influences on social outcomes: The impact of MTV's "16 and Pregnant" on teen childbearing*. Retrieved from https://www.nber.org/papers/w19795

Kim, H. S. (2016). Sexual debut and mental health among South Korean adolescents. *Journal of Sex Research, 53*, 313–320.

Kimberly, C. (2016). Permission to cheat: Ethnography of a Swingers' Convention. *Sexuality & Culture, 20*, 56–68.

Knox, D., Huff, S., & Chang, I. J. (2017). Sex dolls—Creepy or healthy?: Attitudes of undergraduates. *The Journal of Positive Sexuality, 3*(2), 32–37.

Kohut, T., Balzarini, R. N., & Fisher, W. A. (2018). Pornography's associations with open sexual communication and relationship closeness as a function of dyadic patterns of pornography use within heterosexual relationships. *Journal of Social & Personal Relationships, 35*, 655–676.

Montemurro, B. (2014). *Deserving desire: Women's stories of sexual evolution*. New Brunswick, NJ: Rutgers University Press.

Lefkowitz, E., & Wesche, R. (2014, November 8). *Sexual behavior patterns in romantic and nonromantic partnerships*. Paper presented at the Society for the Scientific Study of Sex annual meeting, Omaha, NE.

Levin, D. (2016). *Learning from adults: Exploring the role of teachers in school-based sex education*. Paper presented at Society for the Scientific Study of Sexuality, Phoenix, AZ.

Mark, K. P., Okhotnikov, I. A., & Wood, N. D. (2016, November 4). *Dyadic analyses of couples' daily reports of feeling love and sexual satisfaction*. Poster presented at a conference of the National Council on Family Relations.

Maas, M. K., Vasilenko, S. A., & Willoughby, B. J. (2018). A dyadic approach to pornography use and relationship satisfaction among heterosexual couples: The role of pornography acceptance and anxious attachment. *Journal of Sex Research, 55*, 772–782. Retrieved from https://doi.org/10.1080/00224499.2018.1440281

Masters, W. H., & Johnson, V. E. (1970). *Human sexual inadequacy*. Boston, MA: Little, Brown.

Maxwell, J. A., Muise, A., MacDonald, G., Day, L. C., Rosen, N. O., & Impett, E. A. (2017). How implicit theories of sexuality shape sexual and relationship well-being. *Journal of Personality & Social Psychology, 112*, 238–279.

McKeown, J. K. L., Parry, D., & Penny Light, T. (2018). "My iphone changed my life": How digital technologies can enable women's consumption of online sexually explicit materials. *Sexuality & Culture, 22*(2), 340–354.

Merrill, J., & Knox, D. (2010). *Finding love from 9 to 5: Secrets of office romance.* Santa Barbara, CA: Praeger.

Michael, R. T., Gagnon, J. H., Laumann, E. O., & Kolata, G. (1994). *Sex in America.* Boston, MA: Little, Brown.

Mintz, L. (2017). *Cliteracy.* New York: Harper One.

Molinares, C., Kolobova, I., & Knox, D. (2017). Anal sexual practices among undergraduate students. *Journal of Positive Sexuality, 3*, 21–35.

Morales, E., Gauthier, V., Edwards, G., Courtois, F., Lamontagne, A., & Guérette, A. (2018). Co-designing sex toys for adults with motor disabilities. *Sexuality & Disability, 36*(1), 47–68. Retrieved from https://doi-org.cyrano.ucmo.edu/10.1007/s11195-017-9506-8

Morris, H., I. J., Chang, I. J., & Knox, D. (2016, April). *Threesomes: Data on negotiation and engagement.* Poster presented at the Southern Sociological Society, Atlanta, GA.

Moser, A. (2019). *The influence of cannabis on sexual functioning and satisfaction.* Thesis, Department of Human Development and Family Science, East Carolina University, Greenville, NC.

Muise, A., Boudreau, G. K., & Rosen, N. O. (2017a). Seeking a connection versus avoiding disappointment: An experimental manipulation of approach and avoidance sexual goals and the implications of desire and satisfaction. *Journal of Sex Research, 54*, 296–307.

Muise, A., Kim, J. J., Impett, E. A., & Rosen, N. O. (2017b.) Understanding when a partner is not in the mood: Sexual communal strength in couples transitioning to parenthood. *Archives of Sexual Behavior, 46*(7), 1993–2006.

Muise, A., Schimmack, U., & Impett, E. A. (2015). Sexual frequency predicts greater well-being, but more is not always better. *Social Psychological and Personality Service.* Published online Nov 18.

Muise, A., Maxwell, J. A., & Impett, E. A. (2018). What theories and methods from relationship research can contribute to sex research. *Journal of Sex Research, 55* (4/5), 540–562.

Nagao, K., Tai, T., Saigo, R., Kimura, M., Ozaki, Y., Tanaka, N., Kobayashi, H., & Nakajima, K. (2014). Gaps between actual and desired sex life: Web survey of 5,665 Japanese women. *Journal of Sex & Marital Therapy, 40*, 33–42.

Netting, N. S., & Reynolds, M. K. (2018). Thirty years of sexual behavior at a Canadian university: Romantic relationships, hooking up, and sexual choices. *Canadian Journal of Human Sexuality, 27*, 55–68.

Olmstead, S. B., Davis, K. N., Treadway, K. M., & Anders, K. M. (2018, November 8). *Sex and commitment among college-attending and non-college emerging adults.* Paper presented at the annual meeting at the National Council on Family Relations, San Diego, CA.

Paik, A., K. Sanchagrin, K. J., & Heimer, K. (2016). Broken promises: Abstinence pledging and sexual and reproductive health. *Journal of Marriage & Family, 78*, 546–561.

Palmer, M. J., Clarke, L., Ploubidis, G. B., Mercer, C. H., Gibson, L. J., Johnson, A. M., Copas, A. J., & Wellings, W. (2017). Is "sexual competence" at first heterosexual intercourse associated with subsequent sexual health status? *The Journal of Sex Research, 54*, 91–104.

Peasant, C., Parra, G. R., & Okwumabua, T. M.(2014). Condom negotiation: Findings and future directions. *The Journal of Sex Research.* Retrieved from doi: 10.1080/00224499.2013.868861

Perry, S. L., & Whitehead, A. L. (2019). Only bad for believers? Religion, pornography use and sexual satisfaction among American men. *The Journal of Sex Research, 56*, 50–61.

Perry, S. L., & Schleifer, C. (2018). Till porn do us part? A longitudinal examination of pornography use and divorce. *Journal of Sex Research, 55*, 284–296.

Porter, N. (2014, April 4). *The effects of the sexual double standard on the perceptions of college students towards themselves and their peers.* Paper presented at the Southern Sociological Society annual meeting, Charlotte, NC.

Quinn-Nilas, C., & Kennett, D. J. (2018). Reasons why undergraduate women comply with unwanted, non-coercive sexual advances: A serial indirect effect model integrating sexual script theory and sexual self-control perspectives. *Journal of Social Psychology, 158*, 603–615.

Regnerus, M., Price, J., & Gordon, D. (2017). Masturbation and partnered sex: Substitutes or complements? *Archives of Sexual Behavior, 46*, 2111–2121.

Rosenkrantz, D. E., & Mark, K. P. (2018). The sociocultural context of sexually diverse women's sexual desire. *Sexuality & Culture, 22*, 220–242.

Rosier, J. G., & Tyler, J. M. (2017). Finding the love guru in you: Examining the effectiveness of a sexual communication training program for married couples. *Marriage & Family Review, 53*, 65–87.

Rossi, E., Poulin, F., & Boislard, M. A. (2017). Trajectories of annual number of sexual partners from adolescence to emerging adulthood: Individual and family predictors. *Journal of Youth & Adolescence, 46*, 995–1008.

Rullo, J. E., Lorenz, T., Ziegelmann, M. J., Meihofer, L., Herbenick, D., & Faubion, S. S. (2018). Genital vibration for sexual function and enhancement: a review of evidence. *Sexual & Relationship Therapy, 33*(3), 263–274. Retrieved from https://doi-org.cyrano.ucmo.edu/10.1080/14681994.2017.141955

Sandberg-Thoma, S. E., & Kamp Dush, C. M. (2014). Casual sexual relationships and mental health in adolescence and emerging adulthood. *Journal of Sex Research, 51*(2), 121–130.

Santelli, J. S., Kantor, M., Grilo, S. A., Speizer, I. S., Lindberg, L. D., Heitel, J., Schalet, A. T., Lyon, M. E., Mason-Jones, A. J., McGovern, T., Heck, C. J., Rogers, J., & Ott, M. A. (2017). Abstinence-only-until-marriage: An updated review of U.S policies and programs and their impact. *Journal of Adolescent Health, 61*, 273–280.

Sassler, S., Michelmore, K., & Holland, J. A. (2016). The progression of sexual relationships, *Journal of Marriage & Family, 78*, 587–597.

Satinsky, S., & Jozkowski, K. N. (2015). Female sexual subjectivity and verbal consent to receiving oral sex. *The Journal of Sex & Marital Therapy, 41*, 413–426.

Scimeca, G., Bruno, A., Pandolfo, G., Micò, U., Romeo, V. M., Avenavoli, E., Schimmenti, A., Zoccali, R., & Muscatello, M. R. (2013). Alexithymia, negative emotions, and sexual behavior in heterosexual university students from Italy. *Archives of Sexual Behavior, 42*, 117–127.

Smith, M. B., & Trapp, P. (2017, February). Good sex = happy family. Plum Organics Survey, *USA Today*, 1A.

Sohn, K. (2016). Men's revealed preferences regarding women's promiscuity. *Personality and Individual Differences, 95*, 140–146.

Soller, B., Haynie, D. L., & Kuhlemeier, A. (2017). Sexual intercourse, romantic relationship inauthenticity, and adolescent mental health. *Social Science Research, 64*, 237–248.

Sprecher, S., & Treger, S. (2015). Virgin college students' reasons for and reactions to their abstinence from sex: Results from a 23-year study at a midwestern U.S. university. *Journal of Sex Research, 52*, 936–948.

Stahl, M., K. A., Gale, J., Lewis, D. C., & Kleiber, D. (2018). Sex after divorce: Older adult women's reflections. *Journal of Gerontological Social Work, 61*, 659–674.

Starr, P. (2018, Spring). *Polyamory.* Presentation, Sociology of Human Sexuality, Department of Sociology, East Carolina University, Greenville, NC.

Stein, J. B., Mongeau, P., Posteher, K., & Veluscek, A. (2019, May). Netflix and chill? Exploring and refining differing motivations in friends with benefits relationships. *The Canadian Journal of Human Sexuality*, Advance online.

Stulhofer, A., Traeen, B., & Carvalheira, A. (2013). Job-related strain and sexual health difficulties among heterosexual men from three European countries: The role of culture and emotional support. *Journal of Sexual Medicine, 10*, 747–756.

Sun, W. H., Miu, H. Y. H., Wong, C. K. H., Tucker, J. D., & Wong, W. C. W. (2018). Assessing participation and effectiveness of the peer-led approach in youth sexual health education: Systematic review and meta-analysis in more developed countries. *Journal of Sex Research, 55*, 31–44.

Suschinsky, K. D., & Chivers, M. L. (2018). The relationship between sexual concordance and orgasm consistency in women. *Journal of Sex Research, 55*, 704–718.

Swan, D. J., & Thompson, S. C. (2016). Monogamy, the protective fallacy: Sexual versus emotional exclusivity and the implication for sexual health risk. *Journal of Sex Research, 53*, 64–73.

Thomsen, D., & Chang, I. J. (2000, November). *Predictors of satisfaction with first intercourse: A new perspective for sexuality education.* Poster presented at the 62nd Annual Conference of the National Council on Family Relations, Minneapolis, MN.

Trinh, S. L. (2016). Enjoy your sexuality, but do it in secret. *Psychology of Women Quarterly, 40*, 96–107.

True Love Waits. (2018). Retrieved from https://www.lifeway .com/en/product-family/true-love-waits.

Van de Bongardt, D., Reitz, E., & Dekovic, M. (2016). Indirect over-time relations between parenting and adolescents' sexual behaviors and emotions through global self-esteem. *Journal of Sex Research, 53*, 273–285.

Vannier, S. A., & O'Sullivan, L. F. (2010). Sex without desire: Characteristics of occasions of sexual compliance in young adults' committed relationships. *Journal of Sex Research, 47*, 429–439.

Vasilenko, S. A., Lefkowitz, E. S., & Maggs, J. L. (2012). Short-term positive and negative consequences of sex based on daily reports among college students. *Journal of Sex Research, 49*, 558–569.

Vazonyi, A. I., & Jenkins, D. D. (2010). Religiosity, self-control, and virginity status in college students from the "Bible belt": A research note. *Journal for the Scientific Study of Sex, 49*, 561–568.

Vencill, J., & Christopher, S. (2014, Nov. 7). *"It doesn't matter what I'm wearing": Four perspectives on a qualitative research project examining slutwalk.* Presentation at the annual meeting of the Society for the Scientific Study of Sex. Omaha, NE.

Walsh, S. (2013). *Match's 2012 singles in America survey.* Retrieved from http://www.hookingupsmart.com/2013/ 02/07/hookingupreality/matchs-2012-singles-in America-survey

Willoughby, B. J., Carroll, J. S., & Busby, D. M. (2014). Differing relationship outcomes when sex happens before, on, or after first dates. *The Journal of Sex Research, 51*, 52–61.

Woertman, L., & F. Van den Brink, F. (2012). Body image and female sexual functioning and behavior: A review. *Journal of Sex Research, 49*, 184–211.

Wolfinger, N. (2018, October 22). Does sexual history affect marital happiness? Institute for Family Studies, Retrieved from https://ifstudies.org/blog/does-sexual-history-affect-marital-happiness

Woo, J. T., Brotto, L. A., & Gorzalka, B. B. (2012). The relationship between sex guild and sexual desire in a community sample of Chinese and Euro-Canadian woman. *The Journal of Sex Research, 49*, 290–298.

Wood, J. R., McKay, A., Komarnicky, T., & Milhausen, R. R. (2016). Was it good for you too? An analysis of gender differences in oral sex practices and pleasure ratings among heterosexual Canadian university students. *Canadian Journal of Human Sexuality, 25*, 21–29.

Wright, P. J., Randall, A. K., & Hayes, J. G. (2012). Predicting the condom assertiveness of collegiate females in the United States from the expanded health belief model. *International Journal of Sexual Health, 24*, 137–153.

CHAPTER 10

Aadnanes, M., & Gulbrandsen, L. M. (2018). Young people and young adults' experiences with child abuse and maltreatment: Meaning making conceptualizations and dealing with violence. *Qualitative Social Work, 17*, 594–610.

Agarwal, P. (2019, February 18). In the era of #Metoo are men scared of mentoring women? *Forbes.*

Ahmadabadi, Z., Najman, J. M., Williams, G. M., Clavarion, A. M., d'Abbs, P., & Smirnov, A. (2019). Intimate partner violence in emerging adulthood and subsequent use disorders: findings from a longitudinal study. *Addiction, 114*, 1264–1273

Alvarez, C., Debnam, K., Clough, A., Alexander, K., & Glass, N. E. (2018). Responding to intimate partner violence: Healthcare providers' current practices and views on integrating a safety decision aid into primary care settings. *Research in Nursing and Health, 41*(2), 145–155. Retrieved from DOI: 10.1002/nur.21853

Alvarez-Alonso, M. J., Jurado-Barba, R., Martinez-Martin, N., Espin-Jaime, J. C., Bolanos-Porrero, C., Ordonez-Franco, A., Rodriguez-Lopez, J. A., Lora-Pablos, D., de la Cruz-Bertolo, J., & Jimenez-Arriero, M. A. (2016). Association between maltreatment and polydrug use among adolescents. *Child Abuse & Neglect, 51*, 379–389.

Armenti, N. A., & J Babcock, J. C. (2016, April). Conjoint treatment for intimate partner violence: A systematic review and implications. *Couple and Family Psychology: Research and Practice, 5*(2), 109–123.

Bennhold, K. (2019, January 27). Another side of #MeToo: Male managers fearful of mentoring women. *New York Times.*

Bierie, D. M., & Budd, K. M. (2016). Romeo, Juliet and statutory rape. *Sexual Abuse, 30*(3), 296–321. Retrieved from https:// doi.org/10.1177/1079063216658451

Blag, E. C. (2018, September 27). Can you give sexual consent using an App? *USA Today*, B1.

Bromwich, J. E. (2019, January 19). Why do we hurt robots? *New York Times.*

Buvik, K., & Baklien, B. (2016). "Girls will be served until you have to carry them out": Gendered serving practices in Oslo. *Addiction Research & Theory, 24*, 17–24.

Camperio Ciani, A. S., & Fontanesi, L. (2012). Mothers who kill their offspring: Testing evolutionary hypothesis in a 110-case Italian sample. *Child Abuse & Neglect, 36*, 519–527.

Cecil, C. A. M., Viding, E., Fearon, P., Glaser, D., & McCrory, E. J. (2017). Disentangling the mental health impact of childhood abuse and neglect. *Child Abuse & Neglect, 63*, 106–119.

Centers for Disease Control and Prevention. (2016). *The National Intimate Partner and Sexual Violence Survey*. Retrieved from http://www.cdc.gov/violenceprevention/nisvs/index.html

Chatterjee, R., Doerfler, P., Orgad, H., Havron, S., Palmer, J., Freed, D., Levy, K., Dell, N., McCoy, D., & Ristenpart, T. (2018). The spyware used in intimate partner violence. *IEEE Symposium on Security and Privacy*. Retrieved from https://www.ipvtechresearch.org/pubs/spyware.pdf

Cho, H., & Huang, L. (2017). Aspects of help seeking among collegiate victims of dating violence. *Journal of Family Violence, 32*(4), 409–417.

Choenni, V., Hammink, A., & van de Mheen, D. (2017). Association between substance use and perpetuation of family violence in industrialized countries. *Trauma, Violence & Abuse, 18*, 37–50.

Cohn, A., Zinzow, H. M., Resnick, H. S., & Kilpatrick, D. G. (2013). Correlates of reasons for not reporting rape to police: Results from a national telephone household probability sample of women with forcible or drug-or-alcohol facilitated/incapacitated rape. *Journal of Interpersonal Violence, 28*, 455–473.

Cravens, J. D., Whiting, J. B., & Aamar R. O. (2015, November 13). *Why I stayed/left: An analysis of voices of intimate partner violence on social media*. Paper presented at the National Council on Family Relations annual meeting, Vancouver, British Columbia, CN.

Cunha, O. S., & Goncalves, R. A. (2016). Severe and less severe intimate partner violence: From characterization to prediction. *Violence and Victims, 31*, 235–250.

Daar, D. A., Abdou, S., Wilson, S. C., Hazen, A., & Saadeh, P. B. (2019). "A call to action for male surgeons in the wake of the #MeToo Movement"- Mentor female students. *Annals of Surgery, 20*, 1–3

Dardis, C. M., & Gidycz, C. A. (2017). The frequency and perceived impact of engaging in in-person and cyber unwanted pursuit after relationship break-up among college men and women. *Sex Roles, 76*, 56–72.

Dardis, C. M., Strauss, C. V., & Gidycz, C. A. (2019). The psychological toll of unwanted pursuit behaviors and intimate partner violence on undergraduate women: A dominance analysis. *Psychology of Violence, 9*(2), 209–220.

Davies, C. T. (2019). This is abuse?: Young women's perspectives of what's 'OK' and 'Not OK' in their intimate relationships. *Journal of Family Violence, 34*(5), 479–491.

De Smet, O., Uzieblo, K., Loeys, T., Buysse, A., & Onraedt, T. (2015). Behavior after breakup: occurrence, risk factors, and gender differences. *Journal of Family Violence, 30*(6), 753–767.

Dorahy, M. J., Middleton, W., Seager, L., Williams, M., & Chambers, R. (2016). Child abuse and neglect in complex dissociative disorder, abuse-related chronic PTSD, and mixed psychiatric samples. *Journal of Trauma and Dissociation, 17*, 223–236.

Drouin, M., Jozkowski, K. N., Davis, J., & Newsham, G. (2019). How does alcohol consumption affect perceptions of one's own and a drinking partner's ability to consent to sexual activity? *The Journal of Sex Research, 56*, 740–753

Easton, S. D., & Kong, J. (2017). Mental health indicators fifty years later: A population-based study of men with histories of child sexual abuse. *Child Abuse & Neglect, 63*, 273–283.

Eckenrode, J., Campa, M. I., Morris, P. A., Henderson Jr., C. R., Bolger, K. E., Kitzman, H., & Olds, D. L. (2017). The prevention of child maltreatment through the nurse family partnership program: Mediating effects in a long-term follow-up study. *Child Maltreatment, 22*, 92–99.

Eggett, K. N., & Irvin, M. (2016, April 16). *Sexual violence prevention programs: A meta-analysis*. Poster presented at the Southern Sociological Society annual meeting, Atlanta, GA.

Eke, A., Hilton, N., Harris, G., Rice, M., & Houghton, R. (2011). Intimate partner homicide: Risk assessment and prospects for prediction. *Journal of Family Violence, 26*, 211–216.

Elmquist, J., C. Wolford-Clevenger, C., Zapor, H., Febres, J., Shorey, R. C., Hamel, J., & Stuart, G. L. (2016). A gender comparison of motivations for physical dating violence among college students. *Journal of Interpersonal Violence, 31*, 186–203.

Engel, L. S., Crosson, J., Spencer, C., & Stith, S. (2016, November 3). *Sexual coercion among college students in dating relationships*. Poster, Annual meeting of the National Council on Family Relations, Minneapolis, MN.

Fedina, L., Holmes, J. L., & Backes, B. L. (2018). Campus sexual assault: A systematic review of prevalence from 2000 to 2015. *Trauma, Violence & Abuse, 19*, 76–93.

Foshee, V. A., Gottfredson, N. C., Reyes, H. L. M., Chen, M. S., David-Ferdon, C., Latzman, N. E., Tharp, A. T., & Ennett, S. T. (2016, April). Developmental outcomes of using physical violence against dates and peers. *Journal of Adolescent Health, 58*, 665–671.

Fox, J. A. (2017). Gender differences in patterns and trends in U.S. homicide, 1976–2015. *Violence and Gender, 4*, 37–43.

Freed, D., Palmer, J., Minchala, D., Levy, K., Ristenpart, T., & Dell. (2018). *A stalker's paradise: How intimate partner abusers exploit technology*. Conference Proceedings of the 2018 Conference on Human Factors in Computing Systems. Retrieved from https://www.ipvtechresearch.org/pubs/a046-freed.pdf

French, B. H., Suh H. N., & Arterberry, B. (2017) Explanatory factor analysis and psychometric properties of the Sexual Coercion Inventory. *The Journal of Sex Research, 54*, 962–970.

Gershoff, G. T., & Grogan-Kaylor, A. (2016). Spanking and child outcomes: Old controversies and new meta-analyses. *Journal of Family Psychology*. Retrieved from doi:10.1037/fam0000191

Gibson, R. (2018). Tech Summit 2018 Recap. *Safety Net Project*. Retrieved from https://www.techsafety.org/

Gil, A. P. M., Kislaya, I., Santos, A. J., Nunes, B., Nicolau, R., & Fernandes, A. A. (2015). Elder abuse in Portugal: Findings from the first national prevalence study. *Journal of Elder Abuse & Neglect, 27*, 174–195.

Gill, R., & Orgad, S. (2018). The shifting terrain of sex and power: From the 'sexualization of culture' to #MeToo. *Sexualities, 21*, 1313–1324.

Green, A. E., Trott, E., Willgling, C. E., Finn, N. K., Ehrhart, M. G., & Aarons, G. A. (2016). The role of collaborations in sustaining an evidence-based intervention to reduce child neglect. *Child Abuse and Neglect, 53*, 4–16.

Green, E. L. (2018, July 29). New U.S. sexual misconduct rules bolster rights of accused and protect colleges. *The New York Times*. Retrieved from https://www.nytimes.com/2018/08/29/us/politics/devos-campus-sexual-assault.html

Guadalupe-Diaz, X. L., & Anthony, A. K. (2017). Discrediting identity work: Understandings of intimate partner violence by transgender survivors. *Deviant Behavior, 38*, 1–16.

Herbenick, D., Bartlett, E., Fu, T. C., Paul, B., Gradus, R., Bauer, J. & Jones, R. (2019). Feeling scared during sex: Findings from a U.S. probability sample of women and men ages 14 to 60. *Journal of Sex & Marital Therapy, 45*, 424–439.

Hall, M. & Hearn, J. (2019) Revenge pornography and manhood acts: a discourse analysis of perpetrators' accounts. *Journal of Gender Studies, 28*, 158–170.

Hall, S., & Knox, D. (2019). College Student Attitudes and Behaviors Survey of 13,069 undergraduates. Unpublished data collected for this text. Department of Family, Consumer, and Technology Education Teachers College, Ball State University and Department of Sociology, East Carolina University, Greenville, NC.

Hall, S., & Knox, D. (2012). Double victims: Sexual coercion by a dating partner and a stranger. *Journal of Aggression, Maltreatment & Trauma, 22*, 145–158.

Haelle, T. (2018). Sibling abuse more common than child, domestic abuse combined. *Clinical Psychiatry News.*

Hames, S. E., Herman, J. L., Rankin, S., Keisling, M., Mottet, L., & Anafi, M. (2016). *The Report of the 2015 U.S. Transgender Survey.* Retrieved from http://www.transequality.org/sites/default/files/docs/USTS-Full-Report-FINAL.PDF

Hayes, B., Freilich, J., & Chermak, S. (2016). An exploratory study of honor crimes in the United States. *Journal of Family Violence, 31*, 303–314.

Hellmann, D. F., Stiller, A., Glaubitz, C., & Kliem, S. (2018). (Why) do victims become perpetrators? Intergenerational transmission of parental violence in a representative German sample. *Journal of Family Psychology, 32*, 282–288.

Henry, N., & Powell, A. (2018). Technology-facilitated sexual violence: a literature review of empirical research. *Trauma, Violence, & Abuse, 19*, 195–208.

Hjelmgaard, K. (2018, November 27). 137 women a day killed by family, U.N. study says. *USA Today*, 3 A.

Ho, G. W. K., Gross, D. A., & Bettencourt, A. (2017). Universal mandatory reporting policies and the odds of identifying child physical abuse. *American Journal of Public Health, 107*, 709–716.

Holmes, M. R., Richter, F. G. C., Votruba, M. E., Berg, K. A., & Bender. A. E. (2018). Economic burden of child exposure to intimate partner violence in the United States. *Journal of Family Violence, 33*, 239–249.

Ioannou, M., Hammond, L., & Machin, L. (2017). Male-on-male sexual assault: Victim, offender and offence characteristics. *Journal of Investigative Psychology & Offender Profiling, 14*(2), 189–209. Retrieved from https://doi.org/10.1002/jip.1483

Jacobsen, N., & Gottman, J. (2007). *When men batter women: New insights into ending abusive relationships.* New York: Simon & Schuster.

Javaid, A. (2018). Theorising vulnerability and male sexual victimization. *Australian & New Zealand Journal of Criminology, 51*, 454–470.

Kelman, B. (2018, January 21). Hundreds of journals found in California home. *USA Today*, 4T.

Kennedy, T., & Ceballo, R. (2016). Emotionally numb: Desensitization to community violence exposure among urban youth. *Developmental Psychology, 52*, 778–789.

Kimuna, S., Tenkorang, E. Y., & Djamba, Y. (2018). Ethnicity and intimate partner violence. *Journal of Family Issues, 39*, 2958–2981.

Klipfel, K. M., Claxton, S. E., & Van Dulmen, M. H. M. (2014). Interpersonal aggression victimization within casual sexual relationships and experiences. *Journal of Interpersonal Violence, 29*, 557–569.

Knox, B. (2018). Screening women for intimate partner violence: Creating proper practice habits. *Nurse Practitioner, 43*(5), 14–20.

Knox, D., & Hilliard, T. (2019, November). *The #MeToo Movement: Have we gone too far?* Roundtable, Annual meeting of the Society for the Scientific Study of Sex, Denver, CO.

Koon-Magnin, S., & Schulze, C. (2019). Providing and receiving sexual assault disclosures: Findings from a sexually diverse sample of young adults. *Journal of Interpersonal Violence, 34*(2), 416–441. Retrieved from https://doi-org.cyrano.ucmo.edu/10.1177/0886260516641280

LaMotte, A. D., Meis, L. A., Winters, J. J., Barry, R. A., & Murphy, C. M. (2018). Relationship problems among men in treatment for engaging in intimate partner violence. *Journal of Family Violence, 33*, 75–82.

Lee, M. S., Begun, S., DePrince, A. P., & Chu, A. T. (2016, April 11). Acceptability of dating violence and expectations of relationship harm among adolescent girls exposed to intimate partner violence. *Psychological Trauma: Theory, Research, Practice, and Policy.* Retrieved from http://dx.doi.org/10.1037/tra0000130

Li, Y., Long, Z., Cao, D., & Cao, F. (2017). Maternal history of child maltreatment and maternal depression risk in the perinatal period: A longitudinal study. *Child Abuse & Neglect, 63*, 192–201.

Lin, X., Li, L., Chi, P., Wang, Z., Heath, M. A., Du, H., & Fang, Z. (2016). Child maltreatment and interpersonal relationships among Chinese children with oppositional defiant disorder. *Child Abuse & Neglect, 51*, 192–202.

Liu, W., Mumford, E. A., & Taylor, B. G. (2018). The relationship between parents' intimate partner victimization and youths' adolescent relationship abuse. *Journal of Youth & Adolescence, 47*, 321–333.

Lorber, M. F., & Slep, A. M. S. (2018). The reliability paradox of the parent-child conflict tactics corporal punishment subscale, *Journal of Family Psychology, 32*, 145–150.

Maharaj, N. (2017). Perspectives on treating couples impacted by intimate partner violence. *Journal of Family Violence, 32* (4), 431–437.

Marcum, C., Higgins, G., & Nicholson, J. (2017). I'm watching you: Cyberstalking behaviors of university students in romantic relationships. *American Journal of Criminal Justice, 42*, 373–383.

Marcus, R. E. (2012). Patterns of intimate partner violence in young adult couples: Nonviolent, unilaterally violent, and mutually violent couples, *Violence & Victims, 27*, 299–314.

Maxouris, C., & Ahmed, S. (2018). *Only 8 states require sex education classes to mention consent.* Retrieved from https://www.cnn.com/2018/09/29/health/sex-education-consent-in-public-schools-trnd/index.html

Maxwell, K., Callahan, J., Ruggero, C., & Janis, B. (2016). Breaking the cycle: Association of attending therapy following childhood abuse and subsequent perpetration of violence. *Journal of Family Violence, 31*, 251–258.

McElvaney, R., Greene, S., & Hogan, D. (2014). To tell or not to tell? Factors influencing young people's informal disclosures of child sexual abuse. *Journal of Interpersonal Violence, 29*, 928–947.

Miller, J. D., Zeichner, A., & Wilson, L. F. (2012). Personality correlates of aggression: Evidence from measures of the five-factor model, UPPS model of impulsivity, and BIS/BAS. *Journal of Interpersonal Violence, 27*, 2903–2919.

Monroe, D. (2019, February 6). *kNOw MORE: A journey of rape prevention.* Presentation, Human Sexuality class, East Carolina University, Greenville, NC.

Moser, A., & Ballard, S. (2017, April 5). *Rape myth acceptance among ECU students.* Poster presented at Research and Creative Week. East Carolina University, Greenville, NC.

Muehlenhard, C. L., Peterson, S. D., Humphreys, T. P., & Jozkowski, K. N. (2017). Evaluating the one-in-five statistic: Women's risk of sexual assault while in college. *The Journal of Sex Research, 54*, 549–576.

Murray, C. E., King, K., & Crowe, A. (2016). Understanding and addressing teen dating violence. *Family Journal, 24*, 52–59.

Murray, C. E., Crowe, A., & Flasch, P. (2015). Turning points: Critical incidents prompting survivors to begin the process of terminating abusive relationships. *Family Journal, 23*, 228–238.

Mustapha, A., & Muehlenhard, C. (2014). *Women's and men's reactions to being sexually coerced: A quantitative and qualitative analysis.* Poster session presented at the annual meeting of the Society for the Scientific Study of Sexuality, Omaha, NE.

Nash, C. L., Hayes-Skelton, S. A., & DiLillo, D. (2012). Reliability and factor structure of the psychological maltreatment and neglect scales of the computer assisted maltreatment inventory (CAMI). *Journal of Aggression, Maltreatment & Trauma, 21*, 583–607.

National Network to End Domestic Violence (2018). *Tech abuse: Information from the field.* Retrieved from Survey Findings from the Conference on Crimes Against Women file:///Users/queen/Downloads/2018-09-10-+TAS+GAN+CCAW+Summary.pdf

Negash, S., Cravens, J., Brown, P. C., & Fincham, F. D. (2016). Relationship dissolution and psychologically aggressive dating relationships: Preliminary findings from a college-based relationship education course. *Violence & Victims, 31*, 921–937.

Nybergh, L., Enander, V., & Krantz, G. (2016). Theoretical considerations on men's experiences of intimate partner violence: An interview-based study. *Journal of Family Violence, 31*, 191–202.

O'Brien, C., Keith, J., & Shoemaker, L. (2016). Don't tell: Military culture and male rape. *Psychological Services, 12*, 357–365.

O'Leary, P., Easton, S. D., & Gould, N. (2017). The effect of child sexual abuse on men: Toward a male sensitive measure. *Journal of Interpersonal Violence, 32*, 423–445.

O'Leary, D. K., Foran, H., & Cohen, S. (2013). Validation of fear of partner scale. *Journal of Marital and Family Therapy, 39*, 502–514.

Oriola, T. B. (2017). "Unwilling Cocoons": Boko Haram's war against women. *Studies in Conflict & Terrorism, 40*, 99–121.

Parasidis, E., & Opel, D. J. (2017). Parental refusal of childhood vaccines and medical neglect laws. *American Journal of Public Health, 107*, 68–71.

Perkins, N. H., & O'Connor, M. K. (2016). Physical and emotional sibling violence: A necessary role for social work. *Social Work, 61*, 91–93.

Peterson, C. M., Peugh, J., Loucks, L., & Shaffer, A. (2018). Emotional maltreatment in family of origin and young adult romantic relationship satisfaction: A dyadic analysis. *Journal of Social and Personal Relationships, 35*, 872–888.

Prinz, R. (2016). Parenting and family support within a broad child abuse prevention strategy: Child maltreatment prevention can benefit from public health strategies. *Child Abuse & Neglect, 51*, 400–406.

Proquest Statistical Abstract of the United States. (2019). Online Edition. Bethesda, MD. Retrieved from https://www.proquest.com/products-services/statabstract.html

Roddy, M. K., Georgia, E. J., & Doss, B. D. (2018). Couples with intimate partner violence seeking relationship help: Associations and implications for self-help and online interventions. *Family Process, 57*, 293–307.

Romero-Martinez, Lila, A. M., & Moya-Albiol, L. (2016). Empathy impairments in intimate partner violence perpetrators with antisocial and borderline traits: A key factor in the risk of recidivism. *Violence & Victims, 31*, 347–360.

Rothman, E. F., Exner, D., & Baughman, A. L. (2011). The prevalence of sexual assault against people who identify as gay, lesbian, or bisexual in the United States: A systematic review. *Violence & Abuse, 12*, 55–66.

Russell, B., Kraus, S. W., Chapleau, K. M., & Oswald, D. (2019). Perceptions of blame in intimate partner violence: The role of the perpetrator's ability to arouse fear of injury in the victim. *Journal of Interpersonal Violence, 34(5)*, 1089–1097.

Sandberg, S., & Pritchard, M. (2019, May 17). The number of men who are uncomfortable mentoring women is growing. *Fortune Magazine.*

Salem, S. (2019, Jan. 29). What happens when men are too afraid to mentor women? Ripple effect of #MeToo that women did not ask for: fewer champions. *New York Times.*

Satyanarayana, V. A., Nattala, P., Selvam, S., Pradeep, J., Hebbani, S., Hegde, S., & K. Srinivasan, K. (2016). Integrated cognitive behavioral intervention reduces intimate partner violence among alcohol dependent men, and improves mental health outcomes in their spouses: A clinic based randomized controlled trial from South India. *Journal of Substance Abuse Treatment, 64*, 29–34.

Sell, N. M., Turrisi, R., Scaglione, N. M., Cleveland, M. J., & Mallett, K. A. (2018). Alcohol consumption and use of sexual assault and drinking protective behavioral strategies. *Psychology of Women Quarterly, 42*, 62–71.

Shepard, M. F., & Campbell, J. A. (1992). The Abusive Behavior Inventory: A measure of psychological and physical abuse. *Journal of Interpersonal Violence, 7(3)*, 291–305.

Shorey, R. C., Febres, J., Brasfield, H., &. Stuart, G. L. (2012, August 12). The prevalence of mental health problems in men arrested for domestic violence. *Journal of Family Violence.* Retrieved from doi: 10.1007/s10896-012-9463-z http://www.springerlink.com.jproxy.lib.ecu.edu/content/0g67243666512182/fulltext.pdf

Smeaton, G., & Anderson, P. (2014, November 7). *Gender majority status and tactics used to gain sex from a reluctant partner.* Paper presented at the Society for the Scientific Study of Sex annual meeting, Omaha, NE.

Smith, E., Dominguez, M., Cafferky, B., Spencer, C., & Stith, S. (2014, November). *Military/civilian risk markers for IPV: A meta-analysis.* Paper presented at National Council on Family Relations, annual meeting, Baltimore, MD.

Snowdon, W. (2017). Cyber revenge: Faking dating profiles make woman target of late-night visitors. *CBC.* Retrieved from https://www.cbc.ca/news/canada/edmonton/cyber-revenge-fake-dating-profiles-make-woman-target-of-late-night-visitors-1.4129508

Soklaridis, S., Zahn, C., Kuper, A., Gillis, D., Taylor V. H., & Whitehead C. (2018). Men's fear of mentoring in the #MeToo Era — What's at stake for academic medicine? *The New England Journal of Medicine, 379*, 2270–2274

Soliman, H. H, Alsharqawi, N. I., & Younis, M. A. (2018). Is tourism marriage of young girls in Egypt a form of child sexual abuse? A family exploitation perspective. *Journal of Child Sexual Abuse, 27*, 122–140.

Stanglin, D. (2017, January 28). Russian parliament decriminalizes domestic violence. *USA Today*, front page.

Steuter, E., & Martin, G. (2018, Winter). How militarism teaches our children that violence is normal. *Family Focus, 63(4)* F1–f2.

Temple, J., Choi, H., Brem, M., Wolford-Clevenger, C., Stuart, G., Peskin, M., & Elmquist, J. (2016). The temporal association between traditional and cyber dating abuse among adolescents. *Journal of Youth & Adolescence, 45*, 340–349.

Trabold, N., O'Malley, A., Rizzo, L., & Russell, E. (2018). A gateway to healing: A community-based brief intervention for victims of violence. *Journal of Community Psychology, 46*, 418–428.

Vaillancourt-Morel, M. P., Godbout, N., Sabourin, S., Briere, J., Lussier, Y., & Runtz, M. (2016, January 25). Adult sexual outcomes of child sexual abuse vary according to relationship status. *Journal of Marriage and the Family*. Retrieved from doi: 10.1111/jmft.12154

Vanden Brook, T. (2018). Pentagon hangs on to sexual assault study. *USA Today*, Sept. 10, 3A.

Vil, N. M., Sabri, B., Nwokolo, V., Alexander, K. A., & Campbell, J. C. (2017). A qualitative study of survival strategies used by low-income black women who experience intimate partner violence. *Social Work*, 62, 63–71.

Ward, C. L., Gould, C., Kelly, J., & Mauff, K. (2015). Assessing the impact of parenting on child behaviour and mental health. *SA Crime Quarterly*, 51, 9–22.

Warner, T. D., Allen, C. T., Fisher, B. S., Krebs, C. P., Martin, S., & Lindquist, C. H. (2018). Individual, behavioral, and situational correlates of the drugging victimization experiences of college women. *Criminal Justice Review*, 43, 23–44.

Wong, J. S., & Balemba, S. (2018). The effect of victim resistance on rape completion: A meta-analysis. Trauma, *Violence & Abuse*, 19, 352–365.

Wright, P. J., & Tokunaga, R. S. (2016). Men's objectifying media consumption, objectification of women and attitudes supportive of violence against women. *Archives of Sexual Behavior*, 45, 955–964.

Yang, M., & Maguire-Jack, K. (2018). Individual and cumulative risks for child abuse and neglect. *Family Relations*, 67, 287–301.

Yerke, A., & DeFeo, J., (2016). Redefining intimate partner violence beyond the binary to include transgender people. *Journal of Family Violence*, 31, 975–979.

Zentner, M. (2017). *Child sex abuse treatment using trauma focused cognitive behavioral therapy*. Paper presented at the Sociology of Human Sexuality, East Carolina University, Greenville, NC.

Zia, A. S. (2019). Can rescue narratives save lives? Honor killing in Pakistan. *Signs: Journal of Women in Culture & Society*, 44, 355–378.

CHAPTER 11

Baden, A. L. (2016). "Do you know your real parents?" and other adoption microaggressions. *Adoption Quarterly*, 19, 1–25.

Baden, A. L., Shadel, D., Morgan, R., White, E. E., Harrington, E. S., Christian, N., & Bates, T. A. (2019). Delaying adoption disclosure: A survey of late discovery. *Journal of Family Issues*, 40(9), 1154–1180.

Bailey, S. J. (2015). Transnational adoption challenges: Through the eyes of Eastern European Youth. *Adoption Quarterly*, 18, 85–107.

Baldwin, K. (2018). Conceptualizing women's motivations for social egg freezing and experience of reproductive delay. *Sociology of Health & Illness*, 40, 859–873.

Barclay, K., & Myrskyla, M. (2016). Advanced maternal age and offspring outcomes: Aging and counterbalancing period trends. *Population & Development Review*, 42, 69–94.

Bell, A. V. (2019). "I'm not really 100% a woman if I can't have a kid": Infertility and the intersection of gender, identity, and the body. *Gender & Society*, 33, 629–651.

Bell, M., Edin, K., Wood, H. M., & Crawford Monde, G. (2018). Relationship repertoires, the price of parenthood, and the costs of contraception. *Social Service Review*, (92)3, 313-348.

Bragg, B., Chang, I. J., & Knox, D. (2018, November 8). Some traditions die as slow as molasses: Are sons still preferred? Poster presented at the National Council on Family Relations, San Diego, CA.

Brauer, S. (2018). The surprising predictable decline of religion in the United States. *Journal for the Scientific Study of Religion*, 57, 654–706.

Brown, E., & Patrick, M. (2018). Time, anticipation, and the life course: Egg freezing as temporarily disentangling romance and reproduction. *American Sociological Review*, 83, 959–982.

Bruna, A. (2018). Reproductive decision making in Spain: Heterosexual couples' narratives about how they choose to have children. *Journal of Family Issues*, 39, 3487–3507.

Burge, P., Meiklejohn, E., Groll, D., Burke, N. (2016). Making choices: Adoption seekers' preferences and available children with special needs. *Journal of Public Child Welfare*, 10, 1–20.

Center for Disease Control. *Assisted Reproductive Technology Data for 2015*. Retrieved Oct 1, 2018.

Chung, N. (2018). *All you can ever know*. Catapult. New York.

Colen, C. G., Ramey, D. M., & Browning, C. R. (2016, February 29). Declines in crime and teen childbearing: Identifying potential explanations for contemporaneous trends. *Journal of Quantitative Criminology*, 32(3), 397–426.

Cook, C. T. (2019, February 25). *The social, economic and health status of childless women age 40 and older in the United States*. Paper presented at the American Association of Behavioral and Social Sciences annual conference, Las Vegas, NV.

Cromer, R. (2018). Saving embryos in stem cell science and embryo adoption. *New Genetics & Society*, 37, 362–386.

Datar, A. (2017). The more the heavier? Family size and childhood obesity in the U.S. *Social Science & Medicine*, 180, 143–151.

Daysy. (2018). Retrieved from https://www.ch.daysy.me/effectiveness/

Dvorak, P. (2018). The childfree life: Why so many American women are deciding not to have kids. *Population Connection*, 50, 14–15.

Eeckhaut, M. C. W. (2019). The gendered division of sterilization "fertility work:" The role of educational and racial/ethnic heterogamy. *Journal of Family Issues*, 40, 167–189.

Eeckhaut, M. C. W., & Sweeney, M. W. (2018). Understanding sterilization regret in the United States: The role of relationship context. *Journal of Marriage & Family*, 80, 1259–1270.

Finer, L. B., Frohwirth, L. F., Dauphinne, L. A., Singh, S., & Moore, A. M. (2005). Reasons U.S. women have abortions: quantitative and qualitative reasons. *Perspectives on Sexual and Reproductive Health*, 37, 110–18.

Foster, D. G., Biggs, M. A., Ralph, L., Gerdts, C., Roberts, S., & Glymour, M. M. (2018). Socioeconomic outcomes of women who receive and women who are denied wanted abortions in the United States. *American Journal of Public Health*, 108, 407–413.

Foster, D. Gould, H., Taylor, J., & Weitz, T. A. (2012). Attitudes and decision making among women seeking abortions in one U.S. clinic. *Perspectives on Sexual & Reproductive Health*, 44, 117–124.

Goo, S. K. (2014). *The cost of giving birth varies widely*. Pew Research Center.

Hafner, J. (2019, March 29–31). The "pill" for men: So close, yet so far. *USA Today*, A1.

Hall, S., & Knox, D. (2019). College Student Attitudes and Behaviors Survey of 12,766 undergraduates. Unpublished data collected for this text. Department of Family, Consumer, and Technology Education Teachers College, Ball State University and Department of Sociology, East Carolina University.

Hanna, E., Gough, B., & Hudson, N. (2018). Fit to father? Online accounts of lifestyle changes and help-seeking on a male infertility board. *Sociology of Health & Illness*, 40, 937–953.

Herd, P., Higgins, J., Sicinski, K., & Merkurieva, I. (2016). The implications of unintended pregnancies for mental health in later life. *American Journal of Public Health*, 106, 421–429.

Hunter, L. A., Nelson, L., Chow, J. M., Holt, B. Y., & Bauer, H. M. (2018). Contraceptive method use and chlamydia positivity among California family planning clients: The case for new multipurpose prevention technologies. *Journal of Women's Health*, 27, 768–774.

Jones, C. (2016). Openness in adoption: Challenging the narrative of historical progress. *Child & Family Social Work*, 21, 85–93.

Kageyama, J., & Matsuura, T. (2018). The financial burden of having children and fertility differentials across development and life stages: Evidence from satisfaction data. *Journal of Happiness Studies*, 19, 1–26.

Kashyap, R. (2019). Is prenatal sex selection associated with lower female child mortality? *Population Studies*, 73, 57–78.

Koch, M. C., Lermann, J., van de Roemer, N., Renner, S. K., Burghaus, S., Hackl, J., & Thiel, F. C. (2018). Improving usability and pregnancy rates of a fertility monitor by an additional mobile application: results of a retrospective efficacy study of Daysy and DaysyView app. *Reproductive Health*, 15(1). Retrieved from https://doi-org.cyrano.ucmo .edu/10.1186/s12978–018-0479–6

Koropeckyi-Cox, T., Copur, Z., Romano, V., & Cody-Rydzewski, S. (2018). University students' perceptions of parents and childless or childfree couples. *Journal of Family Issues*, 39, 155–179.

Kotecki, Peter. (2018, August 13). "China's 'one-child' policy led to a demographic time bomb, and now the country is scrambling to undo it." *Business Insider*. Retrieved from www .businessinsider.com

Krishnaswamy, S., Subramaniam, K., Ramachandran, P., Indran, T., & Abdul Aziz, J. (2011). Delayed fathering and risk of mental disorders in adult offspring. *Early Human Development*, 87, 171–175.

Livingston, G., & Horowitz, J. M. (2018, December 12). Most parents—and many non-parents—don't expect to have kids in the future. *Pew Research Center*. Retrieved from https:// www.pewresearch.org/fact-tank/2018/12/12/most-parents-and-many-non-parents-dont-expect-to-have-kids-in-the-future/

Lundberg, O., Berglund Scherwitzl, E., Gemzell Danielsson, K., & Scherwitz, R. (2018). Fertility awareness-based mobile application. *European Journal of Contraception & Reproductive Health Care*, 23(2) 166–168.

Major, B., Appelbaum, M., &, C. (2008, August 13). Report of the APA task force on mental health and abortion. Retrieved from https://www.apa.org/pi/women/programs/abortion/mental-health.pdf

Marshall, E. A., & Shepherd, H. (2018). Fertility preferences and cognition: Religiosity and experimental effects of decision context on college women. *Journal of Marriage and the Family*, 80, 521–536.

Martinez, G. M., Daniels, K., & Febo-Vazquez, I. (2018). Fertility of men and women aged 15–44 in the United States: National Survey of Family Growth, 2011–2015. *National Health Statistics Reports* No. 113, Table 2. Retrieved from www.cdc.gov

Marillier, L., & Squires, D. (2018, December 10–15). Lacking birth control options, desperate Venezuelan women turn to sterilization and illegal abortion. *Population Connection*, 50.

Matias, M., & Fontaine, A. M. (2017). Intentions to have a child: A couple-based process. *Family Relations*, 66, 231–243.

Mathews, T. J., & Hamilton, B. E. (2019, January 10). Total fertility rates by state and race and Hispanic origin: United States, 2017. *National Vital Statistics Reports*, 68, Number 1.

Matthews, R. (2018). *A guide to at-home insemination*. Retrieved from https://www.fertilitysmarts.com/a-guide-to-at-home-insemination/2/476

Margherita, G., Troisi, G., Tessitore, F., & Gargiulo, A. (2017). Teen mothers who are daughters of teen mothers: Psychological intergenerational dimensions of early motherhood. *Children & Youth Services Review*, 83, 294–301.

Monte, L. M. (2019). Multiple-partner fertility in the United States: A demographic portrait. *Demography*, 56, 103–127.

Moore, J., & Abetz, J. S. (2019). What do parents regret about having children? Communicating regrets online. *Journal of Family Issues*, 40, 390–412.

Moore, J. (2017). Facets of agency in stories of transforming from childless by choice to mother. *Journal of Marriage and the Family*, 79, 1144–1159.

Morita, M., Ohtsuki, H., & Hiraiwa-Hasegawa, M. (2016, March 30). Does sexual conflict between mother and father lead to fertility decline? A questionnaire survey in a modern developed society. *Human Nature*, 27(2), 201–219.

Myers, K. (2017). "If I'm going to do it, I'm going to do it right": Intensive mothering ideologies among childless women who elect egg freezing. *Gender & Society*, 31, 777–803.

National Infertility and Adoption Nonprofit. (2016). *Adoption costs*. Retrieved from https://creatingafamily .org/adoption/resources/cost-adoption-us/?gclid=CMDCvIqb7M8CFY07gQodVokOYA

Nebeling Petersen, M. (2018). Becoming gay fathers through transnational commercial surrogacy. *Journal of Family Issues*, 39, 693–719.

Neiterman, E., & LeBlanc, Y. (2018). The timing of pregnancy: Women's interpretations of planned and unplanned pregnancy. *Qualitative Sociology Review*, 14, 52–66.

Newman, L., (2018). Apps for health: What does the future hold? *British Journal of Midwifery*, 26, 561.

Olawole-Isaac, A., Oni, G. A., Oladosun, M., & Amoo, E. O. (2018). Inter-spousal communication: a means for achieving concordant fertility goals. *African Population Studies*, 32, 4068–4079.

Oxford, C. (2017). Coercive population control and asylum in the US. *Social Sciences*, 6(4), 137.

Pedro, J., Brandão, T., Schmidt, L., Costa, M. E., & Martins, M. V. (2018). What do people know about fertility? A systematic review on fertility awareness and its associated factors. *Upsala Journal of Medical Sciences*, 123(2), 71–81.

Persaud, S., Freeman, T., Jadva, V., Slutsky, J., Kramer, W., Steele, M., Steele, H., & Golombok, S. (2017). Adolescents conceived through donor insemination in mother-headed families: A qualitative study of motivations and experiences of contacting and meeting same-donor offspring. *Children & Society*, 31, 13–22.

Picchi, A. (2018, February 26). Raising a child costs $233,610. *USA Today*, A1.

Polis, C. B. (2018). Published analysis of contraceptive effectiveness of Daysy and DaysyView app is fatally flawed. *Reproductive Health*, 15(1), N.PAG. https://doi-org.cyrano .ucmo.edu/10.1186/s12978–018-0560–1

Population Reference Bureau. (2018). 2018 World Population Data Sheet. *Population Reference Bureau*. Washington, DC. Retrieved from www.prb.org

ProQuest Statistical Abstract of the United States. (2019). Online Edition. Bethesda, MD. Retrieved from https://www .proquest.com/products-services/statabstract.html

Puleo, C. M., Schmeidler, J., Reichenberg A., Kolevzon, A., Soorya, L. V., Buxbaum, J. D., & Silverman J. M. (2012). Advancing paternal age and simplex autism. *Autism: The International Journal of Research & Practice, 16*, 367–380.

Reinoso, M., Pereda, N., Van den Dries, L., & Forero C. G. (2016). Internationally adopted children's general and adoption-specific stressors, coping strategies and psychological adjustment. *Child & Family Social Work, 21*, 1–13.

Salazar, A. M., McGowan, K. J., Cole, J. J., Skinner, M. L., Noell, B. R., Colito, J. M., Haggerty, K. P., & Barkan S. E. (2018). Developing relationship-building tools for foster families caring for teens who are LGBTQ2S. *Child Welfare, 96*, 75–97.

Samuelson, K. (2016, September 27). World's first baby born with DNA of three parents. *The New Scientist*. Retrieved from http://time.com/4509565/worlds-first-baby-born-with-dna-from-three-parents/

Santos-Nunes, M., Narciso, I., Vieira-Santos, S., & Roberto, M. S. (2018). Adoptive versus mixed families: Child adjustment, parenting stress and family environment. *Journal of Child & Family Studies, 27*, 1858–1869.

Scott, L. S. (2009). *Two is enough*. Berkeley, CA: Seal Press.

Sharma, R., Agarwal, A., Rohra, V. K., Assidi, M., Abu-Elmagd, M., & Turki, R. F. (2015). Effects of increased paternal age on sperm quality, reproductive outcome and associated epigenetic risks to offspring. *Reproductive Biology & Endocrinology, 13*, 1–20.

Shreffler, K. M. (2017). Contextual understanding of lower fertility among U.S. women in professional occupations. *Journal of Family Issues, 38*, 204–224.

Sifferlin, A. (2019, January 14). The miracle birth that made history. *Time*, 38–39.

Sloan, L. A. (1983). "Abortion Attitude Scale." *Journal of Health Education, 14*(3), 41–42.

Smith, C., Strohschein, L., & Crosnoe, R. (2018). Family Histories and Teen Pregnancy in the United States and Canada. *Journal of Marriage & Family, 80*, 1244–1258.

Soares, J., Ralha, S., Barbosa-Ducharne, M. & Palacios, J. (2019). Adoption-related gains, losses and difficulties: The adopted child's perspective. *Child & Adolescent Social Work Journal, 36*(3), 259–268.

Steenbakkers, A., Ellingsen, I. T., van der Steen, S., & Grietens, H. (2018). Psychological needs of children in foster care and the impact of sexual abuse. *Journal of Child & Family Studies, 27*, 1324–1335.

Steinberg, J. R., Tschann, J. M., Furgerson, D., & Harper, C. C. (2016). Prosocial factors and pre-abortion psychological health: The significance of stigma. *Social Science & Medicine, 150*, 67–75.

Stork OTC. (2018). *How does the Stork OTC work?* Retrieved from https://www.storkotc.com/how-it-works/

Tanaka, K., & Johnson, N. E. (2016). Childlessness and mental well-being in a global context. *Journal of Family Issues, 37*, 1027–1045.

Todd, N. (2017). Infertility and in vitro fertilization. *WebMD*. Retrieved from https://www.webmd.com/infertility-and-reproduction/guide/in-vitro-fertilization#4

Thomas, A., & Karpilow, Q. C. (2018). Long-acting reversible contraception: A silver bullet solution for unintended pregnancy? *American Journal of Public Health, 108*, 1007–1008.

Ugwu, C., & Nugent, C. (2018). *Adoption-related behaviors among women aged 18–44 in the United States: 2011–2015*. (NCHS Data Brief, No 315). Hyattsville, MD: National Center for Health Statistics.

U.S. Department of Health & Human Services. (2017). *Trends in teen pregnancy and childbearing*. Retrieved from https://www.hhs.gov/ash/oah/adolescent-development reproductive-health-and-teen-pregnancy/teen-pregnancy-and-childbearing/trends/index.html.

Wenzel, A. (2017). Cognitive behavioral therapy for pregnancy loss. *Psychotherapy, 54*, 400–405.

Williams, T., & Blinder, A. (2019, May 8) As states race to limit abortions, Alabama goes further, seeking to outlaw most of them. *New York Times*. Retrieved from https://www.nytimes.com/2019/05/08/us/abortion-alabama-ban.html?searchResultPosition=1

Wilson, A. D. (2018). "Put it in your shoe, It will make you limp": British men's online responses to a male pill. *Journal of Men's Studies, 26*, 247–265.

Witwer, E., Jones, R. K., & Lindberg, L. D. (2018, September). Sexual behavior and contraceptive and condom use among U.S. high school students, 2013—2017. *Guttmacher Institute*, Retrieved from https://www.guttmacher.org/report/sexual-behavior-contraceptive-condom-use-us-high-school-students-2013–2017

World Health Organization, (2018). *Adolescent pregnancy*. Retrieved from https://www.who.int/news-room/fact-sheets/detail/adolescent-pregnancy

Wyverkens, E., Provoost, V., Ravelingien, A., Pennings, G., DeSutter, P., & Buysse, A. (2017). The meaning of the sperm donor for heterosexual couples: Confirming the position of the father. *Family Process, 56*, 203–216.

Zacharek, S. (2019, January 14). Why I'm glad I didn't have kids. *Time*, 44–45.

CHAPTER 12

Altenburger, L. E., Schoppe-Sullivan, S. J., & Kamp Dush, C. M. (2018). Associations between maternal gatekeeping and fathers' parenting quality. *Journal of Child and Family Studies, 27*, 2678–2689.

American Academy of Pediatrics. (2016). Media and Young Minds. *Pediatrics, 138*, 1–6.

Ansari, A., & Gershoff, E. (2016). Parent involvement in Head Start and Children's Development: Indirect effects through parenting. *Journal of Marriage & Family, 78*, 562–579.

Barlow, J., & Coren, E. (2018). The effectiveness of parenting programs. *Research on Social Work Practice, 28*, 99–102.

Barry, E. S. (2018, November 8). *Co-sleeping and bioecological theory: An integrative review*. Poster presented at the annual meeting of the National Council on Family Relations, San Diego, CA.

Baig, E. C. (2019, December 6). Obsessed kids are playing "Fortnite" in class. *USA Today*, 2B.

Baumrind, D. (1966). Effects of authoritative parental control on child behavior. *Child Development, 37*, 887–907.

Beato, A., Pereira, A., Barros, L., & Muris, P. (2016). The relationship between different parenting typologies in fathers and mothers and children's anxiety. *Journal of Child Family, 25*, 1691–1701.

Berryhill, M. B., & Durtschi, J. A. (2017). Understanding single mothers' parenting stress trajectories. *Marriage & Family Review, 53*, 227–245.

Bombard, J. M., Kortsmit, K., Warner, L., Shapiro-Mendoza, C. K., Cox, S., Kroelinger, C. D., Parks, S. E., Dee, D. L., D'Angelo, D. V., Smith, R. A., Burley, K., Morrow, B., Olson, C. K., Shulman, H. B., Harrison, L., Cottengim, C., & Barfield, W. D. (2018). Vital signs: Trends and disparities in infant safe sleep practices—United States, 2009–2015. *MMWR Morbidity and Mortality Weekly Report, 67*(1), 39–46.

Borba, M. (2016). Unselfie: *Why empathetic kids succeed in our all-about-me world*. New York: Touchstone Books.

Bouchard, G. (2018). A dyadic examination of marital quality at the empty-nest phase. *International Journal of Aging & Human Development, 86*, 34–50.

Brandel, M., Melchiorri, E., & Ruini, C. (2018). The dynamics of eudaemonic well-being in the transition to parenthood: Differences between fathers and mothers. *Journal of Family Issues*, 39, 2572–2589.

Brett, M. (2017, December 17). More parents track teens online than kids realize. *USA Today*. 6t.

Brummelte, S., & Galea, L. A. M. (2016). Postpartum depression: Etiology, treatment and consequences for maternal care. *Hormones and Behavior, 77*, 153–166.

Burns, R. A., Loh, V., Byles, J. E., & Kendig, H. L. (2018). The impact of childhood parental quality on mental health outcomes in older adults. *Aging & Mental Health, 22*, 819–825.

Cassidy, D. (2017, Spring). The ACEs study and family life education. *NCFR Report*, p. 6.

Census Bureau Current Population Survey. (2017). Annual Social and Economic Survey, 1994–2015.

Centers for Disease Control and Prevention. (2018, January). Safe sleep for babies. *Vital signs*. Retrieved from www.cdc.gov

Clopton, J. (2018, February 12). Baby suffocation deaths from co-sleeping rise. *WebMD HealthNews*. Retrieved from www .webmd.com

Copeland, L. (2012, October 23). Tech keeps tabs on teen drivers. *USA Today*, A3.

Corkin, M. T., Peterson, E. R., Andrejic, N., Waldie, K. E., Reese, E., & Morton, S. M. B. (2018). Predictors of mothers' self-identified challenges in parenting infants: insights from a large nationally diverse cohort. *Journal of Child and Family Studies, 27*, 653–670.

Corralejo, S. M., & Domenech Rodriguez, M. M. (2018). Technology in parenting programs: A systematic review of existing interventions. *Journal of Child and Family Studies, 27*, 2717–2731.

Cote-Arsenault, D., & Denney-Koelsch, E. (2018). "Love is a choice": Couple responses to continuing pregnancy with a lethal fetal diagnosis. *Illness, Crisis & Loss, 26*, 5–22.

Coyne, S. M., & McDaniel, B. T. (2014, November). *Social comparisons on social networking sites predict maternal well-being.* Paper presented at the National Council on Family Relations, annual meeting, Baltimore, MD.

Craft, A. L., & Perry-Jenkins. M. (2017). *Family matters: Long-term consequences of early marital conflict on children's development.* Poster presented at the annual meeting of the National Council on Family Relations, Orlando, FL.

Cubbins, L. A., Sepavich, D., Killpack, S., & Hill, C. V. (2018). Assessing determinants of father's involvement with his partner's pregnancy and his child's well-being. *Men & Masculinities, 21*, 3–34.

Curenton, S. M., Crowley, J. E., & Mouzon, D. M. (2018). Qualitative descriptions of middle-class, African American mothers' child-rearing practices and values. *Journal of Family Issues, 39*, 868–895.

Damen, H., Veerman, J. W., Vermulst, A. A., Nieuwhoff, R., de Meyer, R., & Scholte, R. H. J. (2017). Parental empowerment: Construct validity and reliability of a Dutch Empowerment Questionnaire (EMPO). *Journal of Child and Family Studies, 26*, 424–436.

Daryanani, I., Hamilton, J. L., Abramson, L. Y., & Alloy, L. B. (2016). Single mother parenting and adolescent psychopathology. *Journal of Abnormal Child Psychology, 44*(7), 1411–1423.

Davidson, P. (2017, November 21). More older millennials live with relatives. *USA Today*, B1.

Dervin, D. (2016). Where have all the children gone? *The Journal of Psychohistory, 43*, 262–276.

Durrant, L., & Gillum, N. L. (2018). White fathers and their black-white biracial sons. *Marriage and Family Review, 54*, 374–392.

Eddy, B., Poll, V., Whiting, J., & Clevesy, M. (2019). Forgotten fathers: Postpartum depression in men. *Journal of Family Issues*. Retrieved from doi: 10.1177/0192513X19833111

Edwards, A. L., (2017). Teaching African American children about race: Fostering intergroup relationships through parental racial socialization. *Journal of Child Adolescent Behavior, 5*,1. Retrieved from doi: 10.4172/2375-4494.1000329

Edwards, A. L., & Few-Demo, A. L. (2016). African American maternal power and racial socialization of preschool children. *Sex Roles, 75*, 56–70.

Eanes, R. (2016). *Positive parenting: An essential guide*. New York: Penguin Random House.

Eklund, L., & Roman, S. (2019) Digital gaming and young people's friendships: A mixed methods study of time use and gaming in school. *Young, 27*, 32–47.

Emamzadeh, A. (2018). What factors are associated with positive parenting? *Psychology Today*. Retrieved from https://www.psychologytoday.com/us/blog/finding-new-home/201807/what-factors-are-associated-positive-parenting

Festl, R., & Gniewosz, G. (2019). Role of mothers' and fathers' Internet parenting for family climate. *Journal of Social & Personal Relationships, 36*(6), 1764–1784.

Fletcher, A. C., Benito-Gomez, M., & Blair, B. L. (2018). Adolescent cell phone communications with mothers and fathers: Content, patterns, and preferences. *Journal of Child and Family Studies, 27*, 2125–2137.

Fomby, P. (2018). Motherhood in complex families. *Journal of Family Issues, 39*, 245–270.

Fomby, P., & Osborne, C. (2017). Family instability, multipartner fertility, and behavior in middle childhood. *Journal of Marriage and the Family, 79*, 75–93.

Forbes, E. E., & Dahl, R. E. (2012). Research Review: Altered reward functioning adolescent depression: what, when and how? *Journal of Child Psychology and Psychiatry, 53*, 3–15.

Gabrielli, J., Marsch, L., & Tanski, S. (2018). TECH parenting to promote effective media management. *Pediatrics, 142*(1), 1–4.

Gelabert, E., Subirà, S., García-Esteve, L., Navarro, P., Plaza, A., Cuyàs, E., Navinés R., Gratacòs, M., Valdés, M., & Martin-Santos R. (2012). Perfectionism dimensions in major postpartum depression. *Journal of Affective Disorders, 136*, 17–25.

Gillis, A., & Roskam, I. (2019). Daily exhaustion and support in parenting: Impact on quality of the parent-child relationship. *Journal of Child & Family Studies, 28*, 2007–2016.

Gleditsch, R. F., & Pedersen, D. E. (2017). Mothers' and fathers' ratings of parental involvement: Views of married dual-earners with preschool-age children. *Marriage & Family Review, 53*, 589–612.

Goldfarb, E., Lieberman, L., Santos, P., & Kwiatkowski, S. (2018). Silence and censure: A qualitative analysis of young adults' reflections on communication with parents prior to first sex. *Journal of Family Issues, 39*(1), 28–54.

Golombok, S., Zadeh, S., Imrie, S., Smith, V., & Freeman, T. (2016). Single mothers by choice: Mother-child relationship's psychological adjustment. *Journal of Family Psychology, 30*(4), 409–418.

Green, M., & Piel, J. A. (2010). *Theories and human development*. New York: Psychology Press.

Ginsburg, K. (2014). *Building resilience in children and teens: giving kids roots and wings*. Elk Grove Village, IL: American Academy of Pediatrics.

Grossman, J. M., Richer, A. M., Charmaraman, L., Ceder, I., & Erkut, S. (2018). Youth perspectives on sexuality communication with parents and extended kin. *Family Relations, 67,* 368–380.

Günüç, S., & Atli, S. (2018). Parents' views on the impact of technology on 18- to 24-month old infants. *Addicta: The Turkish Journal on Addictions, 5*(2), 205–226.

Haag, P. (2011). *Marriage confidential.* New York: Harper Collins.

Hamilton, L., Roksa, J., & Nielsen, K. (2018). Providing a "leg up": Parental involvement and opportunity hoarding in college. *Sociology of Education, 91,* 111–131.

Healthy Children. (2018). *Healthy digital media use habit for babies, toddlers and preschoolers.* Retrieved from https://www.healthychildren.org/English/family-life/Media/Pages/Healthy-Digital-Media-Use-Habits-for-Babies-Toddlers-Preschoolers.aspx

Heid, M. (2017, November 6). We need to talk about kids and smartphones. *Time Magazine,* 42–46.

Henchoz, Y., N'Goran, A. A., Deline, S., Studer, J., Baggio, S., & Gmel, G. (2016). Age at cannabis first use and later substance abuse with mental health and depression in young men. *Journal of Substance Use, 21,* 85–91.

Hendrick, S. (2018). The imperative to vaccinate. *The Journal of Pediatrics, 201,* 259–263.

Henretta, J. C., Van Voorhis, M. F., & Soldo, B. J. (2018). Cohort differences in parental financial help to adult children. *Demography, 55,* 1567–1582.

Hickey, G., McGilloway, S., Leckey, Y., Furlong, M., Leavy, S., Stokes, A., O'Connor, S., Bywater, T., & Donnelly, M. (2019). Mothers' well-being, parenting attitudes, and home environment: Cumulative risk and parity in early motherhood. *Child: Care, Health & Development, 45*(4), 523–530.

Hjelmgaard, K. (2017, January 9). Apple urged to help fight kid's phone addiction. *USA Today,* 4B.

Hodge, C. J. (2018, Summer). When time for leisure seems limited, focus on quality. *Family Focus,* FF76 Issue, *63.2.*

Howorth, C. (2017, October 30). The goddess myth. *Time Magazine,* 36–42.

Hutton, J. S., Dudley, J., Horowitz-Kraus, T., DeWitt, T., & Holland, S. K. (2018). Differences in functional brain network connectivity during stories presented in audio, illustrated, and animated format in preschool-age children. *Brain Imaging and Behavior.* https://doi.org/10.1007/s11682-018-9985-7

Ishizuka, P. (2019). Social class, gender, and contemporary parenting standards in the United States: Evidence from a National Survey Experiment. *Social Forces, 98*(1), 31–58.

Jaggers, J. W., Bolland, A. C., Tomek, S., Church, W. T., Hooper, L. M., Bolland, K. A., & Bolland, J. M. (2017). Does biology matter in parent-child relationships? Examining parental warmth among adolescents from low-income families. *Journal of Family Issues, 38,* 225–247.

Janssen, H. J., Eishelsheim, V., Dekovic, M., & Bruinsma, G. J. N. (2016). How is parenting related to adolescent delinquency? A between- and within-person analysis of the mediating role of self-control, delinquent attitudes, peer delinquency, and time spent in criminogenic settings. *European Journal of Criminology, 13,* 169–194.

Jawed-Wessel, S., & Sevick, E. (2017). The impact of pregnancy and childbirth on sexual behaviors: A systematic review. *The Journal of Sex Research, 54,* 411–423.

Johnsen, A., Bjorknes, R., Iversen, A. C., & Sandbaek, M. (2018). School competence among adolescents in low income families. *Journal of Child and Family Studies, 27,* 2285–2294.

Katz, V. S., Moran, M. B., & Ognyanova, K. (2019). Contextualizing connectivity: how interconnection type and parental factors influence technology use among lower-income children. *Information, Communication & Society, 22,* 313–335.

Kılıç, A. O., Sari, E., Yucel, H., Oğuz, M. M., Polat, E., Acoglu, E. A., & Senel, S. (2018). Exposure to and use of mobile devices in children aged 1–60 months. *European Journal of Pediatrics, 1–7.* Retrieved from https://doi.org/10.1007/s00431-018-3284-x

Killoren, S. E., Campione-Barr, N. M., Jones, S. K., & Giron, S. E. (2019). Adolescent girls' disclosure about dating and sexuality. *Journal of Family Issues, 40*(7), 887–910.

Kleiin, V., Becker, I., & Stulhofer, A. (2018). Parenting, communication about sexuality, and the development of adolescent women's sexual agency: A longitudinal assessment. *Journal of Youth & Adolescence, 47,* 1486–1498.

Knox, D., & Milstein, S. (2021). *Human sexuality: Making informed choices,* 6th ed. Redding, CA.: Best Value Publishers.

LaMotte, S. (2018). Limit screen time to protect your child's heart, American Heart Association Says. *CNN.* Retrieved from https://www.cnn.com/2018/08/07/health/screen-time-children-heart-health/index.html

Lee, E.-Y., Hesketh, K. D., Rhodes, R. E., Rinaldi, C. M., Spence, J. C., & Carson, V. (2018). Role of parental and environmental characteristics in toddlers' physical activity and screen time: Bayesian analysis of structural equation models. *The International Journal of Behavioral Nutrition and Physical Activity, 15,* 17. https://doi.org/10.1186/s12966-018-0649-5

Lehr, M., Wecksell, B., Nahum, L., Neuhaus, D., Teel, K., Linares, L. & Diaz, A. (2016). Parenting stress, child characteristics, and developmental delay from birth to age five in teen mother-child dyads. *Journal of Child & Family Studies, 25,* 1035–1043.

Luthar, S. S., & L. Ciciolla, L. (2016). What it feels like to be a mother: Variations by children's developmental stages. *Developmental Psychology, 52,* 143–154.

Maas, M. K., McDaniel, B. T., Feinberg, M. E., & Jones, D. E. (2018) Division of labor and multiple domains of sexual satisfaction among first-time parents. *Journal of Family Issues, 39,* 104–127.

Maroto, M. (2017). When the kids live at home: Coresidence, parental assets, and economic insecurity. *Journal of Marriage and the Family, 79,* 1041–1059.

Mastrotheodoros, S., Van der Graaff, J., Dekovic, M., Meeus, W. H. J., & Branje, S. J. T. (2019). Interparental conflict management strategies and parent-adolescent relationships: Disentangling between-person from within-person effects across adolescence. *Journal of Marriage and the Family, 81,* 185–203.

Martin, E., Roldán, A. D., Haya, P. A., Fernández, G. C., Guzmán, C., & Quintanar, H. (2018). Impact of using interactive devices in Spanish early childhood education public schools. *Journal of Computer Assisted Learning,* Retrieved from https://doi.org/10.1111/jcal.12305

McArthur, M., & Winkworth, G. (2017). What do we know about the social networks of single parents who do not use supportive services. *Child & Family Social Work, 22,* 638–647.

McDaniel, B. T., Teti, D. M., & Feinberg, M. E. (2017). Assessing coparenting relationships in daily life: The Daily Coparenting Scale (D-Cop). *Journal of Child and Family Studies.* Retrieved from doi: 10.1007/s10826-017-0762-0

McDaniel, B. T., & Radesky, J. S. (2018). Technoference: parent distraction with technology and associations with of child behavior problems. *Child Development, 89,* 100–109.

McElwain, A. D., & Bub, K. L. (2018). Changes in parent-child relationship quality across early adolescence: Implications for engagement in sexual behavior. *Youth and Society, 50,* 204–228.

McKinney, C., & Kwan, J. W. (2018). Emerging adult perceptions of and preferences for parenting styles and associated psychological outcomes. *Journal of Family Issues, 39,* 2491–2504.

Meier, A., Musick, K., Fischer, J., & Flood, S. (2018). Mothers' and fathers' wellbeing in parenting across the arch child development. *Journal of Marriage and Family, 80,* 992–1004.

Mellerson, J. L., Maxwell, C. B., Knighton, C. L., Kriss, J. L., Seither, R., & Black, C. L. (2018). Vaccination coverage for selected vaccines and exemption rates among children in kindergarten—United States, 2017–18 school year. *MMWR Morbidity and Mortality Weekly Report, 67,* 1115–1122.

Mikolajczak, M., Raes, M. E., Avalosse, H., & Roskam, I. (2018). Exhausted parents: Sociodemographic, child-related, parent-related, parenting and family-functioning correlates of parental burnout. *Journal of Child and Family Studies, 27*(2), 602–614.

Moilanen, K. L., & Lynn Manuel, M. (2019). Helicopter parenting and adjustment outcomes in young adulthood: A consideration of the mediating roles of mastery and self-regulation. *Journal of Child & Family Studies, 28,* 2145–2158.

Moncada, J., & Natrajan –Tyagi, R. (2018, November 8). *Recollections of peripartum depression: A lived experience storytelling of peripartum depression among Latina women.* Poster presented at the annual meeting of the National Council on Family Relations, San Diego, CA.

Mostafa, T., Gambaro, L., & Joshi, H. (2018). The impact of complex family structure on child well-being: Evidence from siblings. *Journal of Marriage and the Family, 80,* 902–918.

Mowen, T. J., & Schroeder, R. D. (2018). Maternal parenting style and delinquency by race and the moderating effect of structural disadvantage. *Youth and Society, 50,* 139–159.

Murry, V. M., & Lippold , M. A. (2018). Parenting practices in diverse family structures: Examination of adolescents' development and adjustment. *Journal of Research on Adolescence, 28,* 650–664.

Nathanson, A. I., & Beyens, I. (2018). The relation between use of mobile electronic devices and preschoolers. *Behavioral Sleep Medicine, 16*(2), 202–219.

National Conference of State Legislatures. (2017, December 20). *"States with religious and philosophical exemptions from school immunization requirements."* Retrieved from www .ncsl.org

National Institute of Mental Health, (2018). Postpartum Depression Facts. *National Institute of Mental Health.* Retrieved from https://www.nimh.nih.gov/health/ publications/postpartum-depression-facts/index.shtml

Negraia, D. V., Augustine, J. M., & Prickett, K. (2018). Gender disparities in parenting time across activities, child ages, and educational groups. *Journal of Family Issues, 39,* 3006–3028.

Nelson, J. J., & Uecker, J. E. (2018). Are religious parents more satisfied? Individual and couple level religious correlates of parenting satisfaction. *Journal of Family Issues, 39,* 1770–1796.

Neumann, M. M. (2018). Using tablets and apps to enhance emergent literacy skills inyoung children. *Early Childhood Research Quarterly, 42,* 239–246.

Nonoyama-Tarumi, Y. (2017). Educational achievement of children from single-mother and single-father families: The case of Japan. *Journal of Marriage and the Family, 79,* 915–931.

Olivari, M G., Cucci, G., Bonanomi, A., Tagliabue, S., & Confalonieri, E. (2018). Retrospective paternal and maternal parenting styles, regulatory self-efficacy and adolescent risk taking. *Marriage & Family Review, 54,* 282–295.

Overbeek, G., van de Bongardt, D., & Baams, L. (2018). Buffer or brake? The role of sexuality-specific parenting in adolescents' sexualized media consumption and sexual development. *Journal of Youth and Adolescence, 47,* 1427–1439.

Park, H., & Lau, A. S. (2016). Socioeconomic status and parenting priorities: Child independence and obedience around the world. *Journal of Marriage and Family, 78,* 43–59.

Perron, N. C. D. (2018). The four Cs of parenting. *Family Journal, 26,* 48–55.

Petrovic, M., Vasic, V., Petrovic, O., & Santric-Milicevic, M. (2016). Positive parenting attitudes and practices in three transnational eastern European countries: Bosnia and Herzegovina, Macedonia and Serbia. *International Journal of Public Health, 61*(5), 621–630.

Petts, R. J. (2018). Time off after childbirth and mothers' risk of depression, parenting stress, and parenting practices. *Journal of Family Issues, 39,* 1827–1854.

Petts, R. J., Shafer, K. M., & Essig, L. (2018). Does adherence to masculine norms shape fathering behavior? *Journal of Marriage and Family, 80,* 704–720.

Petts, R. J., & Knoester, C. (2018). Paternity leave taking and father engagement. *Journal of Marriage and Family, 80,* 1144–1162.

Pollmann-Schult, M. (2018). Single motherhood and life satisfaction in comparative perspective: Do institutional and cultural contexts explain the life satisfaction penalty for single mothers? *Journal of Family Issues, 39,* 2061–2084.

ProQuest Statistical Abstract of the United States. (2019). Online Edition. Bethesda, MD, Retrieved from https://www .proquest.com/products-services/statabstract.html

Puhlman, D. J., & Pasley, K. (2017, December). The Maternal Gatekeeping Scale: Constructing a measure. *Family Relations, 66,* 824–838.

Qiu, S. (2017, Winter). Chinese "study mothers" in living-apart-together relationships. *Family Focus,* F16-F17.

Ralph, R. (2018). Media and technology in preschool classrooms: Manifesting prosocial sharing behaviours when using iPads. *Technology, Knowledge & Learning, 23*(2), 199–221.

Reis, H. T., Maniaci, M. R., & Rogge, R. D. (2014). The expression of compassionate love in everyday compassionate acts. *Journal of Social and Personal Relationships, 31,* 651–676.

Roopnarine, J. L., & Yildirim, E. D. (2019). *Fathering in cultural contexts.* United Kingdom: Routledge.

Rousseau, S., & Scharf, M. (2018). Why people helicopter parent? An actor-partner interdependence study of maternal and paternal prevention/promotion focus and interpersonal/ self-regret. *Journal of Social and Personal Relationships, 35,* 919–935.

Sacks, A. (2019, April 8). Matrescence: The developmental transition to motherhood. *Psychology Today* online. Retrieved from https://www.psychologytoday.com/us/ blog/motherhood-unfiltered/201904/matrescence-the-developmental-transition-motherhood

Simmins, R. (2019, July 1). Tell kids the truth: hard work doesn't always pay off. *Time Magazine,* p 22.

Schiffrin, H., & Liss, M. (2017). The effects of helicopter parenting on academic motivation. *Journal of Child & Family Studies, 26,* 1472–1480.

Schwartz, A. (2018, January 15). Resolutions: What if self-improvement is making us worse? *The New Yorker,* 65–69.

Shafer, K., Fielding, B., & Holmes, E. K. (2019). Depression, masculine norm adherence and fathering behavior. *Journal of Family Issues, 40,* 48–84.

Shimizu, M., & Teti, D. M. (2018). Infant sleeping arrangements, social criticisms, and maternal distress in the first year. *Infant and Child Development, 27,* 1–16. Retrieved from https://doi-org.jproxy.lib.ecu.edu/10.1002/icd.2080

Smith, M. E., & Gonzalez, A. (2018, September 2). Liberty Mutual survey of 1000 U.S. parents of licensed teenage drivers, *USA Today*, pp. A1.

Smith, M. B., & Loehrke, J. (2018, September 14). Parents monitor child's cell phone. *USA Today*, pp. D1.

Smith, R. (2018, July 21). France bans smartphones from schools. *CNN*, Retrieved from https://www.cnn.com/2018/07/31/europe/france-smartphones-school-ban-intl/index.html

Stewart, S. D. (2017). *Co-sleeping: Parents, children, and musical beds.* New York: Rowman and Littlefield.

Steinberg, L. (2004). *The ten basic principles of good parenting.* New York: Simon and Schuster.

Tokic Milakovic, A., Glatz, T., & and N. Pecnik, N. (2018). How do parents facilitate or inhibit adolescent disclosure? The role of adolescents' psychological needs satisfaction. *Journal of Social & Personal Relationships*, 35, 1118–1138.

Toure, D., Do, K., Ramos, A. K., & Su, D. (2019). Assessing racial and ethnic differences in attitudes towards the use of physical discipline in parenting: A mixed-methods approach. *Journal of Social Service Research*, 45, 455–465.

Turns, B. A., & Sibley, D. S. (2018). Does maternal spanking lead to bullying behaviors at school? A longitudinal study. *Journal of Child & Family Studies*, 27, 2824–2832.

Twenge, J. (2017). *iGen.* New York: Atria Books.

Vincent, C., & Maxwell, C. (2016). Parenting priorities and pressures: furthering understanding of 'concerted cultivation' *Discourse: Studies in the Cultural Politics of Education, 37*, 269–281.

Weithorn, L. A., & Reiss, D. R. (2018). Legal approaches to promoting parental compliance with childhood immunization recommendations. *Human Vaccines & Immunotherapeutics*, 14, 1610–1617.

Wiederhold, B. K. (2018). "Alexa, Are you my mom?" The role of artificial intelligence in child development. (An editorial) *Cyberpsychology, Behavior, and Social Networking*, 21, 471.

Williams, D. T. (2018). Parental depression and cooperative coparenting: A longitudinal and dyadic approach. *Family Relations*, 67, 253–269.

Wilson, K. R., Havighurst, S. S., & Harley, A. E. (2012). Tuning in to kids: An effectiveness trial of a parenting program targeting emotion socialization of preschoolers. *Journal of Family Psychology*, 26, 56–65.

Yadav, S., Chakraborty, P., Mittal, P., & Arora, U. (2018). Children aged 6–24 months like to watch YouTube videos but could not learn anything from them. *Acta Paediatr, 107*(8), 1461–1466.

Yaffe, Y. (2018). Establishing specific links between parenting styles and the S- anxieties in children: Separation, social and school. *Journal of Family Issues*, 39, 1419–1437.

Yahirun, J. J., & Arenas, E. (2018). Offspring migration and parents' emotional and psychological well-being in Mexico. *Journal of Marriage and the Family*, 80, 975–991.

Yang, J., & Trap, P. (2016, September 18). Helicopter parents on job searches. From an Office Team Survey of 608 senior managers. *USA Today*, pp. 6T.

Yahirun, J. J., & Arenas, E. (2018). Offspring migration and parents' emotional and psychological well-being in Mexico. *Journal of Marriage and the Family*, 80, 975–991.

Zabriskie, R. B., & Ward, P. J. (2013). Satisfaction with Family Life Scale. *Marriage & Family Review, 49*(5), 446–463. Retrieved from doi: 10.1080/01494929.2013.768321

CHAPTER 13

Ackert, E., Ressler, R., Ansari, A., & Crosnoe, R. (2018). Maternal employment, community contexts, and the child-care arrangements of diverse groups. *Journal of Marriage and the Family, 80*, 1210–1224.

Ansari, A., & Pianta, R. C. (2018). Variation in the long-term benefits of child care: the role of classroom quality in elementary school. *Developmental Psychology, 54*, 1854–1867.

Balestra, C., R. Boarini, R., & E. Tosetto, E. (2018). What matters most to people? Evidence from OECD Better Life Index users' responses. *Social Indicators Research, 136*, 907–930.

Bongaarts, J., Blanc, A. K., & McCarthy, K. (2019). The links between women's employment and children at home: Variations in low- and middle-income countries by world region. *Population Studies, 73* (2), 149–163.

Brienza, J. P., & Grossmann, I. (2017). Social class and wise reasoning about interpersonal conflicts across regions, persons and situations. *Proceedings of Royal Society B, 284*, (1869): 20171870. Retrieved from http://dx.doi.org/10.1098/rspb.2017.1870

Brockmann, H., Koch, A. M., Diederich, A., & Edling, C. (2018). Why managerial women are less happy than managerial men. *Journal of Happiness Studies, 19*, 755–779.

Bureau of Labor Statistics. (2018, March). Employee benefits survey. Retrieved from www.bls.gov.

Chung, H., & Van der Horst, M. (2018). Women's employment patterns after childbirth and the perceived access to and use of flexitime and teleworking. *Human Relations, 71*, 47–72.

Coontz, S. (2016). *The way we never were: American families and the nostalgia trap* (2nd ed). New York: Basic Books.

Craig, L., & Churchill, B. (2018). Parenting stress and the use of formal and informal child care: Associations for fathers and mothers. *Journal of Family Issues, 39*, 3203–3224.

Davidson, P. (2017, July 31). Tired of the corporate grind? A blue-collar job may be for you. *USA Today*, pp. 1B.

Dinh, H., Strazdins, L., & Welsh, J. (2017). Hour-glass ceilings: Work-hour thresholds, gendered health inequities. *Social Science & Medicine, 176*, 42–51.

Dow, D. M. (2016). Integrated motherhood: Beyond hegemonic ideologies of motherhood. *Journal of Marriage and the Family, 78*, 180–196.

Eberstadt, N. (2016). *Men without work: America's invisible crisis.* West Conshohocken, PA: Templeton Press.

Ellis, C. (2017). Sleeping around, with and through time: An autoethnographic rendering of a good night's slumber. *Qualitative Inquiry, 23*, 287–299.

Fales, M. R., Frederick, D. A., Garcia, J. R., Gildersleeve, K. A., Haselton, M. G., & Fisher, H. E. (2016). Mating markets and bargaining hands: Mate preferences for attractiveness and resources in two national U.S. studies. *Personality and Individual Differences, 88*, 78–87.

Florian, S. M. (2018). Motherhood and employment among Whites, Hispanics and Blacks: A life course approach. *Journal of Marriage and the Family, 80*, 134–149.

Feinberg, L. F. (2018, September). Breaking new ground: Supporting employed family caregivers with workplace leave policies. AARP Public Policy Institute. Retrieved from www.aarp.org

Fulda, B. E., & Lersch, P. M. (2018). Planning until death do us part: Partnership status and financial planning horizon. *Journal of Marriage and Family, 80*, 409–425.

Gault, B., Hartmann, H., Hegewisch, A. Milli, J., & Reichlin, L. (2014). *Paid parental leave in the United States.* Institute for

Women's Policy Research. U.S. Dept. of Labor. Retrieved from www.dol.gov

Gieger, A. (2016). *Sharing chores a key to good marriage, say majority of married adults.* Pew Research Center. Retrieved from http://www.pewresearch.org/fact-tank/2016/11/30/sharing-chores-a-key-to-good-marriage-say-majority-of-married-adults/

Glauber, R., & Day, M. D. (2018). Gender, spousal caregiving, and depression: Does paid work matter? *Journal of Marriage and the Family, 80,* 537–554.

Global Workplace Analytics. (2018). Telecommuting Trend Data. Retrieved from https://globalworkplaceanalytics.com/telecommuting-statistics

Gould, E. (2018, February 1). *Providing unpaid leave was only the first step; 25 years after the Family and Medical Leave Act, more workers need paid leave.* Economic Policy Institute. Retrieved from www.epi.org

Guynn, J. (2018, September 17). Facebook is not as family-friendly as you think, working moms say. *USA Today.* Retrieved from www.usatoday.com

Haines, V. Y., Bilodeau, J., Demers, A., Marchand, A., Beauregard, N., Durand, P., & Blanc, M. E. (2019). Sex, gender dynamics, differential exposure, and work-family conflict. *Journal of Family Issues, 40,* 215–239.

Hall, S., & Willoughby, B. J. (2016). Relative work and family role centralities: Beliefs and behaviors related to the transition to adulthood. *Journal of Family and Economic Issues, 37,* 75–88.

Heller, N. (2017, May 15). The gig is up. *The New Yorker,* 52–63.

Hickman-Evans, C., Higgins, J. P., Aller, T. B., Chavez, J., & Piercy, K. W. (2018). Newlywed couple leisure: Couple identity formation through leisure time. *Marriage & Family Review, 54,* 105–127.

Hochschild, A. R. (1989). *The second shift.* New York: Viking.

Hochschild, A. R. (1997). *The time bind.* New York: Metropolitan Books.

Hodge, C. J., Zabriskie, R. B., Townsend, J. A., Eggett, D. L., &. Poff, R (2018). Family leisure functioning: A cross-national study. *Leisure Sciences, 40,* 194–215.

Horne, R. M., Johnson, M. D., Galambos, N. L., & Krahn. H. J. (2018). Time, money, or gender? Predictors of the division of household labour across life stages. *Sex Roles, 78,* 731–743.

Hwang, W., & Ramadoss, K. (2017). The job demands-control-support model and job satisfaction across gender. *Journal of Family Issues, 38,* 52–72.

Inanc, H. (2018). Unemployment, temporary work, and subjective well-being: The gendered effect of spousal labor market insecurity. *American Sociological Review, 83,* 536–566.

Ingraham, Christopher. (2018, February 5). The world's richest countries guarantee mothers more than a year of paid leave. The U.S. guarantees them nothing. *Washington Post.* Retrieved from www.washingtonpost.com

Ingram, J. & Cangemi. J. (2019). Video games, motivations, effects, and criminal implications on self-esteem. *College Student Journal, 53,* 1–2.

Ishizuka, P. (2018). The economic foundations of cohabiting couples' union transitions. *Demography. 55.* 535–557.

Johnston, T. (2016, June 2). Power couples explain how they juggle career, family and the laundry. *Stanford Business.* Retrieved from https://www.gsb.stanford.edu/insights/power-couples-explain-how-they-juggle-career-family-laundry

Johnson, M. D., Galambos, N. L., & Anderson, J. R. (2016). Skip the dishes? Not so fast! Sex and housework revisited. *Journal of Family Psychology, 30,* 203–213.

Jostell, D., & Hemlin, S. (2018). After hours teleworking and boundary management: Effects on work-family conflict, *Work, 60,* 475–483.

Kamp Dush, C. M., Yavorsky, J. F., & Schoppe-Sullivan, S. J. (2018). What are men doing while women perform extra unpaid labor? Leisure and specialization at the transitions to parenthood. *Sex Roles, 78,* 715–730.

Kaplan, A., & Stier, H. (2017). Political economy of family life: couple's earnings, welfare regime and union dissolution. *Social Science Research, 61,* 43–56.

Kaplan, A., & Herbst-Debby, A. (2018). Fragile employment, liquid love: Employment instability and divorce in Israel. *Population Research and Policy Review, 37,* 1–31.

Kaplan, S., Engelsted, L., Lei, X., & Lockwood, K. (2018). Unpackaging manager mistrust in allowing telework: comparing and integrating theoretical perspectives. *Journal of Business & Psychology, 33*(3), 365–382.

Knox, D., Zusman, M., White, A., & Haskins, G. (2009). Coed anger over romantic partner's video game playing. *Psychology Journal, 6,* 10–16.

Lair, C. D., MacLeod, C., & Budgar, E. (2016). Advertising unreasonable expectations: Nanny ads on Craigslist. *Sociological Spectrum, 36,* 286–302.

Laughlin, L. D. (2013, April). *Who's minding the kids? Child care arrangement: Spring 2011.* U.S. Census Bureau. Retrieved from www.census.gov

Lee, D. J., & Sirgy, M. J. (2018). What do people do to achieve work-life balance? A formative conceptualization to help develop a metric for large-scale quality of life surveys. *Social Indicators Research, 138,* 771–791.

Lee, C., & Kim, O. (2017). Predictors of online game addiction among Korean adolescents. *Addiction Research & Theory, 25,* 58–66.

Lee, Y. S. (2018). Commuter couples' life satisfaction in Korea. *International Sociology, 33,* 107–127.

Lin, W. F., Chen, L., & Li, T. S. (2016). Are "we" good? A longitudinal study of we-talk and stress in dual-earner couples. *Journal of Happiness Studies, 17,* 757–772.

Lindemann, D. J. (2017). Going the distance: Individualism and interdependence in the commuter marriage. *Journal of Marriage and Family, 79,* 1419–1434.

Lindemann, D. J. (2018). Doing and undoing gender in commuter marriages. *Sex Roles, 79,* 36–49.

Lindqvist, E., Ostling, R., & Cesarini, D. (2018). *Long term effects of lottery wealth on psychological well-being.* Research Institute of Industrial Economics. Stockholm, Sweden.

Lup, D. (2018). Something to celebrate (or not): The differing impact of promotion to manager on the job satisfaction of women and men. *Work, Employment and Society, 32,* 407–425.

Ma a tta, K., & Uusiautti, S. (2012). Seven rules on having a happy marriage along with work. *The Family Journal, 20,* 267–271.

Martinez-Marti, M. L., & Ruch, W. (2017). The relationship between orientations to happiness and job satisfaction one year later in a representative sample of employees in Switzerland. *Journal of Happiness Studies, 18,* 1–15.

Matias, M., Ferreira, T., Vieira, J., Cadima, J., Leal, T., & Matos, P. M. (2017). Work-family conflict, psychological availability, and child emotion regulation: Spillover and crossover in dual-earner families. *Personal Relationships, 24,* 623–639.

Mauno, S., Hirvonen, R., & Kiuru, N. (2018). Children's life satisfaction: The roles of mothers' work engagement and recovery from work. *Journal of Happiness, 19,* 1373–1393.

McCann, A. (2019). Best and worst states to raise a family. *WalletHub.* Retrieved from https://wallethub.com/edu/best-states-to-raise-a-family/31065

McDaniel, B. T., & Collins, I. (2018, November). *The impact of relationship commitment on technology use during couple leisure time.* Poster presented at the annual meeting National Council on Family Relations. San Diego, CA.

Miller, A. J., Carlson, D. L., & Sassler, S. (2019) His career, her job, their future: Cohabitors' orientations toward paid work. *Journal of Family Issues, 40*(11), 1509–1533.

Mencarini, L., & Vignoli, D. (2018). Employed women and marital union stability: It helps when men help. *Journal of Family Issues, 39,* 1348–1373.

Minnotte, K. L., Minnotte, M. C., & Pedersen, D. E. (2013). Marital satisfaction among dual-earner couples: Gender ideologies and family-to-work conflict. *Family Relations, 62,* 686–698.

Mirick, R. G., & Wladkowski, S. P. (2018). Pregnancy, motherhood, and academic career goals. *Affilia: Journal of Women & Social Work, 33,* 253–269.

Neilson, J., & Stanfors, M. (2018). Time alone or together? Trends and trade-offs among dual-earner couples, Sweden 1990–2010. *Journal of Marriage & Family, 80,* 80–98.

P, K. (2019). *Study: Average cost of a vacation.* Retrieved from https://www.creditdonkey.com/average-cost-vacation.html

Passias, E. J., Sayer, L., & Pepin, J. R. (2017). Who experiences leisure deficits? Mother's marital status and leisure time. *Journal of Marriage and the Family, 79,* 1001–1022.

Pepin, J. R., Sayer, C., & Casper, L. M. (2018). Marital status and mothers time use: Childcare, housework, leisure, and sleep. *Demography, 55,* 107–133.

Pepin, J. R., & Cotter, D. A. (2018). Separating spheres? Diverging trends in youth's gender attitudes about work and family. *Journal of Marriage & Family, 80,* 7–24.

Petts, R. J., & Knoester, D. (2018). Paternity leave-taking and father engagement. *Journal of Marriage and the Family, 80,* 1144–1162.

PR Newswire. (2018, June 6). Over half of employees say teleworking increases their productivity. PR Newswire US. Retrieved from https://www.prnewswire.com/news-releases/over-half-of-employees-say-teleworking-increases-their-productivity-300660693.html

Preisner, K., Neuberger, F., Posselt, L., & Kratz, F. (2018). Motherhood, employment, and life satisfaction: Trends in Germany between 1984 and 2015 *Journal of Marriage and the Family, 80,* 1107–1124.

Prickett, K. C. (2018). Nonstandard work schedules, family dynamics, and mother-child interactions during early childhood. *Journal of Family Issues, 39,* 985–1007.

ProQuest Statistical Abstract of the United States. (2019). Online Edition. Bethesda, MD. Retrieved from https://www.proquest.com/products-services/statabstract.html

Raub, A., Nandi, A., Earle, A., De Guzman Chorny, N., Wong, E., Chung, P., Batra, P., Schickedanz, A., Bose, B., Jou, J. Franken, D., & Heymann. J. (2018). *Paid parental leave: A detailed look at approaches across OECD countries.* World Policy Analysis Center. Retrieved from www.worldpolicycenter.org

Rodriguez-Muñoz, A., Sanz-Vergel, A. I., Antino, M., Demerouti, E., & Bakker, A. B. (2018). Positive experiences at work and daily recovery: Effects on couple's well-being. *Journal of Happiness Studies, 19,* 1395–1413.

Ruppanner, L., Lee, R., & Huffman, M. (2018). Do mothers benefit from flexible work? Cross-national evidence for work time, job quality and satisfaction. *International Journal of Sociology, 48,* 170–187.

Schoen, R., Astone, N. M., Rothert, K., Standish, N. J., & Kim, Y. J. (2002). Women's employment, marital happiness, and divorce. *Social Forces, 81,* 643–662.

Sharaievska, I., & Stodolska, M. (2017). Family satisfaction and social networking leisure. *Leisure Studies, 36,* 231–243.

Silver-Greenberg, J., & Kitroeff, N. (2018, October 21). Miscarrying at work: The physical toll of pregnancy discrimination. *The New York Times.*

Smith, M. B., & Gelles, K. (2017, April 6). Vacation guilt. *USA Today,* pp. A1.

Smith, M. B., & Gelles, K. (2019, January 11–13). Money versus love. *USA Today,* pp. 1A.

Smith, M. B., & Loehrke, J. (2018, February 25). Credit card debt. *USA Today,* pp. A1.

Sohn, K. (2016). The role of spousal income in the wife's happiness. *Social Indicators Research, 126,* 1007–1024.

State Fact Sheets. (2018). Retrieved from http://usa.childcareaware.org/wp-content/uploads/2018/08/2018-state-fact-sheets.pdf

Strazdins, L., Baxter, J. A., & Li, J. (2017). Long hours and longings: Australian children's views of fathers' work and family time. *Journal of Marriage and the Family, 79,* 965–982.

Telework, V. A. (2018). *How to telework successfully.* Retrieved from http://www.teleworkva.org/forTeleworkers/success.aspx

U.S. Government Accountability Office. (2018). Agencies make some use of telework in space planning but need additional guidance. GAO-18-319. Publicly Released: Mar 22, 2018. Retrieved from https://www.gao.gov/products/GAO-18-319

Valentino, L., Moller, S., Stearns, E., & Mickelson, R. (2016). Perceptions of future career family flexibility as a deterrent from majoring in STEM. *Social Currents,* 3, 273–292.

Van der Lippe, T., & Lippényi, Z. (2018). Beyond formal access: Organizational context, working from home, and work–family conflict of men and women in European workplaces. *Social Indicators Research,* 1–20. Retrieved from https://doi.org/10.1007/s11205-018-1993-1

Vignoli, D., Matysiak, A., Styrc, M., & Tocch, V. (2018). The positive impact of women's employment on divorce: Context, selection, or anticipation. *Demographic Research, 38,* 1059–1110.

Walker, D. (2018). Failing to connect: Studies of remote working in accounting firms show the profession is still struggling to make telework work. Firm leaders need to step up. *Acuity, 5,* 56–59.

Walls, J. K., Helms, H. M., & Grzywacz, J. G. (2016). Intensive-mothering beliefs among full time employed mothers of infants. *Journal of Family Issues, 37,* 245–269.

Westrupp, E. M., Strazdins, L., Martin, A., Cooklin, A., Zubrick, S. R., & Nicholson, J. M. (2016). Maternal work–family conflict and psychological distress: Reciprocal relationships over 8 years. *Journal of Marriage and Family, 78,* 107–126.

Whillans, A. V., & Dunn, E. W. (2019) Valuing time over money is associated with greater social connection. *Journal of Social & Personal Relationships, 36*(8), 2549–2545.

White, E. (2018). USDA cutting down on telework for all employees. *The Washington Post.* Retrieved from https://federalnewsnetwork.com/federal-newscast/2018/01/usda-cutting-down-on-telework-for-all-employees/.

Wise, S., & Trap, P. (2017, March 7). Rise of the home office. *USA Today,* D1.

Wong, J. S. (2017). Competing desires: How young adult couples negotiate moving for career opportunities. *Gender & Society, 31,* 171–196.

Wynn, A. T. (2018). Misery has company: The shared emotional consequences of Everwork among women and me. *Sociological Forum, 33,* 712–734.

Wynn, A. T., Fassiotto, M., Simard, C., Raymond, J. L., & Valantine, H. (2018). Pulled in too many directions: The causes and consequences of work-work conflict. *Sociological Perspectives, 61,* 830–849.

Young, M., & Schieman, S. (2018). Scaling back and finding flexibility: Gender differences in parents' strategies to manage work-family conflict. *Journal of Marriage & Family, 80*, 99–118.

Zabriskie, R. B., & McCormick, B. P. (2001). The influences of family leisure patterns on perceptions of family functioning. *Family Relations, 50*, 281–289.

CHAPTER 14

Aalgaard, R. A., Bolen, R. M. & Nugent, W. R. (2016). A literature review of forgiveness as a beneficial intervention to increase relationship satisfaction in couples therapy. *Journal of Human Behavior in the Social Environment, 26*, 46–55.

Abrahamson, I., Rafat, H., Adeel, K., & Schofield, M. J. (2012). What helps couples rebuild their relationship after infidelity. *Journal of Family Issues, 33*, 1494–1519.

Adams, M. S., Baird, T. C., & Shuler, J. (2018, November 8). *Understanding relationship fidelity.* Poster presented at the annual meeting of the National Council on Family Relations. San Diego, CA.

American Psychiatric Association. (2018). *What is mental illness?* Retrieved from https://www.psychiatry.org/patients-families/what-is-mental-illness

Albuquerque, S., Pereira, M., & Narciso, I. (2016). Couple's relationship after the death of a child: A systematic review. *Journal of Child & Family Studies, 25*, 30–53.

Altgelt, E. E., French, J. E., Meltzer, A. L., McNulty, J. K., & Reyes, M. A. (2018). Who is sexually faithful? Own and partner personality traits as predictors of infidelity. *Journal of Social and Personal Relationships, 35*, 600–614.

Backes, S., Brandstatter, V., Kuster, M., Nussbeck, F. W., Bradbury T. N., Bodenmann, G., & Sutter-Stickel, D. (2017). Who suffers from stress? Action-state orientation moderates the effect of external stress on relationship satisfaction. *Journal of Social and Personal Relationships, 34*, 894–914.

Bakker, D., Kazantzis, N., Rickwood, D., & Rickard, N. (2018). A randomized controlled trial of three smartphone apps for enhancing public mental health. *Behaviour Research and Therapy, 109*, 75–83.

Barnes, H., Knox, D., & Brinkley, J. (2012, March). *CHEATING: Gender differences in reactions to discovery of a partner's cheating.* Paper presented at the Southern Sociology annual meeting. New Orleans, LA.

Beltran, J. (2018) App, brite intervention may be lifesaver for suicidal teens. *UT Southwestern Medical Center.* Retrieved from https://www.utsouthwestern.edu/newsroom/articles/year-2018/brite-app.html

Benuto, L. T., Newlands, R., Ruork, A., Hooft, S., & Ahrendt, A. (2018). Secondary traumatic stress among victim advocates: prevalence and correlates. *Journal of Evidence-Informed Social Work, 15*, 494–509.

Bermant, G. (1976). Sexual behavior: Hard times with the Coolidge Effect. In M. H. Siegel and H. P. Zeigler (Eds.) *Psychological research: The inside story.* New York: Harper and Row.

Bertoncello, C., Colucci, M., Baldovin, T., Buja, A., & Baldo, V. (2018). How does it work? Factors involved in telemedicine home-interventions effectiveness: A review of reviews. *PLoS ONE, 13*, 1–24.

Breitenstein, C. J., Milek, A., Nussbeck, F. W., Davila, J., & Bodenmann, G. (2018). Stress, dyadic coping, and relationship satisfaction in late adolescent couples. *Journal of Social and Personal Relationships, 35*, 770–790.

Brisini, K. S. C., Solomon, D. H., & Nussbaum, J. (2018). Transitions in marriage: Types, turbulence, and transition processing activities. *Journal of Social and Personal Relationships, 35*, 831–853.

Brown, A. R. (2018). A systematic review of psychosocial interventions in treatment of opioid addiction. *Journal of Social Work Practice in the Addictions, 18*, 249–269.

Burke, M. L., Eakes, G. G., & Hainsworth, M. A. (1999). Milestones of chronic sorrow: Perspectives of chronically ill and bereaved persons and family caregivers. *Journal of Family Nursing, 5*, 387–84.

Burr, W. R., & Klein, S. R. (1994). *Reexamining family stress.* Thousand Oaks, CA: Sage.

Bush, N. E., Armstrong, C. M., & Hoyt, T. V. (2018). Smartphone apps for psychological health: A brief state of the science review. *Psychological Services.* Retrieved from doi: 10.1037/ser0000286

Carter, Z. A. (2016). Married and previously married men and women's perceptions of communication on Facebook with the opposite sex: How communicating through Facebook can be damaging to marriages. *Journal of Divorce and Remarriage, 57*, 36–55.

Centers for Disease Control and Prevention. (2018). *Learn about mental illness.* Retrieved from https://www.cdc.gov/mentalhealth/learn/index.htm

Chohaney, M. L., & Panozzo. K. A. (2018). Infidelity and the Internet: The geography of Ashley Madison usership in the United States. *Geographical Review, 108*, 69–91.

Christensen, A. P., Silvia, P. J., Nusbaum, E. C., & Beaty, R. E. (2018). Clever people: Intelligence and humor production ability. *Psychology of Aesthetics, Creativity, and the Arts, 22*, 136–143.

Contreras, S., Porras-Javier, L., Chung, P. J., Zima, B. T., Soares, N., Park, C., &. Coker, T. R. (2018). Development of a telehealth-coordinated intervention to improve access to community-based mental health. *Ethnicity & Disease, 28*, 457–466.

Consoli, A. J., Blears K., Bunge, E. L., Mandil, J., Sharma, H., & Whaling, K. M. (2018). Integrating culture, pedagogy, and humor in CBT with anxious and depressed youth. *Practice Innovations, 3*, 138–151.

Cook-Darzens, S., Gelin, Z., & Hendrick, S. (2018). Evidence base for Multiple Family Therapy (MFT) in non-psychiatric conditions and problems: a review (part 2). *Journal of Family Therapy, 40*, 326–343.

Coppola, E. C., & Wadsworth, S. M. (2017, November). *The role of family functioning on posttraumatic stress disorder symptoms.* Poster presented at the National Council on Family Relations annual meeting, Orlando, FL.

Knox, D., & Crisp, B. (2019, February 25). *Behavioral marriage and family therapy—A best practice review and practical applications.* Paper presented at the American Association of Behavioral and Social Sciences annual conference. Las Vegas, NV.

Crisp, B., & Knox, D. (2009). *Behavioral family therapy.* Durham, NC: Carolina Academic Press.

Daniels, J., Netherland, J. C., & Lyons, A. P. (2018). White women, U.S. popular culture, and narratives of addiction. *Contemporary Drug Problems, 45*, 329–346.

Digital Health Today. (2018). *Four ways technology is helping mental health.* Retrieved from https://digitalhealthtoday.com/blog/technology-and-mental-health/

Donnelly, R., Umberson, D., & Kroeger, R. A. (2018). Childhood adversity, daily stress, and marital strain in same-sex and different sex marriages. *Journal of Family Issues, 39*, 2085–2106.

Doss, B. D., Cicila, L. N., Georgia, E. J., Roddy, M. K., Nowlan, K. M., Benson, L. A., & Christensen, A. (2016). A randomized controlled trial of the web-based OurRelationship program:

Effects on relationship and individual functioning. *Journal of Consulting and Clinical Psychology, 84*, 285–296.

Eaton, E. M., Magill, M., Capone, C., Cramer, M. A., Mastroleo, N. R., Reavy, R., & and. Borsari, B. (2018). Mechanisms of behavior change within peer-implemented alcohol interventions. *Journal of Studies on Alcohol and Drugs, 79*, 208–216.

Ellis, M., & Kleinplatz, P. J. (2018). How contingencies of self-worth influence reactions to emotional and sexual infidelity. *Canadian Journal of Human Sexuality, 27*, 43–54.

Emeka, A. (2018). Where race matters most: Measuring the strength of association between race and unemployment across 50 United States. *Social Indicators Research, 136*, 557–573.

Fan, J. (2017, June 19). The third person. *The New Yorker.*

Finnas, F., Rostila, M., & Saarela, J. (2018). Divorce and parity progression following the death of a child: A register-based study from Finland. *Population Studies, 72*, 41–51.

Frey, L. M., & Cerel, J. (2015). Risk for suicide and the role of family: A narrative review. *Journal of Family Issues, 36*, 716–736.

Frey, L. M., Cerel, J., & Hans, J. D. (2014). *A phenomenological exploration of family reaction after suicide.* Paper presented at the National Council on Family Relations Annual Conference, Baltimore, MD.

Frisby, B. N., Horan, S. M., & Booth-Butterfield, M. (2016). The role of humor styles and shared laughter in the postdivorce recovery process. *Journal of Divorce & Remarriage, 57*, 56–75.

Gardner, T. E. (2017, Fall). *Legal aspects of marriage and divorce,* Presentation to Marriage and Family class, East Carolina University, Greenville, NC.

George, M. J., Russell, M. A., Piontak, J. R., & Odgers, C. L. (2018). Concurrent and subsequent associations between daily digital technology use and high-risk adolescents' mental health symptoms. *Child Development,* 89, 78–88.

Gottman, J. M., & Gottman, J. S. (2018) *The science of couples and family therapy: Behind the scenes at the Love Lab.* New York: W.W. Norton & Company

Hall, S., & Knox, D. (2019). College Student Attitudes and Behaviors Survey of 12,684 undergraduates. Unpublished data collected for this text. Department of Family, Consumer, and Technology Education Teachers College, Ball State University and Department of Sociology, East Carolina University, Greenville, NC.

Hazlett-Stevens, H. (2018). Mindfulness-based stress reduction in a mental health outpatient setting: Benefits beyond symptom reduction. *Journal of Spirituality in Mental Health, 20*, 275–292.

Heffer, T. & Willoughby, T. (2017). A count of coping strategies: A longitudinal study investigating an alternative method to understanding coping and adjustment. *PLoS ONE, 12*(10): e0186057. Retrieved from https:// doi.org/10.1371/journal .pone.0186057

Hendy, H. M., Black, P., Can, S. H., Fleischut, A., & Aksen, D. (2018). Opioid abuse as maladaptive coping to life stressors in U.S. adults. *Journal of Drug Issues, 48*, 60–571.

Hilpert, P., Milek, A., Bodenmann, G., Feng, X., Atkins, D. C., Bradbury, T. N., & Xu, F. (2018). Couples coping with stress: Between-person differences and within-person processes. *Journal of Family Psychology, 32*, 366–374.

Hollis, C., Sampson, S., Simons, L., Davies, E. B., Churchill, R., Betton, V. & Tomlin. (2018). Identifying research priorities for digital technology in mental health care: Results of the James Lind Alliance Priority Setting Partnership. *The Lancet Psychiatry, 5*, 845–854.

Holmes, H. T., & Rahe, T. H. (1967). The Social Readjustment Rating Scale. *Journal of Psychosomatic Research, 11*(2), 213–221.

Hyland, P., Shevlin, M., Fyvie, C., & Karatzias, T. (2018). Posttraumatic stress disorder and complex posttraumatic stress disorder in DSM-5 and ICD-11: Clinical and behavioral correlates. *Journal of Traumatic Stress, 31*, 174–180.

Isanejad, O., & Bagheri, A. (2018, September). Marital quality, loneliness, and internet infidelity. *Cyberpsychology, Behavior, and Social Networking, 21*(9). Retrieved from https://doi .org/10.1089/cyber.2017.0602

Jau. J., & Hodgson, D. (2018). How interaction with animals can benefit mental health: A phenomenological study. *Social Work in Mental Health, 16*, 20–33.

Jeanfreau, M. M., & Michael, M. (2019). Barriers to marital infidelity. *Marriage and Family Review, 55*, 1, 23–37, Retrieved from doi 10.1080/01494929.2018.1518821

Johnson, M. D., & Bradbury, T. N. (2015). Contributions of social learning theory to the promotion of healthy relationships: Asset or liability? *Journal of Family Theory & Review, 7,* 13–27.

Jorolmen, J., & Patel, G. (2018). The effects of animal-assisted activities on college students before and after a final exam. *Journal of Creativity in Mental Health, 13,* 264–274.

Kanter, J. B., & Schramm, D. G. (2018). Brief interventions for couples: An integrative review. *Family Relations, 67,* 211–226.

Kennard, B. D., Goldstein, T.,. Foxwell, A. A., McMakin, D. L., Wolfe, K., Biernesser, C., Moorehead, A., Douaihy, A., Zullo, L., Wentroble, E., Owen, V., Zelazny, J., Iyengar, S., Porta, G., & Brent, D. (2018). As safe as possible (ASAP): A brief app-supported inpatient intervention to prevent postdischarge suicidal behavior in hospitalized, suicidal adolescents. *American Journal of Psychiatry, 175*(9), 864–872.

Kertesz, S. G., & Gordon, A. J. (2019). A crisis of opioids and the limits of prescription control: United States. *Addiction, 114*, 169–180

Kim, H. W., Pepping, C. A., & Petch, J. (2016). The gap between couple therapy research efficacy and practice effectiveness. *Journal of Marital and Family Therapy, 42,* 32–44.

Kish, A. M., Newcombe, P. A., & Haslam, D. M. (2018). Working and caring for a child with chronic illness: A review of current literature. *Child: Care, Health and Development, 44*, 343–354.

Lammers, J., & Maner, J. (2016). Power and attraction to the counternormative aspects of infidelity. *Journal of Sex Research, 53,* 54–63.

Lebow, J. L. (2017). Editorial: Emerging principles of practice in couple and family therapy. *Family Process, 56,* 535–539.

Lee, B. H., & O'Sullivan, L. F. (2018). Ain't misbehaving? Monogamy maintenance strategies in heterosexual romantic relationships. *Personal Relationships, 25,* 205–232.

Lee, Y., Hofferth, S. L., Flood, S. M., & Fisher, K. (2016). Reliability, validity, and variability of the subjective well-being questions in the 2010 American Time Use Survey. *Social Indicators Research, 126,* 1355–1373.

London-Johnson, A. M., Wells, B. A., Smith, A. M., Baity, C., & Grzywacz, J. G. (2017). *Understanding the impact of chronic illness on couples' relationship quality.* Poster presented at the annual meeting of the National Council on Family Relations, Orlando, FL.

Lopez, V. (2016). Love is a battlefield. *Youth & Society, 49*, 23–45.

Lustgarten, S. D., & Elhai, J. D. (2018). Technology use in mental health practice and research: Legal and ethical risks. *Clinical Psychology: Science and Practice, 25*, 1–10.

Maume, D. J., Hewitt, B., & Ruppanner, L. (2018). Gender equality and restless sleep among partnered Europeans. *Journal of Marriage and the Family, 80*, 1040–1058.

Meyer, T. D., Casarez, R., Mohite, S. S., La Rosa, N., & Iyengar, M. S. (2018). Novel technology as platform for interventions for caregivers and individuals with severe mental health illnesses: A systematic review. *Journal of Affective Disorders, 226,* 169–177.

Mitchell, J. M., & Abraham, K. M. (2018). Parental mental illness and the transition to college: Coping, psychological adjustment, and parent-child relationships. *Journal of Child and Family Studies, 27,* 2966–2977.

Molla, E., Tadros, E., & Cappetto, M. (2018). The effects of alcohol and substance use on a couple system. *Family Journal, 26,* 341–350.

Moon, I., & Han, J. (2019). Associations between health risk behaviors and perceived health status among individuals with serious mental illness (SMI). *Social Work in Mental Health, 17*(4), 494–508.

Moore, J., Magee, S., Gamreklidze, E. & Kowalewski, J. O. (2019) Social media mourning: Using grounded theory to explore how people grieve on social media sites. *Journal of Death & Dying, 79*(3), 231–259.

Morell, V. (1998). A new look at monogamy. *Science, 281*(5385), 1982–1983.

Moreno, N., & Kahumoku-Fessler, E. P. (2018). Understanding infidelity: How perceptions of infidelity behaviors vary by sex and one's own infidelity experiences. *American Journal of Family Therapy, 46,* 107–121.

Mrug, S., Tyson, A., Turan, B., & Granger, D. A. (2016). Sleep problems predict cortisol reactivity to stress in urban adolescents. *Physiology & Behavior, 155,* 95–101.

Nabors, L., Cunningham, J. F., Lang, M., Wood, K., Southwick, S., & Stough, C. O. (2018). Family coping during hospitalization of children with chronic illnesses. *Journal of Child and Family Studies, 27,* 1482–1491.

National Institute of Mental Health. (2018). Mental Illness. Mental Health Information. Statistics. Retrieved from https://www .nimh.nih.gov/health/statistics/mental-illness.shtml

Nichols, H. (2018). The top 10 mental health apps. *Medical News Today.* Retrieved from https://www.medicalnewstoday .com/articles/320557.php

Norona, J. C., Olmstead, S. B., & Welsh, D. P. (2018) . Betrayals in emerging adulthood: A developmental perspective of Infidelity. *Journal of Sex Research, 55,* 84–98.

O'Hare, T., Shen, C., & Sherrer, M. (2018). Lifetime trauma and suicide attempts in older clients with severe mental illness. *Social Work in Mental Health, 16,* 505–517.

Owen, J., Rhoades, G. K., Stanley, S. M., Markman, H. J. & Allen, E. S. (2019). Treatment-as-usual for couples: Trajectories before and after beginning couple therapy. *Family Process, 58*(2), 273–286.

Papp, L. M. (2018). Topics of marital conflict in the everyday lives of empty nest couples and their implications for conflict resolution. *Journal of Couple and Relationship Therapy, 17,* 1–17.

Patrick, M. E., & Terry-McElrath, Y. M. (2017). High-intensity drinking by underage young adults in the United States. *Addiction, 112,* 82–93.

Peisch, V., Sullivan, A. D., Breslend, N. L., Benoit, R., Sigmon, S. C., Forehand, G. L., Strolin- Goltzman, J., & Forehand, R. (2018). Parental opioid abuse: A review of child outcomes, parenting, and parenting interventions. *Journal of Child and Family Studies, 27,* 2082–2099.

Perel, E. (2017). *The state of affairs: Rethinking infidelity.* New York: Harper.

Perzow, S. E. D., Bray, B. C., & Wadsworth, M. E. (2018). Financial stress response profiles and psychosocial functioning in low-income parents. *Journal of Family Psychology, 32,* 517–527.

Platt, L. F., & Scheitle, C. P. (2017) Is marriage counseling perceived as scientific? Examining the views of U.S. adults. *Family Journal, 25,* 239–246.

Pritchard, T. R., & Buckle, J. L. (2018). Meaning-making after partner suicide: A narrative exploration using the meaning of loss codebook. *Death Studies, 42,* 35–44

ProQuest Statistical Abstract of the United States. (2019). Online Edition. Bethesda, MD. Retrieved from https://www .proquest.com/products-services/statabstract.html

Rao, A. H. (2017). Stand by your man: Wives' emotion work during men's unemployment *Journal of Marriage and the Family, 79*(3), 636–656. Retrieved from doi: 10.1111/jomf.12385.

Roddy, M. K., Rothman, K., Cicila, L. N., & Doss, B. D. (2019). Why do couples seek relationship help online? Description and comparison to in-person interventions. *Journal of Marital & Family Therapy, 45*(3), 369–379.

Riordan, B. C., Conner, T. S., Flett, J. A. M., Droste, N., Cody, L., Brookie, K. L., Riordan, J. K., & Scarf, D. (2018). An intercept study to measure the extent to which New Zealand university students pre-game. *Australian and New Zealand Journal of Public Health, 42,* 30–34.

Rodriguez-Rey, R., Alonso-Tapia, J., & Hernansaiz-Garrido, H. (2016). Reliability and validity of the Brief Resilience Scale (BRS) Spanish version. *Psychological Assessment, 28,* e101-e110.

Roex, K. L. A., & Rozer, J. J. (2018). The social norm to work and the well-being of the short and long term unemployed. *Social Indicators Research, 139,* 1037–1064.

Rootes-Murdy, K., Glazer, K. L., Van Wert, M. J., Mondimore, F. M., & Zandi, P. (2018). Mobile technology for medication adherence in people with mood disorders: A systematic review. *Journal of Affective Disorders, 227,* 613–617.

Rue, N. (2018). *Is technology good or bad for mental health.* Retrieved from https://thedoctorweighsin.com/is-technology-good-or-bad-for-mental-health/

Sawang, S., & Newton, C. J. (2018). Defining work stress in young people. *Journal of Employment Counseling, 55,* 72–83.

Schauss, E., Howell, K., & Ellmo, F. (2019). How do couples cope with unemployment: Examining relationships among support, undermining, and depression. *Family Journal, 27*(3), 268–277.

Schmidt, S., & Barnes, R. (2019, August 31). Ginsburg says she is 'on my way to being very well' after cancer treatment. *Washington Post.* Retrieved from https://www .washingtonpost.com/politics/courts_law/ginsburg-says-she-is-on-my-way-to-being-very-well-after-cancer-treatment/2019/08

Shaffer, J. (2018, July 27). *Jilted spouse wins 8.8 million in alienation of affection lawsuit.* Retrieved from https://www .newsobserver.com/latest-news/article215633900 .html

Shrout, M. R., & Weigel, D. J. (2018). Infidelity's aftermath: Appraisals, mental health, and health-compromising behaviors following a partner's infidelity. *Journal of Social and Personal Relationships, 35,* 1067–1091.

Smith, T. M., Bertmann, F. M. W., Pinard, C. A., Schober, D. J., Shuval, K., Nguyen, B. T., & Yaroch, A. L. (2017). Factors associated with supplemental nutrition assistance program participation among the working poor: Findings from 2012 American Community Survey. *Journal of Hunger & Environmental Nutrition, 12,* 169–180.

Sotero, L., Moura-Ramos, M., Escudero, V., & Relvas, A.P. (2018). When the family is opposed to coming to therapy: A study on outcomes and therapeutic alliance with involuntary and voluntary clients. *Couple and Family Psychology: Research and Practice, 7,* 47–61.

Stanko, K. E., Cherry, K. E., Marks, L. D., Sampson, L., Ryker, K. S., Barrios, B., Anderson, R., Sanchez, S., & Allen, K. (2018). When reliance on religion falters: Religious coping and post-traumatic stress symptoms in older adults after multiple disasters. *Journal of Religion, Spirituality and Aging, 30,* 292–313.

Swan, D. J., & S. C. Thompson, S. C. (2016). Monogamy, the protective fallacy: Sexual versus emotional exclusivity and the implication for sexual health risk. *Journal of Sex Research, 53,* 64–73.

Theisen, J., Ogolsky, B., & Wiley, A. (2016, November). Fit and happy: How exercise and maintenance buffer the effects of stress. *National Council on Family Relations.* Phoenix, AZ.

Thomas, R., & Matusitz, J. (2016). Pet therapy in correctional institutions: A perspective from relational-cultural theory. *Journal of Evidence-Informed Social Work, 13,* 228–235.

Thorson, A. R. (2017). Communication and parental infidelity: A qualitative analysis of how adult children cope in a topic-avoidant environment. *Journal of Divorce & Remarriage, 58,* 175–193.

Topete, L., Forst, L., Zanoni, J., & Friedman, L. (2018). Workers' compensation and the working poor. *American Journal of Industrial Medicine, 61,* 189–197.

Totenhagen, C. J., Randall, A. K., & Lloyd, K. (2018). Stress and relationship functioning of same-sex couples: The vulnerabilities of internalized homophobia and outness. *Family Relations, 67,* 399–413.

Tuttle, B. M., Giano, Z., & Merten, M. J. (2018). Stress spillover in policing and negative relationship functioning marriages. *Family Journal, 26,* 246–252.

Tyler, K. A., Schmitz, R. M., Adams, S. A., & Simons, L. G. (2017). Social factors, alcohol expectancy and drinking behavior: A comparison of two college campuses. *Journal of Substance Abuse, 22,* 357–364.

Vanman, E. J., Baker, R., & Tobin, S. J. (2018). The burden of online friends: the effects of giving up Facebook on stress and well-being. *Journal of Social Psychology, 158,* 496–507.

Vobemer, J., Gebel, M., That, K., Unt, M., Hogberg B., & Strandh, M. (2018). The effects of unemployment and insecure jobs on well-being and health: The moderating role of labor market policies. *Social Indicators Research, 138,* 1229–1257.

Walker, A. M. (2019). Perception of life satisfaction during outside partnerships. *Sexuality & Culture, 23,* 112–131.

Wang, W. (2018, January 10). *Who cheats more? The demographics of infidelity in America.* The Institute for Family Studies. Retrieved from https://ifstudies.org/blog/who-cheats-more-the-demographics-of-cheating-in-america

Webb, H. J., Zimmer-Gembeck, M J., Scuffham, P. A., Scott, R., & Barber, B. (2018). Family stress predicts poorer dietary quality in children: Examining the role of the parent-child relationship. *Infant and Child Development, 27,* 1–19.

West, A. R., & Haynes-Lawrence, D. (2017, March 16–18). Managing fatigue with parents with multiple sclerosis. Poster presented at the annual meeting of the Southeastern Council on Family Relations, Charlotte, NC.

Whitt-Woosley, A., & Sprang, G. (2018). Secondary traumatic stress in social science researchers of trauma-exposed populations. *Journal of Aggression, Maltreatment and Trauma, 27,* 475–486.

Wiebe, S. A., Johnson, S. M., Lafontaine, M. F., Burgess Moser, M., & Dalgleish, T. L. (2017). Two-year follow up outcomes in emotionally focused couple therapy: An investigation of relationship satisfaction and attachment trajectories. *Journal of Marital & Family Therapy, 43,* 227–244.

Williamson, H. C., Hammett, J. F., Ross, J. M., Karney, B. R., & Bradbury, T. N. (2018). Premarital education and later relationship help-seeking. *Journal of Family Psychology, 32,* 276–281.

Wilson, S. L., Cooper, R. L., Nugent, W. R., & Champion, D. (2016). BASICS, ACT, mindfulness and BMI: Effective evidence-based practices that treat collegiate high-risk drinking. *Human Behavior in the Social Environment, 26,* 81–88.

World Health Organization. (2018). *Mental disorders.* Retrieved from https://www.who.int/mental_health/management/en/

Young, D. K. W. (2018). Cognitive behavioral therapy group for reducing self-stigma for people with mental illness. *Research on Social Work Practice, 28,* 827–837.

Yuan, S., & Weiser, D. A. (2019). Relationship dissolution following marital infidelity: Comparing European Americans and Asian Americans. *Marriage and Family Review, 55*(7), 631–650.

CHAPTER 15

Abetz, J., & Wang, T. R. (2017). "Were they ever really happy the way that I remember?": Exploring uncertainty for adult children of divorce. *The Journal of Divorce and Remarriage, 58*(3), 194–211.

Alba-Fisch, M. (2016). Collaborative divorce: An effort to reduce the damage of divorce. *Journal of Clinical Psychology, 72,* 444–457.

Amato, P., & Patterson, S. (1917). The intergenerational transmission of union instability in early adulthood. *Journal of Marriage and Family, 79,* 723–738.

Amelia, K. (2018). Three co-parenting apps that make life easier. Retrieved from https://thegrapevinegossip.com/co-parenting-apps-that-make-life-easier/

Andresson, J., & Johansson, T. (2019). Becoming a half-time parent: Fatherhood after divorce. *Journal of Family Studies, 25,* 2–17.

Bartle-Haring, S., Shannon, S., Holowicz, E., Patton, R., & Lotspeich-Younkin, F. (2018). Is there the "sweet spot" for age at marriage and positive marital outcomes? *Journal of Family Issues, 39,* 1085–1107.

Beebe, P. C., & Sailor, J. L. (2017). A phenomenological study of parental estrangement. *Journal of Divorce & Remarriage, 58,* 347–357.

Braver, S. L., & Votruba, A. M. (2018). Does joint physical custody "cause" children's better outcomes? *Journal of Divorce & Remarriage, 5,* 452–468.

Brenner, R., & Knox, D. (2018). Recovery from breakup of a romantic relationship. Unpublished data. State University of New York/Albany; East Carolina University, Greenville, NC.

Brenner, R. E., & Vogel, D. L. (2014, November). Measuring thought content valence after a breakup: Development of the positive and negative ex-relationship thoughts scale. Poster presented at American Psychological Association Annual Meeting, Washington, DC.

Brimhall, A. S., & Engblom-Deglmann, M. L. (2011). Starting over: A tentative theory exploring the effects of past relationships on post bereavement remarried couples. *Family Process, 50,* 47–62.

Brons, M. D., & Harkonen, J. (2018). Parental education and family dissolution: A cross-national and cohort comparison. *Journal of Marriage and the Family, 80,* 426–443.

Carlson, M. J., VanOrman, A. G., & Turner, K. J. (2017). Fathers' investments of money and time across residential contexts. *Journal of Marriage and the Family, 79,* 10–23.

Carter, K, Knox, D., & Hall, S. (2019, January 7). Romantic breakup: Difficult loss for some and not for others. *Journal of Loss & Trauma.* Retrieved from https://www.tandfonline.com/doi/abs/10.1080/15325024.2018.1502523?journalCode=upil20

Carter, K., Knox, D., & Hall, S. (2019, April 10–14). Romantic Breakup: Difficult loss for some but not for others. Poster, Southern Sociological Society annual meeting, Atlanta, GA.

Clarke, S. C., & Wilson, B. F. (1994). The relative stability of remarriages: A cohort approach using vital statistics. *Family Relations, 43,* 305–10.

Coontz, S. (2016). *The way we never were: American families and the nostalgia trap* (2nd ed). New York: Basic Books.

Crowley, J. E. (2019a) Does everything fall apart? Life assessments following a gray divorce. *Journal of Family Issues, 40*(11), 1438–1461

Crowley, J. E. (2019). Once bitten, twice shy? gender differences in the remarriage decision after a gray divorce." *Sociological Inquiry, 89,* 150–176.

Cuzzolino, E., & Williams, C. L. (2017). Child support queens and disappointing dads: Gender and child support compliance. *Social Currents, 4*(3), 228–245.

DeAnda, J., Langlais, M., Anderson, E., & Greene, S. (2017, November 16). Mother's emotional attachment to the ex-spouse. Poster presented at the National Council on Family Relations annual meeting.

Di Nallo, A. (2019). Gender gap repartnering: The role of parental status and custodial arrangements. *Journal of Marriage and the Family, 81,* 59–78.

Doherty, W. J., Harris, S. M., & Didericksen, K. W. (2016). A typology of attitudes toward proceeding with divorce among parents in the divorce process. *Journal of Divorce and Remarriage, 57,* 1–11.

Duncan, J. C., Futris, T. G., & Bryant, C. M. (2018). Association between depressive symptoms, perceived partner emotional expression, and marital quality. *Marriage & Family Review, 54,* 507–520.

Fabricius, W. V., Aaron, M., Akins, F. R., Assini, J. J., & McElroy, T. (2018). What happens when there is presumptive 50/50 parenting time? An evaluation of Arizona's new child custody statute. *Journal of Divorce & Remarriage, 59,* 414–428.

Ferraro, A. J., Lucier-Greer, M., & and K. Oehme, K. (2017). *Competing methods of co-parenting post-divorce: A stress process approach.* Annual meeting of the National Council on Family Relations, Orlando, FL.

Ferraro, A. J., Malespin, T., Oehme, K., Bruker, M., & Opel, N. (2016). Advancing co-parenting education: Toward a foundation for supportive post-divorce adjustment. *Child & Adolescent Social Work Journal, 33*(5), 407–415.

Finnas, F., Rostila, M., & Saarela, J. (2018). Divorce and parity progression following the death of a child: A register-based study from Finland. *Population Studies, 72,* 41–51.

Fisher, H., & Garcia, J. R. (2016). Singles in America. Retrieved from http://www.singlesinamerica.com/.

Fisher, H. & Garcia, J. R. (2019). Singles in America. https://www.singlesinamerica.com/#RELATIONSHIPS5

Fonseca, G., Cunha, D., Crespo, C., & Relvas, A. P. (2016). Families in the context of macroeconomic crises: A systematic review. *Journal of Family Psychology, 30,* 687–697.

Fowler, C., & Gasiorek, J. (2017). Depressive symptoms, excessive reassurance seeking, and relationship maintenance. *Journal of Social and Personal Relationships, 34,* 91–113.

Gager, C. T., Yabiku, S. T., & Linver, M. R. (2016). Conflict or divorce? Does parental conflict and/or divorce increase the likelihood of adult children's cohabiting and marital dissolution? *Marriage & Family Review, 52,* 243–261.

Galovan, A. M., & Schramm, D. G. (2017). Initial coparenting patterns and postdivorce parent education programming: A latent class analysis. *Journal of Divorce & Remarriage, 58*(3), 212–226.

Ganong, L., Coleman, M., Chapman, A., & Jamison, T. (2018). Stepchildren claiming stepparents. *Journal of Family Issues, 39,* 1712–1712.

Gardner, R. A. (1998). *The parental alienation syndrome.* 2d ed. Cresskill, NJ: Creative Therapeutics.

Geiger, A., & Livingston, G. (2019). 8 facts about love and marriage in America. Retrieved from https://www.pewresearch.org/fact-tank/2019/02/13/8-facts-about-love-and-marriage

Godbout, E., & Parent, C. (2012). The life paths and lived experiences of adults who have experienced parental alienation: A retrospective study. *Journal of Divorce and Remarriage, 53,* 34–54.

Goetting, A. (1982). The six stations of remarriage: The developmental tasks of remarriage after divorce. *The Family Coordinator, 31,* 213–22.

Gregg, H. (2018). The effect of the new tax bill. *American Journal of Family Law, 32,* 37–38.

Guzmán-González, M., Garrido, L., Calderón, C., Contreras, P., & Rivera, D. (2017). Chilean adaptation and validation of the Fisher Adjustment Scale-Short Form. *Journal of Divorce and Remarriage, 58,* 96–109.

Guzzo, K. B. (2017). Shifts in higher-order unions and stepfamilies among currently cohabiting and married women of childbearing age. *Journal of Family Issues, 38,* 1775–1799.

Guzzo, K. B. (2018). Marriage and dissolution among women's cohabitations: Variations by stepfamily status and shared childbearing. *Journal of Family Issues, 39,* 1108–1136.

Haddad, L., Phillips, K., & Bone, J. M. (2016). High conflict divorce: A review of literature. *American Journal of Family Law, 29,* 243–258.

Hall, S., & Knox, D. (2019). College Student Attitudes and Behaviors Survey of 12,756 undergraduates. Unpublished data collected for this text. Department of Family, Consumer, and Technology Education Teachers College, Ball State University and Department of Sociology, East Carolina University, Greenville, NC.

Halligan, C., Chang, I. J., & Knox, D. (2014). Positive effects of parental divorce on undergraduates. *Journal of Divorce and Remarriage, 55,* 557–567.

Hansson, M., & T. Ahborg, T. (2016). Factors contributing to separation/divorce in parents of small children in Sweden. *Nordic Psychology, 68,* 40–57.

Harris, M., & Crabtree, S. A. (2016, November). *Discernment counseling for couples on the brink of divorce.* Paper presented at the National Council on Family Relations annual meeting. Phoenix, AZ.

Hartman, T. (2019). Men who were left and the high cost of the high road. *Contemporary Family Therapy: An International Journal, 41*(3), 316–325.

Hawkins, A., Galovan, A., & Schramm. (2016, November). *What are they thinking? A national study of stability and change in divorce ideation.* Paper presented at the National Council on Family Relations, annual meeting, Phoenix, AZ.

Hilliard, T., Carter, K., Knox, D., & Hall, S. (2019, November). *Sexual value changes after a romantic breakup*. Poster, Society for the Scientific Study of Sex, Denver, CO.

Hoffnung, M., & Williams, M. A. (2016). Women's postdivorce name choice. *Journal of Divorce & Remarriage, 57*, 2–35.

Hoy, A. (2018). Invisibility, illegibility, and stigma: The citizenship experiences of divorced gays and lesbians. *Journal of Divorce & Remarriage, 59*, 69–91.

Jackson, L. J., & Fife, S. T. (2018). The impact of parental divorce: The relationship between social support and confidence levels in young adults. *Journal of Divorce & Remarriage, 59*, 123–140.

Jensen, T. M., Shafer, K., Guo, S., & Larson, J. H. (2017). Differences in relationship stability between individuals in first and second marriages: A propensity score analysis. *Journal of Family Issues, 38*, 406–432.

Jensen, T. M., Lippold, M. A., Mills-Koonce, R., Fosco, G. M. (2018). Stepfamily relationship quality and children's internalization and externalizing problems. *Family Process, 57*, 477–495.

Kang, Y., Ganong, L. (2018, November 8). *How do divorced fathers decide what to disclose to their children?* Poster presented at the annual meeting of the National Council on Family Relations. San Diego, CA.

Kesselring, R. G., & Bremmer, D. (2006). Female income and the divorce decision: Evidence from micro data. *Applied Economics, 38*, 1605–17.

Killewald, A. (2016). Money, work, and marital stability: Assessing change in the gendered determinants of divorce. *American Sociological Review, 81*, 696–719.

Kerpelman, J. L., McElwain, A. D., Pittman, J. F., & Adler-Baeder, F. M. (2016). Engagement in risky sexual behavior. *Youth and Society, 48*, 101–125.

Klobucar, N. R., & Simonic, B. (2017). Causes of divorce from the perspective of females in Slovenia. *The Journal of Divorce and Remarriage, 58*(4), 263–275.

Kutner, J. (2015). *What nobody tells you about being an adult child of divorce*. Retrieved from https://www.mic.com/articles/127347/what-nobody-tells-you-about-being-an-adult-child-of-divorce

Lamb, M. E. (2018). Does shared parenting by separated parents affect the adjustment of young children? *Journal of Child Custody, 15*, 16–25.

Lawson, E. J., & Satti, F. (2016). The aftermath of divorce: Postdivorce adjustment strategies of South Asian, Black, and White women in the United States. *Journal of Divorce & Remarriage, 57*, 411–431.

Leopold, T. (2018). Gender differences in the consequences of divorce: A study of multiple outcomes. *Demography, 55*, 769–797.

Livingston, G. (2014, November 14). The demographics of remarriage. Pew Research Center. Retrieved from https://www.pewsocialtrends.org/2014/11/14/chapter-2-the-demographics-of-remarriage/

Louis, C. S. (2017, December 20). Debunking myths about estrangement. *New York Times*.

Love, H. A., Durtschi, J. A., Ruhlmann, L. M., & Nelson Goff, B. S. (2018). Army soldiers and suicidal thoughts: The impact of negative relationship dynamics moderated by the dissolution of romantic relationships. *Journal of Marital & Family Therapy, 44*, 265–276.

Mahrer, N. E., O'Hara, K. L., Sandler, I. N., & Wolchik, S. A. (2018). Does shared parenting help or hurt children in high-conflict divorced families? *Journal of Divorce & Remarriage, 59*, 324–347.

Markham, M. S., Hartenstein, J. L., Mitchell, Y. T., & Aljayyousi-Khalil, G. (2017). Communication among parents who share physical custody after divorce or separation. *Journal of Family Issues, 38*(10), 1414–1442.

Marschall, A. (2017). When everyday life is double looped. Exploring childrens' (and parents') perspectives on post-divorce family life with two households. *Children & Society, 31*, 342–352.

Martin-Uzzi, M., & Duval-Tsioles, D.(2013). The experience of remarried couples in blended families. *Journal of Divorce and Remarriage, 54*, 43–57.

Masheter, C. (1999). Examples of commitment in postdivorce relationships between spouses. In J. M. Adams and W. H. Jones (Eds), *Handbook of interpersonal commitment and relationship stability (pp. 293–306)*. New York: Academic/Plenum Publishers.

McKinley Irvin Family Law. (2018). *Useful apps to help with co-parenting*. Retrieved from https://www.mckinleyirvin.com/family-law-blog/2018/september/useful-apps-to-help-with-co-parenting/

Mercadante, C., Taylor, M. F., & Pooley, J. A. (2014). "I wouldn't wish it on my worst enemy": Western Australian fathers' perspectives on their marital separation experiences. *Marriage & Family Review, 50*, 318–341.

Mercer, J. (2019). Examining parental alienation treatments: Problems of principles and practices. *Child & Adolescent Social Work Journal, 36*(4), 351–363.

Mikucki-Enyart, S. L., Wilder, S. E., & Barber, H. (2017). What is all smoke and mirrors?: Applying the relational turbulence model to adult children's experience of late-life parental divorce. *Journal of Social and Personal Relationships, 34*, 209–234.

Miller, R. W. (2019, February 12). Divorced and millennial. *USA Today*, pp. 1B.

Mogilski, J. K., & Welling, L. L. M. (2016). Staying friends with an ex: Sex and dark personality traits predict motivations for post relationship friendship. *Personality and Individual Differences, 115*, 114–119.

Morgan, E. S. (1944). *The Puritan family*. Boston, MA: Public Library.

Morris, M., Halford, W. K., Petch, J., & Harwick, D. (2018). Predictors of engagement in family mediation and outcomes for families that fail to engage. *Family Process, 57*, 131–147.

Nichols, S. (2018). *Custody arrangement and communication style as predictors of parent-child relationships postdivorce*. (Doctoral dissertation). Regent University, Virginia Beach, VA.

Nielsen, L. (2018). Joint versus sole physical custody: Children's outcomes independent of parent-child relationships, income and conflict in 60 studies. *Journal of Divorce & Remarriage, 59*, 247–281.

Osmani, N., Matlabi, H., & Rezaei, M. (2018). Barriers to remarriage among older people: Viewpoints of widows and widowers. *Journal of Divorce and Remarriage, 59*, 51–68.

Papernow, P. L. (2018). Clinical guidelines for working with stepfamilies: What family, couple, individuals and child therapists need to know. *Family Process, 57*, 25–51.

Perrig-Chiello, P., Hutchinson, S., & Morselli, D. (2015). Patterns of psychological adaptation to divorce after a long-term marriage. *Journal of Social & Personal Relationships, 32*, 386–405.

Poortman, A. R. (2018). Postdivorce parent-child contact and child well-being: The importance of predivorce parental involvement. *Journal of Marriage and the Family, 80*, 671–683.

Potarca, G., Mills, M., & van Duijin, M. (2017). The choices and constraints of secondary singles: Willingness to stepparent among divorced online daters across Europe. *Journal of Family Issues, 38*, 1443–1470.

ProQuest Statistical Abstract of the United States. (2019). Online Edition. Bethesda, MD. Retrieved from https://www .proquest.com/products-services/statabstract.html

Reinstein, K. (2018). *Co-parenting after divorce: The relation among forgiveness, empathy, and hostile attribution bias.* (Doctoral Dissertation). Hofstra University, Hempstead, Long Island, New York.

Roberson, P. N. E., Norona, J. C., Lenger, K. A., & Olmstead, S. B. (2018). How do relationship stability and quality affect wellbeing? Romantic relationship trajectories, depressive symptoms, and life satisfaction across 30 years. *Journal of Child & Family Studies, 27,* 2171–2184.

Ruppanner, L., Branden, M., & Turunen, J. (2018). Does unequal housework lead to divorce? Evidence from Sweden. *Sociology, 52*(1), 75–94.

Saether, M. H. (2019). Childhood family dissolution and school outcomes. The timing of dissolution effects. *Marriage & Family Review, 55*(7), 686–7000.

Saini, M., & Polak, S. (2018). The benefits, drawbacks, and safety considerations in digital parent–child relationships: An exploratory survey of the views of legal and mental health professionals in family law. *Family Court Review, 56,* 597–606.

Saleh, R. H., & Luppicini, R. (2017). Exploring the challenges of divorce on Saudi women. *Journal of Family History, 42,* 184–198.

Schramm, D. G., Kanter, J. B., Brotherson, S. E., & Kranzler, B. (2018). An empirically based framework for content selection and management in divorce education programs. *Journal of Divorce & Remarriage, 59,* 195–221.

Shimkowski, J. R., Punyanunt-Carter, N., Colwell, M. J., & Norman, M. S. (2018). Perceptions of divorce, closeness, marital attitudes, romantic beliefs, and religiosity among emergent adults from divorced and nondivorced families. *Journal of Divorce & Remarriage, 59,* 222–236.

Sigurdardottier, S., Juliusdottir, S., & Palsdottir, D. (2018). Children's voices on equal time-sharing arrangement following parents' divorce. *Journal of Social Welfare & Family Law, 40,* 164–180.

Sjöblom, B., Franzén, A., & Aronsson, K. (2018). Contested connectedness in child custody narratives: Mobile phones and children's rights and responsibilities. *New Media & Society, 20*(10), 3818–3835.

Soares, A. L. G., Howe L. D., Matijasevich, A., Wehrmeister, F. C., Menezes, A. M. B., & Goncalves, H. (2016). Adverse childhood experiences: Prevalence and related factors in adolescents of a Brazilian birth cohort. *Child Abuse & Neglect, 51,* 21–30.

Soria, K. M., Morrow, D. J., & Jackson, R. (2018). Parental divorce and college students' persistence and degree attainment. *Journal of Divorce & Remarriage, 59*(1), 25–36.

Spencer, T. A., Cox, R., Brosi, M., & Jones, E. (2018, November 8). *Increasing collaborative co-parenting.* Poster presented at the Annual Conference of National Council of Family Relations, San Diego, CA.

Stephens, C. (2018). Best co-parenting app. Stiles Law. Retrieved from https://www.mynclaw.com/single-post/2016/03/09/5-Apps-That-Will-Make-Co-Parenting-Much-Easier

Sullivan, M. E. (2016). Family law mediation: The master checklist. *American Journal of Family Law, 30,* 58–63.

Theunis, L., Schnor, C., Willaert, D., & Van Bavel, J. (2018). His and her education and marital dissolution: Adding a contextual dimension. *European Journal of Population, 34*(4), 663–687.

Thomas, M. J., Mulder, C. H., & Cooke, T. J. (2018). Geographical distances between separated parents: A longitudinal analysis. *European Journal of Population, 34*(4), 463–489.

Tong, S. T. (2013). Facebook use during relationship termination: Uncertainty reduction and surveillance. *Cyberpsychology, Behavior, and Social Networking, 16*(11), 788–793.

Vaus, D., Gray, M., Qu, L., & Stanton, D. (2017). The economic consequences of divorce in six countries. *Australian Journal of Social Issues, 52,* 180–199.

Vinick, B. (1978). Remarriage in old age. *The Family Coordinator, 27,* 359–63.

Waller, M. R., & Dwyer Emory, A. (2018). Visitation orders, family courts and fragile families. *Journal of Marriage and the Family, 80*(3), 653–670.

Wang, W. (2018, January 10). Who cheats more? The demographics of infidelity in America. *The Institute for Family Studies.* Retrieved from https://ifstudies.org/blog/who-cheats-more-the-demographics-of-cheating-in-america

Watkins, N. K., & Waldron, M. (2017). Timing of remarriage among divorced and widowed parents. *Journal of Divorce & Remarriage, 58*(4), 244–262.

Watkins, N. K., & Waldron, M. (2017, November). Parental divorce during emerging adulthood and risk of depression. Poster presented at the annual meeting of the National Council on Family Relations, Orlando, FL.

Winchester, D., Spencer, J. W., & Baird, D. M. (2018). "I felt so guilty for being so happy": Narrative expressions and management of postdivorce ambivalence. *Sociological Focus, 51*(3), 200–216.

Wong, M. M. C., Ma, J. L. C. & Xia, L. L. (2019). A qualitative study of parents' and children's views on mediation. *Journal of Divorce & Remarriage, 60*(6), 418–435.

Wu, Z., & Penning, M. J. (2018). Marital and cohabiting union dissolution in middle and later life. *Research on Aging, 40*(4), 340–364.

Xu, Y., Lin, L., Yang, L., Zhou, L., Tao, Y., Chen, W., Chai, H., & Wang, W. (2016). Personality disorder and perceived parenting in Chinese students of divorce and intact families. *Family Journal, 24*(1), 70–76.

Zella, S. (2016). Marital status transitions and self-reported health among Canadians: A life course perspective. *Applied Research in Quality of Life, 12*(2), 303–325.

CHAPTER 16

Aarts, S. (2018). Social media and loneliness among community dwelling older adults. *International Journal of Geriatric Psychiatry, 33,* 554–555.

Alltucker, K. (2018, October 30). The hidden side of dementia: End-of-life decisions ignite family feud. *USA Today,* A1.

Azman, A., Jamir Singh, P. S., & Sulaiman, J. (2019). The mentally ill and their impact on family caregivers: A qualitative case study. *International Social Work, 62,* 461–471

Balasubramaniam, M. (2018). Rational suicide in elderly adults: A clinician's perspective. *Journal of the American Geriatrics Society, 66,* 998–1001.

Barbosa Neves, B., Franz, R., Judges, R., Beermann, C., & Baecker, R. (2019). Connectedness among older adults? A feasibility study. *Journal of Applied Gerontology, 38,* 49–72.

Bedor, E. (2016). It's not you, it's your (old) vagina: Osphena's articulation of sexual dysfunction. *Sexuality & Culture, 20,* 38–55.

Bell, L. G., & A. Harsin, A. (2018). A prospective longitudinal study of marriage from midlife to later life. *Couple and Family Psychology: Research and Practice, 7,* 12–21.

Berk, R. A. (2015). The greatest veneration: Humor as a coping strategy for the challenges of aging. *Social Work in Mental Health, 13,* 30–47.

Bildtgard, T., & Oberg, P. (2017). New intimate relationships in later life consequences for the social and filial network? *Journal of Family Issues, 38*, 381–405

Blackburn, J., Locher, J. L., & Kilgore, M. L. (2016). Comparison of long-term care in nursing homes versus home health: Costs and outcomes in Alabama. *Gerontologist, 56*, 215–221.

Brown, R. (2014, March 13). Learn from retirees about biggest regret. *USA Today*, 3B.

Burton-Jeangros, C., & D. Zimmermann-Sloutskis, D. (2016). Life satisfaction trajectories of elderly women living in Switzerland: An age-period-cohort analysis. *Ageing & Society, 36*, 106–132.

Cancino, A. (2016, February 16). More grandparents raising their grandchildren. Associated Press.

Carmel, S., Tovel, H., Raveis, V. H., & O'Rourke, N. (2018). Is a decline in will to live a consequence or predictor of depression in late life? *Journal of the American Geriatrics Society, 66*, 1290–1295.

Caswell, G., & O'Connor, M. (2019). "I've no fear of dying alone": exploring perspectives on living and dying alone. *Mortality, 24*, 17–31.

Chancler, L. L. M., Webb, F. J., & Miller, C. (2017). Role of the black grandmother in the racial socialization of their biracial grandchildren. *Marriage & Family Review, 53*, 444–464.

Chang, I. J., Huff, S., & Knox, D. (2019). Humanoid Robots: Acceptance for personal and family use. *College Student Journal, 53*, 71–77.

Chen, F., Bao, L., Lin, Z., Zimmer, Z., Gultiano, S., & Borja, J. (2018). Double burden for women in mid- and later life: Evidence from time-use profiles in Cebu, the Philippines. *Ageing and Society, 38*, 2325–2355.

Chonody, J. M., & B. Teater, B. (2016). Why do I dread looking old?: A test of social identity theory, terror management theory, and the double standard of aging. *Journal of Women & Aging, 28*, 112–126.

Coco, K., Kangasniemi, M., & Rantanen, T. (2018). Care personnel's attitudes and fears toward care robots in elderly care: A comparison of data from the care personnel in Finland and Japan. *Journal of Nursing Scholarship, 50*, 634–644.

Comas-d'Argemir, D., & Soronellas, M. (2019). Men as carers in long-term caring: Doing gender and doing kinship. *Journal of Family Issues, 40*, 315–339.

Connidis, I. A., Borell, & Karlsson, S. G. (2017). Ambivalence and living apart together in later life: A critical research proposal. *Journal of Marriage and the Family, 79*, 1404–1418.

Costa, A., Martinez-Martin, E., Cazorla, M., Julian, V. (2018). PHAROS—Physical Assistant Robot System. *Sensors, 18*(8), 2633. Retrieved from https://doi.org/10.3390/s18082633

Crowley, J. E., & DePalma Brand, J. (2019). Should it be easy? Divorce process attitudes among those who have split up in midlife. *Journal of Divorce & Remarriage, 60*, 47–68

Dahlberg, L., Andersson, L., & Lennartsson, C. (2018). Long-term predictors of loneliness in old age: Results of a 20-year national study. *Aging and Mental Health, 22*, 190–196.

Diegelmann, M., Jansen, C. P., Wahl, H. W., Schilling, O. K., Schnabel, E. L., & Hauer, K. (2018). Does a physical therapy activity program in the nursing home impact on depressive symptoms? A generalized linear mixed-model approach. *Aging and Mental Health, 22*, 784–793

Dilmaç, J. A. (2018). The new forms of mourning: Loss and exhibition of the death on the Internet. *Omega: Journal of Death & Dying, 77*, 280–295. Retrieved from https://doi.org/10.1177/0030222816633240

Dunifon, R. E., Near, C. E., & Ziol-Guest, K. M. (2018). Backup parents, playmates, friends: Grandparents' time with grandchildren. *Journal of Marriage & Family, 80*, 752–767.

Emery Trindade, P. G., Santos, R. L., Lacerda, I. B., Johannessen, A. & Nascimento Dourado, M.C. (2019). Awareness of disease in Alzheimer's disease: What do patients realize about their own condition? *Aging & Mental Health, 23*(10), 1292–1299.

Ferdows, N. B., Jensen, G. A., & Wassim, T. (2018). Health aging after age 65: A life-span health production function approach. *Research on Aging, 40*, 480–507.

Francis, J. (2018). *"Thanks to Facebook, getting old isn't that bad and I am not all alone in this world": An investigation of the effect of Facebook use on mattering and loneliness among elder orphans* (Order No. 10931229). PhD dissertation. Michigan State University, East Lansing, MI.

Friedman, E. M., Park, S. S., & Wiemers, E. E. (2017). New estimates of the sandwich generation in the 2013. Panel Study of Income Dynamics. *Gerontologist, 57*, 191–196.

Friend, T. (2017, April 3). The God pill: Silicon valley's quest for eternal life. *The New Yorker*, 54–67.

Gilleard, C., & Higgs, P. (2017). Ageing, corporeality and social divisions in later life. *Ageing & Society 37*, 1681–1702.

Granville, L., & Pregler, J. (2018). Women's sexual health and aging. *Journal of the American Geriatrics Society, 66*(3), 595–601.

Hogsnes, L., Melin-Johansson, C., Gustaf Norbergh, K., Danielson, E. (2014). The existential life situations of spouses of persons with dementia before and after relocating to a nursing home. *Aging & Mental Health, 18*, 152–160.

Isherwood, L. M., King, D. S., & Luxzcz, M. A. (2017). Widowhood in the fourth age: support exchange, relationships and social participation. *Ageing and Society, 37*, 188–212.

Iveniuk, J., & Waite, L. J. (2018). The psychosocial sources of sexual interest in older couples. *Journal of Social and Personal Relationships, 35*, 615–631.

Jappens, M. (2018). Children's relationships with grandparents in married and in shared and sole physical custody families. *Journal of Divorce & Remarriage, 59*, 359–371.

Johnson, C. L., & Barer, B. M. (1997). *Life beyond 85 years: The aura of survivorship*. New York: Springer Publishing.

Kalmijn, M., & Leopol, T. (2019). Changing sibling relationships after parent's death: The role of solidarity and kinkeeping. *Marriage and the Family, 81*, 99–114

Koimizu, J., Kokado, M., & Kato, K. (2018). Ethical perspectives of Japanese engineers on ambient assisted living technologies: Semi-structured interview. *Asian Bioethics Review, 10*, 143–155.

Koren, C., Simhi, S., Lipman-Schiby, S., & Fogel, S. (2016). The partner in late-life repartnering: Caregiving expectations from an intergenerational perspective. *International Psychogeriatrics, 28*(9), 1555–1565.

Lee, Y., & Chi, I. (2016). Do cognitive leisure activities really matter in the relationship between education and cognition? Evidence from the aging, demographics, and memory study (ADAMS). *Aging & Mental Health, 20*, 252–261.

Lehoux, P., Grimard, D. (2018). When robots care: Public deliberations on how technology and humans may support independent living for older adults. *Social Science & Medicine, 211*, 330–337.

Lifshitz, R., Nimrod, R., & Bachner, Y. G. (2019) Spirituality and wellbeing in later life: a multidimensional approach. *Aging & Mental Health, 23*(8), 984–991.

Malone Beach, E. E., Hakoyama, M., & Arnold, S. (2018). The good grandparent: Perspectives of young adults. *Marriage & Family Review, 54*, 582–597.

Margolis, R. (2016). The changing demography of grandparenthood. *Journal of Marriage & Family, 78,* 610–622.

McCann, B. R., & Allen, K. R. (2018). Romantic forecasts in later life: Older single women's perspectives on family and kin relationships. *Journal of Family Issues, 39,* 747–770.

McClatchey, I. S. (2018). Fathers raising motherless children: Widowed men give voice to their lived experiences. *Omega: Journal of Death & Dying, 76,* 307–327.

Miller, L. (2019). The perils and pleasures of aging: How women's sexualities change across the life course. *Sociological Quarterly. 60*(3), 371–396.

Miner, B., Gill, T. M., Yaggi, H. K, Redeker, N. S., Van Ness, P. H., Han, L., & Fragoso, C.A. V. (2018). Insomnia in community-living persons with advanced age. *Journal of the American Geriatrics Society, 66,* 1592–1597.

Montemurro, B., & Chewning, L. (2018). Unscripted: Exploring representations of older unpartnered women's sexuality. *Journal of Women & Aging, 30,* 127–144.

Moore, T. J., & Sailor, J. L. (2018). A phenomenological study of romantic love for women in late life. *Journal of Women & Aging, 30,* 2011–126.

Muruthi, B., McCoy, M., Chou, J., & Farnham, A. (2018). Sexual scripts and narrative therapy with older couples. *American Journal of Family Therapy, 46,* 81–95.

Navarro, J., Vidaña-Vila, E., Alsina-Pagès, R. M., & Hervás, M. (2018). Real-time distributed architecture for remote acoustic elderly monitoring in residential-scale ambient assisted living scenarios. *Sensors, 18,* 2492. Retrieved from https://doi.org/10.3390/s18082492.

Nguyen, A., Chatters, L., Taylor, R., & Mouzon, D. (2016). Social support from family and friends and subjective well-being of older African Americans. *Journal of Happiness Studies, 17,* 959–979.

Oraka, E., Mason, S., & Xia, M. (2018). Too old to test? Prevalence and correlates of HIV testing among sexually active older adults. *Journal of Gerontological Social Work, 61,* 460–470.

Paine, E. A., Umberson, D. & Reczek, C. (2019). Sex in midlife: Women's sexual experiences in lesbian and straight marriages. *Journal of Marriage and the Family, 81,* 7–23.

Papernow, P. L. (2018). Recoupling in mid-life and beyond: From love to last to not so fast. *Family Process, 57,* 52–69.

Park, J., Tolea, M. I., Arcay, V., Lopes, Y., & Galvin, J. E. (2019). Self-efficacy and social support for psychological well-being of family caregivers of care recipients with dementia with Lewy bodies, Parkinson's disease dementia, or Alzheimer's disease. *Social Work in Mental Health, 17*(3), 253–278.

Park-Lee, E., Sengupta, M., Bercovitz, A., & Caffrey, C. (2013). Oldest old long-term care recipients: Findings from the national center for health statistics' long-term care surveys. *Research on Aging, 35,* 296–321.

Penning, M. J., & Wu, Z. (2019). Caregiving and union instability in middle and later life. *Marriage and the Family, 81,* 79–98

Pilotto, A., Boi, R., & Petermans, J. (2018). Technology in geriatrics. *Age and Ageing, 47,* 771–774.

Polenick, C. A., Zarit, S. H., Birditt, K. S., Bangerter, L. R., Seidel, A. J., & Fingerman, K. L. (2017). Intergenerational support and marital satisfaction: Implications of beliefs about helping aging parents. *Journal of Marriage and the Family, 79,* 131–146.

ProQuest Statistical Abstract of the United States. (2019). Online Edition. Bethesda, MD. Retrieved from https://www.proquest.com/products-services/statabstract.html

Quan-Haase, A., Mo, G. Y., & Wellman, B. (2017). Connected seniors: How older adults in East York exchange social support online and offline. *Information, Communication & Society, 20,* 967–983.

Rapp, I. (2018). Partnership formation in young and older age. *Journal of Family Issues, 39,* 3336–3390.

Rauer, A. (2013, February 22). From golden bands to the golden years: The critical role of marriage in older adulthood. Presentation at annual meeting of the Southeastern Council on Family Relations, Birmingham, AL.

Rollins, A. (2019). Racial socialization: a developmental perspective. In R. Nazarinia Roy, & A. Rollins (Eds.), *Biracial families: Crossing boundaries, blending cultures, and challenging racial ideologies* (pp. 159–182). New York: Springer.

Rubio, L., Dumitrache, C. G., Garcia, A. J., & Gordon-Pozo, E. (2018). Coping strategies in Spanish older adults: A MIMIC model of socio-demographic characteristics and activity level. *Aging & Mental Health, 22,* 226–232.

Rutagumirwa, S. K., & Bailey, A. (2018). "The heart desires but the body refuses": Sexual scripts, older men's perceptions of sexuality, and implications for the mental and sexual health. *Sex Roles, 78,* 653–668.

Sadana, R., Blas, E., Budhwani, S., Koller, T., & Paraje, G. (2016). Healthy aging: Raising awareness of inequalities, determinants, and what could be done to improve health equity. *Gerontologist, 56,* 178–193.

Sarabia, M., Young, N., Canavan, K., Edginton, T., Demiris, Y., & and Vizcaychipi, M. P. (2018). Assistive robotic technology to combat social isolation in acute hospital settings. *International Journal of Social Robotics, 10,* 607. Retrieved from https://doi.org/10.1007/s12369–017-0421-z

Satorres, E., Ros, L., Melendez, J. C., Serrano, J. P., Latorre, J. M., & Sales, A. (2018). Measuring elderly people's quality of life through the Beck Hopelessness Scale: A study with a Spanish sample. *Aging and Mental Health, 22,* 239–244.

Schafer, M. H., Upenieks, L., & Iveniuk, J. (2018). Putting sex into context in later life: Environmental disorder and sexual interest among partnered seniors. *Gerontologist, 58,* 181–190.

Schimmele, C. M., & Wu, Z. (2016). Repartnering after union dissolution in later life. *Journal of Marriage and the Family, 78,* 1013–1031.

Sheppard, P., & Monden, C. (2019). Becoming a first-time grandparent and subjective well-being: A fixed effects approach. *Journal of Marriage & Family, 81*(4), 1016–1026.

Silva, P., Matos, A. D., & Martinez-Pecino, R. (2018). Confident network and quality of life of individuals aged 50+: The positive role of Internet use. *Cyberpsychology, Behavior, and Social Networking, 21,* 22. Retrieved from https://doi.org/10.1089/cyber.2018.0170

Silver, M. P., & Williams, S. A. (2018). Reluctance to retire: A qualitative study on work identity, intergenerational conflict, and retirement in academic medicine. *Gerontologist, 58,* 320–330.

Silverman, P. R., & Thomson, S. (2018). When men grieve: Widowers' stories of coping with their wives' deaths. *Omega: Journal of Death & Dying, 77,* 133–153.

Simhi-Meidani, S., & Koren, C. (2018). When late-life repartnering and parental death intertwine: Adult children's perspectives. *Journal of Family Issues, 39,* 1639–1663.

Singer, P. (2018, November 30–December 2). Aging, alone, overlooked and in danger. *USA Today,* A1, 2.

Smeaton, D., Di Rosa, M., Principi, A., & Butler, Z. (2018). Reverse retirement—a mixed methods study of returning to work in England, Italy and the United States: Propensities, predictors and preferences. *International Journal of Ageing and Later Life, 12,* 5–40

Smith, S., Spence, L., Diehl, D., & Kail, A. (2017, November). The art of saying goodbye: End of life education. Poster presented at the annual meeting of the National Council on Family Relations, Orlando, FL.

Sniderman, D. (2018). Robotics rise to healthcare challenges: From surgery to rehab, robots are improving patient comfort and cutting costs. *Medical Design Technology, 22,* 14–16.

Steinert, A. & Haesner, M. (2019). Stress in retired adults— Stressors, symptoms and coping strategies. *Ageing International, 44*(2), 129–140.

Stensland, M. L., & Sanders, S. (2018). "It has changed my whole life": The systemic implications of chronic low back pain among older adults. *Journal of Gerontological Social Work, 61,* 129–150.

Stokes, J. E. (2017). Marital quality and loneliness in later life: A dyadic analysis of older married couples in Ireland. *Journal of Social and Personal Relationships, 34,* 114–136.

Stroope, S., McFarland, M. J., & Uecker, J. E. (2015). Marital characteristics and sexual relationships of U.S. older adults: An analysis of national social life, health, and aging project data. *Archives of Sexual Behavior, 44,* 233–247.

Tiilikainen, E., & Seppanen, M. (2017). Lost and unfulfilled relationships behind emotional loneliness in old age. *Ageing & Society, 37,* 1068–1088.

United Nations, Department of Economic and Social Affairs, Population Division (2015). World Population Ageing 2015 (ST/ESA/SER.A/390).

Vandemeulebroucke, T., de Casterlé, B., & Gastmans, C. (2018). How do older adults experience and perceive socially assistive robots in aged care: a systematic review of qualitative evidence. *Aging & Mental Health, 22,* 149–167. Retrieved from doi: 10.1080/13607863.2017.1286455.

Wada, M., Hurd Clark, L., & Mortenson, W. B. (2019). 'I am a busy independent woman who has a sense of humor, cares about others': Older adults' self-presentations in online dating profiles. *Ageing & Society, 39,* 951–976.

Wade, P., & Wild, L. G. (2017). Mother, father, and grandparent. *Journal of Family Issues, 38,* 776–797.

Wilmoth, J. D. (2016, November). *Comparing needs of single parents with single grandparents raising grandchildren.* Paper presented at the National Council on Family Relations annual meeting, Phoenix, AZ.

Wolff, J. L., Mulcahy, J., Roth, D. L., Cenzer, I. S., Kasper, J. D., Huang, J., & Covinsky, K. E. (2018). Long-term nursing home entry: A prognostic model for older adults with a family or unpaid caregiver. *Journal of the American Geriatrics Society, 66,* 1887–1894.

Zhang, H. (2019). Sending parents to nursing homes is unfilial? An exploratory study on institutional care in China. *International Social Work, 62,* 351–362

INDEX